‘Sjef-*Sache*’

AF892140

‘Sjef-*Sache*’

Essays in honour of Prof. mr. dr. J.H.M. (Sjef) van Erp on the occasion of his retirement

Bram Akkermans and Anna Berlee (Eds.)

eleven
international publishing

Published, sold and distributed by Eleven International Publishing
P.O. Box 85576
2508 CG The Hague
The Netherlands
Tel.: +31 70 33 070 33
Fax: +31 70 33 070 30
email: sales@elevenpub.nl
www.elevenpub.com

Sold and distributed in USA and Canada
Independent Publishers Group
814 N. Franklin Street
Chicago, IL 60610, USA
Order Placement: +1 800 888 4741
Fax: +1 312 337 5985
orders@ipgbook.com
www.ipgbook.com

Eleven International Publishing is an imprint of Boom uitgevers Den Haag.

ISBN 978-94-6236-197-3
ISBN 978-90-8974-509-5 (e-book)
NUR 822

© 2021 The authors | Eleven International Publishing

This publication is protected by international copyright law.
All rights reserved. No part of this publication may be reproduced, stored in a retrieval system, or transmitted in any form or by any means, electronic, mechanical, photocopying, recording or otherwise, without the prior permission of the publisher.

Voorwoord

Op 11 januari 2021 ging Sjef van Erp met emeritaat en zwaaide hij af als hoogleraar burgerlijk recht en Europees privaatrecht aan de Universiteit Maastricht, een functie die hij sinds 1997 bekleedde. Het werk van Sjef kenmerkte zich gedurende zijn hele loopbaan door een steeds omvangrijkere hoeveelheid rechtsvergelijkende academische werken met een even zo indrukwekkend onderzoeksnetwerk. Zijn komst naar Maastricht maakte deel uit van een breder initiatief om de rechtsvergelijkende onderzoeksagenda en het onderwijs aan de European Law School te versterken. Met zijn achtergrond in het verbintenissenrecht bracht hij een nieuw perspectief met zich mee toen hij de overstap maakte naar het goederenrecht. Hij ontwierp een van de eerste, zo niet de eerste, Engelstalige rechtsvergelijkende vakken over het goederenrecht, die – in een geëvolueerde vorm – vandaag de dag nog steeds worden gegeven. Hij bracht ook internationale ervaring met zich mee. Hoewel opgeleid en gevormd in Tilburg, bracht Sjef ook een deel van zijn promotietijd door in de Verenigde Staten en het Verenigd Koninkrijk, waar hij een heel andere academische wereld leerde kennen. Aandacht voor, en begrip van, *common law*-systemen heeft sindsdien altijd deel uitgemaakt van zowel zijn onderzoek als zijn onderwijs.

Hij nam het werk als promotor van zijn voorganger over en begeleidde sindsdien een bestendige lijn van promovendi, die elk een deel van zijn zorgvuldig geformuleerde onderzoekslijn uitwerkte en proefschriften schreven die daarin paste. Een lijn waarbij hij de onderliggende principes en spanningen in goederenrechtelijke systemen verkende. Hierdoor heeft zijn onderzoeksagenda geleid tot een Maastrichtse basis voor goederenrechtelijk onderzoek dat in het afgelopen decennium een sterke en stabiele reputatie heeft opgebouwd.

Het betekende echter niet dat het werk geïsoleerd werd uitgevoerd. Integendeel, de connecties met andere goederenrecht geleerden over de hele wereld, zoals met de Leuvense Vincent Sagaert of wijlen André van der Walt uit Stellenbosch en hun respectievelijke onderzoeksgroepen, waren zeer bepalend voor het verenigen van rechtsvergelijkende goederenrechtspecialisten op wereldniveau.

In het laatste decennium werden deze onderzoeksverbanden uitgebreid toen Sjef als stichtend lid betrokken raakte bij het European Law Institute (ELI). Als lid van het American Law Institute kon hij zijn eigen ervaring inbrengen en een grote rol spelen bij de oprichting van de Europese tegenhanger. Als vicepresident van het ELI bleef hij een belangrijke rol spelen in de richting die het instituut in het eerste decennium van zijn bestaan is ingeslagen. Evenzo heeft hij als rapporteur, met name in verband met PropTech, bijgedragen aan de inhoudelijke werkzaamheden van het instituut en zo ook invloed uitgeoefend op toekomstige Europese wetgeving op dit gebied.

Zijn werk wordt ook gekenmerkt door zijn eigen internationale ervaring. In 2006 was als hij Marie Curie-fellow aan de Universiteit van Bremen verbonden en sinds 2017 is hij als gasthoogleraar aan de Universiteit van Trento verbonden. Daarnaast zijn er tal van bezoeken, lezingen en promoties over de hele wereld waar Sjef zich mee heeft bezig gehouden.

Ter ere van deze prachtige carrière presenteren wij deze essaybundel, met niet alleen bijdragen van collega's in Maastricht, maar ook van collega's over de hele wereld. Het moment waarop het boek wordt gepresenteerd komt wanneer de wereld gegrepen is door het COVID-19 virus en daarom waren sommigen niet in staat om een bijdrage te leveren of in staat deze te leveren op de manier zoals zij dat wilden.

Wij presenteren bijdragen zowel in het Nederlands als in het Engels, ook ter ere van Sjef's carrière, waarin hij consequent in zowel het Nederlands als Engels heeft gepubliceerd. Het leveren van een bijdrage aan de ontwikkeling van het Nederlandse recht en het creëren van bewustwording van buitenlandse, Europese en zelfs mondiale debatten is altijd een onderdeel van zijn missie geweest.

De reikwijdte en omvang van Sjef's werk wordt weerspiegeld door de rijkdom aan onderwerpen die de verschillende bijdragen in dit *Liber amicorum* laten zien. Er zijn niet minder dan tien delen waarin we de bijdragen hebben verdeeld, welke variëren van het vermogensrecht in het algemeen, tot bijdragen die specifiek betrekking hebben op het verbintenissenrecht, erfrecht en natuurlijk de vele verschillende facetten van het goederenrecht. Het eerste deel is echter gewijd aan de rechtsvergelijkende methode en methodologie in het algemeen. Sjef's gezaghebbende werk aangaande het 'klassieke' model van het goederenrecht en zijn invloedrijke Walter van Gerwen Lezing zijn van grote invloed geweest op vele generaties studenten goederenrecht aan de Universiteit Maastricht en daarbuiten, omdat de daarin verwoorde methode niet alleen een uitstekend instrument is gebleken om verschillende goederenrechtelijke regimes met elkaar te vergelijken, maar ook om te begrijpen waarom deze verschillen bestaan tussen regimes binnen Europa en daarbuiten. Zoals uit de verschillende bijdragen in Deel I blijkt, is het werk van Sjef op het gebied van rechtsvergelijking ook van grote invloed geweest op de rechtswetenschappelijke literatuur op het gebied van het goederenrecht. Deel II gaat verder met stimulerende bijdragen die verschillende fundamentele goederenrechtelijke begrippen en concepten analyseren, maar ook het goederenrecht testen. Deel III verbindt het goederenrecht met aangrenzende rechtsgebieden en herinnert ons eraan dat Sjef echt een vermogensrecht jurist is en niet alleen een goederenrecht expert. Deel IV brengt ons bij een specifiek element van rechtsvergelijking en bevat bijdragen met betrekking tot legal translations. De delen V-VIII hebben zien op bijdragen die (deels) gewijd zijn aan specifieke gebieden van het goederenrecht of daar nauwe verwantschap mee hebben. Het gaat om bijdragen met betrekking tot zekerheidsrechten (deel V), landregistratie en het notariaat (deel VI), erfrecht (deel VII) en het huwelijksvermogensrecht (deel VIII). Op elk van deze gebieden heeft ook Sjef zijn stempel weten te drukken. Het voorlaatste deel van dit *Liber* bevat bijdragen die ingaan op de relatie tussen het goederenrecht en technologie. Sjef heeft altijd een scherp oog gehad voor technologische ontwikkelingen en wat deze (zouden kunnen) betekenen voor het vermogensrecht in het algemeen en het goederenrecht in het bijzonder, waarbij met name de vraag naar de kwalificatie van data centraal heeft gestaan in zijn werk. Het afsluitende deel X van dit boek bestaat uit twee bijdragen die het indrukwekkende oeuvre van Sjef aan een eigen data analyse onderwerpen.

Tot slot een paar woorden over zijn rol als mentor. Vanaf het begin van zijn samenwerking met een onderzoeksstudent, doctoraatsonderzoeker en daarbuiten, heeft Sjef zich gekenmerkt als een vriendelijke mentor, die zich richtte op zoveel meer dan alleen de inhoud van het onderzoek dat werd uitgevoerd. Door vrijelijk met ons zijn visie te delen op onderwijs, bestuurlijke aangelegenheden in en buiten universiteiten en de manier waarop universiteiten werken over de hele wereld, hielp hij zijn collega's bij hun voorbereiding op een carrière in en buiten de academische wereld. De warmte van de relaties die hij heeft opgebouwd, zal worden doorgegeven als zijn eigen onderzoekers op hun beurt de rol van mentor vervullen.

Bram Akkermans
Anna Berlee
Redacteuren

Preface

On 11 January 2021 Sjef van Erp retired as professor of civil law and European Private Law at Maastricht University, a post he held since 1997. Throughout his tenure, Sjef's work has been characterized by an ever expanding body of comparative work with an accompanying research network. When he came to Maastricht he was part of an effort to strengthen the comparative research agenda and teaching at the European Law School programme. Although he began his career as a contract lawyer, moving to property law meant he brought a fresh perspective. He designed one of the first, if not the first, English language comparative courses on property law, which – in an evolved form – are still taught today.

He also brought international experience with him. Educated and trained in Tilburg, Sjef spend part of his PhD research in the US and the UK, where he came across a whole different academic world. Attention to and understanding of common law systems has always been part of both his research and teaching.

Taking over the PhD supervision of his predecessor, he then proceeded to supervise a steady line of PhD theses, each fulfilling some part of his carefully curated research line, exploring the underlying principles and tension in property law systems. Through this, his research agenda led to a Maastricht base of property research that has gained a strong and steady reputation in the past decades.

It did not mean, however, that the work was carried out in isolation. To the contrary, connections to and with other property law scholars throughout the world, such as with Leuven based Vincent Sagaert, or the late André van der Walt based in Stellenbosch and their respective research groups were very much part of uniting comparative property law scholars at the global level.

In the last decade these research connections were extended when Sjef became involved as a founding member of the European Law Institute (ELI). As a member of the American Law Institute himself, he could contribute his own experience to the founding of the European counterpart. As vice-president of the ELI he continued to play an important role on the direction the institute took for the first decade of its existence. Similarly as rapporteur, especially dealing with issues relating to PropTech, he contributed to the substantive work of the institute, thus also influencing future European legislation in the area.

His work has also been characterized by his own international experience. In 2006 he was a Marie Curie fellow at the University of Bremen and since 2017 he has been visiting professor at the University of Trento. Apart from that, there are numerous visits, lectures and phd examinations across the world in which Sjef took place.

As a testament to his work, we present this collection of essays, not only from colleagues at Maastricht, but from colleagues from all over the world. It comes at a time when the world is in turmoil due to the COVID-19 virus and therefore some were not able to contribute or able to contribute in the manner they wanted to.

We present contributions both in Dutch and in English, also as a testament to Sjef's career, in which he consistently published most frequently in both Dutch and English. Contributing to the development of Dutch law as well as to create awareness of foreign, European and even global debates, has always been a part of his mission.

The breadth of Sjef's work is mirrored by the wealth of topics the different contributions in this book of friends displays. There are no less than ten parts in which we have divided the contributions, which range from patrimonial law in general, to specific contributions regarding contract, tort, succession, and of course the many different elements of property law. The first part is however dedicated to the comparative method, and methodology in general. Sjef's instrumental work on the 'classical' model of property law and his influential Walter van Gerwen Lecture have been a great influence on many generations of property law students at Maastricht University and beyond, by providing not only an excellent tool to compare property law regimes but also to understand why these regimes within Europe (and beyond) are different. Moreover, as the different contributions in Part I show, Sjef's body of work on comparative property law has also been of great influence in property law scholarly literature. Part II continues with stimulating contributions that seek to understand the concept of property but also challenges it. Part III ties property law concepts with adjacent areas of the law and reminds us that Sjef is not only a property lawyer. Part IV brings us to a specific element of comparative law and features contributions regarding legal translations. Parts V-VIII concern contributions dedicated (in part) to specific areas of property law or property law-adjacent areas and feature contributions regarding security rights (Part V), land registration and the notariat (Part VI), succession law (Part VII) and marital property law (Part VIII). Each of these also being an area of the law Sjef is very familiar with and has published extensively about. The penultimate part of this book contains contributions that deal with the relationship between property law and technology. Sjef has always had a keen eye on technological developments and what these mean for property law and how they fit within property law, in particular questions concerning the legal qualification of data. The concluding Part X of this book comprises of two contributions which look at and analyse the impressive body of work Sjef has produced thus far, and as such look at Sjef's published work as data.

A few words, finally, on his role as a mentor. From the start of collaborating with a research student, PhD researcher and even beyond that, Sjef has always served as a kind mentor, focusing on much more than just the content of the research that was carried out. Liberally sharing his views on teaching and management, as well as how universities work throughout the world, he helped prepare his colleagues for careers both in and outside of academia. The warmth of the relations he built will be passed on as his own researchers mentor on their own.

Bram Akkermans
Anna Berlee
Editors

Table of Contents

Part I
Comparative Law and Methodology

(Normative) Models of Property Law

Using Van Erp's Framework to Advance Sustainable Property Law

Bram Akkermans[*]

1 Introduction

It was the year 2000 when Sjef van Erp introduced me to Dutch, comparative and European Property Law. In his innovative course European Property Law, he was amongst the first property scholars to offer an undergraduate comparative property law course. I made more notes than for any other course in my degree and learned not only about the rules of property law, but especially about the underlying thought patterns of systems of property law.

The strength of this approach lies in emphasis of similarities in a field that is traditionally perceived as very fragmented. Through a thematic approach students learned about ownership and fee simple, about limited property rights to use and for security, and – last but not least – about trusts. I was hooked and knew this was the field I wanted to specialize in. Sjef became supervisor of my LLM thesis, where I wrote about South African, English and (non-existing) Dutch trusts law and we began work on a proposal for a PhD Project. Not about trust law, but about one the most problematic areas in civil law property law when it comes to the introduction of trusts: the *numerus clausus* of property rights. It was also the beginning of a 20-year collaboration in which I had the pleasure of working for and with Sjef to discover the systematics of property law.[1]

With someone looking at this fundamental principle of property law this, in Sjef's words, cleared the way for him to take a broader perspective. This led to his Walter van Gerven lecture in 2006 in which Sjef presented a method for analysis of property law systems into fundamental principles, ground rules and technical rules, and his contribution to the festschrift for Konstantin Kerameus in 2009, in which he introduced the framework for analysis in classical system of property law.[2] At the same time, we collaborated with

* Associate Professor of European Private Law and Sustainability at Maastricht University, Faculty of Law.

1 A search of my special "Van Erp" email inbox shows over 25.000 emails we exchanged over the years.

2 Sjef van Erp, From 'classical' to modern European property law, in Essays in Honour of Konstantinos D. Kerameus/Festschrift für Konstantinos D. Kerameus, Vol. I., Athens/Brussels, Ant. A. Sakkoulas/Bruylant, 2009, p. 1517 *et seq.*

many others on the making of the *Ius Commune* Casebook on Property Law, that would become the standard work for comparative property lawyers in the years to come.

The Van Erp-framework of classical property law – as I would name it – has been greatly influential to the descriptive work uncovering various European property law traditions. With the use of his work, we learned more about these fundamental principles and ground rules. Classical systems of property law, mostly formed in the 19th century, all answer to these divisions; or common thought-patterns in Van Erp's terminology.

At the base of this work is the contradiction between the classical model, made at a time and in societies that had very different requirements, and our modern day property law. Van Erp then investigates how modern day challenges, at first in the form of incorporeal assets such as data, lately more with a focus of technological developments in property law, or PropTech, cause us to rethink our fundamental principles, ground rules and technical rules of property law.

This approach raises – in my view – two highly significant questions: (1) can this originally descriptive method also be used to answer normative questions of property law and (2) can this approach also be used to address different challenges to property law beyond PropTech? In this contribution I will explore both of these questions, answering in the affirmative and applying this framework to challenges to property law brought by sustainability.

2 Normative Framework?

Before we can come to applying Van Erp's framework to challenges to property law, there is a methodological question that must be addressed. Sjef van Erp developed his framework on the basis of a descriptive comparative analysis. In this view, in short, all property law systems answer to a threefold division: (1) there are fundamental principles of property law, the principle of numerus clausus and the principle of transparency; (2) there are four ground rules of property law, (a) nemo dat, (b) *prior tempore, potior iure*, (c) limited rights have priority over fuller rights and (d) special protection rules exist.[3] All other property rules, in Van Erp's framework, are technical rules. These can differ from legal system to legal system.[4]

The strength of this framework thus lies not only in the uncovering of similarities at a more abstract level, but also at the inclusion of the diversity (or plurality) of property law

3 Sjef van Erp, European and National Property Law, Osmosis or Growing Antagonism, Walter van Gerven Lecture 6, Groningen, Europa Law Publishing, 2006, p. 15-16.

4 Sjef van Erp, European and National Property Law, Osmosis or Growing Antagonism, Walter van Gerven Lecture 6, Groningen, Europa Law Publishing, 2006, p. 16-17.

systems. The framework allows to analyse legal systems in a similar manner and thus form a base for comparison.[5]

The comparative work subsequently carried out, allowed us to uncover differences and similarities between various European legal systems. It provides us with a method for descriptive research that has helped us uncover how all classical systems of property law struggle with modern day challenges. These challenges include European (economic) integration, dephysicallisation of property, the advances of technology and property law's response to this, and sustainability. It is clear these new challenges require us to critically examine our property law systems and rules. It has also become clear in the past decades that our property law systems as well as our rules need adaptation.

The question that has not often been raised by property lawyers is how to best approach these changes from a methodological viewpoint. Most property scholarship focuses on changing concrete rules of property law, such as the work done in the context of the Draft Common Frame of Reference.[6] However, as Van Erp has shown us, there is much more to property than the technical rules. In fact, I would submit that Van Erp has shown us that the technical rules of property law function in a system that is made by fundamental principles and ground rules. To rise to the challenge therefore, perhaps also these two levels should be addressed?

This immediately raises a methodological question whether a framework that was derived from the existing state of law can also be used as a framework for further development. Sanne Taekema has brought attention to the sensitivities surrounding the use of theoretical frameworks as a normative basis.[7] These frameworks do not only explain the law as it is, but also need to be used to explain how the law should be.[8]

To address this methodological question there are two elements that must be brought to the forefront: (1) the normative nature of the existing framework and (2) the underlying values that provide further content to the framework.

First, the normative elements in Van Erp's framework. I submit that this framework is not entirely descriptive in nature. Although Van Erp uses his framework to describe property law systems, there is an organizational framework that lies at the foundation of this. The distinction in fundamental principles, ground rules and technical rules in Van

5 See Sjef van Erp and Bram Akkermans (Eds.), Text, Cases and Materials on Property Law, Ius Commune Casebooks for the Common Law of Europe, Oxford, Hart Publishing, 2012.

6 See, e.g., Reiner Schulze (ed), Common Frame of Reference and Existing EC Contract Law, 2nd edition, München, Sellier European Law Publishers, 2009, Vincent Sagaert, Matthias Storme and Evelyne Terryn (Eds.), The Draft Common Frame of Reference, national and comparative perspectives, Antwerp, Intersentia 2009.

7 Sanne Taekema, Theoretical and Normative Frameworks for Legal Research, Putting Theory into Practice, Law and Method, 2018, p. 2-3.

8 Sanne Taekema, Theoretical and Normative Frameworks for Legal Research, Putting Theory into Practice, Law and Method, 2018, p. 5-6.

Erp's view are the result of common thought patterns that he distinguishes in property law systems. Although the thought patterns themselves, i.e. the content, are derived using a descriptive method, Van Erp presents the threefold distinction as a normative element when he writes: "when looking for such common thought patterns a distinction should be made between leading principles, ground rules and technical rules".[9]

These thought patterns can – of course – differ from legal system to legal system. However, the structure that Van Erp uses can be applied in a variety of settings. In 2006, when Van Erp developed his framework, the debate in European Private Law centered around the question of the making of rules of European private law. The Draft Common Frame of Reference (DCFR) was still to be published, and the Common European Sales Law had only been mentioned in the form of an optional instrument.[10] For property lawyers, the discussion centered around the question if, and if so what aspects of property law, should be included in this. The approach was one of finding a coherent set of rules that could function as a system at the European level.

In 2021 the field looks very different. The Common European Sales Law proposal was revoked and the systemic approach replaced by a thematic approach. The work on the digital single market brought with it two legislative instruments on the sale of digital assets. The role of property law became very different and was – I would – submit largely ignored in these legislative proposals. The future of European Union development states that rules of business law remain under consideration, but the focus is brought to further technological developments and to sustainability in the context of the European Green Deal.[11]

These developments raise the question if Van Erp's framework can also be applied to these thematic approaches and can form the normative foundation to discuss how property law should respond to these challenges. I think it can and in the next section I will apply the framework to the question of sustainability in property law as a case study (section 3). I will then try to add to Van Erp's framework to make it more sustainable to deal with 21st century challenges (section 4).

---

9 Sjef van Erp, European and National Property Law, Osmosis or Growing Antagonism, Walter van Gerven Lecture 6, Groningen, Europa Law Publishing, 2006, p. 13.

10 Communication from the Commission to the European Parliament and the Council – A more coherent European contract law – An action plan COM(2003) 0068 final.

11 Communication from the Commission to the European Parliament and the Council – the European Economic and Social Committee and the Committee of the Regions – The European Green Deal COM(2019) 640 final.

3 Sustainable Property Law?

Sustainability means taking care of our own needs compromising 'the ability of future generations to meet their own needs.'[12] This means, in particular, an ecological purpose, meaning that we must treat our planet in a sustainable manner. Property law plays a crucial role in this as the vast majority of objects on our planet are privately held.[13] The rules that apply to this property give shape to the way in which this property is treated.

Also here it are the principles, ground rules and technical rules of property that form the legal framework on how we treat our planet; each of the three elements representing a level at which we can analyse property law. (1) At the level of fundamental principles, there are grand ideas that give shape to the system of property law. These are, apart from their substantive content, also organisation principles. (2) At the level of ground rules, the fundamental principles are 'translated' into the system of property law. These ground rules systematize the technical rules that follow. (3) At the level of technical rules, or – perhaps better – property doctrine, the actual rules of property law exist. It is in the collaboration of these three levels, that a system of property law arises.

This system of property law is relatively neutral as regards the application. The rules can be applied in very different settings, ranging for example from family situations, situations of social welfare, to corporate and commercial settings. In recent years, more attention has been given to the underlying values of our systems of property law. At the basis of our current application of property law is both economic and philosophical theory.[14]

In terms of economic foundation, the current leading economic theory is that of neoliberalism.[15] This means that economic growth is the driving force behind our society. In terms of philosophical foundation the current foundation primarily lies in utilitarianism.[16] For property law that means that the exclusivity of ownership is the primary focus. By being able to fence off one's property and to hold exclusive possession over such property, we allow for the accrual of wealth. The assumption is that when I use my property

12 Brundtland Commission, Report of the World Commission on Environment and Development, Our Common Future, Oxford, Oxford University Press, 1987.

13 D. Grinlinton and P. Taylor, Property Rights and Sustainability. The evolution of property rights to meet ecological challenges, Leiden/Boston, Martinus Nijhoff Publishers, 2011, p. 1-2.

14 See Gregory Alexander and Eduardo Peñalver, An Introduction to Property Theory, Cambridge, Cambridge University Press, 2012, p. 1 *et seq.*

15 See, Bram Akkermans, Sustainable Property Law – Towards a revaluation of our system of property law, in Bram Akkermans and Gijs van Dijck (Eds.), Private Law and Sustainability, The Hague, Eleven International Publishing, 2019, p. 37 *et seq.*

16 Gregory Alexander and Eduardo Peñalver, An Introduction to Property Theory, Cambridge, Cambridge University Press, 2012, p. 35 *et seq.*

to accrue wealth that is not only beneficial for me, but – because it also leads to economic growth – is also beneficial for our society as a whole.[17]

At both of these foundational levels there is movement towards new insights. At the level of the economic foundation of our society, more and more economists are moving towards a post-growth based models.[18] This means that in these viewpoints economic growth is no longer the decisive aim, but rather the quality of the economy becomes leading. Kate Raworth is one of the most prominent proponents of such an approach. She proposes a model of doughnut economics, which is a model that provides a bandwidth within which economic development should take place. The core of the doughnut represents a shortage, such as famine, political violence, social inequality or lack of energy and housing. The outer limit of the doughnut represents an overshoot and means pollution, loss of biodiversity or climate change.[19]

Such a new economic basis will also have effect on the way in which property law is applied. In a way a basis of doughnut economics also results – especially considering the important role of property law addressed above – in a doughnut property law. The framework and rules of property should also not lead to shortage or overshoot.

In terms of philosophical foundation utilitarianism, made very popular by the study of law and economics, is receiving more and more criticism. Especially combined with a neoliberal economic perspective, the application of utilitarianism has led to excesses of wealth accumulation and great inequality. Most recently this has been brought to the forefront by economist Thomas Piketty, who shows how the richest 10% has accumulated over two thirds of all capital, including land, over the past centuries.[20] Alternative theoretical foundations of property law exist, such as Gregory Alexander's human flourishing theory. The core of the human flourishing is not to deny the individual, but rather to place the individual in context of the community of which he is a part of.[21] Human flourishing theory, which finds it's basis in Aristotelian virtue ethics, focuses on development as a central concept. Every one of us is a member of one or more communities and between members of communities not only rights, but also obligations exist.[22]

As a result human flourishing theory poses a challenge for property law to respond and offer not only a framework for the rights of the right-holder, but also for the

17 Bram Akkermans, Sustainable Property Law – Towards a revaluation of our system of property law, in Bram Akkermans and Gijs van Dijck (Eds.), Private Law and Sustainability (The Hague, Eleven International Publishing, 2019), p. 37 *et seq.*

18 Peter Victor, Managing Without Growth, second edition, Northampton, MA, Edward Elgar Publishing, 2019.

19 See Kate Raworth, Doughnut Economics, seven ways to think like a 21st century economist, London, Random House, 2018.

20 Thomas Piketty, Capital in the 21st Century, Harvard, Harvard University Press, 2017.

21 Gregory Alexander, Property and Human Flourishing, Oxford, Oxford University Press, 2018, p. xi *et seq.*

22 Gregory Alexander, Property and Human Flourishing, Oxford, Oxford University Press, 2018, p. 75 *et seq.*

responsibility and obligations that come with that. The combination of rights and obligations provides a possibility to look at te application of property principles, ground rules and technical rules in a different light.

This becomes especially so when we consider adding sustainability as a fundamental principle of property law.[23] By incorporating sustainability, especially eco-sustainability as described above, incorporating other insights than (economic) utility become part of the property law decision making framework. By this I mean that when applying property rules, the principles and ground rules that give shape to these rules, should be considered in the light of sustainability. It means, for example, that when considering whether an owner has an action to stop interference with his property, the answer should not only be based on the exclusivity of the owner, but also on the context in which the right of ownership is exercised.[24] More concretely, squatters may be allowed or tolerated on the property.[25] Some of these arguments have been advanced already under the heading of sharing property.[26]

Sustainable property law thus calls for a 'rewiring' of our property law to accommodate a specific purpose.[27] Such purpose, combined with its economic and philosophic foundation, provides the framework in which principles, ground rules and technical rules function. It also shows that application of the framework is not as neutral as the framework may suggest. After all, Van Erp himself uses the framework in the context of the making of European property law.[28]

4 Adding to Van Erp's framework: The Underlying Values of Property Law

The above raises the question how Van Erp's framework could be completed to be applied in different normative settings. I submit that this can be done by incorporating property's

23 See, on this, Benjamin Verheye, Toekomst van de circulaire vastgoedeconomie, Tijdschrift voor Privaatrecht (2019), p. 107 *et seq.*

24 It is difficult to generally state what the difference in outcome will be, as this will depend very much on the actual fact pattern at hand.

25 Lorna Fox O'Mahoney and Marc Roark, Squatting and the State, Cambridge, Cambridge University Press, 2021 (forthcoming).

26 See Rashmi Dyal-Shand, Sharing the Cathedral, 46 Connecticut Law Review 2 (2013), p. 647 *et seq.* and André van der Walt, Sharing Servitudes, 4 European Review of Private Law 3 (2015), p. 162 *et seq.*

27 See Lynda Butler, Property's problem with extremes, 55 Wake Forest Law Review 1 (2020).

28 See Sjef van Erp, European and National Property Law, Osmosis or Growing Antagonism, Walter van Gerven Lecture 6, Groningen, Europa Law Publishing, 2006.

purpose.[29] In this way the normative purpose of the framework becomes evident from the start and we can solve the methodological issue addressed in section 2.

Property's purpose, or the underlying values, provides not only direction for the application of property principles and rules, but also provides a framework to balance different interests involved. Whether the underlying value is utilitarian of Aristotelian in origin, by making this clear in advance, we provide the normative direction of the form that we think property law should take. Adding clarity on the underlying values adds purpose and therefore provides the normative direction we want to take.

Van Erp's framework works – as I tried to demonstrate above – not only as a descriptive but also as a normative model. The difficulty with using a framework that was derived from descriptive research also as a normative framework to discuss the law as it should be can only be achieved methodologically if we are clear and precise about normative elements in that model. Property's purpose, which comprises the underlying values provide exactly that: based on the purpose identified – for example to enable technical developments, to achieve a more fair distribution of wealth, or sustainability – property law systems answer to the common thought patterns that Van Erp has identified. Fundamental principles, ground rules and technical rules will function in service of the purpose that was identified. In the next and final section of this contribution, I will explore what this means for the challenges brought to property law by sustainability.

5 WHAT DOES THIS MEAN FOR SUSTAINABLE PROPERTY LAW?

When the propose of property law is to create sustainable property law, and we provide a human flourishing theory foundation, it becomes clear that the fundamental principles of property – including sustainability – are to provide a law of property that enables us to take care of our current needs, but also of include the needs of future generations.

Human flourishing theory presents us with a view in which we all strive for the same purpose and do so as a member of one or more different communities. These communities are groups of people that we belong to on the basis of shared characteristics. Such characteristics may be defined by family relations, territorial occupancy, but can also be based on other connections such as the religion we identify with, or shared interest we have with others. Communities can therefore include both present as well as future members.[30]

---

29 See Gregory Alexander, Property and Human Flourishing, Oxford, Oxford University Press 2018, p 39 *et seq*.

30 See Gregory Alexander, Property and Human Flourishing, Oxford, Oxford University Press, 2018, p. 103 *et seq*.

Communities are central to human flourishing theory as they provide an organizational mechanism. Apart from the connection to the subject matter of the property right, which provides the traditional connection for property rights as they follow the object on which they are created.[31] In the past, property scholars have brought attention to the relational character of property law; property rights are exercised in relation to an object, but vis-à-vis other persons.[32] The relationalist analysis, however, does not specify which property rights exactly are used against whom. Of course this is part of the *erga omnes* effect we hold our property rights have.

Such *erga omnes* effect, however, is a fiction in the sense that our rights never really work against everyone, but could potentially be invoked against all others. In reality, however, our rights have effect against those that we directly deal with. Those, that enter our community, perhaps even temporarily, are those that are affected by our rights.[33]

Property rights provide us with connection, to the object on which they rest, but also to others who hold property rights around us, and to others that simply are around us. Our communities therefore provide a home in which our rights take their place. It is in that way that they provide an organizational paradigm.

The connections we hold towards our fellow community members provide context to our property rights, they provide the both content and limitations. Moreover, it is human flourishing theory that provides the basis of that content and limitations. Especially in the context of sustainability, the rights and obligations become more concrete.

In terms of the environmental impact of the property rights we hold, science in the last decades has demonstrated how we are all connected and how – for example – CO_2 emissions in one location can have environmental effects on the other side of the planet.[34] The global community in which we hold our rights provides a connection between all property owners.

Apart from the global community there are other territorial committees we belong to, such as the town or the neighborhood we live in.[35] Some other communities are

---

31 This especially applies to property rights created on tangible objects. The effect is also know as *droit de suite*.

32 See Frédéric Zenati, Essai sur la nature juridique de la propriété. Contribution à la théorie du droit subjectif (diss.), Lyon, 1981, S. Ginossar, Droit réel, propriété et créance – élaboration d'un système rationnel des droits patrimoniaux, Paris, LGDJ 1960.

33 This approach also fits the analysis made by Henry Smith in which he analyses different types of third parties. See Thomas Merrill and Henry Smith, Optimal Standardization in the Law of Property, The *Numerus Clausus* Principle, (110) Yale Law Journal, 2000, p. 27. Also see Bram Akkermans, Standardisation of Property Rights in European Property Law, in Bram Akkermans, Ernst Marais and Eveline Ramaekers (eds.), Property Law Perspectives ii, Antwerp, Intersentia, 2013, p. 222 *et seq.*

34 See Eric Holthaus, The Future Earth, New York, HarperOne, 2020.

35 See Gregory Alexander, Property and Human Flourishing, Oxford, Oxford University Press, 2018, p. 75 *et seq.*

non-territorial in nature, such as an association we belong to, or even inter-generational in nature, such as our family.

The core of human flourishing theory is that we hold property rights not just for ourselves, but in the context of the communities we belong to.[36] As all members of society answer to the underlying social thesis that human flourishing means taking care of our own needs, but also of those around us, being a member of a community comes not only with rights, but also with obligations. Especially for those who hold property rights, these obligations affect the way in which these rights may be exercised. Alexander distinguishes two types of obligations: (1) general obligations and (2) specific obligations.

General obligations can be fulfilled by handing over part of our property to the collective in the form of taxes. Alexander uses infrastructure such as roads or utility services as an example of this. Specific obligations are more concrete and arise and exist between members of a community. They cannot be fulfilled by handing over money, but can mean that we must exercise our rights in a certain manner. Although the obligation is moral in nature, there are many ways in which these specific obligations can find a legal form. Examples of such are offered by last wills or trust devices in which a settlor leaves instructions on how property rights are to be exercised.[37] The debate on sharing of property rights fits very much in this framework.[38]

Alexander also mentions a clean environment as an example of a general obligation.[39] By paying taxes, in his view, we can fulfill an obligation to ourselves and our communities to ensurer that a clean environment comes about by way of public policy. Alexander is not alone in this. In his seminar works on capital economist Thomas Piketty also puts the emphasis on the need for taxation to reduce inequality and to ensure a better and clean environment for ourselves and for the generations to come.[40] Piketty is part of a group of progressive French economist who focus on the importance of taxation of the richest 1% of the world to raise funds to strengthen public policy in fields such as education and environment that will greatly reduce inequality without compromising economic growth.[41]

Although this approach has clear merits, it also helps support the current system of property law that has given rise to many of the problems it seeks to resolve. In the context of sustainability, and not just the movement towards a clean environment, a much more

---

36 See Gregory Alexander, Property and Human Flourishing, Oxford, Oxford University Press, 2018, p, 75 *et seq*.

37 See Gregory Alexander, Property and Human Flourishing, Oxford, Oxford University Press, 2018, p, 113-114.

38 See Rashmi Dyal-Shand, Sharing the Cathedral, 46 Connecticut Law Review 2 (2013), p. 647 *et seq*. and André van der Walt, Sharing Servitudes, 4 European Review of Private Law 3 (2015), p. 162 *et seq*.

39 Gregory Alexander, Property and Human Flourishing, Oxford, Oxford University Press, 2018, p. 56-57.

40 Thomas Piketty, Capital in the 21st Century, Harvard, Harvard University Press, 2017, Thomas Piketty, Capital and Ideology, Harvard, Harvard University Press, 2020.

41 See also Gabriel Zucman, The Hidden Wealth of Nations, Chicago, University of Chicago Press, 2016.

holistic approach is proposed in which we also look at the underlying causes of our current problems. In this context, taking care of our own needs without compromising the needs of future generations comes with a critical view on the exclusivity property rights offer. By fencing off our property form others, either literrally in case of land or more fictionally in case of intangible property, property law has offered a system that has allowed a very small group of people to accumulate vast amounts of property, leaving others with none.[42]

We move towards an eco-sustainable society by tackling not only the manifestation of our current way of dealing with property, which is heavily inspired by neoliberalism and utilitarianism, such as Piketty is proposing, but also by critically examining the system of property law that has given rise to this.[43] Our rules of property law are therefore not as neutral as many would like to believe: a 'rewiring' of property law, in other words, can form the foundation on which we can build a new and more sustainable society.[44]

As a manifestation of sustainability, the underlying value for our system of property law in this respect can very well be human flourishing. The social thesis that underlies this is that we are all a member of a (global) society and that for each of us to flourish, we must take care of our own needs, whist taking care of the needs of future generations. Human flourishing read in this way brings a decision scheme with it on the basis of which we can begin to shape a sustainable society.[45]

In such an approach we can and must all contribute towards a more sustainable society. Not only by paying our taxes, thus reducing inequality and allowing for a partial redistribution of wealth through public policy (which must also become sustainability focused), but also in the way in which we treat our property. Farmers can farm their land in different and much more diverse manners, we can invest ourselves in non-fossil sources of energy, such as wind or solar, and we use these proceeds to help our fellow community members do the same.[46]

---

42 See Howard Mansfield, The habit of turning the world upside down, our belief in property and the cost of that belief, Peterborough, Bauhan Publishers, 2018. On the division of ownership in our society see Piketty, Capital and Ideology, Harvard, Harvard University Press, 2020, p. 99 *et seq*. For a more legal point of view see Katharina Pistor, The Code of Capital. How the law creates wealth and inequality, Princeton, Princeton University Press, 2019.

43 See Bram Akkermans, Sustainable Property Law – Towards a revaluation of our system of property law, in Bram Akkermans and Gijs van Dijck (Eds.), Private Law and Sustainability, The Hague, Eleven International Publishing, 2019, p. 37 *et seq*.

44 Lynda Butler, Property's problem with extremes, 55 Wake Forest Law Review 1 (2020).

45 See Jill Robbie, Moving Beyond Boundaries in the Pursuit of Sustainable Property Law, in Bram Akkermans and Gijs van Dijck (Eds.), Private Law and Sustainability, The Hague, Eleven International Publishing, 2019, p. 59.

46 Marjorie Kelly, Owning our Future. The Emerging Ownership Revolution, Oakland, Berrett-Koehler Publishers Inc, 2012, Eric Holthaus, The Future Earth, New York, HarperOne, 2020, Howard Mansfield, The habit of turning the world upside down, our belief in property and the cost of that belief, Peterborough, Bauhan Publishers, 2018, Joseph Singer, The Edges of the Field. Lessons on the Obligations of Ownership, Boston, Beacon Press, 2001.

The framework in which we do this is where we take our fundamental principles, ground rules and technical rules and hold these to the light to see their inner workings. By providing new values of sustainability and human flourishing, we have a defined object van thus can effectively rewire these three levels of Van Erp's framework. This begins, I submit, by accepting that ownership does only come with exclusives powers, but also comes with a responsibility and a context in which the right is to be exercised. That responsibility – and herein lies the strength of the human flourishing approach – is private law based. It is not imposed externally by a state or (local) government, but follows from our membership of our communities. The context in which we hold that responsibility is therefore – at least in some part – also private. It is also public – as is already the case – we must exercise our rights within the limits of the law. Also these public law aspects can be adapted; for example when it comes to mining minerals and other fossil substances.

If we manage to adapt this new approach together, and we find our common value to preserve the earth for generations to come, we begin to alter our common thought pattern. Part of this is already happening in 2021, as the debate on climate change is moving away from climate change denial towards a much more nuanced discussion on what approaches are necessary.[47]

6 Conclusion

Van Erp's work on our common thought patterns has brought about significant change in the study and teaching of property law. During his career the field moved from an almost purely national oriented discipline to a comparative, European and even global field of study. Van Erp's work has offered a substantial contribution towards this. Not only in his substantive research, but also through his methodological work, always focussing on the best possible way to compare legal systems.[48] Finally, his work has had a significant impact on generations of students going through his courses on comparative and European property law in Maastricht, Bremen, Trento and beyond.[49]

47 See Eric Holthaus, The Future Earth, New York, HarperOne, 2020. Global Warming of 1.5°C an IPCC special report on the impacts of global warming of 1.5 °C above pre-industrial levels and related global greenhouse gas emission pathways, in the context of strengthening the global response to the threat of climate change, sustainable development, and efforts to eradicate poverty, available at https,//www.ipcc.ch/sr15/download/.

48 See, for example, Sjef van Erp, Civil and common property law, caveat comparator – the value of legal historical-comparative analysis, in European Review of Private Law (2003), p. 394 *et seq.* and Sjef van Erp, Linguistic diversity and a European Legal Discourse, Electronic Journal of Comparative Law (2003).

49 Instrumental in this is the Ius Commune casebook on property law, Sjef van Erp and Bram Akkermans (eds.), Text, Cases and Materials on Property Law, Oxford, Hart Publishing, 2012.

The framework that underlies all of this is Van Erp's three level analysis. It works, as I have tried to demonstrate, not only as a descriptive approach to carry out comparative legal analysis, but can also be used as a method to tackle normative questions. The methodological risk of using a originally descriptive method to tackle normative questions can be addressed by being transparent about the purpose as well as by incorporating normative elements, such as the values underlying the system of property law.

With that, the road is open towards a normative study of property law. Increasingly, as property law is confronted with major challenges such as technological developments and sustainability, the needs to address these normative issues becomes more and more urgent. Van Erp's model has been around for almost 15 years and has proven to be a useful way to analyse property law systems. Its greatest strength in this respect lies in the incorporation of various levels of scholarship, which are still studied in isolation of each other by many. Van Erp's model looks at fundamental principles, such as numerus clausus and transparency, at ground rules that translate some of these general principles into a concrete rule, such as the relationship between mother and daughter rights, and technical rules, where the actual property practice comes to life, giving content to both the principle and ground rules levels.

By taking a step back, Van Erp showed us in 2006, we can oversee much more of the complexities of property law. In a normative context as I propose we use Van Erp's framework, we step even further away to see the normative context in the form of the underlying values of property law, before we can step forward to make changes to the framework and the rules that result from that.[50]

---

50 An example of such analysis I offered in Bram Akkermans, Sustainable Property Law – Towards a revaluation of our system of property law, in Bram Akkermans and Gijs van Dijck (Eds.), Private Law and Sustainability, The Hague, Eleven International Publishing, 2019, p. 37 *et seq.*

The Nature of Comparing

*Jill Robbie**

1 Introduction

Prof van Erp has explained that studies in comparative property law have, until recently, been rather rare and the number of studies is still relatively small.[1] He blames this on "technocratic conservatism"[2] where property law is seen as "a set of national, fairly rigid, and technical legal rules, either in statutory or case law format, which are largely of a mandatory character, thus limiting the parties' freedom to shape their legal relations, at least as these relations may have an effect *vis-à-vis* third parties."[3] This view has led to a static approach to comparative property law with a focus on the differences between the Common law and Civil law countries. Prof van Erp states that the differences are "seen as an historical accident that has led to the existence of two leading traditions in property law, coherent within themselves but difficult to reconcile."[4]

Prof van Erp disputes this view of property law as a "petrified legal area"[5] through showing how a "dynamic approach to property law using an open-critical comparative analysis can open our minds and help us to find creative and workable solutions."[6] He does this by exploring the issues of recognising new objects of property rights and new types of property rights, drawing on examples such as digital data and CO_2 emission rights, as well as innovations in moveable and immoveable security rights. Prof van Erp places this analysis within the context of national, regional and global developments, which challenge existing property law conceptions and require a change in mentality.[7]

* Senior Lecturer in Private Law, University of Glasgow.

1 S. van Erp, 'Comparative Property Law' in M. Reimann & R. Zimmermann (Eds.), *The Oxford Handbook of Comparative Law*, 2nd ed., Oxford, Oxford University Press, 2019, pp. 1032 and 1037. Prof van Erp does note, however, that comparative property law has been at the heart of scholarship on mixed legal systems.

2 *Ibid.* p. 1037.

3 *Ibid.* p. 1032.

4 *Ibid.* p. 1037. There are exceptions noted by Prof van Erp including Y. Emerich, *Droit commun des biens: perspective transsystématique*, Cowansville, Yvon Blais, 2017, which has now been published in English with amendments as Y. Emerich, *Conceptualising Property Law: Integrating Common Law and Civil Law Traditions*, Cheltenham, Edward Elgar, 2018.

5 S. van Erp, 'Comparative Property Law' in M. Reimann & R. Zimmermann (Eds.), *The Oxford Handbook of Comparative Law*, 2nd ed., Oxford, Oxford University Press, 2019, p. 1032.

6 *Ibid.* p. 1050.

7 *Ibid.* pp. 1054-1057.

One of the reasons that a change of mentality is necessary, according to Prof van Erp, is a growing awareness of climate change, which he states "will, no doubt, have enormous consequences on ownership questions regarding natural resources."[8] In this contribution, I wish to explore this issue in a broader context. In particular, I wish to investigate what the role of environmental factors could be in comparative property law projects and how this may encourage us to re-consider our approach to comparative property law. This is upon the background that humanity is currently having an unprecedented impact on the natural world and the way we are using natural resources is unsustainable.[9] Therefore in this contribution, I will investigate the "nature" of comparing.

2 Static Comparative Property Law

As noted by Prof van Erp, the static approach to comparative property law is focused on the Common law and Civil law divide. Some claim this to be the "most fundamental and most discussed issue in comparative law".[10] This issue is a product of a wider attempt to categorise the world's legal systems into legal families. Ironically, in the context of the argument contained in this contribution, the attempt at classification was apparently originally inspired by the Linnaean taxonomy of animals, plants and minerals with the result of the comparative lawyer as zoologist.[11]

Many different taxonomies of legal families have been suggested over time, and these taxonomies have also regularly been subject to criticism.[12] The factors taken into account to produce the classifications have been listed by Prof Husa as including the history of a legal system, level of codification, process of judicial reasoning, influence of religion or political systems on law, structure of the court system, and so on.[13] Perhaps unsurprisingly, there is a focus on the structure and content of the positive law that comprises the legal

8 *Ibid.* p. 1037.

9 *See* Intergovernmental Science-Policy Platform on Biodiversity and Ecosystem Services, 'Summary for Policymakers of the Global Assessment Report on Biodiversity and Ecosystem Services', 2019. Available here: https://ipbes.net/global-assessment (accessed 14 November 2020).

10 U. Mattei, *Comparative Law and Economics*, Ann Arbour, University of Michigan Press, 1997, p. 70. This claim can, of course, be disputed.

11 M. Siems, *Comparative Law*, Cambridge, Cambridge University Press, 2014, p. 72.

12 *See* the table provided in M. Siems, *Comparative Law*, Cambridge, Cambridge University Press, 2014, p. 76, table 4.1, and summary of the criticisms pp. 80-93.

13 J. Husa, 'Legal Families' in J.M. Smits (Ed.), *Elgar Encyclopaedia of Comparative Law*, 2nd ed., Cheltenham, Edward Elgar, 2012, pp. 492-493.

system, and the influences on this system. An interesting omission is external factors to the legal system such as the geography, climate, or biodiversity in a jurisdiction.[14]

The limitations of the concept of legal families, including that is it reductionist and does not reflect the plurality of influences on different legal systems, have resulted in the suggestion that the taxonomy is only useful as a starting point.[15] At the beginning of a research project, legal families can be used in order to select legal systems to investigate more deeply. This is indeed often the way in which legal families are used for comparative property law projects, where the jurisdictions chosen are seen to be representatives of a particular family.[16] In the context of a European comparative property law project, the systems of France, Germany and England maybe initially selected – representing the Romanistic, Germanic and Common law legal families.

The stumbling block which the comparatist then encounters is the doctrinal dissimilarity between Civil and Common law systems in relation to property issues – the irreconcilability referred to by Prof van Erp above. One of the fundamental differences between Common law and Civil law systems is the conceptualisation of ownership. Generally, Civil law systems consider ownership to be the most comprehensive and complete right a person can have in a thing.[17] Subordinate real rights are strictly defined and grant only limited and partial rights in a thing, which are derivative of the ownership right. In contrast, Common law systems have adopted the concept of relative title, with no single, absolute right that is superior to all other competing claims. Furthermore, there has been the influence of legal realism in Common law systems, which has disaggregated property entitlements into a bundle of rights, which can be held by various people, and these rights are relations between people, rather than rights directly in a thing.[18] Although important scholarly work has been done on how to overcome these differences, including Prof van Erp's work,[19] the divide still dominates comparative property law.

---

14 K. Zweigert & H. Kötz, *Introduction to Comparative Law*, 3rd ed., Oxford, Clarendon Press, 1998, p. 64. In the past, race has been used as a factor for consideration. However, this is now rightly rejected. *See* M. Siems, *Comparative Law*, Cambridge, Cambridge University Press, 2014, p. 77.

15 J. Husa, 'The Future of Legal Families', Oxford Handbooks Online, 2016.

16 *See* S. van Erp & B. Akkermans (Eds.), *Cases, Texts and Materials on National, Supranational and International Property Law*, Oxford, Hart Publishing, 2012.

17 Described in S. van Erp, 'Deconstruction and Reconstruction of European Property Law: A Research Agenda' in E. Cashin Ritaine (Ed.), *Legal Engineering and Comparative Law*, Geneva, Schulthess, 2008, p. 113.

18 These differences are summarised in A.J. van der Walt, *Property in the Margins* Oxford, Hart Publishing, 2009, pp. 32-36.

19 Such as S. van Erp, 'Comparative Property Law' in M. Reimann & R. Zimmermann (Eds.), *The Oxford Handbook of Comparative Law*, 2nd ed., Oxford, Oxford University Press, 2019; S. van Erp & B. Akkermans (Eds.), *Cases, Texts and Materials on National, Supranational and International Property Law*, Oxford, Hart Publishing, 2012; S. van Erp, 'Deconstruction and Reconstruction of European Property Law: A Research Agenda' in E. Cashin Ritaine (Ed.), *Legal Engineering and Comparative Law*, Geneva, Schulthess, 2008; S. van Erp, 'European and National Property Law: Osmosis or Growing Antagonism', 6th Walter van Gerven Lecture, Groningen, Europa Law Publishers, 2006. *See also*, for example, B. Akkermans, *The Principle of*

This focus on doctrinal differences can direct attention away from consideration of the broader implications of property law in a comparative project. For example, when exploring eviction in a comparative context, Prof van der Walt argues that both Common law and Civil law systems attach "the qualities of power and centrality to individual or private property because of its importance for economic liberalism as a social system; the doctrinal differences are technical remainders that should not detract attention from the rhetorical and ideological similarities."[20] I would argue that the current focus on doctrinal questions in comparative property law projects indeed has a role in obscuring larger conceptual issues. In this contribution, I suggest that an important issue which is under-investigated due to a doctrinal focus is the relationship between property law and environmental factors.

To illustrate this point, I will give two examples. In the book *Lawscape: Property, Environment, Law*, Australian scholar Nicole Graham investigates the abstract conceptualisation of property rights and how this creates a blindness to social and environmental consequences.[21] Graham demonstrates this by analysing the imposition of English property laws to England's colonies. She argues that English property laws were the product of particular social and environmental conditions. Important factors were a temperate climate with a high rainfall, which were perceived as being capable of supporting intensive and productive agriculture. These laws were then transposed to arid regions of Australia and the USA, as well as to areas in Canada with a sub-arctic climate. She states:

> From the earliest days of their colonisation, there was an incongruity between the English ideology of property and its practicability in different environmental contexts. The climates and geographies of other countries did not always support intensive agriculture and/or pastoralism without substantial and ongoing changes to the landscape and hydroscape to render English land use practices possible and productive. Property law in the colonies was not responsive to its local environment ... Colonial land law was inappropriate – literally out of place.[22]

Numerus Clausus in European Property Law, Antwerp, Intersentia, 2008 and L.P.W. van Vliet, *Transfer of Movables in German, French, English and Dutch Law*, Nijmegen, Ars Aequi Libri, 2000.

20 A.J. van der Walt, *Property in the Margins* Oxford, Hart Publishing, 2009, p. 37.

21 N. Graham, *Lawscape: Property, Environment and Law*, Abingdon, Routledge, 2011. See also N. Graham, 'Dephysicalised Property and Shadow Lands' The University of Sydney Law School, Legal Studies Research Paper Series, No. 19/84, December 2019.

22 N. Graham, *Lawscape: Property, Environment and Law*, Abingdon, Routledge, 2011, p. 88. Graham also explores the use of property concepts in the dispossession of Indigenous peoples in the process of colonisation in Ch. 4.

Graham argues that property law becomes maladapted when it is disconnected with place, or in other words dephysicalised. A focus on doctrinal questions of comparative property law does not reveal these important observations.

Another example can be found in the Mixed Jurisdiction of Louisiana. Mixed Jurisdictions have been perceived by some comparative property lawyers as potentially overcoming the Common law/Civil law divide mentioned above.[23] Further, there has been interest between the members of various Mixed Jurisdictions to investigate developments in other Mixed Jurisdictions, with some projects including Louisiana.[24] Despite being a State in the USA, Louisiana has a Civil Code, which has been influenced by both French and Spanish law, among other sources.[25] Articles of this Code are arguably maladapted to the environmental context of Louisiana. The coastal region of the State is dominated by swampland and marshland, which are among the most valuable ecosystems in the world, and yet which in recent years have become increasingly submerged due to the encroaching waters of the Gulf of Mexico.[26] There are on-going property law disputes regarding ownership and access to these newly submerged lands.[27] The relevant provisions of the Civil Code regarding the Division of Things into common, public and private things,[28] and the provisions on alluvion,[29] do not provide clear solutions to these disputes, and seem inappropriate to both the particular geography of this coastal region and the accelerating physical transformations taking place. Once again, a focus on doctrinal issues would miss this important controversy in Louisiana's property law.

23 *See*, for example, J.M. Smits (Ed.), *The Contribution of Mixed Legal Systems to European Private Law*, Antwerp, Intersentia, 2001. On Mixed Jurisdictions generally see K.G.C. Reid, 'The Idea of Mixed Legal Systems', *Tulane Law Review*, Vol. 78, 2003, pp. 5-40.

24 *See*, for example, V.V. Palmer and E. Reid (Eds.), *Mixed Jurisdictions Compared: Private law in Louisiana and Scotland*, Edinburgh, Edinburgh University Press, 2009.

25 J.W. Cairns, *Codification, Transplants and History: Law Reform in Louisiana (1808) and Quebec (1866)*, New Jersey, Talbot Publishing, 2015.

26 *See* T.E. Törnqvist *et al.*, 'Tipping points of Mississippi Delta marshes due to accelerated sea-level rise', *Scientific Advances*, Vol. 6, 2020.

27 *See* Report of the Public Recreation Access Task Force to the Louisiana Legislature, 31 January 2020. Available at: http://www.dnr.louisiana.gov/assets/Legal/PublicRecAccessTFReport.pdf (accessed 14 November 2020). *See also* J. Mestayer, 'Saving Sportsman's Paradise: Article 450 and Declaring Ownership of Submerged Lands in Louisiana', *Louisiana Law Review*, Vol. 76, 2016.

28 Arts. 448-456 of the Louisiana Civil Code.

29 Arts. 499-506 of the Louisiana Civil Code.

3 The Nature of Comparing

In what ways could environmental factors be an important element in comparative property law projects? Despite the view that environmental law and property law are enemies,[30] both are components of the system of laws and policies that governs the human relationship with natural resources.[31] Furthermore, property law has an impact on the environment that it seeks to regulate. As stated by Peter Burdon, "all tangible items of property are (in one way or another) derived from nature and our property choices have very real and immediate impacts on our community and the environment."[32]

An example Graham gives to demonstrate the impact property law can have is the enclosure movement in England between the mid-18th century and the beginning of the 19th century. This process of individual appropriation, facilitated by law, had significant ecological effects, and changed the relationship between people and the land.[33] The same can be said of the Highland Clearances in Scotland in the same period, which has continuing ecological consequences.[34] Graham also argues the imposition of English land laws and land use practices on Australia, resulted in physical transformations of the land.[35] This has reflections in contemporary practices, and she highlights the discourse of the Australian farmer "battling the land" as evidencing over-exploitation of the particular natural features of certain areas.[36] Therefore, property laws can have significant environmental consequences and in carrying out a comparison between legal systems and evaluating different property regimes, we could consider these consequences. When comparing property laws, we could consider questions such as: In what ways does property law regulate natural resources? How does this reflect a perception or ideology of the natural world? How are natural resources used or exploited in that jurisdiction? What effects does this have?[37]

---

30 *See* V. Sagaert, 'Property Law, Contract Law and Environmental Law: Shaking Hands with the (Historical) Enemy' in S. Demeyere & V. Sagaert (Eds.), *Contract and Property with an Environmental Perspective*, Antwerp, Intersentia, 2020.

31 P. Taylor and D. Grinlinton, 'Property Rights and Sustainability: Towards a New Vision of Property' in D. Grinlinton & P. Taylor (Eds.), *Property Rights and Sustainability: The Evolution of Property Rights to Meet Ecological Challenges*, Leiden, Martinus Nijhoff Publishers, 2011, p. 9.

32 P.D. Burdon, *Earth Jurisprudence: Private Property and the Environment*, Abingdon, Routledge, 2015, p. 45.

33 N. Graham, *Lawscape: Property, Environment and Law*, Abingdon, Routledge, 2011, Ch. 3.

34 *See*, for example, discussion in C. Warren, *Managing Scotland's Environment*, 2nd ed., Edinburgh, Edinburgh University Press, 2009; R.A. Dodgshon, 'The Scottish Highlands before and after the Clearances: an ecological perspective' in D. Whyte and A.J.L. Winchester (Eds.), *Society, Landscape and Environment in Upland Britain*, Society for Landscape Studies, 2005, and T.C. Smout, *Nature Contested: Environmental History in Scotland and Northern England since 1600*, Edinburgh, Edinburgh University Press, 2000.

35 N. Graham, *Lawscape: Property, Environment and Law*, Abingdon, Routledge, 2011, pp. 123-130.

36 *Ibid*, pp. 181-189.

37 To engage in such projects may require interdisciplinary research teams. I have argued elsewhere that interdisciplinary work would be beneficial to property law research, *see* J. Robbie, 'Moving Beyond

Conversely, the particular environmental conditions of a jurisdiction may result in different legal responses. For example, some take the view that when a resource becomes increasingly scarce, more defined private property rights develop over that resource.[38] This, it is argued, explains the system of prior appropriation in relation to water in the arid Western States of the USA in contrast to the system of riparian rights in the Eastern States.[39] However, this argument has also been subject to critique[40] and other studies show greater control by the state in times of water scarcity, which restricts property rights.[41] Much remains to be explored here through comparative study.

As Prof Robinson states: "Alpine montane legal systems will necessarily be distinct from the management of coastal zones in their environmental problems, forms of land tenure, economic development pressures; it is no surprise that, as a result, different types of environmental legal means can and should be structured for such places."[42] Therefore, in comparative property projects, we could ask: In what ways do external features to the legal system, such as geography, climate and biodiversity, influence property rules? How do different jurisdictions deal with abundance and scarcity of resources? Can any common patterns be discerned? Do countries take paradigms which have been perceived to function well for certain resources and use these paradigms for other resources? What happens when laws that are the product of particular environmental conditions are transplanted to other environments?[43]

Considering environmental factors in this way may open up different possibilities for the exploration of similarities and differences between jurisdictions. Instead of choosing England, France and Germany – the traditional representatives of the various legal families – it could be fruitful to look at two countries with an abundance of a natural resource and one dealing with scarcity. The comparatist could investigate a legal system which allows people to hold water rights in relation to a river, and a legal system where a river itself is

---

Boundaries in Pursuit of Sustainable Property Law' in B. Akkermans & G. van Gijck (Eds.), *Private Law and Sustainability*, The Hague, Eleven, 2019.

38 H. Demsetz, 'Toward a Theory of Property Rights' *The American Economic Review*, Vol. 57, 1967, p. 347.

39 T.L. Anderson and P.J. Hill, 'The Evolution of Property Rights: A Study of the American West', *Journal of Law and Economics*, Vol. 18, 1975, p. 163.

40 *See* C.M. Rose, 'Energy and Efficiency in the Realignment of Common-Law Water Rights', *Journal of Legal Studies*, Vol. 19, 1990, p. 261.

41 *See* overview of the arguments in D. Schorr, 'Water Rights' in M. Graziadei & L. Smith (Eds.), *Comparative Property Law: Global Perspectives*, Cheltenham, Edward Elgar, 2017 and I. Kissling-Näf & S. Kuks, *The Evolution of National Water Regimes in Europe: Transitions in Water Rights and Water Policies*, Dordrecht, Kluwer Academic Publishers, 2004.

42 N.A. Robinson, 'Comparative Environmental Law: Evaluating How Legal Systems Address Sustainable Development', *Environmental Policy and Law*, Vol. 27, 1997, p. 340.

43 Graham's argument here is that they become 'maladapted'. *See* N Graham, *Lawscape: Property, Environment and Law*, Abingdon, Routledge, 2011, p. 206.

recognised as having legal personality.[44] Such projects would transcend the doctrinal Civil law/Common law divide and allow us to investigate more effectively how property law responds to and governs the natural environment, and what consequences this governance has.

4 A Nature-Based Approach to Comparative Property Law?

Taking the argument of the importance of environmental factors to comparative property law even further would be to consider the possibility of nature-based comparative property law. This would mean allowing natural features, species and habitats to determine the legal systems for investigation. Prof Robinson again states: "If the jurisdictions compared each have the same migratory species resident in their lands, airs and waters, the comparison of land use systems to maintain habitat can be made. Similarly, when studying aquifer protection and maintenance, the comparative analysis begins with the location of those jurisdictions where the aquifers are situated."[45]

We are currently losing crucial components of the natural world at an alarming rate, with extinction levels around 100-1000 times higher than in pre-human times.[46] This has significant negative consequences for humanity, which will only worsen if we do not take any action.[47] Therefore, considering how to best protect nature deserves dedicated attention. In the European context, nature-based comparative property law could be fruitful as there is a common framework for nature protection within the European Union under the Wild Birds[48] and Habitats Directives.[49] The Wild Birds and Habitats Directives require Member States to take measures to maintain or restore natural habitats, as well as populations of wild flora and fauna, including all wild birds naturally occurring in the EU.[50] For the purposes of these Directives, Europe has been divided into eleven biogeographical regions – including Alpine, Boreal and Mediterranean – to provide reference areas for

---

44 *See*, for example, A. de Vries-Stotijn, I. van Ham & K. Basteijer, 'Protection through Property: From Private to River-held Rights', *Water International*, Vol. 44, 2019, p. 736; E. O'Donnell, *Legal Rights for Rivers: Competition, Collaboration and Water Governance*, Abingdon, Routledge, 2018; C. Rodgers, 'A New Approach to Protecting Ecosystems: The Te Awa Tupua (Whanganui River Claims Settlement) Act 2017', *Environmental Law Review*, Vol. 19, 2017, p. 266.

45 N.A. Robinson, 'Comparative Environmental Law: Evaluating How Legal Systems Address Sustainable Development', *Environmental Policy and Law*, Vol. 27, 1997, p. 340.

46 European Commission, 'An Advocacy Toolkit for Nature: Biodiversity Loss, Nature Protection and the EU Strategy for Nature', 2020, p. 4.

47 *Ibid.*, pp. 5-7.

48 Directive 2009/147/EC on Conservation of Wild Birds.

49 Directive 92/43/EEC on the Conservation of Natural Habitats and of Wild Fauna and Flora.

50 *See generally* D. Langlet and S. Mahmoudi, *EU Environmental Law and Policy*, Oxford, Oxford University Press, 2016, Ch. 15.

large-scale ecological analyses.[51] A product of these Directives has been the creation of Natura 2000, the largest co-ordinated network of protected areas in the world, which currently covers 18% of the EU's territory.[52] Many of the Natura 2000 sites cross national boundaries in order to fulfil the aspiration to create a "coherent European ecological network of special areas of conservation".[53]

The impact of these Directives has rarely been investigated from the point of view of property law, but it is clear that the implementation of the Directives in the Member States has an effect on the exercise and content of property rights in relation to particular sites, which can vary from country to country.[54] The framework of the Directives could lead to a focused purpose for the comparison – how has property law changed and how is it functioning in relation to these protected areas? A small-scale comparative property law project could investigate a particular transboundary Natura 2000 site, and consider the property law response in relation to the site on either side of the border. A large-scale project could consider a natural feature such as the Alps, which stretch over the EU countries of France, Italy, Germany, Austria and Slovenia, and well as the non-EU countries of Switzerland and Liechtenstein. The mountain range contains rich biodiversity and a multitude of Natura 2000 sites.[55] In these projects we could ask: What has been the property law response to the management of these crucial areas of Europe's natural environment? How do the property laws differ in various countries with respect to these important areas? In what ways are these laws similar? Are any laws more effective than others in maintaining or restoring the natural habitats or species?

Investigating these questions would be in accordance with the aims of the EU Biodiversity Strategy for 2030, which promotes cooperation across borders among the Member States, and between EU Member States and other countries.[56] Researching these issues also recognises that natural features, species and habitats do not respect national

51 *See* the map of the regions provided by the European Environment Agency. Available at: https://www.eea.europa.eu/data-and-maps/figures/biogeographical-regions-in-europe-2 (accessed 14 November 2020).

52 European Commission, 'EU Biodiversity Strategy for 2030: Bringing Nature Back into Our Lives', COM/2020/380, p. 4. The EU has a goal to increase the total area of protected areas to 30% of the EU's land mass and also to provide strict protection to areas of very high biodiversity value or potential by 2030.

53 Art. 3(1) of Directive 92/41/EEC on the Conservation of Natural Habitats and of Wild Fauna and Flora. A. Aragão, 'Transboundary Nature Conservation: Are there no Boundaries within the Natura 2000 Network?' in C-H. Born, *The Habitats Directive in its EU Environ- mental Law Context*, Abington, Routledge, 2015.

54 *See* A. Garcia-Ureta, 'The ECJ Jurisprudence on Nature Protection and Ownership Rights' in G. Winter (Ed.), *Property and Environmental Protection in Europe*, Groningen, Europa Law Publishing, 2016; G. Winter, 'Property Rights and Nature Conservation' in C-H. Born, *The Habitats Directive in its EU Environmental Law Context*, Abington, Routledge, 2015.

55 *See* the range of information on the Alpine Biogeographical Region here: https://ec.europa.eu/environment/nature/natura2000/platform/knowledge_base/134_alpine_region_en.htm (accessed 14 November 2020).

56 European Commission, 'EU Biodiversity Strategy for 2030: Bringing Nature Back into Our Lives', COM/2020/380, p. 5.

boundaries. "Like the rivers, which flow freely across borders, species run, fly, swim, crawl or go with the wind, across borders."[57] To contribute to tackling the issue of biodiversity loss and promote nature conservation, our research methodologies should reflect this reality of the natural world.

5 Conclusion

Prof van Erp's research encourages us to see beyond the traditional Common law/Civil law divide in comparative property law. His work also challenges us to change our mentality in order to contribute to solving some of the world's most pressing problems. Being inspired by his arguments, in this contribution, I have sought to explore how comparative property law projects could consider environmental factors or even adopt a nature-based methodology. Again, within the spirit of Prof van Erp's scholarship, I have investigated the possibility of this type of research in the context of EU law. In doing so, I have developed the argument of Prof van Erp that we need a dynamic approach to property law using an open-critical comparative analysis.

The arguments in this contribution are founded on the acceptance that the transition to sustainability is one of the most pressing challenges facing humanity. We must adapt to living within the Earth's resources. Property law can, and should, have a positive role in this transition. Nevertheless, this transition will not be an easy one, and will require changes to the existing methodologies, logic, assumptions and working practices of the discipline.[58] Involving the environment in comparative property law projects could be a valuable step in the process of the transition to sustainability. As Graham states:

> Integrating the material conditions and consequences of law into law's logic and operation are not only helpful, but vital, to authoritative and sustainable people-place regulation. If we want to know how to reshape our property law, we have to look no further than the landscape because it is the landscape that reveals our place in the world and the opportunities and limits of our connection with it.[59]

---

57 A. Aragão, 'Transboundary Nature Conservation: Are there no Boundaries within the Natura 2000 Network?' in C-H. Born, *The Habitats Directive in its EU Environmental Law Context*, Abington, Routledge, 2015, p. 247.

58 *See also* J. Robbie, 'Moving Beyond Boundaries in Pursuit of Sustainable Property Law' and B. Akkermans, 'Sustainable Property law – Towards a Revaluation of Our System of Property Law' in B. Akkermans & G. van Gijck (Eds.), *Private Law and Sustainability*, The Hague, Eleven, 2019 and J. Robbie & E. van der Sijde, 'Assembling a Sustainable System: Exploring the Systemic Constitutional Approach to Property in the Context of Sustainability', *Loyola Law Review*, Vol. 66, 2020, p. 553.

59 N. Graham, *Lawscape: Property, Environment and Law*, Abingdon, Routledge, 2011, p. 206.

If it is the landscape, containing all its natural features, species and habitats, which provides the limits to the law, perhaps this is where we need to begin our property law research.

The Role of Comparative Law in European Private Law: A Janus-Faced Enterprise?

*Luisa Antoniolli**

1 The Role of Comparative Law in European Private Law

Selecting a topic for my contribution to the Liber Amicorum for Sjef van Erp among the catalogue of Sjef's work has been a tough choice, because of the impressive breadth of his interests, displayed in the long list of books and articles he has written, as well as in his institutional and practice-oriented work.

I have finally decided to write about the role of comparative law in European private law, first of all because this is a hot topic of comparative law,[1] but also because it is the *fil rouge* of my long-lasting collaboration with Sjef, and of his links with the Faculty of Law of my home University, the University of Trento.[2]

The general debate about the role of comparative law is an old one, and yet it is far from settled. In fact, today the situation is more complex and confused than ever: comparative law has gained a prominent role in legal science, and has attracted an increasingly large group of scholars and practitioners, who have significantly expanded the scope (both geographical and substantial) and the methods of the discipline.[3] The consequence of this evolution is that the level of heterogeneity has significantly increased, making it extremely difficult to try and reach a shared understanding of its aims, content and methods.[4]

Comparative law has played and is playing a specific and important role in the European context, particularly in relation to the structure and features of European Union law and

---

* Professor of private comparative law, Faculty of Law/School of international Studies, University of Trento.

1 For a recent comprehensive analysis of the evolution and current trends in comparative law see M. Reimann, 'Comparative law', in *International Encyclopedia of Comparative Law*, Vol. II, *The Legal Systems of the World – Their Comparison and Unification*, Leiden, Brill, 2020. See also M. Reimann, R. Zimmermann, *The Oxford Handbook of Comparative Law*, 2nd ed., Oxford, Oxford University Press, 2019.

2 I have taught with Sjef for many years a course on comparative private law, an experience that has inspired and enriched both the students and me: he is an excellent teacher, gifted with the ability of making complex and highly technical topics both easy to understand and intellectually stimulating, and has greatly contributed to raising a keen interest in comparative law among students.

3 For a recent analysis of the expansion of comparative law see M. Siems, 'The Power of Comparative Law', *American Journal of Comparative Law*, vol. 67, 2019, pp. 861-888.

4 See Reimann, *op. cit.*, pp. 61 and 78.

its interplay with the laws of the Member States. This branch of the law, moreover, is part of a broader picture, related to globalization and the growing connection among different legal systems, national, transnational and international.

From a theoretical point of view, comparative law works can be grouped in two main strands:[5] the first conceives comparative law as a tool of analysis and as a means to acquire wider and deeper knowledge of legal phenomena, their context and their evolution.[6] The second focuses on the use of comparative law to achieve legal change, introduce legal reform, foster legal harmonization or legal integration, or solve conflicts.[7]

While this distinction is clear in theory, in practice it is blurred:[8] in order to pursue legal change, one first needs to know the legal rules that are meant to be changed, as well as those that serve as a model for the change; therefore, knowledge and analysis are necessarily a prerequisite for reform. Yet, the fact that in the first kind of comparison knowledge is an end in itself, while in the second it is instrumental to the achievement of a further goal, marks a crucial distinction: in the first case, every element that has analytical and explanatory value needs to be taken into account; on the contrary, in the second case a selective approach must be adopted, which takes into account only the elements that are relevant in order to shape the proper course of action and achieve the desired result. Therefore, while the two comparative exercises have many elements in common, they remain structurally distinct.

The aim of this contribution is to analyse briefly the evolution of European private law at the cross-road between national private laws and EU law (par. 2), in order to highlight the tension in the use of comparative law as a legal engineering tool or as a yardstick for critical assessment (par. 3). It will then focus on European private regulatory law, a form of law that cuts across traditional legal categories, methods and actors, and is related to phenomena of globalization and transnational law (par. 4). It will conclude with a short discussion of the challenges and opportunities that this scenario opens up for comparative law (par. 5).

5 See P. Glenn, 'Aims of Comparative Law', in J.M. Smits (Ed.), *Elgar Encyclopedia of Comparative Law*, 2nd ed, Cheltenham, Northampton (MA), 2006, pp. 65-74. A comprehensive and authoritative analysis of the aims of comparative law was given by Ernst Rabel, *Aufgabe und Notwendigkeit der Rechtsvergleichung*, reprinted in K. Zweigert, H.-J. Puttfarken, *Rechtsvergleichung*, Darmstadt, Wissenschaftliche Buchgesellschaft, 1978, pp. 85-108.

6 R. Sacco, P. Rossi, *Introduzione al diritto comparato*, 6th ed., Torino, UTET, 2015; K. Zweigert, H. Kötz, *An Introduction to Comparative Law*, 3rd ed., Oxford, Clarendon, 1998; M.A. Glendon, M.W. Gordon, P.G. Carozza, *Comparative Legal Traditions: Texts, Materials and Cases on Western Law*, 3rd ed., St. Paul (MN), Thomson/West, 2007.

7 This activity can focus on legislation, case law, legal doctrine or legal practice. In the 19th century, when the discipline was established as an autonomous subject, the strongest emphasis was on legislative intervention.

8 Reimann, *op. cit.*, p. 181.

2 The Long and Winding Road of European Private Law

The specificities of comparative law in Europe, particularly in the area of private law, derive from a plurality of factors. My contribution will focus on private law, an area where harmonization and integration efforts have been intense and pervasive,[9] and where the bifurcation between the theoretical and practical scope of comparative law had important consequences for European law in general, and for EU law in particular.

Historically, Europe was the area in the West where the scientific study of comparative law first developed, at the end of the 19th century. Although in the European tradition the main seat for the study and development of law have been Universities, the establishment of comparative law as an autonomous legal subject was at the time predominantly related to practical purposes, namely the drive for legal reform and legal unification that developed at the end of the 19th century. This was a time of unlimited faith in progress, and comparative law was considered as a tool to achieve the best law for the whole world. These dreams were tragically dispelled by two successive world wars in the 20th century, but they left an important imprint on comparative law, and its theories and instruments for legal reform, which later came back in a different form, when the European Communities were established, based on the idea of integration through law.[10]

In Europe law, particularly private law, was considered for many centuries as a comprehensive common system, coexisting with manifold local variations: *ius commune* was a repository of shared principles, institutions, concepts and methods, which allowed legal rules (and jurists) to travel across borders.[11] This shared *koine* was gradually overshadowed when, beginning at the end of the 18th century, and accelerating in the 19th century, European nation states consolidated their political, institutional and legal identity by enacting codes (for civil law, as well as for many other substantial and procedural branches of law), focusing on national specificities, rather than on shared transnational features. This fragmentation was strengthened by two factors: the high number of national (and sometimes sub-national) languages, a formidable multiplier of legal complexity, as well as a hallmark of national cultures, and by the fragmentation of legal education,[12] which established different traditions that remain even today, in spite of globalizing trends.

---

9 Reimann, *op. cit.*, p. 81, lists unification of European private law among the five main themes of comparative law today.

10 See the seminal work of M. Cappelletti, M. Seccombe, J. Weiler (Eds.), *Integration Through Law: Europe and the American Federal Experience*, 5 vols., Berlin, New York, De Gruyter, 1985-1987.

11 R. Zimmermann, *Roman Law, Contemporary Law, European Law: The Civilian Tradition Today*, Oxford, Oxford University Press, 2001, ch. 2.

12 H. Dedek, 'Stating Boundaries: The Law, Disciplined', in H. Dedek, S. Van Praagh (Eds.), *Stateless Law. Evolving Boundaries of a Discipline*, Ashgate, Routledge, 2016, pp. 9-22.

This centrifugal trend was countered in Europe by the establishment of the European Communities in the 1950s, an important driver of convergence of national systems, and possibly the most ambitious and successful experiment of regional integration in the world. The final aim of the integration process was political: the Schuman Declaration, which marks its start, openly acknowledged economic integration as the first step towards political integration (i.e. a Europen federation).[13] In spite of the extraordinary success of this gradual process, political integration has not been achieved, and today it seems to be not only in troubled waters, but to have outright disappeared from the horizon. Yet, no matter what the fate of the European political project will be, the common/internal market and the four fundamental freedoms that underpin it have been, and still are, a very powerful engine of legal harmonization in Europe.[14]

The notion of common/internal market is functionally-oriented and cuts across legal categories, and many areas of national private law (for example, contract law and tort law) have been affected by the rules established by the EC, and later the EU, in order to build and regulate it. Harmonization related to the internal market is typically fragmented and unsystematic, being connected to piecemeal needs and interventions, lacking a general design: integration is not aimed at establishing a comprehensive system, but rather at tackling specific problems that hinder the development and working of the internal market, because of the obstacles to a level playing field caused by national legal rules, which can be a barrier to the free flows of goods, services, persons and capital.

In the 1980s this pattern of integration changed due to two related elements. The first was institutional: with the entry into force of the Single European Act in 1987, the internal market was not only reinforced as the cornerstone of the European integration process, but its development was boosted by the introduction of a new law-making procedure,[15] which made the enactment of secondary legislation much easier and quicker than before.

---

13 In the words of Schumann, one of the political fathers of European integration, "The pooling [of coal and steel production] should immediately provide for the setting up of common foundations for economic development as a first step in the federation of Europe". In his vision, "Europe will not be made all at once, or according to a single plan. It will be built through concrete achievements which first create a de facto solidarity"; this is the so-called "Europe des petits pas". Schuman declaration, 9 May 1950 (http://europa.eu/about-eu/basic-information/symbols/europe-day/schuman-declaration/index_en.htm, last visited 21 February 2021).

14 The EU economic constitution has always been heavily oriented towards market values, and while it is certainly true that, over time, social concerns have increasingly made their way into the constitutional fabric of the EU legal system, the predominance of market values seems to be part of the DNA of the EU, with a strong emphasis on functionalism. For a critical position see Study Group on Social Justice in European Private Law, 'Social Justice in European Contract Law: A Manifesto', 10 *European Law Journal*, vol. 10, 2004, pp. 653-674.

15 In the co-operation procedure the Council acted together with the European Parliament, and normally decided by qualified majority, instead of unanimously, as before. This procedure later led to the co-decision procedure (art. 289 TFEU), which further strengthened the role of the EP as a co-legislator, and is today the ordinary law-making procedure.

Second, the aim of market integration was gradually transformed from an instrument for achieving political integration in the long run, into a self-standing and all-encompassing end-goal, becoming an ideological frame that justified interference with, and sometimes trumping on, national systems, with crucial and often disruptive consequences for them, legally, economically and politically.

3 Comparative Law as Legal Engineering or as a Critical Tool of EU Private Law: The Clash Reloaded?

This situation led to a clash between a vision of European private law as an immanent body of principles, concepts and rules, slowly and gradually evolving, which could be tracked and analyzed by expert work in comparative law, and one of private law as a practical tool to be employed to foster legal harmonization of EU private law.[16]

In fact, legal engineering related to the internal market led in the late 1980s and 1990's to a veritable flood of EC legislation,[17] which significantly impacted private law, for example in the area of consumer protection (particularly consumer contracts), but also in areas such as product liability, franchising, agency, company law, etc. An analysis of this extensive body of law is beyond the scope of this contribution, but a shared essential feature related to its impact on national private law in the member States must be highlighted: while EC law was meant to harmonize only selectively national laws, in fact its impact has been much wider and deeper, because its specific market-driven logic gradually led to a revision of the structure and underlying principles of whole areas of law. To those who were in favor of protecting the integrity of national legal systems, this development was criticized as an unwelcome "legal irritant".[18] For those in favor of comprehensive legal integration, this was the first step towards a truly uniform European private law, which would finally develop out of partial harmonization steps.

The theoretical debate about European private law was also evolving in this period. In the mid-1990's the idea of working systematically on European private law, on the basis of a comparative analysis of national legal systems, was gradually gaining momentum. The Commission on European Contract Law, known as the Lando Commission after the name of its President, was established in 1980, gathering a small but prominent group of legal scholars with extensive comparative expertise, that produced the first volume of the Principles of European Contract Law (PECL) in 1995, followed by two further volumes in

16 Reimann, *op. cit.*, p. 131 ff.

17 See list of measures to be enacted to boost the internal market in the 1985 Commission's white book on Completing the Internal market (COM/85/0310 final).

18 See G. Teubner, 'Legal Irritants: Good Faith in British Law or How Unifying the Law Ends Up in New Differences', *Modern Law Review*, vol. 61, 1998, pp. 11-32.

2000 and 2003.[19] The Lando Commission was essentially an academic endeavour, isolated from direct law-making tasks. Yet, the main aim of the PECL as a forerunner for future comprehensive legal harmonization at the European level was openly acknowledged by Lando himself: "The Principles are intended to become part of a future European Civil Code".[20]

While at first this scholarly endeavour remained isolated from the political and institutional debate, in a sort of "scholarly bubble", things started to change at the end of the 1980s, when the issue of comprehensive harmonization of private law came under the radar of the institutions of the European Community. It was the European Parliament that first raised it, and in very bold terms, calling for a codification of the whole of private law (even family law) in a 1989 Resolution, the first time that an institution openly referred to codification, a highly symbolic move.[21] Although it lacked binding legal effects, the political salience of the 1989 Parliament Resolution (backed by several others in the following years) cannot be underestimated, because it opened the door to a debate that, in spite of its uneven and at times obscure evolution, has continued unabated for over 30 years. The next significant institutional step was the Commission Communication on European contract law of 2001, setting out several options in order to remedy to the fragmentary nature of EC law in the area of contract law, one of which envisaged the enactment of a comprehensive legal instrument.[22]

Meanwhile, on the academic side an important development took place in 1998, when the Lando Commission evolved into a larger working group, the Study Group on a European Civil Code, chaired by Christian von Bar. As its very name makes clear, the endeavour was much more ambitious than its predecessor, both because of its wider scope,

19 O. Lando, H. Beale (Eds.), *Principles of European Contract Law Part I, Performance, Non-Performance and Remedies*, prepared by the Commission of European Contract Law, The Hague/London/Boston, Kluwer Law International, 1995; O. Lando, H. Beale (Eds.), *Principles of European Contract Law, Parts I and II (Combined and Revised)*, prepared by the Commission of European Contract Law, The Hague/London/Boston, Kluwer Law International, 2000; O. Lando, H. Beale (Eds.), *Principles of European Contract Law, Part III*, prepared by the Commission of European Contract Law, The Hague/London/Boston, Kluwer Law International, 2002.

20 O. Lando, 'The Structure and the Salient Features of the Principles of European Contract Law', *Juridica International*, vol. 6, 2001, p. 2 (https://www.juridicainternational.eu/). Lando explicitly linked the need for a European Civil Code to the internal market: "The European Union of today is an economic community. Its purpose is the free flow of goods, persons, services and capital. The Union is based on these four flows. They go by way of contracts. (...) The contract law of the Union countries is therefore one (of his) risks. Thus, the existing variety of contract laws in Europe is a non-tariff barrier to trade. It is the aim of the Union to do away with restrictions of trade within the Communties, and therefore the differences of law, which restrict this trade, should be abolished" (pp. 1-2). Along with the Lando group, other study groups have drafted principles related to other areas of private law, such as trust law, insolvency law, tort law and family law.

21 Resolution of 26 May 1989, *O.J.*, 1989, C 158/400.

22 Communication from the Commission to the Council and the European Parliament on European contract law, COM/2001/0398 final.

which covered all private patrimonial law, but also because it openly recognized the enactment of a European Civil Code as its end goal.

The two strands, scholarly and institutional, merged in 2005, when the EU Commission launched and funded a large network of scholars, with the task of preparing a Draft Common Frame of Reference (DCFR), i.e. a body of principles, definitions and model rules that would be used by the EU institutions in their law-making process, in order to guarantee consistency and coherence in the approach to contract law. The final version of the DCFR was completed and published in 2009,[23] and, while the EU mandate was limited to contract law, in fact it covered the whole of private patrimonial law. Commentators stressed that it was, both in terms of substance and form (except for the name) a civil code, namely the European civil code.[24]

The idea embraced by the group was far from being shared by all jurists, both academic and practitioners, as well as by all member states. Consequently, conflict started immediately after its publication, and finally the EU Commission decided to move back to its original plan of working only on contract law, which was considered an essential legal component of the internal market, as well as to the most solid legal basis for enacting comprehensive EU legislation. After a rapid reshuffling work, in 2011 the Commission presented a new proposal for a regulation on a Common European Sales Law (CESL), which would set up a new EU-wide uniform regime, alternative to national contract laws.[25] Yet, even this more limited project failed, due to resistance by several member states and by consumer protection groups. Finally, at the end of 2014 the Commission decided to drop it, and focused its work on two directives on contracts related to the digital internal market, one on digital sales and the other on supply of digital content and services, which were finally approved in 2019.[26]

---

23 *Draft Common Frame of Reference* (DCFR), Outline Edition, prepared by the Study Group on a European Civil Code and the Research Group on EC Private, edited by C. von Bar, E. Clive, H. Schulte-Nölke, Munich, Sellier, 2009. For an assessment of the potential impact in practice of the DCFR see L. Antoniolli, F. Fiorentini (Eds.), *A Factual Assessment of the Draft Common Frame of Reference*, Munich, Sellier, 2011.

24 R. Zimmermann, N. Jansen, 'A European Civil Code in All but Name: Discussing the Nature and Purpose of the Draft Common Frame of Reference', *Cambridge Law Journal*, vol. 69, 2010, pp. 98-112. The DCFR was produced mainly by two working groups, the Study Group on a European Civil Code, and the Research Group on EC Private Law (also called Acquis Group), backed by some other flanking groups working on specific issues (general principles, economic effects, factual impact).

25 Proposal for a Regulation on a Common European Sales Law, COM/2011/0635 final. The regime would have been applicable both to B2B and B2C contracts, and it would have to be selected by the parties through an opt-in mechanism.

26 Dir. 2019/771 of 20 May 2019 on certain aspects concerning contracts for the sale of goods, *OJ L* 136, 22.5.2019, pp. 28-50; Dir. 2019/770 of 20 May 2019 on certain aspects concerning contracts for the supply of digital content and digital services, *OJ* L 136, 22.5.2019, pp. 1-27. See L. Antoniolli, 'From the Draft Common Frame of Reference to the Common European Sales Law: What has gone lost along the way? Some criticial remarks on the Future of European contract law', in A.I. Afonso, *Um direito Europeu des Obrigações? A influência do DCFR*, Porto, Universidade Catòlica Editora, 2015, p. 205.

This made the process come full circle: the effort to overcome legal fragmentation in EC/EU law, with its piecemeal solutions scattered in a plethora of directives and regulations, went all the way up from a comprehensive intervention in the area of contract law, to a full-fledged Civil Code;[27] it then came back to contract law, in particular sales, and was finally restricted to two more scattered and fragmented directives concerning digital contracts.

This leads us to an unavoidable question: why was this process so contorted and unsuccessful? At the end of the day, it seems that the growing complexity and diversification of rules in various sectors at the national and European level cannot be solved by a brand new comprehensive European Civil Code on the model of the national codifications of the 19th and 20th centuries. The idea of a European Civil Code is a path-dependent solution, resting on the implied conviction that, just as in the 19th century many European states proceeded with codification as soon as they were constituted as a nation, or experienced a major change in their fundamental political structure, this was the long-term destiny of the EU. Lurking in the background of the proposal for a European Civil Code was the idea that the European Union was heading towards a state-like structure, and therefore it needed a Civil Code both as a driver and a hallmark for this crucial shift.[28] Yet, this is a highly symbolic but old-fashioned solution, unsuited to the pluralist and multi-level structure of the EU, where the European level complements but does not pre-empt national laws[29] (as it is recognized by the EU motto "united in diversity"). It cannot cope with the increasing

---

27 It must be noted that, apart from the first Resolution of the European Parliament, no other European institution has ever employed the term "Code", a choice having a symbolic, politically sensitive and controversial nature. On the political significance of a European Civil Code see H. Collins, 'Editorial: The Future of European Private Law: An Introduction', *European Law Journal*, vol. 10, 2004, p. 649: "a European civil code will represent a statement of the political values that will govern the basic principles of social justice in the market economy. Such a statement of the ideals of a social market economy requires both democratic endorsement and regulatory legitimacy." (p. 650). See also M. Hesselink, *The Politics of a European Civil Code*, The Hague, Kluwer Law International, 2006.

28 The other symbolic move was the European Constitution, another term clearly referring to the idea of statehood, which never entered into force because of the failure in the ratification after the French and Dutch referenda rejected it in 2005. In fact, the Constitution was a Treaty (its formal title tellingly being Treaty establishing a Constitution for Europe), and its content did not correspond to the highly symbolic move, as it is clear by comparing the rules contained in the Constitution and the Lisbon Treaty: in spite of the radically different form, the content is virtually the same. See J. Ziller, *Il nuovo Trattato europeo*, Bologna, Il Mulino, 2007. Although the failure of the European Constitution was hardly perceived as a relevant event for private law harmonization, it did deeply affect the whole European integration process, marking an entrenchment of member states, and growing skepticism against further expansion of EU competences and powers, which also influenced the debate about the necessity and feasibility of a Civil Code. See H.-W. Micklitz, 'Failure or Ideological Preconcpetions – Thought on Two Grand Projects: The European Constitution and the European Civil Code', in K. Tuori, S. Sankari (Eds.), *The Many Constitutions of Europe*, Burlington (VT), Ashgate, 2010, pp. 109-142.

29 See e.g. C. Joerges, 'Rethinking European Law's Supremacy. A Plea for a Supranational Conflict of Laws', in B. Kohler-Koch, B. Rittberger (Eds.), *Debating the Democratic Legitimacy of the European Union*, Lanham, Rowman & Littlefield, 2007, pp. 311-327.

and diverse pressures on private law. Consequently, it is not surprising that the great expectations placed on the drafting of a Common Frame of Reference as a milestone towards European codification have led to disappointing results in terms of legislative achievements.

While the failure of the project of unifying European private law could be considered as a failure of the ambitions of comparative lawyers to influence the evolution of EU private law, we must broaden our analysis to another component of the community of comparativists working on European private law. In the other lineage of European private law, scholars were not aiming at constructing a uniform or harmonized law, but rather at providing comprehensive knowledge and critical analysis of the content, the similarities and dissimilarities of European private law, working both on national and EU law.

In the 1990's, a number of academic projects sharing this methodological approach developed, with a variety of focuses, aims and audiences. In these culture-oriented projects the focus of the research is not on the practical usefulness of the findings: the aim is not to spot similarities in order to allow meaningful legal harmonisation in the European context. In fact, differences are as relevant as similarities, because the only aim is to provide a realistic description of how law in action works.

A significant example of this kind of enterprise is the Common Core of European Private Law, a large project started in Trento in 1995 under the editorship of Ugo Mattei and Mauro Bussani, whose aim is to "map the law", i.e. to provide a reliable and detailed description of topics related to the three major partitions of private law (contract, tort and property law).[30] There are other projects focused on producing reliable materials on European private law based on a comparative approach, both for teaching and study, such as for instance the *Ius Commune casebooks series*, originally directed by Van Gerven,[31] and

30 The Common core of European private law project merged two paradigmatic comparative methodologies in its research: the factual approach of the common core project on formation of contracts, developed in the 1950s by Rudolph Schlesinger; and the theory of legal formants, developed by Rodolfo Sacco. See M. Bussani, U. Mattei, 'The Common Core Approach to European Private Law', *Columbia Journal of European Law*, vol. 3, 1997-1998, pp. 339-355; M. Bussani, U. Mattei (Eds.), *The Common Core of European Private Law*, The Hague, New York, Kluwer Law International, 2002. In 2019 the project celebrated its 25th anniversary, assessing its achievements and debating its future direction. According to Reimann (*op. cit.*, p. 247), while it has not reached to goal of a comprehensive map of European private law, a task that was unattainable in full, it has produced extensive sampling material.

31 See: http://www.casebooks.eu/welcome/ and https://www.bloomsburyprofessional.com/uk/series/ius-commune-casebooks-for-the-common-law-of-europe/ (last visited 21 February 2021). Among the volumes published are: H. Beale, B. Fauvarque-Cosson, J. Rutgers, S. Vogenauer, *Cases, Materials and Text on Contract Law*, 3rd ed., Oxford, Hart, 2019 (1st ed., 2002); J.H.H. van Erp, B. Akkermans, *Cases, Materials and Text on Property Law*, Oxford, Hart, 2012; W. van Gerven, J. Lever, P. Larouche, *Cases, Materials and Text on National, Supranational and International Tort Law*, Oxford, Hart, 2000.

the *Encylopedia of European private law.*[32] These works are complemented by an increasingly large number of academic journals focusing on European private law, such as the *Zeitschrift für Europäisches Privatrecht* (since 1993), the *European Review of Private Law* (also since 1993), the *Electronic Journal of Comparative Law* (since 1997), *Europa e diritto privato* (since 1998), the *Maastricht Journal for European and Comparative Law* (since 2000), the *European Review of Contract Law* (since 2005), the *Journal of European Tort Law* (since 2010), and the *European Property Law Journal* (since 2011).

Although it is difficult to assess the impact of all these knowledge-based projects, it seems that in the long run their most significant and enduring effect is the gradual formation of a large and growing network of lawyers (mainly scholars, but increasingly also practitioners) who share a knowledge that is made up of common issues, concepts, methods and styles. This is a work in progress, heavily influenced by European multi-linguism, which is both a blessing, because of its richness, and a curse, because of the immense problems of legal translation. Yet, an embryo of a new European culture is clearly developing, and this is particularly relevant for legal education and the training of new generations of lawyers.

Finally, in the result-oriented front of European comparative law a significant novelty has been the founding of the European Law Institute (ELI) in June 2011, an important independent powerhouse aiming "to improve the quality of European law, understood in the broadest sense", which seeks "to initiate, conduct and facilitate research, to make recommendations, and to provide practical guidance in the field of European legal development".[33] This is a crucial task, and a very sensitive one, because of the significant differences among the legal systems of the European States, the variety of scholarly traditions and policy-orientations, as well as linguistic pluralism.

ELI stresses the relevance of comparative law in its activities, and professes an open and comprehensive approach, "striving to bridge the oft-perceived gap between the different legal cultures, between public and private law, as well as between scholarship and practice (...) open to the use of different methodological approaches".[34] Although ELI has clearly

32 J. Basedow, K. Hopt, R. Zimmermann, Stier (Eds.), *The Max Planck Encyclopedia of European Private Law*, 2 vols., Oxford, Oxford University Press, 2012; C. Twigg-Flesner (Ed.), *The Cambridge Companion to European Union Private Law*, Cambridge, Cambridge University Press, 2010.

33 The tasks of the ELI are manifold: evaluation and stimulation of the development of EU law, legal policy, and practice; pan-European research, in particular on principles and rules which are common to the European legal systems; forum for discussion and cooperation of jurists (academics, judges, lawyers and other legal professionals) representing all legal traditions. See the ELI Manifesto: https://www.europeanlawinstitute.eu/about-eli/ (last visited 21 February 2021).

34 "Building on the wealth of diverse legal traditions, its mission is the quest for better law-making in Europe and the enhancement of European legal integration. By its endeavours, ELI seeks to contribute to the formation of a more vigorous European legal community, integrating the achievements of the various legal cultures, endorsing the value of comparative knowledge and taking a genuinely pan-European perspective.

managed to establish itself as an important player at the European level, yet it is hard to detect an underlying coherent vision of and approach to European law in the current agenda of the Institute, which seems to be shaped mainly by the urgency and relevance of specific items (technological developments, problems related to the rule of law and the protection of fundamental rights, etc.).[35]

4 European Private Law 2.0: The Evolution of EU Private Regulatory Law

While comprehensive models for harmonization of private law in Europe are currently in crisis, another form of European private law is gradually developing in different quarters: regulatory private law[36] is a new system, with a mixed character between private autonomy and public regulatory intervention,[37] covering important areas as consumer law, discrimination law, regulated services, unfair commercial practices, public procurements, competition, State aid, standardization, etc.[38] This law consists vertically of a series of bodies of sectoral rules (e.g. energy law, financial services, etc.) that are considered as self-sufficient, both from the point of view of law-making and law enforcement,[39] and tend to displace national regimes. Horizontally, it fosters harmonization of national rules through mechanisms such as mutual recognition, country of origin principle and maximum harmonization of selected aspects of general private law, which must be fitted into national legal systems, often generating frictions and inconsistencies.

As such its work covers all branches of the law: substantive and procedural; private and public.": https://www.europeanlawinstitute.eu/about-eli/ (last visited 21 February 2021).

35 ELI has currently completed twelve projects (ranging from international protection, to family law, ADR, insolvency, copyright, digital single market, sales law, etc.), and has currently eight projects in the pipeline. See https://www.europeanlawinstitute.eu/projects-publications/ (last visited 21 February 2021).

36 See H.-W. Micklitz, 'The Visible Hand of European Regulatory Private Law – The Transformation of European Private Law from Autonomy to Functionalism in Competition and Regulation', *Yearbook of European Law*, vol. 29, 2009, p. 3. See also K. Purhagen, K. Rott, T. Ackerman (Eds.), *Varieties of European Economic Law and Regulation – Liber Amicorum for Hans Micklitz*, Cham (CH), Springer, 2014.

37 See L. Antoniolli, 'The Future of European Private Law at the Crossrodads of Public and Private Law', in Unidroit (Ed.), *Eppur si muove: The Age of Uniform Law – Essays in honour of Michael Joachin Bonell to celebrate his 70th birthday*, Rome, Unidroit, 2016, pp. 481-500.

38 H. Micklitz, Y. Svetiev, G. Comparato, 'European Regulatory Private Law – The Paradigm Tested', *EUI Working Papers*, LAW 2014/04, p. 81: "the piecemeal and fragmentary intervention of EU law in the domain of private law has had unforeseen and unforeseeable ripple effects, producing various experiments of a hybrid nature in both dispute resolution mechanisms and procedures and in the embedding of private regime rule-making into alternative (in the sense of non-legislative) but still publicly-minded structures or processes."

39 For example, co-regulation and self-regulation are forms in which not only public, but also private entities can establish rules. Similarly, regulatory agencies and self-regulatory bodies also involve both public and private actors.

European private regulatory law transforms the traditional autonomy of private law, re-orienting it towards a functional relation to the internal market, based on a self-sufficient body of rules centered on the fundamental tenets of market freedoms and competition,[40] where private autonomy is heavily regulated. Protective mechanism for weaker parties (right to information, transparency, etc.), coupled with specific remedies (such as right of withdrawal, collective redress mechanisms and ADR[41]) are also instrumental to the functioning of the market.[42]

This type of law often operates through a variety of instruments (like co-regulation, standard-setting, benchmarking, etc.),[43] often sector-specific, moving along a continuum between uniformity and flexibility, allowing variable degrees of deviation in the national systems. The features and effects of these new modes of governance[44] have to be compared and assessed against the benchmark of the Community method, which defines the traditional law-making procedure balancing the role of the EU institutions and the member states. Their different rule-making, implementation and control, and the different actors and procedures involved, often cause friction with the EU instruments,[45] and change the forms of accountability and control, deepening the technocratic features of the European Union.[46] This in its turn affects the relationship with national private laws, whose general structure is deeply transformed by the insertion of these new instruments, concepts and rules.

The phenomenon of private regulatory law is not only gradually changing some of the fundamental features of European private law, but of the very paradigm of law in the

40 See Micklitz, 2009.

41 Both collective redress and ADR tend to move away from traditional judicial enforcement, towards administrative and private enforcement.

42 This body of law is underpinned by a peculiar notion of justice, defined by Micklitz as "access justice", which does not aim at social protection through redistributive mechanisms (the traditional notion of distributive justice of national legal systems), but rather guarantees the right to access to goods and services, and the right to protection against discrimination, a hybrid combination between distributive justice and libertarian allocative justice. See H.-W. Micklitz (Ed.), *The Many Concepts of Social Justice in European Private Law*, Cheltenham, Northampton (Mass.), Elgar, 2011.

43 J. Scott, D. Trubek, 'Mind the Gap: Law and New Approaches to Governance in the European Union', *European Law Journal*, vol. 8, 2002, pp. 1-18.

44 European Commission, European Governance: A White Paper, 25 July 2001, COM (2001) 428 fin.: "The Union must renew the Community method by following a less top-down approach and complementing the EU's policy tools more effectively with non-legislative instruments" (p. 4). Nevertheless, the Commission points out that these instruments "must not dilute the achievement of common objectives or the political responsibility of the Institutions", and "should not be used when legislative action under the Community method is possible" (p. 22).

45 This friction can be expressed in binary terms: hierarchy v. network, hard law v. soft law, public institutions v. private actors, judicial review v. accountability, rules v. standards.

46 New forms of governance are essentially related to procedural controls, such as transparency, participation and accountability. See F. Cafaggi, H. Muir-Watt (Eds.), *The Regulatory Function of European Private Law*, Cheltenham, Northampton (Mass.), Elgar, 2009; F. Cafaggi (Ed.), *The institutional framework of European private law*, Oxford, Oxford University Press, 2006.

European integration process, enshrined in the formula "integration through law".[47] Law was originally envisaged as a powerful instrument to achieve legal harmonization in Europe, but was considered as a merely technical tool; political choices were not fully spelled out, and were left in the background, because it was considered that they belonged to the national level. Yet, the dramatic development of EU law in general, and of private regulatory law in particular, requires the re-instatement of the missing link between law and political choices in the European Union, re-embedding law in the European social fabric.[48] Law, also private law, embodies the fundamental set of values and principles that govern any society, also transnational ones, and cannot be considered as a mere a technocratic instrument of governance.[49]

5 The Role of Law of Comparative Law in the Next Stage of European Private Law: Which Way Forward?

The growing but fragmented developments in the area of European private law at the cross-road of national and EU regulatory private law point to the need for new analytical instruments, categories and concepts, which must take into consideration the link with national laws, but at the same time must be able to grasp the specificities of the transnational context in which EU law is placed and evolves. Moreover, legal analysis must openly acknowledged and discuss the political stakes and choices that are at the basis of this system of European private law.[50] Consequently, these new tasks of comparative law in relation to European law must be set in the wider context of the phenomenon of globalization, and its link with transnational law and legal pluralism.[51]

---

47 See the path-breaking work of the "Integration through law project", developed at the European University Institute of Florence under the direction of Mauro Cappelletti. See M. Cappelletti, M. Seccombe, J. Weiler (Eds.), 1986.

48 K. Polanyi, *The Great Transformation*, New York, Farrar and Rinehart, 1944. See also C. Joerges, J. Falke (eds.), *Karl Polanyi and the Potential of Law in Transnational Markets*, Oxford, Portland (OR), Hart, 2011.

49 According to Scott, Trubek, 2002, the instruments of new governance can be a smokescreen for a lack of a vision about the aims of the integration process that characterizes the European Union today: "EU law has emerged as instrumental to a degree that goes beyond the specific objectives pursued by particular norms. It has been instrumental in promoting the transformation of Europe from international, to supranational, or even constitutional, order. Thus the premises underpinning EU law have a symbolic value, and their "tainting" with the values of new governance might be seen to threaten not merely the integrity of "law" as such, but the broader dynamics of integration" (p. 9).

50 On the political stakes hiding behind the apparent neutrality of private law see D. Kennedy, 'The Political Stakes of "Merely" Technical Issues of Contract Law', *European Review of Private Law*, 1, 2001, p. 7; Reimann, *op. cit.*, considers that "taking responsibility" is one the main challenges for comparative law (p. 267).

51 For a comprehensive discussion of the meaning of private law, privatization and globalization in a historical and comparative dimension see R. Michaels, N. Jansen, 'Private Law beyond the State? Europeanization, Globalization, Privatization', *American Journal of Comparative Law*, vol. 54, 2006, p. 843, according to whom it is "clear that private law requires rethinking, especially with regard to its connection to the state"

Globalization[52] is characterized by the compression of time and space, which enlarges the scope of legal (as well as economic, social, etc.) interactions, increasing their speed. State law is no longer fully able to control and discipline these transnational phenomena, and this gap is filled by a plurality of actors producing a variety of norms, which are often not of a strictly legal nature.[53] Consequently, the link between law and the State is no longer absolute:[54] law is increasingly produced and applied outside the State, either by international organisations (as the EU) or by private entities. Also, rules that have legal effects are created outside traditional legal mechanisms,[55] making it difficult to draw sharp dividing lines between legal norms and other social norms.

Globalization is linked to the growth of transnational law,[56] a concept that, although lacking a clear-cut definition (the boundaries between transnational, international and supranational law are not water-tight), refers to all legal phenomena that cannot be comprehensively grasped by applying national legal categories.[57] Transnational law is therefore characterized by legal pluralism,[58] which covers legal sources,[59] as well as enforcement mechanisms.[60] This does not mean that traditional national law disappears,

(p. 873). See also N. Jansen, R. Michaels (Eds.), *Beyond the State - Rethinking Private Law*, Tuebingen, Mohr Siebeck, 2008; C. Joerges, 'The Challenges of Europeanisation in the European Private Law', *Duke Journal of Comparative and International Law*, vol. 24, 2005, p. 149.

52 See S. Cassese, 'The Globalization of Law', 37 *New York University Journal of International Law & Politics*, vol. 37, 2005, p. 973.

53 A.-M. Slaughter, *A New World Order*, Princeton, Princeton University Press, 2004; M. Delmas-Marty, *Les forces imaginantes du droit - Le relatif et l'universel*, Paris, Seuil, 2004.

54 This change is clear in the extensive use of the term "governance", which implies a move away from regulation by the State through traditional legal means. See B. van Vooren, S. Blockmans, J. Wouters (Eds.), *The EU's Role in Global Governance - The Legal Dimension*, Oxford, Oxford University Press, 2013.

55 T. Hale, D. Held, *Handbook of Transnational Governance: Institutions and Innovations*, Cambridge, Malden (Mass.), Polity Press, 2011; F. Cafaggi, 'New foundations of transnational private regulation', *Journal of Law & Society*, vol. 38, 2011, p. 1; D. Wielsch, 'Global law's toolbox: private regulation by standards', *American Journal of Comparative Law*, vol. 60, 2012, p. 1075.

56 The term was coined in the 1950s by Jessup in relation to complex legal situations in which governments, international organisations and private parties are involved, requiring analytical tools that combine instruments from various fields of law (public international law, conflict of laws, private law, procedural law, etc.): P.C. Jessup, *Transnational Law*, New Haven, Yale University Press, 1956. See also P. Glenn, 'A transnational concept of law', in P. Cane, M.V. Tushnet (eds), *The Oxford Handbook of Legal Studies*, Oxford, Oxford University Press, 2003, p. 839

57 See M. Reimann, J. Hathaway, T. Dickinson, J. Samuels, *Transnational Law*, St. Paul (MI), West, 2013. See also the special issue of the *Revue Internationale de Droit Economique* devoted to "Les grandes théories du droit transnational", 2013/1.

58 P. Berman, 'Global Legal Pluralism', *Southern California Law Review*, vol. 80, 2007, p. 1155; J. Griffiths, 'What is Legal Pluralism', *Journal of Legal Pluralism*, vol. 24, 1986, p. 1. In many works, legal pluralism is not only a descriptive device, but a normative concept, which implies the recognition of global legal pluralism as a value to be protected, rather than merely managed.

59 This phenomenon is analysed also under the category of "policentricity": see e.g. H. Petersen, H. Zahle (eds.), *Legal Policentricity: Consequences of Pluralism in Law*, Aldershot, Ashgate, 1995.

60 Transnational law has a relational character, implying acceptance of diversity within a legal space, where rules and institutions regulate the co-existence of the different systems.

but it is challenged in its very foundational elements, i.e. exclusive sovereignty within the national boundaries, and organisation of law according to a hierarchical system.[61] In such a framework, the need for new mechanisms for coordinating and solving conflicts among different systems is crucial.[62]

Other useful analytical categories for this complex and changing legal landscape are those of legal hybrid[63] and hybridization, which focus on the (respectively static and dynamic) features of change, rather than on the definition of borders between legal fields and concepts. This is relevant for transnational law, which is a law that does not fit completely either in national or international law, and EU law can be considered one of the most important and challenging instances of this kind of law.

The same approach is shared also by the concept of "interlegality", which focuses on the overlap, interpenetration and dialogue of legal rules and institutions,[64] implying legal pluralism,[65] where interaction is not merely a normative stance, but an intrinsic feature of law.[66]

61 R. Michaels, 'The re-state-ment of non-state law: the state, choice of law, and the challenge from global legal pluralism', *Wayne Law Review*, vol. 51, 2005, 1209; H. Dedek, S. Van Praagh (Eds.), *Stateless Law. Evolving Boundaries of a Discipline*, Aldershot, Ashgate, 2015.

62 Reimann, *op. cit.*, considers that one of the main challenges for comparative law is to enable to understand, analyse and solve the interplay and friction between national, international and transnational law (pp. 21, 181-182). In the area of EU law, such a model has been proposed by Christian Joerges in his conflicts-law theory, which aims at co-ordinating EU and national laws by constructing EU law as a tool compensating for the failings of national laws (which are due to the gradual erosion of national competences due to the Europeanisation and globalisation process): see C. Joerges, 'Reconfiguring the Politics-Law Relationship in the Integration Project through Conflicts-Law Constitutionalism', *European Law Journal*, vol. 18, 2012, 644; Id., 'Unity in Diversity as Europe's Vocation and Conflicts Law as Europe's Constitutional Form', LEQS Working Papers, 28/2010.

63 K. Tuori, "Transnational law: On legal hybrids and legal perspectivism", in M. Maduro, K. Tuori, S. Sankari (Eds.), *Transnational Law - Rethinking European Legal Thinking*, Cambridge, Cambridge University Press, 2014, pp. 11-57.

64 See B. de Sousa Santos, *Toward a New Legal Common Sense*, London, Butterworths, 2002: "we live in a time of porous legality or of legal porosity, multiple networks of legal orders forcing us to constant transitions and trespassing. Our legal life is constituted by an intersection of different legal orders, that is by interlegality":

65 See P.S. Berman, *Global Legal Pluralism: A Jurisprudence of Law beyond Borders*, Cambridge, Cambridge University Press, 2014; M. Graziadei, 'The many voices of the law in a globalized world - Legal monism, legal pluralism, and the new tasks of comparative law', *Annuario di diritto comparato e di studi legislativi*, vol. 6, 2015, p. 485.

66 "Instead of the either/or logic of dichotomisation, characteristic of radical pluralism, interlegality rather follows a both/and approach": K. Tuori, 2014, p. 41. From a normative point of view, this implies a substantial effort in order to devise new solutions that move beyond a merely confrontational and conflicting logic, and search for compatibility and adjustment: "our late-modern, denationalised legal landscape displays not only signs of fragmentation and disputes of authority, but also counter-tendencies of consensus-oriented dialogue, overlapping and interpenetration", K. Tuori, 2014, p. 49.

Globalization and transnational law are an unavoidable challenge for comparativists,[67] and they pose both opportunities and risks: the risk that by leaving old frames and instruments behind, a cacophony of concepts and ideas will ensue that will hinder the building of a new vision and system of law.[68] On the other hand, there is an opportunity to work in synergy among comparativists, experts of EU law and international law, students of globalization, as well as with other social scientists, in order to frame a new paradigm for law, leaving behind the binary conception of law as either national or international, private or public, and develop taxonomies that are suited to the new features and developments of law.[69]

For comparative lawyers working in the area of European private law, these developments open up important and promising areas of research, both theoretically and practically. Particularly from a theoretical point of view, there is an urgent need to develop research on the essential features of European private law, and its links with national private laws and various forms of transnational and global law. This implies the need to critically scrutinize existing legal concepts and categories, and develop a new analytical framework suited to this new context,[70] which accounts also for its legal process features, focusing on the actors involved, and the methods and procedures applied.[71]

67 D. Gerber, 'Globalization and Legal Knowledge: Implications for Comparative Law', *Tulane Law Review*, vol. 75, 2001, p. 949; H. Muir-Watt, 'Globalization and Comparative Law', in M. Reimann, R. Zimmermann (Eds.), *The Oxford Handbook of Comparative Law*, 2nd ed., Oxford, Oxford University Press, 2019, pp. 599-623; M. Reimann, 'Beyond National Legal Systems: A Comparative Law for the International Age', *Tulane Law Review*, vol. 75, 2001, pp. 1103-1119; G. Teubner (Ed.), *Global Law without a State*, Brookfield, Dartmouth, 1997; W. Twining, 'Globalization and Comparative Law', *Maastricht Journal European Comparative Law*, vol. 6, 1999, 217 (reprinted in W. Twining, *Globalization and Legal Theory*, London, 2000, p. 174).

68 In the 21st century comparative law has greatly expanded its scope both in geographical, substantial and methodological terms, but it has not been able to develop a coherent and scientific status, and risks being lost in heterogeneity and complexity, a veritable "identity crisis". According to Reimann, *op. cit.*, the most recent developments have been a welcome departure from an outdated vision of comparative law, often Western-centric and positivistic, "letting a thousand flowers bloom" (p. 253). Yet, he recognizes that the growing heterogeneity of the discipline has led to excessive specialization and lack of communication, which implies a loss of coherence, and goes as far as stating that it is "pointless to speak of comparative law as an identifiable discipline at all" (p. 270).

69 For an innovative and historically conscious comparative analysis providing new models and categories see P. Glenn, *On Common Laws*, Oxford, Oxford University Press, 2007; Id., 'Transnational legal thought – Plato, Europe and beyond', in M. Maduro, K. Tuori, S. Sankari (Eds.), *Transnational Law - Rethinking European Law and Legal Thinking*, Cambridge University Press, 2014, p. 61.

70 K. Tuori, 2014, p. 55 considers that "Probably "transnational law", "legal pluralism", "interlegality", "legal perspectivism" and, perhaps, "legal hybrid" will belong to the lexis of the new legal Esperanto".

71 For a criticism of the focus on formal rules and systematisation, and the lack of analysis of the relevance of the context and the actors involved, see L. Niglia, 'Europe's Private Law and the Poverty of Orthodoxy', *American Journal of Comparative Law*, vol. 54, 2006, p. 401.

This awareness of the need for a new theoretical legal framework[72] is shared by a growing number of comparativists that consider the role of today's comparative law as that of being a "subversive" discipline, i.e. to be a vehicle for critical assessment of existing concepts, taxonomies and methods, and to point to new directions for the study of law and its relations with other disciplines.[73]

European private law is an ideal testing ground for this new tasks of comparative law: it is highly developed, data and sources are widely accessible, researchers are numerous and highly skilled, stakes (political, social, economic, cultural) are high, room for interdisciplinary research and innovation is wide. This is an opportunity that should not be missed by the community of comparativists.

In his inaugural lecture at Maastricht University on 25th September 1998, Sjef van Erp discussed the dilemmas and choices facing comparative law in the development European private law,[74] and concluded that comparative law has a very important role to play, if it manages to be "adequate comparative law", meaning that comparativists must strive to strike a balance between ideal and reality, and work pragmatically towards a bridge between theory and practice. Sjef has worked for decades for this, together with his colleagues and students. It will be a honour and a pleasure to keep on collaborating with him in this direction also in the future.

---

72 In the words of Micklitz "we are in search of a new theory, a new model, a new toolbox (...). What is needed is a holistic theoretical framework", which requires a fundamental renewal of legal concepts: "Now as before, concepts constitute an integral and indispensable element of our legal *Vorverstaendnis*. But we should accentuate their *heuristic* function. Concepts are necessary for identifying, defining and organising legal issues. But their mutual relations should be seen in terms of clusters and networks rather than as amounting to conceptual pyramids or trees" (p. 304).

73 G. Frankenberg, *Comparative Law as Critique*, Cheltenham, Elgar, 2016; G. Frankenberg, 'Critical Comparisons: Re-thinking Comparative Law', *Harvard International Law Journal*, vol. 26, 1985, pp. 411-455; H. Muir Watt, 'La fonction subversive du droit compare', *Revue International Droit Comparé*, vol. 52, 2000, pp. 503-527.

74 J.H.M. van Erp, 'European Private Law: Postmodern Dilemmas and Choices – Towards a Method of Adequate Comparative Legal Analysis', *Electronic Journal of Comparative Law*, vol. 3, 1999 (https://www.ejcl.org/31/abs31-1.html): "For me, comparative-law method is above all a source of inspiration and creativity, especially when it is employed in the development of a European private law as the object of jurisprudential research".

The Common Patterns of Property Law: A Principled Perspective on the Reform of Belgian Property Law

Vincent Sagaert[*]

1 The Principled Contribution of Sjef van Erp to Comparative and European Property Law

My distinguished colleague and good friend Sjef van Erp is, without any doubt, one of the founders of scientific research in comparative and European property law. He is, in my perspective, with the late André van der Walt (University of Stellenbosch), the founding father of legal research in that area. Being Chairholder on property law at the University of Maastricht, he paved the way to explore and construct the wild and, certainly in the beginning, impenetrable, jungle of European and comparative property law. We can undoubtedly state that Sjef van Erp did not only pave the way through the trees, but he planted the trees himself in order to insure a more rational exploration. We refer, among many other groundbreaking publications, to the Casebook on Property Law, which he co-edited and which gave me the honour to collaborate with him very closely.[1] More than being influential on the level of publications, Sjef van Erp has also been inspiring a whole generation of young to middle-aged property lawyers. He organized conferences and there was no conference on European or comparative property law which he did not organize or which he did not contribute actively to. In that sense, Sjef van Erp is one of the main fathers of the following generation of property law across legal borders.

Along the different research lines which Sjef van Erp analyzed, he always respected the mainstream of a principled comparative approach. We will take as guideline for this article his Walter van Gerven Lecture, which prominently reflects such principled approach.[2] In this article he describes *inter alia* the common patterns of property law across European legal systems. Such approach should serve as legal ground for a bottom-up approach in

---

* Full Professor Property Law, University of Leuven, Belgium.

1 S. van Erp en B. Akkermans (ed.), *Cases, Materials and Text on Property Law*, London, Hart Publishing, 2012, 1256 p.

2 S. van Erp, *European and National Property Law: Osmosis or Growing Antagonism?*, European Law Publishing, Groningen, 2006, 34 p.

elaborating the edifice of a European property law system. Before operating a litmus test of the Belgian property law reform against the common features detected in that article, we will first give a short background of the reform.

2 A Short Background of the Reform of Property Law in Belgium: a Farewell to Napoleon?

The reform of Belgian property law was the result of a period of reflection and political initiatives, beginning about a decade ago. Such reformative ideas have also been present in other national legal systems, favouring a reform of the national system instead of stepping into a European Civil code. Of utmost importance for Belgian law was the substantive reform of private law in French law. The bicentenary of the French Civil Code gave indeed rise, in French law, to a number of substantive reforms,[3] such as the reform of security rights,[4] the reform of succession law,[5] the introduction of a fiducie as a trust-like device in the Civil Code[6] and, in a second stage, the reform of the law of obligations.[7] With regard to property law, the *Association Henri Capitant* took the initiative to elaborate a draft Statute for the reform of property law in French law, which however failed to be approved on a political level.[8]

In the aftermath of the substantive reform movement in French law – a Belgian proverb states that when it rains in Paris, it begins to ooze in Brussels – two major developments in the resurrection of Belgian property law were taken: (1) a first reform initiative in 2011, limited to property security rights on movables, which resulted in the Act of 11 July 2013[9] and (2) a second more comprehensive reform was initiated in 2016, encompassing all general rules with regard to property law, which resulted in the Act of 4 February 2020.[10] As it will emerge, the comparative approach, as promulgated by Sjef van Erp, has played an important role in both these statutory reforms (cf. infra, n°. 9).

3 For an overview of the different reforms and their inspirations: *La réforme du droit privé en France* (ed. V. Sagaert), Brussels, Larcier, 2008, 182 p.

4 French Ordonnance n° 2006-346 of 23 March 2006, official Journal 24 March 2006.

5 Act n° 2006-728 of 23 June 2006 with regard to the reform of succession law and the law of gifts, *Official Journal* 24 June 2006.

6 Act n°. n° 2007-211 of 19 February 2007, introducing the fiducie, *Official Journal* 21 February 2007.

7 Ordonnance n° 2016-131 of 10 February 2016 with regard to the reform of contract law, general law of obligations and evidence law, Official Journal 11 February 2016.

8 Cf. https://www.henricapitant.org/avant-projet-de-reforme-du-droit-des-biens?page=1.

9 *Belgian Official Gazette* 2 August 2013.

10 *Belgian Official Gazette* 17 March 2020.

2.1 The Reform of Property Security Rights in 2013

In 2011, the Belgian Minister of Justice launched a first preliminary stage in the reconstruction of Belgian property law by initiating an expert committee on the reform of the law of property security rights on movables. The initiative had to be seen against the background of the aftermath of the credit crisis and the ensuing credit crunch.

This expert committee, composed of both academics and legal practitioners and presided by Professor Eric Dirix (University of Leuven), was largely inspired by the French reform of property security rights in 2006, introducing a pledge without dispossession which can be registered in an electronic pledge register. The Act of 11 July 2013 approved a reform of property security rights on movables.[11] With this new Act the old provisions regarding pledge in the Civil Code (articles 2071-2091) are replaced by the new "Act on Pledges". The new Act contains a full and far-reaching modernization of the statutory framework regarding security rights on movables including the retention of ownership and the legal lien ('*retentierecht/droit de rétention*'). It takes distance of the requirement of dispossession as means of perfection of a pledge right and introduces the registered pledge in Belgian law. The new Act was introduced in the Civil Code, but with a separate numeration, instead of the former articles 2071 *et seq*. However, due to technical (ICT-)problems of implementation of the register, it took until 1 January 2018 before the Act entered into force.

Apart from introducing the pledge register, the reform also aims to simplify the rules on pledge and to make them coherent. A functional approach, inspired by several legal reforms in Europe but all going back to article 9 of the Uniform Commercial Code, prevails. It is grounded in a rational and integrated approach of security rights aiming to grant identical legal effects to security rights regardless of their conceptual differences.[12]

2.2 The Comprehensive Reform of Belgian Property Law in 2020

The reform of the law on movable property security rights was a preliminary step, directly related to the financial crisis, towards a more global reform. In 2014 a new Minister of Justice was appointed, Koen Geens, who has established a career as an esteemed law

---

11 Act on Property Security rights on moveables, *Belgian Official Gazette* 2 August 2013.The Act is completed by another Act which only encompasses procedural issues (which must be approved in both chambers of parliament). This other Act dates from 24 June 2013 and was also published on 2 August 2013 in the Belgian Official Gazette.

12 See on the reform: E. Dirix and V. Sagaert, "The New Belgian Act on security rights in movable property", European Property Law Journal 2014, 321-355. In French: J. Cataruzza, "Les grands axes de la réforme des sûretés mobilières", Bank Fin.R. 2013, 183-194; W. Derijcke, "La réforme des sûretés réelles mobilières", Revue de Droit Commercial Belge 2013, 691-722; F. Georges, "La réforme des sûretés mobilières", Rev. dr. ULg 2013, 319-368.

professor in company law. He initiated in 2016 a much more ambitious project of reform for several quintessential chapters of Belgian civil law. The project was framed in a policy paper, authored by the Minister of Justice and entitled "*Jump towards the law of tomorrow: re-codification of the foundational statutes*", and approved by the Belgian government on 20 July 2017.[13] This policy paper provides for the foundations of the reform of the basic statutes, not only in civil law but also in commercial law, criminal law and company law.

With regard to civil law, five expert committees – on (1) the law of evidence, (2) property law, (3) general law of obligations, (4) tort law and (5) loan agreements – were established in order to elaborate drafts, which did not start from, or operate within, the framework of the existing texts of the Napoleontic Civil Code, but which started from scratch.[14] With regard to property law, professor Pascale Lecocq[15] and the undersigned author have been appointed as experts in 2016. After having elaborated a first draft, we have submitted it to public consultation in order to enhance the support base and to receive input on the technical and policy dimension of the draft (December 2017 – February 2018).

The statute of 13 April 2019 not only approves the new law on evidence, but also the structure and skeleton of a new Civil Code, consisting of nine books.[16] Each book will be separately numbered, restarting in article 1.

- Book I: General Part (which considers general concepts and principles)
- Book II: Person and Family Law
- Book III: Property Law
- Book IV: Succession Law, Donations and Wills
- Book V: Law of Obligations
- Book VI: Contract Law
- Book VII: Law on Security Rights
- Book VIII: Law of Evidence
- Book IX: Prescription

The new Civil Code has entered into force on 1 November 2020. It entered into force as mere skeleton, which only got body for the rules on evidence in Book VIII.

Property law was the second field of law which was taken on a political level. The Belgian legislator (unanimously) adopted the Act introducing the new Book 3 on Property

13 The paper which is the foundation for the several reform projects provides for the underlying rationale of the reform and is online at https://www.koengeens.be/policy/hercodificatie .

14 Two academics – one from the Flemish-speaking side and one from the French-speaking side – preside and coordinate the several working groups: Eric Dirix and Patrick Wery.

15 Full Professor at the University of Liège.

16 Article 2 of the Act of 13 April 2019 introducing a new Civil Code and a Book 8 "Evidence" in that Code, Belgian Official Gazette 14 May 2019.

Law on the 4th February 2020.[17] This Statute abolishes the book on Property Law in the Napoleontic Civil Code and some ancillary statutes and introduces nothing less than a new comprehensive system on property law. The ambition was fourfold: (1) integration of property law, (2) instrumentalization of property law, (3) modernization of property law and (4) fleixibilization of property law.[18] It is important that the current property law provisions almost all dated from 1804 and have not been amended ever since, so they were construed on the basis of a radically different society than the one 2020 brings us.

The Act introduces 188 statutory provisions[19] and an explanatory memorandum of 450 pages, numbered from article 3.1 to article 3.188, which can be found online on the website of the Belgian Parliament.[20] It will automatically enter into force on 1 September 2021. The 'transition period' of 18 months is being used for the education of legal practitioners, making them familiar with the new legal regime.

The new Book on Property law consists in itself of eight chapters:

- Title 1: General chapter
- Title 2: Goods
- Title 3: Ownership
- Title 4: Co-ownership
- Title 5: Neighbourhood relations
- Title 6: Usufruct
- Title 7: Long lease ('*emphyteusis*')[21]
- Title 8: Building right ('*superficies*')[22]

This structure might, at first sight, seem very classic but in fact contributes to the ambition of integration pursued by the Drafters of the project. Title 5 thus integrates, with Dutch law as main source of inspiration, legal devices which functionally focus on neighbourhood relations: nuisance law, common enclosures and (conventional and legal) servitudes. Moreover, title 1 serves as an umbrella chapter, which we will set out under heading IV (cf. infra, n°. 12 *et seq.*).

---

17 Act of 4 February 2020 introducing a new Book 3 in the Civil Code, Belgian Official Gazette 17 March 2020. For a more comprehensive analysis of the reform: see P. Lecocq, I. Durant, N. Bernard, B. Michaux, J.F. Romain and V. Sagaert (ed.), *Le nouveau droit des biens*, Brussels, Larcier, 2020, 446 p.; V. Sagaert, J. Baeck, N. Carette, P. Lecocq, M. Muylle and A. Wylleman (ed.), *Het nieuwe goederenrecht*, Antwerp, Intersentia, 507 p. ; V. Sagaert, "De hervorming van het goederenrecht", Tijdschrift voor Privaatrecht 2020, 389-654.

18 Explanatory Memorandum, www.dekamer.be, 2019-20, n°. 173/1, p. 5-9.

19 These are numbered from article 3.1 until article 3.188 of the (new) Civil Code.

20 The explanatory memorandum and all other acts which were produces during the parliamentary preparation of the Act can be found in French and in Dutch on https://www.dekamer.be/kvvcr/showpage.cfm?section=/flwb&language=fr&cfm=/site/wwwcfm/flwb/flwbn.cfm?lang=N&legislat=55&dossierID=0173 .

21 In Dutch: *Erfpacht*, in French: *Emphytéose*

22 In Dutch: *Opstal*, in French: *Superficie*

3 The Role of Comparative Law in the Reform of Belgian Property Law

Property law is generally thought as Cinderella of comparative European private law, the field of private law in which comparative and cross-border dimensions are relatively scarce. However, the cross-border mobility of goods has tremendously increased over the last decades. Therefore, it is important to bridge the differences between national legal systems that share trade.

With regard to property security rights, the convergence between national legal systems is important for the freedom of capital within the internal European market. An important innovation underlying the Pledge Act of 11 July 2013 was therefore that it brings Belgian law in line with the international developments regarding the right of secured transactions. There have been, in a comparative perspective, a number of legislative amendments during the last decade in the field of property security rights, which share – in spite of obvious differences – the same features ('*truncus communis*'). This Act also embodies these features and aims to refine them. Thus, the new Act is to a large extent inspired by comparative analysis of *e.g.* Art. 9 Uniform Commercial Code. The drafters also looked at Book IX of the Draft Common Frame of Reference (DCFR, Book IX),[23] the French reform[24] and UNCITRAL Legislative Guide on Secured Transactions.[25] The ambition of the Belgian Act was nothing less than to contribute to a harmonization of the matter.[26]

Also the expert committee on the comprehensive reform of property law elaborated a text for a new property law on the basis of a genuine comparative legal method. The drafters have taken as main source of inspiration three legal systems with recent (draft) acts on property law with a divergent dynamic: Dutch Civil Code, the French system (including the Draft Project Henri Capitant) and the Civil Code of Québec. This comparative research thus covers one fairly recent Western-European Civil Code with German influences (the Netherlands), one traditional and influential legal system with a pure Romanistic perspective (France) and one mixed legal system with a more recent civil code and common law impact (Québec). The comparative perspective was therefore broader than just French law, thereby taking into account that the influence of the French Code in the modern legislative processes all around Europe (especially in the Eastern-European countries) has been in decline. The Draftsmen looked more occasionally into German, Swiss and Spanish law.

23 See, Principles, Definitions and Model Rules of European Private Law Draft Common Frame of Reference (DCFR) Outline Edition (eds. C. von Bar and others), Sellier, 2009, VI volumes.

24 Ordonnance of 23 March 2006 introducing a Book IV in the French Civil Code.

25 http://www.uncitral.org/pdf/english/texts/security-lg/e/09-82670_Ebook-Guide_09-04-10English.pdf.

26 Explanatory Report, *Parl.Doc.* Chamber of representatives, 2012-13, 53-2463-64/001, 9-11 (www.fed-parl.be).

The Explanatory Memorandum reflects this large attention for comparative law: it mentions, prior to the official comments for each provision, the equivalent (similar or opposite) rule from the relevant national legal systems, and the commentaries often mention foreign inspiration on the substance of the provision. The role of legal comparison has thus been pre-dominant.[27]

4 Importance of the Leading Principles of Property Law in the New Belgian Property Law

Time has come, after this introduction, to connect the common features of European property law with the re-codifications in Belgian property law. Sjef van Erp himself makes the distinction in his van Gerven Lecture between leading principles, ground rules and technical rules.[28] We will focus in this article on the former two, leaving the technical rules outside the scope of this article. Leading principles are "*the filters through which a legal relationship must pass before it can be characterized as a property right*". Ground rules "*describe the consequences of a right after it has been established that it has the character of a property right*". What has been the role of the leading principles and ground rules in this codification?

It emerges from the structure of the new property law Act of 4 February 2020 that the common features – both leading principles and ground rules – of property law have had a major role to play in the establishment and elaboration of a new Belgian property law. The first chapter of the new Act, titled "General chapter" and encompassing 37 provisions, serves as an umbrella chapter, covering general features of property law and applying (save for exceptions) to all property rights. Several provisions deal with the enforceability of property rights, such as the priority principle in case of conflict between property rights ('*prior tempore potior iure*') (art. 3.4),[29] the protection against insolvency (art. 3.5) and the power to dispose of property rights (art. 3.6). Other provisions of the general chapter deal with general features of the object of property right: the principle of specificity and unity of the object of property rights (art. 3.8), the rule '*accessorium sequitur principale*' (art. 3.9), the tracing of the object of property rights (real subrogation (art. 3.10)), the effects of the transformation (art. 3.11) and commingling (art. 3.12) of the object of property rights. General rules with regard to the acquisition (art. 3.14) and the termination (art. 3.15-16) of property rights give an overview of the common manner of acquisition and extinction, but are further completed by specific grounds for acquisition and termination in specific

27 Explanatory Memorandum, p. 8-9.

28 S. Van Erp, *European and National Property Law: Osmosis or Growining Antagonism?*, p. 14.

29 The legislator makes a reservation for the good faith of third parties.

property rights. Moreover, the Act contains in this general chapter also provisions with regard to the publicity of property rights. Possession is described as a means of publicity for movables, and in the same development the rules for acquisitive prescription, based on a lawful possession, are inserted in the general chapter (art. 3.18-3.29). Moreover, the general rules on registration of immovables are inserted in this general chapter (art. 3.30-34). Finally, the general chapter contains rules with regard to the unity and indivisibility of the patrimony (art. 3.35-3.37).

The two leading principles on the bone of property law, as described by Sjef van Erp, are (1) the *numerus clausus* principle and (2) the principle of transparency.[30] We will analyze these subsequently below.

4.1 The Closed System of Property Rights

One of the major issues in creating a new property law system is to determine the level of party autonomy which will be allowed and, thus, to take position in the question of standardization of property rights. To phrase it otherwise, the Belgian legislator had to opt between a *numerus clausus* or a full party autonomy, and all shades of grey in between those two. Van Erp sets the scene in the said van Gerven Lecture:

> Legal systems are careful not to accept property rights too easily and therefore limit their number and content. In some legal systems this limitation is stronger than in others, but it can be found in both common as well as civil law, although it has been more theoretically developed in civil law systems.[31]

This was the first, and most fundamental policy choice which had to be taken by the expert committee. It determines the scope, internal structure and external demarcation of property law. Opposing forces meet at a crosspoint in Belgian law with regard to the topic of the closed system of property law.

The traditional starting point of the narrative of Belgian property law is that the freedom of contract of the parties is seriously curtailed by its most fundamental feature, i.e. the numerus clausus principle.[32] This principle states that the number and substance of types

30 S. Van Erp, *European and National Property Law: Osmosis or Growining Antagonism?*, p. 15.

31 S. Van Erp, *European and National Property Law: Osmosis or Growining Antagonism?*, p. 15.

32 For an in depth analysis, *see* V. Sagaert, "Het goederenrecht als open systeem van verbintenissen? Poging tot een nieuwe kwalificatie van de vermogensrechten", *Tijdschrift voor Privaatrecht* 2005, 983-1086. See also H. de Page, *Traité élémentaire de droit civil belge* (Brussel: Bruylant, I), nr. 130; R Derine, F. Van Neste en H Vandenberghe, *Zakenrecht*, in *Beginselen van Belgisch Privaatrecht* (Antwerpen: Standaard 1984), IA, 59, nr. 30; W. van Gerven, *Algemeen Deel*, in *Beginselen van Belgisch Privaatrecht* (Antwerpen: Standaard 1987), 96, nr. 34.

of property rights are limited in the sense that parties cannot create property rights which do not correspond to the essential features of the property rights that have been created by the legislature. Belgian legal scholars regard this principle as a building stone of the property law system. Even if the numerus clausus principle is deeply rooted in Belgian property law, the only possible legal ground for this principle is Article 543 of the (old) Civil Code, as it states that "one may have a right of ownership, or a mere right of enjoyment, or a mere servitude to be claimed on property." The incompleteness of this enumeration is an indication of the fact that the provision is not limitative in nature: long leases and building rights are not mentioned (as these rights were only introduced afterwards), co-ownership is not mentioned either, and the property security rights and liens – which are traditionally considered as property rights in French and Belgian law – have also been omitted. This provision was meant to be a mere introductory provision, announcing generally that the substance of the property rights is dealt with in later provisions.

On the other hand, French case law clearly takes distance from the *numerus clausus* principle. The French Cour de cassation reaffirmed its famous Caquelard-judgment of 1834[33] in 2012, ruling that parties are free to establish property rights under the restriction of mandatory law and public order.[34] We have indicated *supra* the influence of French law as mother law of the Belgian legal system. This is even more the case with regard to this issue, as French law is based on the same statutory rule (e.g. article 543 CC) as Belgian law.

The new Belgian Act of 4 February 2020 unequivocally statutes for the introduction of a closed system of property rights. Article 3.3 of the (new) Civil Code categorizes the acknowledged property rights: (1) (co-) ownership, (2) property rights to use, which are sub-categorized as usufruct, long lease and building rights and (3) property security rights, which are sub-categorized in specific statutory rights of priority, pledge, hypothec, and liens.[35]

The underlying rationale for this strict '*Typenzwang*' is highly comparative:[36] in almost all national legal systems, even in the common law, a standardization of property rights applies to a larger or lesser extent.[37] Some legal-economic arguments have been put forward in favour of the acknowledgment of this principle: it would enhance legal certainty and

33 Cass. fr. (req.) 13 February 1834, *arrêt Caquelard*, S. 1834, I, 205, *D.* 1834, I, 118.

34 Cass. fr. (civ. 3) 23 May 2012, no. 11-13202.

35 Article 3.3 provides as follows: "*Seul le législateur peut créer des droits réels. Les droits réels sont le droit de propriété, la copropriété, les droits réels d'usage et les sûretés réelles. Les droits réels d'usage sont les servitudes, le droit d'usufruit, le droit d'emphytéose et le droit de superficie. Les sûretés réelles, au sens de ce Livre, sont les privilèges spéciaux, le gage, l'hypothèque et le droit de rétention réglés au Livre 7.*"

36 Explanatory Memorandum, pp. 15-16.

37 B. Akkermans, *The principle of numerus clausus in European Private Law*, Antwerp, Intersentia, 2007, 657 p. See also P. Sparkes, "Certainty of Property: *Numerus Clausus or the Rule with No Name?*", *ERPL* 2012, 769-804.

reduce transaction costs.[38] This is the underlying argument for the famous words by Bernard Rudden, "'*Fancies' are for contract, not for property*".[39]

A strict *numerus clausus* principle, as anchored in the new article 3.1 CC, limits the party autonomy to a large extent. However, the counterweight for the closed system of property rights is found in article 3.1 of the new Civil Code: in principle, parties are free to contractually derogate from the statutory provisions. In civil law terms: book 3 is of suppletive law. This provision aims to strengthen party autonomy. This should ensure a flexible system in favour of legal practice. It contradicts the general, but old-fashioned and only historically mistaken, idea that the entire property law must be considered as being of public order. The acknowledgment and integration of contractual freedom within property law is one of the ambitions of the Draft. The draft thereby goes into the opposite direction than the one taken by the first version of the French Draft, developed within the *Association Henri Capitant*, which took as a starting point that the provisions on property law are all of public order.[40] This starting point of the French draft statute proved to be too controversial to survive and probably was one of the reasons why the draft was not brought to the political level.

However, the basic principle of party autonomy in the Belgian Draft is subject to two exceptions:

- Definitions: the draft contains a definition per property right. The definitions mention the core elements of each property right from which parties cannot contractually

38 H. Hansmann and R Kraakman, "Property, Contract and Verification: the *Numerus Clausus* Problem and the Divisibility of Rights", *Journ. L.S.* 2002, 373-451; T.W Merrill, "Introduction: the Demsetz Thesis and the Evolution of Property Rights", *Journ. L.S.* 2002, 331-358; T.W. Merrill and H.E Smith, "Optimal standardisation in the Law of Property: The *Numerus Clausus* Principle", *Yale L.J.* 2000, 1-70; F. Parisi, "Entropy in Property", *Am. Journ. Comp. Law* 2002, 595-632; B. Rudden, "Economic Theory v. Property Law: The Numerus Clausus Problem", in J. Eekelaar en J. Bell (ed.), in *Oxford Essays in Jurisprudence, Third Series*, 239-263; S. Van Erp, "A numerus quasi-clausus of property rights as a constitutive element of a future European property law?", in K. Boele-Woelki, C.H. Brants en G.J.W. Steenhoff (ed.), *Het plezier van de rechtsvergelijking. Opstellen over unificatie en harmonisatie van het recht in Europa aangeboden aan prof. mr. E.H. Hondius* (Deventer: Kluwer 2003), 41.

39 B. Rudden, "Economic Theory v. Property Law: The Numerus Clausus Problem", in J. Eekelaar en J. Bell (ed.), *Oxford Essays in Jurisprudence, Third Series* (Oxford: Clarendon 1987), (239) 243.

40 http://www.henricapitant.org/storage/app/media/pdfs/travaux/Avant-projet_de_reforme_du_droit_des_biens_19_11_08.pdf. The first article of the 2008 draft provided as follows : « Les articles du présent livre sont d'ordre public, sauf disposition contraire. » The Explanatory Memorandum of this French draft statute gives a justification for this rule: ""*L'article, 516, commence par affirmer le caractère d'ordre public du Livre II, sauf dispositions contraires. Ce choix de la commission présente l'avantage de clarifier une question souvent discutée, ambiguë qui oblige le juge à décider, au cas par cas, quels sont les articles impératifs et les autres. Mais, comme il ne saurait être question de supprimer toute marge de souplesse ou de mise à l'écart contractuelle d'un certain nombre de règles du droit des biens, il rend nécessaire la précision expresse, pour chaque article supplétif de volonté, de ce caractère. Cependant, dans la mesure où le nombre d'articles supplétifs de volonté reste néanmoins faible par rapport au total, l'inconvénient est apparu supportable pour les membres de la commission qui ont donc posé le principe du caractère impératif du livre II, sauf exceptions prévues dans les textes*" (*Ibid.*).

deviate. If this exception was not introduced, this would have contradicted the *Typenfixierung* as one dimension of the closed system of property rights. The core of the different property rights must comply with the components of the definition. Definitions are primary rules falling outside party autonomy. To give an illustration: article 3.138, par. 1 CC defines the right of usufruct as follows: "*Usufruct confers on its holder the temporary right to use and enjoy the property of the bare owner, such as a cautious and reasonable person would, in accordance with the destination of that property and subject to the obligation to return the property at the end of his right.*" Hence, it is not possible to contractually agree that the usufructuary can give another destination to the object of the property right.
- Provisions can expressly provide that they are mandatory, so that any contractual derogation would be invalid. In the Draft, this is especially the case for provisions with regard to the duration of the different property rights, especially property rights to use.[41] The mandatory nature of these provisions should safeguard the "attractiveness", in the sense of gravitational force, of the right of ownership. Moreover, the full chapter on so-called compulsory co-ownership is of mandatory law (art. 3.100 CC).[42] The most important example of compulsory co-ownership are the rules on condominium law, which is – in Belgian law – traditionally of mandatory law in order to avoid that a real estate developing company could impose its unilateral intention to other owners in the condominium scheme.

In sum, and to take a comparative perspective, the Belgian legislator adheres in the newly adopted regime to a strict *Typenzwang*, but flexibilizes its system with regard to the *Typenfixieuring*.[43] In other words: it is not possible to create innominate property rights, but there is a large field of contractual freedom within the mandatory borders of the nominate property rights. Parties cannot think out of the box, but the boxes are widened up. In doing so, the Belgian legislator aimed to reconcile the need for legal certainty in the law and economics discourse with the need for flexibility in legal practice.

---

41 The maximum duration of a long lease right is 99 years (art. 3.169 CC). The maximum duration of a right of usufruct is the duration of the life of its holder (usufruct; art. 3.141 CC). The usufruct of a legal person is subject to a double limitation: the existence of the right holder and a maximum of 99 years. For building rights, the maximum duration is, as a matter of principle, also 99 years (art. 3.180 CC). Exceptionally, a building right can be perpetual (1) if it is created for reasons of public domain or (2) to allow for a division in volumes of a complex and heterogeneous immovable property, which includes various volumes which could qualify for independent and varying use and which have between themselves no communal part (cf. art. 3.180, par. 2 CC).

42 It is called compulsory co-ownership because it relates to the nature of the co-owned goods.

43 For these two dimensions of the *numerus clausus* principle, we refer to S. van Erp en B. Akkermans (ed.), *Cases, Materials and Text on Property Law*, pp. 68-72.

4.2 Principle of Transparency

A second leading principle of property law, as promulgated by Sjef van Erp, is the principle of transparency. As property rights are right against the world, others must be able to know about these rights, because of their binding nature.[44] This is the dogmatic approach, starting from the distinction between property rights and personal rights. Three different developments can be analyzed in the mentioned recent Belgian reforms, (1) the growing importance of registration as publicity measure for movables, (2) a functional extension of registration to personal rights and (3) the completion of gaps with regard to registration for property rights.

First of all, the significance of possession as means of publicity is in decline in all European legal systems, and thus also in Belgian law.[45] The Pledge Act of 2011 was a mile stone for Belgian law in this respect: it introduces the registration in a public register as default means for the perfection of a pledge under the new Pledge Act, which has entered into force since 1 January 2018. In order to have third parties effect the security interest needs to be registered in a new Pledge Register (art. 26 Pledge Act). As from the moment of registration the pledge will have third parties effect.[46] However, the legislator has not given exclusive nature to registration as means of publicity. Although registration is under the new regime the default form of publicity, the pledge of a corporeal asset is also effective in relation to third parties if the asset has been handed over to the creditor or a third-party pledgee which has been agreed (art. 39 Pledge Act).

A major exception to the transparency principle within the field of security rights, is the title retention. Although the economic purpose of the retention of title is identical to that of a property security right, it is not made visible to third parties in the same way by the implementation of publicity requirements. The retention of title has in Belgian law third party effect by its mere constitution between parties, without any registration being required. The only formal requirement which has to be fulfilled is that the suspension of transfer of property must be agreed upon at the latest at the moment of delivery of the goods. The legislator mentions only in relation to consumers a requirement of a document

44 S. van Erp, *European and National Property Law: Osmosis or Growing Antagonism?*, 14-15.

45 Kieninger analyses this development as a major development in European private law, and Belgian law confirms this analysis (E.M. Kieninger, "Evaluation: a common core?" in *Security rights in Moveable Property in European Private Law* (ed. E.M. Kieninger), Cambridge, 2004, 652). See also for this development: V. Sagaert, "Security interests", in, *Cases, materials and text on Property Law*, in *Ius Commune Casebooks for a Common Law of Europe*, (eds. S. Van Erp and B. Akkermans) in *Ius Commune Casebooks* (Oxford, Hart Publishing, 2012) 448-450.

46 In doing so, the legislator departs from the dispossession as exclusive means of publicity. The advantages of registration instead of dispossession are multiple: V. Sagaert, "Security interests", in *Cases, materials and text on Property Law*, in *Ius Commune Casebooks for a Common Law of Europe* (ed. S. Van Erp and B. Akkermans), Oxford, Hart Publishing, 2012, 449. See also F. Georges "La réforme des sûretés mobilières", *Rev.dr. Ulg*, 2013, 437.

signed by the buyer (art. 69). A key argument for this solution is a legal-economic one: none of the most important trade partners of Belgium is imposing a registration requirement for the perfection of a title retention.[47] It would have burdened the competitive position of Belgian sellers if they would, contrary to their foreign trade partners, only be entitled to a title retention after registration and would create legal uncertainty in cross border transactions . Moreover, such publicity requirement would burden to a large extent the rapid commercial business transactions.

The new Civil Code does not modify this fairly recent system for property security rights. It sticks to possession as means of publicity for property rights on movables and thus sacrifice the traditional '*possession vaut titre*' rule, meaning that the transferee in good faith who is in possession of a movable is presumed to have title in the good. However, the new Civil Code limits the scope of this provision to the transferee for consideration. A beneficiary of a gift, effected by a non-owner, will not be protected, not even if (s)he is in good faith (art. 3.28 CC). The reason being that in the balance between the evicted owner and the beneficiary of the gift, the former must prevail. Indeed, if the latter has to make restitution of the good, he must restitute what he should never have received. The period for acquisitive prescription for a beneficiary of a gift in good faith is therefore 10 years. The prescription period of a lawful possessor who is in bad faith is 30 years (art. 3.27 CC).

Traditionally, publicity is in most European legal systems limited to property rights. The Belgian legislator has taken a functional approach, making transparency necessary for all rights of which the third-party effectiveness could be desirable for the holder of the right. For instance, the new Act also provides for the registration of rights of pre-emption and purchase options in real estate in the land registers.[48] Although these rights are personal rights in most national legal systems, the holder of these rights can have a legitimate interest to prevent a third person from acquiring in good faith an interest in real estate burdened with (one of) these rights.

Finally, the Belgian legislator has filled some gaps with regard to the real estate registration system. For instance, it was under the old Civil Code not allowed or possible to register the transfer *mortis causa* in traditional Belgian law. This triggered some practical difficulties for public notaries and other actors aiming to know the proprietary status of a real estate. The new Civil Code provides for the possibility to register also acquisitions at the moment

47 Only Swiss law makes an exception: according to Article 715 Swiss Civil Code, a retention of title clause becomes valid only upon registration in a public register, the Retention of Title Clause Register (RTCR), which is kept by the Debt Collection Office in each community. In Swiss law, any third party may fully rely on the absence of registration. Swiss law is, in this sense, closer to the system of Art. 9 UCC, which imposes the registration of the security interest in order to perfect it.

48 Article 3.30, §1, 4° new Civil Code.

of death.[49] The non-compliance with this rules entails, e.g. that the heir or legatee cannot register an act which has to be registered in order to have third party effectiveness. In other words: the non-registration of the acquisition by the legatee or heir has as effect that a '*mainmorte*' is created, the good is immobilized in the hands of the heir of legatee (art. 3.30, §2 CC)

5 Importance of Ground Rules of Property Law in the New Belgian Property Law

Sjef van Erp further analyses in his Walter van Gerven Lecture four ground rules for property rights in a comparative perspective: "the nemo dat (or nemo plus) rule (i), the prior tempore rule (ii), limited rights have priority over fuller rights (iii), protection rules such as the right to (re)claim the object of the property right (iv)."[50]

5.1 'Nemo Plus' Rule

A first ground rule is the rule that nobody can transfer more rights than he has himself. In other words: one must have the power to dispose on the ground of his proper right. If the transferor is not holder of ('entitled to') the rights he transfers, the transfer will remain ineffective, except for some third party protection rules. It is a rule stemming from the dynamic dimension of property law, applying in case of the transfer of a property right. Under the Civil Code of 1804, the Belgian legislator did not give statutory ground to this rule, at least not in a coherent manner, and not with regard to its proprietary dimension.[51]

Article 3.6 of the new Civil Code fills this gap. This section both governs the possibility to transfer property rights within the limits of the own powers of the transferor and the consequences of such transfer with regard to the affiliated obligations:

49 Article 3.30, §1, 7° new Civil Code.

50 S. van Erp, *European and National Property Law: Osmosis or Growing Antagonism?*, p. 16.

51 The only rule connected with 'nemo plus' rule was a provision within the chapter on sales agreements, article 1599 Civil Code: "*The sale of another's good is void. It may open the remedy of compensation if the seller did not know that it was the good of another*". This provision causes more legal uncertainty than it solves problems. First of all, a contract law provision should not determine the property law effects of a defective transfer. Secondly, legal scholars agree that the voidness of article 1599 CC in fact points towards a rescission for non-execution (H. De Page, *Traité élémentaire de droit civil belge*, Brussels, Bruylant, 1958, IV, n°. 128; J. del Corral, *De leveringsplicht bij de overdracht van roerende lichamelijke goederen*, Antwerp, Intersentia, 2013, n°. 333 *et seq.*; R. Jansen, *Beschikkingsonbevoegdheid*, Antwerp, Intersentia, 2009, nr. 585; B. Tilleman, *De totstandkoming en de kwalificatie van de koop*, in *Beginselen van Belgisch Privaatrecht*, Mechelen, Kluwer, 2001, n°. 1025.

> The holder of a property right may dispose of his right. He may only dispose of this right together with the main object to which it is attached, if the nature of the right obliges him to do so. If the holder of a property right transfers his right of use, he shall remain jointly and severally liable with the transferee towards the owner for the personal obligations which constitute the consideration for the creation of this right and which are payable after the transfer. In respect of obligations falling due earlier, the transferor shall be exclusively liable.

If the transferor does not have the power to dispose, the transfer will – from a proprietary point of view – remain ineffective in relation to the person whose rights have been transferred. Third party protection rules – possession with regard to movables (art. 3.28 CC: cf. supra, n°. 20) and registration in the land register for immovables (art. 3.30 CC) – are the traditional exceptions, also taken over in the new Belgian Civil Code.

This provision can be connected to article 3.53 CC, which provides that an owner may give his consent for a restriction of his power to dispose (*'clause d'inaliénabilité / vervreemdingsverbod'*) of the good under the mandatory conditions that (1) the clause is limited in time and (2) the clause corresponds to a legitimate interest. The Civil Code of 1804 took a hostile position towards contractual clauses restricting the right to dispose of goods, as this created in the pre-codification period the phenomenon of the 'death hand' (*'mainmorte'*), which resulted in the donation of important economic assets in favour of religious estates, which could not take part in the economic trade. Such situation was detrimental from a legal-economic point of view.

Case law gradually admitted these clauses under the two said conditions, and they have become part of legal practice, for instance in donations with retention of usufruct. Article 3.53 CC gives statutory ground to this case law. The new Civil Code is not explicit on the legal effects of the violation of such restrictions to the power to dispose. The reason is obvious, at least with regard to corporeals: a violation of the power to dispose is sanctioned on a pure contractual level. It does not result in the ineffectiveness of the transfer, except if contract law provides otherwise.[52]

The obligations connected to property rights are often addressed as 'real obligations'.[53] The idea of the new civil Code is that the holder of a property right cannot discharge

52 For example: if the transferee is also in bad faith, this can result in the voidness of the transfer as reparation in kind for extra-contractual liability (Cour de cassation/Hof van Cassatie 27 April 2006, *Pasicrisie* 2006, I, 976, *Tijdschrift voor Belgisch Burgerlijk Recht* 2008, 507, noot J. Dewez).

53 For a recent in depth analysis in a comparative perspective: S. Demeyere, *Real obligations at the edge between contract and property* (Antwerpen: Intersentia 2020). For an analysis under the old Belgian law: V. Sagaert, "Real rights and real obligations in Belgian and French law", in J. Milo and S. Bartels (ed.), *The content of real rights, Ars notarius*, Deventer, Kluwer Rechtswetenschappen, 2004, 47-70.

himself from obligations which were the counterpart for the creation of a right, such as the compensation in favour of the person vesting the right, an obligation to construct a building, etc. With regard to these obligations, the legislator cannot accept that the creditor can be confronted with a new (exclusive) debtor – the transferee – whose solvency and liquidity is uncertain and has not been taken into account by the creditor. That is different for the obligations of the holder of the property right which do not constitute a counterpart for the creation of the property right. For instance, obligations of maintenance of a usufructuary or (art. 3.153 CC) long lease holder (art. 3.173 CC) are generally not the counterpart for the creation of a proprietary burden. The latter obligations thus follow the property right, discharging the original holder of the property right after the transfer.

5.2 *The 'Priority Rule'*

The second ground rule, according to the system van Erp, is the '*prior tempore, potior iure*' rule. Again, Belgian law was familiar with this rule – often denominated as the "principle of anteriority" – without any statutory ground. The reform of Belgian property law has given firm anchoring to this principle in the legislation: article 3.4 CC provides as follows: "*Without prejudice to Articles 3.28 and 3.30 of this Book and Article 96 of the Mortgage Act, an older property right has priority over a posterior property right. Therefore, subject to the same provisions, a property right confers a right to follow enabling the holder to enforce his right against any successive acquirer of a right to the property.*" The exceptions mentioned in this provision, refer to the third party protection rules with regard to movables (art. 3.28 CC: cf. supra, n°. 20) and with regard to immovables (art. 3.30 CC and article 96 Mortgage Act). With regard to property security rights, this explains why a (registered) pledge or hypothec prevail on a later pledge or hypothec. The latter is, in that case, a security right in second rank.

It is remarkable and theoretically rather innovative that article 3.4 CC conceives the "right to follow" as an application of the '*prior tempore*' rule. If A burdens a good with a property right in favour of B, and A afterwards transfers this good to C, B's property right will be effective against C, subject to third party protection rules. The transferee must, thus, respect, the prior property rights burdening the good. The reason therefore is that the right of A was vested previously to the right of C.

Exceptionally, the Belgian legislator even allows a right holder to dispose of the object of his property right beyond the borders of his own right. That is, for instance, the case for a usufructuary. The latter is normally limited to the borders of his own right, but article 3.148 CC provides for three exceptions: "*A usufructuary may dispose of the burdened property outside the boundaries of his powers if (1) a special legal provision allows so, (2) it is in accordance with the destination of the property that already existed at the time the usufruct was created or was contractually agreed upon between the parties, and is inherent to his obligation of cautious and reasonable management; or (3) the usufruct relates to consumption goods"*.[54] It is an important exception to the "nemo plus" rule, taking a functional approach on the division of powers between the usufructuary and the bare owner.

5.3 *Limited Rights Have Priority over Fuller Rights*

With regard to a third ground rule, Van Erp writes that "*if a new property right has been created with the consent of the holder of the first property right, such a second right will limit the first right*".[55] If the owner grants a usufruct or long lease right on his real estate, the limited property right will burden/restrict the powers of the owner. If the "mother right" is a right of ownership, this rule is self-evident. However, things can get more complicated if the mother right is a limited property right. For instance, A grants a long lease right to B. Can the latter, on his turn, consent with a (sub-)long lease right or usufruct in favour of C?

In Belgian law, such "super-position" of limited property rights has given rise to a lot of legal uncertainty, rooted in often very dogmatic scholarly debates. The reform of Belgian property law has simplified this debate: each holder of a limited property right to use can consent with the burdening of the object of his property right with another property right, under the condition that he does not grant or transfer more powers than he has himself. The object of the second property right is thus not the first property right, but the object of the latter. The '*nemo plus*' rule only imposes that a right holder cannot give away more extensive powers than he has himself and cannot grant powers over a longer time period than the time period of his own right.[56] In doing so, the Belgian legislator has not only made things more straightforward for legal practice, but also opts for the same track as the Dutch legislator in the articles art. 3:84 and 5:93 of the Dutch Civil Code.[57]

54 A usufruct on consumption goods was a difficult issue under the old Civil Code, as it is not possible to use these goods without consuming these. Therefore, such usufruct was often characterized as a quasi-usufruct.

55 S. van Erp, *European and National Property Law: Osmosis or Growing Antagonism?*, p. 16-17.

56 For instance, the holder of a long lease right can grant a (sub-)long lease right, a building right, a right of usufruct or a servitude within the substantive and temporal limits of his own right. A holder of a usufruct can grant a (sub-)usufruct, building right or servitude. He can however not consent with a long lease right, as a long lease right is by nature more extensive than a right of usufruct. We refer to the articles 3.140 (usufruct), 3.117, par.2 (servitudes), article 3.168 (long lease right) and article 3.178 (building right).

57 In Dutch law, this possibility for a limited right holder to burden the object of his property right is generally known as the 'construction-Beekhuis'.

This ground rule in combination with the '*nemo plus*' ground rule demonstrate that there is no necessary connection between the right of ownership and the power to dispose.[58] On the one hand, there are situations in which an owner does not have the power to dispose of the object of his right because his powers to dispose are contractually or inherently restricted. On the other hand, non-owners – such as limited property right holders – can have the right to burden the object of their right with another limited property right.

In our view, this rule is not an autonomous ground rule of property law, but a mere application of the '*nemo plus*' rule. The idea that a limited property right holder can burden the object of his property right with another, more limited right, is in line with the '*nemo plus*' rule, which was mentioned above as separate ground rule (cf. supra, n°. 24 *et seq.*).

5.4 Proprietary Remedies

Once a property right has been created as such it is given special protection on a remedial level.[59] Such special remedies should protect the right holder against any event, such as the insolvency of the one who has possession of the good. The reform of Belgian property law has had particular attention for the remedial dimension of property rights. For instance, article 3.51 CC – the second provision of the chapter on ownership after its definition – pays attention to the remedies of an owner:

> Subject to the other provisions of this Book, the owner may revindicate the object from the person holding it and oppose any infringement or claim by a third party. The right of ownership and claims sanctioning the right shall not extinguish by its non-use.

These special remedies also grant protection in case of insolvency. Property rights should, in the traditional and general formulation, not be affected by insolvency of a third person. This insolvency protection is laid down in article 3.5 of the new Civil Code:

> Without prejudice to Articles 3.28 and 3.30, ownership, co-ownership and property rights to use remain outside the concursus created by the insolvency of third parties. Property security rights give a right of priority over the proceeds of the sale of their collateral.

---

58 See already: R. Jansen, *Beschikkingsonbevoegdheid* (Antwerpen: Intersentia 2009), 931 p.

59 S. van Erp, *European and National Property Law: Osmosis or Growing Antagonism?*, p. 17.

This provision should be read together with article XX.139 of the Belgian Code of Economic Law, which prohibits the bankruptcy trustee to terminate agreements with regard to property rights in case of bankruptcy of one of the parties.[60]

6 Conclusion

Being able to co-author the re-codification of Belgian property law was not in the first place an honour, but a challenge. Seeing that the draft bill on the re-codification was recently approved in Belgian parliament triggers even more modesty towards the enormous heritage Napoleon left us on the level of private law (not necessary on other levels).

This article has given a first analysis of the reform through the eyes of Sjef van Erp, to whom this book is dedicated. Testing a property law system to the principled approach of this outstanding academic can be seen as the ultimate litmus test for the general framework of the legislative work. We have demonstrated, through this article, that both the leading principles and the ground rules which Sjef van Erp has discovered in property law, are prominently present in the new Belgian Civil Code. It is a reinsurance that this litmus test was successful in confronting the new Act with the scholarly analysis made by Sjef van Erp. However, this analysis did not take into account the analysis of the technical rules which elaborate the general rules on a more in-depth level. It only gave a glimpse of some general provisions, to the extent that they were useful to execute this litmus test. A technical analysis of the new Book 3 of the Civil Code requires a much more detailed and comprehensive analysis of the different provisions, which by far exceeds the scope of this article. It is my wish that legal scholarship and legal practice will be two architects for the further edification of the property law building.

60 This provision was introduced in 2017 as a reaction to the case law of the Belgian Cour de cassation / Hof van Cassatie, which ruled that the possibility to terminate ongoing agreements at the moment of the bankruptcy also applied on agreements creating a property right (Cass. 3 december 2015, *Rechtskundig Weekblad* 2016-17, 1113, note V. Sagaert, *Tijdschrift voor Belgisch Handelsrecht* 2016, 846, noot J. Malekzadem: "*Aldus kan de curator wanneer de voorwaarden hiertoe vervuld zijn een einde maken aan overeenkomsten inzake het gebruik en het genot van onroerende goederen ook al beantwoorden de aldus verleende rechten aan een zakelijk recht.*"). Taking this case law to its ultimate effects, it could even trump property rights in case of insolvency, which would of course have endangered legal certainty in real estate transactions.

The Argentine Civil and Commercial Code (2015) and the Contract of *Fideicomiso*: Mapping a De- to Re-Codification Experience

Agustín Parise[*]

1 Introduction

Josephus Henricus Maria van Erp defended his PhD in 1990.[1] That book dealt with the interplay of the law of contract and the law of tort, advocating for a new category of a legal relation. He undertook a comparative study, while also exploring legal history. The epigraph of that book reproduced seminal words by Lord Goff of Chieveley, encapsulating the academic quest that Sjef would undertake ever since the time of publishing that monograph: "in civil law countries as in common law countries, not only are we beset by the same practical problems, but broadly speaking we reach the same practical solutions."[2] The quest of Sjef has taken him to explore problems and solutions in the law of property for a number of decades, attaining worldwide recognition. Legal relations – in many forms – continue to be present in his work.

Friends know that Sjef is passionate about private law codes, and even collects different editions of those *corpora* that shape law and society. Sjef is aware of private law codification in Argentina and supervised the doctoral work of the author of this paper.[3] There, ownership, as encapsulated in the Argentine civil code of 1871, was explored. This paper continues looking at private law in Argentina, yet it deals with the contract of *fideicomiso* as regulated in the civil and commercial code that was adopted in 2015. The paper shows how that trust-like instrument was welcomed by means of de-codification during the 1990s and how it was then moved to the new code as a consequence of re-codification.

Three initial statements are useful. First, revision is hereby understood as a legislative process that results in the amendment of the text of codes. These amendments in the text

* Associate Professor, Faculty of Law, Maastricht University.

1 J.H.M van Erp, *Contract als rechtsbetrekking: een rechtsvergelijkende studie*, Zwolle, W.E.J. Tjeenk Willink, 1990.

2 See the excerpt from *Smith v. Littlewoods* [1987] 2 WLR 480, 511/2, as reproduced in van Erp, 1990, p. v.

3 A. Parise, *Ownership Paradigms in American Civil Law Jurisdictions: Manifestations of the Shifts in the Legislation of Louisiana, Chile, and Argentina (16th-20th Centuries)*, Leiden, Brill Nijhoff, 2017.

are always segmented and limited to autonomous areas of law; and they never aim to replace the code *in totum* by means of a wholesale replacement. In its moderate form, revision aims to introduce isolated changes that will ultimately result in a change of a particular provision, though not necessarily in the adoption of a new code. Second, de-codification is understood as a legislative process that results in the altering of the effect and scope of the text of codes. Those alterations, however, are always included in satellite codes or special legislation that are not part of the original code, but that affect its content. A jurisdiction that experiences de-codification welcomes the enactment of legislative pieces that will eventually make a specific code necessarily depend on those new enactments. A de-codification process weakens the gravitation of codes. Third, re-codification is understood as a legislative process that results in the adoption of an entirely new code. Intense revision may ultimately result in a completely new text, and therefore, qualify as re-codification. Conversely, re-codification can also take place even when intense revision did not precede it, and can happen when a new text replaces *in totum* an existing code.[4]

Fideicomiso links the law of property and the law of contract, hence offering a fertile ground to explore two main pillars in Sjef's work. The paper is divided into two parts. First, the paper summarizes the path towards the adoption of the new code. In that same part, the paper shares information on the place of the law of contract within the new Argentine text. Second, the paper offers an overview of the contract of *fideicomiso* as encapsulated in the 2015 text. Attention is there devoted to a selection of aspects, including, main tenets, parties, effects, and modalities of this trust-like instrument. The aim of this paper is to map de-codification and re-codification as experienced in a specific area of Argentine private law. Looking at *fideicomiso* and its place in the legal framework before and after the enactment of the new code shows that resilience is a characteristic of codification, since it adapts to the needs at different times and places.[5]

2 New Argentine *Corpus*

A national civil and commercial code (ACCC) took effect in the Republic of Argentina on 1 August 2015.[6] The ACCC – entitled *Código Civil y Comercial de la Nación* – replaces the civil and commercial codes that were adopted during the nineteenth century as part of the

4 A. Parise, 'Civil Law Codification in Latin America: Understanding First and Second Generation Codes', *in* J.M. Milo, J.H.A. Lokin & J.M. Smits (eds.), *Tradition, Codification and Unification: Comparative-Historical Essays on Developments in Civil Law*, Cambridge, Intersentia, 2014, pp. 188-189.

5 A. Parise & L. van Vliet, 'Preface', *in* A. Parise & L. van Vliet (eds.), *Re- De- Co-dification? New Insights on the Codification of Private Law*, The Hague, Eleven International Publishing, 2018, p. ix.

6 *Ley 26994, Código Civil y Comercial de la Nación*, available at: http://www.infoleg.gob.ar/infolegInternet/anexos/235000-239999/235975/texact.htm (accessed 14 April 2020).

codification endeavours that multiplied at that time throughout the Western Hemisphere.[7] The adoption of the ACCC brought to an end revision and re-codification efforts that for approximately a century had spread across Argentina. The new text may be considered the final link in the efforts undertaken by hundreds of jurists who saw the need to adopt texts that would better encapsulate private law for Argentine society.

2.1 *Genesis*[8]

The adoption of a national commercial code was delayed in Argentina until 1862. Eduardo Acevedo and Dalmacio Vélez Sarsfield worked on a draft[9] that was approved by the Buenos Aires Congress in 1859.[10] The Argentine Congress extended the application of that draft to all of Argentina on 10 September 1862,[11] with effect as the *Código de Comercio para la Nación Argentina* (Argentine Commercial Code).[12] The Argentine Commercial Code had 1755 articles and was divided into four books.[13] The text spread across Latin America, influencing the likewise influential commercial code of Chile of 1865,[14] and it was adopted by Uruguay (with minor changes) and by Paraguay.[15] Revision and de-codification had a significant impact on the Argentine Commercial Code,[16] a phenomenon also experienced by other commercial codes across the globe.[17] Furthermore, a number of reforms were envisioned, the main one introduced after the work of a codifying commission in 1889.[18]

---

7 A. Parise, 'The Place of the Louisiana Civil Code in the Hispanic Civil Codifications: Inclusion in the Comments to the Spanish Civil Code Project of 1851', *Louisiana Law Review*, Vol. 68, 2008, pp. 826 *et seq.*

8 Parts of this sub-section were previously presented in A. Parise, 'Sources of Law and Legal History', *in* U. Basset (ed.), *Introduction to the Law of Argentina*, Alphen aan den Rijn, Wolters Kluwer, 2018, pp. 1-24.

9 A. Levaggi, *Manual de Historia del Derecho Argentino (Castellano-Indiano/Nacional)*, 3rd ed., Vol. III, Buenos Aires, Abeledo Perrot, 2013, p. 183.

10 Levaggi, 2013, p. 183.

11 A. Levaggi, *Dalmacio Vélez Sarsfield, Jurisconsulto*, Córdoba, Ciencia, Derecho y Sociedad, 2005, p. 164.

12 *Código de Comercio para la Nación Argentina. Sancionado por el Honorable Congreso Nacional. El 10 de Setiembre de 1862*, Buenos Aires, El Nacional, 1863.

13 Book I of persons of commerce, Book II of contracts, Book III of rights and obligations that derive from navigation, and Book IV of insolvency of merchants.

14 Levaggi, 2013, p. 185.

15 H. Cámara, 'Código de Comercio de la República Argentina y reformas o tentativas hasta la actualidad', *in Centenario del Código de Comercio*,Mexico, UNAM, 1991, p. 110.

16 M.C. Araya, 'El contenido del derecho comercial a partir del Código Civil y Comercial', *Revista Jurídica Argentina La Ley*, 20 April 2015, p. 3.

17 J.C. Rivera, 'The Scope and Structure of Civil Codes. Relations with Commercial Law, Family Law, Consumer Law and Private International Law. A Comparative Approach', *in* J.C. Rivera (ed.), *The Scope and Structure of Civil Codes*, Dordrecht, Springer, 2013, p. 21. See G. Medina, 'Argentina on the Eve of a New Civil and Commercial Code', *in* J.C. Rivera (ed.), *The Scope and Structure of Civil Codes*, Dordrecht, Springer, 2013, p. 47; and Cámara, 1991, p. 116 *et seq.*

18 Cámara, 1991, p. 116.

Additional attempts at reform followed, yet they failed. For example, attempts were made in 1935, 1936, and 1959,[19] which paved the way for the eventual adoption of the ACCC.

The adoption of a national civil code began with a similar story. Once again Vélez Sarsfield was appointed,[20] and his draft was approved by the Argentine Congress in 1869, with effect as the *Código Civil de la República Argentina* (Argentine Civil Code) on 1 January 1871.[21] The Argentine Civil Code had 4051 articles and was divided into two preliminary titles and four books.[22] The text spread across Latin America, influencing, for example, the drafters of the civil code of Uruguay of 1868[23] and was adopted *in totum* by Paraguay in 1877.[24] The Argentine text was subject to many alterations that were introduced mainly through revision.[25] Most partial changes dealt with specific areas of the code[26] and lacked a comprehensive approach. The Argentine Civil Code was also eroded by a continuous process of de-codification.[27] Three main efforts were undertaken in 1936, 1954, and 1968 to modify the text, and they assisted in leaving behind a prevailing liberal conception.

Re-codification efforts were launched in Argentina beginning in the 1980s. Projects on unified civil and commercial codes were completed in the years 1987, 1992, 1993, and 1998, though none ever took force of law.[28] The most recent re-codification attempt was presented before the Executive in March 2012.[29] A codifying commission started to work

19 Cámara, 1991, p. 118 *et seq.*

20 A. Levaggi, *Manual de Historia del Derecho Argentino (Castellano-Indiano/Nacional)*, Vol. II, Buenos Aires, Depalma, 1987, p. 266.

21 See the text of the Argentine Civil Code at 'Ley 340', *in Anales de Legislación Argentina*, volume 1852-1880, Buenos Aires, La Ley, 1954, p. 496. See O. Moréteau & A. Parise, 'Recodification in Louisiana and Latin America', *Tulane Law Review*, Vol. 83, 2009, pp. 1143 *et seq.*; and Levaggi, 1987, p. 266.

22 Book I of persons, Book II of personal rights in civil relations, Book III of real rights, and Book IV of real and personal rights dispositions in common.

23 Moréteau & Parise, 2009, p. 1147. A report of 1867 by a codifying commission in Uruguay mentioned amongst its sources the project of Vélez Sarsfield, which was not yet law in Argentina. See Parise, 2008, pp. 850 *et seq.*

24 R. Sapena Pastor, *Fuentes Próximas del Código Civil*, Asunción, Editorial el Foro, 1986, p. 1; A. Levaggi, *Manual de Historia del Derecho Argentino (Castellano-Indiano/Nacional)*, 2nd ed., Vol. I, Buenos Aires, Depalma, 1996, p. 241; and Moréteau & Parise, 2009, p. 1125.

25 J.J. Llambías, *Tratado de Derecho Civil, Parte General*, 6th ed., Vol. I, Buenos Aires, Editorial Perrot, 1975, pp. 199 *et seq.* See A. Cháneton, *Historia de Vélez Sársfield*, Vol. II, Buenos Aires, Editorial "La Facultad", 1937, pp. 335 *et seq.*

26 Levaggi, 1987, p. 271.

27 Moréteau & Parise, 2009, p. 1145.

28 Medina, 2013, p. 58. About some of those drafts see R. Brebbia (dir.), *Estudios sobre el Proyecto de Código Unificado de 1998*, Buenos Aires, Zavalía, 2001; J.C. Rivera, 'El Proyecto de Código Civil para la República Argentina', *Revista Jurídica Universidad Interamericana de Puerto Rico*, Vol. 35, 2001, p. 381; and A.C. Belluscio, 'Le Code civil et commercial argentin de 2014: (aperçu général et droit des personnes et de la famille)', *Revue internationale de droit comparé*, Vol. 2015-3, 2015, pp. 664 *et seq.*

29 E. Louge Emiliozzi, 'El proceso de recodificación y unificación del derecho privado en la Argentina', *Cartapacio de Derecho*, Vol. 29, 2016, p. 1.

in early 2011,[30] and operated under the presidency of Chief Justice Ricardo L. Lorenzetti of the Argentine Supreme Court.[31] Working groups were created to enable an ample participation of specialists from Argentina and other Latin American jurisdictions.[32] The team included more than one hundred experts in different fields, including law professors, practitioners, and judges.[33] That re-codification effort unified the civil and commercial codes into a single body, because on 1 October 2014, the National Congress adopted Law 26994, which approved the text of the ACCC[34] without parliamentary debate.[35] The ACCC has 2671 articles and is divided into a Preliminary Title and six books.[36]

2.2 *Contractual Models*[37]

The re-codification of Argentine private law is sensed especially in the provisions of the ACCC dealing with the law of contract.[38] A unification of civil and commercial contracts had long been demanded by scholars,[39] since many provisions on contracts in general of

---

30 *Decreto 191/2011*, available at: http://servicios.infoleg.gob.ar/infolegInternet/anexos/175000-179999/179643/norma.htm (accessed 14 April 2020). See also J.M. Brodsky & E.E. Donato Brun, 'Aspectos generales de los contratos en el Proyecto de Código Civil y Comercial de la Nación', *Revista En Letra*, Vol. I:1, 2014, p. 82.

31 *Decreto 191/2011.*

32 M.C. Marsili, 'El Código Civil y Comercial y la materia comercial', *Revista Jurídica Argentina La Ley*, 29 June 2015, p. 1 [online].

33 *Fundamentos del Anteproyecto de Código Civil y Comercial de la Nación* available at: http://www.nuevocodigocivil.com/wp-content/uploads/2015/02/5-Fundamentos-del-Proyecto.pdf, at 7 (accessed 14 April 2020). See also R.L. Lorenzetti, 'Presentación del Código Civil y Comercial de la Nación', *Revista Jurídica Argentina La Ley*, 6 October 2014, p. 1 [online].

34 *Ley 26994.*

35 A.P. Monteleone Lanfranco, 'Las asociaciones civiles en el Código Civil y Comercial', *Revista Jurídica Argentina La Ley*, 10 April 2015, p. 1 [online].

36 Book I of the general part, Book II of family relations, Book III of personal rights, Book IV of real rights, Book V of *mortis causa* transmission of rights, and Book VI of dispositions in common for real and personal rights.

37 Parts of this sub-section were previously presented in A. Parise, 'The Argentine Civil and Commercial Code (2015): Igniting a Third Generation of Codes for Latin America', *Zeitschrift für Europäisches Privatrecht*, Vol. 3/2017, 2017, pp. 658-667.

38 Araya, 2015, p. 4.
The law of contract is dealt with in Book III of personal rights of the ACCC. That book consists of five titles, which are: Title I of obligations in general, Title II of contracts in general, Title III of consumer contracts, Title IV of contracts in particular, and Title V of other sources of obligations. Titles II to IV encompass the core of the law of contract across 750 articles, offering a significant reduction in the number of articles dealing with this area of law when compared with the number of articles devoted in the two nineteenth-century codes. For comprehensive studies on the changes in the law of contract, see J.M. Aparicio, 'Contratos en general. Observaciones al Proyecto de Código', *Revista Jurídica Argentina La Ley*, 5 December 2012, p. 1 [online]; and C.A. Hernández, 'Aspectos relevantes de la regulación de los contratos civiles en el Código Civil y Comercial de la Nación', *Revista Jurídica Argentina La Ley – Suplemento Código Civil y Comercial*, 17 November 2014, p. 1 [online].

39 E.M. Favier Dubois, 'La "autonomía" y los contenidos del Derecho Comercial a partir del Código unificado', *Revista Jurídica Argentina La Ley*, 2 February 2015, p. 6 [online].

the Argentine Civil Code also applied to commercial contracts.[40] A commercialization of provisions can be sensed in the ACCC[41] because globalization had triggered significant changes in the law of contract, motivating a need to adapt to new realities by means of different business structures, ultimately surpassing the classical models.[42] There was a need to include contractual models that were not typified in the previous codes and that had developed as a result of de-codification.[43] Many new models had emerged from custom and practice, special legislation, and from the will of the parties.[44]

The law of contract has four pillars in the ACCC, as reaffirmed in the *exposé des motifs*.[45] The first pillar represents freedom of contract, which occupies the paramount place in the new framework. Aspects of freedom, including contractual freedom and binding force, are dealt with in the ACCC.[46] Public order, customs, and imperative norms offer limitations to freedom of contract, however.[47] Freedom of contract was present also in the Argentine Civil Code, and was likewise present in the earlier re-codification efforts.[48] The second pillar represents good faith, which must be present during the entire life of a contract.[49] This principle is also stated in the Preliminary Title,[50] and the interplay of the general part of the ACCC with contract law provisions is important for its full operation.[51] The third pillar represents the supplementation (*integración*) of contracts, which aims at the preservation of contracts.[52] The will of the parties is fundamental for agreements and for business structures, yet contracts may be completed with other sources (e.g. practices of the place of entering into a contract) that exceed that initial will.[53] Finally, the relativity of the effects of contracts is represented by the fourth pillar. The ACCC states that contracts only have effect amongst the parties, and that third parties may be affected only in cases established by law.[54]

40 J.M. Gastaldi & J.M. Gastaldi, 'Los contratos en general', *in* J.C. Rivera (dir.), *Comentarios al Proyecto de Código Civil y Comercial de la Nación 2012*, Buenos Aires, Abeledo Perrot, 2012, p. 524.

41 Marsili, 2015, p. 3 [online].

42 M. Boretto, 'Los llamados "contratos de distribución" en el Código Civil y Comercial', *Revista Jurídica Argentina La Ley*, 6 November 2014, p. 1 [online].

43 Brodsky & Donato Brun, 2014, p. 83.

44 Brodsky & Donato Brun, 2014, p. 83.

45 *Fundamentos del Anteproyecto*, p. 118 *et seq.*; and G. Caramelo, 'Algunos aspectos de la reforma proyectada en la Teoría General de los Contratos Principios, definición, clasificación y categorías contractuales', *Revista Derecho Privado*, Vol. 4, 2013, pp. 5 *et seq.*

46 Articles 958, 959, and 990 of *Ley 26994*. See Aparicio, 2012, p. 2 *et seq.* [online].

47 Article 958 of *Ley 26994*. See Aparicio, 2012, p. 2 [online].

48 Gastaldi & Gastaldi, 2012, p. 528.

49 Article 961 of *Ley 26994*. See Aparicio, 2012, p. 2 [online].

50 Article 9 of *Ley 26994*.

51 Caramelo, 2013, pp. 6 *et seq.*

52 Article 964 of *Ley 26994*. See Caramelo, 2013, p. 6.

53 Aparicio, 2012, p. 2 *et seq.* [online].

54 Article 1021 of *Ley 26994*. See Caramelo, 2013, p. 7.

The ACCC includes contractual models that already existed in Argentine business structures and were recognized by doctrine and jurisprudence.[55] The ACCC typifies an array of contracts in Book III, aiming to offer different models that could accommodate and operate for different needs.[56] Some generic contractual models (e.g. banking), however, include other sub-models (e.g. safe deposit box service, *servicio de caja de seguridad*). Further, Book V of the ACCC includes the contract of assignment of inheritance (*cesión de herencia*). The ACCC unifies the regulation of a number of contracts that were dealt with both in the Argentine Civil Code and in the Argentine Commercial Code (e.g. sale, mutuum, commodatum).[57] The new text also moves some contracts from special legislation into the code (e.g. leasing, which was dealt with in Law 25248 of 2000),[58] and incorporates contractual models that had limited regulation in Argentina (e.g. franchise).[59] This growth can be better sensed by highlighting that the new text duplicates the contractual models that existed in the Argentine Civil Code. The codifying commission looked within its own tradition and beyond: it built on the text of the 1998 draft and included developments available in comparative law.[60]

3 Fideicomiso[61]

Argentina welcomed *fideicomiso* by means of de-codification during the final decade of the twentieth century. Other Latin American jurisdictions, likewise, welcomed different types of *fideicomiso* around the same time. Examples of reception of that instrument can be found, in amongst other jurisdictions, Bolivia, Chile, Colombia, Costa Rica, Ecuador,

55 Favier Dubois, 2015, p. 6 [online].

56 The ACCC includes the contract of *fideicomiso*, which is central to this paper. That same code includes the following contracts: sale (*compraventa*), barter (*permuta*), supply (*suministro*), lease (*locación*), leasing (*leasing*), construction and services (*obra y servicios*), transport (*transporte*), mandate (*mandato*), consignment (*consignación*), brokerage (*corretaje*), deposit (*depósito*), banking (*bancarios*), factoring (*factoraje*), stock exchange (*celebrados en bolsa o mercado de comercio*), bank accounts (*cuenta corriente*), associative (*asociativos*), agency (*agencia*), concession (*concesión*), franchise (*franquicia*), mutuum (*mutuo*), commodatum (*comodato*), donation (*donación*), security (*fianza*), life annuity (*oneroso de renta vitalicia*), gaming (*juego y de apuesta*), assignment of rights (*cesión de derechos*), assignment of contractual status (*cesión de la posición contractual*), settlement (*transacción*), arbitration (*arbitraje*), and fiduciary ownership (*dominio fiduciario*).

57 See 'Modificaciones Relevantes', *in Código Civil y Comercial de la Nación*, Buenos Aires, Infojus, 2015, p. 493.

58 *Ley 25248*, available at: http://infoleg.mecon.gov.ar/infolegInternet/anexos/60000-64999/63283/texact.htm (accessed 14 April 2020).

59 Modificaciones Relevantes, 2015, p. 493.

60 Brodsky & Donato Brun, 2014, p. 84.

61 This section offers information on *fideicomiso*. That information does not aim to be exhaustive, it aims only to offer traits and general rules that may assist in understanding the de- to re-codification experience of that trust-like instrument in Argentina.

El Salvador, Guatemala, Honduras, Mexico, Panama, and Venezuela.[62] It should be stressed that trust law is not part of the Argentine legal system, and that the *fideicomiso* should not be confused with a trust, even when it fulfils many of its functions and presents similarities.[63]

The legislative reception of *fideicomiso* in Argentina was only structured in 1995 by means of Law 24441.[64] Several earlier efforts had advocated, with no success, for a framework for *fideicomiso* in Argentina;[65] since the local economy, especially during the 1990s, called for further regulations on that instrument. Law 24441 addressed *fideicomiso* in its first 26 articles, offering an economic approach towards the development of that model as a business tool.[66] The malleability and ability of that instrument to adapt to the most diverse juridical enterprises may help explain its success and its emergence through de-codification.[67] Law 24441 dealt with financing of housing and construction, yet, as many de-codification counterparts, it regulated tangentially related aspects. *Fideicomiso* was amongst the novelties introduced into the local legal framework, hence being able to grow outside the codes, reacting to the needs of society beyond the seminal *corpora*. In 26 articles, the law regulated many aspects of that trust-like instrument, amongst others, offering a definition,[68] dealing with the different parties,[69] and addressing the effects and its modalities,[70] while mentioning the means of extinction.[71] The use of *fideicomiso* grew exponentially after de-codification took place. For example, Argentina was third, after

62 L.A. Bossini, 'Introducción al fideicomiso', *El Derecho*, Vol. 232, 2009, pp. 1 and 10-11 [online]; and H. Méndez & A.M. Méndez, 'Anteproyecto de Unificación de los Códigos Civil y Comercial de la Nación. El contrato de fideicomiso en garantía. Una visión crítica', *La Ley Online*, AR/DOC/5179/2012, 2012, pp. 8-9 [online].

63 S.V. Lisoprawski, 'Ley de blanqueo. Fideicomiso argentino y trust no son lo mismo', *Revista Jurídica Argentina La Ley*, 5 September 2016, p. 1 [online].

64 *Ley 24441*, available at: http://servicios.infoleg.gob.ar/infolegInternet/anexos/0-4999/812/norma.htm (accessed 14 April 2020).
The Argentine Civil Code had included provisions dealing with fiduciary institutions, however. See for example article 3730 of the Argentine Civil Code. See also J.M. Peire, 'El contrato de fideicomiso. Breve reseña del fideicomiso en distintas etapas', *El Derecho*, Vol. 272, 2017, pp. 10-14 [online].

65 Peire, 2017, pp. 10-14 [online].
For example, the doctoral dissertation of Guillermo Michelson triggered the elaboration of a legislative draft in the 1970s. See generally M.T. Acquarone, 'Trust o fideicomiso de garantía (Aproximación al fideicomiso en la actual ley de financiación de la vivienda)', *Revista Jurídica Argentina La Ley*, Vol. 1995-B, 1995, p. 997.

66 For an overview of Law 24441, see generally F.R. Mantilla, 'Una introducción al fideicomiso', *Revista Jurídica Argentina La Ley*, Vol. 1995-B, 1995, p. 788.

67 Peire, 2017, pp. 10-14 [online]; G.L. Santamaría, M.C. Gómez de la Lastra & A. Monserrat Ortega, 'Fideicomiso: el antes y el después del Código Civil y Comercial. Un análisis comparativo entre la ley 24.441 y las reformas introducidas a partir de la entrada en vigencia del Código Civil y Comercial', *RCCyC*, 6 June 2016, p. 1 [online]; and M.A. Carregal, 'El fideicomiso: su aplicación desde la sanción de la ley 24.441', *Revista Jurídica Argentina La Ley*, 29 March 2007, p. 1 [online].

68 Article 1 of *Ley 24441*.

69 Articles 2-10 of *Ley 24441*.

70 Articles 11-24 of *Ley 24441*.

71 Articles 25-26 of *Ley 24441*.

Mexico and Brazil, in the number of *fideicomisos* that were created in the mid-2000s.[72] The instrument was able to quickly fill a *lacuna* and was adopted spontaneously by the public at large, regardless of legislative deficiencies.[73] This fact returns to the words of Lord Goff of Chieveley that Sjef endorsed, since it shows that practical solutions are reached after facing practical problems.

The ACCC introduced *fideicomiso* to the code of private law. The re-codification experience built on the de-codification precedent; and this is palpable in words of the codifying commission, as expressed in the *exposé des motifs*:

> The proposed text is based on the 1998 draft, which had followed Law 24441. The 1998 draft proposed the incorporation of the [*fideicomiso*] in the unified Code, it systematized the provisions of the law, and proposed the modification of a number of aspects that, at the time of its writing, had been deemed necessary by scholars.
> The current regime does not merit profound changes, since it has not shown major problems of interpretation and application, and has demonstrated efficiency in its application.[74]

3.1 Tenets

The ACCC regulates *fideicomiso*, hence terminating the de-codified period of that instrument, migrating provisions to the new *corpus*. This instrument is now included in chapter 30 of Title IV of Book III of the ACCC, extending through 34 articles.[75] The ACCC replicates the general structure of Law 24441,[76] and scholars have mentioned that the new text improved the old provisions, including aspects advocated for in the literature and that had been stated in court decisions, offering a more precise, clear, and accessible wording.[77]

---

72 L.A. Allende & G.J. Borda, 'Apuntes sobre la práctica del fideicomiso', *Revista Jurídica Argentina La Ley*, 10 August 2007, p. 2 [online].

73 Allende & Borda, 2007, p. 36 [online].

74 *Fundamentos del Anteproyecto*, pp. 173-174.

75 Articles 1666-1700 of *Ley 26994*.
Chapter 31 of the same title deals with fiduciary ownership. The latter was included – not free of doctrinal criticism – in that title since its sole source is found in the *fideicomiso*, being this contractual or testamentary. See R.L. Lorenzetti (dir.), *Código Civil y Comercial de la Nación. Comentado*, Vol. 8, Santa Fe, Rubinzal Culzoni Editores, 2015, p. 257. See also C.M. Kiper & S.V. Lisoprawski, 'El Fideicomiso en el Proyecto de Código', *Revista Jurídica Argentina La Ley*, 27 August 2012, p. 812, p. 14 [online].

76 Peire, 2017, p. 11 [online]. The text was not free from criticism. See, for example, C.A. Molina Sandoval, 'La registración del fideicomiso', *Revista Jurídica Argentina La Ley*, 28 March 2016, p. 1 [online].

77 S.V. Lisoprawski, 'Fideicomiso en el Código Civil y Comercial', *Revista Jurídica Argentina La Ley – Suplemento Especial Nuevo Código Civil y Comercial de la Nación. Contratos en particular*, 21 April 2015, p. 1 [online]; and C.M. Kiper & S.V. Lisoprawski, 'Fideicomiso en el Código Civil y Comercial de la Nación',

They likewise pointed that the new text may settle aspects that had been subject to diverse interpretation.[78] Scholars further pointed that the new text does not present profound changes when compared with the previous regulations.[79] This final point is of interest when looking at the transition from de- to re-codification in that specific area. The working group on *fideicomiso* appointed by the codifying commission stated in these lines that:

> We analysed the criticisms made by the doctrine to the current text and the judicial problems that its application generated. Accordingly, we sent questionnaires to recognized specialists in the field, who expressed their positions on the issues raised and [we] consulted the main judicial decisions that had been rendered since the instrument came into force. [...] We concluded that the current regime does not deserve profound changes, since it has been efficient and has not generated major problems of interpretation and application.[80]

The contract of *fideicomiso* in Argentina involves different parties, and Figure 1 below helps illustrate its structure. The contract entails one party (*fiduciante*) who transfers or commits to transfer the property of goods to a second party (*fiduciario*). Conversely, that second party commits to exercise the right of ownership in benefit of a third party (*beneficiario*) that is identified in the contract. Further, the second party must transfer the goods upon a fix time period or condition to another party (*fideicomisario*). That final party can be the *fiduciante*, the *beneficiario*, or a different person, yet not the *fiduciario*. This contract can extend for a maximum of 30 years, except when the *beneficiario* is incapacitated, since in these occasions the contract will cease to exist at the time the incapacity ends or at the time of death of the *beneficiario*.[81] Law 24441 differed, since the 30-year period could be extended if goods were added to the contract after the original celebration of the contract.[82]

Revista Jurídica Argentina La Ley – Suplemento Código Civil y Comercial, 17 November 2014, p. 125, p. 1 [online].

78 Peire, 2017, p. 11 [online].

79 Kiper & Lisoprawski, 2014, p. 1 [online]; and J.J. Guardiola, 'Fideicomiso: lo que se mantiene y cambia con el nuevo código', *elDial.com – DC1EEA*, 29 April 2015. See the clear comparative chart in Santamaría, Gómez de la Lastra & Monserrat Ortega, 2016, pp. 12-24 [online].

80 J.F. Márquez, 'El fideicomiso en el Proyecto de Código', *Revista Jurídica Argentina La Ley*, 13 August 2012, p. 1 [online].

81 Articles 1666 and 1668 of *Ley 26994*. See J.C. Rivera & G. Medina (dirs.), *Código Civil y Comercial de la Nación. Comentado*, Vol. 4, Buenos Aires, La Ley, 2014, at article 1668.

82 M.A. Carregal, *Fideicomisos*, available at: http://www.marvalnuevocodigo.com/fideicomiso/ (accessed 14 April 2020).

Figure 1. Structure of *Fideicomiso*

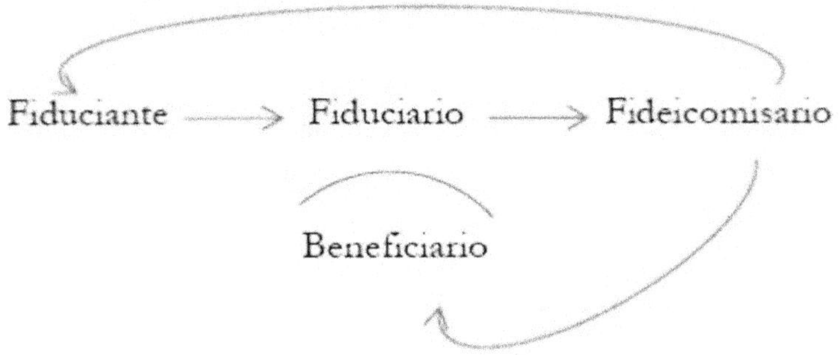

The contract must be registered before a public registry (even when the ACCC is silent on which that registry ought to be),[83] by means of a public or private instrument, and must comply with certain requirements. For example, the instrument must identify the goods that are object of the contract. These goods must be suitable for private legal transactions; and, aiming to bring to an end a long-standing doctrinal debate, the ACCC states that goods can even be universalities, yet cannot include future inheritance.[84] Further, reference must be made of the fix time period or condition that affects the goods. Additionally, the instrument must identify or offer the means to identify the *beneficiario*. Moreover, that instrument must state the fate of the goods after the termination of the contract, together with the *fideicomisario* that must receive them. Finally, such contract requires the indication of rights and obligations of the *fiduciario* and the manner she/he can be substituted.[85]

The main tenets of this instrument were presented both in the de-codification and in the re-codification experiences in Argentina. The codifying commission was able to move to a code an instrument that had not found a place in the previous civil and commercial codes. That tool had grown beyond the nineteenth century codes by means of special legislation. The legislator was able to fill the *lacuna* the codes had generated. The codifying commission then moved the *fideicomiso* to its natural habitat; it returned that instrument to the code that regulates private law.

83 Guardiola, 2015, p. 2 [online]. See also S. Cornet, 'A propósito de la registración de los contratos de fideicomiso', *Doctrina Judicial*, 19 October 2016, p. 1 [online].

84 M.A. Carregal, 'Modificaciones del Código Civil y Comercial al fideicomiso', *Revista Jurídica Argentina La Ley*, 18 April 2016, pp. 3-4 [online].

85 Articles 1667 and 1669-1670 of *Ley 26994*. Sea Kiper & Lisoprawski, 2012, p. 4 [online]; and Cornet, 2016, p. 4 [online].

3.2 Parties

A brief elaboration on the four parties that interact in a *fideicomiso* may, likewise, assist in better grasping the extent of this instrument. In Argentina, according to Law 2441 and the ACCC, a *fideicomiso* involves up to four parties or positions (i.e. *fiduciante, beneficiario, fideicomisario, fiduciario*). Some parties may play more than one role in a single contract, it should be emphasised. The existence of four positions distinguishes the Argentine *fideicomiso* from that of other jurisdictions that accept only three.[86]

A first actor in this instrument is the *fiduciante*. Law 24441 and the ACCC do not offer an extensive definition for this party, yet the rights and duties of this actor are very present and spread across the different articles. Accordingly, the ACCC states briefly that the party who transfers or commits to transfer the property of goods to another party is referred to as the *fiduciante*. This party may be a human or juridical person.[87]

The *beneficiario* may be likewise a human or juridical person, who may or may not exist at the time of entering into the contract. The *fiduciario, fiduciante*, or *fideicomisario* can be appointed *beneficiarios*, hence ending doctrinal debate on that matter;[88] while *beneficiarios* must accept their role in order to receive the benefits of the *fideicomiso*. Acceptance, however, can be presumed and can likewise be requested by court.[89] Multiple *beneficiarios* can be appointed, and there is a presumption of benefiting in equal manner. The right to accession or to appoint substitute *beneficiarios* can be established when *beneficiarios* do not accept, resign, or do not come into being.[90] The characterization of this party to the contract is further elaborated in the ACCC. The new text states that the right of the *beneficiario* can be transferred *inter vivos* or *mortis causa*, even when no acceptance occurred.[91]

Law 24441, encapsulating the de-codification experience of this instrument, was silent in defining the *fideicomisario*.[92] The ACCC now states that *fideicomisario* is the person to whom the property is transferred upon ending the *fideicomiso*. In the same line as the *beneficiarios*, the *fideicomisarios* must accept their role in order to receive the benefits of the *fideicomiso*. Again, acceptance can be presumed and can likewise be requested by court.[93] Special attention merits the fact that the *fiduciante* will be deemed *fideicomisario*

---

86 Márquez, 2012, p. 2 [online]; and Guardiola, 2015, pp. 2-3 [online].

87 J. Amarilla Ghezzi, 'Fideicomiso en garantía. Reflexiones en torno al doble carácter fiduciario/beneficiario del acreedor,' *Doctrina Judicial*, 29 June 2016, p. 1 [online].

88 Carregal, 2016, p. 2 [online]; and Márquez, 2012, p. 3 [online].

89 Articles 1671 and 1681 of *Ley 26994*. See Kiper & Lisoprawski, 2012, p. 5 [online].

90 Article 1671 of *Ley 26994*.

91 Article 1671 of *Ley 26994*.

92 Guardiola, 2015, p. 3 [online].

93 Articles 1672 and 1681 of *Ley 26994*.

upon lack of acceptance, resignation, or non-coming into being of the original *fideicomisario*.[94]

The *fiduciario* may be a human or juridical person according to the ACCC. It is worth noting that the *fiduciario* may be *beneficiario*, yet in such case, the *fiduciario* must avoid conflicts of interests and act in such a way that favours the interests of the other parties involved in the contract.[95] *Fiduciarios*, unless agreed differently, have the right of reimbursement of costs and to opt for retribution.[96] For example, they can use the amounts of money that enter the patrimony to cancel the credits subject to guarantee in a guaranty *fideicomiso*.[97] Notably, guaranty *fideicomisos* were not expressly contemplated in the de-codification experience of Law 24441, and there was doctrinal and jurisprudential consensus about their need.[98] The ACCC further characterises the role of this party to the contract. A *fiduciario* must act as a businessperson, complying with the obligations set by law and the contract. The *beneficiario* and the *fideicomisario* may claim for compliance with the contract and revocation of the acts of the *fiduciario* that were completed in fraud of their interests. Attention should be drawn to the fact that liability is solidary when multiple persons are appointed as *fiduciarios* and acts of disposition–in principle–must be made jointly.[99] *Fiduciarios* can cease in their activities, and the contract may indicate who will or how to replace the *fiduciario*. It bears mentioning that the goods must be transferred to the new *fiduciario*. The ACCC indicates the way in which *fiduciarios* end their participation in a contract of *fideicomiso*. For example, *fiduciarios* will cease in their activities when decided by a judge due to not fulfilling their duties or by material or judicial impossibility to perform their functions.[100]

The re-codification experience in Argentina, differently from the path followed during de-codification, devoted full attention to the characterization of all parties to the contract. Efforts were devoted to explain the rights and duties of each actor, and hence to better depict the possibilities in the interplay amongst parties. That interplay paves the way to better explain the effects and potential application of this instrument.

---

94 Article 1672 of *Ley 26994*. See Kiper & Lisoprawski, 2012, p. 5-6 [online].

95 Article 1673 of *Ley 26994*.

96 Article 1677 of *Ley 26994*.

97 Article 1680 of *Ley 26994*.

98 Amarilla Ghezzi, 2016, p. 1 [online].

99 Articles 1674, 1681, and 1688 of *Ley 26994*. See genearlly Lisoprawski, 2012; and Kiper & Lisoprawski, 2014, p. 8 [online].

100 Articles 1678-1679 of *Ley 26994*.

3.3 *Effects*

A look into the effects of a contract of *fideicomiso* may, likewise, assist in grasping the extent of this instrument. Effects were present in the de-codification experience, and the migration to the code as a result of re-codification preserved these fundamental consequences that are present during the life of a contract.

A pivotal effect deals with the property that is subject to the contract of *fideicomiso*. The ACCC states that a fiduciary property is established on the goods subject to such a contract. The goods within that property comprise an autonomous patrimony that does not fall within the patrimony of any of the parties to the contract.[101] Admittedly, the fiduciary character of the property has effects on third parties once the requirements are met according to the nature of the goods.[102] Inscription of the fiduciary property in the relevant registries is required when the goods are subject to registration. Further, the *fiduciario* must secure civil liability insurance for the damages generated by goods subject to that contractual model. Only the creditors of the *beneficiario* and *fideicomisario* may subrogate on the rights of their debtor, it is worth noting. None of the parties to the contract, however, is liable with their goods for the obligations incurred while performing the *fideicomiso*.[103]

Additional aspects can be mentioned in regards to fiduciary property. The fiduciary property can be used to cancel debts, and if that property does not suffice, liquidation and not bankruptcy may be pursued. Attention should be drawn to the fact that the *fiduciario* may dispose or affect the fiduciary property when the aims of the *fideicomiso* so require; though the contract may indicate limitations.[104] Further, the *fiduciario* may exercise all actions needed to protect the fiduciary property. These actions can be pursued against the other parties to the contract and against third parties. The ACCC likewise states that the other parties to the contract may substitute the *fiduciario* in exercising all actions needed when the latter is inactive due to insufficient reason.[105]

Re-codification was able to benefit from the preceding de-codification.[106] This is evident when looking at fiduciary property in Law 24441 and in the ACCC. The codifying commission also regulated on this important effect, learning from the previous experience, replicating provisions and on occasions improving the text of articles in line with doctrinal

---

101 Article 1682 of *Ley 26994*.

102 Article 1683 of *Ley 26994*. See M. Herrera, G. Caramelo & S. Picasso (dirs.), *Código Civil y Comercial de la Nación Comentado*, Vol. 4, Buenos Aires, Infojus, 2015, p. 390.

103 Articles 1684-1687 of *Ley 26994*.

104 Articles 1687-1688 of *Ley 26994*.

105 Article 1689 of *Ley 26994*.

106 Kiper & Lisoprawski, 2014, p. 1 [online].

and jurisprudential needs. A look into fiduciary property shows that codes are meant for a certain society at a certain time.

3.4 *Modalities*

The ACCC regulates different modalities of *fideicomiso* in chapter 30 of Title IV of Book III. These modalities aim to offer an amalgam of opportunities to parties, aiming to broaden the scope of the *fideicomiso* for the different needs. Scholars have mentioned in those lines that the new text has the potential of offering more certainty in the practical application of this malleable instrument.[107]

A first modality can be found in a *fideicomiso* that relates to financial institutions. The financial *fideicomiso* is a contract in which the *fiduciario* is a financial institution and the *beneficiarios* are the holders of the securities that are guaranteed with the goods that were transferred. The above mentioned securities can be offered to the public within the legal framework that regulates the public offering of securities.[108] The financial *fideicomiso* must meet specific requirements. For example, it must indicate the specific denomination or identification, and must include the terms and conditions of the emission of the securities. Further, the instrument must state the rules for decision making by the *beneficiarios* in case of default or insolvency of the fiduciary property.[109] The financial *fideicomiso* can meet requirements in different manners, as pointed in a reform to the ACCC.[110] For example, this modality will meet registration requirements by attaining authorization for public offering.[111]

A *fideicomiso* can be also established by testament, turning into a useful tool to protect the patrimony and to provide for family needs. That modality was present in Law 24441,[112] and this shows how re-codification does not necessarily require a departure from the path de-codification may have paved. The provisions of the ACCC on this *fideicomiso*, however, offer an improvement when compared with the previous situation.[113] The testator can affect all of the estate, a part subject to indivisibility, or specific goods. In addition, the testator can likewise establish instructions to the fiduciary heir or legatee. Further, in the case of forced heirs, the *fideicomiso* shall not affect their portion of inheritance that is granted by law, except in cases in which there is an improvement in favour of an

107 Kiper & Lisoprawski, 2012, pp. 2-15 [online].
108 Articles 1673, and 1690-1691 of *Ley 26994.*
109 Article 1692 of *Ley 26994.* See Lorenzetti, 2015, pp. 243-244.
110 See article 202 of *Ley 27440*, available at: http://servicios.infoleg.gob.ar/infolegInternet/anexos/310000-314999/310084/norma.htm (accessed 14 April 2020).
111 Article 1692 of *Ley 26994.*
112 Article 10 of *Ley 24441.*
113 Guardiola, 2015, p. 7 [online].

incapacitated heir.[114] Finally, the ACCC does not allow the fiduciary substitution, aiming to avoid the perpetuation of the fiduciary patrimony.[115]

Re-codification of private law in Argentina, building on the de-codification precedent, shows again that practical solutions connect with practical problems. The words of Lord Goff of Chieveley are therefore again present when looking at the modalities of *fideicomiso* that were included in the ACCC. The modalities can indeed serve as tools to deal with different needs of society: they can enable new ways to deal with custom, practice, and the will of the parties.

4 Concluding Remarks

Fideicomiso offered in this paper a playfield to map de- and re-codification experiences of private law that took place in Argentina. The 2015 code that regulates civil and commercial law incorporated institutions that had grown outside of the nineteenth century codes, as part of a process of de-codification. Looking at a selection of aspects of *fideicomiso* may generate awareness on how re-codification can benefit from previous de-codification, since codifiers can build on existing structures, improving provisions by considering sources they have at hand and that had responded to specific needs. These sources include, amongst others, doctrinal writings, court decisions, and special legislation. They likewise offer a mirror of society; they expose the needs that the law should attend. In similar lines, Sjef stated already in his 1990 PhD that "living in a society also means–and this is a condition sine qua non for the existence of society itself–living by rules."[116]

This paper firstly dealt with the ACCC. The adoption of that new code brought to an end efforts that had aimed to adopt texts that would better encapsulate private law for Argentine society. The nineteenth-century commercial (1862) and civil (1871) codes had undergone extensive revision and had been subject to de-codification; while re-codification efforts were launched aiming to unify civil and commercial law in a single fabric. All efforts led towards the adoption of the new code. In that first part, the paper then concentrated in the law of contract, since re-codification is sensed especially in the provisions dealing with that aspect of private law. The mapping of the de- to re-codification experience was further pursued by an analysis of contractual models within the 2015 text. The re-codification of private law welcomed a proliferation of models, since the codifying commission looked within its own tradition and beyond.

114 Articles 1699, 2448 and 2493 of *Ley 26994*. See Kiper & Lisoprawski, 2012, p. 13 [online]; and Kiper & Lisoprawski, 2014, pp. 8-9 [online].

115 Article 1700 of *Ley 26994*. See Lorenzetti, 2015, pp. 255-256.

116 van Erp, 1990, p. 319.

This paper secondly dealt with aspects of the contract of *fideicomiso* as encapsulated in the 2015 text. Argentina welcomed this trust-like instrument by means of de-codification in 1995, with the enactment of special legislation (i.e. Law 24441). De-codification made the reception possible, reacting to the needs of society beyond the seminal codes. Practical solutions were reached after facing practical problems in Argentina. In that second part, the paper addressed a selection of aspects of *fideicomiso*. The tenets were highlighted, indicating that the new text does not present profound changes when compared with the previous regulations: the re-codification experience built on the de-codification precedent. Further, the four parties that interact in a *fideicomiso* were characterized. Efforts were devoted to briefly depict their rights and duties, and hence to better showcase the possibilities in their interplay. This part also dealt with fiduciary property, one of the main effects of the contract of *fideicomiso*. Finally, this part addressed different modalities of *fideicomiso*. Accordingly, the financial and testamentary *fideicomisos* were briefly explained.

Many relations can emerge from a *fideicomiso*. The legislator was aware of that fact, and worked on filling a *lacuna* that was sensed in the nineteenth century codes. Special legislation stepped in and regulated that instrument. Legal relations that emerged from that de-codification experience, together with the doctrinal writings and court decisions that followed, offered necessary sources when the new code was being drafted. On that occasion, the re-codification of private law moved the *fideicomiso* to the orbit of the code. Re-codification was indeed able to move this useful instrument to an optimal place for legal relations to prosper in society.

Global and National Property Law

Osmosis, Antagonism, or a Middle Ground?

Amnon Lehavi[*]

1 Introduction

This chapter pays tribute to Sjef van Erp's lecture, titled: "European and National Property Law: Osmosis or Growing Antagonism?" – which he delivered as the Sixth Walter van Gerven Lecture at the Leuven Centre for a Common Law of Europe in 2006.[1] My contribution reconsiders the key theoretical and doctrinal arguments made by Van Erp in his lecture, and seeks to expand their scope not only to the European level, but also to the global setting. In particular, this chapter builds on the interplay between bottom-up and top-down approaches that Van Erp addressed in his lecture as alternative mechanisms for converging property law within the European Union, and it then offers a broader-based analysis of legal strategies for the globalization of property law.

Legal strategies cannot be detached from political, economic, cultural, and social considerations. Just as the question of "osmosis or growing antagonism" that Van Erp referred to in his lecture extends beyond jurisprudential considerations, so do current trends in the local/global landscape of property law reflect the conflation of legal and extra-legal developments. Today, more than ever before, any attempt at increasing the scope of cross-border norms and institutions pertaining to property law must consider their efficacy in addressing potential extra-legal obstacles. This is so especially because of developments within the European Union and across the globe since 2006, such as the Eurozone debt crisis, Brexit, the immigration crisis, the rise of political populism and isolationism, the U.S.-China trade wars, and currently – the coronavirus. Therefore, the choice of a legal strategy for property law, and for particular subsets of it, is crucial in predicting whether we will move toward osmosis, growing antagonism, or some middle ground.

To illustrate this point, this chapter examines four legal strategies for the globalization of property law: supranationalism, approximation, conflict of laws, and soft law/private

* Dean and Atara Kaufman Professor of Real Estate, Harry Radzyner Law School, and Academic Director, Gazit-Globe Real Estate Institute, Interdisciplinary Center (IDC) Herzliya. Email: alehavi@idc.ac.il.

1 S. van Erp, *European and National Property Law: Osmosis or Growing Antagonism?* (Sixth Walter van Gerven Lecture, Leuven Centre for a Common Law of Europe), Leuven, Europa Law Publishing, 2006.

ordering. It then looks at case studies for the employment of such strategies in the European Union and beyond: unitary patent and the Unified Patent Court; cultural property; and cross-border insolvency. This chapter concludes that the key for cross-border property law may lie in the combination of an effective top-down strategy with bottom-up tools in the form of "soft law" or private ordering.

2 Van Erp on Bottom-Up versus Top-Down Approaches to European Property Law

Van Erp starts his lecture by portraying the concept of "economic constitution" that underlies the European Union and the European Community, and identifies three core economic features embedded in their constitutive documents: (1) freedom to choose a profession or start an enterprise; (2) protection of ownership; and (3) freedom of contract and making individual market decisions. He analyzes the process of economic integration within Europe, and suggests that within this process, the "harmonization of property law is more and more considered to be unavoidable."[2]

Van Erp then discusses the thin body of property law norms in primary and secondary European law (as of 2006), as well as the then early stages of the project on the Common Frame of Reference (CFR) initiated under the responsibility of the Directorate General Health and Consumer Protection, and intended to provide a "toolbox" for future European private law. As Van Erp predicted, although the CFR project originally focused on contract law, "it may prove to be very difficult, not to say impossible, to exclude property law from the CFR, given the already existing law and the work on future European property law."[3] Indeed, the Draft Common Frame of Reference (DCFR), published in 2009, includes Book IX on Proprietary Security Rights in Movable Assets[4] – a property law theme that has long preoccupied scholars and policymakers,[5] but that has not yet been enacted, as of 2020, as part of the formal or top-down European law.

Identifying the gap between the lack of a significant body of property law that applies across the Member States of the European Union, and the need to promote such common norms in order to facilitate a fuller-scale economic integration within Europe, Van Erp

2 Id., pp. 4-6.

3 Id., p. 11.

4 Study Group on a European Civil Code and Research Group on EC Private Law (Acquis Group), *Principles, Definitions and Model Rules on European Private Law: Draft Common Frame of Reference (DCFR)*, Munich, Sellier, 2009, available at: https://www.law.kuleuven.be/personal/mstorme/2009_02_DCFR_OutlineEdition.pdf.

5 See U. Drobnig & O. Boger, *Proprietary Security in Movable Assets*, Munich, Sellier, 2015.

sets out to consider the relative efficacy of two competing methods for doing so: top-down and bottom-up approaches.

Under a top-down approach, the European Union and the European Community should "use the well-known legislative forms of a directive or a regulation to force Member States to change their national laws or, less compelling, use a non-binding recommendation."[6] Van Erp examines the competence to engage in a top-down approach for property law, based on the provisions of the various treaties. These provisions include Article 95 of the Treaty Establishing the European Community ("EC Treaty") [currently, Article 114 of the Treaty on the Functioning of the European Union (TFEU)] that deals with the "approximation of laws,"[7] and Article 295 of the EC Treaty [currently, Article 345 of TFEU], by which "This Treaty shall in no way prejudice the rules in Member States governing the system of property ownership."[8] Van Erp argues that Article 95 EC [Article 114 TFEU] can "only be the basis for harmonization of certain specific areas of property law," while Article 295 EC [Article 345 TFEU] should not be read to mean that "property law cannot be touched at all by European law."[9] As a matter of legal policy, Van Erp claims that harmonization of property law would be useful "in areas which directly affect cross-border business dealings," such as security interests in movables and immovables, but that a bottom-up method is also needed to alleviate potential tensions arising from top-down norms.[10]

What should such a bottom-up approach look like? According to Van Erp, any harmonization attempt should start "with a search for common leading principles and ground rules to establish the *fonds commun* upon which the new European common (property) law can be built."[11] Such an approach should reconsider existing differences between common law and civil law doctrines, by looking under the surface in order to reveal "common thought patterns." Once such patterns are identified, these may alleviate "unnecessary friction" in promoting harmonization measures.

6 Van Erp, 2006, pp. 11-12.
7 Consolidated Version of the Treaty on the Functioning of the European Union, Art. 114, signed on 13 December 2007, OJ (C 326/47), 26 October 2012, available at http://eur-lex.europa.eu/legal-content/EN/TXT/PDF/?uri=OJ:C:2012:326:FULL&from=EN.
8 Id., Art. 345.
9 Van Erp, 2006, pp. 12-13.
10 Id., p. 13.
11 Id., p. 4.

Distinguishing between "leading principles,"[12] "ground rules,"[13] and "technical rules,"[14] Van Erp shows that the first two categories exhibit significant similarities across national property law systems.[15] Thus, a bottom-up approach, based on a meta-juridical view with a historical-comparative perspective, is able to avoid the trap of looking merely at technical rules "under the surface." Accordingly, such an approach creates awareness for underlying common thought patterns, expressed in both leading principles and ground rules. It allows European property law to be perceived not as a *corpus alienum*, but rather as "law that can be received and accepted as a further development of the existing national property law," with the result being a "growing osmosis between national and European property law."[16] In contrast, a top-down approach that is "not based upon thorough research of the national property law traditions in the European Union, is bound to lead to growing antagonism."[17] Van Erp thus concludes his lecture by arguing:

> To promote osmosis and avoid growing antagonism it is submitted that a combined bottom-up / top-down approach will be a *conditio sine qua non*. Based upon a thorough analysis of the national legal systems, a European model could be developed that should have a non-binding nature and could act as an extra jurisdiction next to the legal systems of the Member States. The European model could then prove itself in competition with the existing national law.[18]

Van Erp's analysis entails major lessons for reconsidering the legal relations between national and supranational property law, and for devising appropriate methods in an effort to promote a better synergy between two (or more) layers of legal norms in the face of legal and extra-legal considerations. Accordingly, beyond the important insight by which the risk of antagonism may be present also for less "political" branches of law, a meta-juridical examination of underlying values may actually aid in finding common denominators not initially observed on the surface. Moreover, identifying the appropriate choice of strategy, and in particular, realizing the potential of a bottom-up approach to

---

12 Leading principles are "the filters through which a legal relationship must pass, before it can be characterized as a property right." Id., pp. 13-14.

13 Ground rules "describe the consequences of a right after it has been established that it has the character of a property right." Id., p. 14.

14 Technical rules "provide in more detail how property rights function and are more of a detailed nature (e.g. the requirement of a notarial deed in case of transfer of land"). Id.

15 All European legal systems share two leading principles: (i) *numerus clausus*, and (2) transparency. Id., pp. 14-16. Further, these systems share four ground rules: (i) *nemo dat* rule; (ii) *prior tempore* rule; (iii) priority of limited rights over fuller rights; (iv) protection rules such as the right to reclaim the object of the property right. Id., pp. 16-17.

16 Id., p. 18.

17 Id.

18 Id., p. 19.

lead the way, or at least to be utilized alongside a top-down approach, has a significant bearing on the prospects of moving efficiently toward cross-border property law.

The next sections develop further these ideas, while also shifting the focus to the global setting. Section 3 identifies four globalization strategies for setting up cross-border norms and institutions. Section 4 illustrates the use of such strategies through case studies that deal with various aspects of property law, and examines the efficacy of the globalization strategies chosen.

3 Globalizing Property Law in the Face of Legal and Extra-Legal Constraints

As noted in the introduction, the current forces and counter-forces of globalization are bringing about changes that are even more rapid and fluctuating than those anticipated previously. In an article published in the *New York Times* in March 2020, just as the coronavirus started spreading across multiple borders, Peter Goodman analyzed how "a world defined by deepening interconnection appeared to be reassessing the merits of globalization."[19] While the world today is practically interconnected to such an extent that even the rise of isolationist trends cannot simply undo previous processes, including the flow of goods, services, capital, and persons across borders, it seems clear that the trajectory of local/global market trends and controls is not a one-way route.

Accordingly, just as political, economic, cultural, and social processes of globalization do not follow a single course, so the appropriate legal strategy for addressing various cross-border scenarios that apply to property law should not take a single form. When examining which strategy to adopt, in regard to a specific type of asset, market, or cross-border activity, one should consider an entire array of issues, including normative and extra-legal perspectives.

In my book, *Property Law in a Globalizing World*,[20] I identified four legal strategies that could be employed to decrease the gap between traditionally-domestic property law systems and the cross-border nature of markets, interpersonal networks, and technology.

First is a **soft law/private ordering strategy** – adopting nonbinding principles or institutions, which aim to serve as potential legislative and administrative templates (including model laws), guides to best practices, tools of interpretation, and so forth – alongside arrangements made between non-governmental (i.e., private) actors. Although such principles or institutions are not directly binding on states, and accordingly,

19 P.S. Goodman, 'A Global Outbreak is Fueling the Backlash to Globalization' *The New York Times*, 5 March 2020.

20 A. Lehavi, *Property Law in a Globalizing World*, Cambridge, Cambridge University Press, 2019.

are not enforceable by domestic and supranational institutions – soft law or private ordering mechanisms can influence practically the ways in which both states and private actors design and administer arrangements that pertain to property law. This strategy resonates, therefore, with the bottom-up approach that Van Erp addressed in his lecture.

Second is a **conflict of laws strategy** – advancing new or improved interstate agreements on rules concerning conflict of laws or private international law. This strategy aims at improving certainty about the national forum that would have jurisdiction and the law that would apply, while leaving the mainstay of property ordering to the respective domestic systems. The most notable manifestation of this strategy, employed across various fields of law – including private law, commercial law, and civil procedure – is an array of 40 conventions,[21] concluded by the Hague Conference on Private International Law (HCCH), an intergovernmental organization comprising 84 Member States (plus the European Union) as of 2020.[22]

Third is an **approximation strategy** – requiring states to approximate their substantive and procedural property norms. This is regularly done through treaties or conventions that introduce "minimum standards of protection," while leaving to states the chief power of lawmaking and enforcement of such norms. A prominent example is the Agreement on the Trade-Related Aspects of Intellectual Property Rights (TRIPS).[23] While TRIPS requires all signatory states to introduce certain minimum standards for the protection of patents, copyrights, trademarks, and other intellectual property rights, it enables them to introduce stricter measures to protect intellectual property rights, and more generally, it leaves the ongoing operation, interpretation, and enforcement mostly to domestic institutions – including national courts. The approximation strategy thus goes beyond the conflict of laws strategy, because it intervenes in domestic legal ordering by requiring states to approximate their laws. At the same time, the approximation strategy stops short of directly preempting local lawmaking and enforcement.

Fourth is a **supranationalism strategy** – establishing supranational norms and institutions with binding lawmaking and enforcement powers. Such supranational norms enjoy some type of a superior legal status over national norms in case of conflict, even if the application of such supranational provisions may be tempered or limited by adopting principles that defer to domestic rules in some cases. A leading example is that of property

21 For a full list of HCCH conventions, see Hague Conference on Private International Law, Conventions, Protocols and Principles, available at: www.hcch.net/en/instruments/conventions (accessed on 10 August 2020).

22 For the current list of HCCH member states, see HCCH, HCCH Members, available at: https://www.hcch.net/en/states/hcch-members (accessed on 10 August 2020).

23 Agreement on Trade-Related Aspects of Intellectual Property Rights, 15 April 1994, 1869 UNTS 299, 33 ILM 1197. The TRIPS Agreement is Annex IC to the Marrakesh Agreement Establishing the World Trade Organization, 15 April 1994, 1867 UNTS 154, 33 ILM 1144.

clauses included in human rights treaties, such as Article 1 of the First Protocol of the European Convention on Human Rights.[24] In reviewing the conformity of local lawmaking to the binding provisions of this supranational property clause, the European Court of Human Rights has gradually developed a set of supranational criteria for interpreting and applying this clause. The court has thus established fair balance, proportionality, and other principles as supranational standards for reviewing the validity of local lawmaking, while subjecting such review to some level of deference by introducing a "margin of appreciation" for local norms.[25] Other manifestations of the supranationalism strategy include the introduction of a supranational registry of property, such as the Cape Town Convention on International Interests in Mobile Equipment,[26] and the Protocol to the Convention,[27] which create an international registry of security interests in aircrafts and aircraft equipment. Out of all strategies, supranationalism thus seems to be the quintessential example of a top-down strategy.

What principles should guide us in choosing an appropriate strategy for property law, in the context of a specific type of asset, market, or cross-border activity – and what is the role that normative considerations should play in doing so? I suggest that considering both normative and practical considerations, no single strategy could serve as a panacea for all types of challenges that property law faces in an age of increasing globalization. The choice among the strategies may depend, inter alia, on the specific attributes of the underlying assets; existence of genuine value-based differences in the fundamental features of local legal regimes; *realpolitic* considerations of setting up supranational bodies with binding enforcement power, and so forth. This balance in itself requires us to re-evaluate normative principles and to update them to a changing reality.

In particular, the need for a normative re-evaluation of value-based principles of property law arises when there is growing disparity between such pre-existing normative principles and the changing operation of markets, interpersonal networks, and technology across national borders.

Thus, from a functional perspective, when a certain market for assets becomes dominated by a cross-border activity, the need to create an *in rem* ranking of rights might justify the costs of moving to some sort of a system of property law norms and institutions with a cross-border effect.

---

24 European Convention for the Protection of Human Rights and Fundamental Freedoms, 4 November 1950, 213 UNTS 221, Protocol 1, Art. 1.

25 Y. Arai-Takahashi, *The Margin of Appreciation Doctrine and the Principle of Proportionality in the Jurisprudence of the ECHR*, Antwerp, Intersentia, 2002.

26 International Institute for the Unification of Private Law (UNIDROIT), Convention on International Interests in Mobile Equipment, 16 November 2001, 2307 UNTS 285.

27 Protocol to the Convention on International Interests in Mobile Equipment on Matters Specific to Aircraft Equipment, 16 November 2001, 2307 UNTS 517.

The normative grounding may be, however, more complex and would not always align with the functional consideration. Normative reasons for scaling down supranational pressures posed by functional forces may be multiple and can go beyond general considerations of sovereignty, national pride, or cultural idiosyncrasy. National-security considerations could justify, for example, some limits on the applicability of cross-border norms or on the jurisdiction of supranational tribunals in regard to assets clearly impacted by national-security concerns. Somewhat counterintuitively, protection of human rights or promotion of public health may at times cast doubts on the desirability of introducing a single set of supranational norms.[28]

More broadly, this means that the normative criteria for adopting a certain strategy for the development of property law norms and institutions in a cross-border setting cannot be simply replicated from an analysis that has been made in a certain national setting, or from a "technical" balancing between different value-based preferences promoted by national governments in their various international dealings with each other. A genuine response to the current cross-border reality in markets, technology, and interpersonal networks necessitates a normative re-evaluation. It requires to move beyond paradigms that have been developed in a local context, offering a fresh approach that also recognizes the unrealistic nature of any aspiration to move to wholesale legal unification. Reconstructing property law in the age of globalization – which inherently manifests a fragmented and incomplete phenomenon – requires us to do significant theoretical and policy-oriented work not only in assessing the *end* of globalization, but also the proper *means* to do so.

4 Employing Globalization Strategies: Three Case Studies

This section examines three case studies, and asks if the employment of one or more of the globalization strategies in each such case leads to osmosis, antagonism, or some middle ground.

4.1 Unitary Patent and Unified Patent Court

The European Union is in the process of introducing a unitary patent package, which will include a single registry for patents and a Unified Patent Court. The unitary patent is based on two EU regulations that entered into force in 2013, and were signed by 25 participating states (all EU countries at the time – with the exception of Spain, Poland, and Croatia).

28 For a more detailed analysis, see Lehavi, 2019, pp. 37-41.

The two regulations deal, respectively, with creating a unitary protection for patents granted by the European Patent Office,[29] and with making the translation arrangements required for such a unitary protection.[30]

Both regulations will be applicable once the Agreement on a Unified Patent Court (UPC), signed on February 2013,[31] will have been properly ratified. One threshold has already been met with more than half of the signatories ratifying the agreement.[32] In addition, the agreement must be specifically ratified by the three signatory states in which the highest number of European patents had effect in the year preceding the signature of the agreement.[33] France did so in 2014. The United Kingdom ratified it in 2018, but in 2020, it announced it will not remain in the agreement following its departure from the European Union, declaring that "Participating in a court that applies EU law and is bound by the CJEU would be inconsistent with the Government's aims of becoming an independent self-governing nation."[34] Moreover, in a decision rendered in 2020, the German Constitutional Court (*Bundesverfassungsgericht*) invalidated the German law approving accession to the UPC Agreement. The German Court held that yielding sovereignty to the new court has constitutional implications, and thus has to pass the threshold of a two-thirds majority in the Bundestag required for constitutional amendments – a condition not met by the Bundestag in this case.[35] It is unclear if the Bundestag will act again to meet this requirement. In any case, these setbacks require the Preparatory Committee to make the necessary adjustments.[36]

Once launched, the Unified Patent Court will have exclusive jurisdiction for litigation over European patents with a unitary effect. It will include a Court of First Instance, a Registry, and a Court of Appeal.[37] The Unified Patent Court will thus become the second

29 Regulation (EU) No 1257/2012 of the European Parliament and of the Council of 17 December 2012 Implementing Enhanced Cooperation in the Area of the Creation of Unitary Patent Protection, OJ (L 361/1), 31 December 2012.

30 Council Regulation (EU) No 1260/2012 of 17 December 2012 Implementing Enhanced Cooperation in the Area of the Creation of Unitary Patent Protection with regard to the Applicable Translation Arrangements, OJ (L 361/89), 31 December 2012.

31 Agreement on a Unified Patent Court, available at: https://www.unified-patent-court.org/sites/default/files/upc-agreement.pdf (accessed on 10 August 2020).

32 For the list of ratifications, see European Council, Agreement on a Unified Patent Court (UPC), available at: https://www.consilium.europa.eu/en/documents-publications/treaties-agreements/agreement/?id=2013001&DocLanguage=en (accessed on 10 August 2020).

33 Agreement on a Unified Patent Court, Art. 89(1).

34 Unified Patent Court, 'UK Withdrawal from the UPCA' (20 July 2020), available at: https://www.unified-patent-court.org/news/uk-withdrawal-upca.

35 See 2 BvR 739/19, Rn. (1-21), BVerfG, Beschluss des Zewiten Senats vom 13. Februar 2020, available at: https://www.bundesverfassungsgericht.de/e/rs20200213_2bvr073917.html (in German).

36 A Message from the Preparatory Committee Chair, Alexander Ramsay – March 2020 (5 March 2020), available at: https://www.unified-patent-court.org/news/message-preparatory-committee-chair-alexander-ramsay-march-2020.

37 Agreement on a Unified Patent Court, Art. 6(1).

EU-level supranational court, after the Court of Justice of the European Union, but it will be very different from the latter from an institutional perspective. The Unified Patent Court will deal with a specific type of right – patents – rather than covering the broad array of themes or assets concerning the operation of the European Union. At the same time, however, it will deal with patents in a very comprehensive manner institutionally, relying not only on the legislative function of the underlying agreement, but also on the executive function of the Registry and other administrative bodies in charge of implementing the Agreement on a Unified Patent Court and the regulations. Most importantly, the Unified Patent Court will have exclusive jurisdiction over unitary patents. As such, the European patent package is highly ambitious not only from a normative perspective – establishing its own set of rules on admissibility, registration, and protection of patents – but also institutionally, in that it offers a focused but internally complete mechanism for cross-border governance of patents.

At the same time, the lingering difficulties with finalizing the process of setting up the Unified Patent Court – which will serve as the quintessential example of a top-down approach to supranational (in this case, European) property law – also point to the constant push and pull of extra-legal forces, and mostly political ones. The European Union looked different in 2013, before the immigration crisis, the rise of political populism and isolationism in many Member States, most notably in Hungary and Poland, and culminating in the 2016 Brexit referendum and the consequent decision of Britain in 2020 to withdraw from the UPC Agreement. It remains to be seen whether this ambitious initiative will be able to materialize given these extra-legal trends.[38]

4.2 *Cultural Property*

One setting concerning proprietary disputes over movable property, in which a thick body of norms has emerged internationally, has to do with the cross-border return of cultural artifacts, which have been illegally excavated, stolen, or otherwise illicitly moved away from one country and that end up in the hands of museums, private collectors, or other purchasers in another country.

In fact, in following the development of mechanisms dealing with the cross-border return of cultural artifacts during the past few decades, one can discern the concurrent employment of all four globalization strategies. That said, the most dominant strategy can be typified as one of approximation, as shown below. At the same time, much of the dynamics that aids in turning the "law in the books" into "law in action," meaning that

38 For a more detailed discussion, see A. Lehavi, 'The Role of Innovation in the Globalization of Property Law,' *in* E. Nordtveit (Ed.), *The Changing Role of Property Law: Rights, Values and Concepts*, Cheltenham, Edward Elgar Publishing, forthcoming 2021.

such cultural artifacts are actually returned to their origin states, can be explained by the power of soft law mechanisms, including codes of ethics for museums, collectors, and art dealers. This result seems to support Van Erp's argument, by which a combined top-down/bottom-up approach is required to reduce antagonism and promote synergy, or at least coordination – especially because the subject matter of cultural property is laden with issues of national identity and history, and correspondingly with cross-border tensions.

A full-scale analysis of cross-border legal instruments dealing with cultural property is outside the scope of this chapter.[39] Briefly, the first major milestone is the 1970 UNESCO Convention on the Means of Prohibiting and Preventing the Illicit Import, Export and Transfer of Ownership of Cultural Property ("1970 UNESCO Convention"),[40] ratified to date by 140 states.[41]

According to Article 1, an asset is classified as cultural property only if it is "specifically designated by each State as being of importance for archaeology, prehistory, history, literature, art or science," and it must also fall within one of twelve general categories included in Article 1. Accordingly, each Member State must designate and publicize in its national laws the types of assets it wishes to protect as cultural property. In this respect, the convention may be seen as adopting an approximation strategy, rather than embracing a uniform supranational norm. Moreover, the 1970 UNESCO Convention places the main onus on potentially origin states to set the terms for exporting cultural artifacts, accompanied by an appropriate certificate, such that any cross-border transfer violating such norms established by the state of origin would be considered illicit. Absent such specific norms promulgated by the state of origin, the export or transfer of cultural artifacts is not *per se* prohibited. In contrast, the affirmative duties imposed on potentially destination states are narrower. Most importantly, the duty of a state to return a cultural artifact to its state of origin arises only when the cultural property has been stolen from a "museum or secular public monument or similar institution," and upon the specific request of the state of origin to the destination state, made through "diplomatic offices."[42] The 1970 UNESCO Convention thus applies only among states and it requires them to actively engage in executing the convention.

---

39 See, generally, A. Tadelen, *The Return of Cultural Artefacts: Hard and Soft Law Approaches*, New York, Springer, 2016.

40 United Nations Educational, Scientific and Cultural Organization (UNSECO), Convention on the Means of Prohibiting and Preventing the Illicit Import, Export, and Transfer of Ownership of Cultural Property, 14 November 1970, 823 UNTS 231.

41 For a current list of the Member States, see the 1970 UNESCO Convention website at: www.unesco.org/eri/la/convention.asp?KO=13039&language=E&order=alpha (accessed on 10 August 2020).

42 1970 UNESCO Convention, Art. 7(b)(i)-(ii).

A somewhat different strategy is followed by the 1995 UNIDROIT Convention on Stolen or Illegally Exported Cultural Objects ("1995 UNIDROIT Convention").[43] This convention, aimed at aiding the "fight against illicit trade in cultural objects," seeks to do so by "establishing common, minimal legal rules for the restitution and return of cultural objects between Contracting States."[44] Compared with the 1970 UNESCO Convention, the 1995 UNIDROIT Convention creates a broader system for compelling the return of an illegally exported or stolen cultural artifact. At the same time, the 1995 UNIDROIT Convention is ratified by a smaller number of states – 48 as of 2020 – most of them potential "exporters" of cultural artifacts.[45]

The 1995 UNIDROIT Convention creates a uniform definition of cultural objects, unlike the 1970 UNESCO Convention that allowed each state to establish its scope. In this sense, it applies a strategy that is close to supranationalism in identifying the types of assets governed by the convention. Applying to "claims of an international character" it is designed as a self-executing convention that addresses the prospective proprietary rights of distant parties to a dispute over such assets. As for the illegal export of cultural objects, the 1995 UNIDROIT Convention provides that a court or another competent authority in the destination state must order the return of the object from a buyer, if the state of origin establishes that the removal of the object from its territory "significantly impairs" the physical preservation, integrity of a complex object, preservation of information of a scientific or historical character, or the traditional or ritual use of the object. In such case, the person who acquired the object after its illegal export and "neither knew nor ought reasonably to have known at the time of acquisition that the object had been illegally exported" is entitled to payment of fair and reasonable compensation by the requesting state.

In the case of a stolen object, the 1995 UNIDROIT Convention addresses directly the prospective rights of the possessor and the claimant. According to Article 3(1), "the possessor of a cultural object which has been stolen shall return it." Article 4(1) provides that "the possessor of a stolen cultural object required to return it shall be entitled, at the time of its restitution, to payment of fair and reasonable compensation provided that the possessor neither knew nor ought reasonably to have known that the object was stolen and can prove that it exercised due diligence when acquiring the object." The convention therefore adopts a uniform substantive rule for deciding proprietary disputes between

43 International Institute for the Unification of Private Law (UNIDROIT), Convention on Stolen or Illegally Exported Cultural Objects, June 24, 1995, 34 ILM 1330.

44 *Ibid.*, at Preamble, para. 4.

45 For the current status of signatory states, see UNIDROIT's website at: www.unidroit.org/status-cp (accessed on 10 August 2020).

original owners (claimants) and buyers (possessors), superseding any national norms that govern in the matter.[46]

Another top-down measure taken in the matter, applying to the European Union, is the 2014 European Directive on the Return of Cultural Objects Unlawfully Removed from the Territory of a Member State.[47] The directive enables Member States to secure the return of cultural objects, which are classified as "national treasures" within the meaning of Article 36 of TFEU[48] – which grants the right to identify such national treasures to the Member States – and that have been removed from their territory in breach of national provisions or the 2009 Council Regulation on the Export of Cultural Goods.[49] While restricted to the illegal cross-border transfers of cultural objects within the Member States of the European Union, the directive nevertheless binds countries that are regularly destination states, adding yet another layer of binding top-down norms in regard to such movable goods. According to Article 3 of the 2014 Directive, "cultural objects which have been unlawfully removed from the territory of a Member State shall be returned in accordance with the procedure and in the circumstances provided for in this Directive." Article 10 provides that "where return of the object is ordered, the competent court in the requested Member State shall award the possessor fair compensation according to the circumstances of the case, provided that the possessor demonstrates that he exercised due care and attention in acquiring the object."

How effective are the above-surveyed top-down measures at the European and global levels? I suggest that while these formal mechanisms create a necessary legal framework for coordinating the cross-border governance of return of stolen or illegally exported cultural artifacts, these measures are in themselves insufficient for bringing about the actual return of such goods. To be truly effective, such measures have to be complemented by a bottom-up approach, and in particular by mechanisms that seek to establish informal but significant norms not only among states, but also among non-state actors such as museums, collectors, and dealers.

One should, therefore, consider the actual effects of a series of soft law instruments, such as the ICOM Code of Ethics for Museums,[50] and the UNESCO International Code

46 Tadelen, 2016, pp. 77-87; J. Sprankling, *The International Law of Property*, Oxford, Oxford University Press, 2014, pp. 55-56.

47 Directive 2014/60/EU of the European Parliament and of the Council of 15 May 2014 on the Return of Cultural Objects Unlawfully Removed from the Territory of a Member State (Recast), OJ (L 159/1), 25 May 2014.

48 Consolidated Version of the Treaty on the Functioning of the European Union, Art. 36, signed on December 13, 2007, OJ (C 326/47), 26 October 2012, available at http://eur-lex.europa.eu/legal-content/EN/TXT/PDF/?uri=OJ:C:2012:326:FULL&from=EN.

49 Council Regulation (EC) No 116/2009 of 18 December 2008 on the Export of Cultural Goods, OJ (L 39/1), 10 February 2009.

50 International Council of Museums, *ICOM Code of Ethics for Museums*, 2017, available at: https://icom.museum/wp-content/uploads/2018/07/ICOM-code-En-web.pdf.

of Ethics for Dealers in Cultural Property.[51] The ICOM Code of Ethics, for instance, provides minimum standards of professional conduct carrying the spirit of the conventions to museums in 136 countries and territories, thus reaching many more actors than the 1995 UNIDROIT Convention, including all the major destination states. Recent years have also seen mounting pressure on museums, collectors, and art dealers to avoid clandestine transactions, and on Western governments – to recognize their role in preventing looting.[52] This combination of soft law measures, media attention, and political pressure have indeed resulted in practices of increased enforcement by governmental agencies,[53] as well as in voluntary steps taken by museums to return at least some cultural artifacts to origin states.[54]

The case of cultural property seems, therefore, to illustrate a key point made by Van Erp. To the extent that a certain theme concerning property law also involves extra-legal considerations that have traditionally led to antagonism among states and their respective national cultures, a top-down change must be accompanied by bottom-up measures that may also change informal norms.

4.3 Cross-border Insolvency

A different aspect of property law – and a different type of institutional innovation employed to mitigate substantive and procedural frictions in moving across borders – concerns insolvency. Cross-border insolvencies of individuals and corporations are proving particularly challenging, because no supranational court or tribunal is currently authorized to run a bankruptcy proceeding or otherwise establish a single set of priorities or asset-distribution for cross-border insolvency.[55] This means that a top-down ordering, based on a supranationalism strategy, is currently unrealistic.

To handle this institutional deficiency, the United Nations Commission on International Trade Law (UNCITRAL) developed a soft law mechanism – the Model Law on Cross-Border

51 The United Nations Educational, Scientific and Cultural Organization (UNESCO), *International Code of Ethics for Dealers in Cultural Property*, 1999, available at: https://unesdoc.unesco.org/ark:/48223/pf0000121320.

52 A. Efrat, 'A Major Museum Has to Return Another Looted Artifact. Welcome to the Dark Side of the Art World', *The Washington Post*, 7 August 2017.

53 T. Mashberg, 'Ancient Vase Seized from Met Museum on Suspicion It Was Looted,' *The New York Times*, 31 July 2017.

54 E. Jacobs, 'Across Europe, Museums Rethink What to Do with their African Art Collections,' *NPR*, 12 August 2019, available at: https://www.npr.org/2019/08/12/750549303/across-europe-museums-rethink-what-to-do-with-their-african-art-collections.

55 See Sandeep Gopalan & Michael Guihot, *Cross-Border Insolvency* Law, Chatswood (NSW), LexisNexis Butterworths, 2016, pp. 178-179 (suggesting to set up a supranational insolvency court in The Hague with power to resolve multinational corporate insolvencies).

Insolvency[56] – adopted by 80 states as of 2020.[57] In essence, the Model Law relies on the ability to extend the scope of territorial coverage of the debtor's assets beyond the jurisdiction in which the original (main or non-main) insolvency proceeding was opened, but it relies on the discretion of the local court in deciding whether to assist the foreign proceeding opened in another country. In so doing, the court considers whether the interests of local creditors and other stakeholders are sufficiently protected. This form of cooperation relies, therefore, on the willingness of countries to embrace the Model Law, recognize foreign proceedings, and assist foreign representatives in materializing assets located in the territory. The Model Law thus does not set a binding system of conflict-of-laws rules on jurisdiction, choice of law, or enforcement, but it relies, rather, on the cooperation of states and national courts in facilitating cross-border insolvency proceedings.[58]

A recent study by Wai Yee Wan and Gerard McCormack examines how the Model Law was enacted and implemented in four states in the Asia-Pacific region: Australia, Singapore, Japan, and Korea – with the former two being common law countries and the latter two being civil law countries.[59]

In particular, the authors study the divergences between these states in regard to both the implementation of the Model Law's provisions in their domestic statutes and the interpretation of the legislation enacting the Model Law by the national courts in each one of these states. Thus, for example, Japan and Korea have not introduced in their domestic legislation the provision of Article 20 of the Model Law on an automatic stay with the recognition of foreign bankruptcy proceedings. These two countries have also deviated from the Model Law's provisions in other respects, such as in regard to judicial communication and cooperation, and the priority given to local proceedings. These deviations from the Model Law also have a practical effect, in that they limit the accessible, quick, and predictable outcomes of cases involving relief concerning cross-border insolvency.[60]

What accounts for these differences? While some commentators attribute this divergence to the fact that Australia and Singapore are common law jurisdictions, and Japan and

---

56 UNCITRAL, Model Law on Cross-Border Insolvency (1997), available at: www.uncitral.org/uncitral/en/uncitral_texts/insolvency/1997Model.html; UNCITRAL, Model Law on Cross-Border Insolvency with Guide to Enactment and Interpretation (2013), available at: www.uncitral.org/pdf/english/texts/insolven/1997-Model-Law-Insol-2013-Guide-Enactment-e.pdf.

57 For the list of countries that adopted the Model Law, see UNCITRAL, Status: UNCITRAL Model Law on Cross-Border Insolvency (1997), available at: https://uncitral.un.org/en/texts/insolvency/modellaw/cross border_insolvency/status (accessed on 10 August 2020).

58 Lehavi, 2019, pp. 261-263.

59 W. Yee Wan & G. McCormack, 'Implementing Strategies for the Model Law on Cross-Border Insolvency: The Divergence in Asia-Pacific and Lessons for UNCITRAL,' *Emory Bankruptcy Developments Journal*, 36, 2020, pp. 59-96.

60 Id., pp. 70-89.

Korea are civil law ones,[61] the authors suggest a different explanation that combines legal and extra-legal aspects.

According to Yee Wan and McCormack, where states start from the position of having moderately territorialist approaches towards cross-border insolvency (as is the case with Australia and Singapore), they are more likely to adopt wholesale the moderately universalist approach found in the Model Law.[62] However, where states start from the position of an exclusively territorialist approach (such as in Korea and Japan), they are more likely to adopt a more nuanced version. Such a version would signal these states' commitment to international norms (such as broadly agreeing to give effect to the recognition of foreign insolvency proceedings), but at the same time, these states impose more modifications, carve-outs, or exceptions to give effect to their domestic path dependency, as well as to extra-legal considerations touching on sovereignty.[63] The authors thus conclude by arguing that in determining the strategies for uniform implementation of a Model Law, such as that of UNCITRAL, attention should be paid to the importance of both the "signaling effect" alongside the path dependency of these countries, which will have implications for other jurisdictions considering the adoption of the Model Law or other soft law instruments.[64]

A more promising route for effectively running a cross-border insolvency – one that does not rely on conventional supranational institutions or norms – can be identified in recent practices of coordination advanced directly by national courts or private actors (i.e., debtors and creditors). I survey below one such case, which shows what a bottom-up approach may look like in the context of cross-border insolvency, and how it may work in conjunction with top-down institutions.

In the midst of the subprime crisis, in September 2008, Lehman Brothers Holdings Inc. filed a Chapter 11 petition with the US bankruptcy court. With over $600 billion in assets prior to its insolvency, Lehman Brothers had approximately 900 operating entities in more than 40 countries. Accordingly, the filing resulted in over 80 proceedings, under the purview of 16 Official Representatives. Proceedings were subsequently adjudicated in nine countries, and the laws in each country varied widely. This fragmentation posed an entire array of complicated issues and practical barriers to managing the insolvency

61 See e.g., K. Yamamoto, 'New Japanese Legislation on Cross-border Insolvency as Compared with the UNCITRAL Model Law,' *International Insolvency Review*, 11, 2002, pp. 67-96.

62 As the authors note: "the universalist principle is premised on the view that only the courts of the bankrupt's 'home jurisdiction' have control of, and may administer, the bankrupt debtor's assets and that there should only be one governing law. In contrast, the territorialist principle is one where each country has jurisdiction over the portion of the bankrupt debtor's assets within its territory only ... There are also many combinations and variations between the two dichotomies in practice." Yee Wan & G. McCormack, 2020, pp. 64-65.

63 Id., p. 66.

64 Id., pp. 95-96.

proceedings for the hundreds of Lehman Brothers affiliates, including the dispersion of assets and activities of affiliates across jurisdictions.[65]

Against this background, Official Representatives of many of the affiliates-debtors recognized the necessity for cooperation among bankruptcy administrators and creditors across borders. To promote this goal, they developed a "Cross-Border Insolvency Protocol for the Lehman Brothers Group of Companies," which was submitted to the various courts in May 2009.[66] The Protocol was the result of a thick series of meetings and information-exchange between the Official Representatives, which included the preparation of a Global Close Balance Sheet between November 2008 and January 2009. The Protocol is a nonbinding agreement, aimed at minimizing costs and maximizing fair recoveries for all creditors through information-sharing, coordinating activities, and finding consensual, negotiated solutions wherever possible, in order to keep to a minimum the need to involve courts or other dispute-resolution forums.[67]

The institutional innovation embedded in the Protocol is intertwined with the innovative substantive and procedural approach advanced by the Protocol. It does so through a functional and geographical division of labor between the Official Representatives and creditors in various countries to minimize the risk of inter-jurisdictional friction and incongruent decisions made by local courts and tribunals. One such principle is stated in Section 8 of the Protocol, titled "claims:"

> Without prejudice to secured claims or rights in rem, and subject to applicable law, Official Representatives should adjust distributions so that a creditor who has received payment with respect to its claim in one Proceeding may not receive a payment for the same claim in any other Proceeding as to the same Debtor, so long as the payment to the other creditors of the same class is proportionately less than the payment the creditor has already received in respect of that claim.[68]

In this and other ways, the Protocol seeks to create mechanisms that would coordinate the proceedings across numerous jurisdictions so as to mimic to the best possible extent a

65 J. Altman, 'A Test Case in International Bankruptcy Protocols: The Lehman Brothers Insolvency,' *San Diego International Law Journal*, 12, 2010-2011, pp. 463-496.

66 Cross-Border Insolvency Protocol for the Lehman Brothers Group of Companies, 26 May 2009, available at: http://dm.epiq11.com/#/case/LBH/info under "Key Documents," then "Cross-Border Insolvency Protocol and Reports" (hereinafter: "Lehman Brothers Protocol" or "Protocol").

67 Official Representatives and Other Participating Affiliates Pursuant to the Cross-Border Insolvency Protocol for the Lehman Brothers Group of Companies, "Report of Activities through January 15, 2010," available at: http://dm.epiq11.com/#/case/LBH/info under "Key Documents," then "Cross-Border Insolvency Protocol and Reports" (hereinafter: "Lehman Brothers 2010 Report").

68 Lehman Brothers Protocol, Sect. 8.

single process in which priorities are set, and assets or proceeds from their sale are distributed to creditors.

While the principles set out in the Protocol rely on the goodwill of Official Representatives, creditors and courts to exchange information, coordinate activities and negotiate solutions, the track record of the bankruptcy proceedings, across the various jurisdictions, points to considerable success.[69] Thus, the Lehman Brothers case comes closest to a cross-border bankruptcy that is run *de facto* as a single supranational process. This result was made possible by an innovative combination of a bottom-up approach, initiated by private actors sharing a common goal of running an effective cross-border process, and its execution through the collaboration of national courts. The Protocol thus provides a practical solution for coordinating a cross-border insolvency, without having to rely on an (unrealistic) expectation to set up a purely top-down global insolvency court.

5 Conclusion

At the end of his lecture, Sjef van Erp quotes from Theodor Storm's book *Der Schimmelreiter* ("The Rider on the White Horse"),[70] which portrays the story of a man deeply troubled by rising water and how to contain it through building and maintaining dykes – as a metaphor for challenges that European property lawyers face in dealing with the "incoming tide of European law."[71]

Sjef's contribution to the study of property law within and across the European Union is probably unmatched. His attention to details on the water's surface, alongside his outstanding ability to identify the underlying theoretical and jurisprudential principles that lie at the seabed of European legal systems, make him the ultimate captain of the ship – at least for us, property law scholars – as it navigates through the stormy waters of the European Union and beyond. Especially in times when anti-European, and more broadly, anti-global sentiments are gaining traction, the task of navigating the ship to facilitate the free movement of goods, services, capital, and persons – and correspondingly, to build and maintain the infrastructure of property law for this purpose – is ever more challenging.

As Sjef shows, the way to approach this challenge is by realizing that the means chosen to achieve the end of 'Europization' or globalization of property law must be carefully tailored in order to address both legal and extra-legal considerations. Most importantly,

69 By way of example, for the current state of the bankruptcy proceedings in the US Bankruptcy Court of the Southern District of New York, see Lehman Brothers Holdings Inc. (Chapter 11), Case No. 08-13555, available at: http://dm.epiq11.com/#/case/LBH/info (accessed on 10 August 2020).

70 Th. Storm, *Der Schimmelreiter*, Heide, Boyens & Co., 2003.

71 Van Erp, 2006, p. 19.

sticking solely to a top-down approach – i.e., looking only at regulations or directives in the European Union, or at binding international conventions at the global level – may prove over-ambitious and even counterproductive. Any such top-down method to establish supranational norms and institutions must be complemented by appropriate bottom-up approaches that involve academic scholars, private actors, and voluntary collaborations among non-governmental and governmental agencies. Such a bottom-up approach might not only reveal similarities that are not apparent on the surface, but it may also create opportunities for bridging over existing disparities and lead toward a gradual and incomplete, but consistent process of osmosis – rather than one of a growing antagonism.

Spirits of Law from the Girdle of Emerald

On Adat and Custom in Indonesian, Dutch and Comparative Law

Michael Milo[*]

1 Introduction

Wide and far amicus noster has travelled, with an impressive footprint resulting, of scholarly nature. In his inaugural lecture Sjef pointed to Indonesian law which early on raised his interest in the comparatists' fundamental methodological issue of understanding foreign law in foreign culture.[1] This very domain I will explore further by looking into Indonesian adatlaw, the customary law in the girdle of emerald, the colonial Dutch east-Indies, which once featured prominently in Dutch law itself (2). Customary law finds itself secondary in the western tradition of codified civil law as well as in comparative law (3), which is illustrated by the debate on codifying *adat* (4). Spirits of *adat* property law have a strong presence in this debate as concepts and system of property rights in adatlaw are both strongly related to the objects'societal functions (5). The need for adequate methodologies in understanding customary law makes sociological as well as historical and comparative methodologies appearing early on stage (6). The study of adatlaw in modern history of Dutch law provides an unexpected colorful perspective on comparative understanding. We come to realize perhaps even more: there is no place like home (7).

2 Oriental *Adat*

2.1 *The Struggle for* Adat

'He who enters the study of the law of the Dutch east-indies after having studied Dutch law, enters a new world,'[2] thus the first and foremost Dutch player in the field of *adat* Van

* Associate Professor legal history and comparative law, Utrecht University.

1 J.H.M. van Erp, *Postmoderne dilemma's van de rechtsvergelijking* (1998), p. 3.

2 C. van Vollenhoven, *Het Adatrecht van Nederlandsch Indië* (E.J. Brill 1906, 1918, onveranderde herdruk 1925), p. 3. On Van Vollenhoven see H. de Beaufort, *Cornelis van Vollenhoven* (1954); N.H.M. Roos, 'Cornelis van Vollenhoven,' *Zestig Juristen* (1986), p. 377-385; On Van Vollenhoven's *De ontdekking van het adatrecht* (1928), see N. Efthymiou, in *Juristen die schreven en bleven* (published as *Pro Memorie* 2019/2), p. 181-184.

Vollenhoven remarked in the first line of his magnum opus.[3] In order to come to an understanding of *adat*, the western law tradition, nurtured and natured in the hearts and minds of all colonial officials, administrators, judges and professors alike, happened all too easily to blur Indonesian customary reality. The development of the study of adatrecht in the Netherlands has been described as a gradual shift from neglect to recognition, coined as a discovery, and as a struggle, against the prevailing method and minds of all officials in the legal domain.[4] Scholars such as Wilken, Snouck Hurgronje and Van Vollenhoven carried out extensive ethnological research on these local customs, and sought to have their audience – often lawyers – convinced to take adatlaw seriously.[5] Adatlaw came to have its distinct place, in all legal domains, in all geographic areas, to various extents, particularly since the later decades of the 19th century.[6] These changes in perceptions and position of *adat* took place against a background of Indonesian armed resistance, changing opinions in politics and culture on administering a colony.[7] Public powers indeed were much better armed with law, particularly unwritten local laws.

The formal foundations of adatlaw in the constitutional domain,[8] know two legal provisions of prime importance for the status of adatlaw in Indonesia. The act on general provisions for the Dutch East-Indies accepted adatlaw as a source of objective law next to written law, contrary to its European counterpart;[9] the Regerings-reglement for the Dutch

3 C. van Vollenhoven, *Het Adatrecht van Nederlandsch-Indie*, p. 3. The term adatlaw – *adatrecht* – was coined in the late 19th century by Chr. Snouck Hurgronje, *De Atjehers* (1893) I, p. 16 and 386.

4 C. van Vollenhoven, *De ontdekking van het Adatrecht* (1928), passim; also in *Het adatrecht* (1906, 1925), p. 65 e.v.; earlier C. van Vollenhoven, 'De strijd om het adatrecht,' *De Gids* 1914; see also C. Fasseur, 'Colonial dilemma: Van Vollenhoven and the struggle between adatlaw and western law in Indonesia,' in W.J. Mommsen and J.A. de Moor, *European Expansion and Law* (1992), p. 237-256.

5 G.A. Wilken (1847-1891), *De vrucht van de beoefening der vergelijkende ethnologie voor de rechtswetenschap* (oratie Leiden 1885), passim and p. 11 on a minority of lawyers accepting the sense in applying adat; see also in 'Oostersche en Westersche rechtsbegrippen,' (*Bijdragen tot de Taal-, Land- en Volkenkunde van Nederlandsch-Indie* 1888); this and much more in his *Verspreide geschriften* – 4 parts, published twice 1892 and 1912). Snouck Hurgronje – famous for his research into Islam (*Het Mekkaansche Feest* (1880), *Mekka* (1889) – and on Indonesian adat e.g. *De Atjehers* (1893 – also in English *The Acehnese*, 1906); *Het Gajoland en zijne bewoners* (1903). Beatrice de Graaf pointed to Snouck Hurgronje in *NRC* February 28, 2020.

6 I refer to both works – page-turners! – by Van Vollenhoven, *De Ontdekking* (1929) as well as *Het Adatrecht* – any edition. The education of civil servants was arranged in Delft (from 1843 onward), Leiden (since 1864), Batavia (1867) and in Utrecht (since 1925) – Ph. Kleintjes, *Staatsinstelingen van Nederlandsch-Indië* (6e uitgave 1932), p. 441-443.

7 The Aceh-wars since 1873; the 'ethcal politics' replacing mere economic exploitation, e.g. C. Th. van Deventer in 'Eene Eereschuld,' *De Gids* 1899; Multatuli, *Max Havelaar of de koffijveilingen der Nederlandsche Handelmaatschappij* (1860).

8 On the constitutional arrangements see Ph. Kleintjes, *Staatsinstelingen van Nederlandsch-Indië* (6e uitgave 1932) – with ample room for unwritten *adatstaatsrecht*; J. de Louter, *Handboek van het staats- en administratiefrecht van Nederlandsch-Indië* (6e druk 1914); illustrative is also Kees Briët, *Het hooggerechtshof van Nederlands-Indië 1819-1848.* (2015).

9 'Behoudens de uitzonderingen omtrent inlanders en daarmee gelijkgestelde personen vastgesteld, geeft gewoonte geen recht, dan wanneer de wet daarop verwijst.' G. André de la Porte, *Recht en rechtsbedeeling in Nederlandsch-Indië* (1933), p. 12-13.

East-Indies allowed indigenous to be ruled by 'their religious laws, institutions and customs.'[10] The court-system was a composite of courts for indigenous and for Europeans.[11] Judicial powers of indigenous courts were in the hands of presiding administrative magistrates, and the heads of local villages, *kampung*, who had to apply these customs.[12]

What then is this substantive adatlaw and where to find it? Van Vollenhoven lists about seven sources: the society itself; case-law; government-reports; academic research, indigenous documents, writings and compilations of *adat*.[13] Real life was the first and foremost place where research on *adat* had to happen, before it came to be used in deciding on conflicts, published in reports, journals and books, adding to a variety of already existing indigenous compilations (*undang-undang*) of adatlaw.[14] It was in dire need of accessibility.

A formal national institutional research arrangement was proposed, but a private arrangement did take shape as a commission of adatlaw as well as a commission for assistance was formed – on the initiative of Van Vollenhoven and the Arts and Sciences Society of Batavia.[15] It published from 1910 onward yearbooks on adatlaw – with publications on *adat* of all kinds compiled, with a regional systematization.[16] Excerpts of jurisprudence were substantively systematized in the so-called 'pandects' of adatlaw.[17] Thus an elaborate corpus of adatlaw and institutions came to be established, as a distinct scholarly discipline, in close affinity with the legal domains of colonial legislation, administration and judiciary. The application of adatlaw in caselaw is often disappointing – Van Vollenhoven remarks, yet he advertises a few illustrative cases of

10 Art. 75 Regeringsreglement ' ... worden door den inlandschen regter toegepast de godsdienstige wetten, instellingen en gebruiken der inlanders, voor zover die niet in strijd zijn met algemeen erkende beginselen van billijkheid en rechtvaardigheid.' J. de Louter, *Handboek voor het Staats- en administratiefrecht van Nederlandsch-Indië* (1914), p. 101 e.v.

11 A schematic overview Van Vollenhoven, *Het Adatrecht* (1926), p. 96; Europeans were to be ruled from 1848 onwards by the Civil code, as much as possible in accordance with Dutch law. On the export of the Dutch civil code to the various colonial parts of The Netherlands see H.D. Ploeger, 'Het BW 1838 naar de Oost en de West,' in *BW-krant Jaarboek* (1997), p. 57-82.

12 See e.g. the Reglement tot regeling van het rechtswezen in de residentie Lampongsche districten (Regulation on the Judiciary in the Residence Lampong Districts), in force since July 1, 1879, art. 1. Judicial competence was with 1. the magistrates; 2. Indigenous courts (Inlandsche Rechtbanken – Landraad and Proatins) and 3. The residential court. Art. 11 provides the foundation for heads of *kampung* to be part of the proatin.

13 Van Vollenhoven, *Het adatrecht* (1926), p. 92-115. Written indigenous edicts are often to be found, but do appear often only secondary to adatlaw.

14 These compilations should be treated with caution, as it is by definition not the *adat* as it stands, and often contains metaphors. See e.g. the warnings by Chr. Snouck Hurgronje, *Adatrechtbundel* I (1910), p. 23. Also Van Vollenhoven, *Het Adatrecht* (1926), p. 92 – citing these sources may often be misleading.

15 Bataviaasch Genootschap voor schone kunsten en wetenschappen – an old (1778) and influential society. See H.L. Wesseling, *Indië verloren, rampspoed geboren* (1988, 2nd edition 1995), p. 88.

16 *Adatrechtbundel* I (1910) – LV (1955).

17 *Pandekten van het adatrecht* 1. Het beschikkingsrecht over grond en water (1916); 2. Het voorkeurrecht op grond en het genotrecht van grond (1915); 3.Het Inlandsch bezitrecht van grond en het bewerkingsrecht van grond (1916); 4. De overige rechten op grond en water (1918).

courts taking *adat* seriously.[18] One of these cases finds an origin in the volcanic eruption of the Krakatau in August 1883.

2.2 *Krakatau and Kalianda*

Krakatau coloured western sunsets the years following, but also law. It resulted in the Kalianda-case, a conflict over property entitlements, when the devastated islands and shores of South-western Sumatra were slowly repossessed, step-by-step.[19] Mariam, Raden Mas Inten te Pematan Tembok claimed to be entitled to the remains of the islands of Krakatau, Sabesie Sebuku Besar, Sabuku Ketjil and Pulau Tiga, and several sawahs on the south-shore of Sumatra near Kalianda, against Minak Putra, head of *kampung* Radja Basa, who had these islands and sawahs already a couple of years in factual possession. As Mariam was the only surviving child of Krakatau-victim Pangeran Singa Branta, who was entitled to islands and sawahs, she claimed to have inherited the said lands, and thus consequently entitled to evict the defendant. The procedure was dealt with by the local court, the *Proatin*, presided by a Dutch official, who denied the claim.[20] Subsequently the case was appealed to the Council for Justice in Batavia, who upheld the *Proatin*'s decision.

The reasoning brings adatlaw center-stage at both levels. While the proprietary claim to the land was as such not dealt with and quite easily and western-style was qualified as ownership, the claimants alleged acquisition by inheritance of the land and the proprietary claim was channelled alongside islamic law towards first and foremost local Lampong adatlaw. Indeed, the court held, was Mariam the only surviving child of Branta, who was proprietary entitled to the disputed land, and who had died – as a direct casualty of the Krakatau disaster in 1883. However, Mariam had been married, and the type of marriage precluded her to be a heir of her father's property. The conclusion was reached through an expose of the four types of marriage in South Sumatra Lampong *adat*, with reference to art. 75 Regeringsreglement ('religious laws, institutions and customs'), to the report made by Junghuhn on the Bataks in 1840, which provided the *Proatin* with some comparative support (as Lampongers are no Bataks) in substance of the types of marriages, and further to the treatises of De Louter[21] and Van den Berg.[22] There are various types of marriage distinguished in the *Proatin's* expose, of which the *adat djoedjoer* was the regular

18 Van Vollenhoven, *Het adatrecht van Nederlandsch-Indië* (1926); sometimes cases fall short in knowledge of *adat* – but natural justice is then explicitly referred to, e.g. in the decision by the Landraad Bandjarnegara, August 4, 1923 (Ngabdoellah/ Hoedosenito), *Indisch Tijdschrift van het Recht* 1923, p. 46-49.

19 *Indisch Weekblad van het Recht* 1903, nrs 2082-2083.

20 W.A.C. Whitlau, controleur van Katimbang, comissioned at May 12, 1900 – see the *Regeerings-Almanak voor Nederlandsch-Indië*, 2e deel (Lands-drukkerij Batavia 1903).

21 *Staats- en administratief recht van Nederlandsch-Indië*, p. 264.

22 *Beginselen van Mohammedaansche Recht*, p. 179 ff..

type – marriage by elopement, and a payment of a price, dowry (*djoedjoer*) to the bride's family.[23] Within the *djoedjoer*-marriage again various varieties are distinguished, of which only one seems to be grounded in individual mutual affection – *toewang maling*. In all types: family counts heavily in all respects.[24]

An extensive expose of the provided testimonies, leads us through Mariam's extended family-relations, the various person's whereabouts and their relations to the contested land, and to the proof of Mariam's *toewang maling* marriage, all in a living narrative reflecting the factual and customary oriental scenery. In case of a *djoedjoer*-marriage the bride moves out of her father's family, into the family of her husband – receiving with her all kind of personal property, but further barred from inheriting – also in this case. A call for application of Islamic law[25] does not lead to adjusting the conclusion reached by *adat*. Adatlaw needed to be given its effect as the primary source of indigenous law, and does not have to yield to religious law. In the background: *adat* may help to preserve the traditional Sumatran family-relations.[26]

23 The other types are the *tjamboer soembaij* and the *tjamboer soembaij ngisi*. The first deals with the situation in which the bride's father has his daughter conclude the marriage with the son-in-law, if the father has no sons and if all his male relatives consent, since the son-in-law will then inherit. The latter concerns kind of mariage-on-credit relationship, in which a lower price for the bride is accepted, and the husband-to-be still has sons who need to be taken care of, and undertakes to live with the bride's family and take care of the bride's family until his sons have come of age.

24 *Toewang tjintok, toewang bagoes* and *toewang djagalarangan*; the *Proatin* does not use G.A. Wilken's 'Over het huwelijks- en erfrecht bij de volken van Zuid-Sumatra,' *Bijdragen tot de Taal-, Land-, en Volkenkunde van Nederlandsch-Indië* VI (1891), 149-235, (also in *Verspreide geschriften* II, p. 219-308), which elaborately deals with the varieties in marriages and inheritance-rights.

25 A referral to Soera 4.12 as then was used is conform with 4.11, and provides inheritance rights up to half of the inheritance in case of only one surviving daughter; and a general norm of 'reasonableness and fairness' (words 'billijkheid en rechtvaardigheid' are used) is called upon.

26 See particularly Th.W. Juynboll, *Handleiding tot de kennis van de Mohammedaansche wet volgens de leer der Sjafitische school* (1925); Neglect of this adatrule has been held to have had negative consequences, as impoverishment of Sumatran families. See particularly De Waal van Anckeveen on a decision of the Raad van Justitie te Padang 11 september 1905, *Adatrechtbundel I* (1910), p. 80-84 en 84-85). Van Vollenhoven and Snouck Hurgronje argued strongly against applying islamic law too soon – as it often was not in line with *adat*, and had its presence rather for political reasons.

2.3 *Adat in Contemporary Law*

Adatlaw still has a presence in contemporary Dutch academy,[27] but hardly in the legal domain, not surprisingly. It has no serious presence in recent caselaw,[28] is rarely encountered in contemporary scholarly work.[29] Van Rhee analysed the indigenous rights to land on Java;[30] Smits pointed to the Dutch school of adatlaw as exemplary in contemporary legal methodology.[31] Adatlaw may be found in sociology of law – criticized for overlooking the school of adatlaw.[32] Adatlaw does seem to have an increasing presence in the fabric of contemporary Indonesian law.[33] Life in western law is not easy for custom.

3 Occidental Custom

Customs 'long observed and sanctioned by the consent of those who employ them,'[34] is a component part of the wester legal tradition, yet had to establish its validity in relationship

---

27 In anthropology see e.g. J.A.C. Vel and A.W. Bedner, 'Decentralisation and village governance in Indonesia: the return to the nagari and the 2014 Village Law,' in *The Journal of Legal Pluralism and Unofficial Law*, 2015, 3, p. 493-507; earlier with a long list of literature J. Griffiths, 'Recent anthropology of law in The Netherlands and its historical background,' in K. von Benda-Beckmann and F. Strijbosch, *Essays on Legal Pluralism* (1986), p. 11-66.

28 Only three cases – on family law and inheritance law – can be found where *adat* is referred to. The contribution to the case is rather thin: only references in general, only one a little bit more specific referring to Toradja (Sulawesi) *adat*. See Hof den Bosch, 11 september 2012, ECLI:NL:GHSHE:2012:BX7336; Hof Arnhem-Leeuwarden, 7 mei 2020, ECLI:NL:GHARL:2020:3628; the referral to Toradja *adat* and its acceptance (on the basis of official authority) in Rb Noord Holland 27 augustus 2014, ECLI:NL:RBNHO:2014:8344).

29 F. von Benda-Beckmann, 'Van Vollenhoven over het adatrecht,' *NJB* 1985, pointing to the value Van Vollenhoven's studies still have. On criminal law: Pompe, S. 'De Invloed van het adatrecht bij de toepassing van het strafrecht in Indonesie,' in: *Bijdragen Tot De Taal-, Land- En Volkenkunde*, vol. 143, no. 4, 1987, pp. 499-506. See as well Peter Burns, *The Leiden Legacy. Concepts of law in Indonesia* (2004), passim.

30 C.H. van Rhee, 'Particuliere Landerijen in Nederlands-Indië en het zogenaamde erfpachtsrecht (1836-1912)'. *Ars Aequi*, 1991, 973-983.

31 Jan Smits, *The mind and method of the legal academic* (2012), p. 27.

32 John Griffiths, 'Anthropology of law in The Netherlands,' in K. von Benda-Beckmann and F. Strijbosch, *Essays on Legal Pluralism* (1986), p. 18-24 – as it provides a descriptive richness which is unparallelled and is 'terribly modern' in its method. English and American anthropologists only since the second half of the 20th century 'discovered insights and concepts which had been commonplace in the Dutch adat-law tradition.'

33 Franz von Benda Beckmann and Keebet von Benda-Beckmann, 'Myths and stereotypes about adat law. A reassessment of Van Vollenhoven in the light of current struggles over adat law in Indonesia,' *Bijdragen tot de taal- land- en volkenkunde* 2011, 167-195, p. 168: 'adat-based claims acquired full strenght after the fall of the suharto regime.' On land conflicts in contemporary Indonesia see e.g. K. Szczepanski, 'Land Policy and Adat Law in Indonesia's Forests,' *Pacific Rim Law and Policy Association Journal* 2002, p. 231-256. Bono Budi Priambodo, 'Positioning Adat Law in the Indonesia's Legal System: Historical Discourse and Current Development on Customary Law,' in *Udayana Journal of Law and Culture* 2018, p. 140-164.

34 Institutes I.2.9.

with norms written[35] as well as with ratio and natural law in the middle ages,[36] early modern[37] and modern times.[38] Customary law in the European Netherlands became bridled in the early nineteenth century, where it needed a formal recognition in codified law – opposed to custom in the orient.[39] An underlying legal theory of positivistic legal reasoning similarly made it hard to directly apply customary norms.[40] Custom never stopped to be of importance in legal history, where next to Roman law, a field of research in history of national laws came to be developed, where customary laws were acting front stage – omnipresent in the study of law and scholarly work.[41] The coming of sociological jurisprudence as a reaction to societal needs and positivism can be seen all over western tradition. The law is no longer (only) to be found in positive law, but in society.[42] Nevertheless: even in the first and foremost jurisprudential analysis in Dutch law custom comes only secondary.[43] The importance of attention for customary law may perhaps be on the rise – due to an increasing diversity in national populations – just as custom once needed to be taken serious in a colonial setting.

Are comparatists paying attention to customary law? Not too much, it seems: '[b]eyond statute law and case law comparatists have rarely ventured' and: 'custom, its establishment, its proof and its application never seem to have arrived on the radar of comparative lawyers,' Vogenauer remarks.[44] Only slight attention shows in the Oxford Handbook of Comparative

35 Primacy to custom is provided by D.1.3.32 1. (Julianus, Digest LXXXIV); yet it was subject to written norms and ratio in C.8.52.2 (Constantinus to Proculus, 319). Irnerius argued this text having primacy over the text of Julian: this text [D.1.3.32.1] speaks for its own time, in which the people had the power to issue laws, and hence to abrogate the same by silent consensus of all. But since this power has been transferred to the emperor, nihil faceret desuetudo populi – nothing is established contra custom by the people. On this F.C. von Savigny, *Geschichte des Romischen Rechts im Mittelalter* 4 (Heidelberg, Mohr 1850), p. 459.

36 As Aquinas argued, citing Isidore of Sevilla: pravum usum ratio et lex vincat – see *Summa Theologica* I-II, q. 97.

37 See Grotius in his *Inleidinge* I.2.

38 A wonderful expose of custom, or 'folk law' by G.C.J.J. van den Bergh, 'The concept or folk law in historical context: a brief outline', in *Anthropology of law in The Netherlands. Essays on legal pluralism* (1986), p. 67-89.

39 Custom does not accrue to law, unless a statute refers to it, thus art. 3 Wet AB (1829).

40 See e.g. the theory by C.W. Opzoomer, in which the position of customary law is indeed subjected to formal legislation.See his *Aanteekening op de Wet, houdende Algemeene Bepalingen* (4e druk 1884), p. 67 e.v.; legalism and positivism may be found with different flavours all over the western legal world in the 19th and early 20th century. J.Th. de Smidt, *Rechtsgewoonten* (1954) shows the variety still present in these 'statutory endorsed' customs.

41 J.M. Milo, 'Eigen recht eerst' *Ars Aequi* 2020/6, p. 626-632.

42 A symbolical beginning in The Netherlands in W.L.P.A. Molengraaff, 'De oneerlijke concurrentie voor het forum van den Nederlandschen rechter,' *Rechtsgeleerd Magazijn* 1887, leading to HR January 31, 1919, NJ 1919, 616 (Lindenbaum/Cohen) – the acceptance of unwritten rules as part of the formal legal fabric.

43 Paul Scholten, *Algemeen deel* (1931), par. 24.

44 S. Vogenauer, 'Sources of law and legal method in comparative law,' in M. Reimann and R. Zimmermann, *The Oxford Handbook of Comparative Law* (2006), p. 895-897.

Law, at least in its outward appearance of headings and subject index.[45] The affiliation of comparative law with early legal anthropology is dealt with by Cairns.[46] Mostly, however, it is dealt with only shortly, reluctantly,[47] and sometimes quickly discarded, if not plainly denied.[48] If we are to take a quick closer look, the comparative confrontation of the strange customary *adat* in its large diversity with western civil law gave rise to issues in the core of any comparative agenda, such as codifying unwritten law, the concept of property rights and the methodology underlying law and legal reasoning, all in the domain of *adat*.

4 Codifying *Adat*

Civil law was codified in 1848, for the European part of the population.[49] The possibility it might be extended to the indigenous was immediately topic of debate.[50] Since then, legislative changes favouring a western perspective, courts not sufficiently applying adatlaw, as well as the use of western concepts and systematizations in adatlaw were in discussion nearly until the end of the colonial period.[51] Forceful reactions by Van Vollenhoven in particular sought to clear the orient from occidental prepossessions: no lawyer's law for the indigenous.[52]

Accessibility of adatlaw by continued research, subsequent systematization and publication was hence of importance for adatlaw and its use in legal practice. Many studies

45 In M. Reimann and R. Zimmermann's *The Oxford Handbook of Comparative Law* (2006), 42 chapters of which only one chapter is formally dedicated to (African) customary law (Bennett), but in a 'Comparative law and ...' structure. Some other chapters make clear that custom must be included, e.g. by using words as 'legal traditions' (Patrick Glenn), or 'socio-legal studies' (Annelise Riles). In the extensive index only three entries are provided of custom as well as three of customary law (Bennett), and both refer to the mentioned chapters of Bennett and Riles.

46 John Cairns, 'Development of Comparative Law in Great-Britain,' in Reimann and Zimmermann, *Oxford Handbook*, p. 131-174, at 135-138.

47 Benedicte Fauvarque-Cosson, 'Development of Comparative Law in France,' in *The Oxford Handbook of Comparative Law*, p. 35-68.

48 And quite unjustly so. In particular Ingeborg Schwenzer, 'Development of Comparative Law in Germany, Switzerland and Austria,' in Reimann and Zimmermann, 69-106, where the scholar with an immense authority in *adat*-jurisprudence Kohler is depicted shortly as one who was mistaken: 'In fact, the careless accumulation of sources, the imprudent use of different methods, and the combination of observations and purely speculative thoughts make it difficult to appreciate the work of those authors.'

49 On which see particularly J. van Kan, *Uit de geschiedenis onzer codificatie* (Batavia 1927).

50 J. van Kan (1927), p. 161-180 (chapter 14).

51 On this see Van Vollenhoven, *De Ontdekking van het Adatrecht* (1928), passim, or *Het Adatrecht* (1926), p. 39-64.

52 Among more: *Geen Juristenrecht voor den Inlander* (1905); 'De strijd om het adatrecht,' *De Gids* 1914; *Juridisch Confectiewerk. Eenheidsprivaatrecht voor Indie* (1925). Also others were present, e.g. J.H. Carpentier Alting, Ph. Kleintjes, C. van Vollenhoven, W.A.P.F.L Winckel, *Vierentwintig ontwerpen over Indisch Recht* (1909). See as well V.E. Korn, *Mohammedaansch recht en adatrecht in Britsch – en Nederlandsch-Indië* nr. 104, p. 104.

of adatlaw had by that time been made, local *adat*-compilations as well,[53] but a compilation of *adat* for the whole archipelago could be possible, and would be of help in courts fulfilling their social function.[54] A call for such a non-binding codification of adat had already been made by H.J. Scheuer.[55] Van Vollenhoven made such a code for Indonesian adatlaw, 100 articles long, with an introduction to justify such an all embracing general code, referring to Scheuer, to French authors having comparable stances on codifying and applying law in French colonies, to the study of old Germanic laws, where a similar debate on general systematizations did take place, and as well to *adat*-property laws in particular.[56]

How does this 'customary ius commune' look like? It does follow a kind of institutional system – provisions of a general nature precede those on family-relations, inheritance, land, obligations, common provisions to land and obligations, delict and two last paragraphs on amending existing laws and closing provisions e.g. on the remaining power of the indigenous to change their *adat*. Law of obligations concerns movable property as well. The general provisions make clear that the code is providing a non-binding 'common frame of reference,' and is not meant to be exclusive in any way. Adatlaw is the law to be applied, if conflicts between indigenous are to be dealt with by the court. The code offers guidance as help, but does not in itself state the customary law. *Adat* in action prevails.[57] Particularly the connection between the old customary Germanic laws and contemporary *adat* draws our attention, as the extensive citation of Paul Laband in Van Vollenhoven's introduction centers on the fundamental differences in property law in the Roman and the Germanic tradition – no separation between personal and real rights, and neither can the various civil law real rights be found.

5 PROPERTY

Landlaw was central in developing of the cultivation-system since 1830, until its demise from 1870 onwards. The indigenous were free from forced production and services, while

53 An example of such a regional compilation is J.H. Carpentier Alting, *De regeling van het privaatrecht voor de inlandsche bevolking in de Minahassa-districten der Residentie Menado* (1902) – Carpentier Alting was president of the landraad in Menado (Celebes). Earlier already Snouck Hurgronje in his advices on the codification of Western-Sumatra *adat* (1893) – see *Adatrechtbundel* 1 (1910), p. 21.

54 C. van Vollenhoven, *Juridisch confectiewerk*, Koloniale studien 3 (1925).

55 H.J. Scheuer, 'Hervormingen in de Indische rechtsbedeeling,' *Onze Eeuw* 1910, p. 33 e.v. Likewise G. Andre de la Porte, *Over codificatie van materieel privaatrecht in het bizonder van Ned.-Indisch adatrecht* (1918).

56 C. van Vollenhoven, *Een adatwetboekje voor Indië* (1925), p. 3 e.v.; the French authors: Girault, *Principes de Colonisation*; Morand and his *Projet de Codification du Droit Musulman*. In the domain of germanic law Fruin argued likewise to analyse and systematize all that had been found in archives on old local laws. R. Fruin, *De studie van het oud-vaderlandsche recht en de archieven* (1910), p. 6.

57 See art. 2 Adatcode.

individual entrepreneurs could enter the agrarian market in competition.[58] The state was declared to hold all 'land without owner.'[59] A further act arranged the government to transfer wasteland ('woeste gronden') as 'long-lease.' It came to be backed by research on indigenous laws on Java and Madura, coming to the same conclusion: the sovereign is owner of all land on Java.[60] Indigenous had in areas on Java given an 'indigenous property right' – but that far from cleared the indigenous positions relative to the western property rights in the land.[61] Is the sovereign to be considered 'owner' in a civil law sense? Certainly not according to a Thorbecke, not only prime minister, but eminent scholar in civil, constitutional and administrative law.[62]

In parliamentary debate leading to the acts above, Thorbecke stressed the need to first and foremost protect the indigenous' relation to the land. The public interests at stake in this arrangement, did not just concern the individual entrepreneur's interests, but even more the interests of the indigenous population – drawing on a report by one of the older writers on *adat*, Muntinghe, written once for the Raffles administration. The members of the village-community, the dessa, were entitled to the right to develop and possess parts of the waste-land surrounding the dessa, which is, according to Thorbecke, not just a individual right, but a communal dessa-right as well, which should not be made dependent on a permit, as could be the case in this proposed legislation.[63] Similarly Thorbecke pointed to the various other communal Dessa-lands that faced the danger to be given in long-lease under this proposal – which should be prevented. The argument was comparatively made, alongside the arrangements of old Indo-Germanic villages' common grounds – or *markegronden*.[64] Van Vollenhoven referred very positively to Thorbecke's stance,[65] exemplary also for adatlaw's own terminology. The relationship between the government and indigenous holder of land is not between owner and holder of land, and neither does

58 See the parliamentary debate on June 21, 1867.

59 No. 118. Ordonnancie dd. 9 September 1870 (Koninklijk besluit dd. 20 Julij 1870. nr. 15). Regeling van eenige agrarische aangelegenheden. Art. 1. Behoudens opvolging van de tweede en derde bepaling der voormelde Wet, blijft het beginsel gehandhaafd, dat alle grond, waarop niet door anderen regt van eigendom wordt bewezen, domein van den Staat is.

60 See the citations from this report (*Onderzoek naar de rechten van den Inlander op den grond op Java 1867-1869*) in G.P. Rouffaer, *De Agrarische Rechtstoestand van den Bevolking op Java en Madoera* (1904).

61 C.H. van Rhee, 'Particuliere Landerijen in Nederlands-Indië en het zogenaamde erfpachtsrecht (1836-1912)'. *Ars Aequi*, 1991, 973-983.

62 On Thorbecke's legal position see E. Poortinga, *De scheiding tussen publiek- en privaatrecht bij Johan Rudolph Thorbecke* (1987), p. 207 ff.

63 Thorbecke's strong remarks, translated: 'I will stand as strong as can be, that no right will be taken from the Javan population – the Javan peasant is not to ask for a long-lease! He has a better right: individual and Dessa-like.'

64 TK 1866-1867, 86ste zitting, 21 juli, Regeling der uitgifte in erfpacht van gronden in Nederlandsch-Indie, p. 1225-1239, p. 1236-1237, in which also the previous citation can be found.

65 C. van Vollenhoven, *De Ontdekking van het Adatrecht* (1928), p. 89: '... waarbij vooral Thorbecke het adatrecht in zijn kern weet te vatten ... '

ownership in land exist. Nevertheless it is too often heard, Van Vollenhoven recalls in the introduction to his adatcode.[66]

Of particular interest in the many publications which concern property law issues in adatlaw is the classification of things in accordance with their relationship with man – not according to their physical characteristics as we are more accustomed to. Hence the various communities as families, villages and larger communities, as well as the individual determine the property relations with things primarily. Some things are fit to be held in private, others not, as they serve one of the communities in their various interests. Hence things held by a family (*pusaka*) are not fit to be transferred or inherited by any individual in an individual and exclusive ownership.[67] The variety of social functions lead to a wide variety in powers over the thing, which unsurprisingly occurred particularly in land.[68]

Van Vollenhoven's code of adat deals with property rights, with an open-ended list. I cite article 30. 1. The indigenous rights in immovable property are one or more of the following:

a. rights to control;[69]
b. indigenous rights to possession of immovable property;
c. agrarian ownership on Java and Madoera;
d. rights to work or build on the land;
e. right to enjoy precarious building fields;
f. right to use of communal lands;
g. right to develop;
h. right to gather, to mine and hunt;
i. right to graze;
j. rights to acquire by neighbours;
k. pledge on immovables;
l. right to sharecrop;[70]

66 *Adatwetboekje* (1926), p. 1-2.

67 See above on the reasoning in the Kalianda-case. No inheritance according to Islamic reasonableness and fairness, as it infringes on adatlaw concerning inheritance, against the background of societal consequences for Sumatran families.

68 It is illustrated among many more by G.A. Wilken's publication on rights to land in the Minahasa. G.A. Wilken, 'Het Landbezit in de Minahasa,' *Mededeelingen van wege het Nederlandsche Zendelinggenootschap* XVII (1873), p. 107-137, in *Verspreide Geschriften* II (1912), p. 355-378. Van Vollenhoven is very positive on Wilken's research, but critical on his use of civil law terminology. See *De ontdekking van het adatrecht* (1928), p. 100.

69 Which is a term that does not strongly relate to the legal term of power to dispose concerning contemporary property arrangements.

70 Recht van deelbouw, on which see Van Vollenhoven, *Het adatrecht*, p. 202-203; the dissertation by A.M.P.A. Scheltema (1931), *Deelbouw in Nederlandsch-Indië* (1931) – also known in the European lowlands, fitting in our system – as deelbouw in four decisions (CBB 3 juni 2016, ECLI:NL:CBB:2016:159), as deelteelt 11 decisions.

m. right to lease;
n. waterrights;
o. fishing rights;
p. all other rights which may exist in adatlaw, or come to develop in adatlaw.[71]

A similar open-ended list is to be found in the part of the law of obligations concerning property rights in movables.[72]

Rights to control are only to be held by communities, not by individuals (art. 31); crops do not principally accede to the land (art. 32); indigenous rights to possession originate by clearing land (art. 33). Excluded are the all too familiar western property rights, taken from the Dutch civil code: ownership, possession, servitudes, superficies, emphytheusis, groundrents, tithes, usufruct, use and habitation `are unknown to adatlaw.'[73] Similarly in the part of rights in movable property 'ownership, possessio civilis and usufruct are not known to *adat*.'[74] Adatlaw does not recognize limitation and acquisitive prescription. The relation between *ius proprium* and *iura in re aliena*, individual ownership and limited property rights is absent. If there is a proprietary hypocenter, it is not the individual but the community – the family, the village. There is no numerus clausus. It indeed is an order which clearly deviates from the civil tradition, and hence concepts, rules but also reasoning or methodology needed to be reconsidered.

6 LAW AND METHODOLOGY

How to understand adatlaw and to apply it? In its methodology, the domain of *adat* made use of sociological, comparative as well as historical methods. It is quite likely that the change in legal reasoning towards acceptance of sociological arguments had influence in adatlaw becoming recognized. The commission of adatlaw provided a methodological

71 art. 30. 1) De inlandsche rechten op onroerend goed zijn een of meer der navolgende: a. beschikkingsrecht; b. inlandsch bezitrecht op onroerend goed; c. agrarisch eigendom op Java en Madoera; d. bewerkings- of bouwrecht; e. genotrecht van wisselvallige bouwvelden; f. gebruiksrecht van gemeenschapsgrond; g. recht om te ontginnen; h. recht om te zamelen (te delven, te jagen); i. recht om te weiden; j. naastings- en prioriteitsrecht van geburen; k. pandrecht op onroerend goed; l. recht van deelbouw; m. recht van huur en van leen op onroerend goed: n. waterrecht; o. vischrechten; en p. alle overige rechten op onroerend goed, die in het adatrecht mochten bestaan of door ontwikkeling van het adatrecht (artikel 51) mochten in zwang komen.

72 Art. 53 – starting with the indigenous right to possession, it reveals a variety of rights to use and dispose.

73 2) Recht van eigendom, recht van burgerlijk bezit, recht van erfdienstbaarheid, recht van opstal, erfpachtsrecht, recht van grondrenten en tienden, recht van vruchtgebruik, recht van gebruik (usus) en recht van bewoning op onroerend goed zijn in het adatrecht niet bekend.

74 Art. 53 s. 2.

outline for research in *adat*, in 1910, as one of its first publications. It is a 26-articled roadmap. Facts are primary: observation of behaviour is needed to find *adat*; there may be more than one rule, and all need to be taken into account. New ways need to be recognized and not to be discarded, even if the opinions tend to be negative. Results of research need to distinguish as sharp as possible between facts and the norm.[75] This factual approach very strongly reminds us of the Common core methodology.[76] The need to as well pay attention to *adat* in its dynamics is strongly underlined by Van Vollenhoven and Snouck Hurgronje.[77] It needs to be studied historically, Liefrinck argues.[78] Wilken makes room for evolutionary theory – 'in the age of Darwin.' Changing norms reflect adaptation to new circumstances – in all human societies, 'primitive' and 'developed,' and it thus allows us not just to understand 'primitive' *adat*, but also to understand our own 'more advanced' stage of development. Comparative law and legal history are indeed just around the corner.

Comparative law was already seen as a topic which concerned not just official law, but particularly also customary laws as detected by anthropology in the colonies. Illustrative is the *Zeitschrift für Vergleichende Rechtswissenschaft* (since 1878) which does pay attention to other legal traditions, than the learned Roman and the national-local tradition.[79] Wilken made comparative law the key to his inaugural lecture in Leiden on September 16, 1885, and stressed the need for comparative law to learn from ethnology.[80] 'A point of view as precious as rare,' judged G.A. van Hamel in a review.[81] Van Hamel called upon ethnologists to make use of legal history in particular,[82] referring to the historical school grandmasters Hugo and Von Savigny, but in particular to the 1881 inaugural address of Pijnacker Hordijk to the chair of Germanic law in Utrecht.[83] It indeed is remarkable how analyses of adatlaw very often explicitly refer to similarities to old germanic laws. The underlying idea indeed is the cultural relationship between human societies, and that 'more primitive' societies may provide a window on our own legal history. Van Vollenhoven refers in his Het

---

75 'Adatwijzer, houdende praktische wenken bij onderzoekingen naar adatrecht,' *Adatbundel* I (1910), p. 16-20.

76 U. Mattei and M. Bussani, 'The Common Core Approach of European Private Law,' *Columbia Journal of European Law* (1997), p. 339-356.

77 C. van Vollenhoven, *Het Adatrecht* I (1926), p. 65-66, referring to Chr. Snouck Hurgronje, *De Atjehers* I, p. 9-10 and II, p. 353.

78 Liefrinck, *Tijdschrift Bataviaasch Genootschap* 33 (1890), p. 338

79 See the first article in 1878 by one of its founding fathers, F. Bernhoeft, 'Über Zweck und Mittel der vergleichenden Rechtswissenschaft,' in *Zeitschrift für vergleichende Rechtswissenschaft* 1878, p. 1-38.

80 G.A. Wilken, *De vrucht van de beoefening der ethnologie voor de vergelijkende rechtswetenschap* (1885).

81 G.A. van Hamel, in *Revue Coloniale Internationale* 1886 II, p. 88-101.

82 G.A. van Hamel, o.c. p. 93-96.

83 *De taak van den beoefenaar der Nederlandsche rechtsgeschiedenis* (1881). Pijnacker Hordijk was Governor General of the Dutch East-Indies from 1888-1893.

Adatrecht to Beseler's ground-breaking and highly debated publication *Volksrecht und Juristenrecht* (1843); in his preface of his adatcode to Labands' systematic approach of old Germanic local laws;[84] movable property we have seen systematically placed in the law of obligations, as, just as in Germanic law, in *adat* possession is (some kind of) 'title.' The inaugural lecture at the Batavian law school by Hoetink on understanding of foreign law is remembered for the choice one has as a comparatist or historian, to study the old and strange either in itself for its own sake, or to use it in one's own contemporary analysis – with possibly a so-called 'productive misunderstanding.'[85] But the central theme of Hoetink was built on the conceptual gap between the occidental Roman mind and the oriental *adat*-societies, and concerned the ultimate goal of historians a well as comparatists in law alike: a ius commune as a philosopher's stone.

7 CONCLUSION

Indonesian customary adatlaw once was near Dutch law, colonial-wise. Understanding and applying *adat* was far from self-evident, and was established first and foremost by the forceful and convincing presence of anthropology in the field of law. This corpus of law and its rise to acceptance have been near to forgotten in the western legal domain, unfortunately. Codification, property, methodology are evergreens in our law, just as our everlasting struggle with unofficial customary law. A non-binding customary *ius commune* on adatlaw was drafted, next to a wealth of literature, with indigenous property concepts, using an exemplary method, far ahead of its time. We do not even have to productively misunderstand in order to make a contemporary use of it. The search for the *ius commune* in custom in these days of adatlaw has also affirmed more strongly the seats of legal history and comparative law at the table of brotherhood – aisle or window, always at home.

84 *Het Adatrecht* (1926), p. 4 – to G. Beseler, *Volksrecht und Juristenrecht* (1843); *Een adatwetboekje voor Indië* (1925), p. 4 – to Paul Laband, *Das Magdeburg – Breslauer systematische Schöffenrecht* (1863).

85 H.J. Hoetink, *Over het verstaan van vreemd recht*, inaugural lecture Batavia (1929), also published in *Rechtsgeleerde Opstellen* (1982), p. 21-61.

Part II
Concept of Property

Reflections on the Fluidity of Ownership

An Essay in Honour of Sjef van Erp

Elsabé van der Sijde[*]

Fluid:
a. having particles that easily move and change their relative position without a separation of the mass and that easily yield to pressure: capable of flowing;
b. subject to change or movement[1]

1 Introduction

In 2013, Prof. Sjef van Erp visited Stellenbosch University to deliver the first annual lecture of the South African Research Chair in Property Law. In his address, Prof. van Erp explored the fluidity of ownership as an evaluation of how ownership evolves to respond to social change.[2] Prof. van Erp argued that this fluidity may necessitate that we "revisit and rethink our classical model of property law" to keep up with changing social, economic and technological insights.[3] In so doing, he used the South African experience as a type of lodestar for how property law systems can transform in response to changed social conditions.[4] South Africa was (and remains) a particularly interesting example of this phenomenon given the seismic shifts in its legal system to develop post-Apartheid law.[5]

---

* Research Fellow, South African Research Chair in Property Law, Stellenbosch University. The South African Research Chair in Property Law is funded by the South African national Department of Science and Technology, administered by the National Research Foundation and hosted by Stellenbosch University and the author gratefully acknowledges the financial support of the National Research Foundation. The views expressed in this article are those of the author and should not be attributed to any of these institutions. A sincere word of thanks to Richard Shay and Sameera Mahomedy for their helpful comments on an earlier draft of this article. Remaining errors are my own.

1 "Fluid." Merriam-Webster.com Dictionary, Merriam-Webster, https://www.merriam-webster.com/dictionary/fluid. (Accessed 15 Jul. 2020.)

2 This lecture subsequently was published as S. van Erp, 'Fluidity of Ownership and the Tragedy of Hierarchy. A Sign of a Revolutionary Evolution?', *European Property Law Journal*, Vol. 4, No. 1, 2015, pp. 56-80. Both the lecture and the subsequent article dealt with a variety of topics, but my interest for purposes of this contribution is limited to Van Erp's discussion of the fluidity of ownership and its effects on the hierarchy of rights.

3 Hereafter collectively referred to as "social change" or "changed social conditions" for want of a better term.

4 Van Erp, 2015, p. 79.

5 Van Erp, 2015, p. 58.

In a general sense (as can be seen from the definition above), "fluidity" refers to particles (of a substance) that can change their relative position. What then did Prof. van Erp mean when he discussed "fluidity" in the legal context, and specifically the fluidity of ownership? At a first glance, it seems improbable that he could have meant that the rights or entitlements associated with ownership are subject to change or movement, yield easily, or adjust their relative position, because ownership quintessentially is the opposite. Typically, ownership is perceived as a strong and valuable real right precisely because it is absolutely enforceable and not relative.[6] Moreover, insofar as it is a characteristic of fluidity that something *yields easily*, one has to pause and consider whether, or to what extent, this is true of ownership. Conceptually, ownership is regarded as the most complete, most absolute right, a so-called trump-all right, and therefore a right that does not yield easily to any other rights or interests. Van Erp's characterisation of ownership as fluid therefore challenges the dominant view of modern ownership as a timeless, natural institution that has existed in an essentially unchanged form for centuries.

In his lecture, Van Erp demonstrated that this challenge to the dominant view is warranted. He argued convincingly that changed social conditions already have introduced an element of fluidity in ownership (and with it a degree of uncertainty) in many aspects of property law. Accordingly, this essay reflects on Van Erp's construct of fluidity of ownership and the contribution it can make to discussions of how property law reacts to a whole range of social forces, including technological advancement, inequality concerns, and increased environmental awareness.

2 Four Aspects of Fluidity of Ownership

2.1 *Background*

This essay explores the premise that the fluidity of ownership can be a useful imaginative construct to highlight the aspects of ownership that is responding to social change. To do so, it is necessary first to consider what "fluidity" means in this specific context. Closer scrutiny of Van Erp's argument reveals that he uses "fluidity of ownership" in three interrelated ways. He relies on various examples to indicate where fluidity is already occurring or could occur in the (near) future within ownership and the property law system. The different meanings of fluidity in these examples highlight various facets of

6 This characteristic of ownership is often linked to the response to feudalism, which heralded the end of relative title, and to the legal developments introduced by Hugo de Groot to create a system of rights based on the distinction between ownership (as the only full, complete real right), limited real rights and personal rights. See A.J. van der Walt, Tradition on Trial: A Critical Analysis of the Civil-law Tradition in South African Property Law, *South African Journal on Human Rights*, 1995, Vol. 11, No. 2, pp. 176-179.

ownership that usually is perceived as stable or static, but in fact is subject to a degree of continuous movement as the legal system responds to prevailing social conditions.

Below, I explore these three meanings of fluidity based on Van Erp's lecture and article, and I add to the discussion one further meaning where ownership arguably is already displaying characteristics of fluidity within the broader legal system. This fourth meaning is related to and relevant for the overall analysis of fluidity of ownership. In each category, I briefly consider the type of legal change that can be linked to that specific meaning of fluidity.[7]

2.2 *Fluidity of the Ownership Concept*

Firstly, our modern concept of ownership is not nearly as timeless and unchanging as we would like to believe.[8] Rather, the contemporary conception of ownership as an individual, uniform, exclusive, absolute, complete right is a product of various historical developments, and the importance of these characteristics have been emphasised differently at various points in history.[9] Fluidity in the prevailing ownership paradigm is important as support for the notion that our shared understanding of what ownership means and entails has changed at different points in history and can change in response to new social, economic, political or environmental developments.

"Fluidity" is used in this context by Van Erp as a springboard to discuss other aspects of fluidity in the subjects and objects of property, and the creation of new types (or amended contents) of property rights, which are discussed below. However, fluidity within the broad

---

7 The idea of fluidity has been used in other contexts in legal scholarship that cannot be explored in any detail in this contribution. Consider for instance Henry Smith's phrase "fluid property rights" to consider governance regimes and information-cost theory in water law. See H.E. Smith, Governing Water: The Semicommons of Fluid Poperty Rights, *Arizona Law Review*, Vol. 50, 2008, p. 445.

8 Consider for example the centrality of the right to exclude in property law scholarship in the United States, while the right to exclude was not listed as an incident of ownership in the common law context when Honoré wrote his seminal text on ownership in 1961. See A.M. Honoré, 'Ownership', *in* A.G. Guest (Ed.), *Oxford Essays in Jurisprudence*, Oxford, Clarendon Press, 1961, p. 113. Honoré lists eleven incidents of ownership (the right to exclude is not listed) and expressly states that while the right to exclude does form part of the cardinal features of the institution of ownership, it has been a distortion from the eighteenth century to view the right to exclude and the right of "using as one wishes" as the only legally or socially important characteristics of the owner's position. See also the discussion by P Dhliwayo, *A Constitutional Analysis of Aaccess Rights that Limit Landowners' Right to Exclude* (LLD dissertation Stellenbosch University, 2015) 20-21.

9 This topic has been dealt with extensively by other scholars and is not revisited here. See for instance the overviews offered by A.J. van der Walt, 'Bartolus se Omskrywing van Dominium en die Interpretasies daarvan sedert die Vyftiende Eeu', *Tydskrif vir die Hedendaagse Romeins-Hollandse Reg*, 1986, Vol. 49, pp. 305-321; G. Pienaar, 'Ontwikkelings in die Suid-Afrikaanse Eiendomsbegrip in Perspektief', *Tydskrif vir die Suid-Afrikaanse Reg*, 1986, pp. 295-308; R. Feenstra, 'Historische Aspecten van de Private Eigendom als Rechtsinstituut' *Rechtgeleerd Magazijn Themis*, 1976, pp. 248-275.

understanding of ownership that is conceptualised as individual, uniform and exclusive is worth closer consideration before unpacking the other aspects of fluidity of ownership.

In this respect South Africa is a pertinent example of a jurisdiction engrossed in transforming its dominant ownership concept as part of its process of transformative constitutionalism.[10] Ownership in South African law has Roman and Roman-Dutch roots, but does not mirror the institutions of these times perfectly.[11] Nineteenth-century Pandectism, for example, contributed to the highly conceptualised, absolute character of ownership associated with the (pre-constitutional) South African common law, at least in academic literature, where the absolute character of ownership as the freedom to do with your property whatever you wish (subject to the limits of the law) was stressed as a defining characteristic of ownership.[12]

Subsequently, however, the Constitution of the Republic of South Africa, 1996 has had a remarkable impact on ownership.[13] For instance, the constitutional protection of property has shifted the focus from ownership to property rights,[14] the limitations and obligations that accompany ownership are more important, and while the definition of ownership has remained effectively unchanged, the emphasis has shifted away from enforcing ownership in an absolute, exclusive and abstract manner.[15] The uniformity of ownership (that there is only one single form of "true" or "full" ownership) has also come under pressure given indigenous communities' way of life that does not depend on a Western concept of individual ownership.[16] Many communities in South Africa view their rights and responsibilities in relation to land and other natural resources communally, as a shared asset.[17] Understanding and accommodating these alternative notions of ownership within

10 Karl Klare coined the phrase "transformative constitutionalism" to describe South Africa's "long term project of constitutional enactment, interpretation, and enforcement committed ... to transforming a country's political and social institutions and power relationships in a democratic, participatory, and egalitarian direction." See K. Klare, 'Legal Culture and Transformative Constitutionalism', *South African Journal on Human Rights*, 1998, Vol. 14, p. 150.

11 Van Erp, 2015, p. 66, referring to D. P. Visser, 'The "Absoluteness" of Ownership: The South African Common Law in Perspective' *Acta Juridica*, 1985, p. 39

12 Visser, 1985, p. 39; Van Erp, 2015, p. 67 Here common law is not referring to Anglo-American law, but rather to the hybridised version of Roman-Dutch and English law that constitute South African common law.

13 *Port Elizabeth Municipality v. Various Occupiers* 2005 (1) SA 217 (CC) para 23. (Hereafter '*PE Municipality*'.)

14 The constitutional property clause protects "property" rather than ownership. See section 25 of the Constitution of the Republic of South Africa, 1996.

15 *PE Municipality* para 23.

16 Pienaar, 1986, pp. 305-306.

17 C. Rautenbach, *Introduction to Legal Pluralism in South Africa*, 5th ed., Durban, LexisNexis, 2018, p. 119

the legal system is an important step in South Africa's journey towards creating post-colonial, post-Apartheid property law.[18]

Consider for example the strong protection that the High Court of South Africa afforded to the Umgungundlovu community in *Baleni v. Minister of Mineral Resources.*[19] This case concerned a dispute between the Umgungundlovu community and an Australian mining company who wished to obtain a mining license for titanium mining in the area where the Umgungundlovu community has resided for centuries.[20] The community holds informal rights to the land in terms of the Interim Protection of Informal Land Rights Act 31 of 1996 ("IPILRA"). The dispute turned on whether the community merely had to be consulted by the Minister of Mineral Resources when considering an application for a mining license, or whether the community had to consent before a license could be granted.[21] In its reasoning, the court considered the following:

> In the context of this community, a residential plot represents far more than merely a place to live: it is a symbol of social maturity and social dignity. Each residential plot further serves as a critical conduit for the preservation of relations of inter-linkage and mutual dependence between the living and the dead and it is critically important for the wellbeing of each imizi.[22]

While the court was cognisant of the fact that the community members were not individual owners of their plots of land, the court appreciated that this community did not view their rights to their homes and to the land and resources where they live through the lens of absolute, individual, exclusive ownership. The community's way of life was protected, in part, by their own, very specific view of "ownership" of the land and resources.[23] The court's approach of reading all the applicable legislation together to afford the community a veto right (rather than merely the right to be consulted) led to the community having "the right to decide what happens with their land".[24] In so doing, the court allowed the community's way of life and their cultural and religious practices to be central to the discussion about the use and exploitation of the resources to which the community held (previously informal)

18 H. Scott, 'Absolute Ownership and Legal Pluralism in Roman Law: Two Arguments' *in* H. Mostert & T. Bennett (Eds.), *Pluralism & Development. Studies in Access to Property in Africa*, Cape Town, Juta, 2012, pp. 23, 34.

19 2019 (2) SA 453 (GP) (hereafter '*Baleni*').

20 *Baleni* para 2.

21 The Mineral and Petroleum Resources Development Act 28 of 2002 affords a right to consulted to the community, while IPILRA affords a veto-right to the community to refuse consent for mining activities. See paras 24- 27 of *Baleni*.

22 *Baleni* para 16.

23 *Baleni* para 18: 'They further tell the Court that the proposed mining activities of TEM threatens [sic] to tear their community apart and leave them divided, insecure and vulnerable.'

24 *Baleni* para 83.

legal rights, and chose to protect those rights as strongly as if it amounted to a right of ownership.[25]

Fluidity of the ownership concept means that, in the South African context, a shared understanding of what ownership means and entails should reflect some of these values and principles that highlight a more communal character of ownership, especially in relation to land and other natural resources. Moreover, legal developments acknowledging different types of ownership (or rights closely resembling ownership) raise questions regarding the continued accuracy of describing ownership in South Africa as a single, uniform right. In other jurisdictions, the fluidity of the ownership concept can equally be in need of reconsideration. For instance, the ownership concept may need to change to reflect the recognition of how untenable it is to uphold the individual, exclusive or uniform nature of ownership in light of the climate emergency.[26]

2.3 *Fluidity of the Taxonomy of Property Rights*

The second way in which Van Erp uses "fluidity" relates to the form and content of property rights. Thus, Van Erp connects the fluidity of ownership with the ability to create new property rights. He explains that the "[f]reedom to create limited property rights is a different way of arguing that ownership no longer is "total" or "uniform", but can be fragmented and is losing its function as the sole primary right."[27]

Van Erp thus argues that ownership is fluid if it is possible to create new forms or types of real rights.[28] He shows, with references to developments in global finance, how blurred the line between property law and contract law has become and the very real and devastating effects that can result from a court's decision of having to decide to what degree (if at all) a contract will be given third-party effect.[29]

Jurisdictions may need to determine, in response to various developments, which rights should be given the special status of being recognised as real rights. Each legal system will

---

25 As it stands, the community actually was placed in a stronger position than common law owners, to whom IPILRA would not apply. See *Baleni* paras 68, 74, 78. The Court justified this distinction with reference to the "greater interests of the community" that IPILRA is intended to protect.

26 See for example P. Taylor & D. Grinlinton 'Property Rights and Sustainability: Toward a New Vision of Property' *in* D. Grinlinton & P. Taylor (Eds.), *Property Rights and Sustainability The Evolution of Property Rights to Meet Ecological Challenges*, Leiden, Martinus Nijhoff Publishers, 2011, p. 1-20; F. Capra & U. Mattei, *The Ecology of Law. Toward a Legal System in Tune with Nature and Community*, Oakland, Berrett-Koehler Publishers, 2015, pp. 121-128.

27 Van Erp, 2015, p. 73, citing B. Akkermans, 'Concurrence of Ownership and Limited Property Rights' *ERPL*, 2020, Vol. 2, p. 259. Van Erp thus questions whether many jurisdictions have not already began acknowledging different types of ownership, arguing that ownership of emissions rights or ownership in the virtual world can hardly be said to be "a right of ownership in the sense of the all-embracing classical right."

28 Van Erp, 2015, p. 73.

29 Van Erp, 2015, p. 73-75.

have its own rules in place to make this determination. Generally, the *numerus clausus* principle, which creates a closed list of possible forms of property rights with predetermined content, is said to be a universal feature of most modern property systems, although not all systems recognise the principle by name and some jurisdictions follow the principle more closely than others.[30] Akkermans explains that the effect of strict adherence to the *numerus clausus* principle is "more rigidity in the system, but also a maximum level of legal certainty".[31] However, for certain types of legal developments flexibility is preferred above certainty, particularly in situations demanding a fast and adaptable legal response. Examples include developments in the sharing and circular economies, where the trend is to use contract law to achieve sustainability objectives with private law, but where the predetermined content of property rights would make these initiatives difficult, or in some cases impossible.[32]

2.4 *Fluidity of the Subjects and Objects of Property*

Van Erp uses the idea of the fluidity of ownership in a third and related way to the above. Fluidity of ownership is evident in the subjects and objects of property. While the subjects and objects of property generally is regarded as a stable area of law, there are many examples that illustrate a degree of fluidity in its ability to respond to social change. We now take for granted that women and people of colour can own property as fully recognised legal subjects and that corporations enjoy all the benefits of legal personality, but these legal developments happened in response to social change.[33] Van Erp convincingly highlights further evidence of fluidity in the subject and objects of property in relation to developments

30 See B. Akkermans 'The *Numerus Clausus* of Property Rights', *Maastricht European Private Law Institute Working Paper*, No. 2015/10, p 5 where Akkermans explains that even though certain countries claim not to recognise a *numerus clausus* of property rights (like Spain and South Africa), the creation of new property rights happens very rarely and there are still requirements in place for the recognition of new types of property rights. Also see T. W. Merril & H.E. Smith, 'Optimal Standardization in the Law of Property: The *Numerus Clausus* Principle', *Yale Law Journal*, 2000, Vol. 110, pp. 5, 9 where the authors explain that the general principle that property rights must conform to certain standardised forms does not have a name in common law and is not expressly recognised, and yet courts and commentators in the USA behave in a way that suggests that their property system is characterised by a limited number of forms not subject to contractual or judicial modification.

31 Akkermans, 2015, p. 9. This interplay between rigidity and certainty is revisited in Section 3 below.

32 B. Akkermans, 'Sustainable Poperty Law: Towards a Revaluation of our System of Property Law' in B. Akkermans and G. Van Dijck (Eds.), *Private Law and Sustainability* (The Hague, Eleven International Publishing, 2020), pp. 44-47; B. Verheye, 'Toekomst van de Circulaire Vastgoedeconomie', *TPR*, 2019, pp. 1-90.

33 See B.G. Carruthers & L. Ariovich 'The Sociology of Property Rights', 2004, Vol. 30, *Annual Review of Sociology* pp. 23-46. For a critical perspective on legal personality for corporations, see Capra & Mattei, 2015, pp. 82-84, 117-120.

in technology, questioning for example whether an ATM pays the cardholder (the traditional legal subject) or the card, or asking who the legal subject is in a virtual world.[34]

Van Erp's observations find support from other areas of development as well. Consider for instance the environmental context, where intense pressure to afford better legal protection and recognition to certain areas of the natural world is creating interesting changes to the categories of legal persons. For example, in New Zealand[35] and India,[36] rivers and natural areas of particular cultural and religious significance have been granted environmental personhood.[37] The legal implications of these developments are still being worked out, especially for property law, but it raises important questions surrounding the creation of a new type of legal subject. Similarly, granting rights to nature, such as through the establishment of environmental personhood, shows the interplay that can happen when the objects of property changes to become subjects rather than objects of property.[38]

New objects of property can be recognised and different jurisdictions will give different answers to the question of what can be owned.[39] Jurisdictions continuously have to decide how to treat potential new property objects such as government-granted rights or digital assets.[40] Even established objects of property can change in their scope: for instance, every jurisdiction has had to decide whether land includes what is underneath the surface and overhead. Technology influences which part of "land" as a composite is most valuable. It also has made it necessary for law to determine how parts of an object that were previously not useable or not economically relevant are to be treated in a situation where technology

34 Van Erp, 2015, p. 62

35 The Te Urewera Act 2014 declared Te Urewera a legal person (prior to 2014, Te Urewera was a national park); Te Awa Tupua (Whanganui River Claims Settlement) Act 2017 declared the Te Awa Tupua a legal person. See the discussion by B. Hoops, 'Looking for a Place for the Property of Environmental Persons' (draft article, cited with permission).

36 High Court of Uttarakhand, Judgment of 20 March 2017, *Salim v. State of Uttarakhand*, Writ Petition (PIL) No. 126 of 2014 (legal personality of rivers); Uttaranchal High Court, Judgment of 30 March 2017, *Lalit Miglani v. State Of Uttarakhand and Others*, Writ Petition (PIL) No.140 of 2015 (legal personality of rivers as well as their glaciers and surrounding areas).

37 I use these examples to illustrate the point that there is a debate regarding the best way to protect natural environments, and in at least some jurisdictions, the granting of legal personhood to create a new type of legal subject, has been identified as the appropriate way forward. However, in common law there is no legal concept of "ownership" so the doctrinal aspects of holding property as a legal subject is different from the position in a civil law system. These legal developments have been analysed in more detail by other scholars, who engage with the subtle distinctions of these developments in civil law and common law traditions, although scholarship on the property rights of environmental persons is still sparse. See for instance B. Hoops 'Looking for a Place for the Property of Environmental Persons' (note 35 above).

38 See Hoops 'Looking for a Place for the Property of Environmental Persons' (note 35 above) who explores the question of rivers and forests owning themselves, versus legal personality being granted to flowing water.

39 Carruthers & Ariovich, 2004, pp. 23-46; Van Erp, 2015, p. 63.

40 J.H.M. van Erp, 'Ownership of Digital Assets and the *Numerus Clausus* of Legal Objects', *Maastricht European Private Law Institute Working Paper No. 2017/6*, available at SSRN: https://ssrn.com/abstract=3046402.

changes the value of that part of the asset.[41] Even these limited examples demonstrate that there is a degree of responsiveness to social change in the subjects and objects of property that can be characterised as "fluidity" in ownership.

2.5 *Fluidity of the Position of Ownership within the Broader Legal System*

In my view, there is an additional aspect of the fluidity of ownership that should be addressed, although it was not identified by Van Erp. It pertains to the position that ownership occupies in the legal system. In many jurisdictions, the hierarchy of rights (discussed in Section 3) is so constructed that ownership is the pinnacle right, which functions as a trump-all right in private law (albeit subject to some exceptions). Generally, in the traditional civil law system of rights (that remains influential in South African law and was the dominant tradition prior to the change to a new democratic constitutional legal system), ownership is regarded as the strongest, most important, or most valuable right.[42] However, ownership need not take centre stage (neither descriptively nor normatively) in all disputes involving ownership (or property).

In a seminal article on the marginal systemic status of property, Prof. André van der Walt has shown that there are many cases where ownership yields (or should yield) to democratically or civically important rights.[43] He demonstrated that the position of ownership (as either central or marginal) is surprisingly contextual and can change depending on the priorities of the particular society in which it functions.[44]

An interesting example to explain this proposition can be found in the Constitutional Court of South Africa's approach to reconciling the rights of an owner and the rights of a statutorily protected occupier in *Daniels v Scribante*.[45] In this case, an inimical relationship existed between the parties, which once more led to litigation when Ms Daniels, the occupier, asserted that she had the right to make necessary improvements to her dwelling

41 The airspace above property was significantly less interesting (and valuable) before technology that enabled skyscrapers, airplanes and drones. Similarly, pockets of shale gas underneath land that were not reachable with previous methods of extraction suddenly become more valuable when the technology for fracking was introduced. See D.A. Dana & H.J. Wiseman, 'Fracking as a Test of the Demsetz Property Rights Thesis', *Hastings Law Journal*, 2020, Vol. 71, p. 849.

42 See Van der Walt, 1997, pp. 175-199. This characterisation of the traditional private law method as creating a hierarchy of rights is explored more fully in Section 3.

43 These rights included the right to life, dignity and equality, as well as free movement, free speech and free assembly rights. See A.J. van der Walt, 'The Modest Systemic Status of Property Rights', *Journal for Law, Property and Society*, 2014, Vol. 1, pp. 28-29.

44 Space constraints prevent me from delving into the nuance of the argument. See Van der Walt, 2014, pp. 45-101 for a detailed analysis.

45 2017 (4) SA 341 (CC) (hereafter "*Daniels*").

without the consent of the owner of the property, Chardonne Properties CC.[46] Chardonne Properties argued that as the owner of the property, it had the right to veto any undertaking to facilitate improvements, and that it could prohibit contractors from entering onto the property.[47]

What makes this example interesting is that the Court did not start with an analysis of the technical aspects of the various relevant legal entitlements to determine who had the stronger right to settle the dispute.[48] Seen from the perspective of the civil law tradition (as it functioned in South Africa prior to 1994), the owner's rights would have constituted the point of departure. By virtue of being the owner of the property, it should have been permitted to defeat Ms Daniels's claims unless legislation clearly created a limitation on its rights of ownership. Yet this was neither the Court's approach nor its conclusion.

Instead of using the logic of the hierarchy of rights (discussed in more detail in section 3 below) as point of departure, the Court opted firstly to place this conflict within its broader socio-political history and emphasised the circumstances that led to a significant power discrepancy between Ms Daniels and Chardonne Properties.[49] From there, it looked at the specific circumstances: Ms Daniels was a single mother who lived in deplorable conditions with her children on a farm owned by Chardonne Properties who only tolerated her presence on the property due to her protected statutory status as an occupier in terms of the Extension of Security of Tenure Act 62 of 1997.[50] She sought to make necessary improvements to her home at her own expense to create a more habitable and dignified home for her and her children.[51]

Turning to the applicable legislation, the Court interpreted the applicable legislative provisions broadly and purposively to give occupiers such as Ms Daniels the right to make necessary improvements to a dwelling that was occupied legally in terms of the relevant legislation. The Court held that this interpretation best gives effect to sections 10 and 25(6) of the Constitution, 1996.[52] The Court held that this right would exist even when the improvements would be contrary to the wishes of the owner.[53]

---

46 *Daniels* paras 5-11.

47 *Daniels* paras 5-6, 9.

48 See paras 1-2 of the main judgment, as well as paras 72-78 (Afrikaans version) or paras 109-115 (English version) of the Froneman J concurring judgment for a sense of how the court chose to contextualize the matter within the broader socio-political context.

49 *Daniels* paras 1-2 (main judgment), 72-78 (Afrikaans judgment by Froneman J), 109-115 (English judgment by Froneman J).

50 *Daniels* paras 4, 7.

51 *Daniels* paras 7-8.

52 *Daniels* paras 22-58. The Court expressly held that this interpretation best serves the right to human dignity (section 10) and security of tenure (section 25(6)). The Court held that it was not necessary to engage with arguments pertaining to the right of access to adequate housing (section 26).

53 *Daniels* paras 59-60. The right to make improvements was however subject to an obligation to engage meaningfully with the owner to determine when and in what manner the improvements should be made.

In this case, ownership did not function as a trump-all right, and it was not protected as the most important, most valuable, pinnacle right. The Court did not consider the rights of the owner until after Ms Daniels' fundamental right to dignity and security of tenure had been secured.[54] This approach constitutes a departure from the logic and method of property law as it existed prior to the advent of the new constitutional dispensation in South Africa, which would have prioritised securing the right of ownership (i.e. protecting it as "fully" or strongly as possible) unless there was an express limitation of the right. This approach suggests that the position of primacy that ownership occupies in the South African common law is not static and can change to accommodate the legal system's new normative constitutional commitments to, for example, human dignity.[55]

While the social, political and economic conditions in other jurisdictions differ from that of South Africa, this aspect fluidity of ownership (the fluidity of the position of ownership within the broader legal system) may be evident in many jurisdictions despite these pertinent differences. This fluidity can be identified, for instance, in jurisdictions facing pressure to promote values *other* than wealth maximisation or individual freedom, as is highlighted by the criticism of the dominant position of ownership in works dealing with sustainability.[56]

3 Effects of the Fluidity of Ownership and Avoiding the Tragedy of Hierarchy

The discussion above expands on what Van Erp identified as fluidity in ownership to show that an analysis of the aspects of fluidity of ownership can bring to the fore touch points and fault lines where established property doctrine and changed social conditions meet. Yet, one might question whether this type of illumination of the issues is worth recognising fluidity in ownership. After all, it could be argued that fluidity introduces instability, and in property law, stability is a prized virtue of the classical property law system.[57] Van Erp acknowledged this concern about introducing instability when he considered what the fluidity of ownership means for the hierarchy of rights from the perspective of his functional analysis of property rights as primary, secondary and tertiary rights.[58] In terms of this

54 *Daniels* paras 27-58.

55 See A.J. van der Walt, *Property in the Margins*, Oregon, Hart Publishers, 2009, pp. 230-247.

56 See for example Capra & Mattei, 2015, pp. 131-146; Taylor & Grinlinton, 2011, pp. 1-20.

57 A. Bell & G. Parchomovsky, 'A Theory of Property', *Cornell Law Review*, 2005, Vol. 90, p. 538.

58 Van Erp, 2015, p. 79 raises the following concerns regarding the effects of fluidity and the hierarchy of rights: "Do older (existing) property rights really have priority over newer (younger) rights? Do (existing) limited rights have priority over (younger) fuller rights, such as new forms of ownership? The classical model resulted in a clear, well settled, hierarchy of property rights. It created security and predictability, but does it still create an acceptable outcome in light of a rebalancing of interests?"

functional summary of how the hierarchy operates, Van Erp explains that primary rights "give their holder within a given property law system the maximum of rights, powers, privileges and immunities", secondary rights are property rights that are less strong than primary rights and can be divided into two major types: security rights and use rights. In turn, tertiary rights are those that exist on the border of the law of property and the law of obligations.[59] The functioning of the hierarchy can be simplified as follows: ownership trumps all rights (as the sole primary right), limited real rights (secondary rights) trump personal rights (tertiary rights), and personal rights trump "no rights" (usually interests or informal rights).[60]

All four aspects of fluidity mentioned above pose some risk to the effective functioning of this hierarchy. Fundamentally, the hierarchy of rights relies on an individual, uniform, and exclusive concept of ownership as a shared understanding. This implicates the first aspect of fluidity (fluidity in the ownership concept). The hierarchy of rights further requires a clear distinction between personal and real rights, and equally requires any innovation to fit in with the predefined categories of primary, secondary and tertiary rights (the second aspect of fluidity). Prevailing uncertainty regarding what can be owned and by whom will similarly inhibit the simple application of the methodology of the hierarchy in a legal dispute. The shape that innovation can take is therefore constrained by the structure and method underlying the hierarchy of rights. Finally, the hierarchy (which represents the reasoning, method or logic of private law) comes under pressure if ownership is no longer the sole primary right. Fluidity in the position of ownership in the legal system requires the application of the hierarchy of rights to be called into question, since its point of departure is ownership's status as the pinnacle right that can function as a "trump all" right. If that is no longer the case, the hierarchy cannot be applied in an abstract manner, which means that certainty and predictability within the property law system would decrease.

In his lecture, Van Erp focused primarily on the disruption in the taxonomy of property rights (the second aspect of fluidity discussed above) and fluidity in the subjects and objects of property (the third aspect of fluidity discussed above). That is why, in my discussion, I expanded on the fluidity of the ownership concept and fluidity of the position of ownership in the legal system, to show that all these aspects of fluidity pose a threat to the functioning of the hierarchy of rights. Yet, as Van Erp pointed out, if the outcomes that follow from the application of the hierarchy of rights do not reflect our modern "rebalancing of interests", the "threat" that fluidity poses should not be seen in a negative light.[61] Part of what makes any process of legal transformation complex is that a certain measure of

59 See Van Erp, 2015, pp. 61-63.
60 Van der Walt, 1995, pp. 178-179.
61 Van Erp, 2015, p. 79.

continued stability (usually in the form of protection for vested rights) is needed for many economic and social institutions to function, but not so much as to undermine necessary reform measures. Van Erp describes this paradox as the "tragedy of the hierarchy": what he views as the need to abandon, but also to preserve.[62] Instability arising from recognising fluidity of ownership can be regarded as a type of guideline to determine what to abandon and what to preserve, rather than as a threat to the effective functioning of the property law system.

Some instability in the hierarchy is inevitable, not only because the classical system of property law has always had exceptions but also because, as society changes and becomes more complex, a degree of fluidity not only in ownership but also in the functioning of the hierarchy itself becomes necessary. Van der Walt attempted to work out an example of such a modified hierarchy, when he argued that ownership cannot adopt a position of primacy in the face of certain types of rights, particularly, the right to life, dignity and equality.[63] He also considered the relative position of ownership in the hierarchy of rights vis-à-vis democratically important rights such as the right to assemble and freedom of speech.[64] Such a modified hierarchy can balance the need for some degree of certainty and predictability with the aspects of fluidity of ownership and property law in a contextual manner that gives effect to the normative commitments of a particular jurisdiction.[65]

There is a risk that property lawyers may shy away from the challenge of working out conflicts that arise from introducing new rights, interests and values within the logic of the rights hierarchy. This avoidance could result in a property law system that is less able to adapt to changes in society. Consequently, if the property law system cannot adapt or "evolve" (as Van Erp characterised it), it could lead to property-dispute outcomes that are not aligned with the values and objectives of a particular society, or to archaic rules of property doctrine that cannot regulate complex property relationships effectively.[66]

4 Concluding Remarks

There are many who will lament the loss of certainty that accompanies the significant technological, environmental, political, and economic changes to which the legal system

62 Van Erp, 2015, p. 79.
63 Van der Walt, 2014, pp. 45-62.
64 Van der Walt, 2014, pp. 62-101.
65 See for example AJ van der Walt, *Property and Constitution*, 2012, Pretoria, Pretoria University Press, 2012, pp. 23-24 where Van der Walt sums up the characteristics of the broader constitutional legal framework that the hierarchy of rights must fit into to be in line with the normative commitments of the democratic South African legal order.
66 Van Erp makes this point in particular detail in relation to global finance, but his argument holds sway more broadly. See Van Erp, 2015, pp. 74-76.

must respond. Yet Van Erp recognised in this loss tremendous power for development: the opportunity for the legal system, and for property law and ownership specifically, to adapt and "to lead us into the future".[67] In his lecture, he brilliantly demonstrated that various aspects of social change represent fundamental challenges for our conceptualisation of ownership as a single, uniform right that exists within a fixed hierarchy of rights. It struck me as particularly insightful that, in his lecture, Van Erp was not arguing that ownership *should* be fluid, but rather that it *already is* fluid. Additionally, Van Erp did not conclude that the "tragedy of hierarchy" is as simple as its existence being threatened by the effects of fluidity in ownership: rather the tragedy is the paradox of needing to preserve some aspects of the hierarchy, while amending or abandoning other parts of it. In so doing, he successfully brings to the fore a significant challenge to the structure and logic of the classical system of property law.

This essay proposes that further aspects of ownership and the property law system exhibit fluid characteristics than was first identified by Van Erp, and consequently, that the implications of fluidity for the hierarchy of rights is even more significant than first anticipated. This essay thus finds support for Van Erp's contention that ownership exhibits fluid characteristics in response to social change and that this places the effective functioning of the hierarchy of rights under pressure.

Fluidity of ownership reflects areas of interaction between social change, property doctrine and methods of legal reasoning in property law. To this end, the essay concludes that the fluidity of ownership is a useful imaginative construct to identify and investigate aspects of ownership and the property system that is responding to social change. "Fluidity" has the potential to challenge existing beliefs regarding the nature of ownership and the logic of the classical property law system: a possibility that is much needed right now, as many legal systems struggle to respond to various urgent social challenges.

---

67 Van Erp, 2015, p. 79.

The Metamorphosis of the Right to Property

James Gordley[*]

1 Introduction

Jurists and philosophers began to speak of a "right to property" only in the 16th century. Some scholars have thought that this innovation must have been accompanied by a change in the conception of rights. It was merely a change in vocabulary.

The real change began in the Middle Ages when philosophers such as Thomas Aquinas drew upon Aristotelian philosophy to explain what was later called the right to property. The Roman jurists and the medieval civil and canon lawyers had interpreted the law without benefit of philosophy. The change that began with Aquinas culminated in the 16th and 17th centuries in the work of a group centered in Spain and known to historians as the late scholastics. They synthesized Roman and Canon law as interpreted by medieval jurists with Aristotelian philosophy as interpreted by Thomas Aquinas. According to this approach, property was not an absolute right. It was established to avoid the disadvantages of common ownership. The owner's rights were therefore limited by the purposes it served. Their approach influenced the founders of the northern natural law school of the 17th and 18th centuries, Hugo Grotius and Samuel Pufendorf.

It was replaced by one that has become far more familiar. A private right such as property is defined in unqualified terms: as a zone of freedom in which the right-holder can do as he chooses. We associate that conception of rights with 19th century liberals such as Immanuel Kant. Yet it was held by 18th century rationalists such as Gottfried Wilhelm Leibniz and Christian Wolff. It was also held by 19th century jurists who seemed to have arrived at it independently of the influence of philosophers, liberal or otherwise. The common feature was not a philosophical commitment but an attempt to define property rights without regard to the purposes served by the institution of private property.

Since the 19th century, many jurists have believed that they have escaped this earlier approach by insisting the that private rights to property must give way to public interests. Yet their idea of private rights remains much the same: a zone of freedom in which the right-holder can act as he chooses. If they defined the owner's rights in terms of the purpose that property serves, they would recognize that sometimes the reason the owner cannot act as he chooses is that his right to property does not extend that far. He cannot exercise

* W.R. Irby, Professor of Law, Tulane University Law School, New Orleans, USA.

a right that he never had. It is important to distinguish such situations from those in which an owner is deprived of rights that he otherwise would have in order to promote public interests. We cannot draw that distinction, unless, like the late scholastics and Aquinas, we analyze the purposes of private property before defining the rights that belong to an owner.

2 Changes in Vocabulary

2.1 A Miscellany of Rights: Roman Law

Much of modern private law is based on concepts that were first identified and refined by Roman jurists. Nevertheless, modern private law has a systematic doctrinal structure. It is organized by topics such as property, tort, contract and unjust enrichment. Each topic is developed by introducing basic concepts, defining them, and then presenting a series of rules. Roman law did not have a systematic doctrinal structure. Because of their method, the Roman jurists did not feel the need for one.

Their method was to explore the content of a concept by putting particular cases. For example, they distinguished ownership from possession. When Ulpian considered whether a person could retain possession even after he had relinquished physical control, he asked what would happen "if someone has gone away from his field or house leaving none of his household there, and on his return was ... prevented from entering the premises."[1] Ulpian answered that he retained possession even after he had left and so could recover it from the intruder. When Paulus discussed what sort of physical control is necessary to establish possession, he said "that should not be taken to mean that one seeking to possess an estate must go round every part of it. It is enough it that he enters some part of the estate, but with the intent and awareness that he seeks to possess the estate to its furthest boundaries."[2] According to Celsus, "[i]f I instruct the seller to leave what I bought at my house, it is certain that I possess it, even though no one has yet touched it. Again, if my seller points out to me from my turret the neighboring land which I have bought, and declares that he is giving me vacant possession, I begin to possess it no less than if I set foot within its boundary."[3] A buyer of wine is in possession when he is given the key to the cellar.[4] The buyer of a pile of logs who has been told by the seller to take them away is in possession as soon as he puts a guard on them.[5]

1 D. 43.16.1.24.
2 D. 41.2.3.1.
3 D. 41.2.18.2.
4 D. 18.2.1.21.
5 D. 18.2.51.

Similarly, they did not try to define the concept of property. They described particular rights that accompany particular kinds of property. The sea and seashore are "common things" that belong to everyone, and so everyone can use them.[6] But an individual owns gems or pebbles he takes from the shore.[7] Moreover, an individual can build a hut on the shore.[8] Others must keep clear of the hut.[9] But his ownership lasts only as long as the building remains. If it collapses, someone else can build on the site.[10] Wild animals, birds and fish belong to no one, but become the property of the person who captures them.[11] Rivers and harbors are "public things." They belong to the public, and everyone can fish or boat on them.[12] The banks are owned by those whose lands border them, yet everyone using the river is free to beach boats, dry nets, and haul fish onto the banks, and to tie up to trees there even though the trees belong to the owner of the land.[13] Theaters and stadiums are "civic things." They belong the citizen body as a whole, not to the citizens as individuals.[14] An individual citizen, however, has a right of action against anyone who prevents him from using them.[15] Some things cannot become private property: consecrated things (*res sacrae*), which cannot become consecrated and hence incapable of private ownership through the act of a private person;[16] hallowed things (*res religiosae*) such a tombs which can cease to be private property by the act of a private person who buries a corpse on a plot;[17] and city walls and gates (*res sanctae*) which are not only incapable of private ownership[18] but of private use by a person who wishes to build against them.[19]

Through the use of this method, the Romans were able to give a sophisticated account of the incidents of ownership without ever speaking of a right to property. Indeed, they used the term *ius* or right only to speak of particular rights. A person's rights in another's land could include the right to walk across it (*ius ambulandi*),[20] to drive animals across it (*ius agenda*),[21] to have water flow across it (*ius aquaeductus*),[22] to burn limestone on it (*ius*

6 I. 2.1.1; I. 2.1.5. D. 1.8.2.1.
7 D. 1.8.3.
8 I. 2.1.5; D. 1.8.3.
9 D. 1.8.4.
10 D. 1.8.6.pr.
11 I. 2.1.12.
12 I. 2.1.2; D. 1.8.5.pr.
13 I. 2.1.4; D. 1.8.5.pr.
14 I. 2.1.6; D. 1.8.6.1.
15 D. 47.10.15.7.
16 I. 2.1.8; D. 1.8.6.3.
17 D. 1.8.6.4; I. 2.1.9.
18 I. 2.1.10; D. 1.8.6.2; D. 1.8.8.2.
19 D. 1.8.8.2.
20 J. 2.3.pr.
21 J. 2.3.pr.
22 J. 2.3.pr.

calcis coquendae)[23] and to take sand from a sandpit (*ius harenae foedienae*).[24] A person with a usufruct had the right to use and take produce from the land (*ius utendi fruendi*).[25] A debt was a *ius debiti*.[26] A creditor had a *ius crediti*.[27] The Romans spoke of particular rights such as these, but not of a right to property.

Because, like Greek philosophers, the Roman jurists were concerned with concepts, some modern scholars have thought that they must have been influenced by Greek philosophy. But their method was quite different.[28] They did not clarify their concepts by definition, like the Greeks, or ask what was the justification for private property.

2.2 *A Shorthand Term for Subjective Rights: Canon Law and Thomas Aquinas*

The Canon lawyers were concerned with the sins a person might commit through an ungenerous use of his own property or wrongful taking of another's. They addressed these concerns without speaking of a "right to property." When they wished to refer to whatever a person was entitled to have or to do, they did not use the term "right" (*ius*). They used the term *res* which literal means a "thing" that one may own or possess.

St. Augustine used the term *res* when he said that a thief cannot be forgiven unless he returns what he stole.

> If the thing (*res*) of another person, for which a sin was committed, is not returned when it can be returned, there is not penance but rather pretense. If indeed it is truly done, the sin is not forgiven unless restitution *(restitutio)* is made of the thing (res) that was taken away.[29]

This passage was incorporated in the *Decretum*, a 12th century compilation of sources that Christians regarded as authoritative that became the basis for the study of Canon law.

The Canon lawyers read the passage from St. Augustine to mean that one who had wrongfully harmed another could not be forgiven without *restitutio*, that is, without compensating the victim for the harm he had suffered. In Roman law, *restituere* meant to restore something, such as a damaged building or road, to its former condition. *Restitutio in integrum* was an extraordinary remedy which allowed a person to set aside a transaction

23 J. 2.3.2.
24 J. 2.3.2.
25 D. 7.1.1.
26 D. 4.2.13.
27 D. 4.2.13.
28 James Gordley, *The Jurists A Critical History* (Oxford, 2013), 12-18.
29 C. 14 q. 6 c. 1.

and be placed in his former position when he had suffered an inequitable loss. The Canonists broadened the meaning of the term. It meant making compensation for any kind of loss one person had wrongfully caused another. In doing so, they also broadened the term *res*. It meant, not only a thing that a person owned, but whatever belonged to him. One who took or harmed what belonged to another had to make *restitutio*, if, for example, the harm had been done to the other person's reputation.[30]

Thomas Aquinas, like the Romans, rarely used the term right (*ius*) to mean anything that a person is entitled to have or to do. In discussing harms to other people, he had not asked whether a "right" was violated but whether the conduct in question was allowed (*licet*). For example, in discussing murder, he asked whether one person is allowed to kill another.[31] In discussing property, Aquinas asked whether one person is allowed to possess a thing as his own.[32]

Like the Canonists, he used the term *res* in discussing *restitutio*. "*Restitutio* appears to be nothing else than to reinstate someone in the possession or ownership of his own thing (*res*)."[33] He used the Aristotelian concept of commutative justice to explain the need for *restitutio*. *Restitutio* is an act of commutative justice.[34] According to Aristotle, in involuntary transactions in which one person deprives another something that belongs to him, commutative justice requires that the victim be compensated. In voluntary transactions, the parties exchange resources and commutative justice requires that they do so at price that enriches neither party at the expense of the other.[35] Aquinas used the term res when he described commutative justice in buying and selling: one person "voluntarily transfers his thing (*res*) to another."[36]

2.3 *Subjective Rights and the Right of Property: the Late Scholastics*

When Aquinas and the Canonists spoke of a *res* or thing, they meant not just a physical thing but honor, reputation and whatever else belonged to a person. Late scholastics such as Francesco de Vitoria, Leonard Lessius and Luis de Molina recognized that the word *res* was awkward. Literally, it meant "thing. They substituted the word *ius* or "right." In Latin, the word *ius* can mean either a right to have or to do something, such as a right of way

30 Raimundus de Penafort, *Summa de poenitentia*, eds. Xaverio Ochoa & Alosio Díez (Rome, 1978), II.5.42; Hostiensis, *Summa aurea* (Lyon, 1556), lib. V, *Quibus et qualiter*; *Quid de accusatoribus*. See Karl Weinzierl. *Die Restitutionslehre der Frühscholastik* (Munich, 1936), 132-46.

31 *Summa theologiae* II-II, Q. 64, aa. 2-7.

32 *Ibid.* Q. 66, a. 2.

33 *Ibid.* Q. 62 a. 1.

34 *Ibid.*

35 Aristotle, *Nicomachean Ethics* V.ii 1130^b-1131^a; V.i 1131^b-1132^b.

36 *Summa theologiae* II-II, Q. 61, a. 3.

(*ius ambulandi*), or it can mean a body of law such as the *ius* civile. The same is true European languages other than English: for example, *Recht* in German, *droit* in French and *diritto* in Italian. When non-English speakers wish to make it clear that they are using the term in the first sense, the speak of "subjective rights." As we have seen, the Roman spoke of particular subjective rights. The late scholastics used the term *ius* to refer to subjective rights in general, to whatever a person was entitled to do or to have.

Vitoria did so in his commentary on Aquinas: "a right (*ius*) ... is nothing other than what one is allowed to do or what the law (*lex*) allows. ... We say, indeed, "I do not have the right of doing this," that is, "it is not allowed for me to do it," and again, "I am using my right," that is, "it is allowed.""[37] Lessius defined right, in this sense, as a "legitimate power ... the violation of which constitutes an injury."[38] According to Molina, a right is a "faculty or power to something a man has ... or the to use something of by his own right." "Nor do I see it possible to define this meaning of *ius* more appropriately than if we say, it is a faculty to do something, to obtain something, to or to claim it or in another way to have it, such that, it is contravened, without a legitimate ground (*sine legitima causa*), one suffers an injury (*iniuria*)."[39]

Some scholars believe that the late scholastic used the term "rights" in this sense because they rejected a medieval concept of rights in favor of a modern one. Some Catholic authors have argued that they betrayed a medieval idea that one could not speak of a person's rights apart from the principles of justice they reflected. Some secular authors congratulated the late scholastics for founding a modern conception of individual rights.[40]

Brian Tierney has shown that neither of these views is correct. Vitoria was not launching a new concept of law but using the terms "rights" to state the doctrine of *restitutio* more clearly. "Vitoria's problem was that he could not discuss restitution adequately without considering the concept of *ius* as a subjective right. the definition he had earlier accepted from Aquinas did not include any such concept."[41]

37 Francisco de Vitoria, *Commentarios a la Secunda Secundae de Santo Tomas*, ed. Vicente Beltrán de Heredia (Salamanca: Apartado 17, 1932), to II-II Q. 61, a. 1.

38 Leornardus Lessius, *De iustitia et iure* (Paris, 1628), lib. 1, cap. 2, dub. 1, no. 3.

39 Ludovicus de Molina, *De iustitia et iure tractatus* (Venice, 1614), II, disp. I, no. 2.

40 See Brian Tierney, *The Idea of Natural Rights Studies on Natural Rights, Natural Law, and Church Law 1150-1625* (William B. Eerdman, Grand Rapids, MI, 1997), 259.

41 *Ibid.*

3 A QUALIFIED RIGHT: ARISTOTLE, THE LATE SCHOLASTICS AND THE NORTHERN NATURAL LAWYERS

A more far-reaching change began when Aquinas considered the implications of Aristotelian philosophy for private property. That innovation culminated in the work of the last scholastics who self-consciously attempted to synthesize Roman and Canon law with Aristotelian philosophy as interpreted by Aquinas. Many of their conclusions were adopted by the founders of the northern natural law school, Hugo Grotius and Samuel Pufendorf, and spread throughout Europe, paradoxically, during the centuries when Aristotelian philosophy was losing its once unchallenged authority.

Aristotle rejected the view of his teacher Plato that all property should be in common. If it were, Aristotle said, "[t]hose who labor much and get little will necessarily complain of those who labor little and receive or consume much."[42] Aquinas gave a similar explanation.[43] The late scholastics concluded that, although all things were in common ideally or in principle or in the beginning private property was instituted to remedy the defects of common ownership that Aristotle and Aquinas had described.

It followed that the right to property was not absolute. It was limited by the purposes for which private property was instituted. The late scholastics explained the Canonists, doctrine of necessity in terms of those purposes, borrowing again from Aquinas. He had said that despite "the division of things ... man's needs have to be remedied by these very things ..." Therefore, if the need was "manifest and urgent" then "it is lawful for a man to meet his own need by means of another's property ..."[44] Lessius explained:

> [O]ne may take another's thing when one is in extreme necessity because, in extreme necessity, one needs what is necessary to preserve one's life. ... The reason for this is that the end of inferior things is to serve men through necessity, so that through them men may preserve and maintain their lives. Therefore this right belongs to all by nature. Nor can the division of things introduced by the law of peoples take away this right, for the law of peoples presupposes the law of nature and does not destroy it particularly as to what is necessary to preserve life. The division of things must therefore be deemed to have been made with a reservation to each person of this natural right to whatever is necessary to maintain his life. Otherwise the division would not have been done in a rational way.[45]

42 *Politics* II. v.
43 *Summa theologiae* II-II Q. 66, a. 2.
44 *Ibid.* a.7.
45 Lessius, *De iustitia et iure*, lib. 2, cap. 12, dub. 12.

Soto and Molina took the same view.[46] Their conclusion about the right to use another's property in time of necessity was adopted by the 17th century founders of the northern natural law school, Hugo Grotius and Samuel Pufendorf,[47] whence it passed into later law.

As a result, the scholastics and the founders of the northern natural law school conceived of the right to property rights differently than most modern writers. They recognized that an owner is free to exercise his rights as he chooses. Nevertheless, the content of his rights is determined by the reasons that it is just for a person to own property.

4 Property as an Unqualified Right: a Modern Innovation

Today, we are more familiar with a modern conception of property rights as a zone of freedom within which the owner can do as he will with his own. The innovation was not to introduce the concept of the will. It was to leave out the considerations of justice, anchored in the social order, that once defined the content and therefore limited the exercise of rights.

We identify this concept of property with 19th century liberal philosophers such as Immanuel Kant. Yet it had been introduced by the rationalist philosophers of the previous century, and it was used by the 19th century jurists, liberal and conservative, who were not influenced by liberal philosophers.

4.1 The Rationalists

Rationalists such as Gottfried Wilhelm Leibniz and Christian Wolff believed that to reach conclusions with certainty one must use the method of mathematicians. One should begin with definitions and trace their logical implications. By beginning with definitions of higher-level moral concepts, the rationalists hoped to a derive conclusions about moral law.

They began with the concept of "perfection." According to Leibniz, "the true good" is "whatever serves the perfection of intelligent substances."[48] Therefore "justice" is "charity" and "charity" is "universal benevolence"[49] which is to seek the perfection of oneself and of

46 Domenicus Soto, *De iustitia et iure libri decem* (Salamanca, 1553), lib. 5, q. 3, a. 4; Molina, *De iustitia et iure* disp. 20.

47 Hugo Grotius, *De iure belli ac pacis libri tres* (de Kanter-van Hetting Tromp, eds., Leiden, 1939), II.ii.6-7; Samuel Pufendorf, *De iure naturae et gentium libri octo* (Amsterdam, 1688), II.vi.5.

48 Gottfried Wilhelm Leibniz, "Reflections on the Common Conception of Justice," in Leibniz, *Philosophical Papers and Letters* Leroy E. Loemaker, ed., 1 (Chicago, 1956), 911 at 917.

49 Gottfried Wilhelm Leibniz, "Codex iuris gentium diplomaticus," Praefatio, in Leibniz, *Philosophical Papers and Letters* 690 at 690. Similarly, "the good man is one who is benevolent toward all.... The ultimate rule of law is everything is directed to the maximum general good or common happiness." "De tribus juris

all others. Borrowing from Leibnitz,[50] Wolff said: "Without doubt, every man as an ultimate end should seek his perfection and that of others, and therefore to make all use of his faculties that is required for this end to be pursued. The perfection of others, then, should be no less dear and of concern to us than our own."[51] The moral standard by which people were supposed to act was one of complete altruism.

As Klaus Luig observed, the difficulty was to bridge the gap between this principle of complete altruism and the concept of private rights.[52] Rather than doing so, they defined private rights negatively by opposition to altruism. They are private in the sense that they belong to particular right-holders and self-regarding in the sense that the right-holder is not obligated to follow the principle of altruism. He can use his rights any way that he wishes. The relationship between altruism and private rights as one of radical disjunction.

Consequently, for Leibnitz and Wolff, a property right is unlimited by definition. The owner can do whatever he wishes with his property According to Klaus Luig, in Leibnitz" view, "the thing [is] the object of an absolute right."[53] Wolff said that "the owner "has the right to dispose of rights over a thing subjected to him according to his own judgment (*arbitrio*). The right "of disposing of a thing by one's own decision, indeed, as one sees fit, we call ownership."[54] "By nature, no one is held to give another a reason concerning in what way a thing is used, nor does anyone have the right to impede an abuse of things, so long as whoever is abusing the thing does nothing against the right of another."[55]

Although such a right is conceptually unlimited, its exercise may be limited by some extrinsic principle. Yet such a limitation does not arise from the purposes for which property rights are established. It is an interference with property justified by some other principle or concern. Leibnitz said that even though a right was conceptually unlimited, the law might have a reason, extrinsic to the definition of the right, for limiting it. Thus, what belongs to the owner of property is "what is in his power, or what he may deal with in every way according to his will unless for some particular reason there is an exception."[56] Wolff tried to find such a reason when he dealt with the right to use another's property in time of necessity. He said that there is a right extraneous to the law of property that trumps

praeceptis sive gradibus," in Gottfried Wilhelm Leibnitz, *Textes inédits*, Gaston Grua, ed. (N.Y., 1985), 606 at 607.

50 Clemens Schwaiger, "Ist Wolffs Ethik leibnianisch? Ein Beitrag zur Wiederbelebung der Glücksthematik," in *Leibnitz und Europa VI. Internationaler Leibnitz-Kongress* (Langenhagen 1994), 727 at 728.

51 Christian Wolff, *Jus naturae method scientific pertracta*, published as *Jus naturae* in Christian Wolff, *Gesammelte Werke* (M. Thomann, ed., Hildescheim, 1972 –), vols. 17-24 , I, § 609.

52 Klaus Luig, "Leibnitz als Dogmatiker des Privatrechts," in Okko Behrends, Malte Diesselhorst, Wulf Eckart Voss, *Römishes Recht in der europäischen Tradition Symposion aus Anlass des 75 Geburtstages Franz Wieacker* (Ebelsbach, 1985), 213 at 220.

53 *Ibid.* 231.

54 Wolff, *Jus naturae* I, § 609, cited II, § 496; II, § 118.

55 *Ibid.* II, § 169.

56 Leibnitz, "De iustitia et novo codice," *Textes inédits* 2, 621 at 621.

property rights. It is the right of self-preservation. That right can never be given up because it is "connatural,"[57] in the sense that it is inseparably joined to human nature.[58] Therefore, one could use another's property but only when one's life was at stake.

4.2 *Immanuel Kant*

Kant believed that it is impossible to derive moral rules, as the rationalists thought, from the concept of "perfection."[59] That concept "turns in a circle and inevitably though clandestinely presupposes the morality that it ought to explain ...."[60] Nevertheless, he believed that morality is based on reason. It is based on what he called the categorical imperative which can be formulated: "So act that the maxim of your will could always hold at the same time as a principle in a giving of universal law."[61] Or: "I ought never to act otherwise than in such a manner that I could also will that my maxim should become a universal law."[62]

Kant's critics have claimed that it is impossible to derive and moral conclusions from the categorical imperative. Kant gave examples of how it can be done. Christian Schnoor and Kenneth Westfall suggested that the reason his examples seem plausible is that if we look at them closely, we find beneath the surface an independent reason supporting his conclusions, a reason that does not depend on the categorical imperative but can be formulated without regard to it.[63] Such is the case with the right to property.

To steal or appropriate a deposit, according to Kant, violates what he called a person's "strict or narrow (inflexible) duties." Another such duty is to keep a promise. Such duties arise "when actions are so constituted (*beschaffen*) that their maxim cannot without contradiction even be thought (*gedacht*) as a universal law of nature, let alone that one could will that it should be one."[64] If someone were to ask, "why should I keep a promise," the answer, according to Kant, is that "[i]t is utterly impossible to give a proof of this

57 Wolff, *Jus naturae* I, § 609, cited II, § 496; VI, § 562.

58 *Ibid.* II, § 10; I, § 64.

59 Immanuel Kant, *Kritik der praktischen Vernunft* in *Kant's gesammelte Schriften*, Königlich Preussischen Akademie der Wissenschaft (5th ed., Berlin,1913), 1 at 40.

60 Immanuel Kant, *Grundlegung zur Metaphysik der Sitten* in *Kant's gesammelte Schriften* 4:385 at 443.

61 Kant, *Kritik der praktischen Vernunft* 40.

62 Kant, *Grundlegung* 492.

63 Christian Schnoor, *Kants Kategorischer Imperativ als Kriterium der Richtigkeit des Handelns* (Tübingen,1989), 47, 54-55; Kenneth R. Westphal, "How 'Full' is Kant's Categorical Imperative?" *Jahrbuch für Recht und Ethik / Annual Review of Law and Ethics* 3 (1995), 467.

64 Kant, *Grundlegung* 424.

categorical imperative just as it is impossible for a geometrician to prove by logical inference that to make a triangle I must take three lines...."[65]

So it is with taking another's property. Like Leibniz and Wolff, Kant defined property as the right of the owner to use a thing as he chooses and to exclude others from doing so. "Anything is rightfully mine (*meum juris*) when I am so connected with it, that if any other person should make use of it without my consent, he would do me an injury."[66] By definition, anyone who uses another's property without his consent violates the owner's rights. Therefore, according to Kant, one cannot will as a universal law that to keep a deposit against the owner's will or to steal another's property.

This argument is plausible only if one believes that an owner, by definition, has an unlimited right to use his property as he chooses and to exclude others from using it. Unless the right is unlimited, the rules that govern property cannot not be a matter of "universal law" which "must hold always and necessarily" as the categorical imperative requires. Instead, they would be "rules that on the average are most often correct."[67] Consequently they would rest on a "hypothetical imperative." They would be rules to be followed only to achieve a particular end.

Thus, Schnoor and Westfall would say, beneath the surface of Kant's argument is an independent principle that does not depend on the categorical imperative and can be formulated without regard to it. The principle is that by definition property is an unlimited and exclusive right of the owner to do as he chooses with what he owns. The principle does not follow from the categorical imperative. It is supposed to be true in the same way as the definition of a triangle. As Kant himself said of the duty to keep a promise, in his view, one could not more prove such a definition than a geometrician can prove by "that to make a triangle I must take three lines." Kant opposed the rationalists. Yet to explain the categorical imperative, he explained private rights in the same way.

4.3 *The Jurists*

In the 19th century, the work of the northern natural lawyers and of the rationalists was discredited. It was an age of legal positivism. Jurists claimed that their conclusions were derived from the texts that were legally in force in their own jurisdictions. In Germany, where they had not been displaced by codes or statutes, the authoritative texts were still those of Roman law contained in the *Corpus iuris civilis* of Justinian. They remained in

---

65 *Die Metaphysik der Stitten Erster Theil. Metaphysische Angangsgründe der Rechtslehre* in *Kant's gesammelte Schriften*, ed. Königlich Preussischen Akademie der Wissenschaft (Berlin: Deutsche Akademie der Wissenschaften zu Berlin, 1914), 6: 203 at 273.

66 *Ibid.* 245.

67 Kant, *Kritik der praktischen Vernunft* 36.

force until displaced by the German Civil Code of 1900. In France, the authoritative texts were those of the French Civil Code enacted in 1804. In England and the United States, they were the decisions of judges.

Although the 19th century jurists rejected rationalism, their work bore a closer resemblance to it than they acknowledged. The rationalists" method was to derive conclusions logically from definitions as mathematicians do. Their conclusions were supposed to have the same certainty as the definitions. The positivists" method was to derive conclusions logically from authoritative texts. Their conclusions were supposed to have the same authority as the texts. If an interpreter were to add anything that did not logically follow from the texts, his conclusions would lack the authority of his sources. He would be usurping authority by making law.

Another resemblance was that the 19th century jurists defined basic legal concepts in much the same way as the rationalists. Thus we speak of the 19th century as an age of conceptualism. Property is an example. Supposedly, the German jurists derived their conclusions from the Roman texts, the French from their Civil Code, and the common lawyers from their decided cases. To do so, they identified basic legal concepts in the texts, such a property, and drew conclusions from them. They typically defined property in the same way as the rationalist, as the exclusive right of the owner to do as he chooses with what belongs to him.[68]

As with the rationalists, that right was unqualified. Any limits there might be arose not from the law of property but from some extrinsic principle or concern. A striking example is the law governing interference among neighboring landowners which the common lawyers call nuisance, the French *troubles de voisinage*, and the Germans *Immissionenrecht*. By definition, an owner can use his property as he chooses. How then can a body of law be justified that prevents him from using his land in certain ways that bother his neighbors?

The common lawyers did not explain. French jurists acknowledged that a landowner's right to use his own land as he chooses is violated when he is restrained from using it in a way that interferes with his neighbors. The violation must be tolerated because life would become impossible if owners could exercise in practice the rights that belonged to them in principle. According to Charles Aubry and Charles Rau, the "respective rights of [the] proprietors" of adjacent land were in a "conflict [that] cannot be resolved except by means of certain limits imposed on the natural exercise of the powers inherent in property."[69]

---

68 *E.g.*, Christopher Columbus Langdell, "Classification of Rights and Wrongs" (pt. 1), *Harvard Law Review* 13 (1900), 537, 537-38; Pollock, *First Book of Jurisprudence* 160; Aubry & Rau, 2: § 190; François Laurent, *Principes de droit civil français*, 6 (Paris, 1869 – 78), 1875), § 101; Charles Demolombe, *Cours de Code Napoleon* 9 (Paris, 1854-82), § 543; Bernhard Windscheid, *Lehrbuch des Pandektenrechts* 1 (7th ed., Düsseldorf, 1891), § 167.

69 Charles Aubry & Charles Rau, *Cours de droit civil français d'après la méthode de Zachariae*, 2 (4th ed., Paris, 1869-71), 2, § 194.

Charles Demolombe observed that if all proprietors could "invoke their absolute right, it is clear that none would have one in reality." What would be the result? "It would be war! It would be anarchy!" Similarly, François Laurent believed that "[a]ccording to the rigor of the law, each proprietor would be able to object if one of his neighbors released on his property smoke or exhalations of any kind, because he has a right to the purity of air for his person and his goods."[70] If that were so, he admitted, the existence of towns would be impossible.[71] Thus they arrived at the conclusion that, in principle, the law conferred rights on proprietors that they should not have and which the law would not allow them to exercise.

The German jurists were interpreting a Roman text that prevented the owner of a cheese shop from smoking cheese and so interfering with a person who lived upstairs.[72] Typically, they described the Roman text as a limitation of the right of property by positive law (*gesetzliche Beschränkung des Eigenthums*)."[73] According to Bernhard Windscheid, the limitation was a good one because "reckless realization of the consequences of the concept of ownership is not possible without serious disadvantages."[74] But it was still a limitation by positive law of the owner's rights, as though the law no sooner conferred property rights on the owner than it had to take some of them back.

4.4 *The Common Thread*

The jurists" idea of property rights was congenial to the liberalism of the 19th century. Historians have often assumed that the jurists were influenced by 19th century liberal ideas. There is no reason to think that they were.

Nineteenth century jurists defined the right to property in much the same way whether or not they were committed to liberal philosophy. Indeed, the jurists claimed that their conclusions were based on an interpretation of authoritative texts that was independent of any philosophical commitments. An example is Friedrich Karl von Savigny, one of the most philosophically-minded jurists. Like Kant, he said that law existed to protect freedom.[75] Yet he said that "[w]e in the area of law are not at all occupied with the speculative difficulties of the concept of freedom. For us, freedom is based simply on the appearance, that is, on the capacity, of making a choice among several alternatives."[76] In 19th century

70 Laurent, *Principes* 6: § 144.
71 *Ibid.*
72 D. 8.5.8.5-6.
73 2 G.F. Puchta, *Cursus der Institutionen* 2 (3d ed. 1851)k, § 231; Karl von Vangerow, *Leitfaden für Pandekten-Vorlesungen* (Marburg, 1847), § 297 Anm. II; Windscheid, *Lehrbuch* 1: § 169.
74 Windscheid, *Lehrbuch* 1: § 169.
75 Karl Friedrich von Savigny, *System des heutigen Römischen Rechts* 1 (Berlin, 1849), 331-32.
76 *Ibid.* 3:102.

France, as Valérie Ranouil noted, jurists were hostile to philosophy, never cited Kant, and, until the end of the century, never spoke of the autonomy of the will.[77] In England, Sir Frederick Pollock said that jurists should leave alone "topics which ... may be philosophical, or ethical, or political, but are distinctly outside the province of jurisprudence."[78] The "business" of jurists is simply "to learn and know ... what rules the State does undertake to enforce and administer, whatever the real or professed reasons for those rules may be."[79]

Moreover, as we have seen, the rationalists defined the right to property in much the same way as Kant even though they were not liberals. A liberal such as Kant did not invent his conception of property rights but borrowed it from them. Except in Germany, the jurists were unlikely to have been influenced by the rationalists. They arrived as the same conception of property rights on their own.

Thus philosophers and jurists arrived at the same conception even though their professed concerns were quite different. The rationalists began with a principle of extreme altruism and defined private right by its opposition to altruism. Kant wished to show that it was actions such as theft or the appropriation of a deposit "cannot without contradiction even be thought" to be consistent with a "universal law of nature." The only concern of jurists, they said, was to interpret their authoritative texts.

The best explanation is that all of them were trying to explain the right to property while abstracting from the purposes that the institution of property serves. When they did so, nothing was left but the idea that the owner can do as he wills with his own.

5 Whither?

Since the late 19th century, few jurists have defended the idea that property is an unqualified right. Yet few have escaped its influence. Sometimes it has re-emerged simply because it is familiar. Sometimes it has been perpetuated by the very jurists who claim to have repudiated it. The problem is that there is no generally accepted alternative. To arrive at one, we, like the late scholastics, would have to ask ourselves what purpose property rights serve.

In the United States, the idea of property as an unqualified right slumbers on. At unfortunate moments it awakes. In 1986, in *Loretto v. Teleprompter Manhattan CATV Corp.*,[80] the Supreme Court held that a local government could not require a landlord to permit a cable to be installed on his property for the convenience of his tenants even though

77 Valérie Ranouil, *L'Autonomie de la volonté: Naissance et évolution d'un concept* (Paris, 1980), 9, 53-55, 79.

78 Sir Frederick Pollock, "The Nature of Jurisprudence Considered in Relation to some Recent Contributions to Legal Science," in Sir Frederick Pollock, *Essays in Jurisprudence and Ethics* (London, 1882), 19-20.

79 Pollock, *First Book* 26-27.

80 458 U.S. 419 (1982).

the inconvenience to himself was trivial. In explaining that result, the court described property as though it were an unqualified right: "Property rights in a physical thing have been described as the rights 'to possess, use and dispose of it.' To the extent that the government permanently occupies physical property, it effectively destroys *each* of these rights."[81] The court did not ask what purposes are served by recognizing the right to possess, use and dispose of property, and how the owner of an unqualified right to physical possession serves those purposes.

Often, especially in continental Europe, jurists have disavowed the idea that property is an unqualified right. Yet the way that they have done so entrenches this idea. They have said that that private rights to property must yield to the public interest. What they mean by a private right, however, is still the unqualified right of an owner to do as he chooses with what he owns.

An early example is the justification of the drafters of the German Civil Code for § 904 which allows a person in distress to use another's property to save himself. A prior draft had not allowed him to do so. According to the Drafting Commission, the justification of the doctrine of necessity is that

> action taken through necessity ... manifests the importance of higher interests over lower ones, that is, to the extent that it is a function performed as a duty to the community. There should be no contradiction between rights and laws of morality. Every private right carries the inherent limitation that it must give way to the general interest, and when such a higher interest is present is decided by the judgment of the community.[82]

Paradoxically, this description of the "inherent limitation" of property rights assumes that property rights are conceptually unlimited. Without that assumption it would be unintelligible. The Drafting Commission cannot have meant that an owner must always exercise his rights to promote the general interest. If that were so, private property would cease to exist. The Commission must have meant that sometimes the owner's right to do as he chooses with his property must "give way to the general interest." The right that sometimes must give way has not changed. It is a right that in itself is conceptually unqualified. The limitation is that it can be trumped by considerations of public interest. The philosophers and jurists who first explained property as an unqualified right would have agreed. Leibniz said that the owner may deal with his property "in every way according to his will unless for some particular reason there is an exception."[83] Nineteenth century

81 *Ibid.* 436.
82 *Protokolle der Kommission für die zweite Lesung des Bürgerlichen Gesetzbuches* VI, § 419, 214 (Berlin, 1899).
83 Leibnitz, "De iustitia et novo codice," *Textes inédits* 2, 621 at 621.

French and German jurists acknowledged that the law could stop a landowner from interfering with his neighbors even though to do so abridged his right to property.

A striking example is the controversy in France in the mid-19th century over whether to recognize the doctrine of abuse of rights (*abus de droit*). According to proponents of the doctrine, French courts had implicitly accepted the idea that rights are inherently limited. An illustration was a decision of the Court of Appeal of Colmar[84] which they regarded as path-breaking. The court refused to allow a property owner to build a false chimney in order to block his neighbor's window. René Demogue explained that "the expression ... abuse of rights" indicates "a problem of the limits of every right. ... Does it not have limits of a kind which are teleological or social? Is it not necessary to understand, as included in every provision of law, [the qualification that] the right hereby recognized can only be exercised for motives in accordance with good social order?"[85] According to Louis Josserand, "to abuse [a right] is to proceed, intentionally or unintentionally, against the purpose of the institution of which one has misunderstood the finality and the function."[86]

Nevertheless, Demogue and Josserand did not analyze the *telos* or the purpose of the institution of private property. Consequently, their defense of abuse of rights raised the spectre that courts could require any owner's exercise of his rights to be socially beneficial. Critics of the doctrine of such as Marcel Planiol and George Ripert did not defend the idea that property rights are "absolute."[87] They feared, however that a judge would try to "remedy every wrong,"[88] to "ask of each man an account of the motives of his acts ..."[89]

Perhaps advocates of the doctrine of abuse of rights wanted judges to have the power to do so. Demogue said that the doctrine was "in harmony with the reaction which is taking place against individualistic ideas. Today, one wants the individual to act in the general interest."[90] Josserand said that the doctrine "constitutes a living and moving theory of great suppleness, an instrument of progress, a method of adapting law to social needs."[91] Did they mean that, in principle, a property owner could exercise his rights only when he was "act[ing] in the general interest? If a property owner were always required to act in the general interest, private property would cease to exist.

84 Colmar, 2 May 1855, D. 1856.II.9.

85 René Demogue, *Traité des obligations en général* 4 (Paris, 1924) no. 679.

86 Louis Josserand, *De l'esprit des droits et de leur relativité Théorie dite de l'abus des droits* 2nd ed. (Paris, 1939) no. 245.

87 Marcel Planiol & Georges Ripert, *Traité pratique de droit civil français* 6 (Paris, 1930), no. 573.

88 *Ibid.* no. 574.

89 Georges Ripert, *La Règle morale dans les obligations civiles* 3rd ed. (Paris, 1935), no. 103 bis.

90 Demogue, *Traité des obligations* no. 679.

91 Josserand, *De l'esprit des droits* no. 247.

Today in France, although the doctrine is widely accepted, it has been defanged and declawed.[92] It means that regulations made in the general interest can trump private property rights. Planiol and Ripert never claimed otherwise. The difficulty, however, is that the property right that may be trumped is still regarded as an unqualified right of the owner to do as he will with this own.

To escape the difficulty, like the late scholastics, we would have to consider carefully the purposes which private property serves. Then we would be able to distinguish two very different limits on what the owner can do. One limit concerns the extent of the right to property: the owner should have only those rights that serve the purposes for which private property is established. A second limit is a restriction of one person's property rights in the interest of someone else, whether another individual or the public. In the first case, the owner is merely preventing from exercising a right that he never had. In the second, his right is sacrificed from the benefit of someone else. It matters which is which.

92 Anna di Robilant, "Abuse of Rights: The Continental Drug and the Common Law," *Hastings Law Journal* 687 61 (2010), 687.

Vermogensongelijkheid: heeft het goederenrecht een antwoord op Piketty?

Jan Smits[*]

1 Inleiding

In een opmerkelijk redactioneel commentaar riep de *Financial Times* – geen krant die bekend staat om zijn linkse signatuur – op 1 januari 2018 op tot een nieuw sociaal contract voor onze kapitalistische samenleving.[1] Het terugdringen van de uitwassen van globalisering en neoliberalisme, waaronder belastingontwijking door grote bedrijven, groeiende macht van *big tech*, sterk toegenomen inkomensverschillen en scheve vermogensgroei, zouden een nieuw maatschappelijk verdrag tussen bedrijfsleven en maatschappij vereisen.

Dit pleidooi, dat drie jaar later nauwelijks aan belang heeft ingeboet, is slechts één van de stemmen die opgaan voor een radicale verandering van de manier waarop onze economie is georganiseerd. In het internationale publieke debat is de Franse econoom Thomas Piketty de bekendste vertolker van dit geluid.[2] Ook Piketty bepleit een nieuwe ideologie. Zoals de premoderne standenmaatschappij, het Europa van na de Franse Revolutie en de naoorlogse verzorgingsstaat elk een eigen politiek-filosofische onderbouwing kenden, zo bestaat volgens hem nu de noodzaak om het huidige "hyperkapitalistische" en "inegalitaire neoproprietaristische mondiale systeem"[3] opnieuw te herijken willen we in staat blijven tot vreedzaam samenleven. De huidige, op liberale beginselen geënte, maatschappij is immers niet langer in staat om te grote ongelijkheid – historisch gezien de belangrijkste reden voor revoluties en bloedvergieten, maar op de kortere termijn ook verantwoordelijk voor maatschappelijke neergang – tegen te gaan.[4] Dat is overigens een constatering die niet alleen door een links georiënteerde econoom als Piketty, maar ook door juristen aan de rechterkant van het politieke spectrum wordt gedaan.[5]

---

* Hoogleraar Privaatrecht aan de Universiteit Maastricht en decaan van de Faculteit der Rechtsgeleerdheid.

1 'The FT View: A better deal between business and society', *Financial Times*, 1 januari 2018.

2 T. Piketty, *Kapitaal in de 21ste eeuw*, Amsterdam, De Bezige Bij, 2014 (*Le Capital au XXI siècle*, Paris, Seuil, 2013).

3 T. Piketty, *Kapitaal en ideologie*, Amsterdam, De Geus, 2020 (*Capital et idéologie*, Paris, Seuil, 2019), p. 732.

4 Wetenschappelijke Raad voor het Regeringsbeleid, *Hoe ongelijk is Nederland? Een verkenning van de ontwikkeling en gevolgen van economische ongelijkheid*, WRR-verkenning 28, Den Haag 2014.

5 Zie bijv. E.A. Posner & E.G. Weyl, website Radical Markets: "wealthy countries are at a moment of fundamental crisis that threatens the legitimacy and stability of our values and institutions. (...) the coming years

In deze bijdrage bij het afscheid van Sjef van Erp – die zijn Maastrichtse hoogleraarschap wijdde aan het vergelijkend goederenrecht – wil ik ingaan op één specifiek aspect van pleidooien zoals dat van de *Financial Times* en Piketty.[6] Het betreft de vraag welke rol het goederenrecht precies speelt bij het in stand houden, of versterken, van scheve vermogensgroei én of het goederenrecht een rol kan spelen bij het tegengaan daarvan. Dat van ongelijke vermogensverhoudingen sprake is, behoeft daarbij geen betoog. In veel landen bezit de rijkste tien procent van de bevolking de helft van het totale vermogen, terwijl de armste helft het vaak moet doen met niet meer dan tien procent daarvan.[7] In Nederland bezit de rijkste één procent een derde van het vermogen, internationaal beschouwd een van de meest ongelijke vermogensverdelingen.[8] Het hangt zonder meer van iemands persoonlijke politieke opvattingen af of dit ook een probleem is, maar zodra ongelijkheid de stabiliteit van de samenleving in gevaar brengt – zoals de FT en Piketty betogen – is er een publiek belang bij betrokken om daar iets aan te doen. Een recht dat dit niet langer kan, verliest zijn legitimiteit.

2 Vermogensongelijkheid en recht: hyperkapitalisme "n'est pas une fatalité"

De eerste, fundamentele, vraag is of het goederenrecht een rol speelt bij het in stand houden of versterken van vermogensongelijkheid. Zoals elke deskundige op een bepaald terrein wellicht geneigd is om het belang van het eigen specialisme te benadrukken, zo zal ook de jurist deze vraag zonder meer bevestigend beantwoorden. Het recht maakt mogelijk dat eigendom, en andere rechten, kunnen worden gevestigd op al dan niet fysieke voorwerpen en beschermt degenen aan wie deze rechten toekomen. Weinig verbazingwekkend is dan ook dat juist in pleidooien voor een minder scheve groei van vermogen eigendomsrechten (inclusief rechten op niet-materiële objecten, zoals voortbrengselen van de geest en data) een centrale rol hebben. In de afgelopen tweehonderd jaar is door generaties van juristen aan studenten voorgehouden dat dit type rechten in beginsel jegens iedereen (*erga omnes*) kan worden gehandhaafd, voortdurend is (in die zin dat het recht op het goed niet teniet gaat, maar op de zaak blijft rusten zolang die zaak bestaat), een exclusief genot geeft aan de rechthebbende, en alomvattend, overdraagbaar (dus verhandelbaar) en overerfbaar is. Zo beschouwd ligt de toekenning van eigendom, en andere rechten, aan al dan niet fysieke

hold great peril for wealthy societies." http://radicalmarkets.com/why-radical-markets (bezocht op 5 september 2020).

6 Zie ook R. Bregman, *Gratis geld voor iedereen*, Amsterdam, De Correspondent, 2014.

7 Piketty, 2014, p. 257.

8 S. Toussaint, B. van Bavel, W. Salverda & C. Teulings, 'Nederlandse vermogens schever verdeeld dan gedacht', *ESB* 1 juli 2020.

objecten ten grondslag aan de verdeling van welvaart. Als deel van het vermogensrecht beschermt het goederenrecht de status quo.[9] Het rechtvaardigt de bestaande rechtstoestand en staat remedies zoals revindicatie toe in geval van feitelijke afwijking daarvan. Dit betekent dat ook het toenemen van vermogensongelijkheid in die zin door het goederenrecht wordt veroorzaakt dat het door koop, schenking, erfenis of creatieve uitvinding gegroeid vermogen beschermt.

In zijn meest recente boek stelt Piketty dan ook terecht dat het bestaan van hyperkapitalisme niet onvermijdelijk is.[10] Verschillen in rijkdom worden niet veroorzaakt door economie, technologie, creativiteit of handig zakendoen, maar door politieke keuzes. Die keuzes komen op hun beurt voort uit een bepaalde politiek-filosofische opvatting en worden vervolgens neergelegd in rechtsregels. Dat de bescherming van eigendom direct is geënt op zo'n ideologie, behoeft voor de lezers van deze bundel weinig betoog. Zoals uiteengezet wordt in par. 3 is met name problematisch indien daarin wordt uitgegaan van eigendom als een natuurlijk, pre-juridisch, recht.

Dat het recht verantwoordelijk is voor de verdeling van vermogen wordt ook benadrukt in een recent geruchtmakend boek van Katharina Pistor.[11] Pistor laat zien dat kapitaal altijd bestaat uit twee ingrediënten: een al dan niet materieel object (zaak, vordering, uitvinding, data) en de, wat zij noemt, "legal code." Alleen dankzij die codering (de juridische regeling) krijgt het overgrote deel van objecten hun waarde. Direct beschikbaar voedsel en de feitelijke toestand van een dak boven het hoofd hebben een intrinsieke waarde omdat zij de mens in staat stellen te overleven, maar zij worden deel van het vermogen zodra het recht daar bescherming aan verleent. Goederenrechtelijk betekent die bescherming immers dat ieder ander tot in lengte van dagen van dat voedsel en huis moet afblijven en dat zij kunnen worden overgedragen aan anderen.[12] De ongebreidelde vermogensgroei van de afgelopen decennia komt daarbij overigens vooral door de juridische bescherming van financiële instrumenten, intellectuele eigendom en digitale informatie: "with the right legal coding, any of these assets can be turned into capital and thereby increase its propensity to create wealth for its holder(s)."[13] Pistor stelt terecht dat het recht, en het recht alleen, bepaalt welk bezit bescherming verdient en daarmee geldt als vermogen. Zonder recht geen kapitaal.

9 Zie recent bijv. J.W.A. Biemans & A.G. Castermans, *Barmhartigheid in het burgerlijk recht*, preadvies Nederlandse Vereniging voor Burgerlijk Recht, Zutphen, Paris, 2017, p. 21.

10 Piketty, 2019, p. 1112: "le nouveau récit hyperinégalitaire (...) n'est pas une fatalité."

11 K. Pistor, *The Code of Capital: How the Law Creates Wealth and Inequality*, Princeton, Princeton University Press, 2019.

12 Pistor, 2019, p. 183: "Law is code; it turns a simple asset into a capital asset by bestowing the attributes of priority, durability, universality, and convertibility on it."

13 Pistor, 2019, p. 3.

Dit inzicht, hoewel door Pistor met veel tamtam gepresenteerd, is uiteraard niet nieuw. Evident is dat het recht bepaalt welke subjectieve rechten bescherming verdienen en daarmee in iemands vermogen vallen. Voor de continentale jurist is dit gesneden koek, en niet alleen omdat die gewenst is aan het gebruik van de term "vermogensrecht." De nadruk die Pistor legt op het recht als basis voor de economie – waarbij de "code" niet alleen door het goederenrecht, maar ook door het contracten- en ondernemingsrecht wordt gevormd – valt alleen te verklaren vanuit haar wens om dit inzicht ook over te brengen aan niet-juristen, inclusief economen.[14]

Wat Pistor wel blootlegt, is dat in een geglobaliseerde samenleving individuele staten niet langer in staat lijken om het ontstaan en de verspreiding van kapitaal te controleren. Dat is omdat partijen vrijelijk kunnen kiezen voor het recht van één staat (de bekende jurisdictionele competitie). Zolang die staat bereid is om de door een partij gewenste juridische bescherming te bieden, kan het recht – en kunnen gespecialiseerde advocaten en belastingadviseurs als "masters of the code"[15] – de rol vervullen van dienaar van het kapitaal. De dominantie in het internationale zakenleven van Engels recht en dat van de staat New York valt daarmee te verklaren vanuit de grote vrijheid die deze jurisdicties aan partijen laten. Dankzij rechtskeuze is vervolgens ook op grote schaal belastingontwijking mogelijk. Omdat unificatie of harmonisatie van recht op de hier relevante rechtsgebieden grotendeels is mislukt, prevaleert dan die rechtskeuze boven het publieke belang.[16] Voor Pistor dient het recht hiermee de rijken, die ter rechtvaardiging van hun vermogenspositie altijd kunnen verwijzen naar het recht en critici kunnen voorhouden: "but it is legal."[17] Dat er vele varianten van kapitalisme bestaan, en sommige landen wel degelijk beperkingen opleggen aan te ongelijke vermogensgroei, is hierbij minder relevant: zolang diezelfde landen de keuze voor een ander rechtsstelsel toestaan, heeft dat geen effect.

Het punt dat Piketty maakt voor ideologie, en Pistor voor het recht, kan niet serieus genoeg worden genomen. Waar Piketty benadrukt dat kapitaal ongelijkheid creëert, stelt Pistor dat recht bepaalt wat kapitaal is. Wie welvaart in de samenleving effectief wil verdelen, moet daarom de macht hebben over het coderen van vermogen. Toenemende vermogensongelijkheid door globalisering is hiermee geen noodzakelijkheid, maar het gevolg van een keuze van *nationale* rechtsordes om daar in het eigen recht geen paal en perk aan te stellen én de keuze voor buitenlandse normen te erkennen.

---

14 Pistor bouwt voort op het werk van onder meer O.E. Williamson, *The Economic Institutions of Capitalism*, New York, The Free Press, 1985.

15 Pistor, 2019, p. 158.

16 Pistor, 2019, p. 21, 134, 160. Vgl. p. 221: "for roving capital, the law of a given state is just an option, which its holders and their master coders will exercise only if it promises greater wealth than the laws of another state."

17 Pistor, 2019, p. 161.

3 Wat vermag het goederenrecht? Voorbij obstakels

Indien het vermogensrecht, door de bescherming van eigendom en andere rechten, verantwoordelijk is voor groeiende vermogensongelijkheid, kan het dan ook worden ingezet om die tegen te gaan? Wie de redenering zoals uiteengezet in de voorgaande paragraaf volgt, kan die vraag niet anders dan bevestigend beantwoorden. Hierbij zijn wel enige obstakels te overwinnen.

Het huidige goederenrecht is nog altijd geënt op de idee dat eigendom, zodra men het eenmaal heeft, een onvervreemdbaar recht is waar het positieve recht slechts bij uitzondering afbreuk aan mag doen. Dat is de lange slagschaduw van het idee van eigendom als een pre-juridisch recht dat ten minste teruggaat tot Locke.[18] In deze opvatting bevestigt eigendom de status quo, zoals de Verklaring van de Rechten van de Mens en de Burger van 1789 deed door het als natuurlijk en onweerlegbaar, onschendbaar en heilig te kwalificeren. Uiteraard wordt de sociale functie van eigendom al heel lang volop en overal erkend, in sommige landen zelfs in die mate dat het ook volgens de grondwet altijd moet worden uitgeoefend in overeenstemming met "social justice" of "dem Wohle der Allgemeinheit",[19] maar ook dat blijft gebaseerd op het uitgangspunt dat eigendom *in beginsel* als absoluut en exclusief moet worden beschermd. Uitzonderingen daarop moeten steeds worden gerechtvaardigd.

Voor het overgrote deel van de juristen betekent deze nadruk op bescherming van de status quo dat het vermogensrecht geen rol heeft te spelen bij de herverdeling van bezit.[20] Met het redresseren van vermogensongelijkheid houdt het zich niet bezig. Uiteraard is de premisse dat de wijze waarop goederen werden verkregen juist was, maar als dat het geval is, bemoeit het privaatrecht zich niet met de mate waarin dit ook leidt tot een rechtvaardige verdeling. Beter uitgedrukt: de rechtvaardige verdeling is die, die volgt uit een correcte verkrijging van goederen. Het privaatrecht functioneert niet als een Robin Hood die neemt van de rijken en geeft aan de armen.

In deze heersende opvatting vindt herverdeling van welvaart plaats op een andere manier, namelijk via progressieve belastingen. Belasting van vermogen, schenkingen en erfenissen wordt in die visie beschouwd als effectiever. Piketty laat zien dat tussen 1900 en 1980 de financiële gelijkheid in de wereld daardoor inderdaad sterk toenam. Dat

18 J. Locke, *Two Treatises of Government*, 1689, ed. P. Laslett, Cambridge, Cambridge University Press 1988, p. 298. Aldus ook nog bij H.L.A. Hart, *The Concept of Law*, 1961, 2nd ed., Oxford, Oxford University Press, 1994, p. 196 die "enige" bescherming van eigendom beschouwt als deel van het minimale natuurrecht.

19 Resp. art. 43 Constitution of Ireland en art. 14 Grundgesetz für die Bundesrepublik Deutschland. Vgl. J.M. Smits, *Advanced Introduction to Private Law*, Cheltenham, Edward Elgar, 2017, p. 65 v. en C.J.H. Jansen, 'Het eigendomsrecht en het gemeenschapsdenken', *Groninger Opmerkingen en Mededelingen* XXV (2008), pp. 1-12.

20 Zie Biemans & Castermans, 2017, p. 21 en (meer genuanceerd) W.H. van Boom, *Privaatrecht en markt*, Den Haag, BJU, 2020, p. 163 v. met verwijzingen naar auteurs.

veranderde na 1980 toen hoge belastingtarieven in de VS[21] en veel andere landen allengs verdwenen. Er is dan ook geen gebrek aan pleidooien om de groeiende kloof tussen rijk en arm opnieuw te lijf te gaan met een hoge progressieve belasting op vermogen en erfenissen.[22] In het bijzonder erfbelasting is daarbij een interessant instrument nu het doorgeven van bezit aan de volgende generatie één van de belangrijkste oorzaken is van groeiende vermogensongelijkheid.[23] Een confiscatoire erfbelasting van 100% zou veel meer leiden tot gelijke kansen voor iedereen en een vermogensverdeling die veel meer is gebaseerd op prestaties. De Amerikaanse activist Orestes Brownson formuleerde het in 1840 zo: "Een man mag alles houden wat hij op eerlijke wijze heeft verworven, zolang hij deel uitmaakt van de wereld waarin hij het heeft verworven. Echter, zijn macht over dit eigendom moet samen met zijn leven eindigen, waarna het staatseigendom dient te worden en een rechtvaardige wet ervoor zorgt dat de generatie die zijn plaats inneemt erover kan beschikken."[24] In onze geïndividualiseerde samenleving is dat een nog aantrekkelijker gedachte dan zij in het midden van de negentiende eeuw was, waarbij uiteraard denkbaar is om die confiscatie alleen boven een bepaalde waarde of voor bepaalde goederen te laten plaatsvinden.

Toch kent belastingheffing als instrument om vermogensongelijkheid tegen te gaan belangrijke bezwaren. Eén bezwaar werd reeds genoemd: de mogelijkheid om door rechtskeuze belastingen te ontwijken, een optie die vooral voor de werkelijk vermogenden gemakkelijk valt te realiseren. Pistors remedie om rechtskeuze minder gemakkelijk te maken en op de koop toe te nemen dat een land zich – vrij letterlijk – uit de markt prijst, is niet heel realistisch.[25] Een bezwaar tegen een hoge erfbelasting is bovendien dat vermogen dan waarschijnlijk al bij leven wordt weggeschonken.[26] Ten slotte kan een hoge belasting de eigenaar belemmeren om nog te investeren. Dat bevestigt de noodzaak om na te gaan hoe het goederenrecht zelf kan bijdragen aan de herverdeling van bezit. Dat is overigens ook vanuit theoretisch perspectief een gerechtvaardigde exercitie.

---

21 Beroemd is de slogan dat miljardairs in de VS tegenwoordig minder belasting betalen dan hun secretaresses. Zie inmiddels E. Saez & G. Zucman, *The Triumph of Injustice*, New York, Norton, 2019.

22 Zie behalve Piketty, 2020, p. 1051 bijv. OECD, *Taxation of Household Savings*, OECD Tax Policy Studies No. 25, 2018; vgl. D. Kamin, 'How to Tax the Rich', *Tax Notes* 146 (2015), No. 1.

23 Zie de diverse bijdragen aan P. de Beer e.a. (red.), *Voor wie is de erfenis?*, Amsterdam, Van Gennep, 2018. Voor Nederland is dit betwist door het CPB: zie S. Groot, M. Lever & J. Möhlmann, *Effect van erfenissen en schenkingen op vermogensongelijkheid en de rol van belastingen*, CPB-Notitie december 2019.

24 Geciteerd in J. Beckert, 'Zijn wij nog wel modern?', *in* De Beer e.a., 2018, pp. 201-216, p. 207.

25 Pistor, 2019, p. 225.

26 Hoewel een optimaal tarief kan worden bepaald om dat te voorkomen; vgl. T. Piketty & E. Saez, 'A Theory of Optimal Inheritance Taxation', *Econometrica* 81 (2013), pp. 1851-1886.

4 Van voortdurende en exclusieve eigendom naar tijdelijke gebruiksrechten

Buiten twijfel moet worden gesteld dat het goederenrecht, zoals het gehele vermogensrecht, wel degelijk *mede* een instrument is van verdelende rechtvaardigheid. Het is dat ook altijd geweest, niet door afbreuk te doen aan bestaande rechten maar wel door te bepalen wie welke rechten mag hebben en wat die rechten inhouden (de "code" van Pistor). Zo is het onschendbaar en heilig verklaren van eigendom een keuze voor een bepaalde allocatie van goederen die wel degelijk is gebaseerd op een verdelingsmaatstaf,[27] net zoals de politieke filosofie van Rawls of Sen leidt tot een andere verdeling.[28] Zoals eerder aangegeven handhaaft de huidige maatstaf in sterke mate de status quo en reproduceert die daarmee bestaande rijkdom. De keuze om *niet* te herverdelen is ook een opvatting over verdelende rechtvaardigheid.

Hiermee kan het goederenrecht wel degelijk een rol vervullen bij het redresseren van vermogensongelijkheid. Indien eigendom – hoeveel afbreuk daaraan in de afgelopen twee eeuwen ook is gedaan – nog altijd *in beginsel* een absoluut, alomvattend, exclusief, voortdurend en overerfbaar recht is, is nu de tijd gekomen voor een fundamenteel doordenken van dat recht opdat het beter past bij de huidige tijd. Dit impliceert dat komaf gemaakt wordt met de zojuist genoemde karakteristieken.

Aanzetten hiertoe ontbreken niet. Zo bepleitte Van Maanen op het voetspoor van anderen dertig jaar geleden al voor een differentiatie van typen eigendom naar de aard van het gebruik. Naast maatschappelijke eigendom (die van productiemiddelen, grond en water) en persoonlijke eigendom (ter vervulling van materiële en culturele behoeften) onderscheidt hij eigendom van woonruimte. Elk van deze vormen kent eigen regels die worden ingegeven door wat voor het type eigendom in kwestie rechtvaardig of in het belang van de gemeenschap is.[29] Hiermee wordt vooral de karakteristiek van de alomvattendheid van de eigendom gerelativeerd: de eigenaar mag niet alles met de eigendom. Wat hij wel mag, wordt bepaald door de aard van de zaak.

Mijns inziens moet voor het tegengaan van ongewenste ongelijke vermogensgroei vooral het temporele aspect van het eigendomsrecht worden gerelativeerd. De eerder genoemde karakteristiek van de voortdurendheid ziet erop dat eigendomsrechten op de

27 Vgl. Smits, 2017, p. 9.

28 Resp. J. Rawls, *A Theory of Justice*, Cambridge Mass., Harvard University Press, 1971 en A. Sen, *Commodities and Capabilities*, New Delhi, Oxford University Press, 1999, uitgewerkt in G.S. Alexander, *Property and Human Flourishing*, Oxford, Oxford University Press, 2018, waarover B. Akkermans, 'Duurzaam goederenrecht: naar een herijking van ons goederenrechtelijk stelsel?, *Tijdschrift voor Privaatrecht* 55 (2018), pp. 1437-1470, p. 1446.

29 G.E. van Maanen, *Eigendomsschijnbewegingen*, Nijmegen, Ars Aequi Libri, 1987, p. 157.

zaak zich in beginsel onbeperkt uitstrekken in de tijd;[30] dat is de belangrijkste reden waarom kapitaal groeit. Erfbelasting kan dienen om die groei te remmen,[31] maar ook het goederenrecht zelf kan dit bewerkstelligen door de periode gedurende welke gebruik kan worden gemaakt van een goed, of van de waarde daarvan kan worden geprofiteerd, te beperken. Dat verhoogt de omloopsnelheid van het goed in kwestie. Voortdurende en alomvattende eigendomsrechten worden daarmee ingeruild voor tijdelijke gebruiksrechten.

Dit kan op verschillende wijze worden gerealiseerd. Eén radicaal voorstel, waarin "possessors become lessees from society", werd onlangs gedaan door Posner en Weyl.[32] Hun uitgangpunt is dat de eigenaar het beste in staat is om voor goederen te zorgen. Ook in een andersoortig goederenrecht moet de gebruiker daarom een prikkel houden om in het goed te investeren. Publiek bezit loopt het risico te worden verwaarloosd. Deze *investment efficiency* moet echter worden afgewogen tegen *allocative efficiency*. Aan dat laatste ontbreekt het, ook volgens hen, op dit moment door een te grote opeenhoping van bezit bij een te kleine groep personen. Posner en Weyl bepleiten daarom een systeem van "partial common ownership" dat beide vormen van efficiëntie verenigt: alle bezit gemeenschappelijk maken voorkomt dat één persoon een monopolie heeft op (materiële of immateriële) goederen (verdelende efficiëntie) terwijl het voor de rechthebbende nog wel loont om te investeren (investeringsefficiëntie).[33] Over de wijze waarop zij dit willen bereiken – namelijk door alle gebruiksrechten ondergeschikt te maken aan het prijsmechanisme, gekoppeld aan een belasting op de waarde die de gebruiker zelf aan het object geeft[34] – valt veel te zeggen. De waarde van de exercitie van Posner en Weyl ligt er in dat zij laten zien dat eigendomsverhoudingen op een radicaal andere manier kunnen worden vormgegeven zonder te vervallen in een centrale verdeling van eigendomsverhoudingen zoals in communistische samenlevingen het geval is.

De visie van Posner en Weyl is vooral aansprekend omdat het goederenrecht daarin niet langer dient om de status quo te rechtvaardigen, maar wordt ingezet om verandering teweeg te brengen.[35] Dat bevestigt het eerder gemaakte punt dat bescherming van eigendom geen natuurlijk pre-juridisch recht is, maar het product van maatschappelijk en politiek

---

30 Voor de term R. Dekkers-E. Dirix, *Handboek Burgerlijk Recht deel II*, 3de dr., Antwerpen, Intersentia, 2005, no. 132; S.E. Bartels & A.A. van Velten, *Asser's Handleiding deel 5 Zakenrecht: eigendom en beperkte rechten*, 16de dr., Deventer, Kluwer, 2017, no. 20 noemen dit de onbeperkte duur van de eigendom.

31 Zie daarvoor ook Piketty, 2020, p. 1055 met een pleidooi om "sociaal en tijdelijk bezit" via belastingen te realiseren.

32 E.A. Posner & E.G. Weyl, *Radical Markets: Uprooting Capitalism and Democracy for a Just Society*, Princeton, Princeton University Press, 2018, p. 62.

33 Posner & Weyl, 2018, p. 52.

34 Posner & Weyl, 2018, p. 61: een "common ownership self-assessed tax (COST)."

35 Voor een werk dat dit vanuit geheel ander perspectief ook bepleit: C. Menke, *Kritik der Rechte*, Berlin, Suhrkamp, 2015; zie voor een poging tot concretisering A. Fischer-Lescano, H. Franzki & J. Horst (red.), *Gegenrechte*, Tübingen, Mohr Siebeck, 2018.

debat dat in het recht wordt neergelegd. In mijn optiek kan een systeem van tijdelijke gebruiksrechten ook zonder een radicaal marktdenken worden gerealiseerd. Het vereist de principiële keuze alleen dat type rechten op bepaalde goederen zoals huizen en auto's te aanvaarden. Dat is een mogelijke oplossing voor de situatie dat huiseigenaren nu door stil te zitten worden beloond met een waardestijging van hun woning terwijl minder vermogenden geen toegang hebben tot de huizenmarkt. Het nut van privébezit van auto's[36] kan vanuit een ander oogpunt, namelijk duurzaamheid, in twijfel worden getrokken. Dat past bij een trend waarin goederen steeds meer worden gedeeld, zoals wanneer gebruik wordt gemaakt van deelauto's (bijvoorbeeld via Greenwheels) of van bemiddeling tussen reizigers en aanbieders van vervoer (zoals bij Uber).[37] Het creëren van dergelijke tijdelijke rechten past bij de regulering van rechten op voortbrengselen van de geest, die ook is gebaseerd op het idee dat waardevolle goederen na verloop van tijd moeten worden teruggegeven aan de gemeenschap.

5 TEN SLOTTE

Het doel van deze bijdrage is niet om uit te werken hoe een systeem van tijdelijke gebruiksrechten er precies uit moet zien. De vraag voor welke goederen zo'n systeem moet worden ingevoerd, en gedurende welke termijn het goed mag worden gebruikt om voldoende investeringsefficiëntie te bewerkstelligen, vereist nadere uitwerking. Wat deze bijdrage wel beoogt duidelijk te maken, is dat het goederenrecht een antwoord heeft op het alom gesignaleerde fenomeen van toenemende vermogensongelijkheid. Het is tijd voor het opnieuw fundamenteel doordenken van eigendom. Het conservatieve argument dat privé-eigendom nu eenmaal een bestaand en onschendbaar recht is, heeft daarbij definitief afgedaan.[38] Indien we Pistor en Posner & Weyl geloven, duldt die herbezinning op de grondslagen van het goederenrecht geen uitstel. Daarmee laat het voorafgaande zien hoe praktisch relevant, volgens sommigen zelfs essentieel voor blijvend vreedzaam leven, een grondslagendiscussie kan zijn.

36 Door Posner & Weyl, 2018, p. 77 niet ten onrechte een "fetish" genoemd.

37 Zie ook Akkermans, *TPR* 2018, p. 1454 en T. Piketty, 'Pour une économie circulaire', *Le Monde* 12 oktober 2019 met een pleidooi voor "circulation permanente du pouvoir, de la richesse et du savoir."

38 Zie ook nog Piketty, 2020, p. 1056: "Het idee dat er strikt privébezit zou bestaan (...) is nauwelijks staande te houden."

Is Our Concept of Property Sustainable?

A Catholic Social Teaching Perspective

Katja Zimmermann[*]

"The principle of the subordination of private property to the universal destination of goods, and thus the right of everyone to their use, is a golden rule of social conduct and 'the first principle of the whole ethical and social order'."

Laudato si' *93*[1]

When we think about property rights, we are easily tempted to restrict our view to the powers that they bestow on us while we too eagerly forget the duties that form their counterparts.[2] Yet, against the background of climate change and the ongoing debate on how to create a more sustainable world, it seems that we are beginning to become more sensitive again to the duties attached to property, especially when considering property rights on land. The morality of property rights and specifically the balancing of rights and obligations has already been analyzed through various angles, most prominently through the lenses of law and philosophy. However, and this is perhaps rather surprising in more secular societies, one of the most influential writings in the sustainability debate to date is a publication of a church leader; five years after its publication, Pope Francis' encyclical *Laudato si'*, has received wide attention far beyond Catholic circles. How can his perspective enrich the sustainability debate outside the Catholic context? Without a doubt, tackling the sustainability problem demands creative solutions and lawyers have proven their ability to think outside the box to provide tailor-made methods to address pressing issues.[3] Considering the wide-reception of *Laudato si'*, the need for creative solutions, and the fact

* LL.M. Lecturer in Private Law at Maastricht University.

1 Francis, *Laudato si'* (Encyclical on Care for our Common Home), May 24, 2015, 93. Accessed on October 5, 2020. http://www.vatican.va/content/francesco/en/encyclicals/documents/papa-francesco_20150524_enciclica-laudato-si.html.

2 Benedict XVI, *Caritas in veritate* (Encyclical on Integral Human Development), June 29, 2009, 43. Accessed on 5 October 2020. http://www.vatican.va/content/benedict-xvi/en/encyclicals/documents/hf_ben-xvi_enc_20090629_caritas-in-veritate.html.

3 Reference could for instance be made to the famous Whanganui river in New Zealand that has received legal personhood. See: K. Warne, 'A Voice for Nature', *National Geographic*, 2019. Accessed on October 5, 2020. https://www.nationalgeographic.com/culture/2019/04/maori-river-in-new-zealand-is-a-legal-person/.

that the Roman Catholic Church is one of the largest private land owners in Europe, it seems defendable to explore how the Catholic Church's position on the concept of property can enrich the sustainability debate. After all, theologians have been thinking about the question of how to balance the right to property with the common good for centuries.[4] From a modern perspective, when considering the existence of the seventh commandment ("You shall not steal.") and the specific legal provisions governing the protection of movable property that God himself communicated to Moses on Mount Sinai, it becomes quite clear that God generally legitimizes private property.[5] After all, if this was not the case, these rules would have simply been superfluous. However, it is not self-evident that the question about the legitimacy of private property was formulated at all when one considers that the early Christians were anticipating that Christ would soon return to Earth and that they, when the day would come, were to give themselves up to His judgment.[6] As such, they were primarily focused on preparing themselves for the heavenly kingdom to come and, compared to mankind nowadays, to a much lesser extent concerned with the here and now.[7] In particular, given that Scripture declares that the heavenly kingdom belongs to the "poor in spirit", this entailed that pursuits to accumulate wealth and fortune were practically non-existent in the early Christian community.[8] Yet, as more time passed after the resurrection of Christ, this fundamental approach became increasingly fragile.[9] Slowly but steadily, the way was paved for a "charitable humanistic interpretation of property rights and wealth", which implied that Christians could hold private property as long as they lived up to their Christian obligation to make a contribution to charity.[10] Among the first and most Catholic influential thinkers who went beyond this apocalyptical presumption by acknowledging private property were St. Augustine of Hippo and St. Thomas Aquinas who, being inspired by Aristotle, much influenced the Christian social doctrine in this

4 The concept of the 'common good' refers to "the sum of those conditions of social life which allow social groups and their individual members relatively thorough and ready access to their own fulfillment". See: Paul VI, *Gaudium et spes* (Pastoral Constitution on the Church in the Modern World), December 7, 1965, 69. Accessed on October 5, 2020. http://www.vatican.va/archive/hist_councils/ii_vatican_council/documents/vat-ii_const_19651207_gaudium-et-spes_en.html.

5 Exodus 20:15, 22:1-14 and Deuteronomy 5:19. Also see H.J. Berman, *Faith and Order: The Reconciliation of Law and Religion*, Grand Rapids/Cambridge, William B. Eerdmans Publishing Company 1993, p. 168.

6 T.P. Rausch, *I Believe in God: A Reflection on the Apostles' Creed*, Collegeville, Minn., Liturgical Press (e-book), 2008, p. 100. Also see H. Chroust and R.J. Affeldt, 'The Problem of Private Property According to St. Thomas Aquinas', *Marquette Law Review* Volume 34, Issue 3, 1950-1951, p. 152. Also see Matthew 16:27-28 and Revelation 22:12.

7 *Ibid.*

8 Matthew 5:3. Also see Pope Francis, 'Message of Pope Francis for the Twenty-Ninth World Youth Day' 2014. Accessed on October 6, 2020. http://w2.vatican.va/content/francesco/en/messages/youth/documents/papa-francesco_20140121_messaggio-giovani_2014.html. Also see Chroust and Affeldt, 1950-1951, pp. 152-153, 159.

9 Chroust and Affeldt, 1950-1951, p. 156.

10 *Ibid.*

regard.[11] However, it was not until 1891, when Pope Leo XIII's encyclical *Rerum Novarum* was published, that considerations on the legitimacy of private property found their way in a papal encyclical and Catholic social teaching saw the light of day.[12] Papal encyclicals are circulars that are penned by the popes and that are, though not exclusively, directed to all Christians.[13] Despite the fact that they are not automatically given the 'ex cathedra' status, which means that it is in principle possible to challenge them, they are binding on Catholics and considering that the popes address societal problems against the background of the Christian faith in these writings, they constitute a prime source of Catholic social teaching.[14] It is for this reason that in the following, the Roman Catholic position on property shall be outlined on the basis of Catholic social teaching, as established and reaffirmed by the Compendium of the Social Doctrine of the Church, the Catechism of the Catholic Church, and the relevant papal encyclicals from *Rerum Novarum* to *Fratelli Tutti*.

Leo XIII – *Rerum Novarum*: Encyclical on Capital and Labour (1891)

The first social papal encyclical stems from Pope Leo XIII.[15] In his encyclical, he takes a stand for the working class that suffers under the exploitation by the rich.[16] To solve this societal incongruity, the socialists at that time advocated the liquidation of private property into common property so that each person would receive what they are entitled to.[17] Pope Leo XIII however firmly criticizes this approach as "emphatically unjust, for they would rob the lawful possessor, distort the functions of the State, and create utter confusion in the community".[18] According to his social teachings, private property is a natural right

11 Chroust and Affeldt, 1950-1951, pp. 151-152, 178-179. Also see R.J. Dougherty, 'Catholicism and the Economy: Augustine and Aquinas on Property Ownership', *Journal of Markets & Morality*, Volume 6, Number 2, 2003, p. 479 and D. Lametti, 'The Objects of Virtue', *in* G.S. Alexander and E.M. Penalver, *Property and Community*, New York, Oxford University Press, 2010, pp. 24-25.

12 A. Kim, *An Introduction to Catholic Ethics since Vatican II*, New York, Cambridge University Press, 2015, p. 119.

13 G.J. Schwab, 'Social Encyclicals of the Catholic Church', *in* J.E. Tropman (Ed.), *The Catholic Ethic and the Spirit of Community*, Washington, D.C., Georgetown University Press, 2002, p. 231. Also see F.G. Morrissey, 'Encyclical', *in New Catholic Encyclopedia*, 2nd ed., vol. 5, Detroit, Gale, 2003, p. 205. Also see M. Dillon, 'Encyclical', *in Contemporary American Religion*, vol. 1, New York, NY, Macmillan Reference USA, 1999, p. 220-221.

14 *Ibid.*

15 *Ibid.*

16 Leo XIII, *Rerum Novarum* (Encyclical on Capital and Labor), May 15, 1891, 3. Accessed on October 5, 2020. http://www.vatican.va/content/leo-xiii/en/encyclicals/documents/hf_l-xiii_enc_15051891_rerum-novarum.html.

17 *Rerum Novarum* 4.

18 *Ibid.*

and its limits are to be governed by secular law.[19] The acquisition of property (especially land) is considered to be the workers' driving force and that depriving them of this possibility would not only be counterproductive but also strictly against their interests.[20] Moreover, it is argued that while both humans and animals can transitionally possess goods, it must be possible for mankind to also possess goods on a continuous basis.[21] This is due to the fact that mankind is distinct from animals as God conferred reason only upon His own image.[22] The deprivation of the right to private property would thus constitute injustice.[23] Also, if human beings are dispossessed of the benefit of the instalment of common property, their livelihood is taken away given that they must survive on the fruits that they cultivate on their land.[24] Connected herewith, Pope Leo XIII argues that "when man thus turns the activity of his mind and the strength of his body toward procuring the fruits of nature, by such act he makes his own that portion of nature's field which he cultivates".[25] Last, it is established that the strength of the right to private property increases in the context of the family, considering that "it is a most sacred law of nature that a father should provide food and all necessaries for those whom he has begotten".[26] Arguably, private property plays a key role in the fulfilment of the father's duty of parental care; only if he is able to bequeath property on his children after he passes away, can he provide them with the equipment for a secure life.[27]

Pius XI – *Quadragesimo Anno*: Encyclical on Reconstruction of the Social Order (1931)

The second social encyclical dates from the eventful period between the two world wars. Its title shows its strong relation to Pope Leo XIII's encyclical, which was published 40 years earlier.[28] As a main point of departure, Pope Pius XI reminds his audience about the fact that the right to private property has always been believed to be a concept that is derived not only from natural law but even from God himself.[29] As such, this right is

19 *Rerum Novarum* 6, 8, 13.
20 *Rerum Novarum* 5.
21 *Rerum Novarum* 6.
22 *Ibid.*
23 *Ibid.*
24 *Rerum Novarum* 7, 9.
25 *Rerum Novarum* 9.
26 *Rerum Novarum* 13.
27 *Ibid.*
28 Pius XI, *Quadragesimo Anno* (Encyclical on Reconstruction of the Social Order), May 15, 1931, 1. Accessed on October 5, 2020. http://www.vatican.va/content/pius-xi/en/encyclicals/documents/hf_p-xi_enc_19310515_quadragesimo-anno.html.
29 *Quadragesimo Anno* 45.

double-sided: on the one hand, it allows man not only to care for themselves but also for their family while on the other hand it must not be forgotten that those goods that God intended for mankind as a whole must be used for common benefit.[30]

As has already been established by Pope Leo XII, the right to property must be differentiated from the use of that property.[31] This is due to the fact that the latter is regulated by Christian virtues which are not as a whole governed and enforceable in a secular man-made legal system.[32] Further, it is considered impossible for a property right to be "destroyed or lost by reason of abuse or non-use".[33] Pope Pius XI also cedes certain duties to the State. If the owners' duty to use their property to the benefit of the common good is not sufficiently governed by natural law while such regulation is deemed necessary, then the State is entitled to regulate the use of private property to this end in line with both divine and natural law.[34] This competence conferred to mankind is necessary as it is noted that the concept of ownership is not carved in stone but has been subject to changes in the course of history.[35] The abolition of private property and its transfer by means of succession are however expressly excluded from the State's entitlement.[36] Lastly, Pope Pius XI responds to the title of acquisition by mankind by restating that property is originally acquired by occupying a *res nullius* and by the performance of labour on their own behalf.[37]

John XXIII – *Mater et Magistra*: Encyclical on Christianity and Social Progress (1961)

The encyclical letter *Mater et Magistra* was issued exactly 30 years after *Quadragesimo Anno* and 70 years after *Rerum Novarum*.[38] The rather elaborate explanations regarding the right of (private) property are found in its second chapter. First and foremost, Pope John XXIII responds to the change of societal values and necessities. Three main developments are identified. First, within the industrial sector, a "distinction has been growing between the ownership of productive goods and the responsibility of company managers".[39] This development hampers the State in its task of ensuring that the latter's

30 *Quadragesimo Anno* 45-46.
31 *Quadragesimo Anno* 47.
32 *Ibid.*
33 *Ibid.*
34 *Quadragesimo Anno* 49.
35 *Ibid.*
36 *Ibid.*
37 *Quadragesimo Anno* 52.
38 John XXIII, *Mater et Magistra* (Encyclical on Christianity and Social Progress), May 15, 1961. Accessed on October 5, 2020. http://www.vatican.va/content/john-xxiii/en/encyclicals/documents/hf_j-xxiii_enc_15051961_mater.html.
39 *Mater et Magistra* 104.

goals can be conciliated with the common good.[40] Second, the role of private property as a means to secure one's future has decreased as a result of the emergence of insurances and social security.[41] At the same time, in people's minds, the learning of a profession has overtaken the value once attached to the acquirement of private property, which is evaluated as a further societal progress.[42]

After having set out the changed circumstances, Pope John XXIII addresses the question whether these changes influence the right to private property.[43] In essence, he concludes that this question must be answered in the negative given that "the right of private ownership of goods, including productive goods, has permanent validity. It is part of the natural order, which teaches that the individual is prior to society and society must be ordered to the good of the individual".[44] History shows that the non-recognition of private property comes together with other fundamental restrictions of the right of freedom.[45] Therefore "private ownership must be considered as a guarantee of the essential freedom of the individual, and at the same time an indispensable element in a true social order".[46] It is thus of utmost importance that the enjoyment of this right is not restricted to those who stand high enough in the societal hierarchy but is instead granted to all members of society.[47]

While emphasizing the necessity of private property, the validity of public property, which was gaining importance at the time, is also expressly acknowledged.[48] When deciding whether a certain good is to be declared public property, States must take into account the "principle of subsidiarity", according to which the common good must always be balanced with individual interests.[49] Last, we are reminded that while the Gospel confirms the right to private property it also admonishes us to not accumulate fortunes but to transfer them to the poor instead.[50]

40 *Ibid.*
41 *Mater et Magistra* 105.
42 *Mater et Magistra* 106-107.
43 *Mater et Magistra* 108.
44 *Mater et Magistra* 109.
45 *Ibid.*
46 *Mater et Magistra* 111.
47 *Mater et Magistra* 113.
48 *Mater et Magistra* 116-117.
49 *Mater et Magistra* 117.
50 *Mater et Magistra* 121.

Paul VI – *Gaudim et spes*: Pastoral Constitution on the Church in the Modern World (1965)

Gaudium et Spes is one of the four constitutions that resulted from the Second Vatican Council.[51] In the context of the Catholic teachings, the term "pastoral constitution" was at the time a newly invented term to describe a document that not only contains the binding truths of the Catholic faith but also identifies misconceptions.[52] By the same token, pastoral constitutions are characterized by the fact that they do not portray the church in isolation but relate theological considerations to current affairs.[53]

The pastoral constitution reiterates the perception of the right to private property as elaborated in the social encyclicals that were published prior to it. It thus affirms that God has entrusted the earth to all humans.[54] Two sub-principles can be derived from this main principle. First of all, while acknowledging the legitimacy of private property, mankind must not forget that even private property can and must contribute to the common good.[55] Therefore, the ownership of private property is paired with a wide charitable duty to support the poor.[56] Yet, the simple provision of goods that fall within one's surplus is considered to be insufficient.[57] Under grave circumstances it is even legitimate for the poor to "procure for what [they need] out of the riches of others".[58] Second, considering that the earth was given to mankind as a whole, each human being is entitled to a part of the earth and its fruits, which allows them to provide for themselves and for their family.[59] This entitlement is "necessary for the autonomy of the person and the family, and it should be regarded as an extension of human freedom".[60] This principle has both a temporal and geographical dimension in the sense that future generations and developing countries deserve special attention.[61] It is stressed that the negligence of this social dimension of the right to private property leads to the situation in which "property often becomes an occasion

---

51 L.D. Lefebure, Is There Reason for Hope?: The Second Vatican Council and Catholic Interreligious Relations, in: L. Van Rompay, S. Miglarese & D. Morgan (eds.), The Long Shadow of Vatican II: Living Faith and Negotiating Authority since the Second Vatican Council, Chapil Hill: The University of North Carolina Press, 2015, p. 14.

52 M. Belok, Die Pastoralkonstitution Gaudium et spes.: Anliegen und bleibende Verpflichtung, in: M. Belok and U. Kropač (eds.), Volk Gottes im Aufbruch: 40 Jahre II. Vatikanisches Konzil, Zürich: Theologischer Verlag Zürich, 2005, p. 158.

53 *Ibid.*

54 *Gaudium et spes* 69.

55 *Ibid.*

56 *Ibid.*

57 *Ibid.*

58 *Ibid.*

59 *Ibid.*

60 *Gaudium et spes* 71.

61 *Gaudium et spes* 70.

of passionate desires for wealth and serious disturbances, so that a pretext is given to the attackers for calling the right itself into question".[62] Furthermore, it must not be forgotten that private property, next to modern security mechanisms such as security funds, still provides an important source of security.[63]

In addition to private property, the existence of public property is also legitimate.[64] Three conditions apply to the creation of public property: first, the party that transfers the property to the State must be legally entitled to do so, second, public property can only be created in accordance with "the demands and within the limits of the common good", and third, it must be accompanied by "fair compensation".[65]

Paul VI – *Populorum Progressio*: Encylical on the Development of Peoples (1967)

Pope Paul VI's encyclical *Populorum Progressio* is comparatively short on considerations regarding the right to property, but certainly not less interesting.[66] As follows from Scripture, God has given the earth to mankind as a whole.[67] Therefore, each human being is entitled to what they need.[68] All rights, including the right to property, must comply with this central maxim.[69] In other words, the individual's right to property must always be in accordance with the common good and is thus not an "absolute and unconditional" right.[70] As Pope Paul VI clearly states that "no one may appropriate surplus goods solely for his own private use when others lack the bare necessities of life".[71] It is specifically stressed that this principle bans the transfer of financial resources to a destination abroad by the rich.[72] Further, expropriation of land for the benefit of the common good, as confirmed by the Second Vatican Council, might form a legitimate tool.[73] Yet, the use of this tool is only acceptable under certain conditions.[74] To be precise, plots can be expropriated only if they "impede the general prosperity because they are extensive, unused or poorly used,

62 *Gaudium et spes* 71.
63 *Ibid.*
64 *Ibid.*
65 *Ibid.*
66 Paul VI, *Populorum Progressio* (Encyclical on the Development of Peoples), March 26, 1967, 22-24. Accessed on October 5, 2020. http://www.vatican.va/content/paul-vi/en/encyclicals/documents/hf_p-vi_enc_26031967_populorum.html.
67 *Populorum Progressio* 22.
68 *Ibid.*
69 *Ibid.*
70 *Populorum Progressio* 23.
71 *Ibid.*
72 *Populorum Progressio* 24.
73 *Ibid.*
74 *Ibid.*

or because they bring hardship to peoples or are detrimental to the interests of the country".[75]

John Paul II – *Laborem Exercens*: Encyclical on Human Work (1981)

In *Laborem Exercens*, Pope John Paul II situates the right to private property on the scale of two opposing economic systems: collectivism and capitalism.[76] On the one hand, Catholic social teaching, given that it had already acknowledged the validity and importance of private property, does not advocate collectivism.[77] On the other hand, the right to private property is not so strong as to be capable to justify capitalism.[78] As outlined before, the right to private property must operate under the maxim that all goods are to serve the common good. Eventually, Pope John Paul II takes the discussion on capitalism a step further by paying special attention to the divide between those who are entitled to the means of production and those who provide the labor.[79] After all, in accordance with Catholic Social Teaching, private property is the result of human labor and is thus in principle accorded to those who provide this labor.[80] Against this background, he argues that "[i]solating these means (of production) as a separate property in order to set it up in the form of "capital" in opposition to "labour"-and even to practice exploitation of labour-is contrary to the very nature of these means and their possession".[81] For this reason, the Catholic Church has actively lobbied to enhance the position of the workers with regard to the entitlement to the means of production.[82]

John Paul II – *Sollicitudo Rei Socialis*: Encyclical for the twentieth anniversary of Populorum Progressio (1987)

In his encyclical *Sollicitudo Rei Socialis*, Pope John Paul II calls on all "people of good will" and especially on all those who are active in economy and politics, to position humanity and the "immense multitudes of the hungry, the needy, the homeless, those without medical

75 *Ibid.*
76 John Paul II, *Laborem Exercens* (Encyclical on Human Work), September 14, 1981, 14. Accessed on October 5, 2020. http://www.vatican.va/content/john-paul-ii/en/encyclicals/documents/hf_jp-ii_enc_14091981_laborem-exercens.html.
77 *Ibid.*
78 *Ibid.*
79 *Ibid.*
80 *Ibid.*
81 *Ibid.*
82 *Ibid.*

care and, above all, those without hope of a better future" in the centre of their decision-making and actions.[83] It considers private property as a "social mortgage" because private property has an intrinsically social function.[84] Within this context, the principle of the universal destination of goods is reaffirmed.[85] At the same time, this principle is emphasized as the foundation and justification for the necessity of private property.[86]

JOHN PAUL II – *CENTESIMUS ANNUS*: ENCYCLICAL ON THE HUNDRETH ANNIVERSARY OF RERUM NOVARUM (1991)

Unlike his earlier encyclicals, the right to private property is given a prominent place in *Centesimus Annus*. Pope John Paul II reaffirms that the right to private property is not an absolute right, but must always thrive to benefit the common good.[87] The underlying reason is that God, being the creator of the earth and of mankind, has given the earth to those made in His image.[88] The earth thus constitutes a gift from God, which is essential to enable human life in first place.[89] Yet, in order to turn the earth into a proper living environment with clean water to drink, nutritional food to eat and adequate shelter for protection, mankind has to fulfill its own side of the bargain and invest the necessary work, through which "he makes part of the earth his own, precisely the part which he has acquired through work; this is the origin of individual property".[90] Therefore, "besides the earth, man's principal resource is man himself".[91] The relation between work and labor is not a constant one and has been subject to changes.[92] Thus, while land in previous centuries used to play a dominating role in this relation, it can be observed that the importance of labor is increasing.[93] At the same time, the concept of labor has undergone changes.[94]

---

83 John Paul II, *Sollicitudo Rei Socialis* (Encyclical for the twentieth anniversary of *Populorum Progressio*), December 30, 1987, introduction and 42. Accessed on October 5, 2020. http://www.vatican.va/content/john-paul-ii/en/encyclicals/documents/hf_jp-ii_enc_30121987_sollicitudo-rei-socialis.html.

84 *Ibid.*

85 *Ibid.*

86 *Ibid.*

87 John Paul II, *Centesimus Annus* (Encyclical on the Hundreth Anniversary of Rerum Novarum), May 1, 1991, 30. Accessed on May 5, 2020. http://www.vatican.va/content/john-paul-ii/en/encyclicals/documents/hf_jp-ii_enc_01051991_centesimus-annus.html.

88 *Centesimus Annus* 31.

89 *Ibid.*

90 *Ibid.*

91 *Centesimus Annus* 32.

92 *Centesimus Annus* 31.

93 *Ibid.*

94 *Ibid.*

Connected with the evolution of labor, a new form of possession has gained importance; the "possession of know-how, technology and skill".[95]

The Catechism of the Catholic Church (1992)

The intention of the Catechism is to provide "an organic synthesis of the essential and fundamental contents of Catholic doctrine, as regards both faith and morals, in the light of the Second Vatican Council and the whole of the Church's Tradition" and functions as a benchmark.[96] The right to private property is dealt with in the context of the seventh commandment. In its very first provision, the right to private property is expressly acknowledged while it is also emphasized that the goods of the earth must benefit the common good.[97] In particular, private property must keep the socially disadvantaged in good stead, leading to the owners' duty to use their own goods "with moderation, reserving the better part for guests, for the sick and the poor".[98] In providing for the poor, "we give them what is theirs, not ours. More than performing works of mercy, we are paying a debt of justice".[99] Therefore, the right of ownership is not absolute in nature.[100] To ensure that owners comply with their duty to fulfill this social obligation, the political power is authorized to monitor the proper exercise of ownership rights.[101]

Moreover, the concept of theft according to Catholic social doctrine deserves attention. Theft is defined as the taking of possession of another's property against the latter's "reasonable will".[102] On the contrary, theft cannot be established in the case of a presumption of consent or "if refusal is contrary to reason and the universal destination of goods".[103] Thus, to provide an example, if a homeless person were to pick apples in an apple orchard to prevent him from starving, they might commit theft according to secular civil law, but they would not commit theft under the definition of the Catholic Church.[104] On the basis of these considerations, one might be led to the belief that the definition of theft as applied in Catholic social teaching is more limited than under the secular civil law. This would be a misconception. The Catholic definition of theft also comprises acts that are not necessarily included in the concepts of theft employed in the secular civil law traditions.[105] Examples

95 *Centesimus Annus* 32.
96 CCC 11. Accessed on October 5, 2020. https://www.vatican.va/archive/ENG0015/_INDEX.HTM.
97 CCC 2401-2403, 2452. On the duty to work, see: CCC 2427.
98 CCC 2405.
99 CCC 2446.
100 CCC 2404.
101 CCC 2406.
102 CCC 2408.
103 *Ibid.*
104 *Ibid.*
105 CCC 2409.

that are provided include "deliberate retention of goods lent or of objects lost; business fraud; paying unjust wages; forcing up prices by taking advantage of the ignorance or hardship of another."[106]

COMPENDIUM OF THE SOCIAL DOCTRINE OF THE CHURCH (2004)

In addition to the papal encyclicals and the CCC, the Compendium of the Social Doctrine of the Church, published in 2004 by the Pontifical Council for Justice and Peace, addresses the Church's stand on the right to private property.[107] Placing private property within the context of the universal destination of goods, its great importance for the sustainability of all layers of society is acknowledged.[108] Yet it also stresses that every human being must share in the privilege of acquiring private property "so that all may become, at least in some measure, owners".[109] At the same time, such a right can never be absolute as its existence is never a goal in itself but is simply an instrument to realize the universal destination of goods.[110] As such, private property must also always be understood in the context of the common good.[111] By this, it is meant that owners, rather than solely considering their own advantage, must not neglect to contemplate the consequences that follow from the exercise of their property right.[112] Therefore, private property fulfills a "social function".[113] However, a focus on the common good also benefits the individual owners as it prevents them from "becom[ing] owned and enslaved by" their possessions.[114] It is highly interesting to note then that the concept of "goods" that can be owned must not be restricted to the well-established categories of goods, but must also embrace "new goods that were completely unknown until recent times".[115] In particular, the discussion on the ownership of data takes a fascinating twist when analyzed through the lens of the universal destination of goods.

106 *Ibid.*
107 Pontifical Council for Justice and Peace, *Compendium of the Social Doctrine of the Church*, 2004, 176-181. Accessed on October 5, 2020. http://www.vatican.va/roman_curia/pontifical_councils/justpeace/documents/rc_pc_justpeace_doc_20060526_compendio-dott-soc_en.html.#The%20universal%20destination%20of%20goods%20and%20private%20property.
108 *Compendium of the Social Doctrine of the Church* 176.
109 *Ibid.*
110 *Compendium of the Social Doctrine of the Church* 177.
111 *Compendium of the Social Doctrine of the Church* 178.
112 *Ibid.*
113 *Ibid.*
114 *Compendium of the Social Doctrine of the Church* 181.
115 *Compendium of the Social Doctrine of the Church* 179.

Benedict XVI – *Deus caritas est*: Encyclical on Christian Love (2005)

Referring to Acts 2:44-45,[116] Pope Benedict XVI takes his audience back to the community of the early Christians, in which the private property of its members became communal property, thereby establishing a real communion in which any material inequalities were obsolete.[117] Although this exceptional form of practising communion still forms a cornerstone of religious life, it is evident that it cannot be upheld on a larger scale in today's Church. However, this does not take away the fact that the Church still adheres to the same elementary principle according to which "within the community of believers there can never be room for a poverty that denies anyone what is needed for a dignified life".[118] Even stronger, as a dictate of love, this principle is a leitmotif for the Church "at all levels, from the parishes, through the particular Churches, to the universal Church" and its individual followers to support, like the Good Samaritan, the needy wherever they are found and independently of whether they form part of the community of believers.[119]

Benedict XVI – *Caritas in veritate*: Encyclical on Integral Human Development in Charity and Truth (2009)

As its title already suggests, Pope Benedict XVI outlines the Christian duty to practice charity in truth in the context of justice, whereby the latter constitutes an essential component of the former.[120] After all, "I cannot "give" what is mine to the other, without first giving him what pertains to him in justice".[121] In addition, the practice of charity and justice necessitates not only the concern for the specific individual good but also a devotion to the common good.[122] Against this background, Pope Benedict XVI discusses different aspects of human development and societal structures, which are too numerous to be addressed here. Arguably of most interest from a property law perspective, is the fourth chapter in which the interwovenness of right and duties is highlighted. Referring to his predecessor Pope John Paul II, Pope Benedict XVI reiterates that "rights presuppose duties, if they are not to become mere licenses" and argues that especially in our modern world,

---

116 Acts 2:44-45: "All the believers were together and had everything in common. They sold property and possessions to give to anyone who had need." (NIV)

117 Benedict XVI, *Deus caritas est* (Encyclical on Christian Love), December 25, 2005, 20. Accessed on October 5, 2020. http://www.vatican.va/content/benedict-xvi/en/encyclicals/documents/hf_ben-xvi_enc_20051225_deus-caritas-est.html.

118 *Ibid.*

119 *Deus caritas est* 25, 30, 32.

120 *Caritas in veritate* 6.

121 *Ibid.*

122 *Caritas in veritate* 7.

where some live in great abundance and claim that their rights to receive even more are recognized, others are left without the bare necessities of life such as clean water and food and without a recognition of their right to receive what they are entitled to under the common good.[123] It is thus time to acknowledge and realize our duties which "set a limit on rights because they point to the anthropological and ethical framework of which rights are a part".[124]

Francis – *Laudato si'*: Encyclical on Care for our Common Home (2015)

Pope Francis reminds the reader that all people, independent of their religious affiliations, recognize that the earth and its fruits are destined for mankind as a whole.[125] For this very reason the secular world order must especially guard the socially deprived.[126] To be able to live up to this "golden rule of social conduct", private property must always be subordinated to the common good and can thus under no circumstances be qualified as an absolute right.[127] A concrete illustration of the relative nature of private property provided by Scripture can be found in Leviticus 19:9-10:

> "When you reap the harvest of your land, do not reap to the very edges of your field or gather the gleanings of your harvest. Do not go over your vineyard a second time or pick up the grapes that have fallen. Leave them for the poor and the foreigner".[128]

Francis – *Fratelli tutti*: Encyclical on the Fraternity and Social Friendship (2020)

As already suggested by its title, Pope Francis reminds us that as being created in the image of God, every human being is entrusted with equal dignity.[129] As such, everyone is entitled to the world and its resources to live a dignified life.[130] Therefore, it is our common duty

123 *Caritas in veritate* 43.
124 *Ibid.*
125 *Laudato si'* 93.
126 *Ibid.*
127 *Ibid.*
128 *Laudato si'* 71.
129 Kim, 2015, p. 120.
130 Francis, *Fratelli tutti* (Encyclical on Fraternity and Social Friendship), October 3, 2020, 118. Accessed on October 5, 2020. http://www.vatican.va/content/francesco/en/encyclicals/documents/papa-francesco_20201003_enciclica-fratelli-tutti.html.

to realize the "common destination of created goods".[131] In this context, quoting St. Gregory the Great, Pope Francis reminds us that "[w]hen we provide the needy with their basic needs, we are giving them what belongs to them, not to us".[132] This implies that private property is not understood as an absolute right, but as a right that at all times must be subordinated to the "universal destination of created goods".[133] It is for this reason that Pope Francis argues that "[t]he right to private property can only [take the place of] a secondary natural right".[134]

Conclusion

Private property is good. This essential conclusion that follows from the discussion of Catholic social teaching certainly puts property lawyers at ease. However, in addition to acknowledging the validity of private property, Catholic social teaching aims to go a step further and make private property not only fruitful for the person holding a property right on a good, but, in a way, also fruitful for everybody else. It is for this reason that owners of private property must not lose sight of the common good and respect the universal destiny of goods. In theory of course, it is arguably rather difficult to disagree with the proposition that all human beings deserve a fair share in the resources that this world has to offer. But the reality in which we live in tells us a different story. Although traces of acknowledging the social function of private property and its relationship with the common good is not limited to theological discussions but can to some extent also be found in secular laws (a prominent example is article 14(2) of the German constitution), we should ask ourselves whether property law is overly focused on the property rights of such a select group against the entire world and not concerned enough with the duties attached to these rights, with the common good, and ultimately with the fair distribution of resources across the universal community of humanity. Perhaps the time has come then for us to bid farewell to understanding property rights predominantly as rights that are enforceable against the entire world, and instead radically strengthen our understanding of them as duties that the entire world in return can enforce against those who are privileged enough to be entitled to a property right.

131 *Fratelli tutti* 119.
132 *Ibid.*
133 *Ibid.*
134 *Fratelli tutti* 120.

Part III
Patrimonial Law

Lindenbaum/Cohen in de Bouillonstraat

*Gerrit van Maanen**

Opgedragen aan André van der Walt (1956-2016)

Proloog

Onder het decanaat van Jan Smits hebben verschillende lokalen aan de Bouillonstraat in Maastricht de naam van illustere juristen gekregen. Slechts één *arrest* fungeert als naamgever: *Lindenbaum/Cohen*. Dat geeft aan hoe belangrijk dat arrest is in ons collectieve juristengeheugen. Sjef van Erp zal wellicht nog college gegeven hebben in die ruimte. Maar dat was voordat die zaal de naam kreeg van dat beroemde arrest van 31 januari 1919. Met dit opstel, ter ere van Sjef van Erp en ter nagedachtenis aan ons beider vriend André van der Walt,[1] keer ik nog eenmaal – en dan nu echt voor het laatst – terug naar de zaak die mij een leven lang geboeid heeft. De belangrijkste reden om nog eenmaal terug te keren naar Lindenbaum en Cohen, is gelegen in de schuld die ik na veertig jaar wil inlossen. Daarover gaat het slot van deze bijdrage.

1 Van Zutphen naar Amsterdam

De Zutphense Juffrouw

Voor eeuwig verbonden: Max Lindenbaum[2] en Samuel Cohen. Zonder Lindenbaum geen Cohen.[3] Maar zonder Juffrouw De Vries geen *Lindenbaum/Cohen*! Het was tien jaar vóórdat de Hoge Raad arrest wees in de zaak *Lindenbaum/Cohen*, het vroor dat het kraakte in Zutphen in de nacht van 4 op 5 januari 1909, waardoor de waterleiding bevroor en ging

* Prof. Mr. Gerrit van Maanen (1949) is emeritus-hoogleraar privaatrecht aan de Universiteit Maastricht.

1 http://www.mepli.eu/2016/11/in-memoriam-professor-andre-aj-van-der-walt-1956-2016/.

2 Max Lindenbaum (Essen, 29 maart 1871 – Theresienstadt, 17 november 1944). Voor meer informatie over de hoofdpersonen verwijs ik naar het slot van deze bijdrage.

3 In mijn leven heb ik al heel veel geschreven over dit onderwerp. Ik ontkom daarbij dan ook nu niet aan enige herhaling. Voor dit essay maak ik gebruik van twee eerdere publicaties, te weten 'Lindenbaum/Cohen', in: *Canon van het Recht*, Nijmegen (*Ars Aequi*) 2010, p. 85-89 en 'De Nederlandse Kelderluikarresten. Al meer dan honderd jaar – rechtseconomisch (!) – op de goede weg in Europa!', *Nederlands Tijdschrift voor Burgerlijk Recht* 2008/1, p. 42-50.

lekken. Pakhuiseigenaar Nijhof maant zijn huurster Juffrouw De Vries om nu eindelijk de hoofdkraan dicht te draaien om verdere schade aan zijn eigendommen te voorkomen. Ze doet het niet. De rechtbank wijst de schadevordering toe omdat

> de begrippen onrechtmatige daad en onrechtmatige nalatigheid niet zoo beperkt moeten worden opgevat, dat daaronder alleen zouden vallen zulke daden of nalatigheden, welke "inbreuk maken op eens anders recht of in strijd zijn met des daders rechtsplicht", maar dat er tevens onder vallen zoodanige, waarbij de noodige eerbied voor eens anders persoon, goederen of arbeid uit het oog wordt verloren.

De Hoge Raad acht deze uitleg van de term "onrechtmatige daad" in art. 1401 (oud) BW, in zijn arrest van 10 juni 1910 (*W.* 9038) veel te ruim:

> dat door zoodanige daden en nalatigheden (...) wel in strijd met hetgeen zedelijk en maatschappelijk betaamt kan zijn gehandeld; dat echter de toepasselijkheid van de artt. 1401 en 1402 BW niet daardoor wordt bepaald, maar afhangt van de bevinding of hetzij de daad, hetzij het verzuim al dan niet in strijd is met des daders rechtsplicht of inbreuk maakt op eens anders recht.

Naar Amsterdam: Lindenbaum/Cohen

De houdbaarheid van deze beperkte en legistische uitleg van de art. 1401 en 1402 (oud) BW, de voorgangers van artikel 6:162 BW, wordt op de proef gesteld door de Amsterdamse heren Lindenbaum en Cohen. Zij vechten hun geschil uit voor de Hoge Raad.[4] De aanleiding was dat Lindenbaum in 1915, toen nog gevestigd aan de Reguliersdwarsstraat 10, later onder meer aan de Heerengracht 457, ontdekte dat zijn oud-werknemer Samuel Cohen zijn bediende had overgehaald om aan Cohen de door Lindenbaum aan diens relaties uitgebrachte offertes voor zijn drukwerken, door te spelen. Daardoor kon Cohen met zijn drukkerij "Cohen & co" net onder de prijs van Lindenbaum gaan zitten. Dat was dus oneerlijke concurrentie. Volgens de rechtbank heeft Cohen daarmee onrechtmatig gehandeld tegenover Lindenbaum. De bediende handelde in strijd met zijn contractuele verplichting voortvloeiende uit zijn arbeidsovereenkomst en verzaakte dusdoende zijn rechtsplicht. Hetzelfde gold voor Cohen die hem hiertoe overhaalde. Het hof ziet *geen* schending van een rechtsplicht door Cohen, hoewel Cohen wel de bediende van

4 Cohen heeft ook nog een strafklacht tegen Lindenbaum ingediend wegens smaadschrift. Die zaak is echter geseponeerd, zie Sjoerd Faber, 'Lindenbaum. Herinneringen, gebouwen en een strafzaak', in: *Pro Memorie* 10.2 (2008), p. 236/237.

Lindenbaum heeft aangezet tot verzaking van diens plichten tegenover zijn werkgever. De Hoge Raad denkt daar in zijn uitspraak van 31 januari 1919[5] anders over:

> onder onrechtmatige daad is te verstaan een handelen of nalaten, dat òf inbreuk maakt op eens anders recht, òf in strijd is met des daders rechtsplicht of indruischt, hetzij tegen de goede zeden, hetzij tegen de zorgvuldigheid, welke in het maatschappelijk verkeer betaamt ten aanzien van eens anders persoon of goed, terwijl hij door wiens schuld tengevolge dier daad aan een ander schade wordt toegebracht, tot vergoeding daarvan is verplicht.

Deze beslissing heeft het juridische landschap – het is immers een *landmark case* – ingrijpend beïnvloed en staat sindsdien symbool voor de *openheid* van ons rechtssysteem; niet de wettelijke regelingen bepalen wat rechtmatig of wat onrechtmatig is, maar óók en vooral datgene wat maatschappelijk gezien zorgvuldig is.

De receptie en perceptie van Lindenbaum/Cohen

Mijn oude leermeester Jan Wiarda vertelde, vijftig jaar geleden, de volgende anekdote:

> Mijn vader (...) stond eens naar zijn gewoonte te wachten bij de tramhalte, schuin tegenover ons huis, op lijn 2. Dat moet geweest zijn op zaterdag, zondag of maandag 1, 2 of 3 februari van het jaar 1919. Daar ziet hij opeens iemand hollend en met armen zwaaiend op hem afkomen, en hoort hij dezen opgewonden toeroepen: "Mijnheer Wiarda, heeft U de krant al gelezen, het arrest van de Hoge Raad over de onrechtmatige daad..".[6]

5 *NJ* 1919, p. 161.

6 Gepubliceerd in *Terecht Gesteld. Groninger juridisch studentenblad.* Jrg. 1, nr. 4 (februari 1969), p. 19. Jan Wiarda (5 maart 1909 – 18 mei 1993) was destijds hoogleraar handelsrecht en burgerlijk procesrecht aan de Groninger Juridische Faculteit.

Jan Wiarda (5 maart 1909 - 18 mei 1993)

We weten dat de *receptie* in de juridische literatuur in overeenstemt met deze reactie van de vader van Jan Wiarda; het was een beslissing waarnaar iedereen had uitgekeken. Vooral omdat de *Zutphense Juffrouw* zoveel verontwaardiging had opgeroepen. Molengraaff zegt hierover, in een noot onder *Lindenbaum/Cohen* in het *Weekblad van het Recht*, dat de arresten van 1905 (*Singer/Ivens*)[7] en 1910 (*Zutphense Juffrouw*)[8] qua uitkomst "verbijsterend" waren. Met de uitspraak inzake *Lindenbaum/Cohen* heeft de Hoge Raad gedaan, wat de wetgever in gebreke bleef te doen:

> Er is door ons hoogste rechtscollege zelden een arrest gewezen, waarvan zoo heilzame invloed op ons rechtsleven mag worden verwacht.[9]

De *perceptie* nadien van de betekenis van artikel 1401 (oud) BW in bijna alle handboeken - tot in de jaren tachtig van de twintigste eeuw - was, dat men in de hele negentiende eeuw onder invloed van het "starre legisme" onder onrechtmatig slechts onwetmatig verstond en dat het arrest van *Lindenbaum/Cohen* de bevrijding bracht van de knellende banden van deze enge opvatting.

---

7 *Weekblad van het recht*, (1905) 8168, p. 1.

8 HR 10 juni 1910, *W.* 9038.

9 W.L.P.A. Molengraaff, noot in *Weekblad van het Recht*, (1919) 10 365, p. 2/3.

De relativering van Lindenbaum/Cohen

Het is echter onjuist om te stellen dat in de *hele* negentiende eeuw onder invloed van het "starre legisme" de heersende opvatting was dat onrechtmatig uitgelegd moest worden als on*wet*matig. Alles wijst erop dat tot aan het einde van de negentiende eeuw de Hoge Raad en het merendeel van de schrijvers een *ruime* opvatting van de aansprakelijkheid uit onrechtmatige daad voorstonden. Tot 1883 bestond er in Nederland duidelijk een ruime aansprakelijkheid voor buitencontractuele schade door de zelfstandige rol van artikel 1402 (oud) BW, waarbij aan de termen "nalatigheid of onvoorzigtigheid" een betekenis werd toegekend vergelijkbaar met de "maatschappelijke onzorgvuldigheid" uit *Lindenbaum/Cohen.*

In *Singer/Ivens* van 6 januari 1905[10] werpt de Hoge Raad een dam op tegen de praktijk van de lagere rechters om oneerlijke concurrentie te bestrijden door middel van een ruime uitleg van 1401 en 1402 (oud) BW.

De Singernaaimasjien[11]

De zeer beperkte uitleg van artikel 1401 en 1402 (oud) BW in *Singer/Ivens*, als reactie op deze praktijk, is te verklaren tegen de achtergrond van verschillende visies op de industriële

10 *Weekblad van het recht*, (1905) 8168, p. 1.

11 Naar Paul van Ostaijen, HULDEGEDICHT AAN SINGER. *'Een Singer? Jawel jawel jawel jawel ik zeg het u een Singer versta-je geen nederlands mijnheer Circulez Bitte auf Garderobe selbst zu achten ik wil een naaimasjien iedereen heeft recht op een naaimasjien ik wil een Singer iedereen een Singer'.*

ontwikkeling op dat moment; moet oneerlijke concurrentie worden tegengegaan of juist niet?

W.L.P.A. Molengraaff (10 mei 1858 - 7 juli 1931)

Molengraaff wil deze oneerlijke concurrentie bestrijden ofwel door toepassing van artikel 1402, ofwel door een ruime uitleg van de term "onrechtmatig" uit artikel 1401 (oud) BW. Eyssell[12] - als president van de Hoge Raad medeverantwoordelijk voor *Singer/Ivens* - was een uitgesproken tegenstander van de bestrijding van oneerlijke concurrentie en dus ook van de daarmee verbonden ruime opvatting van onrechtmatig. In een opstel in Themis uit 1911 gaat hij stevig te keer tegen het ontwerp Regout dat deze ruimere aansprakelijkheid uit 1401 voorstond: *"eene ontwrichting van ons burgerlijke regtsstelsel, (...) eene civielregtelijke ramp"*.

12 1837-1921, lid HR 1886-1912.

A.Ph.Th. Eyssell (1837-1921, lid HR 1886-1912)

De conservatief Eyssell

Eyssell was als president van de civiele kamer verantwoordelijk voor de arresten van de Hoge Raad waarin de enge leer met grote volharding werd doorgevoerd. Eyssell is trots op het feit dat hij aan deze rechtspraak (*Singer/Ivens* en de *Zutphense Juffrouw*) heeft meegewerkt:

> Naar mijne vaste overtuiging is het der maatschappij in haar geheel véél dienstiger dat af en toe een op zich zelf weinig sympathiek arrest gewezen moet worden dan dat de wet Regout, zoodanige uitspraak keerende, de algemeene regtszekerheid prijs geeft aan eenen stortvloed van "onregtmatigheidsgedingen" Af en toe eischt de regtszekerheid dat in onze onvolmaakte maatschappij berust worde in hetgeen op zich zelf aanstotelijk is.

Over de ruggen van de Zutphense Juffrouw en de pakhuiseigenaar werd dus een rechtspolitiek conflict uitgevochten over de vraag of de rechter in mocht grijpen in de vrije concurrentie in handel en industrie. Uiteindelijk heeft Molengraaffs opvatting na deze nederlaag in 1910 toch gezegevierd; de rechter màg ingrijpen en Molengraaffs uitleg van de term "onrechtmatig" wordt in 1919 door de Hoge Raad definitief omarmd; ons recht wordt verrijkt met een uitspraak die voortleeft in het collectieve geheugen van alle juristen: *Lindenbaum/Cohen.*[13]

2 Rechtsvergelijkend en historisch kader

Toetsen aan ongeschreven rechtsnormen

Wat is de juridische betekenis van deze uitspraak van 31 januari 1919? Dat is, dat door *Lindenbaum/Cohen* nòg duidelijker wordt dan uit artikel 1402 (oud) BW reeds bleek, dat

> onder onrechtmatige daad is te verstaan een handelen of nalaten, dat óf inbreuk maakt op eens anders recht, òf in strijd is met des daders rechtsplicht of indruischt, hetzij tegen de goede zeden, hetzij tegen **de zorgvuldigheid, welke in het maatschappelijk verkeer betaamt ten aanzien van eens anders persoon of goed**, ...

Voor de vraag of bepaald concreet schadeveroorzakend gedrag tot aansprakelijkheid leidt, is de rechter dus niet gebonden aan het toetsen van dat gedrag aan geschreven rechtsnormen (*strijd is met des daders rechtsplicht*) of het schenden van andermans subjectieve rechten zoals eigendomsrechten (*inbreuk maakt op eens anders recht*), maar mag ook toetsen aan ongeschreven zorgvuldigheidsnormen (*de zorgvuldigheid, welke in het maatschappelijk verkeer betaamt ten aanzien van eens anders persoon of goed*). Dat laatste biedt een ongekend aantal mogelijkheden, maar de vraag is dan hoe we daaraan invulling geven. Hoe doe je dat?

Het openstaande kelderluik als archetype van de gevaarzettende handeling

Hoe doe je dat, toetsen aan ongeschreven zorgvuldigheidsnormen? Welke handvatten biedt ons recht daarvoor? Voor situaties waarin iemands gedrag gevaarlijk is voor anderen, biedt het klassieke *Kelderluikarrest*[14] een mooi, hanteerbaar toetsingskader.

De *dramatis personae* zijn Mathieu Duchateau die een biertje drinkt in het Amsterdamse café De Munt, en een werknemer van Coca-Cola, zeer toepasselijk genaamd Sjouwerman,

13 Zie ook het mooie opstel van F.C.J. Ketelaar, 'De schepping van het arrest Lindenbaum-Cohen', in: *Kabaal in Holland* 1993, p. 15-24 over de wordingsgeschiedenis. Ketelaar heeft het concept van het arrest uit het archief opgedoken.

14 HR 5 november 1965, *NJ* 1966/136.

die het kelderluik had geopend, maar verzuimd heeft de nodige veiligheidsmaatregelen te nemen. Er waren wel wat kratjes neergezet. Op weg naar het toilet belandt Duchateau – door het openstaande kelderluik – in de kelder en uiteindelijk in het ziekenhuis. Duchateau vordert schadevergoeding van Coca-Cola.

Hoe moeten we vaststellen wat de vereiste zorgplicht is in een dergelijke situatie? Als de omstandigheden daartoe aanleiding geven, moeten bepaalde veiligheidsmaatregelen worden genomen, omdat er rekening mee moet worden gehouden dat niet iedereen even voorzichtig is. Welke omstandigheden zijn daarbij relevant? De Hoge Raad geeft een aantal *gezichtspunten* waarop men zou moeten letten:

- naarmate het waarschijnlijker is dat potentiële slachtoffers minder oplettend en voorzichtig zijn, dient een hogere zorgplicht betracht te worden;
- naarmate de kans op schade groter is, dient een hogere zorgplicht betracht te worden;
- naarmate de ernst en de omvang van de mogelijke schade groter is, dient een hogere zorgplicht in acht genomen te worden;
- naarmate de gedraging gevaarlijker is, dient een hogere zorgplicht in acht genomen te worden;
- naarmate het nemen van bepaalde voorzorgsmaatregelen, zowel op zichzelf beschouwd als in relatie tot de mogelijke schade, minder bezwaarlijk is qua kosten, tijd en moeite, bestaat een sterkere gehoudenheid tot het treffen van preventieve maatregelen.

Bij dit alles is niet van belang of men het *specifieke* gevaar dat zich heeft verwezenlijkt, concreet heeft voorzien.[15] Voldoende is dat met het nemen van bepaalde veiligheidsmaatregelen in het algemeen – naar objectieve maatstaven – bepaalde (gezondheids-)gevaren worden voorkomen.[16]

Effectiviteit van de waarschuwing

Nog één punt. De genomen veiligheidsmaatregelen en waarschuwingen moeten wel *effectief* zijn, althans er moet een reële verwachting zijn dat de waarschuwing het beoogde gevolg zal hebben. Dat wordt nog weer eens duidelijk gemaakt in het *Jetblast*-arrest, waar toeschouwers zich aan het hek vasthielden om door de kracht van de straalmotor in de lucht te hangen:

> Voor het antwoord op de vraag of een waarschuwing kan worden beschouwd als een afdoende maatregel met het oog op bescherming tegen een bepaald

15 HR 8 januari 1982, *NJ* 1982, 614 (Dorpshuis Kamerik).

16 HR 29 november 2002, *NJ* 2003, 549 (JBMV)(Legionellabesmetting Westfriese Flora).

> gevaar, is van doorslaggevende betekenis of te verwachten valt dat deze waarschuwing zal leiden tot een handelen of nalaten waardoor dit gevaar wordt vermeden.[17]

De gevergde mate van zorg is echter weer afhankelijk van de bijzondere omstandigheden van het geval.[18] Zo zal van belang zijn of iemand zelf de gevaarlijke situatie in het leven heeft geroepen of kennis had van die gevaarlijke situatie.

Maar ... we mogen ook van burgers verwachten dat ze zelf een zekere zorgplicht aan de dag leggen zonder daar specifiek op geattendeerd te zijn. Met andere woorden, als de verwachting is dat potentiële slachtoffers onvoldoende zorg voor hun eigen veiligheid betrachten, bijvoorbeeld omdat ze wat gedronken hebben (Duchateau in café De Munt) of aangetrokken worden door de spanning om aan een hek te hangen in de luchtstroom van de straalmotoren (*Jetblast*), dan zullen de voorzorgsmaatregelen steviger moeten zijn.

In ons collectieve juristengeheugen zijn dit de belangrijke kaders: de *kelderluikfactoren* en de *effectiviteit* van de waarschuwing.[19] Mijn (juridisch geschoolde) intuïtie zegt me dat de genoemde vuistregels ontwikkeld voor gevaarzettingssituaties op basis van het Kelderluikarrest van 1965, zodanig basaal en *common sense* zijn, dat ieder aansprakelijkheidsstelsel ze zal kennen. Ik zal hieronder een klein rechtsvergelijkend, zowel diachroon als synchroon, onderzoekje doen om deze hypothese te testen. Eerst de diachrone vergelijking.

Terug naar 1906: het eerste Kelderluikarrest

Wie denkt dat voormelde inzichten pas in 1965 of zelfs pas in 2004, tot ontwikkeling zijn gebracht, vergist zich. Nog vóór het arrest *Lindenbaum/Cohen* uit 1919 met zijn expliciete opening naar ongeschreven zorgvuldigheidsnormen,[20] lag er al een uitspraak van de Hoge Raad uit 1906 die reeds de kernelementen van het *Kelderluik-arrest* van 1965 bevat en die bovendien de inzichten uit het *Jetblast*-arrest heeft geïncorporeerd.

De plaats van handeling is ook hier een café, ditmaal de Amsterdamse stationsrestauratie. Daar bevond zich ene H.F. Smith, van beroep "*professeur de biljard*". Deze biljartleraar had zijn trein gemist en stond op 13 november 1902 de dienstregeling te bekijken, niet wetende dat op datzelfde ogenblik een van de personeelsleden van de stationsrestauratie

17 HR 28 mei 2004, *NJ* 2005, 105 (Jetblast); Gem. Hof Ned. Antillen en Aruba 18 maart 2005, *NJ* 2005, 302.

18 Het plaatsen van barkrukken voor een keldergat in – alweer – een Amsterdams café is niet altijd afdoende; het zijn volgens de Amsterdamse rechtbank in een café geen voorwerpen waarvan een waarschuwing uitgaat (Rb Amsterdam 10 juni 2003, *VR* 2003, 174).

19 Zie ook Hartlief in zijn AA-noot onder Jetblast (*AA* 2004, p. 1027).

20 Vergelijk over de achtergrond van deze ontwikkeling mijn rechtshistorisch cahier: *De Zutphense juffrouw en de ontrouwe bediende van Lindenbaum.* Nijmegen (Ars Aequi) 1999, 2e druk.

achter zijn rug het luik van de daar aanwezige kelder had weggenomen. De zich van geen gevaar bewuste biljartleraar deed enkele stappen achteruit en is in het keldergat gevallen, heeft zwaar lichamelijk letsel opgelopen en is "*zoodanig gekwetst, dat daaruit een tijdelijke verhindering in de uitoefening zijner beroepsbezigheden is ontstaan*".

De conclusie van de Advocaat-Generaal Jhr. Rethaan Macaré

A-G Rethaan Macaré schetst het juridisch kader op een heldere wijze. Als slechts de hiervoor geschetste feiten aan de orde zouden zijn, zo stelt hij, dan was de uitkomst simpel: de gedaagde partij – de Buffet-maatschappij E. Pluribus Unum – zou aansprakelijk zijn, aangezien het verwezenlijkte gevaar voor "ieder met gezonde hersenen begaafd persoon" te voorzien is geweest. Maar de zaak wordt anders nu is vastgesteld dat de bediende, het gevaar voorziende, een poging heeft gedaan om dat gevaar af te wenden: "*Zij hebben eene waarschuwing doen hooren.*" Maar die waarschuwing heeft kennelijk – gelijk de uitkomst heeft geleerd – niet haar doel bereikt. De hamvraag is nu of het doen uitgaan van deze waarschuwing – de anders onbetwistbare verplichting tot schadevergoeding – heeft opgeheven.

Het wettelijk kader waarbinnen deze vraag moet worden beantwoord, zijn de art. 1401 en 1402 (oud) BW, die tezamen de voorlopers van ons art. 6:162 BW vormen. Met name art. 1402 is hier van belang. Daarin worden als criteria gegeven "nalatigheid" en "onvoorzichtigheid". Is hier van één van beide sprake?, zo vraagt de A-G zich af.

> 'Onvoorzichtig, het woord duidt het reeds aan, is hij die niet voorziet, die de mogelijke gevolgen van zijne daden, die hij had kunnen en behooren te voorzien, niet overweegt. Die gedachtenloos een gevaarwekkende daad onderneemt.' 'Nalatig', zo vervolgt de A-G, is hij 'die de mogelijke gevolgen van zijn daad wel voorziet, doch nalaat het noodige te verrichten, om derden voor de hen bedreigenden schade te behoeden; die, hetzij uit gemakzucht, hetzij uit berekening, 't er op waagt, in de hoop, dat 't ergste, wat gebeuren zou kunnen, nu juist niet zal gebeuren. Menigmaal zal die hoop verwezenlijkt worden en hij dus de goede vruchten plukken van zijn berekening of gemakzucht, maar juist daarom is het billijk en recht, dat wanneer een enkel maal het waagstuk niet gelukt, hij die de goede kansen voor zich heeft genomen, ook de kwade draagt.'

Het is opmerkelijk dat we hier in eenvoudige bewoordingen in feite precies dezelfde afweging zien die ook ten grondslag ligt aan het *Kelderluikarrest* van 1965. Wie nalaat preventieve maatregelen te treffen die mogelijk en geboden waren, moet aansprakelijk zijn voor de schade. Hoe stellen we nu vast of de gekozen maatregelen voldoende zijn? De A-G heeft daarop een eenvoudig antwoord: het gaat er niet om of de voorzorgsmaatregelen in abstracto als voldoende of onvoldoende te beschouwen zijn, maar men moet

> enkel op grond van de uitkomst aannemen, dat ze *in casu concreto* onvoldoende waren, om te voorkomen, dat de schade tot wier vergoeding de onvoorzichtige of nalatige krachtens de wet gehouden was, ontstond.

Dat betekent derhalve, in de visie van de A-G, dat in alle gevallen waarin iemand een gevaarzettende handeling onderneemt zonder dat (afdoende) maatregelen worden genomen om het dreigende gevaar af te wenden, er sprake is van een nalatigheid of onvoorzichtigheid in de zin van art. 1402 (oud) BW.

Zijn slachtoffervriendelijke redenering toepassend op de voorliggende casus, leidt dit hem tot de gevolgtrekking dat de bediende verantwoordelijk is voor het *ontstaan* van het gevaar, terwijl de uitkomst van deze zaak leert dat de getroffen maatregelen *ondoeltreffend* zijn gebleken. Dat betekent voor de A-G dat de beslissing van het hof – dat de vordering had afgewezen – niet in stand kan blijven en dat het toewijzende vonnis van de rechtbank kan worden bevestigd.

Wat doet de Hoge Raad?

In cassatie spitst de zaak zich toe op de door de bediende gegeven waarschuwing en op hetgeen daarover precies is komen vast te staan. De rechtbank was van oordeel dat een "behoorlijke" waarschuwing nodig is, én dat komt vast te staan dat die waarschuwing ook door degene voor wie zij is bedoeld is verstaan en begrepen. De rechtbank is van oordeel dat dit laatste niet met voldoende zekerheid is af te leiden uit de getuigenverklaringen en wijst daarom de vordering toe.

Het hof zou – volgens het cassatiemiddel – het arrest vernietigende, hebben gesteld dat naar de mening van de rechtbank een waarschuwing slechts behoorlijk is als die ook is begrepen. Daarop voortbouwend zou het hof – nog steeds volgens het middel – hebben beslist dat eiser op grond van de afgelegde getuigenverklaringen wél behoorlijk is gewaarschuwd.

De Hoge Raad overweegt dat het middel op een onjuiste feitelijke grondslag berust, voor zover "*daarbij wordt gesteld, dat het Hof zou hebben beslist, dat men bij het doen eener waarschuwing zich in geen geval zou behoeven te vergewissen, of de waarschuwing tot den gelaedeerde doorgedrongen is;*". Dat heeft het hof niet gesteld. Het hof heeft wél, zo gaat de Hoge Raad verder, uitdrukkelijk aangenomen dat deze vraag niet in zijn algemeenheid kan worden beantwoord en heeft zich verder gericht op de vraag of in dit concrete geval voldoende gewaarschuwd was. Die vraag heeft het hof op grond van de verklaringen van getuigen bevestigend beantwoord. Dat is een beslissing die berust op de gebleken feiten en omstandigheden. Daardoor kunnen de artikelen 1401 en 1402 dus niet geschonden zijn, aldus de Hoge Raad.

Wat betekent dit nu?

Het gaat in de visie van de Hoge Raad uitsluitend nog om de vraag of het hof wel of niet terecht heeft geoordeeld dat er *in casu* behoorlijk was gewaarschuwd. De rechtbank vond van niet, het hof vond kennelijk op basis van eigen onderzoek, dat er wel voldoende was gewaarschuwd. Dat is een feitelijk oordeel waar de Hoge Raad verder buiten blijft.

De A-G staat een meer slachtoffervriendelijke benadering voor, dat áls de schade niet is voorkomen door de waarschuwing, dat deze dan kennelijk niet doeltreffend was. De waarschuwing was dan niet *effectief*, zouden wij na *Jetblast* zeggen. De Hoge Raad gaat echter niet mee met de door de A-G gevolgde redenering en diens voorstel tot vernietiging van het arrest van het hof.

Wat blijft, is dat de door de A-G gevolgde benadering grote gelijkenis vertoont met die van het *Kelderluikarrest* van 1965. Dat daarbij het hof kennelijk wat minder coulant was voor het slachtoffer en oordeelde dat er wél voldoende was gewaarschuwd, is een gevolg van een *feitelijke* appreciatie van de afgelegde getuigenverklaringen. Dat een waarschuwing ook moet doordringen tot het potentiële slachtoffer is in alle instanties eigenlijk vanzelfsprekend. Maar, met name het hof en Hoge Raad gaan niet zover dat uit het enkele feit dát de schade die door de waarschuwing had moet worden voorkomen tóch is ontstaan, kan worden afgeleid dat de waarschuwing dus niet behoorlijk is geweest, zijnde immers niet doeltreffend gebleken. Door middel van getuigenverklaringen moet worden vastgesteld dat er behoorlijk is gewaarschuwd.

3 Hoe doet men het elders?

Engelse kelderluikuitspraken

Op een regenachtige en winderige dag – het is kort na het middaguur op 20 april 1937 – loopt Mevr. Daniel met opgestoken paraplu over het trottoir. Plotseling stapt ze in een gat. Het blijkt de opening naar de kolenkelder van de aangrenzende woning. De (alleen werkende) kolenboer heeft het luik opengezet om de eerste zak met kolen van de vrachtauto te halen. Hij had het slachtoffer wel aan zien komen, maar keerde haar de rug toe om de zak te pakken en liet zodoende het niet afgedekte keldergat voor een ogenblik onbewaakt.

Pas op het moment dat Daniel in het gat stapte, liet de kolenboer een waarschuwingskreet horen: te laat…

Precies een jaar later komt de zaak voor de King's Bench Division.[21] De rechter oordeelt – in het kader van de *Tort of Negligence*[22] – dat voetgangers er van uit mogen gaan dat het trottoir normaal te gebruiken was, tenzij ze gewaarschuwd zijn voor een specifiek gevaar. Dat betekent dat als het trottoir – door het openen van een kelderluik – niet meer de normale veiligheid biedt, dat het dan de plicht is van degene die daarvoor verantwoordelijk is, om bepaalde voorzorgsmaatregelen te nemen:

> it [then] became the duty of the person who had altered the footpath from one on which the plaintiff might pass and repass with ordinary safety into one on which a person could pass and repass only by taking sufficient care to avoid the hole to take precautions of those using it, and to see that they would, so to speak, have fair and sufficient warning of the danger, so as to protect them against it.

Wàs er in deze situatie een noodzaak om dergelijke voorzorgsmaatregelen te treffen? Dat is zeker het geval, vindt Judge Hilbery. Hij is er absoluut niet van overtuigd dat het te bezwaarlijk zou zijn om verplaatsbare waarschuwingsborden mee te nemen met de kolenwagen. Die kunnen dan om het keldergat geplaatst worden. Bovendien, zo gaat hij verder, zou je ook een paar kolenzakken rond het geopende keldergat kunnen zetten (dat heeft hij zelf wel eens gezien). Maar dat moet dan wel tijdig!

> No doubt he would in time have put some sacks around the hole, but unfortunately he created the danger first, and, before he could establish effective measures of precaution, this accident occurred.

"*Effective measures of precaution*", dus. De kolenboer heeft dat nagelaten en is dus tekortgeschoten in zijn zorgplicht.

Maar hoe zit het de eiser zelf, met Mevr. Daniel? Heeft zij niet zelf ook schuld aan het ongeval? De rechter is daar niet van overtuigd. De eiser gebruikte immers het trottoir op normale wijze. Het is niet zo dat het enkele feit dat er kelderluiken in het trottoir zijn aangebracht, mee zou brengen dat men verdacht moet zijn op het openstaan van die luiken. Ook het feit dat ze een paraplu op had gestoken, die misschien het zicht wat belemmerde, doet daar niet aan af, omdat het normaal is een paraplu te gebruiken als het regent. De

21 [1938] 2 *ALL ER* 631, Daniel v Rickett Cockerll & Co Ltd and Raymond.

22 Zie voor een helder overzicht het prachtige boek van Cees van Dam, *European Tort Law*, Oxford 2013, met name nr. 503.

kolenboer, dat wil zeggen zijn baas, is dus aansprakelijk. De huiseigenaar wordt als opdrachtgever voor één tiende medeaansprakelijk gehouden.

Een Duits kelderluikarrest

Wat zou een Duitse rechter doen? Bij een lagere school is een ondergrondse nooduitgang, uitkomend in de tuin naast de speelplaats, afgedekt met een metalen luik van 70 bij 80 cm. Het luik is niet afgesloten, maar gaat wel enigszins verscholen achter struikgewas. Deze nooduitgang is ook van buiten de school en speelplaats te bereiken. In de zomervakantie van 1995 openen spelende kinderen het luik. Doordat het (zware) luik door zwiepte naar achteren verloor het - zevenjarige - kind zijn evenwicht en viel in de bijna 3 meter diepe schacht en raakte zodanig gewond dat hij 6 weken lang in het gips moest liggen.

Het kind vordert smartengeld op grond van het feit dat de school de *Verkehrssicherungspflicht* - wij zouden zeggen in strijd met de maatschappelijke zorgvuldigheid heeft gehandeld - niet is nagekomen.[23]

Zowel in eerste aanleg als in hoger beroep wordt de vordering afgewezen. De redenering - in het kader van par. 823 BGB - is dat de school haar *Verkehrssicherungspflicht* niet heeft geschonden. Hoewel duidelijk is dat van zo'n "geheim" luik een grote aantrekkingskracht op kinderen zal uitgaan, mocht de school er niettemin van uit gaan dat kinderen een dergelijk gevaar "*aus ihrem natürlichen Angstgefühl heraus nicht bewusst aussetzen würden*". Alleen al de constructie van het luik zou het kind moeten doen beseffen dat het niet "*befugt war*" het luik te openen (we zijn in Duitsland...). Maar ook zou het kind bij een gedeeltelijke opening van het luik het gevaar van de diepe schacht hebben moeten zien. Dat zou aanleiding geweest moeten zijn om het luik weer dicht te doen, in plaats van het nog verder te openen.

Ook het BGH[24] acht de *Verkehrssicherungspflicht* in dit geval niet geschonden. Ook al was een technische constructie mogelijk geweest die zou voorkomen dat het luik verder naar achteren door klapte.[25] Dat zou anders zijn als de school *bekend* zou zijn met het feit dat kinderen regelmatig op die bewuste plek zouden spelen. Maar iets dergelijks is door de eiser niet gesteld.

---

23 Deze *Verkehrssicherungspflicht* is een technisch/juridisch instrument om in gevallen van *nalaten* toch tot een schending van par. 823 BGB te komen, ondanks het feit dat er geen sprake is van een 'echte' directe inbreuk op één van de beschermde rechtsgoederen. Het nalaten wordt als het ware getransformeerd tot een schending van een positieve gedragsnorm. In dit geval het moeten nemen van bepaalde voorzorgsmaatregelen. Zie voor meer info Van Dam, a.w., nr. 403.

24 BGH 4 Mai 1999, *VI ZR* 379/98.

25 Het BGH overweegt - ten overvloede - dat het enkele feit dat de bouwvoorschriften in acht zijn genomen de school niet zou vrijpleiten; er kunnen andere redenen zijn om in zo'n geval toch van schending van de *Verkehrssicherungspflicht* te spreken. Evenmin zou het enkele feit dat het luik zich op een afgezonderde plaats bevindt buiten de speelplaats, voldoende om de school vrij te pleiten.

De plicht om kinderen te behoeden voor eigen lichtzinnigheid heeft echter, zo overweegt het BGH, zijn grenzen. Die plicht bestaat wel in gevallen waarin kinderen als gevolg van hun jeugdige onbezonnenheid het gevaar niet kennen of onvoldoende onderkennen (hoogspanningsleiding van een trein, bijvoorbeeld). Dat ligt echter anders in deze zaak:

> Es würde eine Überspannung der Sorgfaltsanforderungen bedeuten, wollte man von den Beklagten verlangen, den Deckel des Notausstiegs mit einer Vorrichtung zu versehen, die die Arretierung des angehobenen Deckels in der Senkrechten sicherstellt.

Niet is vast komen te staan dat een dergelijke constructie die voorkomt dat het luik naar achter door kan klappen – vanwege eerdere ervaringen – geboden zou zijn. Zonder dergelijke ervaringskennis hoeft de school er geen rekening mee te houden dat een kind het luik zover naar achteren toe zou kunnen openen. Integendeel, de school mocht ervan uitgaan dat een kind bij het gedeeltelijk openen van het luik door zijn "natuurlijke angstgevoel" zou laten weerhouden om verder te gaan. Dat in deze zaak het kind toch het luik verder opende, is zo ongewoon dat de school daar geen rekening mee hoefde te houden. Ook kan men de schoolleiding niet verwijten dat ze er geen rekening mee hebben gehouden dat het kind wel sterk genoeg was om het luik te openen, maar niet om tegen te gaan dat het luik naar achteren door zou klappen.

Deze uitkomst is begrijpelijk, nu er in deze Duitse casus geen sprake is van een kelderluik dat is *opengezet* door de gevaarzetter, maar slechts van een luik dat – met enige moeite – opengemaakt kon worden door het slachtoffer. Dat verklaart in belangrijke mate het verschil in uitkomst met de Engelse zaak.

Een Frans kelderluik

Waar Engelse rechters de geïnteresseerde lezer voorzien van een overdaad aan feitelijke details en juridische argumentatie, is de Franse rechter extreem bondig en apodictisch. Hij is nog steeds de "*bouche de la loi*". Met name de uitspraken van de *Cour de Cassation* zijn uiterst kort en geven nauwelijks inzicht in wat er precies aan de hand was. Toch wil ik de lezer kennisname van een Franse kelderluik zaak niet onthouden.

Ene Popoff was bij het binnengaan van een *Café-Tabac*, eigendom van Bouchede, in de kelder gevallen. Ook hier was het luik opengezet om de aflevering van bepaalde goederen mogelijk te maken. Popoff had in feitelijke instantie maar een deel van zijn schade vergoed gekregen, omdat er sprake zou zijn van onvoorzichtigheid aan zijn kant. Hij is het daar niet mee eens en gaat in cassatie.

Het *Cour de Cassation* geeft aan dat Bouchede heeft nagelaten om voorzorgsmaatregelen te treffen om te voorkomen dat klanten binnen de gevaarzone zouden komen.[26] Daarvoor is hij zowel op grond van art. 1382 CC (eigen fout) als op basis van de algemene zorgplicht voor zaken die men onder zijn opzicht heeft (art. 1384 aanhef CC), aansprakelijk. Maar Popoff die goed bekend was met dit café, heeft zelf ook onvoldoende opgelet en heeft zo zelf aan het ontstaan van zijn schade bijgedragen.

Hoewel de Franse hoogste rechter ons weinig inzicht biedt in de weging van de argumenten, weten we uit de literatuur dat ook in Frankrijk dezelfde factoren in de afweging betrokken worden als die wij in Nederlandse, Engelse en Duitse rechtspraak aantreffen.[27]

Anders en eender

Het is overal dezelfde gedachtegang:
- de *mate van waarschijnlijkheid* waarmee de niet-inachtneming van de vereiste oplettendheid en voorzichtigheid door het slachtoffer, kan worden verwacht, gecombineerd met
- de *grootheid van de kans* dat daaruit ongevallen ontstaan, en
- de *ernst die de gevolgen daarvan kunnen hebben*, in het licht van
- de *bezwaarlijkheid* van te nemen veiligheidsmaatregelen, en
- de *effectiviteit* van deze veiligheidsmaatregelen.

De invulling en weging van deze factoren in de omstandigheden van het concrete geval leiden tot een bepaalde uitkomst. Soms had het slachtoffer zelf voorzichtiger moeten zijn, waardoor aansprakelijkheid ontbreekt (het Duitse kelderluik) of gedeeltelijk vervalt (de Franse Popoff; Duchateau die 50% eigen schuld heeft). Soms had de dader meer en effectievere voorzorgsmaatregelen moeten treffen (de Engelse kolenboer; de Coca-Cola bezorger in het Amsterdamse café De Munt). De technisch-juridische kaders zijn (een beetje) anders, maar de redenering en de afweging is eender.

---

26 Het Hof: *'Mais attendu qu'après avoir constaté que Bouchede avait négligé de prévenir sa clientèle des risques courus et n'avait pris aucune precaution pour interdire la circulation aux abords de la zone dangereuse, laquelle était proche d'une porte d'entrée dont l'accès était libre et en avoir déduit que cette faute d'abstention était à l'origine de l'accident, les juges du second degré ont énoncé que Popoff qui a reconnu bien connaitre les lieux "n'a pas veille suffisamment à sa propre sécurité en ne prenant pas toutes les precautions utiles et qu'il a ainsi contribue à la réalisation de son dommage"; Attendu qu'en l'état de ces constations et énonciations, la cour d'appel à pu admettre à l'encontre de Popoff que l'omission de veiller à sa propre sécurité et l'absence de precaution étaient constitutives d'une faute, en rapport direct avec l'accident et à ainsi donne une base légale à sa decision.'*

27 C.C. van Dam, *European Tort Law*, Oxford 2013, nr. 805-2.

4 Lessen uit het verleden en van de buren

Singer/Ivens van 1905 heeft samen met de *Zutphense Juffrouw* uit 1910, niet definitief de enge leer gevestigd, maar was juist de directe aanleiding voor een voorstel tot verruiming in het wetsvoorstel Regout van 1911 (gevolgd door een aangepast ontwerp Heemskerk in 1913). In 1919 komt de Hoge Raad in *Lindenbaum/Cohen* met een ruime uitleg van de term "onrechtmatig" uit artikel 1401, naadloos aanhakend bij de omschrijving uit het wetsvoorstel Heemskerk uit 1913. In het arrest van 1919 wordt de functie van artikel 1402, zoals die was in de periode voor 1883, overgenomen door de nieuwe uitleg van de term "onrechtmatig" uit artikel 1401, waardoor artikel 1402 in feite overbodig wordt als zelfstandig artikel. De rechtspraktijk – ook die van de Hoge Raad – was ondertussen zijn eigen gang gegaan, en had al in een aantal gevallen afstand genomen van de extreme uitspraak van 1910. Het arrest van 31 januari 1919 is vooral de *symbolische* breuk met die opvatting.

De kern van onze onrechtmatige daads-aansprakelijkheid blijft heel eenvoudig en *common sense*: als je voorzienbare en substantiële schade kunt vermijden door niet al te ingewikkelde of al te kostbare voorzorgen, dan moet je dat doen! Anders handel je onzorgvuldig en ben je aansprakelijk voor de schade. Dat neemt niet weg dat ook een potentieel slachtoffer aan zijn eigen veiligheid moet denken. Dat geldt niet alleen in Frankrijk, in Engeland, in Duitsland, maar overal… En ook niet pas de laatste vijftig jaar, maar eigenlijk altijd al, ook al in 1906 in de zaak van de biljartleraar. Het Nederlandse *Kelderluikarrest* uit 1965 verwoordt dit alles op eloquente wijze en kan daarom een klassieker genoemd worden, die een plaats verdient in de eregalerij met op nummer één het meer dan honderd jaar oude *Lindenbaum/Cohen* arrest.

5 Hoe is het verder met Max Lindenbaum en Samuel Cohen gegaan?

Tijdens mijn rechtenstudie werd nooit ingegaan op het tragische lot van de hoofdpersonen uit het arrest Lindenbaum/Cohen. Als onderzoeker heb ik mij – gek genoeg – ook zelf niet deze vraag gesteld. Dat had ik eigenlijk wel moeten doen… Het is pas nadat ik een jaar of twee geleden de indrukwekkende biografie over Max Moszkovicz[28] van Marcel Haenen[29] had gelezen, dat ik mezelf de vraag stelde hoe het eigenlijk met Lindenbaum en Cohen tijdens de Duitse bezetting is gegaan. Zijn ze ook, net als vrijwel alle Joodse Nederlanders afgevoerd naar de concentratiekampen? Tijdens mijn zoektocht stuitte ik op meer

28 5 oktober 1926, Essen, Duitsland.

29 https://www.standaardboekhandel.be/p/de-bokser-9789021408064 (laatstelijk geraadpleegd op: 21 november 2020).

informatie over Max Lindenbaum. Deze informatie heb ik vooral ontleend aan de website van *Joodsamsterdam.*[30]

Vader Max Lindenbaum (Essen, 29 maart 1871 – Theresienstadt, 17 november 1944) was de oprichter van het bedrijf. Hij huwde op 24 december 1900 met Bertha Gundelfinger (Stuttgart, 30 november 1874 – Theresienstadt, 3 november 1944), waarna ze als gezin op 26 januari 1901 naar Amsterdam kwamen. Het gezin krijgt de Nederlandse nationaliteit. Zoon Erwin werd vertaler van beroep en trouwde met Bella Schiff (Gladenbach, 20 november 1893 – Auschwitz, 3 september 1943). In hun huis op de Wouwermanstraat 16 in Amsterdam voerde Bella een pension.

Erwin Simon Lindenbaum (25 september 1901 - 31 maart 1944)

Naast Erwin kregen Max en Bertha een dochter Hertha Jenny op 31 maart 1905. Hertha Jenny trouwde met koopman Erich Hans Carow (Frankfurt am Main, 2 mei 1893 – Auschwitz, 16 augustus 1942) en zij kregen een dochter Marga Grete Carow (Frankfurt am Main, 17 juli 1930 – Auschwitz, 25 oktober 1944). Hertha werd op 30 september 1942 in Auschwitz vermoord.

In 1899 woonde het gezin van Max Lindenbaum op het Singel 459 te Amsterdam. De Stoomdrukkerij Lindenbaum was aanvankelijk op de Reguliersdwarsstraat 10 gevestigd.

30 https://www.joodsamsterdam.nl/gebbedrijfstoomdrukkerijlindenbaum/(laatstelijk geraadpleegd op: 21 november 2020).

Op 25 september 1912 plaatste de 11-jarige Erwin Simon Lindenbaum (Amsterdam, 25 september 1901 - Auschwitz, 31 maart 1944) de eerste steen voor het bedrijf van zijn vader en deze eerste steen is er nog steeds.

Eerste steen gelegd door Erwin Lindenbaum

Max Lindenbaum was al voordat hij zijn gezin naar Amsterdam haalde, begonnen met het bedrijf, en wel in 1896. Naast de drukkerij verkocht Max ook schrijfmachines en kantoorbenodigdheden. Hij was ook hoofdredacteur van het Drukkersweekblad in Nederland. Het ging niet altijd goed met het bedrijf, het drukkerij-gedeelte moest door de crisis in 1929 op een laag pitje gezet worden en in 1935 sprak de rechter het faillissement uit. Er werd echter een doorstart gemaakt, samen met de heer S. S. Korthuis onder de naam Drukkerij M. Lindenbaum & Co N.V. Gedurende de oorlog stond het bedrijf onder de leiding van K.A. Weeda.

De kantoren waren op de Herengracht 457 gevestigd, dat is aan de achterkant van Reguliersdwarsstraat 10. Drukkerij Lindenbaum is nu gevestigd op de Admiraal de Ruyterweg 545 (tegenwoordig stadsdeel Bos en Lommer) in Amsterdam.

Bijzonder is nog dat Jules Schelvis, overlevende van Vernietigingskamp Sobibor,[31] zijn opleiding bij drukkerij Lindenbaum heeft gevolgd. Jules Schelvis werd in 1921 geboren als tweede kind van Joodse ouders. Ze hadden de godsdienst afgezworen, waren humanist en lid van de Sociaal Democratische Arbeiderspartij. Een diamantwerkersgezin, zoals er in die tijd wel meer waren in Amsterdam. Hij volgde de driejarige hbs, waarna hij als drukker in 1939 zijn vakdiploma haalde bij Drukkerij Lindenbaum op de Heerengracht. Vanwege zijn Joodse afkomst werd hij na de Februaristaking ontslagen en kwam uiteindelijk terecht in verschillende Duitse concentratiekampen.[32] Jules Schelvis overleed op 3 april 2016 in Amstelveen. Hij was in 1999 de oprichter van de Stichting Sobibor[33] waarmee hij het verhaal van Sobibor op de kaart zette. Sobibor was tot ver na de oorlog in het collectieve geheugen in Nederland minder bekend dan Auschwitz. Koning Willem-Alexander gaf een eerbetoon aan Schelvis in zijn toespraak van 4 mei 2020 op een, vanwege het Corona-virus, lege Dam. Dat Jules Schelvis, net als Max Moszcovitz, deze concentratiekampen heeft overleefd, is miraculeus. Zij zijn de uitzonderingen op de regel dat vrijwel de volledige Joodse gemeenschap werd uitgeroeid. Zo ook Max Lindenbaum en zijn familie.

En Samuel Cohen dan? Sam Cohen zoals hij zich noemde, blijkt al voor de uitspraak van de Hoge Raad naar Indië te zijn vertrokken en zich in *Hotel des Indes* in Batavia

31 https://www.sobiborinterviews.nl/nl/nederlandse-overlevenden/jules-schelvis (laatstelijk geraadpleegd op: 21 november 2020).
32 https://www.joodsamsterdam.nl/jules-schelvis/ (laatstelijk geraadpleegd op: 21 november 2020).
33 www.sobibor.org (laatstelijk geraadpleegd op: 21 november 2020).

gevestigd te hebben.[34] In een kort stukje in "Het nieuws van den dag voor Nederlandsch-Indië"[35] wordt verhaald dat deze Sam Cohen een van de hoofdpersonen was in het arrest Lindenbaum-Cohen. Voorts wordt erop gewezen dat hij een aanhanger zou zijn van (de communist) David Wijnkoop.[36]

> "Sedert eenigen tijd woont hier in het Hotel des Indes een zekere Heer Sam Cohen, iemand met uiterst geavanceerd staatkundige – en commercieele – begrippen. Men deelde ons mede, dat hij een zendeling van David Wijnkoop was, en hier gekomen om Bolsjewiksche propaganda te voeren. Bevestiging van dit gerucht hebben wij tot nog toe niet kunnen krijgen, ofschoon wij natuurlijk in het algemeen belang de politie van een en ander op de hoogte hebben gesteld, en deze ons beloofde een wakend oog op den sinjeur te zullen houden.
> Dat dit ook uit anderen hoofde noodig is, bleek ons uit een nummer van het Weekblad van het Recht, dd. 21 Februari ISI9, No. 10365, waar wij o.m. het volgende lezen:
> (N. B.: het gold hier eene klacht van de firma M. Lindenbaum & Co., drukkers, te Amsterdam, tegen dezen Sam Cohen, daar de laatste een bediende van Lindenbaum voor geld had overgehaald om aan hem, Cohen, inlichtingen te verstrekken omtrent al hetgeen ten kantore van Lindenbaum gebeurde, hem copie te geven van de door laatstgenoemde gedane offerten, en opgaaf te doen van klanten, die bestellingen deden of prijsopgaven vroegen.)
> De Hooge Raad der Nederlanden was van oordeel dat Sam Cohen hiermee "eene onrechtmatige daad" had gedaan – (nog-al! zouden wij zoo zeggen.) – daar:
> onder onrechtmatige daad is te verstaan een handelen of nalaten, dat of inbreuk maakt op eens anders recht, of in strijd is met des daders rechtsplicht, of indruischt, hetzij tegen de goede zeden, hetzij tegen de zorgvuldigheid, welke in het maatschappelijk verkeer bestaat ten aanzien van eens anders persoon of goed, terwijl hij, door wiens schuld tengevolge dier daad aan een ander schade wordt toegebracht, tot vergoeding daarvan is verplicht; dat onder dit begrip zeker valt de daad van hem, die tot eigen baat door giften en beloften den

34 Mijn goede collega Prof. Corjo Jansen heeft me op dit spoor gezet! Zie ook C.J.H. Jansen, *De wetenschappelijke beoefening van het burgerlijke recht in de lange 19e eeuw*, Wolters Kluwer 2015, p. 310, noot 280.

35 "Waar wij in Indië al zoo mee worden opgescheept.". "Het nieuws van den dag voor Nederlandsch-Indië". Batavia, 1919/10/10 00:00:00, p. 1. Geraadpleegd op Delpher op 30-07-2020, http://resolver.kb.nl/resolve?urn=ddd:010180326:mpeg21:p001.

36 https://socialhistory.org/bwsa/biografie/wijnkoop (laatstelijk geraadpleegd op: 21 november 2020).

bediende van een concurrent overhaalt de beroepsgeheimen van zijn meester aan dezen afhandig te maken en aan hem zelven te openbaren; ...
Wel, de zaak werd dus door den Hóogen Raad naar het Hof terugverwezen, om recht te doen. Maar de Heer Sam Cohen vond het toch beter om de eindbeslissing liever niet af te wachten en naar Indië te trekken. En nu hebben wij hier het voorrecht van zijne aanwezigheid ...!
"Intusschen" – zoo zegt de Redactie van het Weekblad van het Recht, bij monde van Prof. Mr. Molengraaff – intusschen "moet men er zich in verheugen, dat de "Hooge Raad in dit ergerlijk geval de opvatting van art. 1401 heeft aanvaard, die "het den Rechter mogelijk maakt, het gedrag van eenen mensch tegenover den anderen te toetsen, ook aan de onbeschreven "regels, welke men naar onze door ons "zedelijk en ons rechtsbewustzijn gedragen "begrippen van hetgeen in het maatschappelijk verkeer betaamt, tegenover elkander "behoort in acht te nemen". "Er is door ons hoogste rechtscollege "zelden een arrest gewezen, waarvan zoo heilzame invloed op ons rechtsleven mag worden verwacht".
Jawel, jawel!... dat kan best zijn! Maar wij zitten er toch maar mee in Indië, met zulke indelicate perceeltjes."

Sam Cohen blijkt dus naar Nederlands-Indië te zijn vertrokken. Hij is in 1916 een vennootschap aangegaan met Herman Smalhout die in Nederlands-Indië een onderneming drijft.[37] Deze Smalhout is in 1912 in ondertrouw gegaan met Adele Krouwer (met de handschoen; hij in Semarang zij in Amsterdam). Volgens een krantenbericht opent

"De heer Smalhout (...) den len Januari 1916 een nieuwe importzaak, met kantoren te Batavia en te Amsterdam. De nieuwe firma zal zich speciaal toeleggen op den import van machines en materialen voor drukkerijen en den import van moderne kantoormachines enz. De naam der firma zal luiden: Herm. E. Smalhout."[38]

Smalhout was eerder administrateur van de drukkerij Mercurius in Batavia en blijkt dus een samenwerking met Cohen te zijn aangegaan. De firma verkoopt van alles, van

37 *'Bij onderhandsche akte, dd. 1 Juni 1916, is tusschen de heeren Samuel Cohen, koopman, wonende te Amsterdam, en Emanuel (zich schrijvende Herm. E.) Smalhout, koopman, wonende te Batavia, aangegaan eene vennootschap onder de firma Herm. E. Smalhout & C°., gevestigd te Amsterdam, en ten doel hebbende den import- en exporthandel, zoowel voor eigen rekening als voor rekening van derden. De vennootschap wordt geacht te zijn ingegaan den eersten Januari 1900 zestien, en is aangegaan voor onbepaalden tijd.'*

38 "Nieuwe importzaak. – De heer Herm. E". "Bataviaasch nieuwsblad". Batavia, 1915/12/16 00:00:00, p. 1. Geraadpleegd op Delpher op 21-11-2020, http://resolver.kb.nl/resolve?urn=ddd:011037357:mpeg21:p005.

typemachines, brandkasten tot sleepboten aan toe. Maar of Cohen daar nog een rol in heeft gespeeld, is niet duidelijk. Smalhout was ook redacteur van de *Grafische Revue.*[39]

Andere traceerbare sporen heeft Samuel Cohen niet nagelaten, afgezien dan van een berichtje in *Het nieuws van den dag voor Nederlandsch-Indië* enkele weken na het bericht van 10 oktober 1919 dat hiervoor werd geciteerd.[40]

> "De Heer S. Cohen heeft tegen het N v. d. Dag een aanklacht ingediend, wegens het "in het openbaar aanranden van zijn eer en goeden naam." Het is de Javabode die het bericht meedeelt. En al willen wij, op gezag van dat orgaan, gaarne aannemen dat de Heer Sam Cohen in het bezit is van de beide kostbare geestelijke goederen welke hij door ons „aangerand" acht, – zoodat er hier naar het schijnt geen non liquet behoeft te volgen wegens manifeste onmogelijkheid om het geïncrimineerde feit te plegen – wij verklaren volmondig: niet te begrijpen hoe de simpele overname van een oordeel van den Hoogen Raad der Nederlanden over de faits et gestes van zeker individu, aan den beoordeelde aanleiding kan geven tot een aanklacht. Als de Heer S. Cohen den Hoogen Raad eens aanklaagde? Want die was nog-al héél erg onvriendelijk jegens hem..."[41]

Voor altijd aan elkaar verbonden. Zelfs in Nederlandsch-Indië werd Cohen nog in verband gebracht met Lindenbaum. Die laatste is vermoord in Theresienstadt op 17 november 1944. Hoe het met Samuel Cohen is afgelopen weten we niet.

39 "Van hier en daar.". "Sumatra-bode". Padang, 1928/11/12 00:00:00, Geraadpleegd op Delpher op 21-11-2020, http://resolver.kb.nl/resolve?urn=MMKB19:002130062:mpeg21:p00006.

40 "Een aanklacht.". "Het nieuws van den dag voor Nederlandsch-Indië". Batavia, 1919/10/14 00:00:00, p. 2. Geraadpleegd op Delpher op 21-11-2020, http://resolver.kb.nl/resolve?urn=ddd:010180329:mpeg21:p002.

41 "Een aanklacht.". "Het nieuws van den dag voor Nederlandsch-Indië". Batavia, 1919/10/14 00:00:00, p. 2. Geraadpleegd op Delpher op 21-11-2020, http://resolver.kb.nl/resolve?urn=ddd:010180329:mpeg21:p002.

Wonderen verwachten van crisiscontractenrecht?

Ton Hartlief[*]

1 Afscheid *in extremis*

De hoofdrolspeler in dit vriendenboek neemt afscheid *in extremis*. Niet in blessuretijd natuurlijk, maar in een bizarre periode die ook (de wereld van) juristen en het recht raakt. Uiteraard hebben we eerder crises meegemaakt, maar de coronacrisis is niet te vergelijken met bijvoorbeeld de kredietcrisis uit, zeg maar, 2008. Anders dan toen ligt de oorsprong nu niet in economie of markt. We zitten in een wereldwijde ernstige gezondheidscrisis die ook tot enorme economische en financiële problemen heeft geleid en nog steeds leidt juist vanwege in dit verband getroffen overheidsmaatregelen die in vredestijd ongekend zijn: al dan niet intelligente *lock downs* met daarmee gepaard gaande sluiting van grenzen en van bedrijfstakken als de horeca, verbod op evenementen en sportactiviteiten, sluiting van scholen, drastische beperking van de mobiliteit, instelling van een avondklok et cetera. Het verschil met eerdere crises merken we ook in de juridische wereld.

2 Contractenrecht in nood

De kredietcrisis heeft het contractenrecht destijds bijvoorbeeld nauwelijks beroerd:[1] een beroep op onvoorziene, dat wil zeggen: niet in de overeenkomst verdisconteerde, omstandigheden in de zin van art. 6:258 BW in dat verband werd in de gepubliceerde rechtspraak eigenlijk steeds afgewezen ("ondernemersrisico").[2]

Dat lijkt in corona-tijd wel anders. Ondernemingen zien zich geconfronteerd met gedwongen sluiting, met drastisch teruggelopen orderaantallen, met een kelderende omzet

* Advocaat-Generaal bij de Hoge Raad der Nederlanden en hoogleraar privaatrecht aan de Universiteit Maastricht.

1 Zie onder meer T. Hartlief, 'Crisis? What crisis?', *NJB* 2013, p. 1765.

2 Zie bijvoorbeeld Rb. Arnhem (vzr.) 24 oktober 2008, ECLI:NL:RBARN:2008:BG3630 (*Giesbers Gebiedsontwikkeling/B&S Vastgoed*), Rb. Zutphen (vzr.) 30 september 2009, ECLI:NL:RBZUT:2009:BK3761 (*Nieuwwaerde Projecten BV*), Rb. Dordrecht 14 juli 2010, ECLI:NL:RBDOR:2010:BN1443, Rb. Amsterdam 5 december 2012, ECLI:NL:RBAMS:2012:BY7459 en ook hof 's-Hertogenbosch 30 mei 2017, ECLI:NL:GHSHE:2017:2299.

en/of met financiële problemen (minder inkomsten, debiteuren in betalingsproblemen). Het juist voor bijzondere situaties bedoelde algemene contractenrechtelijke arsenaal zoals een beroep op overmacht of op onvoorziene omstandigheden wordt in de corona-crisis nadrukkelijk van stal gehaald[3] en, zo lijkt uit de tot nu toe gepubliceerde rechtspraak te kunnen worden afgeleid, nu meer kans te maken.[4] Zelfs in gewone media wordt bericht over afgedwongen huurprijsverlagingen in de vastgoedsector bijvoorbeeld. Zo besteedde *NRC* op 20 augustus 2020 niet alleen aandacht aan het exclusieve W Hotel in Amsterdam dat "tonnen minder" huur zou hoeven te betalen, maar ook aan de zaak van voetbalclub Vitesse die minder succes boekte in haar relatie met de verhuurder van stadion de Gelredome.[5]

Art. 6:258 BW lijkt nu voor het eerst werkelijk inzetbaar in vredestijd, althans in niet (na)oorlogse tijden.[6] Dat onderstreept natuurlijk hoe bijzonder de huidige situatie is. Ook het contractenrecht zelf staat onder druk. Zo wordt in de doctrine inmiddels niet alleen hardop gesteld dat in deze tijd aan klassieke beginselen als contractvrijheid en trouw aan het gegeven woord (*pacta sunt servanda*) moet kunnen worden getornd,[7] maar wordt ook geopperd financiële problemen onder omstandigheden toch als overmacht te zien.[8]

---

3 Zie in dit verband onder meer H. Schelhaas & J. Spanjaard, 'Contract en coronacrisis', *NJB* 2020, p. 956 e.v. (hierna: Schelhaas & Spanjaard 2020), M. Ruygvoorn, 'Kan ik van mijn overeenkomst af met een beroep op de coronacrisis?', *NJB* 2020, p. 970 e.v., C.E. Drion, 'Corona en het recht', *NJB* 2020, p. 813 en K.L. Maes & J. den Hartog, 'Corona en commerciële contracten: een schets van de (reikwijdte van de) juridisch relevante remedies', *Bb* 2020, p. 159 e.v. (Maes & Den Hartog 2020). Verder is een aantal bijdragen verschenen waarin meer specifiek op de invloed van de corona-crisis op contracten in bepaalde sectoren wordt ingegaan. Zie bijvoorbeeld V. Mak, 'Consumentenrecht in tijden van crisis. Moet de consument kiezen tussen recht en solidariteit?', *TvC* 2020, p. 116 e.v., J.A. Tuinman & T.Q. de Booys, 'De coronapandemie en huur van bedrijfsruimte: *don't believe the hype*', *WR* 2020, p. 197 e.v., S.A. Kruisinga, 'Internationale koop en de Coronacrisis', *Bb* 2020, p. 224 e.v., R.P.J.L. Tjittes & A. Hogeterp, 'De coronacrisis en MAC-clausules in M&A-contracten', *Ondernemingsrecht* 2020, p. 366 e.v., T. Rijkse, ''Ordinary course' in tijden van corona', *Ondernemingsrecht* 2020, p. 607 e.v., A. ter Mors en H. Plas, 'Coronacrisis en bouwcontracten', *BR* 2020, p. 249 e.v., J. Meesters, 'COVID-19 en bouwprojecten: the show must go on – maar wie betaalt de rekening?', *Vastgoedrecht* 2020, p. 88 e.v. en J. Meesters, 'COVID-19 in de bouw: laveren tussen juridische risicoverdeling en praktische oplossingen', *Bb* 2020, p. 202 e.v.

4 Daarbij moet overigens worden aangetekend dat het hier om uitspraken in kort geding gaat. Van werkelijk constitutieve uitspraken in de zin van art. 6:258 BW is nog geen sprake.

5 Zie respectievelijk Rb. Amsterdam (vzr.) 17 juli 2020, ECLI:NL:RBAMS:2020:3494 (*Palace Hotel/Deka*) en Rb. Gelderland (vzr.) 29 mei 2020, ECLI:NL:RBGEL:2020:2768 (*Vitesse/Exploitatiemaatschappij Gelredome*).

6 Zie in dit verband ook W.H. van Boom, 'De Grote Oorlog en het Nederlandse Overeenkomstenrecht – Neutraliteit, Weerstand en Responsiviteit', *TPR* 2018, p. 55 e.v.

7 Vergelijk Schelhaas & Spanjaard 2020, p. 958.

8 Zie in dit verband C.E. Drion, 'Corona en het recht', *NJB* 2020, p. 813 die de vraag stelt waarom we in deze crisistijd wel eventueel bereid zijn leveranciers tegemoet te komen maar niet hun afnemers. Ook afnemers in ketens hebben nu eenmaal massaal te maken met bedrijfssluitingen van hun eigen afnemers waardoor hun *cash flow* zwaar wordt aangetast. Zou hen in die omstandigheden niet toch een beroep op overmacht jegens hun toeleveranciers moeten kunnen toekomen? Anders R.P.J.L. Tjittes & J.V. Tetelepta, 'Lessen uit de eerste rechterlijke uitspraken over de COVID-19-criss en onvoorziene omstandigheden en overmacht bij commerciële contracten', *Contracteren* 2020, p. 101 e.v. (hierna: Tjittes & Tetelepta 2020) die er niet

In deze bizarre tijd kan en zal in nieuwe af te sluiten contracten rekening worden gehouden met crises van een orde als de huidige coronacrisis.[9] In zoverre is dan wellicht sprake van een tijdelijk probleem, een vluchtig verschijnsel, al kunnen ook hier nog steeds zaken misgaan. Zo is niet ondenkbaar dat onder druk van de omstandigheden bepaalde voorwaarden worden afgedwongen bijvoorbeeld. Mogelijk is daarbij sprake van misbruik van omstandigheden.

De aandacht gaat vooralsnog echter uit naar (de consequenties voor) lopende contracten.[10] Wat het crisiscontractenrecht hier inhoudt en wie daarbij de leiding heeft, is voorwerp van discussie. Zo is inmiddels door Rinkes en Van Wechem in het *NJB* gepleit voor een specifieke Corona-wet en een Corona-rechter juist omdat het bestaande arsenaal onvoldoende ruimte zou bieden voor een adequate oplossing.[11] Anderen zien dat (kennelijk) niet voor zich en zetten hun geld wel degelijk op de mogelijkheden die het bestaande stelsel en dan in het bijzonder het leerstuk van de onvoorziene omstandigheden te bieden heeft. In die gevallen waarin partijen er al dan niet na heronderhandeling niet uitkomen, verwachten zij vooral heil van rechterlijke *wijziging* van de overeenkomst op basis van art. 6:258 BW. In dat verband gaat de aandacht uiteraard uit naar de vraag of aan de verschillende toepassingsvoorwaarden is voldaan. Hoewel er wel enkele hordes te nemen zijn, is de rode draad in verschillende publicaties dat de coronacrisis (en/of de in dat verband genomen maatregelen) in principe als onvoorziene omstandigheid kwalificeert en niet als "ondernemersrisico" kan worden afgedaan. Hier wordt het verschil met eerdere crises gemaakt. Interessant is dan de vervolgvraag: wat bepaalt de door de rechter door te voeren aanpassing van de overeenkomst? Is daarbij verdeling van de lasten bij helfte (*share the pain*; *share the burden*) uitgangspunt, zoals Tjittes in verschillende publicaties heeft betoogd?[12]

Deze lijn blijkt een zekere aantrekkingskracht in de rechtspraak te hebben en kan ook op steun in de doctrine rekenen, zij het dat het beeld wat lijkt te kantelen. Nadat

---

alleen op wijzen dat Drions suggestie om wat soepeler om te gaan met een beroep van de debiteur op financiële problemen (nog) niet is gevolgd in de rechtspraak, maar daarvan ook afstand nemen, omdat dit 'een flinke bijl zou zetten aan de nakoming van contracten' (Tjittes & Tetelepta 2020, p. 103).

9 Denk bijvoorbeeld aan clausules die voorzien in verplicht overleg, een eventuele maximum aanpassing van de prijs of aan geactualiseerde overmacht- of *material adverse change*-clausules.

10 Ik ben nu tamelijk ongenuanceerd over wat lopende en nieuwe contracten zijn. Waar in bepaalde literatuur wel wordt aangenomen dat 20 maart 2020 een kantelpunt zou zijn voor de vraag of de coronacrisis een onvoorziene omstandigheid is, is het waarschijnlijk ingewikkelder zowel waar het (kort) vóór genoemde datum afgesloten contracten betreft als na die datum afgesloten contracten. Ik verwijs in dit verband naar M.V.R. Snel, 'Coronacrisis als onvoorziene omstandigheid in het overeenkomstenrecht', *WPNR* 7300 (2020), p. 766-767 (hierna: Snel 2020).

11 T.H.M. van Wechem & Jac. Rinkes, 'Kroniek van het vermogensrecht', *NJB* 2020, p. 2615-2616.

12 Zie vooral R.P.J.L. Tjittes, 'Commerciële contracten en corona: uitgangspunt 50/50 verdeling nadeel' op https://www.barentskrans.nl/nieuws/commerciele-contracten-en-corona-uitgangspunt-50-50-verdeling-nadeel/ (laatstelijk geraadpleegd op: 2 november 2020).

aanvankelijk enkele schrijvers slechts kanttekeningen plaatsten, wordt inmiddels meer of minder nadrukkelijk afstand genomen. Zo heeft Van Boom een duidelijk tegengeluid laten klinken.[13] Art. 6:258 BW is wat hem betreft geen panacee; Van Boom benadrukt juist ook het belang van de bijdrage van andere rechtsgebieden zoals het insolventierecht aan een oplossing die recht doet aan de problemen waarmee contractspartijen zich geconfronteerd zien. Wordt art. 6:258 BW dan al ingezet dan is volgens hem eerder *ontbinding* dan wijziging aangewezen. Van het crisiscontractenrecht mogen we kennelijk eerder de botte bijl dan wonderen verwachten. In dezelfde hoek zit ook Snel die recent in *WPNR* de verwachtingen heeft getemperd: hij betoogt dat art. 6:258 BW ook in deze crisis maar beperkt inzetbaar zal zijn, dat dan bovendien ontbinding eerder dan wijziging in beeld zou moeten komen en dat in die gevallen waarin wijziging door de rechter wel aan de orde is van een 50/50-verdeling uiteindelijk vaak toch geen sprake zal zijn. Het gaat om maatwerk in de specifieke omstandigheden van het geval.[14]

Deze korte blik van afstand – als in vogelvlucht – op de status quo leert in ieder geval dat over betekenis en inhoud van het contractenrecht in nood én over de rol van de rechter in dit verband uiteenlopend wordt gedacht. Laten we, om de jubilaris eer te bewijzen, nu wat beter naar het zojuist geschetste palet kijken. Kunnen we in deze crisistijd wonderen verwachten van ons contractenrecht of is dat teveel gevraagd?

3 CORONA-RECHTER IN EEN CORONA-CONTRACTENRECHT?

Het lijkt mij goed daarbij te beginnen met het misschien meest opmerkelijke geluid: omdat het bestaande contractenrecht niet voor deze situatie is toegerust, is het volgens Rinkes en Van Wechem tijd voor een door de wetgever afgekondigd crisiscontractenrecht en een door hem aangewezen corona-rechter.

Tot deze conclusie zijn zij niet meteen gekomen. De kiem is gelegd in hun eerste aan de ontwikkelingen in het Vermogensrecht gewijde *NJB*-kroniek uit 2020 waarin Rinkes en Van Wechem zich hardop afvragen of het wel aan de rechterlijke macht is om de gevolgen van de corona-crisis vast te stellen. Is dat niet meer een taak van wetgever die net als in de donkere dagen van de Eerste Wereldoorlog bijvoorbeeld met een Betalingsuitstelwet op de proppen zou kunnen komen?[15] In hun tweede, meest recente, *NJB*-kroniek van 2020 komen zij met verdere uitwerking. Naar hun mening zou de rechter zich op politiek terrein begeven wanneer hij een oordeel geeft binnen het vermogensrecht, terwijl dat voor *deze* situatie geen oplossing biedt. Het in het vermogensrecht verankerde

13 W.H. van Boom, 'Onvoorziene omstandigheden en coronacrisis: *#sharetheburden*?', *NTBR* 2020, p. 85 e.v. (hierna: Van Boom 2020).

14 Snel 2020, p. 763 e.v.

15 T.H.M. van Wechem & Jac. Rinkes, 'Kroniek van het vermogensrecht', *NJB* 2020, p. 1029.

redelijkheid en billijkheid-instrumentarium is namelijk enkel geschikt voor toepassing in het specifieke en concrete geval. Wanneer de rechter desondanks aan de hand van dat instrumentarium een oplossing voor het *generieke* geval zou geven, zou sprake zijn van een optreden dat aan de wetgever is voorbehouden. Daarom bepleiten Rinkes en Van Wechem nu invoering van een Corona-wet en het aanwijzen van een Corona-rechtscollege.[16]

Het gaat vooral om de inhoud van de Corona-wet. Volgens de chroniqueurs zou in deze regeling afstand moeten worden genomen van de *pacta sunt servanda*-gedachte die in andere publicaties over de consequenties van de corona-crisis nog altijd centraal staat. Zolang aan dat uitgangspunt wordt vastgehouden, wordt, zo betogen Rinkes en Van Wechem, in iedere corona-situatie steeds één der contractspartijen op achterstand gezet. De correctiemogelijkheden die het BW biedt, zien op het geval dat één der partijen – buiten haar toedoen – in een positie wordt gemanoeuvreerd die om aanpassing van de normale rechtsgevolgen van het *niet* nakomen van gemaakte afspraken vraagt. De correctiemogelijkheden zouden minder zijn toegesneden op de situatie dat de "tsunami van onheil" tegelijkertijd over beide partijen wordt uitgestort. Het ligt in die situatie meer voor de hand om *niet* één der partijen aan te rekenen dat zij haar contractuele verplichting niet nakomt. In plaats daarvan zou het uitgangspunt dat gemaakte afspraken moeten worden nagekomen "fluïde gemaakt moeten worden". Het klassieke uitgangspunt impliceert namelijk een situatie onder normale omstandigheden: de belofte dat partijen zich volgens de regelen van het recht jegens elkaar zouden gedragen in de (wederzijdse) veronderstelling dat de maatschappij slechts binnen een bepaalde bandbreedte zal veranderen. Nu *dat* uitgangspunt door de gevolgen van de corona-crisis, volstrekt onhoudbaar is, komt de vraag op of deze situatie niet meebrengt dat beide partijen hun "over en weer"-verwachtingen *moeten* bijstellen zodat pas van een wanprestatie kan worden gesproken wanneer zij zich buiten een bepaalde bandbreedte bevindt. De situatie is dermate a-typisch dat het "shamen en blamen" van één van de contractspartijen in principe achterwege zou moeten blijven, aldus nog steeds Rinkes en Van Wechem.

De kans dat een dergelijke Corona-wet wordt opgetuigd, lijkt niet erg groot; het aanwijzen van een speciale Corona-rechter zie ik evenmin gebeuren. Ook inhoudelijk valt wel een vraagteken te plaatsen: als de niet-nakoming door een der partijen *nu*, in deze crisistijd, geen wanprestatie is, terwijl dat volgens de oorspronkelijke afspraak "onder normale omstandigheden" wél het geval zou zijn, krijgt toch nog steeds één van beide contractspartijen de rekening gepresenteerd? In ieder geval blijft de partij die door het uitblijven van (deugdelijke) nakoming schade heeft geleden daarmee zitten, omdat in deze bijzondere situatie uiteindelijk toch geen sprake zou zijn van wanprestatie.

16 T.H.M. van Wechem & Jac. Rinkes, 'Kroniek van het vermogensrecht', *NJB* 2020, p. 2615-2616.

Een eventuele betalingsuitstelwet daargelaten,[17] zal het dus "gewoon" op toepassing van het reguliere contractenrechtelijke arsenaal door de civiele rechter aankomen. Daarbij is de aandacht gericht op de mogelijkheden die art. 6:258 BW te bieden heeft en dan vooral de wijziging van de (inhoud van de) overeenkomst door de rechter. Een interessante vraag in dat verband is dan natuurlijk, in zoverre is het betoog van Rinkes en Van Wechem wel illustratief, of de rechter moet aansturen op verdeling van lasten. Is een dergelijke crisissolidariteit een wenkend perspectief en, zo ja, ook een haalbare kaart?

4 Art. 6:258 BW

Dat art. 6:258 BW in beeld komt, heeft er onder meer mee te maken dat de coronacrisis maar in een beperkt aantal gevallen aanleiding geeft voor het aannemen van overmacht (art. 6:75 BW). Dat kan namelijk alleen wanneer de wettelijke maatregelen de desbetreffende schuldenaar beletten de prestatie zelf (tijdig) te verrichten, zoals bijvoorbeeld het geval is bij een import- of exportverbod of wanneer een evenement geen doorgang kan vinden omdat het door de overheid is verboden.[18] De primaire gevolgen van overmacht zijn bekend: de debiteur is geen schadevergoeding verschuldigd (art. 6:74 BW), maar kan wel met (al dan niet gedeeltelijke) ontbinding door de crediteur ex art. 6:265 BW worden geconfronteerd. Op zijn beurt kan de debiteur eventueel een beroep doen op art. 6:258 BW.[19] Een beroep op overmacht is echter gedoemd te mislukken in gevallen waarin *nu* presteren heel ongunstig is in verband met veranderde omstandigheden waardoor het contractuele evenwicht ernstig is verstoord (bekende voorbeelden zijn de sterk gestegen prijs voor de door de debiteur te verrichten prestatie en het geval waarin de waarde van deze prestatie voor de crediteur sterk is gedaald). In een dergelijk geval kan mogelijk wel een succesvol beroep worden gedaan op art. 6:258 BW.[20]

Het primaat ligt overigens ook dan bij partijen: we hebben het over gevallen waarin het geschil tussen partijen niet wordt bepaald door een specifieke clausule (*hardship*,

---

17 Ten tijde van het schrijven van deze bijdrage is een wetsvoorstel Tijdelijke betalingsuitstelwet (*Kamerstukken II* 2020-2021, 35 557) aanhangig waarin de rechter tijdelijk (steeds voor 2 maanden te verlengen) de bevoegdheid krijgt de behandeling van faillissementsverzoeken aan te houden en andere verhaalsacties te schorsen en een schuldenaar een tijdelijk betalingsuitstel te verlenen. Zie in dit verband kort T. Hartlief, 'Insolventierecht in nood', *NJB* 2020, p. 1711 en J.J. van Hees & T.V.J. Bil, 'Kroniek van het insolventierecht', *NJB* 2020, p. 2723-2724 en overigens ook C.J.H. Jansen, 'Noodwetgeving en privaatrecht. Ervaringen naar aanleiding van eerdere mondiale crises', *NJB* 2020, p. 1508 e.v.

18 Zie bijvoorbeeld Asser Verbintenissenrecht/C.H. Sieburgh, *Deel 6-I. De verbintenis in het algemeen*, Deventer: Wolters Kluwer 2017, nr. 340 (hierna: Asser/Sieburgh 6-I) en Tjittes & Tetelepta 2020, p. 102.

19 Asser/Sieburgh 6-I, nr. 379.

20 Asser/Sieburgh 6-I, nr. 340.

material adverse change), zij er onderling niet uitkomen[21] en één van hen dan de gang naar de rechter maakt om wijziging of ontbinding ex 6:258 BW af te dwingen. Of dat lukt, hangt uiteraard in de eerste plaats af van de vraag of de toepassingsvoorwaarden zijn vervuld. Ik ga nu niet op alle finesses in, nu dat in verschillende recente bijdragen al is gebeurd.[22] Ik beperk me nu tot de hoofdlijnen.

Uiteraard moet sprake zijn van onvoorziene, dat wil zeggen niet in de overeenkomst verdisconteerde, omstandigheden. In de kern komt dat neer op de vraag of met deze omstandigheden rekening is gehouden in het contract.[23] Dat is de eerste horde. In de recente rechtspraak is herhaaldelijk aangenomen dat de coronacrisis vanwege haar omvang en gevolgen voor samenleving en economie in beginsel als een onvoorziene omstandigheid te beschouwen is, waarmee partijen in beginsel geen rekening hebben gehouden in hun contract.[24] Vervolgens moet in verband met art. 6:258 lid 1 BW (dat nader ingevuld wordt door de risicoverdeling van het tweede lid; wanneer de betrokken omstandigheden krachtens aard van de overeenkomst of verkeersopvattingen voor rekening komen van degene die zich daarop beroept, blijft rechterlijk ingrijpen buiten beeld[25]) gezegd kunnen worden dat

---

21 Tjittes heeft al eerder, onder verwijzing naar HR 19 oktober 2007, ECLI:NL:HR:2007:BA:7024, *NJ* 2007/565 (*Vodafone/ETC*), een heronderhandelingsplicht voor partijen bepleit en die gebaseerd op de gehoudenheid van partijen rekening te houden met elkaars gerechtvaardigde belangen. Zie R.P.J.L. Tjittes, 'Spoediger wijziging van commerciële contracten', *Contracteren* 2012, p. 97. Hij krijgt op dit punt zekere steun van Schelhaas & Spanjaard 2020, p. 964 en van Maes & Den Hartog 2020, p. 162-163, maar wordt bestreden door Snel 2020, p. 771-772.

22 Zie bijvoorbeeld Tjittes & Tetelepta 2020, p. 103 e.v., Van Boom 2020, p. 86 e.v. en ook Snel 2020, p. 763 e.v.

23 Asser Verbintenissenrecht/C.H. Sieburgh, *Deel 6-III. Algemeen overeenkomstenrecht*, Deventer: Wolters Kluwer 2018, nr. 441 (hierna: Asser/Sieburgh 6-III).

24 Zie Rb. Amsterdam (vzr.) 20 mei 2020, ECLI:NL:RBAMS:2020:2647 (*Coltavast/Metroprop*), rov. 4.7, Rb. Noord-Nederland (vzr.) 27 mei 2020, ECLI:NL:RBNNE:2020:1979 (*Sigismund/InBev*), rov. 4.8, Rb. Gelderland 29 mei 2020 (vzr.), ECLI:NL:RBGEL:2020:2768 (*Vitesse/ Exploitatiemaatschappij Gelredome*), rov. 4.1, Rb. Amsterdam (vzr.) 11 juni 2020, ECLI:NL:RBAMS:2020:2914, rov. 3.5, Rb. Rotterdam (vzr.) 18 juni 2020, ECLI:NL:RBROT:2020:5583, rov. 5.5, Rb. Rotterdam (vzr.) 18 juni 2020, ECLI:NL:RBROT:2020:5585, rov. 5.5, Rb. Amsterdam (vzr.) 17 juli 2020, ECLI:NL:RBAMS:2020:3494 (*Palace Hotel/Deka*), rov. 5.1, Rb. Amsterdam (vzr.) 17 juli 2020, ECLI:NL:RBAMS:2020:3508 (*EHM/Museum Hotel*), rov. 4.4, Rb. Noord-Nederland (vzr.) 21 juli 2020, ECLI:NL:RBNNE:2020:2540 (*D-rt Retail*), rov. 4.5, Rb. Amsterdam (vzr.) 28 juli 2020, ECLI:NL:RBAMS:2020:4280, rov. 11, Rb. Amsterdam (vzr.) 27 augustus 2020, ECLI:NL:RBAMS:2020:4253, rov. 16, Rb. Amsterdam (vzr.) 1 september 2020, ECLI:NL:RBAMS:2020:4274 (*CSU/Conservatorium Hotel*), rov. 4.6, Rb. Amsterdam (vzr.) 1 september 2020, ECLI:NL:RBAMS:2020:4414 (*Nimatrasco/NS Stations*), rov. 35, Rb. Noord-Holland (vzr.) 21 oktober 2020, ECLI:NL:RBNHO:2020:8300, rov. 5.2, Rb. Amsterdam (vzr.) 7 oktober 2020, ECLI:NL:RBAMS:2020:4904 (*Hotshots BV*), rov. 14, Rb. Amsterdam (vzr.) 9 oktober 2020, ECLI:NL:RBAMS:2020:4924 (*Naked Espresso Dam BV/Netterdam Beheer BV*), rov. 5.2 en overigens Gerecht Eerste Aanleg (GEA) Curaçao (KG) 8 juni 2020, ECLI:NL:OGEAC:2020:156, rov. 3.7, GEA Curaçao (KG) 26 juni 2020, ECLI:NL:OGEAC:2020:162 (*Zhenghao/Peru Fusion*), rov. 3.9 en GEA Aruba (KG) 27 augustus 2020, ECLI:NL:OGEAA:2020:358 (*Aruba Hotel Enterprises/WRS International*), rov. 4.9.

25 Zie bijvoorbeeld voor een geval waarin in verband met de coronacrisis de aard van de overeenkomst roet in het eten gooit Rb. Overijssel (vzr.) 6 mei 2020, ECLI:NL:RBOVE:2020:1688 (*Gemeente Enschede/Projectontwikkelaar*), rov. 4.9. In verschillende uitspraken is geoordeeld dat de coronacrisis niet als ondernemers-

ongewijzigde nakoming van het contract onaanvaardbaar is naar maatstaven van redelijkheid en billijkheid. De rechter dient hierbij, zo is duidelijk uitgangspunt, terughoudendheid te betrachten, juist omdat redelijkheid en billijkheid in de eerste plaats trouw aan het gegeven woord verlangen.[26] Dat zien we ook terug in de corona-rechtspraak.[27] Marktschommelingen maar ook een economische crisis worden in beginsel als ondernemersrisico gezien, maar dat geldt niet (meteen) voor de grote problemen waarvoor een onderneming zich door de (maatregelen vanwege de) coronacrisis gesteld ziet.

Is aan deze voorwaarden voldaan, dan zal de rechter op verlangen van een der partijen de overeenkomst moeten wijzigen of (al dan niet gedeeltelijk) moeten ontbinden.[28] Bij wijziging is het aan hem om het contractuele evenwicht te herstellen met inachtneming van de gewijzigde situatie waarbij zoveel mogelijk wordt aangesloten bij de aanvankelijke bedoelingen van partijen en de aanvankelijke in het contract neergelegde risicoverdeling.[29] In een invloedrijke vroege bijdrage over de invloed van de coronacrisis op contracten heeft Tjittes ten behoeve van de praktijk een viertal gezichts- en uitgangspunten geformuleerd (in mijn parafrase):[30]

- bij duurcontracten ligt een tijdelijke wijziging (waaronder een opschorting) of gedeeltelijke ontbinding meer voor de hand dan een blijvende wijziging of gehele ontbinding. Invloed en gevolgen van het coronavirus op de nakoming van contracten zijn immers tijdelijk van aard;
- als uitgangspunt kan worden aanvaard dat nu beide partijen geen blaam treft van de coronacrisis de tegenvaller gelijkelijk over hen verdeeld moet worden;

risico valt te beschouwen en daarom niet naar verkeersopvattingen voor rekening komt van de partij die zich op onvoorziene omstandigheden beroept. Zie Rb. Gelderland (vzr.) 29 mei 2020, ECLI:NL:RBGEL:2020:2768 (*Vitesse/Exploitatiemaatschappij Gelredome*), rov. 4.1, Rb. Amsterdam (vzr.) 11 juni 2020, ECLI:NL:RBAMS:2020:2914, rov. 3.5, Rb. Rotterdam (vzr.) 18 juni 2020, ECLI:NL:RBROT:2020:5583, rov. 5.5, Rb. Rotterdam (vzr.) 18 juni 2020, ECLI:NL:RBROT:2020:5585, rov. 5.5 en 5.6 en Rb. Noord-Nederland (vzr.) 21 juli 2020, ECLI:NL:RBNNE: 2020:2540 (*D-rt Retail*), rov. 4.5. De rechtspraak is er wel scherp op dat het nadeel van de partij die zich op onvoorziene omstandigheden beroept, daadwerkelijk is toe te schrijven aan de coronacrisis en niet aan tekortschietend ondernemerschap of een marktbeweging die geen verband houdt met de coronacrisis. Zie bijvoorbeeld Rb. Amsterdam (vzr.) 17 juli 2020, ECLI:NL:RBAMS:2020:3508 (*EHM/Museum Hotel*) waarin huurprijsverlaging werd afgewezen, omdat (ook) sprake is van een uit de hand gelopen verbouwing.

26 Vergelijk *Parl. Gesch. Boek 6*, p. 974 (MvA II) en zie verder onder meer Asser/Sieburgh 6-III, nr. 444 en ook HR 20 februari 1998, ECLI:NL:HR:1998:ZC2587, *NJ* 1998/493 (*Briljant Schreuders/ABP*) en HR 13 oktober 2017, ECLI:NL:HR:2017:2615, *RvdW* 2017/1099 (*Gemeente Bronckhorst*).

27 Zie bijvoorbeeld NCC (KG) 29 april 2020, ECLI:NL:RBAMS:2020:2406 (*Tennor Holding*), rov. 3.25.

28 Bij de vraag voor welk ingrijpen hij kiest, is de rechter uiteraard gebonden aan de eis. Daarop wijst Snel 2020, p. 765 terecht.

29 *Parl. Gesch. Boek 6*, p. 970 (TM) en 974 (MvA II).

30 Het gaat om de al eerder genoemde bijdrage: R.P.J.L. Tjittes, 'Commerciële contracten en corona: uitgangspunt 50/50 verdeling nadeel' op https://www.barentskrans.nl/nieuws/commerciele-contracten-en-corona-uitgangspunt-50-50-verdeling-nadeel/ (laatstelijk geraadpleegd op: 2 november 2020).

- de tussen partijen aanvankelijk overeengekomen contractuele risicoverdeling moet echter wel gehandhaafd blijven. Een partij mag niet commercieel profiteren van de aanpassing van het contract. Wie een commercieel voordelig of onvoordelig contract heeft gesloten, moet dat voordeel of nadeel bij wijziging of ontbinding proportioneel behouden. Dat is een reden om van de 50/50-verdeling van het nadeel af te wijken;
- bij het vaststellen van het nadeel moeten ook eventuele voordelen betrokken worden als gevolg van eventuele compenserende overheidsmaatregelen. Dat kan nopen tot een heraanpassing (met terugwerkende kracht) op het moment dat een partij dit voordeel heeft genoten.

Met deze "vuistregels" heeft Tjittes niet alleen richting gegeven aan de actuele rechtspraak, maar ook het debat in de literatuur sterk bepaald.

5 Share the pain

Dat geldt in het bijzonder voor zijn pleidooi, in het spoor van Nieuwenhuis, om de lasten van de tegenvaller gelijkelijk over beide partijen te verdelen, juist omdat geen van hen blaam treft.[31]

"Share the pain" of "share the burden" is in deze opvatting dus het devies. Verdeling van de pijn bij helfte dus, zij het als vuistregel, want afwijking is aangewezen indien het contract zelf een andere risicoverdeling in zich bergt, zoals wanneer het is gesloten op (on)gunstiger voorwaarden dan de toenmalige marktcondities. In dit verband kan worden verwezen naar de opmerking in de parlementaire geschiedenis dat de benadeelde in geval van een ernstige verstoring van de waardeverhouding tussen de wederzijdse prestaties wel aanpassing van zijn verplichtingen kan eisen, maar ook zelf een zeker aandeel in het risico moet dragen.[32] Tjittes haakt als gezegd aan bij Nieuwenhuis die al eerder betoogde dat wanneer geen van beide partijen blaam treft van de onvoorziene omstandigheid, het daarmee verband houdende financiële nadeel in beginsel gelijkelijk over partijen verdeeld zou moeten worden.[33]

Samen met Tetelepta heeft Tjittes nog als voordeel van het hanteren van dit uitgangspunt genoemd dat het richting geeft aan de onderhandelingen van partijen over aanpassing van

31 In zijn zojuist genoemde bijdrage verwijst Tjittes in dit verband naar J.H. Nieuwenhuis, 'Vernietigen, ontbinden of aanpassen (II)', *WPNR* 6165 (1995), p. 41 die al eerder steun kreeg van M.E.M.G. Peletier, *Rechterlijke vrijheid en partij-autonomie*, diss., Den Haag: Bju 1999, p. 118-120 en E.J.M. van Beukering-Rosmuller, 'Imprévision en zelfregulering', *NTBR* 2006, p. 43.

32 *Parl. Gesch. Boek 6*, p. 970 (TM).

33 J.H. Nieuwenhuis, *WPNR* (1995) 6165, p. 41. Overigens vinden Tjittes & Tetelepta 2020, p. 108-109 ook steun in de (toelichting op) art. 6:111 van de Principles of European Contract Law en in par. 313 BGB.

hun contractuele relatie hetgeen juist in een tijd waarom talloze contractuele relaties worden geconfronteerd met ontwrichting van het economische systeem, kan voorkomen dat partijen blijven hangen in juridische geschillen.[34]

Dit betoog kan rekenen op een zekere steun in de recente aan de corona-crisis gewijde literatuur[35] en heeft ook zijn weg gevonden naar de rechtspraak.[36] Er is echter ook aanleiding voor relativering. Zo wordt in de rechtspraak, ook in gevallen waarin melding wordt gemaakt van het 50/50-uitgangspunt,[37] regelmatig voor een andere verdeling gekozen. Ook de ontvangst in de literatuur is bij nadere beschouwing niet onverdeeld enthousiast. Hoewel het 50/50-uitgangspunt een zekere logica en ook aantrekkingskracht heeft, ziet niet iedereen het werkelijk zitten. Zo klinkt 50/50 volgens Drion aantrekkelijk, maar zal in aan een aldus in te richten aanpassing van de overeenkomst niet steeds eenvoudig vorm te geven zijn, al was het maar omdat het nadeel in veel contractuele verhoudingen (bijvoorbeeld leverancier – afnemer) ongelijksoortig zal zijn.[38] Dit punt wordt door Schelhaas & Spanjaard onderschreven, maar zij achten de 50/50-verdeling desondanks een handzaam richtsnoer, waarvan kan worden afgeweken als blijkt dat de contractuele verhoudingen en verdeling van risico's over en weer anders liggen.[39] Jagtenberg & Van Leynseele noemen 50/50 echter te kort door de bocht, omdat geleden nadeel zal variëren al naar gelang de specifieke contractuele relatie in kwestie. Zij benadrukken daarom dat steeds maatwerk geboden is.[40]

Het krachtigste tegengeluid komt uit Leiden en Curaçao.

6 TEGENGAS

De Leidse hoogleraar Van Boom en de Curaçaose wetenschappelijk hoofdmedewerker Snel hebben er kort geleden namelijk niet alleen op gewezen dat aan het betoog van Tjittes

---

34 Tjittes & Tetelepta 2020, p. 110.

35 Zie bijvoorbeeld Schelhaas & Spanjaard 2020, p. 966-967 en Maes & Den Hartog 2020, p. 163.

36 Zie bijvoorbeeld Tjittes & Tetelepta 2020, p. 108 e.v. die onder meer wijzen op NCC (KG) 29 april 2020, ECLI:NL:RBAMS:2020:2406 (*Tennor Holding*), rov. 3.42 e.v., Rb. Amsterdam (vzr.) 11 juni 2020, ECLI:NL:RBAMS:2020:2914, rov. 3.8 en Rb. Amsterdam (vzr.) 17 juli 2020, ECLI:NL:RBAMS:2020:3494 (*Palace Hotel/Deka*), rov. 5.4. Toe te voegen zijn Rb. Amsterdam (vzr.) 28 juli 2020, ECLI:NL:RBAMS:2020:4280, rov. 14, Rb. Amsterdam (vzr.) 1 september 2020, ECLI:NL:RBAMS:2020:4414 (*Nimatrasco/NS Stations*), rov. 42 en ook Rb. Amsterdam (vzr.) 7 oktober 2020, ECLI:NL:RBAMS:2020:4904 (*Hotshots BV*), rov. 19.

37 Een veel genoemd voorbeeld is NCC (KG) 29 april 2020, ECLI:NL:RBAMS:2020:2406 (*Tennor Holding*), rov. 3.42 e.v.

38 Zie C.E. Drion, 'Corona en het recht', *NJB* 2020, p. 813.

39 Schelhaas & Spanjaard 2020, p. 966-967. Dit sluit aan bij het eerder genoemde betoog van Tjittes & Tetelepta 2020, p. 110.

40 R. Jagtenberg & P. Van Leynseele, 'Corona: de nood moet vindingrijk maken', *Nederlands-Vlaams tijdschrift voor Mediation en conflictmanagement* 2020, p. 49.

veelal moeilijk uitvoering te geven zal zijn (hoe bijvoorbeeld, zoals Tjittes nadrukkelijk in het kader van één van zijn uitgangspunten heeft bepleit (hiervoor onder 4 vierde gedachtestreepje), eventuele steunverlening door de overheid mee te wegen?[41]), maar ook dat bij rechterlijke wijziging ex art. 6:258 BW niet alle tegenvallers waarmee de crisis partijen opzadelt in aanmerking kunnen worden genomen. In de kern is hun betoog dat er geen plaats is voor hooggespannen verwachtingen: in deze crisissituatie zijn andere rechtsgebieden en maatregelen belangrijker dan aanpassing van contracten via art. 6:258 BW. Mocht deze bepaling al in beeld zijn, dan is volgens hen ontbinding van de overeenkomst bovendien vaak eerder aangewezen dan wijziging ervan.[42]

Van Boom zet zijn bijdrage over art. 6:258 BW meteen op scherp:

> "In een aantal blogs dat onlangs verscheen, is (...) gesuggereerd dat bij wijze van terugvaloptie een soort standaardverdeling aangehouden kan worden: *fifty-fifty*. Of, in tijden van "warme communicatie": *share the burden.*" ... Die suggestie behoeft naar mijn mening (veel) nuancering. Ik denk dat de rol die art. 6:258 BW kan spelen in tijden van corona, eigenlijk redelijk beperkt is. Of art. 6:258 BW iets kan bijdragen aan het "verdelen van smart" is namelijk afhankelijk van de context waarin het artikel wordt ingeroepen. In veel gevallen heeft een contractspartij er, kort gezegd, niets aan, en een panacee voor alle coronamalaise is het in elk geval niet."[43]

Van Boom is weliswaar van oordeel dat een systeemontwrichting zoals die in deze crisis aan de orde is, aanleiding kan zijn voor toepassing van art. 6:258 BW, maar de meerwaarde is volgens hem beperkt.

In een aantal gevallen zal de bepaling *feitelijk* buiten beeld blijven, omdat partijen reeds hebben voorzien in een contractuele "nooduitgang" zoals een annuleringsmogelijkheid, een uitdrukkelijke wijzigingsbevoegdheid of de mogelijkheid om de overeenkomst aan het einde van de looptijd niet te verlengen.[44] En waar art. 6:258 BW feitelijk wel in beeld komt, is deze bepaling volgens Van Boom geen alomvattend instrument van maatschappelijke solidariteitspolitiek. Het nadeel waar art. 6:258 BW zich op richt, is wat anders dan de "algehele malaise" waardoor contractspartijen nu getroffen worden.

Treffend is Van Booms voorbeeld van een café dat zich voor jaren verplicht heeft minstens een bepaald bedrag (X) aan bestellingen te doen bij een leverancier. In het kader van een beroep door de afnemer op art. 6:258 BW is dan het in aanmerking te nemen

41 Van Boom 2020, p. 89.
42 Van Boom 2020, p. 85 e.v. en Snel 2020, p. 763 e.v.
43 Van Boom 2020, p. 85-86.
44 Van Boom 2020, p. 87. Hij acht het niet erg waarschijnlijk dat zulke nooduitgangen met een beroep op art. 6:258 BW door de wederpartij kunnen worden geblokkeerd.

nadeel in dat verband ten hoogste dat bedrag X. Ander nadeel (zoals loondoorbetalingen en de huur van het bedrijfspand bijvoorbeeld) kan langs deze weg niet ten laste van de leverancier worden gebracht; dat heeft immers met het contract niets te maken. Zulke nadelen worden dus niet (50/50) verdeeld. De via wijziging ex art. 6:258 BW te realiseren verdeling ziet enkel op één aspect van de malaise die partijen treft. Voor de leverancier geldt bijvoorbeeld dat hij ook niet al zijn "tegennadeel" in verrekening kan brengen; het kan bijvoorbeeld zijn dat hij wordt geconfronteerd met het faillissement van andere klanten. Ook de gevolgen daarvan voor hem houden geen verband met het contract met dit café. Het brengt Van Boom tot de conclusie dat van art. 6:258 BW bij systeemontwrichting als deze geen alomvattende of eenvormige oplossingen te verwachten zijn: dat heeft niet alleen te maken met het specifieke toepassingsbereik van art. 6:258 BW, maar ook met feit dat de betekenis van deze bepaling sterk afhankelijk is van de specifieke omstandigheden van het geval. Meer heil valt bij een systeemschok te verwachten van gerichte wettelijke ingrepen. Daarbij valt te denken aan wettelijke moratoria en aan de introductie van op schulduitstel en schuldsanering gerichte instrumenten (zoals de op 6 oktober 2020 ook door de Senaat aanvaarde Wet homologatie onderhands akkoord).[45] Ook andere acties hebben meer te bieden dan art. 6:258 BW: het toestaan van vouchers in plaats van terugbetaling om acute *cash flow* problemen te voorkomen,[46] verlenen van uitstel (of zelfs kwijtschelding) door verhuurders van woningen, afstand doen door werknemers van (een deel van het) loon of vakantiedagen. Cruciaal is ten slotte de inzet van de overheid die onder meer met loonsubsidies, overbruggingsregelingen en borgstellingen op de voorgrond is getreden.

In die gevallen waarin art. 6:258 BW wel echt in beeld komt, zal, aldus Van Boom, juist ontbinding in plaats van wijziging aan de orde zijn, omdat een wijziging die goed aansluit bij de oorspronkelijke risicoverdeling lastig te realiseren is. Ook op dit punt geeft hij een sprekend voorbeeld met als kenmerkende gegevens:

- een importeur verbindt zich in december 2019 bij contract tegenover een ziekenhuis tot het leveren van 1 miljoen mondkapjes, te leveren op 31 maart 2020 tegen een stukprijs van € 1;
- de inkoopprijs voor de importeur schommelde tussen 2010 en maart 2020 tussen de € 0,40 en € 0,80 en was in december 2019 € 0,60. De importeur verwacht in december 2019 dus met de transactie een winst van € 400.000 te maken;
- de importeur koopt de mondkapjes normaal altijd twee weken voor leverdatum in bij zijn fabrikant in Frankrijk;
- in de tweede week van maart 2020 blijkt dat de fabrikant wel wil leveren, maar alleen tegen een stukprijs van € 5 (inmiddels een normale marktprijs vanwege de enorm gestegen vraag).

45 Zie uitvoerig F.M.J. Verstijlen, 'Whoa: omkering van waarden', *NJB* 2020, p. 1943 e.v.

46 Van Boom 2020, p. 88.

Als de importeur zich aan zijn afspraken met het ziekenhuis houdt, legt hij € 4 miljoen toe op de transactie. Dat zou zijn ondergang inhouden. Ontbinding zou het ziekenhuis juist in problemen brengen.

Waar komt wijziging op grond van art. 6:258 BW die het nadeel wegneemt en zo dicht mogelijk bij de oorspronkelijke overeenkomst blijft, op neer? Van Boom brengt verschillende relevante vragen in beeld. Is het te verdelen nadeel hier € 4 miljoen of moet de oorspronkelijke prijs van € 1 miljoen bij de vaststelling van het te verdelen nadeel worden betrokken? Is bij een verdeling 50/50 reëel? Ligt het niet meer voor de hand om de oorspronkelijke omzet/winstverhouding aan te houden: 60 te dragen door ziekenhuis en 40 door importeur? Of is de omzet/winstverhouding een omstandigheid die het ziekenhuis juist weer niet aangaat? Wat Van Boom betreft is wijziging hier geen optie. Ontbinding doet juist het meeste recht aan de zaak.[47]

Uiteindelijk is zijn conclusie sterk relativerend:

> "Kortom: de coronacrisis is heel ingrijpend. Natuurlijk heeft het de voorkeur om "er samen uit te komen", maar *#sharetheburden* als motto is echt te kort door de bocht. Voor wat betreft de toepassing van art. 6:258 BW lijkt mij een "vijftig-procentsregel" *à la IZA/Vrerink* niet aan de orde te zijn. Een dergelijke regel zou arbitraire uitkomsten geven en kan ook voor veel gevallen helemaal geen zinvolle oplossing bieden. De rol van art. 6:258 BW is als geheel bovendien beperkt en ik denk dat we meer heil kunnen verwachten van andere maatregelen en uitlaatkleppen in geval van een systeemontwrichting als deze."[48]

Van Boom staat niet alleen. Hij krijgt inmiddels steun van Snel die ook serieuze kanttekeningen heeft geplaatst bij verschillende van de door Tjittes geformuleerde uitgangspunten (hiervoor onder 4):[49]

- ook Snel is van oordeel dat in veel gevallen ontbinding in plaats van wijziging aan de orde zal zijn, juist omdat wijziging in lijn met de oorspronkelijke aan art. 6:258 BW ten grondslag liggende gedachte (zoveel mogelijk recht blijven doen aan de oorspronkelijke risicoverdeling) in deze crisissituatie niet goed mogelijk is;
- daar waar rechterlijke wijziging wel een serieuze optie is, lijkt het 50/50-verdelingsuitgangspunt hem lastig houdbaar;
- dat geldt in ieder geval wanneer het nadeel voor partijen ongelijksoortig is, maar ook wanneer dat anders is, is afwijking van het uitgangspunt eerder regel dan uitzondering.

---

47 Van Boom 2020, p. 88-89. Deze ontbinding zou dan op art. 6:265 BW kunnen worden gebaseerd in het geval aangenomen zou kunnen worden dat sprake is van overmacht aan de kant van de importeur en anders op art. 6:258 BW.

48 Van Boom, p. 89.

49 Snel 2020, p. 770-771.

Niet alleen moet daarbij worden gedacht aan het reeds door Tjittes genoemde geval dat het oorspronkelijke contract een andere risicoverdeling inhield, maar Snel denkt ook aan andere tot afwijking nopende factoren als de maatschappelijke positie en onderlinge verhouding van partijen en de aard en ernst van de belangen van partijen betrokken belangen.[50] Zo zou bij een verzoek om verlichting van betalingsverplichtingen kunnen worden gedacht aan de omvang van het verlies dat betrokkene lijdt als gevolg van de coronaepidemie bijvoorbeeld, zijn financiële positie voor aanvang daarvan en de afhankelijkheid van zijn wederpartij van de betalingen voor zijn eigen bedrijfsvoering;
- net als Van Boom ziet Snel niet goed voor zich hoe met eventuele steun door de overheid in kader van art. 6:258 BW rekening kan worden gehouden juist omdat deze steun vaak niet ziet op het nadeel waar het in het kader van art. 6:258 BW om gaat, maar eerder op de "algehele omzetmalaise die met de coronaepidemie gepaard is gaan".

Het verbaast niet dat ook Snels slotsom is dat art. 6:258 BW in de huidige crisistijd geen panacee is. Is in een voorkomend geval wel aan de toepassingsvoorwaarden voldaan, dan zal het echter voor de rechter nog niet zo eenvoudig zijn de gevolgen daarvan te bepalen:

> "Het daarbij hanteren van een uitgangspunt als het 50/50-verdelen van het nadeel klinkt aanlokkelijk, maar is bij nadere beschouwing toch niet erg gelukkig, zodat er niks anders opzit dan, telkens op grond van alle omstandigheden van het geval, tot een maatwerkoplossing te komen."[51]

7 VOORTSCHRIJDEND INZICHT ÉN BESCHEIDENHEID

Het is met (de opvattingen over de meerwaarde van) art. 6:258 BW een beetje zoals met de coronacrisis zelf. Waar tijdens de eerste golf sprake was van grote saamhorigheid en algemene steun voor de getroffen overheidsmaatregelen, is dat nu (we zitten inmiddels in de tweede golf) duidelijk minder: er is inmiddels veel meer bekend, niet alleen over het virus, behandeling van getroffenen en mogelijke vaccins, maar ook over de gevolgen voor de samenleving van overheidsmaatregelen en dat merken we ook bij de waardering ervan. Wat voor de een onvermijdelijk en goed is, is voor de ander onaanvaardbaar. Ook in de

50 Zie bijvoorbeeld ook Rb. Amsterdam (vzr.) 11 juni 2020, ECLI:NL:RBAMS:2020:2914, rov. 3.8 en Rb. Amsterdam (vzr.) 28 juli 2020, ECLI:NL:RBAMS:2020:4280, rov. 14.

51 Snel 2020, p. 772. Dat in het kader van art. 6:258 BW enkel maatwerk te leveren is en geen standaardoplossingen voor één of meer groepen van gevallen, wordt ook in verschillende andere actuele bijdragen benadrukt. Zie in dit verband T.H.M. van Wechem & Jac. Rinkes, 'Kroniek van het vermogensrecht', *NJB* 2020, p. 2615-2616 en ook C.E. Drion, 'Corona en onvoorziene omstandigheden', *NJB* 2020, p. 1443 die stelt dat het bij een beroep op art. 6:258 BW steeds om een 'enorm feiten-gedreven exercitie' zal gaan.

wereld van het recht maken we, zelfs al in deze korte periode, een verschuiving mee: het aanvankelijke vrij breed zichtbare enthousiasme voor de mogelijkheden die art. 6:258 BW voor contracten zou kunnen bieden juist ook bij de verdeling van de pijn, lijkt inmiddels plaats te maken voor relativering, terughoudendheid en zelfs scepsis. In de eerste fase heeft Tjittes de agenda sterk bepaald met verschillende (al dan niet samen met anderen geschreven) bijdragen. Hoe aanstekelijk zijn enthousiasme ook is en hoe sympathiek de door hem aangeprezen 50/50-gedachte in deze tijd ("samen moeten we het doen") ook klinkt, inmiddels ben ik – in het spoor van Snel en vooral Van Boom en dus profiterend van voortschrijdend inzicht – ook geneigd te concluderen dat in deze grootste crisis sinds de Tweede Wereldoorlog geen wonderen mogen worden verwacht van het (vooral) in art. 6:258 BW verankerde crisiscontractenrecht.

Weliswaar komt art. 6:258 BW nu, anders dan bij de kredietcrisis, nadrukkelijker in beeld en lijken zowel feitenrechtspraak als doctrine ervan doordrongen te zijn dat we niet zomaar van "ondernemersrisico" kunnen spreken, nog steeds is de werkelijke meerwaarde van art. 6:258 BW beperkt. Het instrumentarium van deze bepaling biedt, als al aan de toepassingsvoorwaarden is voldaan, slechts beperkt soelaas, immers alleen in individuele verhoudingen waarbij ook dan nog steeds niet werkelijk alle nadelen waarmee beide partijen zich in deze crisistijd geconfronteerd zien kunnen worden meegewogen.

Meer heil en vooral ook meer structuur (en dus zekerheid) valt te verwachten van niet tot het contractenrecht beperkte noodwetgeving (betalingsuitstel, (tijdelijke) aanpassing van het insolventierecht) én van andersoortige al dan niet door de markt zelf ontwikkelde oplossingen (vouchers in plaats van terugbetaling, bevriezing van schulden en (tijdelijk) staken van incassomaatregelen (denk bijvoorbeeld ook aan de "pauzeknop" waarmee de gemeente Amsterdam wil voorkomen dat schulden van Amsterdammers te hoog oplopen: er komen geen incasso's of aanmaningen meer bij totdat een uitweg is gevonden)[52] en uiteraard steunverlening door de overheid). Het crisiscontractenrecht én ook de crisisrechter past bescheidenheid.

Dat brengt me bij de slotwoorden. Ik heb wel even getwijfeld. Wordt de in dit liber bejubelde, een coryfee op het terrein van het goederenrecht die zijn mannetje staat in het internationale discours (rechtsvergelijking en EU-goederenrecht) en zich daarbij vlekkeloos bedient van de taal van Shakespeare, wel voldoende eer bewezen met een in het Nederlands gestelde relativerende bijdrage over de rol van het Nederlandse contractenrecht bij het aanpakken van de gevolgen van een "vluchtig", naar wij immers allen hopen in de categorie "eens maar nooit weer" vallend, fenomeen? Ik heb toch voor dat thema gekozen. In ieder geval zou een bijdrage over crisiscontractenrecht recht doen aan Sjefs brede belangstelling die zich, zowel in onderwijs als onderzoek, niet beperkt tot "internationaal en Europees goederenrecht" maar zich uitstrekt over kwesties van nationaal vermogensrecht, daaronder

52 *Het Parool* 26 oktober 2020.

begrepen, zo blijkt reeds uit zijn vroegste geschriften, het contractenrecht.[53] Dat de beoefenaar van een specifiek rechtsgebied bescheidenheid past, omdat andere rechtsgebieden soms nu eenmaal een zinvoller bijdrage leveren en zelfs dat de jurist bescheidenheid past, omdat de rol van het recht ook maar betrekkelijk is, weet de jubilaris bovendien als geen ander. Dat gaf de doorslag.

53 Zie bijvoorbeeld J.H.M. van Erp, *Contract als rechtsbetrekking*, diss., Zwolle: W.E.J. Tjeenk Willink 1990 (in de taal van Vondel maar niet tot het Nederlandse recht beperkt).

Pandbelening, gestolen goederen en derdenbescherming

*Jan Biemans**

1 Inleiding

In een universiteitsstad die zo dicht bij de landsgrenzen ligt kan het bijna niet anders dan dat de aldaar werkzame hoogleraar goederenrecht zich verdiept het internationaal privaatrecht, het Europees privaatrecht en in de privaatrechtelijke rechtsvergelijking en dat hij bovendien een graag geziene gast en spreker is op toonaangevende internationale congressen en andere bijeenkomsten. Sjef van Erp heb ik dan ook het meest mogen zien tijdens internationale bijeenkomsten in en buiten Nederland, zoals *Ius Commune* en ALPS.[1] De keer dat ik Sjef van Erp tegenkwam op een "Nederlandse bijeenkomst in Nederland" (een KNB-jaarcongres waar hij als spreker optrad) sprak hij, het mag niet verbazen, over een Nederland-overstijgend onderwerp (de Europese Erfrechtverordening). Het is een genoegen om naar Sjef van Erp te luisteren en met hem te spreken: zijn enthousiasme over het goederenrecht is onuitputtelijk en werkt aanstekelijk. Hetzelfde geldt voor zijn grote toewijding aan de academie in de brede zin van het woord: onderzoek, organisatie en onderwijs.

Hoewel in deze bijdrage geen rechtsvergelijking aan bod komt, en de bijdrage evenmin over de landsgrenzen heen gaat, heeft het onderwerp zijn historische wortels in het Europese privaatrecht, en meer in het bijzonder in de Europese brandhaard van COVID-19 (namelijk Lombardije, Italië). Dat maakt het onderwerp overigens niet (zonder meer) geschikt voor rechtsvergelijking. In de parlementaire geschiedenis bij titel 7.2D BW, waar de pandbelening is ondergebracht, worden geen voorbeelden genoemd van regels voor pandhuizen in de ons omringende landen. Volgens de wetgever verschilt dat recht onderling zo sterk, en is het kennelijk zozeer afgestemd op de specifieke situatie en tradities in die landen, dat ervan afgezien is daarbij in enigerlei vorm aansluiting te zoeken.[2] In deze bijdrage wordt ingegaan op de goederenrechtelijke aspecten van pandbelening, in het bijzonder van verpandingspandbelening en overdrachtsbelening en derdenbescherming bij gestolen

---

* Prof. Mr. J.W.A. Biemans, hoogleraar Burgerlijk recht, Universiteit Utrecht.

1 Association for Law, Property and Society, waarvan de laatste bijeenkomst in New Orleans (mei 2020) helaas is afgelast vanwege COVID-19.

2 Zie Kamerstukken 2011-2012,33 334, nr. 3, p. 11-12.

goederen. De materie wordt daarbij zowel vanuit het privaatrecht, als het strafrecht benaderd.

2 Overeenkomst van pandbelening

Per 1 juli 2014 is titel 7.2D BW inzake de overeenkomst van pandbelening (art. 7:130 t/m 7:140 BW) aan het Burgerlijk Wetboek toegevoegd en zijn de Pandhuiswet 1910 (oud) en De wet van 28 oktober 1946 betreffende opheffing particuliere banken van leening (oud) ingetrokken.[3] Pandbelening en pandhuizen kennen een lange geschiedenis, die teruggaat op de kraam van Lombarden, waar ook het woord "lommerd" als equivalent voor pandhuis van is afgeleid. Handelaars en zakenlieden reisden vanaf de twaalfde eeuw rond als kredietverleners met deze kraam, bestaande uit een tafel met weegschaal en zakken met munten, welke tafel ten grondslag ligt aan de benaming "bank".[4] Pandhuizen voorzien thans in de behoefte van mensen die acuut contanten nodig hebben, maar geen geld willen of kunnen lenen, en ook geen bezittingen wensen te verkopen.[5] Vóór de invoering van Titel 7.2D BW was de overeenkomst van pandbelening geregeld in de Pandhuiswet 1910 (oud),[6] welke wet sterk verouderd was.[7]

Art. 7:130 lid 1 BW definieert de overeenkomst van pandbelening als de overeenkomst waarbij de ene partij, het pandhuis, aan de andere partij, de pandbelener, een geldsom ter beschikking stelt en de pandbelener daartegenover een roerende zaak, niet zijnde een registergoed, in de macht van het pandhuis brengt. Hoewel niet opgenomen in de definitie van art. 7:130 lid 1 BW is het essentiële kenmerk van de overeenkomst van pandbelening dat de pandbelener geen restschuld heeft (art. 7:139 BW).[8] Art. 7:130 lid 1 BW onderscheidt tussen twee soorten van pandbelening, namelijk de verpandingspandbelening (onder a) en de overdrachtspandbelening (onder b).

---

3 Wet van 11 september 2013, Stb. 2013/350 (Wet op de pandbelening); Kamerstukken 33 334; en art. 3 Besluit van 13 maart 2014, Stb. 2014/123 (Besluit op de pandbelening).

4 Bank is afkomstig van het Italiaanse woord 'banco' of 'banca' voor tafel. Aldus ontstonden de 'tafels van lening' of 'banken van lening'. In de Pandhuiswet 1910 (oud) worden pandhuizen aangeduid als 'banken van beleening'. Het begrip 'lommerd' (of bank van lening of pandhuis) is een verbastering van Lombard. Zie voor de geschiedenis en regulering van pandhuizen in Nederland vóór de invoering van de Pandhuiswet 1910 C. olde Heuvel, 'Strafrechtelijke handhaving van pandbelening', NJB 2013/795, par. 4.1; en W. Ruys, 'Toe-eigening bij pandbelening: terug bij de Lombarden', MvV 2020/4, par. 7.

5 Kamerstukken II 2011-2012, 33 334, nr. 3, p. 1-2.

6 Zie Wet van 8 november 1910, houdende wettelijke bepalingen tot regeling van de banken van leening, Stb. 1910/321 (Pandhuiswet 1910).

7 Zie Kamerstukken II 2011-2012, 33 334, nr. 3, p. 2-4.

8 Zie Kamerstukken II 2011-2012, 33 334, nr. 3, p. 1 en 15; en A.F. Salomons, 'Goederenrechtelijke aspecten van de voorgestelde wettelijke regels inzake pandbeleningen', WPNR 2013/6986, p. 653-655, i.h.b. p. 653, r.k.

Bij een *verpandingspandbelening* bevat de overeenkomst van pandbelening het beding dat het pandhuis de zaak aan de pandbelener teruggeeft indien deze binnen de beleentermijn de geldsom volledig aan het pandhuis heeft terugbetaald en de pandbeleningsvergoeding volledig heeft voldaan, en dat het pandhuis eigenaar van de zaak wordt, indien volledige terugbetaling van de geldsom en volledige voldoening van de pandbeleningsvergoeding binnen de beleentermijn uitblijft. Bij een *overdrachtspandbelening* bevat de overeenkomst van pandbelening het beding dat de pandbelener de zaak terstond aan het pandhuis in eigendom overdraagt, maar het pandhuis gehouden is de zaak aan de pandbelener terug in eigendom over te dragen, indien deze binnen de beleentermijn de geldsom volledig aan het pandhuis heeft terugbetaald en de pandbeleningsvergoeding volledig heeft voldaan. Het onder a bedoelde beding komt erop neer dat de pandbelener aan het pandhuis een bijzonder soort pandrecht verschaft. Het onder b bedoelde beding komt erop neer dat de pandbelening de vorm van een koopovereenkomst krijgt.[9] Op grond van art. 7:130 lid 2 BW zijn de bepalingen van titel 7.2D BW mede van toepassing op iedere overeenkomst, aangegaan onder welke vorm of benaming dan ook, met dezelfde strekking als een overeenkomst van pandbelening als bedoeld in art. 7:130 lid 1 BW.

3 VERPANDINGSBELENING NADER BEZIEN

Bij een verpandingsbelening is sprake van een pandrecht op een roerende zaak, niet-registergoed, met dien verstande dat art. 7:130 lid 1 onder a BW daaraan een bijzondere toepassing geeft. Bij een verpandingspandbelening bevat de overeenkomst van pandbelening het beding dat het pandhuis de zaak aan de pandbelener teruggeeft, indien deze binnen de beleentermijn de geldsom volledig aan het pandhuis heeft terugbetaald en de pandbeleningsvergoeding volledig heeft voldaan, en dat het pandhuis eigenaar van de zaak wordt, indien volledige terugbetaling van de geldsom en volledige voldoening van de pandbeleningsvergoeding binnen de beleentermijn uitblijft (art. 7:130 lid 1 onder a BW). Deze vorm is vergelijkbaar met de klassieke verpanding zoals geregeld in de Pandhuiswet 1910. Volgens Salomons is dit een verpanding gecombineerd met een overdracht "bij voorbaat onder opschortende voorwaarde".[10]

Bij een verpandingsbelening is sprake van een bijzonder soort pandrecht. Art. 7:138 BW verklaart een aantal bepalingen uit de regeling in Boek 3 BW buiten toepassing. De bepalingen van toepassing zullen zijn op het pandrecht op de beleende zaak als zodanig zijn art. 3:227 t/m 3:231, 3:236 lid 1, 3:238, 3:243 lid 1, 3:245, 3:257 en 3:258 BW.

9 Zie Kamerstukken II 2011-2012, 33 334, nr. 3, p. 12; Asser/Hijma 7-I 2019/199. Vgl. voorts voor de begrippen verpandingspandbelening en overdrachtspandbelening, Salomons, WPNR 2013/6983, p. 653.

10 Zie Salomons, WPNR 2013/6986, p. 655.

Uit art. 7:138 BW volgt dat op een pandrecht op grond van een verpandingspandbelening slechts een aantal bepalingen van de regeling van pandrecht op roerende zaken, niet-registergoederen van Boek 3 BW in beginsel van toepassing zijn. Art. 7:138 BW bepaalt dat op een verpandingspandbelening (een overeenkomst van pandbelening als bedoeld in art. 7:130 lid 1 aanhef en onder a BW) de regels betreffende pandrecht op roerende zaken, niet-registergoederen van toepassing zijn *behoudens* de artikelen 3:233 t/m 3:235, 3:237, 3:241, 3:242, 3:243 lid 2, 3:244, 3:248 t/m 3:254 en 3:256 BW. Omdat in de bepalingen over rechten van pand (afd. 3.9.1 en 3.9.2 BW) art. 3:232 BW ontbreekt en omdat art. 3:236 lid 2, 3:239, 3:246, 3:246, 3:247, 3:255 BW naar hun aard niet van toepassing zijn op pandrechten op roerende zaken, niet-registergoederen (maar bijvoorbeeld alleen op verpande vorderingen op naam), zijn op de verpandingspandbelening *in beginsel* alleen de volgende pandrechtbepalingen van Boek 3 BW van toepassing: art. 3:227 t/m 3:231, 3:236 lid 1, 3:238, 3:243 lid 1, 3:245, 3:257 en 3:258 BW. Volgens Salomons is het de vraag of bij de verpandingspandbelening nog wel van een pandrecht kan worden gesproken, aangezien het gaat om een zéér primitieve variant, "gespeend van zowat alle verfijningen die in een eeuwenlange rechtsontwikkeling zijn gaan behoren tot de essentialia van het pandrecht".[11]

Het merendeel van de algemene bepalingen inzake pand- en hypotheekrechten is van toepassing, waaronder de substitutiebepaling van art. 3:229 BW, dat tot een pandrecht op een vordering kan leiden. Indien de beleende zaak bijvoorbeeld door brand teniet zou gaan, verkrijgt het pandhuis een pandrecht op de vordering tot vergoeding die in de plaats van de verbonden zaak treedt. Bij een substitutiepandrecht ex art. 3:229 BW is onder andere art. 3:246 BW van toepassing. Hiermee zouden de bepalingen inzake pandrechten op vorderingen alsnog toepasselijk worden bij verpandingspandbelening. De bepalingen inzake derdenpand (art. 3:233-3:234 BW) zijn uitgezonderd. Uit de parlementaire geschiedenis lijkt te volgen dat de reden hiervoor is dat zij gelden voor de verhaalbaarheid van de door het pandrecht gedekte vordering op de zaak en/of de wijze waarop dat verhaal moet worden uitgeoefend, terwijl dergelijke bepalingen bij een verpandingspandbelening niet aan de orde zijn. Zie Kamerstukken II 2011-2012, 33 334, nr. 3, p. 15. Zo bezien zijn deze bepalingen alleen uitgezonderd omdat ze betrekking hebben op de uitwinning van een eenmaal gevestigd pandrecht. Dat laat de mogelijkheid van een derdenpandrecht als zodanig onverlet: degene die de zaak in de macht van het pandhuis brengt (de pandgever) kan een andere partij zijn dan degene aan wie de geldsom ter beschikking wordt gesteld. De bijzondere rechtsgevolgen daarvan (art. 3:233-3:234 BW) blijven bij verpandingspandbelening buiten toepassing. Van de algemene bepalingen is het toe-eigeningsverbod (art. 3:235 BW) evenmin van toepassing.

11 Zie Salomons, WPNR 2013/6983, p. 654, r.k.

Het pandrecht dat tot stand komt op grond van een verpandingsbelening kwalificeert als een vuistpandrecht. De totstandkoming van het pandrecht vindt plaats doordat de pandgever (de pandbelener) de roerende zaak in de macht van de pandhouder (het pandhuis; of van een derde omtrent wie partijen zijn overeengekomen) brengt (art. 3:236 lid 1 BW). De verplichting van de pandbelener[12] om de zaak in de macht van het pandhuis te brengen (vuistpand) volgt tevens uit art. 7:130 lid 1 aanhef BW. Stille verpanding langs de weg van art. 3:237 BW is in art. 7:138 BW uitgesloten. Art. 3:237 BW is daarom niet van toepassing.

Een aantal bepalingen dat betrekking heeft op de bescherming van het belang van de pandbelener als pandgever en als eigenaar van de beleende zaak zijn van toepassing. Het betreft art. 3:243 lid 1, 3:245 en 3:257 BW inzake de zorgverplichting ten opzichte van de verpande zaak en het instellen van rechtsvorderingen tegen derden.

De pandbelener behoudt op grond van met name art. 3:243 lid 1, 3:245 en 3:257 BW bepaalde rechten en bevoegdheden die zijn belang als pandgever beschermen ten opzichte van de in vuistpand gegeven zaak. Het pandhuis (of algemener, hij die uit hoofde van een pandrecht een zaak onder zich heeft) moet als een goed pandhouder voor de zaak zorgdragen (art. 3:243 lid 1 BW). Tot het instellen van rechtsvorderingen tegen derden ter bescherming van het verpande goed is zowel de pandhouder als de pandgever bevoegd, mits hij zorg draagt dat de ander tijdig in het geding wordt geroepen (art. 3:245 BW). Indien het pandhuis (meer algemeen, ook een derde: degene die uit hoofde van een pandrecht een zaak onder zich heeft) in ernstige mate in de zorg voor de zaak tekortschiet, kan de rechtbank op vordering van de pandbelener (de pandgever, of indien bewaard door een derde: of het pandhuis, als pandhouder) bevelen dat de zaak aan een van hen wordt afgegeven of in gerechtelijke bewaring van een derde wordt gesteld (art. 3:257 BW).

Op de verpandingspandbelening zijn art. 3:238 BW en van art. 3:86 lid 2 BW van toepassing. In art. 7:138 BW is noch art. 3:238 BW noch art. 3:86 lid 2 BW van toepassing uitgesloten. Voor bijzondere (kunst)voorwerpen is art. 3:238 lid 4 BW van toepassing: art. 3:238 lid 1 t/m 3 BW kunnen niet worden tegengeworpen aan degene die de zaak opeist, indien volgens art. 3:86a leden 1 en 2 of 3:86b lid 1 BW of volgens art. 6.15 Erfgoedwet ook art. 3:86 BW niet aan hem tegengeworpen zou kunnen worden. Indien de zaak reeds (stil) verpand was aan een andere pandhouder, kan op grond van art. 3:238 lid 2 BW een rangwisseling optreden. Omdat art. 3:253 BW niet van toepassing is op een verpandingspandbelening (art. 7:138 BW) ligt het voor de hand dat de tweede pandhouder niet zal delen in een eventueel overschot in de executieopbrengst. De tweede pandhouder kan dat voorkomen door de beleensom en de pandbeleningsvergoeding te betalen aan het pandhuis.

12 Zie Kamerstukken II 2011-2012, 33 334, nr. 3, p. 15.

Uit het feit dat art. 3:253 BW niet van toepassing is, volgt ook dat het pandhuis gevrijwaard is van aanspraken van schuldeisers van de pandbelener met betrekking tot de beleende zaak.[13] Dat is mogelijk anders indien het pandhuis aan de pandbelener een recht toekent op afdracht van (een deel van) de verkoopopbrengst. Zo bepaalt het *Reglement op de Stadsbank van Lening 2006* van de gemeente Amsterdam dat het "overschot" een jaar lang beschikbaar blijft voor degene die beschikt over het bij de belening afgegeven "pandbewijs".[14] Een schuldeiser van de pandbelener kan zich niet op grond van art. 3:253 BW op dit overschot verhalen, maar dient dat te doen door een beslag op de (contractuele) aanspraak van de pandbelener jegens het pandhuis.

Het pandrecht bij een verpandingspandbelening wordt gevestigd voor één bepaalde vordering en kwalificeert moet daarmee als een vast pandrecht worden gekwalificeerd. Indien de vordering waarvoor het pandrecht is gevestigd door betaling tenietgaat, vervalt dit vaste pandrecht op grond van zijn accessoire karakter. Het pandhuis dient op grond hiervan de verpande zaak af te geven aan de pandbelener (art. 7:135 BW, vgl. art. 3:256 BW). De verpandingspandbelening is naar haar aard een "vast" zekerheidsrecht. Het pandrecht wordt verstrekt als zekerheid voor de terugbetaling van één vaste vordering, die bestaat uit de betaling van de geldlening en de voldoening van de pandbeleningsvergoeding. Dit vaste pandrecht staat tegenover bijvoorbeeld een bankpandrecht, dat strekt tot zekerheid voor alle vorderingen van de pandhouder op de schuldenaar (vgl. art. 3:231 BW). De geldlening is een bestaande vordering; de pandbeleningsvergoeding bestaat uit een of meer toekomstige vorderingen uit hoofde van de pandbeleningsvergoeding, waaronder de rente.

De omstandigheid dat sprake is van een zogenaamd vast pandrecht, sluit aan op art. 7:135 lid 2 BW, waarin is bepaald dat de pandbelener te allen tijde, gedurende de beleentermijn en, in geval van verlenging, gedurende de verlengde beleentermijn, recht heeft op onverwijlde afgifte van de beleende zaak tegen terugbetaling van de ter beschikking gestelde geldsom en voldoening van de pandbeleningsvergoeding. Door het tenietgaan van de gezekerde vordering komt het pandrecht als afhankelijk recht en nevenrecht (vgl. art. 3:7, 3:82, 6:142 e.v. BW) te vervallen. Door dat tenietgaan heeft de pandbelener als eigenaar recht op onverwijlde afgifte van beleende zaak (vgl. art. 5:2 BW). Art. 3:256 BW is niet van toepassing verklaard. Uit deze bepaling volgt in beginsel hetzelfde rechtsgevolg als dat van art. 7:135 BW, namelijk dat wanneer een pandrecht is tenietgegaan, de pandhouder (het pandhuis) verplicht is te verrichten hetgeen zijnerzijds nodig is opdat de pandgever (de pandbelener) de hem toekomende feitelijke macht over het goed herkrijgt. Art. 7:135 lid 2 BW is, in het voordeel van de pandbelener, zwaarder aangezet dan art. 3:256 BW, in het voordeel van de pandbelener, omdat daaruit volgt dat het pandhuis verplicht

13 Zie Salomons, WPNR 2013/6986, p. 654.

14 Salomons, WPNR 2013/6986, p. 654, nt. 7.

is tot "onverwijlde afgifte" van de zaak. Naast art. 7:135 BW bestaat aan art. 3:256 BW geen behoefte.[15]

Omdat het gaat om een naar zijn aard "vast" pandrecht, en mede gelet op art. 3:258 lid 1 BW, is het niet noodzakelijk dat het pandhuis desverlangd aan de pandbelener een schriftelijk bewijs verstrekt dat het pandrecht is geëindigd. Art. 3:258 lid 1 BW, dat van toepassing is op de verpandingspandbelening, bepaalt dat het pandrecht eindigt wanneer een in vuistpand gegeven goed (als bedoeld in art. 3:236 lid 1 BW) in de macht van de pandgever komt. Gelet op het feit dat de pandbelener geen restschuld heeft, ligt het voor de hand dat art. 3:243 lid 2 BW niet van toepassing is.

In afwijking van de regeling in Boek 3 BW geeft het pandrecht aan het pandhuis geen recht zich op de zaak te verhalen. In strijd met wat gewoonlijk geldt (art. 3:235 BW, het toe-eigeningsverbod), wordt het pandhuis eigenaar van de zaak indien de geldsom met de pandbeleningsvergoeding niet binnen de beleentermijn wordt terugbetaald respectievelijk voldaan (art. 7:130 lid 1 onder a BW). Vanwege dit rechtsgevolg zijn de bepalingen die gelden voor de verhaalbaarheid van de door het pandrecht gedekte vordering op de zaak en de wijze waarop dat verhaal moet worden uitgeoefend uitgesloten.

Het rechtsgevolg dat het pandhuis de eigenaar van de beleende zaak wordt, indien de beleensom met de pandbeleningsvergoeding niet volledig binnen de beleentermijn wordt terugbetaald respectievelijk voldaan, geldt ook wanneer de overeenkomst aan de daar gegeven omschrijving voldoet, maar niet van pand of verpanding spreekt.[16] Het pandhuis wordt eigenaar, doordat het na het ongebruikt verstrijken van de beleentermijn niet alleen de macht over de zaak, maar ook het bezit van de zaak verkrijgt, waarmee voldaan is aan de eis voor overdracht, gesteld in art. 3:90 BW.[17] Volgens Salomons verkrijgt het pandhuis de zaak omdat de pandbelener deze zaak heeft overgedragen onder opschortende voorwaarde, en in dat kader de macht van de zaak aan het pandhuis heeft verschaft (art. 3:91 BW). Indien de beleentermijn onbenut verstrijkt, wast deze macht volgens Salomons van rechtswege aan tot bezit. Bij het intreden van de opschortende voorwaarde verkrijgt het pandhuis de eigendom, en gaat het pandrecht van het pandhuis teniet door vermenging ex art. 3:81 lid 2 sub e BW. De zienswijze dat de verpanding van de zaak wordt gecombineerd met een overdracht onder opschortende voorwaarde delen wij niet. De eigendomsverkrijging door het pandhuis volgt uit art. 7:130 lid 1 onder a BW en uit de buitentoepassingverklaring van art. 3:235 BW (verbod van toe-eigening).

Vanwege het bijzondere karakter zijn de bepalingen die gelden voor de verhaalbaarheid van de door het pandrecht gedekte vordering op de zaak en de wijze waarop dat verhaal

15 Zie Kamerstukken II 2011-2012, 33 334, nr. 3, p. 15.
16 Zie Kamerstukken II 2011-2012, 33 334, nr. 3, p. 15.
17 Zie Kamerstukken II 2011-2012, 33 334, nr. 3, p. 12. Zie hierover kritisch Salomons, WPNR 2013/6986, p. 653-654 en vgl. p. 655.

moet worden uitgeoefend, uitgesloten. Bij het onderhavige pandrecht vindt immers in het geheel geen verhaal plaats. Ook dienen de bepalingen te vervallen die verbieden dat de pandbelener zich de zaak toe-eigent. Dit brengt mee dat de artikelen 3:233, 3;234, 3:235, 3:248, 3:249, 3:250, 3:251, 3:252, 3:253 en 3:254 BW niet van toepassing behoren te zijn.[18]

De bepalingen die betrekking hebben op de uitwinning van de verpande zaak of daarop voortbouwen (art. 3:248 t/m 3:255 BW), alsmede het toe-eigeningsverbod (art. 3:235 BW), zijn, zoals uit het voorgaande volgt, naar hun aard niet van toepassing (art. 3:255 BW) of zijn op grond van art. 7:138 BW niet van toepassing verklaard op de verpandingspandbelening (de overige genoemde bepalingen).[19]

Een aantal bepalingen is buiten toepassing verklaard, omdat deze bepalingen volgens de wetgever niet goed passen of overbodig zijn. Het betreft art. 3241, 3:242, 3:243 lid 2, 3:244 en 3:256 lid 3 BW. Dat het pandhuis een verklaring moet afgeven als bedoeld in art. 3:241 BW is volgens de wetgever overbodig naast zijn informatieverplichting die uit artikelen 7:133 en 7:134 BW voortvloeit. Het pandhuis behoort in het onderhavige geval niet de bevoegdheid te hebben te kunnen bedingen dat tot herverpanding als bedoeld in art. 3:242 BW wordt overgegaan. Het pandhuis behoort geen kosten tot behoud of onderhoud als bedoeld in art. 3:243 lid 2 BW in rekening te kunnen brengen, anders dan wellicht als onderdeel van de pandbeleningsvergoeding. Hetzelfde geldt voor het in rekening brengen van rente als bedoeld in art. 3:244 BW. Aan art. 3:256 BW 3 is geen behoefte naast de verplichting tot teruggave die uit de pandbeleningsovereenkomst voortvloeit. Zie Kamerstukken II 2011-2012, 33 334, nr. 3, p. 15.

4 Overdrachtspandbelening nader bezien

Bij een overdrachtspandbelening bevat de overeenkomst van pandbelening het beding dat de pandbelener de zaak terstond aan het pandhuis in eigendom overdraagt, maar het pandhuis gehouden is de zaak aan de pandbelener terug te geven indien deze binnen de beleentermijn de geldsom volledig aan het pandhuis heeft terugbetaald en de pandbeleningsvergoeding volledig heeft voldaan (art. 130 lid 1 onder b BW).

De levering waardoor de overdracht bedoeld in art. 7:130 lid 1 onder b BW aan het pandhuis kan plaatsvinden, dient te geschieden overeenkomstig art. 3:90 BW (bezitsverschaffing). De wetgever verwijst in dit kader tevens naar de verplichting op grond van art. 7:9 BW (koop). Zie Kamerstukken II 2011-2012, 33 334, nr. 3, p. 12. Volgens Salomons impliceert het voorschrift dat tegelijkertijd (feitelijke) machtsverschaffing en

18 Zie Kamerstukken II 2011-2012, 33 334, nr. 3, p. 15.

19 Zie uitgebreid over toe-eigening bij pandbelening, ook in (intern en extern) rechtsvergelijkend en rechtshistorisch perspectief, W. Ruys, 'Toe-eigening bij pandbelening: terug bij de Lombarden', MvV 2020/4, p. 150-158.

(juridische) bezitsverschaffing moet plaatsvinden, zodat een levering *longa manu* of *constituto possessorio* (art. 3:115 BW) is uitgesloten. Zie Salomons, WPNR 2013/6986, p. 654.

Bij overdrachtsbelening (of een daarmee gelijk te stellen figuur) heeft volledige terugbetaling van de geldsom en volledige voldoening van de pandbeleningsvergoeding tot gevolg dat de pandbelener de eigendom van de zaak van rechtswege de zaak herkrijgt, als ware de overdracht aan het pandhuis onder de ontbindende voorwaarde van deze terugbetaling geschied, aldus art. 7:136 BW.

Indien de geldsom met de pandbeleningsvergoeding binnen de beleentermijn wordt terugbetaald respectievelijk wordt voldaan, wordt de pandbelener op grond van art. 7:136 BW van rechtswege weer eigenaar van de aan hem terug te geven zaak. Art. 7:136 BW voegt daaraan toe dat het rechtsgevolg erop neerkomt dat de oorspronkelijke overdracht aan het pandhuis geacht moet worden te hebben plaats gevonden onder de ontbindende voorwaarde van de terugbetaling binnen de beleentermijn. Een dergelijke ontbinding heeft blijkens art. 3:38 lid 2 BW geen terugwerkende kracht, maar heeft wel vanaf het tijdstip van ontbinding goederenrechtelijke werking. De ontbinding werkt vanaf dat tijdstip dus ook jegens derden.[20] De regeling past volgens de wetgever aldus in het stelsel van de Boeken 3 en 6 BW. De regeling waarborgt dat de pandbelener die binnen de beleentermijn heeft terugbetaald, in geval van faillissement van het pandhuis toch de zaak als eigenaar kan opvorderen. Zou het pandhuis de zaak gedurende de beleentermijn aan een derde overdragen dan werkt de ontbinding ook tegen deze derde, tenzij deze zich kan beroepen op art. 3:86 BW. Zie Kamerstukken II 2011-2012, 33 334, nr. 3, p. 14. Art. 7:136 BW spreekt van de verkrijging door pandbelener van de eigendom van de zaak van rechtswege "als ware de overdracht aan het pandhuis onder de ontbindende voorwaarde van deze terugbetaling geschied". Daaruit kan worden afgeleid dat geen sprake is van een overdracht van ontbindende voorwaarde als zodanig. De verkrijging door de pandbelener vindt plaats op de grond van de wet (art. 7:136 BW). Door de verwijzing naar de overdracht onder ontbindende voorwaarde ligt overeenkomstige toepassing van deze rechtsfiguur evenwel voor de hand. Op grond van HR 3 juni 2016, NJ 2016/290 (Rabobank/Reuser) heeft de pandbelener tegenover het eigendomsrecht onder ontbindende voorwaarde van het pandhuis een eigendomsrecht onder opschortende voorwaarde (van volledige terugbetaling van de geldsom en volledige voldoening van de pandbeleningsvergoeding) heeft.[21] Zie voor een andere opvatting Salomons, WPNR 2013/6986, p. 655, die de zienswijze huldigt dat de voorwaarde, ook al is ze niet uitdrukkelijk overeengekomen, onderdeel uitmaakt van de overeenkomst op grond van de wet. In de parlementaire geschiedenis wordt opgemerkt dat de in art. 7:130 lid 1 onder b BW bedoelde teruggave aan de pandbelener geschiedt

20 Zie Parl. Gesch. Boek 3, p. 186 en Parl. Gesch. Boek 6, p. 146 en 149.

21 Zie in deze zin tevens W.H. van Boom, 'Beschikken over voorwaardelijke eigendom', AAe mei 2017, p. 422.

overeenkomstig art. 7:136 BW door vervulling van de daar bedoelde ontbindende voorwaarde. Zie Kamerstukken II 2011-2012, 33 334, nr. 3, p. 12. Dat is minder nauwkeurig. De eigendomsovergang geschiedt van rechtswege op grond van de wet (art. 7:136 BW). De verplichting van het pandhuis om de zaak aan pandbelener terug te geven, ligt in de overeenkomst van pandbelening besloten en kan daarnaast worden aangemerkt als een goederenrechtelijke verplichting die voortvloeit uit de overgang van de eigendom naar de pandbelener (art. 5:2 BW).

Volgens de wetgever is de overdrachtsbelening (art. 7:130 lid 1 sub b BW) niet in strijd met het fiduciaverbod van art. 3:83 lid 3 BW. Het gaat volgens de wetgever immers niet om een zekerheidsrecht, dat gericht is op verhaal van een vordering op de beleende zaak, maar om een overdracht die de strekking heeft de zaak in het vermogen van het pandhuis te doen vallen, tenzij de pandbelener de eigendom van de zaak herkrijgt omdat hij tijdig gebruik maakt van zijn recht afgifte van de zaak tegen terugbetaling van de geldsom te verlangen. Fiduciaire eigendom heeft dus niets met overdrachtsbelening te maken.[22] Volgens Salomons is overdrachtsbelening niet in strijd met het fiduciaverbod omdat het pandhuis "na de totstandkoming van de overeenkomst niets meer te vorderen heeft van de pandbelener".[23] De overdrachtsbelening vormt echter een uitzondering op het fiduciaverbod aangezien de overdracht van de zaak wel degelijk strekt tot zekerheid.

5 DERDENBESCHERMING EN GESTOLEN GOEDEREN

Het risico bestaat dat pandhuizen goederen aangeboden krijgen die afkomstig zijn van diefstal.[24] Anders dan de Pandhuiswet 1910 bevat titel 7.2D BW geen bijzondere bepalingen ten aanzien van gestolen goederen. De regeling daaromtrent is overgelaten aan de algemene regelingen in het strafrecht en het goederenrecht. Op grond van art. 5 lid 3 onder b en art. 28 onder b Pandhuiswet 1910 kon een gemeentelijk respectievelijk particulier pandhuis geen zaken tot pand aannemen die, met duidelijke omschrijving bij de houder van het pandhuis als door diefstal verloren waren aangegeven. Deze bepalingen zijn niet in titel 7.2D BW teruggekeerd, op de grond dat titel 7.2D BW een privaatrechtelijke regeling bevat die voorwerp is van toezicht door de ACM. Het toezicht op de pandhuizen met betrekking tot in- en verkoop van gestolen goederen dient in het kader van het strafrecht te worden bezien. De wetgever verwijst naar art. 416-417ter WvSr (opzet- en schuldheling), art. 437-437ter WvSr, alsmede art. 420bis t/m 420quater WvSr (witwassen). Zie Kamerstukken II 2012-2013, 33 334, nr. 6, p. 6-7.

---

22 Zie Kamerstukken II 2012-2013, 33 334, nr. 6, p. 13.
23 Zie Salomons, WPNR 2013/6986, p. 655.
24 Zie Kamerstukken II 2012-2013, 33 334, nr. 6, p. 6, 7-8 en 11.

Art. 437 WvSr is van toepassing op particuliere pandhuizen. De bepaling is indirect van belang voor de vraag of een pandhuis te goeder trouw is in de zin van art. 3:86 BW. Uit art. 437 WvSr jo art. 1 van het daarbij behorende Uitvoeringsbesluit ex art. 437 lid 1 WvSr blijkt dat art. 437 WvSr van toepassing is op "opkopers en handelaren in gebruikte en ongeregelde goederen, metalen (legeringen en metalloïden), edelstenen, uurwerken, kunstvoorwerpen, auto's, motorfietsen, bromfietsen, fietsen, foto-, film-, radio, audio- en videoapparatuur en apparatuur voor automatische registratie." Particuliere pandhuizen vallen onder deze omschrijving. Art. 437 WvSr is niet alleen van toepassing op het pandhuis in het geval dat sprake is van overdrachtspandbelening, maar ook in het geval dat het pandhuis na zijn eigendomsverkrijging de zaken op commerciële basis verder verhandelt.[25] Het ligt het voor de hand dat art. 437 WvSr steeds van toepassing is op een verpandingspandbelening, ongeacht de vraag of het pandhuis eigenaar wordt van de beleende zaak.

De kern van art. 437 WvSr is als volgt. Een particulier pandhuis mag geen goederen verwerven van iemand die niet zijn identiteitsgegevens heeft opgegeven en van wie het deze gegevens niet in zijn administratie heeft aangetekend. Het particuliere pandhuis dient aantekening te houden van alle gebruikte of ongeregelde goederen die het heeft verworven of voorhanden heeft in een doorlopend en door of namens de burgemeester gewaarmerkt register, waarin het pandhuis onverwijld vermeldt: a. het volgnummer van de aantekening met betrekking tot het goed; b. de datum van verkrijging van het goed; c. een omschrijving van het goed, daaronder begrepen – voor zover dat mogelijk is – soort, merk en nummer van het goed; d. de koopprijs of andere voorwaarden van verkrijging van het goed; en e. de naam en het adres van degene van wie het goed is verkregen.[26] Een pandhuis is strafbaar indien het een zaak verwerft of voorhanden heeft die door of vanwege de politie met een duidelijke schriftelijke omschrijving als door misdrijf aan de rechthebbende is onttrokken of als verloren is aangegeven.[27] Deze strafrechtelijke bepalingen doen denken aan de wettelijke plicht voor particuliere pandhuizen om onderpanden op een voorgeschreven manier te nummeren en de bladen van het register waarin de onderpanden worden bijgeschreven door of vanwege de burgemeester te laten waarmerken (art. 18 Pandhuiswet 1910) en de bijzondere regeling voor zaken die vóór het in pand geven van de zaak met duidelijke omschrijving als door diefstal verloren bij het pandhuis zijn aangegeven (art. 11 van de Pandhuiswet 1910).

Indien een particulier pandhuis niet voldoet aan de hiervoor gestelde, toepasselijke strafrechtelijke bepalingen van art. 437 lid 1 onder b en onder e WvSr zal het pandhuis niet te goeder trouw zijn in de zin van art. 3:86 lid 1 BW. Het pandhuis wordt vanwege

25 Zie Kamerstukken II 2012-2013, 33 334, nr. 6, p. 7-8.
26 Zie art. 437 lid 1 WvSr en art. 2 lid 2 Uitvoeringsbesluit ex art. 437 lid 1 WvSr.
27 Zie Kamerstukken II 2012-2013, 33 334, nr. 6, p. 7-8 en p. 11.

het gebrek aan beschikkingsbevoegdheid niet de eigenaar van de gestolen zaak. Uit de aard van de bepaling volgt dat art. 3:86 lid 1 BW op een overdrachtspandbelening (art. 7:130 lid 1 onder b BW) van toepassing is, aangezien het pandhuis de verkrijger van de zaak is. Art. 3:86 lid 1 BW is ook van toepassing op een verpandingspandbelening (art. 7:130 lid 1 onder b BW), indien het pandhuis op grond daarvan de eigenaar wordt van de zaak. Vgl. Kamerstukken II 2012-2013, 33 334, nr. 6, p. 7-8.

Een pandhuis is niet te goeder trouw in de zin van art. 3:86 BW als het niet gedurende drie jaren de werkelijke identiteit van de pandbelener kan aangeven (art. 3:87 BW). Het pandhuis is daartoe op grond van art. 437 lid 1 onder b BW verplicht. Een pandhuis is voorts niet te goeder trouw indien het door raadpleging van de website www.stopheling.nl van de politie en het Openbaar Ministerie had kunnen achterhalen dat een goed bij de politie als gestolen was geregistreerd (art. 437 lid 1 onder e WvSr). Dat geldt in het bijzonder voor de raadpleging van specifieke nummers van motoren e.d. Het pandhuis is op grond van art. 437 lid 1 aanhef en onder e WvSr wettelijk verplicht om de gegevens uit zijn register (zoals bedoeld in art. 2 lid 2 Uitvoeringsbesluit ex art. 437 WvSr) te vergelijken met de gegevens die zijn te vinden via de bedoelde van de politie en het Openbaar Ministerie.

Indien het pandhuis niet te goeder trouw is, kan het pandhuis geen eigenaar worden van de beleende zaak en zal het deze zonder enige vergoeding aan de eigenaar moeten afgeven. Bij eventuele (door)verkoop handelt het pandhuis onrechtmatig jegens de eigenaar en is het schadevergoeding verschuldigd.[28]

Indien de pandbelener beschikkingsonbevoegd is, bijvoorbeeld omdat de zaak die hij in pand geeft, gestolen is, is art. 3:238 lid 1 BW van toepassing zolang het pandhuis geen eigenaar van de zaak is geworden. Art. 3:238 lid 1 BW geeft een vergelijkbare regeling als art. 3:86 lid 1 BW, die beschermt tegen de beschikkingsonbevoegdheid van de pandgever. Als het pandhuis pandhouder is en (nog) geen eigenaar van de zaak (art. 7:130 lid 1 onder a BW) is art. 3:238 lid 1 BW van toepassing, zoals ook uit art. 7:138 BW volgt. Art. 3:238 lid 1 BW bepaalt dat ondanks onbevoegdheid van de pandgever de vestiging van een pandrecht op een roerende zaak geldig, indien de pandhouder te goeder trouw is op het tijdstip waarop de zaak in zijn macht of in die van een derde is gebracht. In art. 3:238 lid 3 BW is alleen art. 3:86 lid 3 aanhef en onder b en lid 4 BW van overeenkomstige toepassing verklaard, en niet art. 3:86 lid 3 aanhef en onder a BW. In de periode tussen de verkrijging door het pandhuis op grond van verpandingspandbelening en de verkoop door het pandhuis van de beleende zaak aan een derde, kan de bestolen eigenaar zich beroepen op art. 3:86 lid 1 BW.

De eigenaar van de zaak die het bezit daarvan door diefstal heeft verloren, kan de gestolen zaak opeisen bij het pandhuis waar de dief de gestolen zaak heeft beleend ongeacht

28 Zie Kamerstukken II 2012-2013, 33 334, nr. 6, p. 7-8.

de goede trouw van het pandhuis, indien het pandhuis de zaak nog niet heeft verkocht aan een derde (art. 3:86 lid 3, eerste zinsdeel, BW).

De wetgever vermeldt deze mogelijkheid niet. Omdat het pandhuis de zaak verkrijgt van een consument (de dief), kan het pandhuis geen beroep doen op de uitzonderingsbepaling van art. 3:86 lid 3 aanhef en onder a BW. De eigenaar van een gestolen zaak kan derhalve in alle gevallen de zaak revindiceren bij het pandhuis, ongeacht of sprake is van goede trouw, zolang de revindicatie plaatsvindt binnen drie jaren, te rekenen vanaf de dag van de diefstal. Is het pandhuis te goeder trouw, dan wordt het pandhuis na drie jaren alsnog eigenaar van de zaak op grond van verkrijgende verjaring (art. 3:99 BW).

Het voorgaande handelde over de onbevoegdheid van de pandbelener in zijn verhouding tot het pandhuis. De eigenaar van de gestolen zaak kan de zaak niet meer revindiceren, als het pandhuis de zaak heeft verkocht nadat de pandbelener (de dief) de beleensom en/of de pandbeleningsvergoeding niet tijdig heeft betaald, en het pandhuis op grond daarvan tot verkoop van beleende zaak overgaat in de winkel. In dat geval zal een koper te goeder trouw zich kunnen beroepen op art. 3:86 lid 1 jo lid 3 onder a BW. De koper die te goeder trouw een gestolen zaak van het pandhuis heeft gekocht, komt – in tegenstelling tot het pandhuis zelf – wél een beroep toe op art. 3:86 lid 3 aanhef en onder a BW, indien hij de gestolen zaak in een tweedehands winkel van het pandhuis heeft gekocht die voldoet aan de eisen van art. 3:86 lid 3 aanhef en onder a BW. De bestolen eigenaar zal zich voor schadevergoeding kunnen verhalen op het pandhuis. Het pandhuis heeft op grond van art. 3:87 BW bovendien de verplichting om onverwijld aan de bestolen eigenaar de identiteitsgegevens te verschaffen van de pandbelener (de dief).

Limitation Periods and Works of Art

Lars van Vliet[*]

1 Introduction[1]

Ownership of works of art is a fairly uncertain right of ownership. Only in the last few decades has more attention been paid to *provenance research* of artwork. More than in the past, a buyer has an obligation to investigate the provenance of an artwork. In the case of older works of art, their provenance can often only be reconstructed for their recent past. Sales, inheritances and other transfers in the distant past can often no longer be determined with certainty. Both bona fide purchaser protection and limitation periods can provide protection against these uncertainties. The more restrictive a legal system is in granting protection to bona fide acquirers, the more important the limitation periods become. The limitation period then determines the starting point from which the provenance research must be carried out. Certain countries, such as the United States of America, which are extremely reluctant to grant third-party protection, are also extremely reluctant to allow limitation of actions blocking the action to reclaim possession. As a result, a stolen work of art can be claimed back even hundreds of years after the theft. To many lawyers in continental Europe this outcome is unacceptable, because it is impossible to analyse the provenance of artwork over a time span of centuries.

The central dilemma is whether a limitation period or prescription period should run against an owner who is unable to reclaim possession, because he does not know where the thing is located and who is in possession. Internationally, this question is answered very differently. Often the owner does not know, and cannot know, where his artwork is located. In several continental European jurisdictions the requirement of "open possession" (also called "public possession") is used to prevent a limitation period from running against an owner as long as the owner cannot know who is in possession of the artwork. The requirement of open possession finds its roots in Roman law, was adopted in the *ius commune* and the 1804 French civil code, and thus also influenced modern Dutch law. The research will focus on the development in Roman law and the adoption in French

* Maastricht University.

1 This essay, dedicated to Professor Sjef van Erp, is based on a much larger comparative study published in 2018: Lars van Vliet, Verjaring en kunstvoorwerpen, *in*: M.A. Loth and L.P.W. van Vliet, *Recht over tijd, Hoever reikt het privaatrecht in het verleden?* Preadviezen Nederlandse Vereniging voor Burgerlijk Recht 2018, Zutphen, Paris, 2018, pp. 83-154.

law. In addition, it will show that the application of the requirement of open possession is not suitable to prevent a prescription or limitation period from running against an owner of a stolen movable thing. New Jersey law offers a better alternative to this requirement.

2 THE TRADITIONAL JUSTIFICATION FOR PRESCRIPTION[2]

Limitation periods, both liberating and acquisitive, are based on at least the following two rationales. The first is legal certainty, which is the argument that, over time, the law must adapt to the facts. In the art trade, this relieves the buyer of the obligation to carry out research from the moment the work of art was created. The second rationale is the accusation to the owner that he did not take any action for a long time to reclaim possession, even though he did have the opportunity to do so.

The first ratio, legal certainty, has already been emphasised in Roman law. In D. 41,3,1 (Gaius) we can read the following:

> "Acquisitive prescription has been introduced in the public interest, namely to prevent that ownership of certain goods would remain uncertain for a long time or almost permanently, whereas a fixed time period would be sufficient for the owners to search for the goods that belong to them."

The second rationale, the reproach of negligence or idleness on the part of the owner, is the basis for the rule in property law that no limitation period may run against a person who is not aware of it because he cannot know that his right has been infringed and that he must protect his right in order to avoid a loss of right or action.

The owner of immovable property always knows where his property is located, so he is able to inspect his property.[3] In the *ius commune* and in the original version of the French *Code civil* (the version in force until 2008), the owner even had a longer period of time to reclaim possession if he lived further away from the property (*inter absentes*) than an owner who lived in the same province where the property was located (*inter praesentes*).[4] This

2 See in general M. Schermaier, 'Contemporary use of Roman rules: Prescription and Limitation in the Usus Modernus Pandectarum', *in*: J.H. Dondorp, D.J. Ibbetson & E.J.H. Schrage (eds.), *Limitation and Prescription: A Comparative Legal History*, Berlin, Duncker & Humblot, 2019, *Comparative Studies in Continental and Anglo-American Legal History*, vol. 33., ch. 10, par. II.2 and par. III.2.

3 Cf. Scottish Law Commission, *Discussion paper on Prescription and Title to Moveable Property*, 2010, nr. 144, par. 6.13.

4 See C. 7,35,7. Art. 2265 (old number and old text): 'Celui qui acquiert de bonne foi et par juste titre un immeuble en prescrit la propriété par dix ans, si le véritable propriétaire habite dans le ressort de la cour royale [la cour d'appel] dans l'étendue de laquelle l'immeuble est situé; et par vingt ans, s'il est domicilié hors dudit ressort'. As this distinction no longer serves any purpose, in 2008 the prescription period was uniformly set at ten years. See L. Béteille, *Rapport portant réforme de la prescription de matière civile*, Sénat,

difference in term can only be explained if culpability is one of the rationales on which the limitation period is based.[5]

The second rationale, the reproach that the owner has been idle too long, is difficult to apply to movable property. In contrast to immovable property, the owner of movable property that has been stolen or lost often does not know where the property is located. What effect should this lack of knowledge have on the prescription period? If one were to apply this reproach rationale consistently, no prescription period should run against an owner who cannot stop the course of the prescription period: no reproach = no prescription. However, this line of reasoning is at odds with the rationale of legal certainty. For that reason the Dutch Supreme Court rejected this approach and holds that the limitation period for reclaiming possession of stolen movables is not tolled when possession is not open.[6] As a consequence, the possessor may acquire ownership after twenty years of possession, even though the owner cannot prevent this loss of ownership by initiating legal proceedings.[7]

The rules of acquisitive prescription and the rules of limitation of the action of revindication originated in immovable property law. Many institutions of property law were developed in immovable property law, at least strongly influenced by the immovable property. A reason may have been that for centuries land ownership was considered to be of greater social importance[8] than the ownership of movable property and other investments.[9] Since the rules of acquisitive prescription and limitation of actions were also necessary for movable property, these rules, developed for immovable property, were then applied to movable property by way of analogy. This analogous application to movable property has already been codified in the French civil code for the acquisition without good faith after thirty years of possession. Here the problem arises that these rules do not fit in well with movable things, because they are not easy to trace.

Session ordinaire 2007-2008, nos. 83, 54. The reason, which was left unmentioned, is likely to be that nowadays greater distances do not reduce the visibility of infringements and the possibility of taking action against them.

5 These two rationales are discussed in detail in: *Motive zu dem Entwurfe eines Bürgerlichen Gesetzbuches für das Deutsche Reich, vol. 1, Allgemeiner Teil, Amtliche Ausgabe*, Berlin/Leipzig, J. Guttentag, 1888, p. 291 and in the South African judgment Pienaar v. Rabie, 1983 (3) SA p. 126. See about this case C.G. van der Merwe, 'Original acquisition of ownership', *in*: R. Zimmermann & D. Visser (eds.), *Southern Cross*, Oxford: Oxford University Press, 1996, p. 701-725; E.J. Marais, *Acquisitive Prescription in View of the Property Clause*, diss. Stellenbosch 2011, p. 148-149 and 156.

6 Hoge Raad 8 May 1998, ECLI:NL:HR:1998:ZC2644 (Land Sachsen/C.).

7 Artt. 3:105 read with 3:105 Dutch civil code.

8 See for example P.-A. Fenet, *Recueil complet des travaux préparatoires du Code civil*, vol. 15, Paris: Videcoq 1836, p. 591.

9 The great *financial* importance of movable goods was, of course, obvious to the lawyers of that time.

3 Techniques for Not Letting the Prescription Period Run

Legal systems that choose not to allow the prescription or limitation period to run against an owner who is unable to reclaim possession (to revindicate), may achieve this effect in different ways. One method is to toll the limitation or prescription period as long as the possession is not open or public. This technique is used in French law. However, the requirement is not really suitable to the purpose. Many US States take a more nuanced approach with their so-called discovery rule. Even if possession of the stolen thing is not open, the limitation period is not tolled if the owner knew or could have known where his property was. It often requires the dispossessed owner to be active in searching auction and museum catalogues.

A historical analysis will show that originally the requirement of open possession was not developed to prevent a prescription period from running. Without any clear reason the requirement of open possession was introduced into the law of prescription. It may be a perfect match for immovable property, by coincidence, but it is not suitable to stolen movables.

4 Some Historical Remarks About the Requirement of Publicity

4.1 *From Roman Law via the French Code Civil*[10]

Article 2229 (old) *Code civil* read: "Pour pouvoir prescrire, il faut une possession continue et non interrompue, paisible, publique, non équivoque, et à titre de propriétaire." Troplong and Duranton, among others, indicate that the requirement of *possession publique* is a translation of the Roman law requirement that possession is not covert (*nec clam*).[11]

Then there is a question where this requirement *nec clam* comes from. In Roman law we do not encounter this requirement as a requirement for acquisitive prescription, neither in classical Roman law nor in Justinianian law. Under classical Roman law, there are two legal institutions that are similar to our acquisitive prescription: the *usucapio* and the *longi temporis praescriptio*. Neither institution requires open ownership. However, we find the

10 For the prescription in Roman law in general, see: J.E. Jansen, *Bezit te kwader trouw, verkrijgende en bevrijdende verjaring* (diss. Groningen), The Hague, Boom Juridische Uitgevers, 2011; H. Dondorp, 'Limitation and prescription in Justinian's Corpus Iuris Civilis', in: J.H. Dondorp, D.J. Ibbetson & E.J.H. Schrage (eds.), *Limitation and Prescription: A Comparative Legal History*, Berlin, Duncker & Humblot, 2019, *Comparative Studies in Continental and Anglo-American Legal History*, vol. 33., chapter 1.

11 R.Th. Troplong, *Le droit civil expliqué suivant l'ordre du code, De la prescription*, vol. 1, Brussels, Tarlier, 1835, nr. 351; A. Duranton, *Cours de droit français: suivant le code civil*, vol. 21, Paris, Thorel, 1837, nr. 206 and 213.

requirement in a completely different area, namely in the interdicts for the protection of possession. Both the interdict for the protection of possession of immovables and the interdict for the protection of possession of movables require that possession of the thing should not have been taken by force, or secretly or as a mere detentor (so-called precarious possession): *nec vi, nec clam, nec precario*, or in full *nec vi nec clam nec precario ab adversario*. This interdict could even be invoked against the true owner. Precarious possession means that someone is in possession of the thing with the revocable consent of someone else. In the system of the French civil code, this precarist could be regarded as a possessor. In doing so, the code stands in a long Roman law tradition. In Dutch law, however, this person would be called a detentor (*houder*) and cannot be regarded as a possessor because he does not possess *as of right* but rather possesses for another person. The original function of these possessory interdicts was to prevent people from taking the law into their own hands. The owner was not allowed to take the property from another person by self-help, but he was forced to recover possession by proving his right of ownership in a legal proceeding of *rei vindicatio*. However, if the possessor of the object had acquired the object by force or secretly, or if he was only the precarious possessor for the revindicating owner, the owner could take possession of the object by means of self-help, so that he could benefit from the presumption that the possessor is the owner in a proceeding of revindication.

While servitudes can be obtained by *usucapio* under pre-classical law, they are prohibited by the Lex Scribonia under classical law. Later, however, a way was found to obtain a protected position through the long user of servitudes. This protection is based on the actual exercise of a servitude (*usus*). As under classical law the possession of a right is impossible, this possession is called *quasi possessio*. It must comply with the requirements of the *possessio ad interdicta*, so that the requirements *nec vi, nec clam, nec precario* are also set for the protection of this user. It is controversial whether this long-term user led to the *acquisition* of the right of servitude or only to *protection* by an *actio utilis* or interdict.[12]

For the *usucapio* and the *longi temporis praescriptio* it was unnecessary to impose these three requirements of *nec vi, nec clam, nec precario*. Both *usucapio* and *longi temporis praescriptio* require a *iusta causa*, or *iustum initium*, and *bona fides*. The requirement of *iusta causa* or *iustum initium* meant that possession had to be based on a legal ground that could lead to acquisition. And *bona fides*, although not entirely, largely corresponds to the current concept of good faith. A thing that had been taken by force or secretly could not be obtained by prescription due to a lack of *iusta causa* and *bona fides*. As a result, it makes no sense to demand, in addition, that the possession be *nec vi* and *nec clam*. The precarist

12 Zie D. Nörr, *Die Entstehung der longi temporis praescriptio*, Cologne/Opladen, Westdeutscher Verlag, 1969, p. 56.

cannot obtain by prescription because he has no possession. It is therefore no longer necessary to make this requirement explicit.

The only places in the Digest where the three *necs* are mentioned in the context of long-term user is the protection of servitudes, exercised for a long time, for which no act of grant can be proven. These places are D. 8,5,10 pr. and D. 39,3,1,23. In the latter passage these servitudes are called *quasi servitus*. The rules on the long-term use of servitudes fulfilled practically the same function as acquisitive prescription. Doctrinally, however, it must be distinguished from acquisitive prescription. Although prescription of servitudes was possible under pre-classical law,[13] this possibility had been abolished by the Lex Scribonia.[14] In later centuries, however, this protected long-term use of servitudes was interpreted as acquisitive prescription. The long-term use was not only protected against the owner of the servient property but also against third parties who infringed the right of use, says Ulpian in D. 8,5,10 pr. The protection takes various forms. In D. 8,5,10 pr. Ulpian indicates that the actual use is protected by an *actio utilis*. In D. 39,3,1,23 he speaks of an *actio utilis in rem* and an interdict. Because, strictly speaking, the long-term user of a servitude does not lead to acquisitive prescription, the requirements of *iusta causa*, or at least *iustum initium*, and *bona fides*[15] do not apply here. Perhaps the requirements *nec vi, nec clam, nec precario* partly took over the function of good faith. And the requirement of *nec precario* prevents that a limitation period will run against an owner who has given permission for the user. In the case of acquisitive prescription of *ownership*, acquisitive prescription in favour of a detentor would already be prevented by the requirements of *iustum initium* and *bona fides*.

The Code of Justinian does recognise the acquisitive prescription of servitudes (C. 3,34 and C. 7,33,12,4) but does not require *nec vi, nec clam, nec precario* (see also C. 7,33,2). D. 8,5,10 is more akin to protection of possession, i.e. possession which the owner can no longer oppose (hence the requirements *nec vi, nec clam, nec precario*).

Classical Roman law has never used the requirement of open possession to prevent the revindication of the owner of stolen property from being time-barred when the owner could not know where the property and its possessor were located. Stolen goods (*res furtivae)* were excluded from *usucapio* by the Lex Atinia (Paulus D. 41,3,4,6).[16] They could only be acquired by prescription when they had returned into the power of the owner (*reversio*). For our subject it is important to know that such a *reversio* was not only deemed present when the thing was actually returned into the owner's possession but also when

13 C. Möller, *Die Servituten*, Göttingen, Wallstein Verlag 2010, p. 185-186 and 190.

14 C. Möller, *Die Servituten*, Göttingen, Wallstein Verlag 2010, p. 235-250 and 326.

15 D. Nörr, *Die Entstehung der longi temporis praescriptio*, Cologne/Opladen, Westdeutscher Verlag, 1969, p. 56.

16 J.E. Jansen, *Bezit te kwader trouw, verkrijgende en bevrijdende verjaring* (diss. Groningen), The Hague, Boom Juridische Uitgevers, 2011, nr. 11.

the owner had the opportunity to revindicate but did not make use of this opportunity (Paulus D. 50,16,215). In such a case, there was apparently no longer any good reason to exclude prescription.[17]

4.2 *The Old French Customary Law, Pothier and the* Code Civil[18]

Many centuries later in the French *Code civil* we find "the three *necs*", as I will call them, in the law of prescription. It is not possible, in the context of this study, to ascertain when and how these three *necs* were introduced into French law. The first version of the Paris *coutumes* from 1510 mentions the requirement of open possession (possession publique) already in their French-language counterpart in article 68: "Saucun a joüy usé & possedé daucun heritaige par lespace de trente ans continuellement tant par luy que par ses prédecesseurs franchement publicquement & sans aucune inquietation; supposé quil ne face apparoir de titre il a acquis prescription entre aagez & non previlegiez."[19,20] Du Moulin also mentions the three *necs* in his treatise on the *Coutume de Paris.*[21] They are also mentioned by Le Camus d'Houlouve in his treatise on the *coutumes de Boulonnais.*[22] Pothier, then finally, mentions the three *necs* as requirements for acquisitive prescription of ownership in his book on the customary law of Orléans.[23] In the French *droit coutumier*

17 It was only under Justinianian law that stolen things (but not things taken by force) could be acquired by prescription after 30 years of possession. See C. 7,39,8,1 and 2; M. Kaser, *Das römische Privatrecht*, vol. 2, *Die nachklassischen Entwicklungen*, 2nd edition, Munich, C.H. Beck'sche Verlagsbuchhandlung, 1975, par. 243.

18 See in general: D. Deroussin, 'Praescriptione omnia iura tolluntur. Les prescriptions dans l'Ancien Droit français', and: D. Deroussin, 'Le droit français des prescriptions depuis 1804, ou l'impossible simplicité', in: J.H. Dondorp, D.J. Ibbetson & E.J.H. Schrage (eds.), *Limitation and Prescription: A Comparative Legal History*, Berlin, Duncker & Humblot, 2019, *Comparative Studies in Continental and Anglo-American Legal History*, vol. 33., ch. 12 and 14.

19 Th. Baillet & R. Barme (ed.), *Les coustumes generalles de la prevoste et viconte de Paris*, Paris, Guillaume Eustace, 1513 (http://catalogue.bnf.fr/ark:/12148/cb33333042k). This Article later became Article 118 of the revised *coutume*, adding a few words to the text.

20 In the *coutume of* Paris, however, the requirement of *nec vi* has disappeared. This *coutume* does state that the possession must be 'sans aucune inquiétation', but that term does not mean 'without violence' but 'without interruption'. C. de Ferrière, *Commentaire sur la coutume de la prévôté et vicomté de Paris*, part 1, Paris, Le Boucher, 1787; Pothier (Bugnet, ed.), *Traité de la prescription*, vol. 9, Paris : Videcoq Père et Fils/ Cosse et N. Delamott 1846, 1re partie, ch II, nr. 51, p. 334-335.

21 Du Moulin, *Coutumes de la prévôté et vicomté de Paris avec les notes de M. C. Du Moulin*, vol. I, Paris, H. Charpentier, 1691, Titre VI, De Prescription: 'C'est la prescription légale ou de droit (...) En elles sont requises trois choses, titulus, bona fides, continuatio possessionis temporis lege definiti (...). Davantage entre âgez & non privilegiez, nec vi, nec clam, nec precario.'

22 B.-L. Le Camus d'Houlouve, *Coutumes du Boulonnois, conférées avec les coutumes de Paris, d'Artois, de Ponthieu, d'Amiens & de Montreuil*, vol. 2, Paris, F.-A. Didot, 1777, p. 122.

23 Pothier (Bugnet, ed.), *Œuvres de Pothier*, vol. 1, *Coutume d'Orléans*, XIV, 16, Paris, Videcoq Père et Fils / Cosse et N. Delamott, 1845, p. 333.

we come across the three *necs*, or at least the requirement of open possession, in the rules on prescription.

Already in classical Roman law the concept of "defective possession" can be found and discussions are taking place when possession is to be labelled as covert.[24] When we make a small leap in time, we see that Bartolus[25] and Balbo[26] subdivide defects in possession into *vitia personalia* (personal defects) and *vitia realia* (real defects that run with the thing when transferred to another person).

In his *Traité de la possession*, Pothier has classified the requirements *nec vi* and *nec clam* together with, among other things, bad faith under the term defects of possession (*vices de possession*), so that these defects also indirectly block the acquisitive prescription.[27] Pothier argues that in order to acquire ownership by way of prescription, it is necessary to have "une possession civile et de bonne foi, qui procède d'un juste titre, qui a été publique, paisible, et non interrompue."[28] Although the three *necs* are not literally mentioned here, they can be found in other words.[29]

In article 2229 *Code civil*, now renumbered 2260, we find at least two of the three *necs*, namely *nec clam* (*publique*) and *nec precario* (*titre de propriétaire*). We also find the term *paisible* here, but a separate provision is devoted to the absence of violence, namely article 2233, now renumbered as 2263: "*Les actes de violence ne peuvent fonder non plus une possession capable d'opérer la prescription. La possession utile ne commence que lorsque la violence a cessé.*"

According to the *travaux préparatoires* of the *Code civil*, the term *violence* here has the same meaning as in the Roman law rule, which excluded stolen and looted goods from acquisitive prescription. However, the French legislator explicitly rejected the Roman rule that things that had been removed by force from their owner were completely excluded from acquisitive prescription, even if the things had later come into the hands of a possessor

24 D. 41,2,6.

25 Comment on D. 41,2,13, in: *In I Partem Digesti Novi Bartoli A Saxoferrato Commentaria*, Basel, Episcopius, 1588, p. 264-265.

26 J.F. Balbo, *Tractatus de praescriptionibus*, Speyer 1610, p. 148-150.

27 Pothier (Bugnet, red.), *Œuvres de Pothier*, vol. 9, *Traité de la possession, I, III*, Paris, Videcoq Père et Fils / Pod et N. Delamott 1846, p. 273-275.

28 Pothier (Bugnet, red.), *Œuvres de Pothier*, vol. 9, *Traité de la prescription*, nr. 26, Paris, Videcoq Père et Fils / Pod et N. Delamott 1846, p. 327.

29 Pothier indicates that the Roman law rule that *res furtivae* and *res vi possessae* (objects obtained by theft or violence) cannot be obtained by means of *usucapio*, not even by successive acquirers in good faith, has probably not been adopted in French law. Pothier (Bugnet, ed.), *Œuvres de Pothier*, vol. 9, *Traité de la prescription*, Paris, Videcoq Père et Fils/ Cosse et N. Delamott, 1846, 2e partie, art. III, nr. 204, p. 388. This is also accepted by Berroyer and Laurière in their adaptation of Duplessis' comment on the *coutume*: 'Traité des prescriptions', I, 1, in: *Traitez de Mr Duplessis sur la Coutume de Paris*, Paris, Gosselin, 1699, p. 230. This also confirms that these prescription requirements also apply to movable property.

(in good faith or in bad faith) who had *not* been guilty of violence. Hence the rule in article 2263 that violence only tolls the prescription period as long as the violence lasts.[30]

4.3 *The Usefulness of the Three* Necs *in the Absence of Good Faith*

What is the purpose of the above description of the three *necs* and the requirement of open possession? In the realm of acquisitive prescription the requirement of open possession is in any case useful from the moment that the law also allows acquisitive prescription without *iusta causa* and *bona fides*. Covert possession is hardly conceivable if it is based on a legal ground and if it is bona fide.[31] This leads to the conclusion that it makes little sense to impose the requirement of open possession in addition to the requirement of good faith. At the very most, it could be said that openness or publicity of possession (which, unlike covertness, does not indicate intent) is easier to demonstrate than a lack of good faith. In protecting the long user of a servitude under Roman law, the *nec clam* requirement ensured that no limitation period could run against the owner of the servient property without that owner being aware of it, a function that the *nec clam* requirement still has in modern Dutch law of servitudes.[32] The protection of long user was not subject to the requirements of a *iusta causa* and *bona fides*. In the case of acquisition of prescription of the *property* where requirements *iusta causa* and *bona fides* did apply, the requirement of *nec clam* had little added value. This is different if the law also allows for prescription without a legal ground and good faith. Only then can *nec clam* acquire its own meaning. In any case, the requirement of open possession is spelled out in the French Code and in the old Dutch Civil Code as a general condition for all cases of acquisitive prescription. In doing so, it may have been overlooked that the requirement only has an independent role in the absence of a legal ground and good faith.

Under French law, the owner of a movable property acquires ownership of the property after thirty years, even if he did not begin to own it in good faith.[33] In the original version of the *Code civil* this was laid down in article 2262. It codified what was already in force in France according to Roman law and many *coutumes*.[34] When French prescription law was revised in 2008, this article was replaced by article 2227. Strictly speaking, that article

30 P.-A. Fenet, *Recueil complet des travaux préparatoires du Code civil*, vol. 15, Paris, Videcoq, 1836, p. 582.

31 This is probably the reason why Domat considers the person who secretly takes possession of a thing as being in bad faith and, as a result of his bad faith, as being unable to acquire by prescription. Domat, *Les loix civiles*, Paris, Robustel, 1723, Part 1, III, VII, I (De la nature de la possession), 12.

32 L.P.W. van Vliet, 'Verjaring en erfdienstbaarheid', NTBR 2004, nr. 5, p. 206-225.

33 As far as the right of prescription prior to 2008 is concerned, still confirmed by Cour d'Appel d'Aix-en-Provence, 26 October 2006, no. 719 (*Alexander Calder* case). It is understandable that there was no cassation complaint against this holding in *Cour de Cassation*, civ 1er, 19 March 2009, no. 07-12.290.

34 P. van Bemmelen, *Le système de la propriété mobilière*, Leiden/Paris, Brill/Larose et Forcel, 1887, p. 339-345.

refers only to immovable property. However, according to a majority opinion in the literature, the thirty-year prescription also applies to movable property, so that the old rule has continued to apply.[35] It is true that French law holds that the action of revindication does not underlie any limitation period (article 2227 *Code civil*), but when even a mala fide possessor becomes the owner after thirty years, this statement means less than it seems at first glance. The right of ownership which forms the basis of the action of revindication lapses when the possessor becomes the owner by virtue of the acquisitive prescription. It is then somewhat misleading to say that the revindication is not time-barred. Although the revindication is not subject to any limitation period, it lapses when the possessor acquires ownership through prescription. The imprescriptibility of the revindication therefore only means that ownership and the revindication do not lapse as a result of non user.[36]

In applying the requirement of open possession to the revindication of movables French courts struggle with the question what constitutes open or covert possession. The French *Court of Cassation* does not allow the limitation period to run as long as the thing is *deliberately* hidden and remains hidden.[37] Within the category of covert possession, French case law therefore makes a distinction according to whether the possessor *intended* to conceal possession from the owner. This subjective element is understandably deduced from the facts of the case, as the following judgments show.

In a case involving the possession of bearer papers, the *Cour de Cassation* considered the issue:

> Attendu cependant que la détention de titres au porteur, non susceptibles d'un usage commun, dans un coffre qu'elle avait loué sans se dissimuler n'est pas de nature à vicier la possession de Mme Z ... , qui, défenderesse à l'action en revendication exercée au nom de la succession, n'avait pas à prouver l'origine de ces meubles, sa seule possession valant titre.[38]

---

35 Ph. Malaurie and L. Aynès, Les *biens, 6th* edition Paris : LGDJ 2015 nr. 582; B. Grimonprez, *Répertoire de droit civil, Prescription acquisitive*, January 2010 (actualisation: March 2018), no. 12. See on this subject J. Van de Voorde, *De verkrijgende verjaring, De nalatenschap van Rome heroverwogen* (diss. Antwerpen 2017), Brugge, Die Keure, 2018, nr. 766-767 and 1302.

36 L.P.W. van Vliet, in: S. van Erp & B. Akkermans (eds.), *Ius Commune Casebooks for the Common Law of Europe, Cases, Materials and Text on Property Law*, Oxford/Portland, Oregon, Hart Publishing, 2012, explanation of case nr. 7.45.

37 This is in line with the old French law prior to the code. See D. Deroussin, 'Praescriptione omnia iura tolluntur. Les prescriptions dans l'Ancien Droit Français', in: J.H. Dondorp, D.J. Ibbetson & E.J.H. Schrage (eds.), *Limitation and Prescription: A Comparative Legal History*, Berlin, Duncker & Humblot, 2019, *Comparative Studies in Continental and Anglo-American Legal History*, vol. 33., chapter. 12, par. V3b.

38 *Cour de Cassation*, civ. 1re, 11 June 1991, no 89-20422, Bull. civ. I, no 199.

What plays a role here is the question of how open the possession of such items tends to be in the given circumstances and, when the item is in a vault, whether a bona fide possessor might also have a reason to keep the item in a vault. The term "*possession viciée*" means that possession does not have the normal consequences, such as protection of bona fide third parties or acquisitive prescription. On the other hand, in a case where a suspect had hidden bearer documents in his house where the police found them during a search, the *Cour de Cassation* assumed that the possession was defective because the possessor had intended to keep his possessions hidden.[39] It is unclear from which facts the *Cour de Cassation* derives this intention.

No intention of concealment was assumed in the following case. It concerned the revindication of a rare first edition of the complete works of Balzac, dedicated by the author to the Marquise de Castries, bound in uniform Morocco bindings bearing in gold the coat of arms of Baron d'Aldenburg. They were first placed in a private library and then placed in cardboard boxes in a cave. The *Tribunal de Grande Instance*, Paris held:

> La simple circonstance que des ouvrages rares aient été conservés dans une bibliothèque familiale, puis placés dans des cartons et rangés dans une cave, ne révèle qu'une précaution de conservation et des modalités de garde et, en tout cas, aucune tentative de dissimulation de nature à rendre suspecte la possession (...).

The revindication was therefore rejected.[40]

The heirs of the famous Parisian art dealer Ambroise Vollard wanted to reclaim some of the paintings from the heirs of Erich Slomovic, who had taken them with him on his flight to Yugoslavia in 1940. The plaintiffs tried to refute the defence of acquisitive prescription by arguing that the possession was covert. It was established that the possession was initially open, and the *Cour d'Appel* of Paris concluded from this that the possession would not quickly become covert if the paintings were stored in a vault:

> Considérant qu'il est ainsi établi que la possession d'Erich Slomovic sur les oeuvres en litige s'est exercée publiquement, en janvier 1940, et même en 1939, qu'elle n'était pas ignorée des ayants droit d'Ambroise Vollard, des lors que le frère de celui-ci, Lucien, était un familier d'Erich Slomovic; que dans sa lettre du 1er mars 1940, M. Milosaljevic fait état d'informations recueillies auprès de M. Martin Fabiani, qui participait alors à l'administration de la galerie Vollard, et qui a déclaré qu'Erich Slomovic n'avait « qu'un petit nombre de choses »,

39 *Cour de Cassation*, civ. 1re, 8 March 2005, no 03-14.610, Bull. civ. I, no 123, JCP 2005. I. 181, no 4.

40 TGI Paris, 30 November 1988, D. 1990. Somm. 87.

> appréciation explicable par l'immensité de la collection Vollard; que la publicité n'a pu disparaitre par la détention des objets dans un coffre de banque, alors que celle-ci a été commandée par les circonstances exceptionnelles de l'époque de guerre, et le voyage en Yougoslavie d'Erich Slomovic qui a d'ailleurs signalé l'existence du coffre dans la lettre adressée à Matisse le 17 mars 1941 (...).[41]

Due to the presence of many factors that argue in favour of the open nature of the possession, it is difficult to determine what, without these factors, the influence of storage in the vault would have been on the open nature of the possession.

Since a court will never be able to ascertain the possessor's subjective intention, the possessor's intention is simply inferred from the facts of the case. However, the function of this element of intention is already covered by the much broader concept of bad faith. What is more, introducing this "possessor's intention" may run counter to the choice of the legislator. If the French code allows acquisition of ownership by a bad faith possessor after thirty years' possession, that deliberate choice may be undermined if the courts hold that no prescription period runs as long as the possessor had the intention to hide the thing.

In Dutch law open possession is also a requirement of limitation of the action of revindication and acquisitive prescription. However, the Dutch Supreme Court does not apply the requirement to the revindication of *movables*, and allows the limitation period to run against an owner who is unable to reclaim possession because he does not know where his thing is and who is in possession of it.[42]

A middle position is taken by some of the US States, such as Ney Jersey, where a limitation period may start to run against the owner despite the fact that he does not know where his thing is located. A limitation period starts running from the moment he could have discovered the location of the thing and its possessor after careful research.

5 The New Jersey Discovery Rule

5.1 Farewell to the Regime of Adverse Possession

In the past, the US also applied to movable property the regime of prescription as it had developed in real estate law. This regime is called "*adverse possession*", referring to property

41 Cour d'Appel Paris, October 3, 1990, Gaz. Pal. 1991. 1. 113, note P. Frémond.

42 Hoge Raad 8 May 1998, ECLI:NL:HR:1998:ZC2644 (Land Sachsen/C.).

that infringes another person's right of ownership (adverse).[43] In the meantime, for movable property this doctrine has been exchanged for the *discovery rule* or, in the state of New York, for the *demand and refusal rule.*[44] In the *O'Keeffe v. Snyder* case, the Supreme Court of New Jersey applied the *discovery rule* for the first time to a stolen painting.[45] The Court held:

> Similarly, we conclude that the discovery rule applies to an action for replevin of a painting under N.J.S.A. 2A:14-1. O'Keeffe's cause of action accrued when she first knew, or reasonably should have known through the exercise of due diligence, of the cause of action, including the identity of the possessor of the paintings.

One could argue that the *discovery rule* is a more sophisticated instrument than openness of possession because it not only takes into account the openness of possession, but also the attempts that the owner has made, or could have made, to trace the thing.

With the transition to the *discovery rule*, US law moved in the direction of Roman law, which had a similar rule based on *actual knowledge*. A stolen thing was excluded from prescription under classical Roman law and only became subject to prescription again after the thing had returned into the power of the owner (*reversio*). However, this *reversio* was interpreted extensively. D. 50,16,215 (Paul) indicates: "Further Sabinus and Cassius say that in the case of the Lex Atinia a stolen thing is considered to have already come into the power of the owner, if he has the possibility to reclaim it with the revindication." Acquisitive prescription was therefore possible if the owner had the possibility to revindicate but had not done so.[46]

5.2 *Restrictions on the Right of Return*

Under New Jersey law, the limitation period may start to run before the owner knows who is in possession of his thing. New Jersey law is not based on the moment of *actual discovery* but on the moment of *constructive discovery*: the moment at which a reasonably cautious

43 Cf. New Jersey Court of Errors and Appeals, 8 September 1942 *Redmond v. New Jersey Historical Society*, 132 N.J. Eq. 464, 28 A.2d 189.

44 All States except New York apply the discovery rule in some form. New York law gives the owner even more protection against prescription by applying *the demand and refusal rule* instead. Under the latter doctrine the limitation period does not begin until the owner has reclaimed the thing from the possessor and this return has been refused.

45 *O'Keeffe v. Snyder*, Supreme Court of New Jersey, July 17, 1980, 83 N.J. 478, 416 A.2d 862.

46 J.E. Jansen, *Bezit te kwader trouw, verkrijgende en bevrijdende verjaring (diss. Groningen)*, Den Haag: Boom Juridische Uitgevers, 2011, nr. 11 and 38.

owner could and should have discovered where his thing is located and who the possessor is. The law thus imposes a so-called *duty of due diligence* on the plaintiff. The owner must therefore make sufficient efforts to trace the thing after the loss of possession. In the case of artwork that often demands continuous research of auction catalogues, exhibition catalogues, museum catalogues and other relevant publications. To avoid any misunderstanding: this *due diligence* has nothing to do with the duty of care and investigation that a buyer must observe in order to be considered a bona fide buyer.

6 Conclusion

In many jurisdictions based on Roman law, acquisitive prescription requires open or public possession. It is unclear what the origin and what the rationale of this requirement is. In classical Roman law open possession was not a requirement for acquisitive prescription of ownership. It was a requirement for the protection of someone who had exercised a servitude for a long time. For some reason the requirement founds its way into the rules on acquisition of ownership. Actually, it fits well into the rules on immovable property. However, the requirement becomes problematic when applied to movables. What does it mean to have open possession of a movable thing? In the case of stolen movables, adhering strictly to the requirement of openness could easily make limitation of actions and acquisitive prescription virtually impossible. French case law shows how French law struggles to apply the requirement to stolen movables. The Dutch Supreme Court even took the decision to disregard the requirement regarding stolen movables. It holds that a limitation period may run against the owner despite the fact that the owner does not know where his thing is located and who is in possession. Ney Jersey takes a middle position. It abolished the old doctrine of adverse possession and applies the discovery rule. Even if possession of the movable thing is not open, a limitation period may run against the owner from the time he should have known where his thing is located. It imposes on the owner a certain duty to search for his thing.

PROPERTY TORTS AND THE RESTATEMENTS

Peter B Kutner[*]

Among Sjef van Erp's many distinctions is membership in the American Law Institute. The ALI is primarily a body of American judges, legal academics and practicing lawyers, but it also includes a number of eminent jurists from other countries. Since his election to membership in 2011, Professor van Erp has been an active participant in ALI projects and meetings. He has also been active in the interaction of the European Law Institute with the American Law Institute.

The ALI is best known, both within the United States and internationally, for its publication of Restatements of the Law. Restatements are intended to be comprehensive statements of American common law – the law developed and articulated by judges in the course of deciding cases – in various fields of law. Some Restatements also reflect statutory enactments.[1] Work on a Restatement of Property and a Restatement of Torts commenced in the 1920s and resulted in publication of multiple volumes in the 1930s and 1940s. A comprehensive Restatement (Second) of Torts was completed in 1979. There are also second and third Restatements of Property, but they do not include all of the subjects covered in the first Restatement. For some years the ALI has been engaged in producing a Restatement (Third) of Torts for segments of tort law, and work has commenced on a Restatement (Fourth) of Property. The Property and Torts Restatements have been among the ALI's largest and most influential projects.

Many tort actions involve interference with property interests. Property concepts and rights have a great bearing on tort liability, and a number of torts are specifically torts to property. The Restatement rules of liability are to be found in the Restatements of Torts rather than the Restatements of Property. Nevertheless, rules for property torts are to be included in the Restatement (Fourth) of Property.

This contribution examines connections between tort law and property and the Restatements' treatment of tort liability for loss of, damage to or interference with property interests.

---

* Hugh Roff Professor of Law Emeritus, The University of Oklahoma; Life Member, The American Law Institute.

1 See American Law Institute, *Capturing the Voice of the American Law Institute*, Philadelphia, American Law Institute, 2015, at pp. 4-6.

1 Tort Law and Property Interests

Tort law provides individuals and juristic persons with a claim for monetary damages when they have suffered harm or loss. In some circumstances a tort cause of action can also be a ground for an injunction issued to prevent harm or loss. Whether a plaintiff can maintain a tort action depends primarily upon the type of interest affected and the nature of the defendant's conduct. Potential liability protects many types of interests from conduct intended to cause harm and other intentional interference. Relatively few interests are protected against unintentional harm, but these include bodily safety, ownership or possession of tangible property, and personal reputation.[2]

A long-held traditional view was that tort law protected only interests of person and property. An outgrowth of this was an artificially extended concept of property interests to support recognition of a cause of action or the grant of an equitable remedy, such as an injunction. Examples included interests in reputation, in the conduct of a trade or business, in controlling the publication of unpublished writings, and even the enjoyment of spousal consortium. This was trenchantly criticized by the prominent scholar Leon Green, who contended that most intangible interests should be viewed as "relational" interests for purposes of tort liability rather than as property interests. He would treat as property interests only interests in tangible property.[3]

The first Restatement of Torts contained provisions for torts pertaining to most of the interests identified by Green. It did not adopt Green's classifications of interests, but it refrained from characterization as a property interest anything other than an interest in land or chattels.[4] Specific property torts in the Restatement were some type of interference with land (including water and air rights) or chattels. The general tort of negligence and the strict liability torts applied when there was physical harm to property, so the property would be tangible in form rather than an intangible "property" interest of some type.

2 See C. Sappideen & P. Vines, *Fleming's The Law of Torts*, 10th ed., Sydney, Thomson Reuters, 2011, at pp. 5-7.

3 L. Green, 'Relational Interests', *Illinois Law Review*, Vol. 29, No. 4, 1934, pp. 460-490, at pp. 460-462; L. Green, 'Basic Concepts: Persons, Property, Relations', *American Bar Association Journal*, Vol. 24, No. 1, 1938, pp. 65-69, at pp. 65-66. Green classified the relational interests relevant to tort liability as (1) family relations, (2) trade relations (commercial and employment relations), (3) political and professional relations, and (4) general social relations.

4 The provisions on liability for disparagement (injurious falsehood) included disparagement of property in intangibles as well as land and chattels, but disparagement was not characterized as an invasion of a property interest. Rest. Torts §§ 624-629.

This is now the conventional view, reflected in subsequent Restatements[5] and the leading American treatises on tort law.[6] The application of tort law to "property" is in torts that apply to tangible property – land and chattels – either as specific torts to property or negligence and strict liability torts. It is also conventional in American law to treat liability for interference with intellectual property rights as a subject outside tort law, at least as to intellectual property rights created by statute.[7] Interference with what could be viewed as common law intellectual property rights was included in the first Restatement of Torts. However, it was excluded from the second Restatement. It is now in the Restatement of Unfair Competition.[8]

2 Negligence and Strict Liability for Harm to Property

Physical harm to property caused by negligent conduct is a very common instance of tort liability. As explicitly stated in both the first and second Restatements of Torts,[9] the rules on what constitutes negligence or contributory negligence and causation of harm are the same in cases of physical harm to land or chattels as in cases of bodily harm. The Restatement (Third) of Torts: Liability for Physical and Emotional Harm applies common principles of liability for "negligence causing physical harm".[10] "Physical harm" includes physical impairment of real property and tangible personal property – what is typically termed "property damage" – but not impairment of intangible property interests.[11]

The first and second Restatements' provisions on strict liability – that is, liability without proof of the defendant's negligence or intent – have been very influential in shaping American tort law.[12] It can be broadly stated that for strict liability, as for negligence, the rules of liability for tangible property damage are the same as for liability for personal

5 Rest. 2d Torts; Rest. 3d Torts – Physical Harm.

6 D.B. Dobbs, P.T. Hayden & E.M. Bublick, *Hornbook on Torts*, 2nd ed., St. Paul, West Academic, 2016; F.V. Harper, F. James, Jr. & O.S. Gray, *Harper, James and Gray on Torts*, 3rd ed., New York, Aspen, 2006; W.P. Keeton, *Prosser and Keeton on the Law of Torts*, 5th ed., St. Paul, West, 1984.

7 Primarily the federal copyright, patent and trademark statutes and state trademark laws.

8 The Restatement of Unfair Competition contains provisions on liability for unfair competition (wrongful use of trade names, designs, etc.), disclosure or use of trade secrets, and infringement of the right of publicity. It also contains references to common law copyright and to the misappropriation doctrine of *International News Service v. Associated Press*, 248 U.S. 215 (1918), which the Restatement disapproves.

9 Rest. Torts §§ 497-499; Rest. 2d Torts §§ 497-499.

10 Rest. 3d Torts – Physical Harm § 6.

11 Rest. 3d Torts – Physical Harm § 4.

12 Rest. Torts §§ 504-524 (harm caused by animals and ultrahazarous activities); Rest. 2d Torts §§ 402A-402B (harm caused by product defects and misrepresentations in sales of products), §§ 504-524A (harm caused by animals and abnormally dangerous activities). In the third Restatement: Rest. 3d Torts – Physical Harm §§ 20-25 (harm caused by animals and abnormally dangerous activities); Rest. 3d Torts – Products Liability (harm caused by product defects and misrepresentations in sales of products).

injury and that strict liability does not extend to intangible interests, including intangible property interests.[13] But some qualifications to the first proposition are necessary. Liability for harm caused by "trespass" on land by livestock, like the regular action for trespass to land, has been a tort to property maintainable by the possessor or occupier of the land.[14] However, the third Restatement apparently extends the tort to other persons injured by an animal's intrusion onto land.[15] An action under the rule in *Rylands v. Fletcher*[16] for harm caused by an escaping substance is, at least in the English understanding of the rule, limited to the occupier of the land where the damage occurred, as in an action for private nuisance.[17] The Restatements do not have a provision corresponding to the rule in *Rylands v. Fletcher*. Instead, there is strict liability for harm caused by an "ultrahazardous" or "abnormally dangerous" activity, extending to anyone who suffered personal injury or property damage because of the dangers of the activity.[18]

A prominent issue of negligence and strict liability for harm caused by a product defect is whether harm to the defective product itself is to be treated as damage to property. The Restatement (Third) of Products Liability,[19] with the support of a decision of the United States Supreme Court in an admiralty case,[20] treats harm to the defective product itself as an economic loss for which any liability must be found in contract or commercial law, not property damage for which there can be tort liability. Some state cases have allowed an action if the defect created a danger that would be grounds for liability if personal injury or other property damage resulted, or if there was "sudden and calamitous" damage to or destruction of the product because of the defect.[21]

Tort actions requiring physical harm for liability, including negligence and strict liability, require proof of physical impairment to property, not simply physical interference with property.[22] In some instances it is clear that there was physical interference but no impairment of property, and thus no negligence or strict liability – for example, when the plaintiff's machines stopped operating because of a power failure for which the defendant

13 See, in the third Restatement, Rest. 3d Torts – Physical Harm § 4, comments *c*, *e*; Rest. 3d Torts – Products Liability § 1, comment *d*.

14 Rest. Torts § 504(1); Rest. 2d Torts § 504(2).

15 See Rest. 3d Torts – Physical Harm § 21, comment *g*, Reporters' Note.

16 (1868) L.R. 3 H.L. 330, aff'g (1866) L.R. 1 Ex. 265 (Ex. Ch.).

17 See W.E. Peel & J. Goudkamp, *Winfield and Jolowicz on Tort*, 19th ed., London, Sweet & Maxwell, 2014, at pp. 503-504.

18 Rest. Torts §§ 519-520; Rest. 2d Torts §§ 519-520; Rest. 3d Torts – Physical Harm § 23.

19 Rest. 3d Torts – Products Liability § 21.

20 *East River Steamship Corp. v. Transamerica Delaval, Inc.*, 476 U.S. 858 (1986).

21 See J.M. Zitter, 'Strict Products Liability: Recovery for Damage to Product Alone', *American Law Reports (4th)*, Vol. 72, 1989, pp. 12-42. Damage to property other than the defective product might be found if the defect was in a distinct product that was installed on what was damaged or destroyed but not "integrated" into it – for example, a defective window that caused damage to the building it was installed in, or a defective tire that caused destruction of the vehicle it was on.

22 See Rest. 3d Torts – Physical Harm § 4, comments *a*, *c*.

was responsible but there was no damage to the machines or other property.[23] But there are other instances in which it is debatable whether impairment of or harm to property occurred. For example, is there property damage if the defendant caused debris or a flammable substance to spill onto a road, requiring its removal because of the danger, but the road surface was not damaged?[24] Is there impairment of property if a power failure or product defect caused loss of computer data?[25] Or if "contamination" of food products or agricultural land by genetically modified varieties prevented sale of food to organic food markets or to countries which ban imports of genetically modified food?[26] The Restatements do not provide specific guidance on this. When the plaintiff's claim is for harm caused by a defective product, the tendency is to categorize the harm as economic rather than as property damage when this is not clear.[27]

3 PROPERTY TORTS

Tort law contains a number of distinct causes of action that are torts to property. In the first and second Restatements, these are identified as trespass to land,[28] trespass to chattels,[29] conversion,[30] trespass by livestock,[31] private nuisance,[32] withdrawing support from land,[33] and interference with water rights.[34] The individual torts conform to the familiar property

---

23 *E.g. Byrd v. English*, 117 Ga. 191, 43 S.E. 419 (1903). Compare *A.J. Decoster Co. v. Westinghouse Electric Corp.*, 333 Md. 245, 634 A.2d 1330 (1994) (negligence and strict liability action when power failure caused suffocation of over one hundred thousand chickens).

24 See *Attorney General for Ontario v. Fatehi*, [1984] 2 S.C.R. 536, (1984) 15 D.L.R.(4th) 132, rev'g (1981) 34 O.R.(2d) 129, 127 D.L.R.(3d) 603 (C.A) (held to be property damage rather than pure economic loss).

25 See *Transport Corp. of America, Inc. v. International Business Machines Corp., Inc.*, 30 F.3d 953 (8th Cir. 1994) (held to be economic loss).

26 See *Sample v. Monsanto Co.*, 283 F. Supp. 2d 1088 (E.D. Mo. 2003) (treated as economic loss); *In re Genetically Modified Rice Litigation*, 666 F. Supp. 2d 1004 (E.D. Mo. 2009) ("economic loss doctrine" not applied).

27 See *Transport Corp. of America, Inc. v. International Business Machines Corp., Inc.*, *supra* note 25; *Neibarger v. Universal Cooperatives, Inc.*, 439 Mich. 512, 486 N.W.2d 612 (1992) (defective milking machines that caused cows to produce less milk).

28 Rest. Torts §§ 157-166; Rest. 2d Torts §§ 157-166.

29 Rest. Torts §§ 216-222; Rest. 2d Torts §§ 216-222.

30 Rest. Torts §§ 223-243; Rest. 2d Torts §§ 222A-243.

31 Rest. Torts §§ 504-505; Rest. 2d Torts §§ 504-505.

32 Rest. Torts §§ 822-840; Rest. 2d Torts §§ 821A-840E.

33 Rest. Torts §§ 817-821; Rest. 2d Torts §§ 817-821.

34 Rest. Torts §§ 841-864; Rest. 2d Torts §§ 841-864. The Restatements also have a provision on liability for interference with the body of a deceased person. Rest. Torts § 868; Rest. 2d Torts § 868. This could be regarded as interference with the property interest of the person entitled to control the disposition of the body, but more realistically it recognizes liability for family members' emotional distress on account of a body's being mishandled or wrongfully withheld. As noted earlier (in text at notes 14-18), the Restatements do not have a provision for liability on the basis of *Rylands v. Fletcher*, and the third Restatement apparently treats liability for damage caused by animal "trespass" as a strict liability tort extending to any physical harm.

categories of interests in land and interests in chattels (tangible property other than land), with trespass to chattels and conversion being the torts applicable to chattels.[35]

The Restatements' concepts of trespass to land, trespass to chattels and private nuisance differ in important respects from older common law. The distinct rules of liability for trespass to land apply only to intentional entries into the plaintiff's land. An unintentional entry may be labelled as a trespass, but liability is governed by the law of negligence and strict liability.[36] In the second Restatement, flight by aircraft above the land is a trespass only if it enters into the immediate reaches of the air space next to the land and interferes substantially with use and enjoyment of the land.[37] Trespass to chattels is also defined so as to be exclusively an intentional tort, requiring an intentional "intermeddling" with a chattel.[38] Liability for trespass to chattels is limited to instances in which the plaintiff was dispossessed of the chattel or deprived of its use for a substantial time, or where harm to the chattel, other property or the possessor resulted from the trespass. There is no liability for only a brief and harmless trespass to a chattel[39] (unlike a trespass to land).[40] Liability for private nuisance is limited to an interference with the use and enjoyment of land that is either intentional or actionable on grounds of negligence or strict liability (liability for ultrahazardous or abnormally dangerous activities).[41] The second Restatement allows family members living with the possessor of the land to sue for nuisance or trespass when they are harmed in person or property.[42]

The Restatements do maintain the traditional – and sound – position that trespass to chattels and conversion apply only to tangible property that can be physically possessed or interfered with, not to purely intangible property rights.[43] The rules of liability for trespass and conversion ("trover" in older common law) developed over the centuries in

35 The Torts Restatements do not delineate the distinction between chattels and property that is part of land, such as a fixture – defined by Professor E.H. Warren as "realty with a chattel past and the fear of a chattel future". A.J. Casner & W.B. Leach, *Cases and Text on Property*, 2nd ed., Boston, Little, Brown, 1969, at p. 618 n.1.

36 See Rest. Torts §§ 158, 166; Rest. 2d Torts §§ 158, 166.

37 Rest. 2d Torts § 159(2). In the first Restatement, intentional intrusion into air space at any height was trespassory, but reasonable use of air space at heights permitted by legislative regulation was privileged. Rest. Torts § 159, comments *e-f*.

38 Rest. Torts § 217; Rest. 2d Torts § 217.

39 See Rest. Torts § 218; Rest. 2d Torts § 218.

40 See Rest. Torts § 163; Rest. 2d Torts § 163.

41 Rest. Torts § 822; Rest. 2d Torts § 822.

42 Rest. 2d Torts § 162, § 821E, comment *d*. A somewhat obscure provision of the first Restatement allowed a trespass action when the trespass resulted in harm to members of the possessor's household. Rest. Torts § 380.

43 See Rest. Torts §§ 216-217, 221 (trespass to chattels), §§ 223, 242 (conversion); Rest. 2d Torts §§ 216-217, 221 (trespass to chattels), §§ 223, 242 (conversion). The second Restatement does recognize a "liability similar to that for conversion" when one "prevents the exercise of intangible rights of the kind customarily merged in a document" as well as liability when a document into which intangible rights are "merged" has been converted. Rest. 2d Torts § 242.

the context of tangible property. In modern American tort law, under the guidance of the Restatements, trespass and conversion are intentional torts. Trespass to chattels requires intentionally using or "intermeddling" with the chattel or causing its "dispossession".[44] Conversion liability arises from an intentional interference with a chattel,[45] typically described as "intentional exercise of dominion or control over a chattel" inconsistent with the plaintiff's right to control it.[46] But either tort can be committed without any intent to cause harm or violate another's property rights. There is liability for using, taking or delivering the property in the good faith belief that the defendant is entitled or authorized to do this.[47] Conversion liability is for what is assessed as the full value of the property. It is not limited to compensation for interference with the plaintiff's use of the property or other actual loss.[48]

These rules were not formulated for intangible property and are not suitable for infringements of rights in intangibles.[49] In reality, claims of infringement of intangible property rights, such as rights to exclusive commercial use of a name or design, to control or use confidential information, or to receive money or property belonging to someone else, are claims for interference with economic interests that properly come within the law of economic torts such as "unfair competition", interference with contract, interference with economic expectation, slander of title, and misappropriation of trade secrets or other confidential information.

The property torts can provide a remedy for harm to non-property interests, and the intentional torts can provide a remedy for harm not intended or anticipated by the defendant. This is because liability includes responsibility for consequential damage. The most typical example is personal injury resulting from trespass to land, trespass by livestock or nuisance.[50] There can also be liability if trespass to chattels results in personal injury,[51] as when interference with the plaintiff's animal or vehicle causes the plaintiff to be injured,[52]

---

44 Rest. Torts § 217; Rest. 2d Torts § 217.

45 See Rest. Torts § 223; Rest. 2d Torts § 223.

46 Rest. 2d Torts §§ 222A.

47 See Rest. 2d Torts §§ 217, 223, 244.

48 Rest. 2d Torts § 222A, comment *c*.

49 See Sappideen & Vines, 2011, p. 68; Harper, James & Gray, 2006, § 2.13 at pp. 211-213; D.B. Dobbs, 'An Introduction to Non-Statutory Economic Loss Claims', *Arizona Law Review*, Vol. 48, No. 4, 2006, pp. 713-733, at p. 722; V.D. Ricks, Comment, 'The Conversion of Intangible Property: Bursting the Ancient Trover Bottle with New Wine', *Brigham Young University Law Review*, Vol. 1991, No. 4, 1991, pp. 1681-1715.

50 This is recognized in the second Restatement explicitly for trespass to land (§ 162) and trespass by livestock (§ 504), and by implication for private nuisance (§ 821D, comment *b*; § 829A, comment *b*). See also Rest. 3d Torts – Physical Harm § 21, comment *g* (animal trespass).

51 Rest. 2d Torts § 218.

52 *Cf. Glidden v. Szybiak*, 95 N.H. 318, 63 A.2d 233 (1949) (plaintiff interfered with defendant's animal).

or if trespass to land accidentally causes damage to or loss of personal property of the plaintiff,[53] as when the trespass results in a fire[54] or disappearance of valuable items.[55]

4 Required Interest in Property

A plaintiff has a tort action for damage to, loss of or interference with property only if the plaintiff had a legal right in the property that is a property interest rather than some other type of economic interest or expectation. If, for example, the defendant allegedly deprived the plaintiff of an inheritance by fraud or other wrongful conduct, the relevant tort action (if any) is for intentional interference with inheritance,[56] not conversion.[57] This rule applies to negligence and strict liability actions for damage to property as well as to the property torts. If the defendant's negligence damaged property that the plaintiff had a right to use or receive under a contract, the plaintiff does not have an action for property damage. That action belongs to the person with title to the property or possession of it. The harm to the plaintiff is economic loss, for which there is usually no negligence liability.[58]

Tort law specifies the type of interest in or connection with the property a plaintiff must have to maintain a certain type of action. Generally, ownership as such is not required. Most tort causes of action are maintainable by the person with possession of the property at the time of the damage, loss or interference with the property. However, a right to immediate possession is sufficient for torts to land when no one else is in actual possession,[59] and for conversion the basic requirement has been a right to immediate possession of the chattel.[60] A reversionary right to the possess the property, such as the lessor's right to recover it at the end of the lease, may be sufficient when there is physical harm affecting

53 Rest. 2d Torts § 162.

54 *E.g. Brown v. Dellinger*, 355 S.W.2d 742 (Tex. Civ. App. 1962).

55 *E.g. Renairie Corp. v. Vaughn*, 142 A.2d 148 (D.C. App. 1958).

56 See Rest. 2d Torts § 774B; Rest. 3d Torts – Economic Harm § 19.

57 See *Anderson v. Meadowcroft*, 339 Md. 218, 661 A.2d 726 (1995). There might, however, be a valid conversion claim if, because of the defendant's fraud, the plaintiff was entitled to claim the property itself rather than only compensation for its loss.

58 See *Leigh and Sillavan Ltd. v. Aliakmon Shipping Co. Ltd.*, [1986] A.C. 785 (H.L.). A notable example, not American except for the species of insect involved, is *Margarine Union G.m.b.H. v. Cambay Prince Steamship Co. Ltd.*, [1969] 1 Q.B. 219, in which the defendants' failure to fumigate a vessel caused cargo en route to the plaintiffs to be damaged by giant American cockroaches. In *Norsk Pacific Steamship Co. Ltd. v. Canadian National Railway Co.*, [1992] 1 S.C.R. 1021, (1992) 91 D.L.R.(4th) 289, where there was damage to a railway bridge primarily used but not owned by the plaintiffs, an action was allowed as a claim for economic loss.

59 Rest. 2d Torts § 157 (trespass to land), § 821E, comment *c* (private nuisance, applying § 328E).

60 Rest. 2d Torts § 225. Actual possession carries with it a right to possession against others with no superior right. See Rest. 2d Torts §§ 224A, 895.

that interest.[61] Owners of easements and other "nonpossessory estates" can sue for a nuisance that interferes with the use or enjoyment of these property rights.[62]

These are rules of tort law. However, it is property law that provides details on the property interest needed to maintain the cause of action – for example, what is a property interest in land or chattels, what establishes an easement, and what creates a right to possess property. In many cases, especially actions for trespass to land (or ejectment) or conversion, there is an intentional entry into land or exercise of power over property that is clearly a basis of tort liability; the real issue determining liability is whether the plaintiff or the defendant had the right to the property. That depends on the application of property law and relevant contracts, not tort law.

5 Restatement Revision

The American Law Institute decided late in the twentieth century that a third Restatement of Torts should be produced but that it would not be done as a single project. Instead, there would be a number of separate projects addressing different parts of tort law.[63] To date, Restatements (Third) of Apportionment of Liability, Liability for Economic Harm, Liability for Physical and Emotional Harm, and Products Liability have been published in final form. This has largely replaced the provisions of the second Restatement concerning strict liability, but not most of the sections concerning liability for intentional torts, negligence and nuisance. A Restatement (Third) project for intentional torts commenced in 2012. It has been limited to intentional torts to the person. Torts to property, including the intentional torts, are to be addressed in a separate project to create a Restatement (Fourth) of the Law of Property. This project will also restate the law on concepts of property law that bear on liability for torts to property, such as ownership, possession, license, right to possession and easement, much of which has not been revised in a Restatement since the first Restatement of Property.

Inclusion of property torts in a Restatement of Property project may have the advantage of consistency with property law concepts, but it has the disadvantage of dividing between two Restatements the group of intentional torts that originated in the common law trespass action (battery, assault, false imprisonment, trespass to land and trespass to chattels) and continue to share a distinct structure of liability and set of defenses. It also has the consequence that drafts will not be examined by ALI members and others who specialize in tort law or have a particular interest in it. However, the provisions of the Restatement

61 See Rest. 2d Torts § 220 (trespass to chattels), § 243 (conversion), § 821E, comment *f* (nuisance); Dobbs, Hayden & Bublick, 2016, pp. 90-91 (trespass to land).

62 Rest. 2d Torts § 821E.

63 See Rest. 3d Torts – Physical Harm, at p. xi.

(Fourth) of Property on torts to property are being drafted by an associate reporter who is a prominent tort law scholar (Professor John Goldberg) and it is intended that they will eventually form part of the Restatement (Third) of Torts.[64]

The sections of the Restatement (Second) of Torts on the torts to property remain valid and accepted restatements of the law and do not, in my view, need either substantial revision or tinkering with language in the "black letter". It is to be hoped that this will be the prevailing view in the development of the Restatement (Fourth) of Property. That said, a number of "tweaks" would be useful. These include:

- Specifying actual possession as the basic "title to sue" for trespass to land and trespass to chattels, before explaining when and why an immediate right of possession or other right in the property may be sufficient.
- Providing more detail and clarity on liability for property damage to a person who has a reversionary or other future interest in property.
- Including more on liability for consequential damages in torts to property, including liability for resulting injury to a person or other property.
- Specifying substantial interference with use of the chattel (as well as deprivation of use of the chattel) as a basis for trespass to chattels liability.
- Recognizing that trespass to land actions, as well as private nuisance actions, are limited to possessors of the land and family members who reside on the land.
- Removing the provision of the second Restatement that a trespass action for flight by aircraft immediately above the land requires a substantial interference with use and enjoyment of the land,[65] which confuses trespass with nuisance.

6 Conclusion

Property torts and actions for damage to property are important parts of tort law. Whatever the Restatement (Fourth) of Property provides for tort actions involving property, it is likely to have considerable influence in the courts and be included in treatises and articles on tort liability. Uniquely for a Restatement of a common law subject, the ALI has established an international advisory panel for the Restatement (Fourth) of Property project. The distinguished members of this panel include both Sjef van Erp and his

64 Rest. 4th Property, Tentative Draft No. 1, at pp. 17-18. A desire to complete work on a topic more expeditiously has apparently prevailed, in the allocation of torts to new Restatements, over adherence to conventional categories of liability. For example, malicious prosecution and abuse of process, which are not economic torts, are included in the Restatement (Third) of Liability for Economic Harm. Public nuisance will be in the Restatement (Fourth) of Property, although it is not a property tort, together with private nuisance, which is a property tort.

65 Rest. 2d Torts § 159(2)(b).

Maastricht University colleague Bram Akkermans. The project, including the drafting of provisions bearing on tort liability for interference with property, should greatly benefit from the expertise and comparative perspectives of Professors van Erp and Akkermans and the other members of the international advisory panel. I await the results with considerable interest.

Part IV
Legal translations

Uniform Legal Languages and Comparative Law: Seeking for the National Criptotypes

Elena Ioriatti[*]

1 Introduction

Comparative law as the "basis for a common legal system for all humanity"[1] has, ever since its beginning, attracted the attention not only of specialists, but of jurists in general. The attitude of this science to create interest in the world of law was probably favoured by its nature, for which encountering diversity is a key element.

Nevertheless, if diversity – whether it be legal, cultural, linguistic or geographical – might have been the first element of interest for jurists approaching comparative law, over time this discipline has become the actual object of analysis either. Even if past discussions on the existence of comparative law methodology have been overcome, nowadays its nature still remains at the centre of a very lively debate. Particularly over the last twenty years, consistent literature has been specifically dealing with observations on the past, the present and the future of comparative law, as a consolidated scientific discipline:[2] thus, since the beginning of this century, comparative law has been observed by comparatists from "outside", as a stimulating and challenging field of research.

In this framework, scholars' interest actually includes studies concerning current or possible objects of comparative law. Despite the different approaches, recently published collective works show some deal of agreement: firstly, while in the past comparative analysis, mainly micro-comparison, was carried out in a limited number of countries, today there is a growing field of expansion of studies at the regional, international, transnational and global level.[3] Secondly, the difference between "traditional comparative law" and a number

* Elena Ioriatti, Professor of Comparative law, Trento University (Italy), Faculty of Law.

1 C. Jamin, 'Saleilles' and Lambert's Old Dream Revisited', *The American Journal of Comparative Law*, Vol. 50, 2002, pp. 701-718.

2 K. Boele – Woelki & D.F. Arroyo (Eds.), *The Past, Present and Future of Comparative Law – Le passé, le présent et le futur du droit comparé*, Springer, 2018.

3 M. Reimann & R. Zimmermann, *The Oxford Handbook of Comparative Law*, Oxford, Oxford University Press, 2019. M. Siems, 'New Directions in Comparative Law', *in* M. Reimann & R. Zimmermann (Eds.), *The Oxford Handbook of Comparative Law*, Oxford, Oxford University Press, 2019, p. 866.

of alternative approaches like postmodern, socio-legal and numerical comparative law is becoming one of the starting points of current analysis.[4]

Furthermore, the undeniable contribution of this science is that of bridging the gap with other disciplines: comparative law methodology is particularly important in those areas of research in which different methodologies are in increasingly close contact, as, for instance, in the case of law and language, law and sociology, law and economics, law and technology.[5]

Here, even if the level of interdisciplinary studies is constantly increasing, the simple juxtaposition between the object and the directions of comparative law does not exhaust the debate: the question of method remains nevertheless a core issue of this field of literature.[6] This still interesting discussion is delimitated by a high number of studies dealing specifically with methodological aspects from the point of view of the different, possible approaches[7] and by others that go so far as to hypothesize that no method actually does exist, since comparative law is the result of research itself: in such extreme forms, the methodological perspective seems to be inverted and simply to focus on the legitimization of the research.[8]

By contrast, studies also develop methods that aim at a possible extension of the scope of comparative law to new non-conventional "units" of comparison,[9] or even, from an American perspective, calling for a central methodological discussion on a possible *common core* of comparative law worldwide.[10]

Alongside the actual methodological matter, much has started to be written on comparative law as a teaching subject too.[11] Here, studies underline a lack of systematic analysis about teaching techniques and educational contents: outside some established parts of the law – such as comparative private law, mainly focusing on tort, property and contract – practice and curriculum demonstrate that worldwide method, choice and teaching subjects mostly depend on the individual teacher or on the specific curricula of the law course. Thus, this lack of common core in research is mirroring the difference of

4 Siems, 2019, pp. 852 *et seq.*

5 J. Husa, 'Interdisciplinary Comparative Law – Between Scylla and Charybdis', *J. Comp. L.* 28, 2014.

6 M. Van Hoecke, 'Methodology of Comparative Legal Research', *Law and Method*, 2015, pp. 1 *et seq.*

7 M. Adams, *The Method and Culture of Comparative Law: Essays in Honour of Mark Van Hoecke*, Hart Publishing 2014.

8 The positions are collectively denominated "contextual comparative law" by Kischel: U. Kischel, *Comparative Law*, Oxford University Press, 2019, pp. 152 *et seq.*

9 M. Siems, 'The Power of Comparative Law: What Types of Units Can Comparative Law Compare?', *The American Journal of Comparative Law*, Vol. 67, Issue 4, 2019, p. 861.

10 D. J. Gerber, Method, 'Community & Comparative Law: An Encounter With Complexity Science', *Roger Williams University law Review*, Vol. 16, 2011, p. 127.

11 N.V. Demleitner, 'Comparative law in legal education', *in* M. Reimann & R. Zimmermann (Eds.), *The Oxford Handbook of Comparative Law*, Oxford, Oxford University Press, 2019, pp. 321 *et seq.*

teaching and educational approaches in comparative law, which still "represents the quintessential manifestation of academic freedom".[12]

Based on the foregoing thoughts, the abovementioned attempt to find a "common core" of comparative law - equally from a methodological point of view as well as with regard to the research content and legal education - might sound as the future of this science.

However, invoking the need for a common core should also take into account that it may not be easy for comparative law scholars to adapt worldwide, even simply in terms of terminology and definitions, to an idea of comparative law that considers a shared methodology, a common plan for analysis and a number of shared educational goals in legal education. At first glance, a search for unification seems hardly unfamiliar to comparative law, which inevitably responds to constant challenges leading it to face the complexity of global phenomena and the need to converse with other disciplines and cultures;[13] this does in fact favour and imply the establishment of an ever-growing methodological pluralism, also in legal education. As the historic debate on method shows, if the origin of the "undisciplined discipline" of comparative law may have been a weakness for many years, nowadays, also thanks to its methodological flexibility, it is finding its place in the identification of issues and methods that respond to a new and rapidly changing world.

No matter how things stand, thinking about how comparative law should and will evolve worldwide is a fundamental matter and cannot be exhaustively discussed in this context. What is however undeniable is that comparative law now has a history and that from that history we can learn, also in order to encourage its development.

One lesson, in particular, seems undisputed: in the world of law, in the past like today, comparative law is a discipline with unique characteristics. Due to its nature of no enacted law, comparative law is mainly the product of its own scientific community since a comparatist is at the same time the scholar applying comparative methodology, as well as the one who guarantees its existence and survival. The world of comparative law is, in its purest essence, a world of science and knowledge, and for this reason its evolution and existence depends entirely on the scientific community of comparative law scholars. Using a more didactical rather than scientific metaphor, we could say that while scholars of, for instance, private, constitutional or administrative law deal with a field of law that was formulated outside its scientific circle of reference, comparative scholars produce what they observe. Thus, comparative law "is a comparatist made law".

12 *Ibid.*, p. 322.

13 R. Scarciglia, 'Storia e diritto globale. Intersezioni metodologiche e comparazione', *in* M. Butti & A. Somma (Eds.), *Diritto: storia e comparazione. Nuovi propositi per un binomio antico*, Max Planck Institute for European Legal History, 2018, p. 482.

Therefore, observing the personal and academic story of comparatists is not a nostalgic mannerism or point of view from which comparative law should be studied, but a way to understand and comprehend a science that holds the potential and the tools to accompany the world through its rapid changes, more than any other. It is in this direction that some well-known collective works go, gathering contributions that the authors believe have made the history and evolution of the past fifty years of comparative law for many reasons, and in different fields.[14]

Among the comparatists, Sjef van Erp's academic and professional life is undoubtedly an example of completeness. It is somewhat surprising that one single professor of comparative law could join so many roles in his person: scholar, law faculty administrator, researcher, advisor, judge, research projects coordinator, holder of seats in prestigious international organizations, among which Vice – president of the European Law Institute in Vienna. However, among his many qualities, one in particular impressed me ever since the first time we met, twenty years ago, on occasion of a guest lecture of mine, at the Faculty of Law of Maastricht University: his capability to adapt the right linguistic register to any context, in any of the many languages he knew. His ability in fact to fluently speak Dutch, English, French, German, as well as his knowledge of Italian and Indonesian are not just linguistic abilities, but cultural means and tools.

As everybody knows, language is not just a communication tool, but also a system of penetration of different worlds and cultures. Among these, the world of law is probably one of the most complex environments, not simply because legal terminology actually forms a language itself, but also because its environment is made of various legal discourses, each corresponding to its many components: the case law discourse, for instance, with its performative register, differs from the scholarly discourse, that is more assertive, and from the legislator's one, which is mostly prescriptive. On a closer inspection, each of these registers changes from one legal system to another, as is obvious, going from the narrative and fluid style of the judges' *opinion* in common law, to the technical and rhythmic style of the judgements of the European Court of Justice, given the filter of multilingualism.

All in all, plurilingualism is a very useful tool in comparative law, but it is often heavily burdened by the origin of the polyglot comparatist. A scholar with a high knowledge in a foreign language may act in the unfamiliar environment where this language is spoken without really penetrating that realty. Sjef is an exception and a model. In a highly simplified description, his knowledge of language includes the ability to understand not only the word, but also the concept which stands behind the linguistic expression, together with its meaning in a specific context. His ability is instinctive, because it is innate, but also

14 See for all: M. Bussani & U. Mattei (Eds.), *The Cambridge Companion to Comparative Law*, Cambridge: Cambridge University Press, 2012.

supported by constant studying and a never-ending form of curiosity, that he succeeded in transferring to his pupils, with his own example.

This is only one of the reasons why I am pleased and honoured to participate in the Liber Amicorum and to dedicate to Sjef these thoughts on the experience of a European multilingual legal language as a possible model for a uniform Asian legal discourse.

2 Law and language

The relationship between language and law is an example that shows how, ever since the beginning, comparatists have been able to stimulate studies in specific fields of law, bordering with other disciplines. As verbalized and written law is made of language, and comparing the law assumes the transposition of concepts from one language to another, legal translation has always been a fundamental aspect of comparative law analysis.

Nevertheless, when the comparatists' research approach developed around the uncovering of expected commonalities underneath rules of different legal systems, legal translation was simply innominate, perceived as an implicit activity of comparative law methodology and having no dignity of existence as a discipline.

But it soon became clear that the capacity to compare requires an ability to translate, but also the ability to translate implies the capacity to compare. Thus, it was comparative law in the end to draw attention on the circumstances that translating a legal concept does not simply call for linguistic knowledge, but also legal cultural adaptation and that translation must convey not only the linguistic, but the legal meaning too.

Legal translation went from being a simple, even if vital, tool of comparatists in the study of foreign law, although taken for granted, to becoming one of the main subjects of comparative law research.[15] Over time comparatists started to develop some techniques that could be used as a method and guideline, even in different cultural backgrounds, for all those who were dealing with the translation norms and concepts from one language to another. Simplifying a much more complex evolution, as imagined by Susan Šarčević,[16] scholars shifted attention in the field of legal translation from literal to idiomatic translation, to dedicate efforts today particularly to the study of multilingual legal translation.

From this point of view, the European Union is an interesting and absolutely original phenomenon to be observed, since it is the result of a social, institutional and constitutional

15 P.M. Tiersma & L.M. Solan (Eds.), *The Oxford Handbook of Language and Law*, Oxford University Press, 2016. K. Malmkjær & K. Windle, *The Oxford Handbook of Translation Studies*, Oxford University Press, 2011.

16 This evolution of translation techniques for legal information can be seen in the chapter "History of legal translation" by S. Šarčević, *New Approach to Legal Translation*, Kluwer Law International, 2000, pp. 23 *et seq.*

situation that is constantly evolving. If observed from its origins, Europe is a work in progress with its foundations in the solid tradition of its Member States, but that at the same time is gradually building its own linguistic and legal architecture.[17]

This process is not new "on the radar" of the scientific community, that has proven awareness and interest in reflecting upon its own role.[18] However, comparatists as well as jurists in general did not simply observe European law as it is, but also enhanced and guided its development. With various degrees of awareness, they inevitably and crucially contributed to the evolution of its language, particularly in the research of methods for the application and interpretation of European law in the various EU Member States.

In this framework, comparative law research on EU legal language, once again, was the catalyst for a new field of research in the Asian area too, where considerations on a possible uniform Asian legal terminology have recently begun.[19]

3 Asia and Europe Seeking for Their Own Uniform Legal Language

A growing surge of interest in legal translation has been trigged in Europe by the ongoing effort to enhance the understanding of the Eastern legal systems and their legal languages in the international scientific and professional community.

Examples are the projects launched to translate Japanese Law[20] into English; beyond making the Japanese legal system more accessible to foreigners, the aim of these efforts is that of establishing a uniform way of translating Japanese law. By means of advanced tools and methodologies,[21] the goal of the Minister of Justice is to create a unique, agreed Japanese legal terminology, improved both in text quality and coherence.

In China legal translation has been considered a highly sensitive area due to increasing contact with the legal expressions of the global (and consequently) north American legal

17 D. Manf, K. Malacek, É. Muir, *Langues et construction européenne*, Bruxelles, 2010.

18 See for all: R. Van Gestel, H.W. Micklitz, *Why Methods Matter in European Legal Scholarship*, European Law Journal, Vol. 20, Issue 3, pp. 292-316, 2014.

19 See as an example the seminar held at Bologna University in 2016, "Comparing legal languages and creating common/uniform terminologies" organized by Asiatic comparatists with the aim of gathering the research outcomes of the European colleagues on multilingual law and language. For an overview of comparative law in China and Japan see: T. Zhane, "The development of comparative law in Modern China", in M. Reimann & R. Zimmermann (Eds.), *The Oxford Handbook of Comparative Law*, Oxford, Oxford University Press, 2019, p. 228 and L. Nottage, "The development of comparative law in Japan", in M. Reimann & R. Zimmermann (Eds.), *The Oxford Handbook of Comparative Law*, Oxford, Oxford University Press, 2019, p. 201.

20 I. Kitamura, 'La traduction juridique. Un point de vue japonais', *Les Cahiers de droit*, Vol. 28, No. 4 (1987), in *Materiali per una storia della cultura giuridica*, 2/2003, pp. 359-405.

21 See the Japanese Law Translation Database System http://www.japaneselawtranslation.go.jp (Ministry of Justice Website). K. Takeda & Y. Sekine, 'Translation of Japanese Laws and Regulations', *in* L. Cheng, K. K. Sin, A. Wagner (Eds.), *The Ashgate handbook on legal translation*, Ashgate, 2014, pp. 223 *et seq.*

process, leading to a profound need to include foreign neologism in the Chinese legal language. This rather recent inter linguistic phenomenon coexists with the need to recover old legal terms and expressions which accompany the rediscovery of traditional values of the Chinese and east Asian legal cultures.[22] The referential portraying of these new legal concepts can rely on a new representation of a traditional ideogram, enriched of a suffix: in this scenario the use of the suffix "hua" has led to the creation of the words "sirenhua" and "siyouhua", transferring the western legal concept "privatization" into the Chinese taxonomy.[23]

The ongoing developments in translation projects might suggest a separate approach of each of the abovementioned Asian countries to the problem of making internal law accessible from outside and permeable to the global legal process; nevertheless Japan and China share the challenge of finding a unique legal language, common to the legal systems having ideograms as their form of expression of written law. Moreover, Japanese and Chinese legal scholars are struggling with parallel problems regarding the suitable vocabulary to describe common aspects of different legal orders in the non-Western legal systems.

Indeed, it seems that not only legal translation, as suggested by Alwazna,[24] but the uniformization of the legal language itself is becoming a crucial means for global communication, as in different areas of the world there is a pressing need for solutions, without which business and economy between countries would be hindered.[25]

Against this background, the Asian countries and the Member States of the UE, although separated by an ocean of differences, are facing similar challenges in formulating their own unique, uniform legal language.

The most visible complexity lies in the fact that both those legal systems have to accommodate very different languages and legal cultures within the same vocabulary. Likewise, many difficulties that might appear to be technical-linguistic problems of the ideographic legal systems turn out to be matters of the cultural construction of meanings, common to Europe and to Asian at the same time.[26]A second element that a European and a possible Asian legal language unification efforts have in common is the form in

22 On the infra language translation see: M. Timoteo, 'Il diritto per immagini. Aspetti del linguaggio giuridico cinese contemporaneo', *in* B. Pozzo (Ed.), *Lingua e diritto: oltre l'Europa*, Giuffrè, 2014 pp. 83 *et seq*. See also: D. Cao, *Chinese law. A language perspective*, Ashgate, Aldershot, 2004 and D. Cao, *Translating Law*, Bristol, ed. Multilingual Matters, 2007.

23 Timoteo, 2014, p. 82.

24 R.Y. Alwazna, 'Important Translation Strategies Used in Legal Translation: Examples of Hooper's Translation of the Ottoman Majalla into English', *in* L. Cheng, K. K. Sin, A. Wagner (Eds.), *The Ashgate handbook on legal translation*, Ashgate, 2014, p. 252.

25 *Ibid.*

26 L.C. Wolff, Comparing Chinese Law ... But with Which Legal Systems?, *The Chinese Journal of Comparative Law*, Volume 6, Issue 2, December 2018, p. 151.

which law is expressed, as nowadays European and Asian countries rely principally on written sources for the formulation of norms.[27]

This makes it a matter of simple observation that, as regards the uniform legal terminology, the final and official outcome in both spheres will be expressed in a written form,[28] regardless of all efforts, whether they be intellectual, scientific or technical.

Sharing a written form is a similarity which seems to lead to a deep difference at first sight, because of the two rather opposite writing systems which characterize the Asian and European systems: "ideographic" and "phonetic".[29] Ideograms belong to a system of writing in which words are represented by a sign that is not related – or is only partially related – to the sounds of the words themselves. Although ideograms might sometimes symbolize isolated sounds, normally a sign stands for a whole word, and consequently they represent ideas, rather than sounds.[30] Differently, the phonetic system reproduces a succession of sounds that make up the word and is the basis of written language.

If transposed to legal language, these two writing systems have a different and precise impact on the way the rule is transmitted. In the ideographic system the ideogram is much more than a sign that is meant to indicate a legal concept, as a general and abstract term. It is a complex of specific images, which lead to a visual perception of the meaning of the different legal terms.[31] On the other side, in the phonetic systems law is inevitably expressed through a linguistic means, which aims at a specific semantic meaning.[32]

The way in which the law is expressed in these two writing systems is different in the form (graphic or linguistic), in the perspectives (visual or phonetic), as well as from a semantic, textual point of view and in the same way in which the command is expressed and communicated.

Thus, whereas monolingualism evokes a huge distance between ideographic and phonetic written legal languages, the situation slightly changes when it comes to multilingual legal regimes: "conceptualization means not only translation, but materializing notions and concepts into another framework!"[33] stressed Wagner and Gémar describing the role

27 H. Oda, *Japanese Law*, Oxford University Press, 2009.

28 As Colin Robertson has noted, actually, there is a separate oral dimension of the EU legal language, but it can probably be regarded as subordinated to the creation and interpretation of written texts. See C. Robertson, 'EU Legislative texts and Translation', *in* L. Cheng, K.K. Sin, A. Wagner (Eds.), *The Ashgate handbook on legal translation*, Ashgate, 2014, pp. 159 et seq.

29 F. Coulmas, *The Writing Systems of the World*, Blackwell Pub, 1991.

30 M. Shibatani, *The languages of Japan*, Cambridge, 1990. Y. Horie, 'The roots of Japanese legal terminology', *Comparative Legilinguistics 4*, 2010, pp. 81 *et seq.*

31 Timoteo, 2014, p. 73.

32 Coulmas, *Ibid.*

33 A. Wagner & J.C. Gémar, 'Materializing Notions, Concepts and Language into Another Linguistic Framework', *International Journal for the Semiotic of Law*, 2013, p. 732.

of form when, as in legal multilingualism, the expression of the law becomes a symbolic construction.[34]

A further element of complexity is a problem that has not even been discussed enough in Europe regarding national court interpretations and applications of any uniform or harmonized legal terminology. Due to the supranational character of the text, this legal language faces a specific challenge, which is to make the resulting normative expression as uniform as possible in all of the national legal systems involved.[35]

This last aspect is the "Achille's heal" of the European harmonization process, under discussion in Europe,[36] where the opportunity for inconsistencies among the various language versions is so profound that it has led a scholar[37] to say, from an American perspective, that it would not be surprising if the entire system collapsed under its own weight.

4 Europe

How the familiar problems of bilingualism or multilingualism have been managed by the variety of experiences of normative pluralism around the world is interesting and stimulating and might be a useful point of reference; however, the ordeal of the European Union is certainly the main world effort for the creation of a uniform legal means of expression and unique system of law. Beyond the policy and democratic reasons which have led the Union to go for the theoretical absolute multilingualism,[38] on a purely technical basis, the core of the matter is how the tension among the institutional duties of translation and the technical complexity, if not impossibility, of such an effort to translate normative acts in all the 24 official languages has been taken on.

In general, legal scholars tend to emphasize the role of translation, that is considered not only as an essential technique integrated in the drafting process,[39] but a harmonization tool reducing the multi-language complexity to a common meaning.[40] However, it is by

---

34 *Ibid.*, p. 739.

35 See on this point E. Ioriatti, Comparative Law and Eu Legal Language: Towards a European Restatement? Global Jurist, 2021 (published online).

36 See paragraph n. 6 of this Chapter.

37 L.M. Solan, 'The interpretation of Multilingual Statutes by the European Court of Justice', *Brooklyn Journal of International Law*, 2009, p. 276.

38 See S. Van Der Jeught, *EU Language and Law*, Groningen (NL), Europa Law Publishing, 2015.

39 C. Robertson, 'EU Legislative texts and Translation', *in* L. Cheng, K. K. Sin, A. Wagner (Eds.), *The Ashgate handbook on legal translation*, Ashgate, 2014, pp. 159 *et seq*.

40 See S.E. Pommer, 'Interpreting Multilingual EU Law: What the Role of Legal Translation?', *European Review of Private Law*, 2012, p. 1254, who evokes translation as the meta-language of EU legal integration.

now clear in the scientific environment that EU legal translation is so specific that it cannot be sufficiently explained by traditional criteria like the function of the legal texts.[41]

When it comes to EU legal terminology, particularly, the tension between the institutional duty of enacting the harmonized legislation in all the 24 official languages[42] and the technical impossibility of translation have been managed through an autonomous "dictionary" in which EU law is constantly developing "by distilling new meanings into former words and creating new ones".[43] Each term is shaped so that all languages have the same EU definition in common;[44] this "translation" strategy leads a single concept to acquire 24 labels, each one meaning the same thing, like forms of inter-lingual synonyms.[45] The underlying idea is that each of the authentic texts contribute to the meaning of the EU autonomous rule and turn the signified as the ideal, ultimate meaning of this rule. Therefore, uniformity is reached across languages, horizontally, among these synonyms and through the form of the linguistic expression.[46]

With the passing of time, the EU legal language has become a specialized domain of growing importance and the initial limited understanding of the nature of this legal language has been gradually improved by both linguists and jurists.[47]

However, despite the ongoing developments in translation studies, the European legal language is still in want of responses with regards to its own characteristics.

In order to widen the scientific observation point, quite a number of scholars have pointed out the need for an interdisciplinary approach, by analyzing semantic, legal and linguistic aspects.[48]

This field of literature underlines an insufficient understanding of the linguistic nature of EU languages and a consequent impossibility of mapping this new phenomenon with scientific intention: adhering to a strict juridical and substantial approach to each single concept expressed in each language version, obscures to the interpreter a more general, flexible and formal overview of this unique phenomenon.[49] According to Robertson, particularly with regard to EU language, there is still an insufficient understanding of its

41 S. Šarčević, *New Approach to Legal Translation*, Kluwer Law International, 2000, pp. 5 *et seq.*

42 For an analysis of the aim of the multilingual regime of the European Union particularly focusing on legal drafting see Van Der Jeught, 2015, pp. 103 *et seq.*

43 Wagner & Gémar, 2013, p. 739.

44 C. Robertson, 'LSP and EU Legal Language', *in* C. Heine & J. Engberg (Eds.), *Reconceptualizing LSP*, On line proceedings of the XVII European LSP Symposium 2009.

45 *Ibidem.* The example is the concept "regulation" – "règelement"- "Verordung" (etc.).

46 J.G. Turi, 'Le droit linguistique et les droits linguistiques', *Les Cahiers de droit*, Vol. 31, n. 2, 1990, pp. 641 *et seq.*

47 See paragraph n. 6 of this Chapter.

48 C.D. Robertson, *Multilingual Law. A Framework for analysis and understanding*, Abingdon Oxon (UK), New York (USA), Routledge, 2016, p. 172.

49 L. Cheng, W. Cheng & K. Sin, 'Revisiting legal terms: A semiotic perspective',*Semiotica*, Issue 202, 2014, p. 179.

linguistic nature and a consequent impossibility of mapping this new phenomenon with scientific intention.[50]

Thus, a different, suggested perspective is that of semiotics, which is precisely the study of signs.[51] In this field of research, EU law is observed from the semiotic point of view as a sign system[52] and a horizontal meta-juridical law;[53] from this perspective, EU legal terms form a horizontal system of linguistic signs, in which each one formally and ideally bears the same legal concept as containing an inter-lingual synonym.[54] It is up to the form to give the same meaning to a new multilingual reality expressed in all official languages.[55]

Form is therefore not only important in the creation of an EU legal terminology, but definitively part of it, as the language is, at the same time, the object and the subject of the law. As a consequence, each concept acquires meta-juridical features[56] and form is an unavoidable tool for harmonization.

Joseph Turri's research further clarifies the content of the legal language of the EU from the linguistic point of view; the norm enacted on the European level is so specific that it cannot be sufficiently described as an act communicating a social message, as is for the internal, national sources of the law. Turri suggests the term *language law*, as a set of legal rules having the aim of using one or more languages within a certain cultural and supranational context. This is a meta-juridical law, to the extent that language becomes both the subject and the object of the law. Thus, the aim of *language law* is "the language medium" (the form of the linguistic expression) and not "the language – message" (the social message).[57]

According to Gérard Cornu's[58] theory on multilingual legislation, this language medium is composed by rules expressed in the different language versions, representing a unique linguistic item (*linguistic form of the signifier* or *signifier of the linguistic sign)* of a new concept,[59] that is uniform and common to different legal languages and supposed to transmit the same content in all linguistic versions.

50 Robertson, 2016. On the legal concept as a sign see Cheng, Cheng & Sin, 2014, p. 179.

51 Semiotics emerged as an independent science at the beginning of the 20th century with the studies of, among others, Charles Sander Pierce and Ferdinand de Saussure.

52 Robertson, 2016, p. 144.

53 Turi, 1990, p. 642.

54 E. Ioriatti, "Formulation of rights and European legal discourse: any theory behind it?" in *International Journal of Legal Discourse*, 2016.

55 Robertson, 2009, p. 3.

56 On this concept see Turi, 1990, p. 641.

57 Turi, 1990, p. 643.

58 G. Cornu, *Linguistique juridique*, Montchrestien, Paris, 2005.

59 In the background, clearly, the theory of the famous linguist De Saussure, who describes language features referring to two well-known expressions: the *signifier* and the *signified*, which compose the linguistic *sign* (F. De Saussure, *Cours de linguistique générale*, 1916). In the words of Louis Hjelmslev's (*Principes de grammaire générale*, 1928) these two terms are renamed respectively *expression* and *content*. Therefore, the

Within an even more complex debate, a point of arrival is that EU legal language is composed by neologisms, which are *inter-lingual synonyms* and horizontally form a *meta-juridical law* in the different language versions, which represent a unique linguistic depiction (*linguistic form of the signifier*) that transmits the autonomous, uniform, EU rule.

If these categories are applied to EU Law, they all appear as attempts aimed at expressing a legal meaning, as a unit of law at the EU level and it becomes clear that these formulations are nothing more than an approximation of the ideal expression of a rule that pre-exists and of its transferability into a linguistic framework, common to all the official language versions.

In order to highlight this aspect of the reality of the EU legal process, the qualification of Eu legislation as a "meta-language", composed by "meta-norms" proved to be useful as it constructs a mental image that helps to objectively observe the phenomenon.

Thus, with the aim of introducing a parallel qualification of EU concepts as components of the EU language to be completed and consolidated at the national level we here suggest the term (EU) *Meta-concept.*

The Meta-concept is embodied in the EU legal rule on a high level of abstraction.

It is not contained in a single language text, neither the content is the sum of all the different linguistic versions of an EU legislative act. Thus, national case law is not the elaboration of the Meta-concept, but its discovery, identification, completion and consolidation by means of an act of interpretation.

By making reference to De Saussure's theory[60] in the definition of the language, reducing language to a sign (being linguistic or graphic) makes it something artificial, since it only includes the individual part of the reality leaving language outside its social context. A community of speakers is also necessary for the realization of a language. De Saussure calls the outcome of speakers' social interaction the *parole.*

When observed from the EU legal point of view, la *parole* is the word created by the translators, jurists – linguists, EU civil servants, lawmakers, in order to express the Meta – concept and the uniform law.[61]

linguistic *sign* is composed by a *signifier/expression* and a *signified/content*, which separate *form* from *substance.*

60 F. De Saussure, *Cours de linguistique générale*, Paris: Payot & Cie., 1916.

61 It must be noted that Ferdinand De Saussure described language structure and form as arbitrary; in every language the meaning of a word emerges not because of an objective relation between a sign indicating an object and the concrete object itself, but by comparing this specific word to all the other words, as words are collective results of social interaction. ("*la parole*", in the De Saussure's word). However, according to other scholars the connection of signifier (term) and signified (concept) is only relatively arbitrary, as related to a specific system of signs (e.g. that of the European Union): Cheng, Cheng & Sin, 2014, p. 179. See recently E. Ioriatti, 'Comparative Law and EU legal language: Towards a European Restatement?', Global Jurist, 2021.

There might be a real tension between the Meta – concept and la *parole;* the most frequent situation is the presence of divergences in one or some of the language versions. If this occurs, the Meta – concept is not expressed in la *parole* simply because of the limit of the language. In this case, as we will see later, the Meta-concept might simply be implicit in one or more linguistic versions.

5 A Glance to Asia

The role of form is likewise similar when it comes to the formulation of a common legal language through the ideographic writing system. Chinese and Japanese legal languages developed through the mutual circulation of models of inter and intra linguistic translation, not so seldom taken from the West. Therefore, it is necessary to re-conceptualize meanings, languages and culture in order to create a legal taxonomy able to cope with the complex interaction of the divergent legal traditions. Furthermore, the separate, often divergent, evolution of the spoken and the written language is a common feature of the historical development of these legal systems.[62] Although ideograms are often the only form of visual reference, clarifying words that are pronounced in the same way but have different meanings, all this leads to an asymmetric and hybrid use of the legal terms, often carrying different legal effects even if traditionally expressed under the same ideogram. Therefore within the Asian legal systems the creation of a common legal terminology leads to a specific experience of uniformization, in which the role of the ideogram is the graphic form of the legal words (*graphic form of the signifier* or *signifier of the graphic sign*) and of a new concept, (uniform as common to different legal languages Chinese, Japanese…) and supposed to transmit the same content in all the linguistic versions.

These aspects seem suggest that EU and Asian uniform legal texts are proceeding in some sort of parallel fashion as regards the establishment of a formal status. That in turn raises the inference that there is a close relationship between these two uniform legal languages, regardless of the difference between the ideographic and the phonetic system of written law.

62 In the ideographic system the written form is a second language and it has evolved separately from the spoken language. One of the consequences of these peculiarities – based on the fact that the Chinese writing is not syllabic – is the presence of homophones, two different words having the same pronunciation. Thus, the written word expressed in the ideogram can be the visual, figurative reference through which the problem can be solved. In Japanese too, sometimes spoken communication must be clarified by means of the written character and everywhere the same graphic symbol can stand for words from different dialects or languages: M. Timoteo, 2014, pp. 85 *et seq.* For Japanese see: A. Ortolani, 'La lingua del diritto in Giappone', *in* G. Ajani, A. Serafino, M. Timoteo (Eds.), *Il diritto dell'Asia Orientale* (in *Trattato di Diritto Comparato,* directed by Rodolfo Sacco), Torino, 2007, pp. 24-43.

The EU and the Asian legal languages are inconceivable without form and form is represented by a *linguistic* or a *graphic sign*. Regardless of this difference, from a linguistic point of view both the Asian and the European *signs* are aimed at structuring a legal meaning, a *Meta – concept*, that transmits the uniform, autonomous common rule.

6 Back to Europe

In general terms, the role of law is to resolve disputes and settle relationships within a specific social group. EU law turns out to be somehow peculiar in the legal world, as the aim of the EU multilingual legislation is the harmonization of the law, so as to eliminate the different norms enacted by the various Member States, in specific areas, particularly private law. Because the EU principally relies on written sources for the production of its laws – and so on language – the EU legal language has an inescapably instrumental character: as the ideal, ultimate expression of the EU Meta – concept, each EU legal term is meant to lead to a positive outcome of the harmonization process.

However, even if the development of a European Union – specific legal language is gradually surfacing, no clear guidance has ever been given to the national interpreter as regards how to apply the *acquis communautaire*. This is particularly relevant for the national courts, as the judges have no background against which to interpret EU legislation: no system of rules or concepts, no common culture, no general referents.

Despite the ongoing development in translation studies suggesting recent elaborate approaches and the increasing level of awareness, the interpreters at the national level are still in want of responses to this long-standing challenge. The lack of support to national judges in giving a meaning to EU concepts is particularly problematic. True is that the Court of Justice of the EU is more and more sensitive to language issues and the number of cases in which its judgements do - directly or indirectly - contribute to clarify and consolidate EU concepts is constantly increasing. Nevertheless, the awareness that the CJEU is the authority deciding on the meaning of the European autonomous concepts, in the light of the EU law harmonization process, is very low in national courts and, with the exclusion of specialists, in academic circles too.

Moreover, although of high quality,[63] scholars' contributions were merged by the European Commission into the well-known *Draft common frame of reference (DCFR)*,[64] as a set of principles, model rules and definitions which, among its other functions, was

---

63 See as an example the results of the Acquis group (http://www.acquis-group), the "Principles of Existing Contract Law", edited by Sellier.

64 *Principles, Definitions and Model Rules of European Private Law: Draft Common Frame of Reference (DCFR).* Outline Edition by Study Group on a European Civil Code (Editor), Research Group On The Existing EC Private Law (Acquis Group), Sellier European law publisher, 2009.

aimed at guiding the national justices in the interpretation and application of EU law. As far as the content of the DCFR is concerned, the high level of abstraction of the terminology and its use of concepts with German civil law origin (e.g. the "juridical act", which homologates the German "Rechtsgeschäft") has lead to the creation of an instrument that is in part disconnected with the terminology composing EU regulations and directives.[65]

7 National Courts' First Aid: Theories

Several proposals have been constructed in European legal theory in order to support national judges to interpret and apply EU law.

One of the very first monographic works is the German language analysis of the problems of interpretation of community law by Schübel-Pfister (2004);[66] the work was soon followed by Creech's[67] contribution on the language regime of Europe (2005). Few years later, Derlén's essay (2007 and 2009)[68] focused on the attitude towards the multilingual interpretation of Community law of the national courts of Denmark, England and Germany. The interest for EU multilingual law in dedicated volumes returned fruitful in 2013, thanks to Paunio's book on the impact of multilingualism on the judicial reasoning of the Court of Justice of the European Union.[69] "Eu Language and Law" by Van der Jeught (2015) soon followed, as a work having a wider aim of analysis and focusing on the regulation of languages then followed;[70] a year later was the time of Robertson's interdisciplinary opera "Multilingual law. A Framework of Understanding", (2016)[71] addressed especially to EU lawyer linguists, and academics too.

65 See on the discussion E. Ioriatti, 'Draft common frame of reference and terminology', *in* L. Antoniolli & F. Fiorentin, *A factual assessment of the draft common frame of reference*, Munich, Sellier, 2011, p. 343.

66 I. Schübel-Pfister, *Sprache und Gemeinschaftsrecht – Die Auslegung der Mehrsprachig verbindlichen Rechtstexte durch del Europäischen Gerichtshof*, Berlin: Duncker & Humblot, 2004.

67 R.L. Creech, *Law and Language in the European Union: The Paradox of a Babel "United in Diversity"*, Amsterdam, Europa Law Publishing, 2005.

68 M. Derlén, *A Castle in the Air: The Complexity of the Multilingual Interpretation of European Community Law*, Umeå (Sweden): Umeå Studies in Law, 2007 and M. Derlén, *Multilingual Interpretation of European Community Law*, The Hague, New York: Kluwer Law International, 2009.

69 E. Paunio, *Legal certainty in multilingual EU law. Language, discourse and reasoning at the European Court of Justice*, Farnham, Surrey (UK): Ashgate, 2013. In the same period of time, a book written by the author of this Chapter was meant to introduce Italian academics and professionals to EU legal language: E. Ioriatti, *Interpretazione comparante e multilinguismo europeo*, Padua: Cedam, 2013.

70 Van der Jeught 2015.

71 Robertson 2016.

The very last contributions of Baaij (2018)[72] analyze the specific difficulties of interpreting EU law uniformly from the point of view of translation, in order to address proposals and policy advice.

As one can guess, the object of interest of the studies mentioned above is not identical, and every work studies a different aspect of European legal multilingualism.

Schübel-Pfister's work focuses on the problems of interpretation of Community law with particular attention to the case law of the CJEU on conflicting language versions; the national level is analyzed from the point of view of the case law of the Court providing the duty of national judges to compare all different language versions of EU legislation. According to the Author's analysis, this case law is qualified as inconsistent and incompatible with the general principles of Community law. In her research outcome, Schübel-Pfister then suggests a model in which the duty of national courts to go through a language comparison of EU legal concepts should be graduated accordingly with the area of Community law and the *ratio legis* of each specific provision.

Three years later, the purpose of the well-known work by Derlén was the examination of how the institutional mandate to national courts to compare the different language versions in interpreting European community law (EC law) was actually performed. After having examined an impressive number of national decisions of German, Danish and English Courts, the Author demonstrated that, at the time of his research, the multilingual character of EC law had a limited impact in national courts as frequently EC norm was interpreted without the support of any foreign language version. The study also suggests a reform of the multilingual interpretation of EC law, where only few languages, preferably English and French, should be qualified as the only mandatory consultation languages by national courts to reach a uniform interpretation and application of EU law.[73]

While the essay of Creech and that of Van der Jeught do not concentrate efforts specifically on the interpretation of EU multilingual law, in both volumes the interesting research outcomes do however contribute to the issue of determining the language meaning of EU law, because policies on multilingualism are often interlocking reasons behind an EU concept and neologism choice.

Creech observes EU law from the point of view of language regulation – linguistic regimes of EU organs, case law of the CJEU, EU programs of legal education, language regulation in the Member States, EU language rights – in the light of the EU policy; in his interesting concluding remarks the Author argues that language is primarily understood

---

72 C. Baaij, *Legal Integration and Language Diversity. Rethinking translation in EU lawmaking*, New York: Oxford Studies in Language and Law, 2018.

73 Derlén, 2007.

and regulated by the EU as an economic affair, a medium through which commerce is conducted.[74]

In a similar, even though more detailed essay, Van der Jeught analyses the same areas and underlined a fragmented EU and national language policy approach, in which the different levels sometimes hamper EU integration itself. As a conclusion, the Author calls for the adoption of one single vehicular language of communication in the EU, combined with equal status of all others in specific areas of EU law.[75]

From a different perspective, Paunio's main aim is to analyze the concept of legal certainty in Multilingual EU law, qualified as predictability and acceptability, with particular attention to the uncertainty surrounding EU multilingual legislation and the consequences of multilingualism on the judicial reasoning of the CJEU. The intensive and extensive idea accompanying every chapter of the book suggests a conception of legal certainty not based on objectivity or the immutability of the language, but on a "discursive legal certainty", based on acceptability of judicial decision-making and dialogue within the EU legal community.

The insight of Robertson's volume on multilingual law relates specifically to different disciplines – law, language, semiotics, translation, technology – in connection with multilingualism, and so, by extension, to interdisciplinarity. As such, the book is an extensive source of inspiration and information.

In order to favour a uniform interpretation and application of EU law, Baaij places emphasis on the role of English as a *lingua franca*. By clearly observing the reality of the EU multilingual environment, the Author suggests the English language version as the original and only authentic legislative English-based text, according to a source-oriented technique of EU translation illustrated in details.

As noted already, in general, the majority of the studies on EU law multilingualism have their focus of attention on the EU level, mainly analyzing the environment of multilingual translation or the judicial reasoning and case law of the CJEU.

From this perspective, theoretical research has taken out the nature of multilingual text of European provisions from obscurity and this is one crucial aspect of the complex nature of the EU multilingual law process.

Other authors use different approaches, such as Engberg, whose suggestions focus on the importance of maintaining a constant dialogue among the different actors involved in this process.[76]

74 Creech, 2005, pp. 157-158.

75 Van Der Jeught, 2015, pp. 272 – 274.

76 J. Engberg, 'Autonomous EU Concepts – Fact or Fiction?', *in* S. Šarčević (Ed.), *Language and Culture in EU Law: Multidisciplinary Perspectives*, Ashgate, 2015, pp. 169 *et seq*.

Of particular interest is the work of Pommer, who proposes to include translation among the criteria for interpretation. Although difficult to be traced within the process of EU legal drafting, translation should be a necessary stage of the work of a judge who applies EU law. Pommer defines translation as the method according to which reconciliation is undertaken as a way of expressing the thought that can be faithful to a text without being entirely literal.[77]

Furthering this line of reasoning, comparative law might be used as a means of interpretation of multilingual legislation too. This raises the question of the concrete relevance of this proposal, which might sound naïve, as clearly the interpretation of multilingual legislations expressed in different language versions passes through an inevitable process of comparison: however, the use of comparative law as an interpretation criterion entails a step further and presumes the use of all the methodological instruments of comparative law as a science.

8 COMPARATIVE LAW AS AN (IMPLICIT) MEANS OF INTERPRETATION

In her interesting article "Comparative law and language"[78] Vivian Grosswald Curran underlines that one of the reasons that make comparative law our best bet today, is because it is the field with the biggest head start towards detecting the unseen that lurks beneath the seen.

It is well-known that, unlike the traditional and positivist approach, which simply identifies law as the product of the official sources of a given legal system, the methodology involved in comparative law science presupposes the existence of a plurality of legal rules, which are active components – "formants"[79]– of a legal system and contribute to its actual feature. Specifically, it is the theory of the formants and particularly the criptotype which attracted Grosswald Curran, as a tool able to uncover what is present as a rule, but in unexpressed form: "the comparatist knows that legal orders reside as much beneath and aside from words, as they do in the words that purport to embody them".[80]

Among formants, criptotypes are rules not explicitly formulated, but nevertheless implicitly applied by jurists. They exist in all legal systems and are intrinsically part of a legal culture and transferred from one generation of jurists to the next one; for this reason they are mostly invisible to jurists belonging to that culture who have a tendency to consider

---

77 Pommer, 2012, p. 1241

78 V. Grosswald Curran, *Comparative law and language, in* M. Reimann & R. Zimmermann (Eds.), *The Oxford Handbook of Comparative Law*, Oxford University Press, 2006-2012.

79 R. Sacco, 'Legal Formants. A Dynamic Approach to Comparative Law', *American Journal of Comparative Law*, 1991, pp. 1-35 and 343-401.

80 Grosswald Curran, 2006-2012, p. 40.

them a kind of obvious component. A famous example provided by Sacco is how the discipline on transfer of movable property provided in former art. 1138 of the French Civil Code was applied by French courts. Even if the norm explicitly stated that "consent" is the only necessary element for transfer, case law constantly required for a valid transfer the "consent based on a justification or *cause*".[81] European law is an environment where rules might be implicit in one or more language versions.[82] They might get in contact with material facts or rules which are explicit in one or more other language versions and this makes the formulation of the previous implicit rules necessary. Since there are many rules or latent linguistic patterns under the surface of the EU language that are more permanent than visible, uncovering implicit criptotypes might be the key to understanding more about the nature and the functioning of the EU legal discourse.

Let us examine art. 18 of the directive 2011/83/EU on consumer rights in various language versions. We can notice a shift in the Italian version in the definition of "delivery".

> *Article 18*
> **Delivery**
> Unless the parties have agreed otherwise on the time of delivery, the trader shall deliver the goods by **transferring the physical possession** or **control of the goods** to the consumer without undue delay, but not later than 30 days from the conclusion of the contract.
>
> *Artikel 18*
> **Lieferung**
> Sofern die Vertragsparteien hinsichtlich des Zeitpunkts der Lieferung nichts anderes vereinbart haben, liefert der Unternehmer die Waren, indem **den physischen Besitz an den Waren** oder **die Kontrolle über die Waren** dem Verbraucher unverzüglich, jedoch nicht später als dreißig Tage nach Vertragsabschluss, überträgt.
>
> *Articolo 18*
> **Consegna**
> Salvo che le parti abbiano concordato altrimenti in merito al termine di consegna, il professionista consegna i beni mediante il **trasferimento del possesso** o **del controllo fisico dei beni** al consumatore senza indebito ritardo e comunque non oltre trenta giorni dalla conclusione del contratto.

81 See Sacco, 1991, p. 30.
82 Ioriatti, 2016.

Article 18
Livraison
Sauf si les parties en disposent autrement concernant le moment de la livraison, le professionnel livre les biens en en transférant la **possession physique** ou **le contrôle** au consommateur sans retard injustifié, mais au plus tard trente jours après la conclusion du contrat.

The Italian definition is different from all the other versions, as instead of **transferring the physical possession** or **control of the goods** the key sentence provides "**transferring of possession** or **physical control of the goods".**

This version seems the only one admitting that the delivery may be replaced by a legal relationship being agreed between the owner and the acquirer by which the acquirer obtains indirect possession. It is the so called "constructive delivery"[83] ("costituto possessorio", "Besitzkonstitut").

Therefore, according to Italian law, the delivery of the goods involves both the concrete transfer of the goods (*physical control of goods*), as well as the legitimate possession (*transfer of possession*). The English, German and French versions are apparently different as the literal meaning leaves no space to any concept of delivery besides that of an actual material disposition.

However, when other language versions are read in the light of the Italian one it is clear that the "constructive possession" is simply implicit, for instance, in the sentence "die Kontrolle über die Waren" (control over the goods). When read through the presence of criptotypes the Italian version is not isolated, but the text referring to constructive delivery is explicit, whereas in the other versions (German)[84] it is simply present as a *criptotype*, and becomes visible as soon as the text is set against the Italian one.

Why are some concepts implicit in EU law?

A possible explanation is that legal concepts have a peculiar tenacity and an "ability" to reach stability within a particular legal system. However, in order to achieve this result, language needs ties between words and ideas and these relationships are compromised if the denotation of the concepts is not well established.[85]

83 *Constructive delivery.* "If the owner is in possession of the object, the delivery may be replaced by a legal relationship being agreed between the owner and the acquirer by which the acquirer obtains indirect possession".

84 § 930 BGB *Besitzkonstitut.* "Ist der Eigentümer im Besitz der Sache, so kann die Übergabe dadurch ersetzt werden, dass zwischen ihm und dem Erwerber ein Rechtsverhältnis vereinbart wird, vermöge dessen der Erwerber den mittelbaren Besitz erlangt".

85 R. Sacco, 'Language and Law', *in* G. Zaccaria (Ed.), *Übersetzung im Recht / Translation in Law*, in *Ars interpretandi*, 2000, p. 1.

The legal language of the European Union is a melting pot of intrinsic and extrinsic influences and it is not possible to decipher the language through an analysis of the historical dimension of words.[86] However, on the other side, the EU is an area that is characterized by a certain homogeneityy from a cultural point of view and the EU text is a rather recent composition and the jurist's knowledge is often supported by similar conceptions.[87] Sometimes there are concepts that are simply implicit.

As noted above, the Meta-concept is the EU rule elevated at a high level of abstraction. However, these concepts must be somehow expressed through the language. It might occur that one or more languages are not equipped to express the Meta-concept. Words – *la parole* (in the word of De Saussure) – have their own limit.

As noted already, there might be a tension between the Meta-concept and *la parole*, the word created by the EU legislator – translator, jurist linguists, experts – and contained in EU legal acts.

This might be the reason why "constructive delivery", as being an expression of a Meta-concept related to possession and the transfer of possession, although part of the common background of the EU jurists – is explicit in the Italian version and implicit in the German one.

9 Europe, Asia and the Tenacity of the Form

It might be interesting to note that these tensions are present in both the main world legal languages, the phonetic and the ideographic ones.

As Authors tell us referring to Chinese legal language[88] and to Japanese,[89] both idioms have passed through an inter-linguistic and intra-linguistic translation; their main feature is the fact that law drafters made use of semantic borrowings.

Asian languages are not monolingual. Furthermore, written form is a second language in the ideographic system and has evolved separately from spoken language.

As to Chinese, in particular, the consequences of these peculiarities – based on the fact that Chinese writing is not syllabic – is the presence of homophones, two different words having the same pronunciation. Thus, the written word expressed in the ideogram can be the visual, figurative reference through which the problem can be solved.

86 A. Wagner, K. K. Sin & L. Cheng, 'Cultural transfer and Conceptualization in Legal Discourse', *in* L. Cheng, K.K. Sin & A. Wagner (Eds.), *The Ashgate handbook on legal translation*, Ashgate, 2014, p. 35.

87 Sacco, 2000.

88 Timoteo, 2014, p. 85.

89 A. Ortolani, 'Riflessioni in materia di diritto e lingua in Giappone', *in* B. Pozzo (Ed.), *Lingua e diritto: oltre l'Europa*, Giuffrè, 2014, pp. 103 *et seq.* and A. Ortolani, 'La lingua del diritto in Giappone', in G. Ajani, A. Serafino, M. Timoteo, *Il diritto dell'Asia Orientale* (in *Trattato di Diritto Comparato* directed by Rodolfo Sacco), Torino, 2007, pp. 24-43.

However, in Japanese too, sometimes spoken communication must be clarified by means of the written character and everywhere the same graphic symbol can stand for words from different dialects or languages.

From a linguistic point of view, language and writing are two distinct systems of signs and the second one, in theory, exists only for the sole purpose of representing the first.

Nevertheless, as de Saussure already noted, the spoken word is so intimately linked to the written image that the latter manages to usurp the main role. As a consequence, in general more importance is given to the written image of a vocal sign than to the sign itself. This is particularly true in the field of law, as the written form of a legal concept is attached to the authority of the text in which the law is expressed and enforced.

For all these reasons, uncovering of criptotypes could be a relevant step in the creation of an Asian legal language – and in the EU language too – as long term models of the Chinese or Japanese tradition might be implicitly operating behind recent legal taxonomies. Here, the contribution of comparative law methodology is particularly relevant, Once more, in the words of Vivian Grosswald Curran "Comparative law is nothing more than a lantern that makes visible how 'every mode of meaning' signifies".

Between Pragmatism and Perfectionism in Legal Translation

*Patrick O'Callaghan**

1 Introduction

The thoughts I develop in this short essay are inspired by an important argument Professor van Erp pursued in his inaugural lecture delivered at Maastricht University on 25th September 1998.[1] In this lecture, Van Erp focussed on the 'tension between comparative law in practice and comparative law as it should ideally be.'[2] In comparative research, he explained, there is a tension between idealism and pragmatism but, in the end, the comparative lawyer is faced with 'the inevitability of having to make a choice when confronted with [this] dilemma.'[3]

In this essay, I would like to reflect on Van Erp's remarks in the context of the challenges of legal translation. Like many comparatists, I have attempted translations of legal texts from time to time but I have never been entirely satisfied with my results, usually feeling that my translations have fallen short in some way. At the same time, I seek to remind myself that an uncompromising commitment to perfectionism can easily become the enemy of progress. In order to proceed with a comparative study, I must make pragmatic choices so that the translation is good enough for the purposes at hand. Yet, as I will seek to argue in this essay, perfectionism or the idea of a 'true translation' nonetheless plays an essential role in the enterprise of legal translation.

In reflecting on these issues and questions, I will draw on an intriguing book edited by Dr Simone Glanert in 2014. This book, *Comparative Law – Engaging Translation*, includes chapters written by leading legal theorists interested in translation theory.[4] The authors throw light on the problems or dilemmas translators encounter when going about their difficult work and several chapters suggest helpful ways of dealing with these problems. In what follows, I will focus on some insights in this book that intersect with the theme of

* College Lecturer in Law, University College Cork, Ireland and Visiting Research Fellow, Leuphana Law School, Leuphana Universität Lüneburg, Germany.

1 J.H.M van Erp, 'European Private Law: Postmodern Dilemmas and Choices: Towards a Method of Adequate Legal Analysis (1999) 3(1) *Electronic Journal of Comparative Law*, http://www.ejcl.org/31/abs31-1.html.

2 *Ibid.*

3 *Ibid.*

4 S. Glanert (ed), *Comparative Law – Engaging Translation*, Abingdon, Routledge, 2014.

my essay, as inspired by Van Erp's inaugural lecture: the tension between perfectionism and pragmatism in legal translation.

2 Comparative Lawyers as Pragmatists

In her introductory remarks, Glanert poses an important question: why do so few comparatists engage with translation theory? Glanert speculates that there are at least four reasons.[5] First, comparative lawyers tend not to have enough 'interdisciplinary knowledge'.[6] Second, there are some comparatists who think that interdisciplinary research is of no practical use to lawyers.[7] The third explanation stems from what Glanert calls the 'ascendancy of law'.[8] Glanert presents this idea in the following way: 'Traditionally, law has been envisaged as more prestigious than other disciplines such as anthropology, sociology or linguistics.'[9] On her account, this explains, at least in part, why comparatists are more interested in law than the other disciplines. Finally, in legal systems where the emphasis is on a scientific understanding of law, 'there is little epistemological room left for the interaction of law with other fields of knowledge.'[10]

These are good explanations, but I think the second one, or at least a variation of it, has the most explanatory power. I think the pragmatist would accept that there is no such thing as a 'perfect translation' but would argue that we can reasonably agree on pragmatic solutions that allow us to communicate in a meaningful way. It is our shared experience of things that allows us to communicate with each other; the verb 'to communicate' has its roots in the Latin verb *communicare*, meaning 'to share'. After all, as McGilchrist reminds us, '[b]ecause we do not experience precisely the same world does not mean that we are condemned not to meet in the world at all.'[11] Against this background, for the pragmatist, theory is of little or no use to the practical task of translation. In my view, this is the most convincing explanation for the lack of engagement with translation theory.

I think most comparative lawyers are also pragmatists in this sense. Indeed, this is a view that seems to be widely shared: Van Erp opens his inaugural lecture with the question, '[w]hy are almost all comparative lawyers such pragmatists?'[12] I am almost certain that I

5 S. Glanert, 'Chapter 1: Translation Matters', *Ibid.* It is instructive to read Glanert's four reasons alongside Bercea's thought-provoking discussion of 'legal hermeticism' ('Chapter 9: The Powerless Translator', *Ibid.* pp. 140-142) as both passages complement each other.

6 *Ibid.* p. 2.

7 *Ibid.* p. 3.

8 *Ibid.*

9 *Ibid.*

10 *Ibid.*

11 I. McGilchrist, *The Master and his Emissary: The Divided Brain and the Making of the Western World*, New Haven, Yale University Press, 2009, p. 141.

12 Van Erp, 'European Private Law: Postmodern Dilemmas and Choices', n. 1 above.

do not know of any comparatists who think that a 'perfect translation' is achievable in practice. But it should not follow, even for the most pragmatic of pragmatists, that theory is superfluous to the task at hand. Theory is in fact essential because it helps us to detach ourselves from our immediate experience, what McGilchrist calls the 'terrain', and encourages us to rise above it and survey the 'territory' instead.[13] Theory provokes 'aha moments', as McGilchrist puts it, those occasions when suddenly we gain a new insight that helps us see a problem in a new light.[14] We need theory because, among other things, it helps reveal blind-spots in our thinking. Might the 'pragmatic solution', as espoused by the pragmatist, not mask challenges in translation? What does it mean to reach a 'reasonable agreement', as the pragmatist might put it? Might we still be talking past each other though we think we have found a solution? Theory helps reveal problems such as these and, when put to good use, can enrich both our understanding and practice of translation. So, when Legrand, in his contribution to Glanert's book, laments the 'woeful under-theorisation that continues to plague the field [of comparative legal studies]',[15] I think he has a point. But I believe we need the *right* sort of theory (and the right amount of it) if we are to entice comparative lawyers to engage with theory.

What, then, is the right sort of theory for comparative legal studies? The short answer is that it depends. It depends, naturally enough, on the aims and objectives of the research project, the research questions and the target readership. My starting point is that we should encourage a plurality of approaches in the field of comparative legal studies, intersecting as it does with other disciplines such as sociology and anthropology. Generally speaking, then, usefulness in the practical world should not be the only criterion by which we judge the merit of a theory in comparative legal studies. But where the subject of the theorising is the comparative *method* or the actual *practice* of translation, then I think the results of the theorising need to prove practically useful in some way if we expect comparative lawyers to engage with the theory. Take postmodern-style theorising as an illustration of this point. I admit that the metaphorical use of language, the contradictions as well as the *isms* and *isations* of postmodern theories are sometimes helpful because they provoke 'aha moments' in McGilchrist's sense. But often postmodern discourse constructs framework questions for research that ultimately prove to be unhelpful in the practical world because they lead us to 'dead-ends'.[16] If comparative lawyers were to heed all of the warnings emphasised by postmodern scholars, this would lead, as Van Erp put it, to the 'death of comparative law, [methodologically-speaking].'[17] If our aim is to undertake the best comparative research, we need the sort of theory that brings back down to the ground

13 McGilchrist, *The Master and his Emissary*, n. 11 above pp. 21-22.
14 *Ibid.* p. 47.
15 P. Legrand, 'Chapter 13: Withholding Translation' in n. 4 above, p. 208.
16 See J.D. Caputo, *Truth*, London, Penguin, 2013.
17 Van Erp, 'European Private Law: Postmodern Dilemmas and Choices', n. 1 above.

what we have learned from surveying the territory. In this way, as McGilchrist explains, we can 'incorporate [the theory] in such a way that it enriches experience'.[18] Put differently, when the subject of a study is something as practical as the comparative method or the art of translation, we need theories that offer solutions as opposed to those that simply identify problems. Less important in this context – though it may be important in other contexts – is the sort of theorising that is never brought back down to the ground in McGilchrist's sense. The problem with this sort of theorising is that it risks alienating most comparative lawyers.[19] Consider, in this vein, Legrand's idea of *overtranslation* as he explains it in Glanert's book. By this, he writes, he means the following:

> 'I have in mind situations where the transformation to which the source-text is being subjected acts as an unacceptable betrayal of it. As it defects from the source-text, as it fails to abide by the cardinal translative goals of recognition and respect, as it does so much violence to the source-text as to move to a beyond of the inescapable translative disjointure, "translation" emerges as the enemy of singularity.'[20]

The gist of this argument, if I understand it correctly, is that we should avoid bad translations not least because they do injustice to the distinctive character of the source text. Inspired by Legrand's use of words here, I would like to introduce the idea of *overtheorisation.* I want to suggest that in theorising about anything, there is always the risk of *overtheorising* thc subject matter. Again, while postmodern-style theorising has inspired important insights for comparative legal scholars (consider, for example, Legrand's idea of *mentalité*),[21] *overtheorising* risks alienating all but those few scholars interested in similar pursuits. This was a risk that Van Erp identified in his inaugural lecture. As he eloquently put it:

> 'As Legrand has argued, it is of great importance that comparative lawyers should also, as far as possible, compare cultural factors. What I greatly regret,

18 McGilchrist, *The Master and his Emissary*, n. 13 above, p. 22.

19 In his discussion of the postmodern challenges to the comparative law method, Van Erp argues that they often lead to 'all or nothing reactions': 'either comparative lawyers treat the questions so seriously that they no longer get around to undertaking – or dare to undertake – practical comparative studies, or they view the questions as so alien to the practical world that it is better to let them well alone.' Van Erp proposes a 'middle course' where 'comparative lawyers should not only expressly observe various substantive standards when undertaking comparative analysis but should also explain their procedure.' See Van Erp, 'European Private Law: Postmodern Dilemmas and Choices', n. 1 above.

20 Legrand 'Chapter 13: Withholding Translation' in n. 4 above, p. 209.

21 P. Legrand, 'European Legal Systems Are Not Converging' (1996) 45 (1) *International and Comparative Law Quarterly* 52.

however, is that the proponents of this view- and I say this with due respect for those who defend it – have the tendency to withdraw into intellectual isolation, where they may be able to find confirmation of the correctness of their positions, but at the same time leave those involved in the practice of comparative law to their fate.'

3 THE USES OF THEORY

Notwithstanding concerns about overtheorisation, Glanert's book is a collection of brilliant essays, each of which, in one way or another, demonstrates the usefulness of theory for legal translation in comparative research. Hendry, one of the contributors, sums up the book's core question: 'considering the restrictions under which it necessarily has to take place, how can translation be satisfactorily operationalised?'[22] Translation is challenging and has to take place under difficult conditions. How best do we go about our task?

Most of the chapters in the book engage with Hendry's question providing many important insights. For reasons of space, I can give only a flavour of these insights. Take, for example, Boyne's fascinating chapter advocating that the day-to-day realities of legal practice should inform translation.[23] Of particular interest is her analysis of how mistakes in translation can affect what we might call 'meta-claims' that are made about a legal system.[24] Another important question, raised by several authors, concerns the style of translation that is most appropriate for comparative research. In what follows I pay particular attention to this question as it maps neatly onto the theme of my essay.

In her introductory chapter, Glanert introduces Schleiermacher's essay '*Über die verschiedenen Methoden des Übersetzens*' ('On the Different Methods of Translation').[25] She explains that Schleiermacher proposed two methods of translating and quotes him as follows:

> 'Either the translator leaves the writer in peace as much as possible and moves the reader toward him; or he leaves the reader in peace as much as possible and moves the writer toward him.'[26]

22 J. Hendry 'Chapter 6: Legal Comparison and the (Im)possibility of Legal Translation' in n. 4 above, p. 99.
23 S.M. Boyne 'Translating Civil Law "Objectivity" with an Adversarial Brain: An Ethnographic Perspective' in n. 4 above.
24 *Ibid.* pp. 131-132.
25 Glanert 'Chapter 1: Translation Matters' in n. 4 above, p. 9.
26 *Ibid.*

This quote sums up the translator's dilemma. When the translator leaves the writer in peace, she normally adopts a literal approach, trying to remain as faithful as possible to the actual words the writer used. The translation will not read as smoothly as the source text does and this has the benefit of maintaining *strangeness* in the text, as Glanert neatly puts it, in that the reader is continually reminded that he is reading a foreign text.[27] But a drawback is that it can 'give the reader a hard time.'[28] In contrast, when the writer leaves the reader in peace, the translator's focus is to ensure that the 'spirit' of what the writer had to say is carried across to the reader. This encourages a freer translation where, as Hendry succinctly explains, the meaning is supposed to be rearticulated but not necessarily the form.[29] The risk here is obvious. The resulting text may have too much of the translator in it but too little of the original writer.

I think it accurate to say that the majority of contributors to the book – to the extent that I can identify their position on this point – lean towards the side of freer translation. One notable exception is Baaij who develops a sophisticated defence of the literal approach in comparative legal research.[30] Like other contributors, Baaij argues that comparative legal research and translation are inextricably linked but argues that we should work hard to ensure as little 'contamination' as possible in our translations. For Baaij, a literal or a source-oriented approach to translation is more conducive to comparative legal research than a freer or recipient-oriented approach. This is because the latter risks too much contamination whereas the former 'leaves it as much as possible to the comparatist to draw his own comparative conclusions from translated legal texts.'[31]

Though Baaij offers a convincing argument, there are still some lingering questions. These questions stem from the inevitable fact that translation, even when done literally, always involves making choices. This becomes clear when Baaij discusses the example of translating the word *Bezit* from a provision in the Dutch Civil Code. A literal translation might suggest the word 'possession' as an equivalent. But according to Baaij, this word is 'legally loaded' so, in order to be as neutral as possible, it might be better to use the word 'having' instead. What this means, as Baaij admits, is that even for literal translation, the 'legal translator needs at least a rudimentary level of comparative knowledge of the legal systems involved; just enough to avoid accidentally hitting on legally loaded words.'[32]

But surely determining whether a particular word is 'legally loaded' or not presents its own difficulties? To use the example above, it is one thing to assess the provision from the Dutch Civil Code in the abstract; the word 'having' might not be legally loaded in this

27 *Ibid.* pp. 7-10.
28 C.J.W. Baaij 'Translation and the "Contamination" of Comparative Legal Research' in n. 4 above, p. 114
29 Hendry 'Chapter 6: Legal Comparison and the (Im)possibility of Legal Translation' in n. 4 above, p. 91.
30 Baaij 'Translation and the "Contamination" of Comparative Legal Research' in n. 4 above.
31 *Ibid.* p. 115.
32 *Ibid.* p. 116.

abstract context but does it follow that it remains so in every context in which the rule is applied? Moreover, the word the translator chooses might not be 'legally loaded' in Baaij's sense but could be loaded in other ways or could just be too malleable to be useful. The idea of engaging in a neutral literal translation is appealing but choices will always have to be made and, in the end, it will come down to what the translator deems appropriate or inappropriate. In my view, the "inevitability of having to make a choice", as Van Erp put it in his inaugural lecture,[33] underscores the importance of ensuring that the right person is doing the translation; that this same person has an extensive knowledge of the law as well as the appropriate linguistic skills. Baaij is right to point to the risk of contamination but the better approach, I suggest, is for translators to remain vigilant about risk, and to remind themselves that they are situated in a 'horizon' as Gadamer might say.[34] In this way translators should draw on their experience and expertise to make difficult choices, whether this means a literal or freer translation strategy in any given case.

4 Why the Idea of a 'True Translation' is Important

Before I conclude, I would like to reflect on one of the 'threshold questions' Glanert identifies in her introductory chapter: is a true translation possible?[35] Several authors in her book refer to the impossibility of such and criticise those comparatists who seem to think it is possible. At times, this feels like a 'straw man' argument. Again, I am almost certain that I do not know of any comparatists who believe that a perfect translation is possible. But I do believe that most comparatists think that the *idea* of a 'true translation' is important. This is because, as I will now seek to explain, it is integral to the whole translating endeavour.

In the final chapter of the book, Legrand writes: "While I hold that there cannot be a translation that could ever be called 'true' ... I defend the view that there can be mistranslations ...".[36] But it surely follows from Legrand's remarks that if it is possible to identify mistranslations, then it is at the same time possible to identify more accurate translations. This means that it is possible to compare, to say that one translation is better than another. Various translations of the same source text are in that sense commensurable. But, if we can confidently assert that there are mistranslations or more accurate translations, against what standard are we measuring the quality of translation? The standard we measure it against, I suggest, is this: to what extent does the translation carry across the meaning

33 Van Erp, 'European Private Law: Postmodern Dilemmas and Choices', n. 1 above.
34 H.G Gadamer, *Truth and Method*, New York, Continuum, 1977.
35 S. Glanert, 'Chapter 1: Translation Matters' in n. 4 above, p. 11.
36 Legrand 'Chapter 13: Withholding Translation' in n. 4 above, p. 209.

of the original text without doing injustice to it? It is here that the idea of a true translation becomes important.

A true translation might not be achievable in practice. Indeed, quite apart from the misgivings about translating from one language to another, given the scope for disagreement internally within a linguistic community, how would we even know if we achieved perfect equivalence in any given case?[37] But it does not follow that we should abandon the idea of a true translation. The idea remains an important aspiration that gives structure and direction to the translating endeavour.[38] In this way, the aspiration of achieving of a true or perfect translation acts as a 'regulative ideal' and thus has a similar function to 'objective truth' in the natural sciences.[39] As the philosopher of science, Karl Popper has written, while it not might be possible to identify with certainty the criteria of truth, the 'very idea of error – and of fallibility – involves the idea of an objective truth as the standard of which we may fall short.'[40] Popper illustrates this point with a metaphor about a climber ascending a mountain, the peak of which is permanently covered by cloud.[41] Because he cannot see the peak, the climber remains unsure whether he has reached the true summit or a subsidiary peak. But the fact that the climber cannot see the mountain peak does not affect the 'objective existence' of the summit. While the climber can never be sure he has reached the top, he can determine that he has not reached it: where he comes up against an overhanging wall, for example. Put differently, though translators can never be sure that they have arrived at a true translation, they can edge towards it by critically reflecting on what they have done wrong and always seeking to do better.[42]

Most translators set out in their difficult task aiming to produce the best possible translation. Few translators are content with doing a job that is only adequate. But even in this latter category, the idea of a 'true translation' is relevant because how do we determine what is 'adequate' without some sort of standard against which we can measure it? My argument, then, is that perfectionism or the idea of a true translation is important for all translators, even those who regard themselves as pragmatists, whether they realise it or not. That is not the same as saying that translators believe a perfect translation is

37 For a similar point about arriving at truth in the natural sciences, see generally K. Popper, *Conjectures and Refutations*, London, Routledge, 2002.

38 Indeed, it would seem that even prominent postmodernists would accept this point. Interpreting the work of Jacques Derrida, one of the best-known postmodernists, Caputo argues that for Derrida, it is the 'promise of *becoming* true' that gives us something to aim for. See Caputo, *Truth*, n. 16 above, p. 77.

39 For broadly similar arguments in law, see Fuller on legality being a 'morality of aspiration': L. Fuller, *The Morality of Law*, New Haven, Yale University Press, 1964 and Dworkin on the 'right answer thesis': R. Dworkin, *Taking Rights Seriously*, Cambridge, Harvard University Press, 1977.

40 Popper, n. 37 above, p. 311.

41 *Ibid.* pp. 306-307.

42 This argument is shaped by Popper's ideas about falsification, *Ibid.* Consider too, in this context, Samuel Beckett's line from *Worstward Ho* (1983): 'Ever tried. Ever failed. No matter. Try again. Fail again. Fail better.'

achievable in the practical sense – most do not. But even if there are comparatists out there who believe that a true translation is within their grasp, is this really such a terrible thing? At worst, I admit, this could lead to hubris. But in most cases surely, the aspiration of a true translation will motivate translators to do the best job they can do.

5 Conclusions

In his insightful inaugural lecture, Professor van Erp brings to the foreground the issues emerging from the "gap between what, ideally, comparative law should be and what, in practice, comparative law often is."[43] Translation for the purposes of comparative research is challenging work but it is possible to produce translations that are good enough for the purposes at hand, as long as the translator is willing to maintain a pragmatic attitude. But being pragmatic in this way does not mean that perfectionism or idealism becomes irrelevant to the translating endeavour. As I have argued in this essay, perfectionism or the idea of a true translation is in fact an integral part of the enterprise of legal translation.

In concluding, I would like to refer to another metaphor, one provided by Alexis Nouss in his contribution to Glanert's book. It reads as follows:

> "The translator or the reader of a translation are like mariners standing on the deck of a ship crossing the water: what is behind and what is in front are simultaneously separated and united by the progress of the moving vessel. In a sea of contingencies, agitated by waves and waves of possible choices, where to head to is a matter of interpretation."[44]

This is a wonderful metaphor because it draws our attention to the role of 'movement' in translation, as Schleiermacher emphasised. It reminds us too that translation is a practical exercise; it is about getting the job done rather than just theorising about the implications of doing it – the ship, after all, has to set out on its journey no matter how choppy the waters appear to be. But I would like to suggest a few changes to the wording so that it aligns more neatly with the arguments I have made in this essay. I suggest that it should be the translator only who is the mariner steering the ship. The translator is crossing the water, leaving the source text behind and moving towards her destination: the best possible translation she can achieve. I accept that in crossing the water, there will be a 'sea of contingencies' and 'waves of possible choices' but I do not think that the ultimate destination is 'a matter of interpretation'. The mariner may have to steer different courses and the

43 Van Erp, 'European Private Law: Postmodern Dilemmas and Choices', n. 1 above.
44 A. Nouss, 'Chapter 2: Translation as Ethics', see n. 4 above, p. 27.

journey may take longer than she originally anticipated but, in my view, the ultimate destination (i.e. the goal of a perfect or true translation) is firmly fixed, even if it always seems just out of reach.

Part V
Security Rights

Fixtures, Accessories and the MAC-Protocol

The Cape Town Convention Touches Ground

Eva-Maria Kieninger[*]

1 Introduction

In his numerous publications and lectures on Comparative Property Law, Sjef van Erp has never tired of demonstrating that property law, including land law, is far from being old-fashioned or apolitical; rather it is up to property law scholars themselves to broaden their perspectives and explore new, fascinating and politically important subjects such as virtual property, land grabbing or co-ownership and the share economy, to name but a few topics on which Sjef has extensively written and taught.[1] In the same vein, Sjef has educated a whole generation of young academics who in turn have founded the 'Young Property Lawyers Forum', a worldwide research network of junior and senior comparativists specialising in property law.[2] Moreover, Sjef has – almost single-handedly – established 'European Property Law' as a sub-discipline of European private law. The most visible fruit of this endeavour is the European Property Law Journal[3] which he has founded and whose editor-in-chief he has been from the very beginning.

It is therefore with some hesitation that I have chosen 'fixtures and accessories' as a topic for this *Festschrift*.[4] It is not a subject which is likely to be taken up by the European legislator. Nor can the definition of essential components of land or the question under which prerequisites a mortgage extends to equipment which serves the economic purposes of the land, be classified as scientifically stimulating or politically thrilling. It may rather

---

* University of Würzburg. The author was a member of the German delegation at the two sessions of the Committee of Governmental Experts and the Diplomatic Conference which adopted the Pretoria Protocol. The views expressed in this article are purely personal.

1 As a prominent example see S. van Erp, 'Comparative Property Law', *in* M. Reimann & R. Zimmermann (Eds.), *The Oxford Handbook of Comparative Law*, 2nd ed., Oxford, Oxford University Press, 2019, pp. 1031-1057.

2 See http://yplf.net/about/ and the book series 'Property Law Perspectives' (last visited 07.09.2020).

3 The journal, published by de Gruyter, appears since 2012.

4 However, I take some comfort in the fact that the Case Book on European Property Law also devotes a few pages to fixtures, see S. van Erp & B. Akkermans (Eds.), *Cases, Materials and Text on Property Law, Ius Commune Casebooks for the Common Law of Europe*, Oxford & Portland, Hart Publishing, 2012, pp. 640-641, 643-644, 648-650, 659-660.

qualify as a nightmare for law exam candidates.[5] But I nevertheless hope to be able to show at least how important comparative property law can become for the practice of legal unification[6] once the latter leaves the realms of air and space and touches ground.

2 Cape Town in a Nutshell

The 2001 Cape Town Convention (CTC) on International Security Interests in Mobile Equipment is one of the most successful international conventions in the field of commercial law. It has become the gold standard of international aircraft financing. The number of registrations which the International Registry in Dublin receives every year, has risen from an initial 50.000 in 2008 to about 136.000 in 2018.[7] To date, the Cape Town Convention has more than 81 Contracting States plus the EU. Due to its two tier structure, it has to be complemented by an equipment-specific Protocol in order to become practically applicable. Next to the Aircraft Protocol, which was prepared and concluded in parallel to the Convention and has now 78 Contracting States plus the EU, three further Protocols have been finalised: the Luxemburg Protocol 2007 on Railway Rolling Stock, the Berlin Protocol 2012 on Space Assets, and the Pretoria Protocol 2019 on Mining, Agricultural and Construction Equipment, the so-called "MAC-Protocol".[8] None of the three later Protocols is yet in in force.

---

5 Here, I refer specifically to §§ 1120 to 1122 *Bürgerliches Gesetzbuch* on the question when and how fruit, fixtures and accessories cease to be encumbered property under a mortgage.

6 On the role of comparative law for law-making generally and legal unification and harmonisation especially see J. Basedow, 'Comparative Law and its Clients', *American Journal of Comparative Law*, Vol. 62, No. 4, 2014, pp. 821-858 at 842 et seq.

7 Cf. www.internationalregistry.aero/ir-web/annualStatisticalReport/ (last visited 01.09.2020).

8 All legal texts and status charts are available at the website of Unidroit (www.unidroit.org). As to the history and development of the CTC and its Protocols see most recently H.-G. Bollweg, 'Die Übereinkünfte von Kapstadt: beschlossene und künftige Protokolle – Innenansichten aus deutscher Perspektive', *in* C. Benicke & S. Huber (Eds.), *Festschrift für Herbert Kronke*, Bielefeld, Gieseking Verlag, 2020, pp. 707-724. R. Goode's contribution to the same *Festschrift* places the Cape Town Convention in a larger context, see: R. Goode, 'Creativity and Transnational Commercial Law: from Karkhemish to Cape Town', *in* C. Benicke & S. Huber (Eds.), *Festschrift für Herbert Kronke*, Bielefeld, Gieseking Verlag, 2020, pp. 847-870 at 866 et seq. On the economic theory underlying the Cape Town concept see S. Kozuka, 'The Cape Town Convention and the "Fitness" to the Context: Considering the Features of Aircraft, Rail and Space Financing', *in* C. Benicke & S. Huber (Eds.), *Festschrift für Herbert Kronke*, Bielefeld, Gieseking Verlag, 2020, pp. 1005-1016. On the draft Protocol immediately prior to the diplomatic conference see *B.* von Bodungen & O. Böger, 'Neue Regeln für den kreditfinanzierten Handel mit Ausrüstungsgegenständen für Landwirtschaft, Bauindustrie und Bergbau', *WM*, Vol. 26, 2017, pp. 1241-1252; B. von Bodungen & O. Böger, 'The draft MAC Protocol to the UNIDROIT Cape Town Convention on International Interests in Mobile Equipment: A New International Regime for Security Interests in Mining, Agricultural and Construction (MAC) Equipment', *Uniform Commercial Code Law Journal*, Vol. 49, 2019, pp. 45-122. The most comprehensive information on the Cape Town Convention and its Protocols are to be found in the Official Commentaries by R. Goode (see https://www.unidroit.org/official-commentary), who acted as *rapporteur* throughout the whole project.

In essence, the Cape Town System enables parties[9] to create an international security right in the specific piece of equipment as far as it falls in one of the categories covered by a protocol, and to register this interest internationally.[10] Roughly speaking, this interest, once it is duly registered, will take priority over any national or international security right which has been registered subsequently, as well as over any prior security right, whether national or international that was not previously registered in the international register, irrespective of any subjective element, such as knowledge, on the part of the secured creditor.[11] The central rules are to be found in Art. 29 Cape Town Convention which reads as follows: "(1) A registered interest has priority over any other interest subsequently registered and over an unregistered interest. (2) The priority of the first-mentioned interest under the preceding paragraph applies: (a) even if the first-mentioned interest was acquired or registered with actual knowledge of the other interest; and (b) even as regards value given by the holder of the first-mentioned interest with such knowledge."[12] In the event of the debtor's insolvency, the Cape Town Convention, as a matter of principle, guarantees that the international interest remains effective, subject to the applicable national rules on avoidance, and the rules and options contained in the equipment-specific Protocols (Art. 30 CTC).

3 Pretoria or: The Cape Town System Touching Ground

It was not without hesitation that Unidroit set out to include agriculture, mining and construction equipment into the Cape Town system since these categories may cover a huge variety of objects ranging from a rake to a tractor, from a pick to an excavator and from a hammer to a crane. Not all of these objects are necessarily very valuable, highly

---

For further in-depth reading on specific issues see the publications in the *Cape Town Convention Journal* and within the framework of the *Cape Town Convention Academic Project* (https://ctcap.org/).

9 In order for the Cape Town Convention to be applicable, only the debtor must be situated in a Contracting State, see Art. 3 Cape Town Convention: "(1) This Convention applies when, at the time of the conclusion of the agreement creating or providing for the international interest, the debtor is situated in a Contracting State; (2) The fact that the creditor is situated in a non-Contracting State does not affect the applicability of this Convention." According to Art. 4, the debtor is situated in any Contracting State "(a) under the law of which it is incorporated or formed; (b) where it has its registered office or statutory seat; (c) where it has its centre of administration; or (d) where it has its place of business."

10 The register for security rights in aircraft runs fully electronically, see https://www.internationalregistry.aero/ir-web/aboutUs.

11 R. Goode, 'Creativity and Transnational Commercial Law: from Karkhemish to Cape Town', *in* C. Benicke & S. Huber (Eds.), *Festschrift für Herbert Kronke*, Bielefeld, Gieseking Verlag, 2020, pp. 847-870 at 868.

12 In retrospect, the 'father' of the Cape Town Convention, R. Goode, wonders that is was possible to regulate the highly contested issue of priorities in one single article, see R. Goode, 'Creativity and Transnational Commercial Law: from Karkhemish to Cape Town', *in* C. Benicke & S. Huber (Eds.), *Festschrift für Herbert Kronke*, Bielefeld, Gieseking Verlag, 2020, pp. 847-870 at 868.

mobile and uniquely identifiable and hence would not match the general criteria for equipment to be placed under the umbrella of the Cape Town system, see the Preamble of the Convention.[13] To overcome this problem, Unidroit and its advisers resorted to using the classification system of the World Customs Organisation, the Harmonized Commodity Description and Coding System (so-called HS Codes). After intense and detailed work, stretching well into the deliberations at the diplomatic conference, 56 of these codes were at last selected to define the substantive sphere of application of the Pretoria Protocol.[14] This innovative approach however, created the need for highly detailed and well-nuanced rules on procedures for future Treaty changes since the Protocol must on one hand be continuously kept in line with the dynamics of the HS-Code-System in order to avoid the Annexes to become outdated or even obsolete, while on the other hand, Contracting States cannot be forced to be bound by amendments to which they have not consented.[15]

Another new and legally challenging issue relates to MAC-equipment becoming attached or associated to land. In essence, this is again a question of priorities, but in this case between the holder of a mortgage or other legal interest in land and the party secured by an international interest in MAC-equipment under the Cape Town Convention. Two factual scenarios can be distinguished: (i) equipment that becomes physically attached to land. In fact, from consultations with the relevant industry, it became apparent that some of the equipment which was finally included in the Annexes even needed to be – at least partly – affixed to land in order to be operable, for example rock drilling tools or concrete mixers.[16] (ii) A second category consists of equipment that is not necessarily physically affixed to land but is functionally connected to it, and may therefore become legally associated to it even if it is not necessarily always present on the land. One example cited in the preparatory work was a combine harvester used on a farm.[17]

---

13 "AWARE of the need to acquire and use mobile equipment of high value or particular economic significance and to facilitate the financing of the acquisition and use of such equipment in an efficient manner [...]".

14 The Codes are listed with their numbers and verbal descriptions in three separate Annexes to the MAC-Protocol. Each Contracting State can choose whether to apply the Protocol to one, two or all three annexes, see Art. II: "(1) The Convention shall apply in relation to mining equipment, agricultural equipment and construction equipment as provided by the terms of this Protocol and Annexes 1, 2 and 3 irrespective of any intended or actual use of the equipment. (2) A Contracting State may, at the time of ratification, acceptance, approval of, or accession to this Protocol, declare that it will limit the application of this Protocol to the entirety of the equipment comprised in one or two of the Annexes."

15 See the final amendment provisions in Arts. XXXIV to XXXVI, which distinguish between amendments due to adjustments in the HS-Codes initiated by the World Customs Organisation (Art. XXXV), other changes to the HS Codes (Art. XXXVI) and other changes to the Protocol (Art. XXXIV).

16 See Unidroit 2016 – Study 72K – SG4 – DOC.8, p. 50 (Annex III, no. 3). These include HS Code 820713: Rock drilling or earth boring tools, and parts thereof; HS Code 843039: Coal or rock cutters and tunnelling machinery; HS Code 843049: Other boring or sinking machinery; HS Code 847431: Mixing or kneading machines: Concrete or mortar mixers; HS Code 847432: Mixing or kneading machines: Machines for mixing mineral substances with bitumen.

17 See Unidroit 2017 – Study 72K – CGE1 – Report, para. 52.

4 The Comparative Survey

The need to regulate this type of priority conflict and the consequential need for some in-depth comparative work was recognised at a very early stage.[18] With help from Study-Group members and the Unidroit network of correspondents, the Secretariat produced a comparative survey covering fifteen jurisdictions from five continents, roughly representing the major legal traditions.[19] The survey was submitted to the Study Group in December 2015 and – as expected – revealed considerable diversity, not only between jurisdictions belonging to different legal families,[20] but even among the various sister states of the US:[21] Three different border lines can be derived from the reports:[22] The first relates to the criteria for accession through physical attachment.[23] The jurisdictions apply different tests concerning the degree and duration of physical attachment, the severability of the object from the land, and the role, which the intention of the parties are allowed to play. An even greater gulf however, exists between those jurisdiction which require at least a certain degree of physical attachment in order to terminate the separate legal existence of the movable and render it immovable, and others, like for example France, where a movable object can turn into an immovable purely by "destination".[24] Furthermore, a third group of jurisdictions, represented in the study by Germany, does not turn movables into immovables if they serve the economic function of the land, but treats them as a separate category of 'accessories': they retain their separate legal identity but if the land they are serving is charged by a mortgage (*Hypothek* or *Grundschuld*) those movables become part of the so-called '*Haftungsverband*', meaning that they too become encumbered by the mortgage. Hence, it is not only the requirements for turning into an immovable or an accessory which differ from one jurisdiction to another, but also the legal consequences.

---

18 See Unidroit 2019 – DCME-MAC – Doc. 5 corr. – Appendices, Appendix II para 2.

19 See Unidroit 2019 – DCME-MAC – Doc. 5 corr. – Appendices, Appendix II paras. 14 et seq.

20 As to the concept of legal families in Comparative Law, see P. Glenn, 'Comparative Legal Families and Comparative Legal Traditions', *in* M. Reimann & R. Zimmermann (Eds.), *The Oxford Handbook of Comparative Law*, 2nd ed., Oxford, Oxford University Press, 2019, pp. 423-441.

21 See Unidroit 2019 – DCME-MAC – Doc. 5 corr. – Appendices, Appendix II paras. 77 et seq.

22 The Unidroit survey itself was not supplemented by a comparative summary or analysis.

23 See in this respect also S. van Erp & B. Akkermans (Eds.), *Cases, Materials and Text on Property Law, Ius Commune Casebooks for the Common Law of Europe*, Oxford & Portland, Hart Publishing, 2012, pp. 618-660 at 659 et seq.

24 See Art. 524 Code civil: *"Les objets que le propriétaire d'un fonds y a placés pour le service et l'exploitation de ce fonds sont immeubles par destination."*

5 Definition of 'Immovable-Associated Equipment' in the MAC-Protocol and Issues of Private International Law

Given this diversity, the first issue that had to be resolved by the drafters of the MAC-Protocol related to terminology: they needed to avoid any predetermination of the legal outcome through the use of national, pre-fixed terminology.[25] It was therefore decided to use the neutral notion of 'immovable-associated equipment', which is now defined in Art. I (2) (k) of the MAC-Protocol as meaning "equipment that is so associated with immovable property that an interest in the immovable property extends to the equipment under the law of the State in which the immovable property is situated".

Yet, although the terminology may be neutral, the definition is not without legal content, but rather embodies a conflicts rule: Whether and under which conditions equipment becomes so associated as to either legally form part of the land or be included in a proprietary security right encumbering the land, is to be determined by the law of the state in which the land is situated. As long as the equipment stays within the territory of the state in which the immovable is situated this is a clear and logical rule which is in conformity with the probably globally accepted *lex situs* rule for immovables.[26]

But what happens if MAC-equipment which is immovable only by destination such as a tractor, is removed from the territory of the state in which the land is situated, and crosses the border to another jurisdiction which does not know the concept of "immovables by destination"?[27] On the level of Private International Law, different solutions seem possible: either the *lex situs* of the land continues to apply to (or to shape) the legal condition of the movable as long as the functional bond between the two pieces of property continues to exist, or the new *lex situs* of the equipment applies exclusively, with the possible consequence that the interest in the land ceases to extend to the equipment. An intermediate solution is proposed for German Private International Law pursuant to Art. 43 EGBGB: As a matter of principle, the *lex situs* of the land under which the movable has been classified as legally forming part of the land continues to apply, but the new *lex situs* of the movable can reject this result as being contrary to its own property law rules (see Art. 43 (2) EGBGB). In that case, the new *lex situs* will prevail.[28]

25 See Unidroit 2019 – DCME-MAC – Doc. 5 corr. – Appendices, Appendix II paras. 4 et seq.

26 See H.-P- Mansel, 'Internationales Sachenrecht', *in Staudinger BGB*, Berlin, Sellier de Gruyter, 2015, Art. 43 EGBGB para. 34 with further references.

27 This scenario might seem rather hypothetical, yet, during the COVID pandemic which temporarily led to a closure of borders even within the EU, it turned out that many farmers in Bavaria owned fields in Austria and continuously moved their equipment from one side of the border to the other.

28 See H.-P. Mansel, 'Internationales Sachenrecht', *in Staudinger BGB*, Berlin, Sellier de Gruyter, 2015, Art. 43 EGBGB paras. 480 et seq.

Art. I (2) (k) of the MAC-Protocol seems to render the *lex situs* of the immovable exclusively applicable to the legal condition of the associated equipment. But the wording of Art. VII which is the *sedes materiae* for the priority rules concerning immovable-associated equipment may point into a different direction. The sections that are relevant in our context read as follows: "(1) Where immovable-associated *equipment is situated in a non-Contracting State*, this Protocol does not affect the application of any law of that State that determines whether an international interest in the immovable-associated equipment cannot be created, has ceased to exist, is subordinated to any other rights or interests in the immovable-associated equipment, or is otherwise affected by the association of the equipment with immovable property. (2) A Contracting State shall, at the time of ratification, acceptance, approval of, or accession to this Protocol, declare that the entirety of Alternatives A, B, or C of this Article will apply in relation to an international interest in immovable-associated *equipment which is situated in the Contracting State.*" (*Emphasis added*).

Taking Art. VII (1) and (2) MAC-Protocol literally, the rules seem to apply the law at the place where the equipment is situated: this may either be the law of a non-Contracting State in which case the MAC-Protocol cannot say anything about the treatment of fixtures or the continuance or priority of an international interest; or it is that of a Contracting State, so that the applicable rules depend on which alternative (A, B or C) that State has chosen when it became a party to the MAC-Protocol.

Yet, on the other hand, Art. VII (3) in the Alternative B clearly refers to the *lex situs* of the immovable when stating: "This Protocol does not affect the application of any law of the State where immovable property is situated that determines whether an international interest in immovable-associated equipment cannot be created, has ceased to exist, is subordinated to any other rights or interests in the immovable-associated equipment, or is otherwise affected by the association of the equipment with immovable property if the equipment has lost its individual legal identity *in accordance with the law of that State.*" (*Emphasis added*). "That State" at the end refers to "the State where immovable property is situated" in the beginning of the sentence. The same applies to Alternative C which also clearly refers to the "State where immovable property is situated" and not to the situs of the equipment.

To resolve the matter, regard must therefore be had to the *travaux préparatoires*. The question of the applicable law was discussed in the context of Art. VII Alternative B at the first session of the Committee of Governmental Experts (CGE). The report says the following: "It was noted that such an approach could lead to the application of the private international law rules for movable property or immovable property, depending on the jurisdiction and this could result in different outcomes. The Committee requested that the Drafting Committee revise paragraph 3 of Alternative B to ensure that it referred *to the lex situs of the immovable property in all cases*. This approach was found to be consistent with the rule found in the definition of "immovable-associated equipment" in Article I (2) (f)." *(Emphasis added).*[29]

In addition, one should look at the relative weight of the rules in question and the scrutiny they underwent. By exempting immovables situated in non-Contracting States from the priority rules of the Protocol, Art. VII (1) states something that is quite obvious. In the first session of the CGE, it was even questioned whether this provision was needed at all.[30] Art. VII (2) merely introduces the different alternatives. The focus is on the obligation of States to choose one of the three options. In sum, the present author would therefore suggest to take the wording of the definition article and of Alternative B as decisive and conclude that the Protocol rests on the applicability of the *lex situs* of the immovable only.

6 A Uniform, Fact-Based Protocol Standard for Physically Attached Equipment?

In light of the strong affiliation of land law with the nation-state, and in view of the deeply-rooted traditions of real estate financing, it is unsurprising that comprehensive uniform rules on priority conflicts between an international interest and interests in land under national law were unattainable.[31] But a uniform Protocol standard for the treatment of fixtures, perhaps still attenuated by an opt-out possibility, seemed not completely out of reach. A uniform rule or even a reduction to a binary choice between the Protocol standard and national law would have been advantageous especially for financiers of equipment which needs to be physically attached in order to become operable (see supra, 3.). They would have had some chance of legal certainty without having to resort to national law.

However, for political reasons, the hurdles for a uniform solution proved to be unsurmountable. Therefore, Contracting States, if they do not apply domestic law altogether (Alternative C), now have to choose between the factual test of severability as contained in Alternative A, sections 3 to 5, and the legal test of "loss of separate legal identity" (Alternative B). But whereas the test for severability is spelled out in the text of Alternative A itself (see section 4: "Immovable-associated equipment is severable from the immovable

29 Unidroit 2017 – Study 72K – CGE1 – Report, para. 56.

30 Unidroit 2017 – Study 72K – CGE1 – Report, para. 40.

31 See inter alia Unidroit 2019 DCME-MAC – Doc. 21 rev. (Summary report for 12 November 2019), para. 30: "One delegation noted that the MAC Protocol would be the first Protocol within the Cape Town Convention system to cover equipment that could become associated with immovable property. The delegation explained that immovable property was the subject of national law regimes and that it was important for the treaty to strike a balance between preserving the priority of international interests and respecting national law."

property only if its estimated value after physical disconnection of the equipment from the immovable property would be greater than the estimated cost of the disconnection and of any restoration of the immovable property") the legal test of Alternative B is not defined by the Protocol but is left to the *lex situs* of the immovable. Contracting States now have a three-fold choice as regards fixtures: factual test of severability (A), legal test according to the *lex situs* (B) or a complete opt out of any Protocol standard (C). Further comparative work on the exact content of the legal test of 'loss of separate legal identity' might have revealed that the practical differences between the approaches in A and B are marginal, but such further study was not carried out.

7 The Solution of the MAC-Protocol for Accessories and 'Immovables by Destination'

The said Alternatives A, B and C of Art. VII MAC-Protocol not only cover equipment that is physically attached to land, but also accessories and 'immovables by destination'. However, under Alternative A, if the equipment stays severable, the international interest in the equipment will not be affected by the association of the equipment with land. Any further rule on accessories is therefore superfluous if a Contracting State opts for Alternative A. Alternative C also provides a clear-cut answer: the solution of the priority conflict is wholly governed by the *lex situs* of the immovable.

Only Alternative B provides a mid-way, Protocol-based priority rule which forms an exception to the general priority rule in Art. 29 CTC: if both conditions contained in Art. VII Alternative B (4) (a) and (b) are cumulatively fulfilled, the interest in the land will prevail over the international interest in the equipment. Letter (a) requires that the interest in the land has been registered prior to the international interest in the equipment; letter (b) demands that the association of the equipment with the land took place prior to the registration of the international interest in the equipment. The purpose of Alternative B is to protect the legitimate expectations of the holder of the interest in the land, who has contracted on the assumption that at least the equipment which is presently associated with the land, will form part of the encumbered estate. The financier of the equipment will be able to protect himself, since knowing that he is financing equipment which is serving land in a state that has opted for Alternative B, he will be able to search the land register prior to lending money against the equipment.

In sum, the Protocol, by providing three options, give States maximum flexibility in a politically sensitive area. Yet, this flexibility which is also present in numerous other respects (see the list of possible or mandatory declarations in Art. XXVIII MAC-Protocol), is also endangering the economic success of the Cape Town System which aims at providing a *uniform* international security interest.[32]

8 Epilogue

During the diplomatic conference, numerous delegates and observers voiced their concern that the Cape Town system is already suffering from too many alternative solutions and opt-out possibilities for too many important issues. While it is true that practice may push Contracting States to adopt the most creditor-friendly option, for example with respect to insolvency remedies where the so-called OECD-discount on the interest rate[33] is only available to debtors located in States that have opted for Art. XI Alternative A Aircraft Protocol, other choices do not have such an immediate and visible impact on the level of security for creditors and will probably not lend themselves to getting streamlined so easily and rapidly. Furthermore, all declarations and options made by every Contracting State must be recorded by the depositary. Unidroit's General Secretary pointed out on various occasions that the administrative burden which the Secretariat is performing was steadily rising with each new Protocol, and that Unidroit should in the future be reimbursed for those costs via the registration fees.[34] No such decision was taken for the time being but the issue is sure to rise to the surface again in due course.

Perhaps this inflation of opt-outs and alternatives is the logical consequence of engaging in the unification of property law which is, as a matter of principle, mandatory, and has strong links with foreclosure and insolvency law. Unification of contract law is comparably easy; the CISG has only one practically important possibility for a reservation (Art. 95). But of course, parties enjoy freedom of contract and may derogate from nearly every provision of the CISG (Art. 6). It is precisely the absence of such freedom which makes property law so fascinating.

---

32 See the preamble of the Cape Town Convention: "[...] RECOGNISING the advantages of asset-based financing and leasing for this purpose and desiring to facilitate these types of transaction by establishing *clear rules* to govern them, MINDFUL of the need to ensure that interests in such equipment are recognised and protected *universally*,[...]." (Emphasis added).

33 See http://www.oecd.org/trade/topics/export-credits/arrangement-and-sector-understandings/aircraft-specific-rules/ (last visited 04.09.2020).

34 See Unidroit MAC Protocol, Study 72K – CGE1 – Report of the Committee of Governmental Experts, First session Rome, 20-24 March 2017, para. 151: "The Secretary-General explained that the role of UNIDROIT as the Depository under the Cape Town Convention was becoming an ever-increasing cost burden for the Institute. He noted that in contrast to the right of the Supervisory Authority to recover costs associated with its role under the Convention, the Depositary had no such right to cost recovery. He noted that the role of Depositary encompassed the duties of receiving instruments of ratification, assessing ratifications to ensure all mandatory declarations were made, advising States on requirements related to the deposit of an instrument of ratification and liaising with Embassies. He concluded that the role was occupying approximately one-third of the time of a Senior Officer at the Institute."

Retention of Title Clauses, Their Enforceability and the Free Movement of Goods

Björn Hoops[*]

1 Introduction

In the autumn of 2009, Sjef jointly taught the course "Comparative Property Law" with Prof. Christine Godt at the Hanse Law School (an innovative Bachelor's and Master's programme of the universities of Bremen and Oldenburg in Germany, with its Dutch counterpart at the University of Groningen in the Netherlands). I happened to be one of the lucky students to attend Sjef's passionate lectures on issues around the then awfully omnipresent financial crisis, ownership, limited property rights, and the constitutional protection of property rights. His extraordinary skill of explaining complex matters with ease in accessible Dutch, English, and German has made these lectures the most memorable of my student career.

For this subject, the students had to write a paper. I do not remember how the topics of the papers were allocated to the students, but my paper had to address an ECJ case between the European Commission and Italy. The dispute ensued over the EU rules on the retention of title or, in civil law parlance, reservation of ownership by sellers of goods. Art. 4 of Directive 2000/35/EC (now: Art. 9 of Directive 2011/7/EU) obliged EU Member States to give effect to express clauses in which the seller and the buyer agree that the seller will retain their ownership of the sold good until the purchase price is paid. Under Italian law, the seller can only invoke the retention of title as against creditors of the buyer if the retention of title is laid down in a written document dated before the creditors attach the sold good and other documentation requirements are met.[1] The then European Court of Justice found that the Directive did not concern the enforceability of retention of title

* Prof. Dr. B. (Björn) Hoops, Associate Professor of Private Law and Sustainability, Department of Private Law and Notarial Law, University of Groningen.

1 Art. 1524 of the Italian Civil Code (*Codice civile*; CC); Art. 11(3) of the Decree (*Decreto legislativo*) No. 231 of 9 October 2002.

clauses as against third parties. The additional formal requirements therefore did not violate the Directive.[2]

Europeanisation and harmonisation of property law and cross-border situations are fields of particular interest to Sjef. As a tribute to Sjef, this contribution revisits the paper that I wrote at the end of 2009. Reading through my paper again, I thought that something was missing. As the enforceability of retention of title clauses has so far been untouched by harmonisation, additional requirements under the *lex rei sitae* for the enforcement of such clauses as against third parties pose an obstacle to intra-EU trade. These obstacles trigger the question of whether the EU's fundamental freedoms, in particular the free movement of goods, require the receiving state to enforce retention of title clauses from other Member States against third parties without any additional requirements. The influence of the fundamental freedoms on the recognition of property rights from other Member States has been discussed in the literature,[3] but we are still waiting for an answer from the Court of Justice of the EU. A 2019 judgment of the Austrian Supreme Court (*Oberster Gerichtshof*; OGH) on the fate of German non-possessory security ownership in German-Austrian transactions suggests that at least the Austrian judiciary would find a violation of the free movement of goods where the *lex rei sitae* does not recognise a property right from another Member State.[4]

This contribution first sketches the background of Art. 9 of Directive 2011/7/EU (ex-Art. 4 of Directive 2000/35/EC) and the case between the European Commission and Italy. It then discusses the judgment of the European Court of Justice. Finally, it analyses the enforceability of retention of title clauses as against third parties in light of the Free Movement of Goods and the 2019 judgment of the Austrian Supreme Court.

2 Retention of Title Clauses and Article 9 of Directive 2011/7/EU

Retention of title clauses are essential to trading with goods. Buyers cannot always pay for delivered goods immediately because they first have to sell them to a third party to receive the funds needed to pay the seller. For this reason, the parties to the contract of sale agree that the seller will remain owner of the goods until the buyer pays the purchase price.

---

2 ECJ, Judgment of 26 October 2006, *Commission of the European Communities v. Italian Republic*, ECLI:EU:C:2006:683, paras. 29 *et seq.*

3 Most notably by: B. Akkermans & E. Ramaekers, 'Free Movement of Goods and Property Law', *European Law Journal* 2013, 237-266.

4 OGH, Judgment of 23 January 2019, ECLI:AT:OGH0002:2019:0030OB00249.18S.0123.000.

2.1 Retention of Title in Cross-Border Transactions

In most EU Member States, retention of title is not subject to any publicity requirements. In the Netherlands, for instance, the parties agree on an obligation for the seller to transfer the ownership of the goods under the condition precedent (*opschortende voorwaarde*) that the buyer pays the purchase price. The seller/owner then hands over the physical control of the goods to the buyer. This form of delivery is unconditional. In line with Art. 3:84(4) and 3:92(1) of the Dutch Civil Code (*Burgerlijk wetboek*; BW), the buyer thereby receives the ownership of the goods under the condition precedent of the payment of the purchase price, while the seller retains the ownership of the goods under the condition subsequent (*ontbindende voorwaarde*) that the purchase price is paid.[5]

If and when the sold good crosses the border, the law applicable to the retention of title and the property rights of the buyer and the seller changes. Under the rule of *lex rei sitae*, the law of the jurisdiction in which the good is located governs property rights, for example their definition, creation and transfer. The *lex rei sitae* also decides on the extent to which it recognises foreign property rights,[6] such as a conditional right of ownership based on a retention of title clause.

Crossing the border will not pose a problem if the good is moved to a jurisdiction that sets the same or more lenient requirements for the execution of retention of title clauses. Under German law, for instance, § 449 of the German Civil Code (*Bürgerliches Gesetzbuch*; BGB) does not provide for any publicity of the conditional nature of the buyer's right. In German-Dutch trade, the conditional rights of ownership based on retention of title will thus be recognised.[7]

Before the Directive 2000/35/EC was adopted, however, five out of 15 Member States imposed additional publicity or other formal requirements for the validity of a retention of title or its enforcement against third parties.[8] If a German seller had sold goods under a retention of title clause to a Spanish buyer, the retention of title would have ceased to exist when the good crossed the Spanish border unless additional publicity requirements under Spanish law had been observed.[9]

5 See on the recognition of the buyer's conditional right of ownership: Hoge Raad, Judgment of 3 June 2016, ECLI:NL:HR:2016:1046.

6 Akkermans & Ramaekers 2013, p. 250; and B. Akkermans, '*Lex Rei Sitae* and the EU Internal Market – towards mutual recognition of property relations', *European Property Law Journal* 2018, 246-266.

7 Art. 43(2) of the Introductory Act to the German Civil Code (*Einführungsgesetz zum Bürgerlichen Gesetzbuche*); and Art. 10:128(1) BW.

8 E.-M. Kieninger, *Mobiliarsicherheiten im Europäischen Binnenmarkt. Zum Einfluss der Warenverkehrsfreiheitauf das nationale und internationale Sachenrecht der Mitgliedstaaten*, Baden-Baden: Nomos, 1996, pp. 52 *et seq*.

9 Kieninger 1996, pp. 41 *et seq* and 65.

2.2 *Art. 9 of Directive 2011/7/EU and its History*

To ensure that retention of title clauses in B2B, B2G, and G2B transactions would be recognised throughout the EU, the Council and Parliament adopted Art. 4 of the Directive 2000/35/EC. It was re-cast in Art. 9 of Directive 2011/7/EU with the same wording. Art. 9(1) reads as follows:

> Member States shall provide in conformity with the applicable national provisions designated by private international law that the seller retains title to goods until they are fully paid for if a retention of title clause has been expressly agreed between the buyer and the seller before the delivery of the goods.

To understand the judgment of the Court of Justice in the case between the European Commission and Italy, it is important to appreciate the history of the final version of Art. 4 of Directive 2000/35/EC. The background of the Directive 2000/35/EC was that following many transactions, buyers failed to pay on time. This led to additional administrative and financing costs. Differences between the legal systems of the EU Member States made it difficult for sellers to enforce their claims in cross-border situations. Around a third of all companies felt that delayed payments threatened their existence. The European Commission linked a quarter of all bankruptcies in the EU to delayed payments.[10] The goal of the Directive is therefore to promote punctual payments.

The goal of Art. 4 proposed by the Commission was to guarantee that sellers could rely throughout the EU on a retention of title clause for validly reserving ownership for cases of delayed payments.[11] In the original proposal of the European Commission, Art. 4(1) obliged the Member States to allow the seller to retain title if the seller notified the buyer in writing no later than the date of the delivery of the goods, and to reclaim the good if the buyer has not paid by the due date. Section 2 provided that section 1 was only applicable to debts payable in a single instalment. Section 3 of the proposed Art. 4 expressly excluded the effect of the retention of title on third parties acting in good faith from the scope of the Directive.

The European Parliament approved the Commission's proposal with substantial amendments on the enforceability of the retained ownership as against third parties. Parliament further specified the goal of Art. 4 by adding that Art. 4 sought to prevent the

10 Official Journal of the European Communities, 1998, C 168, pp. 13 *et seq. Cf.* W. Lehr, 'Neuer Vorschlag für eine EU-Richtlinie über Zahlungsverzug und Eigentumsvorbehalt im Handelsverkehr', *Europäisches Wirtschafts- und Steuerrecht* 1999, 241-244.

11 See recital 13 of the Commission's proposal.

internal market from being affected by delayed payments.[12] The amended Art. 4 no longer required a written notice by the seller, but an agreement between the seller and the buyer. Moreover, the right to reclaim the good in case of late payment also applied to the relationship between the seller and a third party in case of the buyer's insolvency or similar situations.[13] Section 2 was removed so that Art. 4 also applied to debts payable in more than one instalment.[14]

The Council removed Art. 4 altogether in its common position. It considered that the Member States did not see the need to harmonise the rules on the retention of title and that the right to reclaim the good from third parties unduly interfered with national property and insolvency law.[15]

The final version of the Directive adopted by the Council and Parliament eventually featured Art. 4. The Directive defines the retention of title in Art. 2 No. 3 as a "contractual agreement according to which the seller retains title to the goods in question until the price has been paid in full". While the Commission's proposal sought to oblige Member States to recognise the effects of a retention of title clause between the seller and the buyer, the Directive merely considers in recital 21 that "[i]t is desirable to ensure that creditors are in a position to exercise a retention of title on a non-discriminatory basis throughout the Community, if the retention of title clause is valid under the applicable national provisions designated by private international law." Just as the version adopted by Parliament, Art. 4 does not incorporate any publicity or formal requirements. However, unlike that version, Art. 4 no longer includes explicit rules on the relationship between the seller and third parties.

3 THE COMMISSION OF THE EUROPEAN COMMUNITIES V. ITALIAN REPUBLIC

The European Commission brought an action for failure to fulfil obligations against Italy because the Commission had found that Italy had not fully transposed Art. 4 of the Directive into national law.

3.1 *The Italian Legislation*

The Italian legislation on retention of title clauses concerned by this action were Art. 1523 and 1524 of the Italian Civil Code (*Codice civile*; CC) as well as Art. 11(3) of the Decree

12 Recital 13 of the version adopted by Parliament, Official Journal of the European Communities, 1998, C 313, p. 142.
13 Official Journal of the European Communities, 1998, C 313, p. 144.
14 Official Journal of the European Communities, 1998, C 313, p. 146.
15 Official Journal of the European Communities, 1999, C 284, pp. 6 *et seq.*

(*Decreto legislativo*) No. 231 of 9 October 2002, which concretises Art. 1524 CC. Art. 1523 CC reads as follows:

> Nella vendita a rate con riserva della proprietà, il compratore acquista la proprietà della cosa col pagamento dell'ultima rata di prezzo, ma assume i rischi dal momento della consegna.

This article gives effect to retention of title clauses for debts payable in more than instalment. Buyers will acquire ownership of the good when they pay the last instalment. There is no formal requirement for the validity or effect of the retention of title clause. Art. 1524(1) CC reads as follows:

> La riserva della proprietà è opponibile ai creditori del compratore, solo se risulta da atto scritto avente data certa anteriore al pignoramento.

This article provides that a retention of title in terms of Art. 1523 CC can only be invoked as against the creditors of the buyer if the retention of title was laid down in a written document dated before the good was attached by a creditor. Art. 11(3) of the Decree further provides that the retention of title will only be effective as against third parties if it is confirmed on individual invoices for successive supplies bearing a specific date prior to any attachment procedure and duly entered in the accounting records.

3.2 *The Case and the Judgment of the ECJ*

The Commission brought an action for failure to fulfil obligations because it found that Art. 11(3) of the Decree was inconsistent with Art. 4(1) of Directive 2000/35 and with the spirit of the Directive. In the Commission's view, Italian law subjected the effectiveness of retention of title clauses to additional formal requirements.[16] This contention pre-supposed that the Directive also concerned the relationship between the seller and third parties. Italy responded that the additional requirements served legal certainty, particularly to protect third parties doing business with the buyer who has physical control over the goods, and could be easily met.[17] However, it did not address the issue of the scope of the Directive.

The Court of Justice starts out by noting that the Directive 2000/35/EC does not harmonise all rules relating to late payments. On the contrary, it only harmonises specific

16 ECJ, Judgment of 26 October 2006, *Commission of the European Communities v. Italian Republic*, ECLI:EU:C:2006:683, paras. 14 *et seq.*

17 ECJ, Judgment of 26 October 2006, *Commission of the European Communities v. Italian Republic*, ECLI:EU:C:2006:683, paras. 18 *et seq.*

rules on interest for late payments, retention of title and procedures for recovery of unchallenged claims.[18] From Art. 4, the Court infers that the provision governs the form of a retention of title clause, express agreement, and the effects of retention of title clauses on the parties to the contract of sale, namely that the seller will remain owner until the purchase price is paid.[19] The Court added that the reference to the law applicable under private international law in Art. 4 concerns the conditions for the validity of retention of title clauses and that, if the clause is valid under that law, the Council and Parliament considered in recital 21 that it is desirable that sellers are able to exercise a retention of title on a non-discriminatory basis throughout the EU. In this way, retention of title clauses can contribute to combating late payments.[20] However, the Court finds that the Directive does not govern in any way the relationship between the seller and a third party. It infers this from the wording of Art. 4 and the purpose of the Directive,[21] which is to reduce late payments in commercial transactions. Italy was thus free to adopt additional requirements for the enforceability of the retention of title as against third parties.

3.3 *The Role of the* Lex Rei Sitae?

The findings of the Court of Justice are plausible. Unlike the version adopted by Parliament, the wording of the Directive does not contain any reference to the relationship between the seller and third parties.[22] Also, it is not evident why a right to reclaim the sold good from a third party would promote the Directive's goal, which is to prevent late payments in commercial transactions.

The reference of Art. 9 of Directive 2011/7/EU to the law applicable under private international law and the considerations of the Court about that reference may still cause confusion. On the one hand, the Court holds that the law applicable under private international law governs the validity of the retention of title. If the Court and the Directive refer to the property law regime of the *lex rei sitae*, it is arguable that the retention of title clause will still be ineffective if the *lex rei sitae* sets stricter requirements for the clause's

18 ECJ, Judgment of 26 October 2006, *Commission of the European Communities v. Italian Republic*, ECLI:EU:C:2006:683, para. 23.

19 ECJ, Judgment of 26 October 2006, *Commission of the European Communities v. Italian Republic*, ECLI:EU:C:2006:683, paras. 26 and 29.

20 ECJ, Judgment of 26 October 2006, *Commission of the European Communities v. Italian Republic*, ECLI:EU:C:2006:683, paras. 27 *et seq.*

21 ECJ, Judgment of 26 October 2006, *Commission of the European Communities v. Italian Republic*, ECLI:EU:C:2006:683, para. 29.

22 B. Gsell, 'EG-Verzugsrichtlinie und Reform der Reform des Verzugsrechts in Deutschland', *Zeitschrift für Wirtschaftsrecht* 2000, 1861-1876, 1875; J. Schmidt-Räntsch, 'Zur Zahlungsverzugsrichtlinie der EU', *Zeitschrift für Immobilienrecht* 2000, 484, 485.

effectiveness than the country of origin, even if it complies with Art. 9 of the Directive.[23] On the other hand, the Court also rules that it is the obligation of the Member States to give proprietary effect to an expressly agreed retention of title.[24] There seem to be two ways to resolve this conflict. First, the reference to the applicable law is not construed as reference to the property law regime,[25] but, in particular, the contract law rules on the validity of the agreement. Second, the *lex rei sitae* is only applied insofar as it promotes the goal of Art. 9 and the whole Directive, which is to ensure the reliable use of retention of title clauses throughout the EU and, thereby, to discourage late payments. This would mean that only if private international law refers to a property law regime with more lenient conditions for the validity of the retention of title than under the Directive, would that regime be applicable.

4 Enforceability of Retained Ownership as Against Third Parties

Art. 9 of Directive 2011/7/EU thus obliges EU Member States to give effect to expressly agreed retention of title clauses and allow the seller to remain owner until the purchase price is paid. As for its effectiveness as against third parties, the general conclusion from the judgment of the Court of Justice seems to be that the Member States can set additional requirements for the owner's right to reclaim the good from a third party in case of the buyer's default.[26]

4.1 Difficulties in German-Italian Trade

Additional requirements for the effectiveness of retention of title clauses with respect to third parties may cause the seller substantial costs. For instance, a seller in Germany sells a good to an Italian buyer. The parties expressly agree on a retention of title clause, and the Italian buyer receives the goods. Whether or not the goods are delivered in Germany or in Italy is of no relevance. Italian law gives effect to retention of title clauses without

23 R. Schulte-Braucks, 'Zahlungsverzug in der Europäischen Union', *Neue Juristische Wochenschrift* 2001, 103-108, 107.

24 H. Heinrichs, 'EG-Richtlinie zur Bekämpfung von Zahlungsverzug im Geschäftsverkehr und Reform des Verzugsrechts nach dem Entwurf eines Schuldrechtsmodernisierungsgesetzes', *Betriebs-Berater* 2001, 157-164, 164; and M. Schmidt-Kessel, 'Die Zahlungsverzugsrichtlinie und ihre Umsetzung', *Neue Juristische Wochenschrift* 2001, 97-103, 102.

25 Gsell 2000, p. 1873.

26 See, for instance, T. Juutilainen, *Secured Credit in Europe: From Conflicts to Compatibility*, Oxford: Hart, 2018, p. 131.

any formal requirements under Art. 1523 CC and would also recognise a conditional transfer effectuated under German law as *lex rei sitae* at the moment of the transfer.[27]

Should the Italian buyer be in default, the seller/owner could reclaim possession of the good. However, what would happen if a creditor of the Italian buyer attached the goods because the buyer did not pay that creditor on time either? As the good is located in Italy, Italian law would be applicable as the *lex rei sitae* to the third-party effect of the retention of title. If the parties have not laid down the retention of title clause in a written document in line with Art. 1524 CC or have not furnished the documentation required under Art. 11(3) of the abovementioned decree, the seller will not be able to invoke their right of ownership as against the buyer's creditor.

4.2 *The Free Movement of Goods*

When selling goods across borders, sellers exercise their rights under the free movement of goods. Additional requirements for the enforceability of retention of title clauses as against third parties may violate this fundamental freedom of the seller, more specifically Art. 34 of the Treaty of the Functioning of the European Union (TFEU). Art. 345 TFEU is immaterial to this analysis. The fact that the EU has no competence to adopt rules on the system of property ownership, does not mean that national property law can freely pose obstacles to the functioning of the internal market.[28] Art. 34 TFEU reads as follows:

> Quantitative restrictions on imports and all measures having equivalent effect shall be prohibited between Member States.

The issues at hand are whether the additional requirements constitute measures having equivalent effect and, if so, whether they can be justified.

4.2.1 Measures Having Equivalent Effect

The famous *Dassonville* judgment of the Court of Justice defines measures having equivalent effect as all rules that "are capable of hindering, directly or indirectly, actually or potentially, intra-community trade [...]".[29] Subsequent judgments show that there are three categories

27 Art. 51 and 55 of the Act of 31 March 1995, No. 218 (Riforma del sistema italiano di diritto internazionale privato).

28 B. Akkermans & E. Ramaekers, 'Article 345 TFEU (ex Article 295 EC). Its meaning and interpretations', *European Law Journal* 2010, 292-314.

29 ECJ, Judgment of 11 July 1974, Case C-8/74, *Procureur du Roi v. Benoît and Gustave Dassonville*, ECLI:EU:C:1974:82, para. 5.

of measures having equivalent effect.[30] Measures that treat products from another Member State less favourably, in law or in effect, than domestic products,[31] rules on product characteristics (*Cassis de Dijon*),[32] and rules that factually hinder the access of products from another Member State to the domestic market.[33] The regulation of selling arrangements does not constitute a measure having equivalent effect, unless the regulation differentiates between domestic and foreign products or has, in law or in fact, less favourable effects on foreign products (*Keck*).[34] Moreover, measures whose impact is 'too uncertain and indirect' do not constitute measures having equivalent effect.[35]

Additional requirements for the enforceability of retention of title clauses as against third parties constitute a measure having equivalent effect. Compared to an internal German transaction, German sellers lose an important part of the right that they created under German law. The seller would have to incur substantial costs to obtain legal advice and comply with the formal requirements under Italian law.[36] For these reasons, these additional requirements constitute a measure having equivalent effect.

The literature supports this conclusion. German and Austrian scholars have produced a rich literature on property law obstacles to intra-EU trade because the non-possessory transfer of ownership for security purposes under German law was, until recently, not recognised by Austrian law when the good used as collateral was moved to Austria.[37] These scholars argue that the stricter *lex rei sitae* confines the non-possessory security owner to their country of origin and makes exporting goods substantially more expensive.[38] In a recent judgment, the Austrian Supreme Court (*Oberster Gerichtshof*) ruled that the German security ownership had to be recognised in Austria. Although this ruling was based on statutory interpretation and not on an application of Art. 34 TFEU, the Court referred to

30 See for a more detailed analysis: B. Akkermans & E. Ramaekers, 'Free Movement of Goods and Property Law', *European Law Journal* 2013, 237-266, 243 *et seq*; and C. Barnard, *The Substantive Law of the EU, The Four Freedoms*, 6th edition, Oxford: Oxford University Press, 2019, II.3 and 4.

31 ECJ, Judgment of 10 February 2009, Case C-110/05, *Commission of the European Communities v. Italian Republic*, ECLI:EU:C:2009:66, para. 37.

32 ECJ, Judgment of 20 February 1979, Case C-120/78, *Rewe-Zentral v. Bundesmonopolverwaltung für Branntwein*, ECLI:EU:C:1979:42.

33 ECJ, Judgment of 10 February 2009, Case C-110/05, *Commission of the European Communities v. Italian Republic*, ECLI:EU:C:2009:66, para. 37.

34 ECJ, Judgment of 24 November 1993, Cases C-267/91 and C-268/91, *Criminal proceedings against Bernard Keck and Daniel Mithouard*, ECLI:EU:C:1993:905, para. 16.

35 ECJ, Judgment of 7 March 1990, Case C-69/88, *H. Krantz GmbH & Co. v. Ontvanger der Directe Belastingen and Netherlands State*, ECLI:EU:C:1990:97, para. 11.

36 *Cf.* Akkermans & Ramaekers 2013, pp. 242 and 265.

37 T. Rauscher, *Internationales Privatrecht*, 3rd edition, Heidelberg: C.F. Müller, 2009, pp. 329 *et seq*. See, however, OGH, Judgment of 23 January 2019, ECLI:AT:OGH0002:2019:0030OB00249.18S.0123.000.

38 See, for instance, B. Lurger & M. Melcher, *Handbuch Internationales Privatrecht*, Vienna: Verlag Österreich, 2017, pp. 393 *et seq*; Kieninger 1996, p. 122; and J. Basedow, 'Der kollisionsrechtliche Gehalt der Produktfreiheiten im europäischen Binnenmarkt: favor offerentis', *Rabels Zeitschrift für ausländisches und internationales Privatrecht* 1995, 1-55, 41 *et seq*.

the literature and seemed to agree with the authors' conclusion.[39] Although Austrian law fully deprived the German security owner of their right and Italian law merely subjects the exercise of the ownership as against third parties to additional requirements, these scholarly works and the Austrian judgment strongly indicate that property law can hinder intra-EU trade and that the additional requirements under Italian law constitute a measure having equivalent effect.

4.2.2 Can the Measure Having Equivalent Effect Be Justified?

Under Art. 36 TFEU, measures having equivalent effect can be justified on grounds of

> public morality, public policy or public security; the protection of health and life of humans, animals or plants; the protection of national treasures possessing artistic, historic or archaeological value; or the protection of industrial and commercial property.

As the rules on retention of title do not have a discriminatory character, 'mandatory requirements' in the public interest can justify these measures having equivalent effect.[40] The national protection of creditors seems to be the most obvious public interest that could be invoked to justify the additional requirements for the enforceability of retention of title clauses as against third parties.[41]

The adverse impact of these requirements need to be suitable, necessary, and proportionate with respect to the public goals pursued.[42] Additional documentation requirements for retention of title clauses certainly contribute to the protection of creditors because they make it easier for creditors to detect a retention of title. They are necessary as well because less invasive means, such as the written form of retention of title clauses or no publicity requirements at all, would not protect creditors as extensively as the documentation requirements. The disadvantages suffered by the seller do not seem to be disproportionate because the additional costs incurred by creditors for detecting a retention of title from another Member State would not be lower than the expenses of the seller. The additional requirements under Italian law thus constitute measures having equivalent effect, but they can be justified on grounds of the protection of creditors.

39 OGH, Judgment of 23 January 2019, ECLI:AT:OGH0002:2019:0030OB00249.18S.0123.000, para. 6.3.4.

40 ECJ, Judgment of 20 February 1979, Case C-120/78, *Rewe-Zentral v. Bundesmonopolverwaltung für Branntwein*, ECLI:EU:C:1979:42.

41 Akkermans & Ramaekers 2013, pp. 248 *et seq.*

42 Barnard 2019, II.5.

5 Conclusion

EU law has only harmonised the rules on retention of title clauses with respect to the relationship between the seller and the buyer. The Member States have to recognise an expressly agreed retention of title and allow the seller to retain ownership until the purchase price is paid. However, Member States may impose additional requirements for the clause's enforceability as against third parties. Such measures make intra-EU trade more expensive and fuel legal uncertainty because they create a patchwork. However, they are likely to be justified means to protect creditors.

Sjef has been advocating for the harmonisation of security instruments at EU level.[43] To protect creditors and, simultaneously, ensure legal certainty in cross-border transactions, the enforceability of retention of title clauses would be an obvious candidate for such harmonisation. Wishing him all the best for this new part of his life, I sincerely hope that he will continue to stay and get involved.

43 See, for instance, B. Akkermans, A.F. Salomons & J.H.M van Erp (Eds.), *The Future of European Property Law*, Munich, Sellier, 2012.

Securing Debt in a World Without Collateral

Willem Loof[*]

1 Introduction

Having been an early adopter of technological innovations all his life (outpacing myself, more than 30 years his junior, in all respects), Sjef was also early to write about the challenges that the digital economy presents to traditional property law. When I started out as his research-assistant in 2009, I remember Sjef already discussing the possibilities of having property rights in digital object in online worlds such as Second Life (which was a popular online world at that moment). Since 2009 the importance of digital assets, and the challenge they pose to property lawyers, has exponentially increased. Sjef has continued to take up that challenge with publications in the area of bitcoins, blockchain and digital land registration.

In this contribution I would like to approach the topic from the point of view of creditors who finance investments in the production of digital assets. To which assets can they have recourse and which assets can function as collateral, given the nature of digital assets? It is important, however, to look beyond just digital assets. After all, the 21st century economy can be characterized as an intangible economy – a world 'without collateral' – not just with respect to the investments taking place in the production of digital assets, but also with respect to the investments that take place in production of data, investments in branding, business processes, R&D, etc. In modern economies these types of 'intangible' investments are now the dominant form of investment. And the intangible goods[1] that are being produced (data, software, economic competencies) all share similar economic characteristics that make them unsuitable to function as collateral (in short: they tend to lose value fast, are difficult to valuate and difficult, or impossible, to liquidate). In the following I will explore work done by economists on the intangible economy and the challenges of financing it and I will discuss some of the legal challenges involved.

* Willem Loof is a judge in training at the District Court of Limburg.

1 In this contribution I use the term intangible in the economic and not legal sense.

2 The Intangible Economy and the Challenges of Financing It

Economists define investment as the thing that happens when a producer either acquires a fixed (nonfinancial, long-term) asset or spends resources (money, effort, raw materials) to improve it.[2] Investments can be made in tangible fixed assets: buildings, equipment and vehicles. Investments can also be made in intangible fixed assets. There are three broad categories of intangible investment: Investments in (i) *computerized information*: software or databases; (ii) *innovative property*: R&D, mineral exploration, artistic works or design; and (iii) *economic competences*: training, market research, branding and business process engineering. In many advanced economies the balance of business investment has shifted from tangible to intangible investment. In their book *Capitalism without Capital*, Jonathan Haskell and Stian Westlake offer an enlightening example of this shift. Compare a commercial gym in 1977 with one in 2020. The 2020 gym will have made investments in the same things that 1977 gym would have invested in: buildings, fitness machines, weights, showers, lockers, mats, mirrors. However, on closer inspection, there are some major differences: The computer on the front desk of the 2020 gym contains software that enables booking and scheduling of classes and staff. The 2020 gym will have invested vastly more resources and effort in the development of its brand. Perhaps most importantly, the 2020 gym will have trained key staff members to put on regular exercise classes and might, for instance, have invested in a license to offer "Bodypump" in its facility. This shift from tangible to intangible investment has occurred in all industries, and often to a much greater degree than is the case in the fitness industry.

Intangible investment is characterized by, what Westlake and Haskell call, the four S's, namely *scalability*, *sunkenness*, *spillovers* and *synergies*. In short, intangible assets can be reproduced at relatively low cost (*scalability*); investment in intangibles tends to be irrecoverable (*sunkenness*);[3] it is relatively easy for third parties to benefit from intangible investment (*spillovers*); and intangible assets tend to be worth more when combined (*synergies*). As a result of these characteristics, the outcome and value of intangible investment can be uncertain[4] and the benefits more open to contestation or appropriation by other businesses. In two interesting chapters of their book, Haskell and Westlake argue that there might be a relationship between the rise of intangible investment and the phenomena of secular stagnation[5] and growing inequality: As industry leaders become

2 J. Haskel & S. Westlake, Capitalism without Capital, Princeton, Princeton University Press, 2018, p. 20.

3 For instance: Pets.com, a famous victim of the dot.com bubble crash, invested tens and tens of millions of dollars in the marketing of their puppet mascot, their domain name and other content. After it went bankrupt, these assets were sold for a mere $ 375.000,- to its competitor petsmart.com.

4 The sunkenness of the investment may mean that the investment is worthless, alternatively the return on investment may be high as a result of synergies and scalability.

5 The coincidence of low interest rates, low investment and low consumer demand over a longer period.

increasingly successful in scaling their investment, appropriating spillovers from their competitors and exploiting synergies (all while avoiding taxation on their much more mobile capital), their highly-skilled and highly sought-after employees are paid much better wages and congregate in cities where spillovers and synergies abound.[6] More relevant to this contribution, however, are Westlake and Haskell observations on the (legal) challenges of *financing* an intangible economy. As a result of the *sunkenness* of intangible assets, it may be hard or even impossible to liquidate individual intangible assets (think of, for instance, the investments Toyota has made in its famed lean production system or the investments made by any food retailer in software regulating its supply chain). Intangible assets are also hard to value because, unlike many *tangible* assets, they are often unique and no liquid market for them exists. Finally, given that intangible assets tend to be worth more when combined (synergies) and, therefore, tend to require more intricate cooperation, it becomes more and more important to have clear legal rules and standards to regulate such cooperation.[7] All of this means that it is hard for lenders to obtain security in return for financing the production of intangible property. There is no legal innovation that will definitively solve this problem. It is a structural characteristic of the intangible economy. Nonetheless, certain incremental improvements may be possible.

3 INTANGIBLE INVESTMENT AND (PROPERTY) LAW

The intangible investment category of *computerized information*, as defined by economists, encompasses databases and software. One could define data simply as information which may or may not have been stored on any carrier. Software can be defined as binary data that is stored on a carrier which, through interpretation by a computer, can have a certain functionality for its user (game, music, video, text, etc.).[8]

Investments in the production of software are adequately protected by intellectual property rights such as copyrights and trademarks, which can be used as collateral to pledge to lenders. Investments in licenses for the use of software are more or less adequately protected through the rights that arise out of the license-agreement.[9] These rights can be

6 Haskell & Westlake, 2018, chapters 5 and 6.

7 Haskell & Westlake, 2018, p. 155.

8 The term 'digital content', which is used in the context of European consumer law, is synonymous to the term software as defined in this article, *cf.* art. 2 (11) of the Directive on Consumer Rights, 2011/83/EU of 25 October 2011, OJ 2011 L 304/64.

9 In those jurisdictions in which the use rights arising out of a software license agreement have a quasi-proprietary nature this protection might be more effective. In general, a licensee of software is vulnerable in cases of insolvency of the licensor, because the insolvency trustee, though generally obliged to allow the continued use of the software by the licensee, might not be obliged to make efforts to allow such continued use (i.e. keep servers running, etc.). If economically feasible, parties might agree to keep updated copies of

offered as collateral to lenders to the extent that they are transferable, though I imagine such rights may not, *on their own*, be considered adequate collateral (for instance, because they may require continued periodical payments to the holder of the intellectual property right).

Investments in the production or gathering of data are not generally protected by (property) law. Such investments may be protected through copyrights if the collection of data constitutes an intellectual creation by virtue of the selection or arrangement of the data. A small number of jurisdictions (notably those in the EU) also provide for a *sui generis* database right in cases where a substantial investment is made in the selection or arrangement of the data, even if there is no creative aspect to the compilation.[10] Much of the data that is gathered in our data economy is not, however, structured in a database. It consists, rather, of raw data. Though these compilations of raw data can be extremely valuable (think of data gather by sensors in cars or data gathered by cookies tracking our online behavior), they are not protected by any type of (intellectual) property right. A proposal by the European Commission for the creation of a right for data producers (data ownership[11]) has, it seems, been quietly dropped.[12] Rightfully so, since data as such – abstract information – cannot be specified and, therefore, cannot function as an object of property rights.[13] It is, in any case, questionable whether one would want to award property rights

---

source codes in escrow, allowing the licensee to make continued use of the software if the licensor does not perform his side of the bargain.

10 Cf. Directive 96/9/EC of the European Parliament and of the Council of 11 March 1996 on the legal protection of databases, articles 3 and 7.

11 European Commission, 'Building A European Data Economy', Communication from the Commission to the European Parliament, the Council, the European Economic and Social Committee and the Committee of the Regions, 10 January 2017, COM(2017) 9 final, 13. See also: European Commission, 'Staff Working Document on the free flow of data and emerging issues of the European data economy', Brussels, 10 January 2017, SWD(2017) 2 final, 33-38.

12 European Commission, 'Towards a free flow of data', Communication from the Commission to the European Parliament, The Council, the European Economic and Social Committee and the Committee of the Regions, 25 april 2018, COM(2018) 232 final, p. 9.

13 Cf. P.B. Hugenholtz, 'Against "Data Property"', in: H. Ullricht et al. (eds.), *Kritika: Essays on Intellectual Property*, Cheltenham, Edward Elgard, 2018, p. 48-71. Hugenholtz also remarks that the introduction of data ownership would disrupt the existing system of intellectual property rights and would impact the free flow of information. Any practical need for the introduction of such a right has not been proven. Indeed, the public consultation conducted by the European Commission shows that stakeholders viewed the existing framework as fit for purpose. They indicate that question surrounding data in business do not center so much around the ownership of data but around how access to data is (contractually) organized, see European Commission, 'Towards a free flow of data', Communication from the Commission to the European Parliament, The Council, the European Economic and Social Committee and the Committee of the Regions, 25 april 2018, COM(2018) 232 final, p. 9. See also: J.H.M. van Erp & W. Loof, 'Eigendom in het algemeen: eigendom van digitale inhoud', in: *Boek 5 BW van de toekomst*. Preadviezen KNB 2016, p. 23-63; T. Hoeren & J. Völkel, 'Eigentum an Daten', in: T. Hoeren (ed.), Bi Data und Recht, München, Beck 2014, p. 11-37; E. Tjong Tjin Tai, 'Privaatrecht voor de Homo Digitalis: eigendom, gebruik en handhaving', in: *NJV-preadviezen* 2016, Deventer, Wolters Kluwer 2016, p. 241-306.

to the Facebooks, Googles and Tesla's of our world – being the types of companies that would inevitably benefit most from such rights – on top of the factual control that these companies already enjoy over the immense amount of information that they have gathered.

In conclusion, it seems that a good portion of investment in the production of *computerized information* (namely investment in the production of raw data) does not result in any property or ownership rights in that computerized information. To the extent that such investments do lead to the acquisition of intellectual property rights, these may be offered as collateral. This is of course also true for the category of *innovative property* and to an extent for the category of *economic competences*. Many investments in the latter category will not result in any intellectual property rights; think of investments in training of employees or perhaps investments in business process engineering. This is not necessarily to say that such investments do not result in anything that can be offered as collateral. But it would have to be in the shape of so-called general security rights, which cover an enterprise or floating mass of assets as a whole and not a specific, individual property right. I will make some remarks on the possibilities of general security rights later on, but first I would like to examine the most prominent form of collateral for the intangible economy, namely intellectual property rights.

4 THE CHALLENGES OF USING INTELLECTUAL PROPERTY AS COLLATERAL

In the context of her dissertation on intellectual property rights as collateral, Keur interviewed dozens of lawyers, notaries and bailiffs in the Netherlands, to get some insight into the use of intellectual property as collateral. She found that most of them had never seen intellectual property being used successfully as collateral. Some of them had some experience with attachment of intellectual property rights but primarily as a means of pressuring the other party. Where security was vested in intellectual property rights this was done mostly in the context of financial transactions, in which parties did not envisage such security to be in fact utilized.[14] In short, intellectual property is rarely used as collateral, despite its importance to the intangible economy.

Why is that so? In her general report on security rights in intellectual property, Kieninger notes that there is a lack of (harmonized) statutory law specifically directed toward the admissibility of security rights intellectual property and their creation, perfection and

14 A.I. Keur, *Intellectuele eigendomsrechten als verhaalsobject*, The Hague, Boom juridisch, 2016, p. 2 and 3. See also P.G. Picht, *Vom materiellen Wert des Immateriellen – Immaterialgüterrechte als Kreditsicherungsmittel im nationalen und internationalen Rechtsverkehr*. Mohr Siebeck, Tübingen, 2018, who comes to the same conclusion.

priority.[15] Intellectual property rights often need to be registered and are limited in territorial scope. Registrations might be organized on the level of the state or on a federal or supranational level, whereas security rights might need to be registered on a different level, which creates uncertainties and high transactions costs. The substantial differences in intellectual property regimes in various jurisdictions, even on such fundamental issues as the transferability of intellectual property rights, further compounds this problem. An issue that is inherent to intellectual property rights, but complicates their use as collateral, is that they are open to challenges by third parties and may be limited in duration. Some intellectual property rights might also require "maintenance" such as renewals of registration or payment of taxes, which might be difficult for security right holders to monitor or do themselves without cooperation of the intellectual property right holder. Given the *sunkenness* of most investments in intellectual property, it is difficult for creditors to value intellectual property rights and, indeed, a widely recognized standard for such valuation is non-existent. Almost all collateral is worth more as a going concern and less upon liquidation of the enterprise, but this is especially true for intellectual property rights give the characteristic of *sunkenness* and also that of *synergy*, as discussed above. Therefore, As Kieninger notes, security rights in intellectual property may be worth the least when it is needed the most (i.e. upon insolvency of the intellectual property holder).[16]

Many of the challenges that arise in using intellectual property as collateral, are inherent. The economical function of intellectual property rights is primarily to stimulate further innovation whereas the economical function of 'normal' property rights is primarily to facilitate production.[17] That difference has implications for the legal regimes governing both types of rights and, as a result, for the way in which these rights can function as collateral. Not all challenges are inherent however. Some of the problems discussed above could, it seems, be addressed by way of more harmonized legislation, for instance in the field of requirements for registration.

5 THE ENTERPRISE AS A WHOLE

On the 6th of December 2019 the Dutch Supreme Court ruled on the question whether a portfolio of insurance policies held by an insurance agent, qualifies as 'property' in the sense of art. 3:1 of the Dutch Civil Code and can be pledged to creditors.[18] Such a portfolio consists of the agreements between the insurance agent and the insurance companies and

---

15 E.-M. Kieninger, 'Security Rights in Intellectual Property: General Report', in: E.-M. Kieninger (ed.), *Security rights in Intellectual Property*, Springer, Zürich, 2020.

16 Kieninger, 2020, p. 6.

17 Cf. Keur, 2016, p. 203.

18 HR 6 December 2019, ECLI:NL:HR:2019:1909, NJ 2020/357.

the agreements between the insurance agent and his clients, the insured parties. Pursuant to art. 3:1 all corporeals and all patrimonial rights are to be considered 'property'. The system of the Civil Code presupposes, according to the Supreme Court, that only individualized corporeals or patrimonial rights can be considered property and can function as objects of proprietary transactions. The combination of all contracts in the portfolio and the goodwill that is inherent in it, does not qualify as an individual corporeal or individual patrimonial right, even though in economic traffic the portfolio might be treated as such (also by bank extending credit to insurance agents). Therefore, the portfolio in question was never successfully pledged to the creditor (ING Bank). The ruling made it effectively impossible, or at least very difficult and costly, to use an insurance portfolio and the goodwill that is inherent in it, as collateral.

Many of the companies that operate in the intangible economy might not be so different from an insurance agent. Their business might effectively consist of a set of contracts, such as various license-agreements, agreements with clients, etc., which cannot be pledged to creditors individually, but are of substantial value as a whole. Various legal systems allow for security rights to be vested in an enterprise as a whole or in a mass of assets. The English floating charge covers all present and future assets of a debtor, but only attaches to the property at the moment of crystallization. In France and Belgian however, it is possible to create a fixed charge over classes of assets of an enterprise, without having to specify the individual asset. Such types of security rights might enable creditors to capture the value that is inherent in an enterprise as a whole.

Even if it is possible for creditors to obtain security in the enterprise as a whole, such security will only be of additional benefit to creditors if the value of the whole is higher than the value of the parts. This not normally the case in insolvency. Moreover, the value of an enterprise that operates in the intangible economy often lies primarily in the key employees that it manages to attract and retain. In case of insolvency, or even the remote possibility of insolvency, such employees will be quick to look for greener pastures. The insertion of strong non-compete clause in employment contracts is therefore vital to any company that operates in the intangible economy. But such clauses might be of limited use in case of insolvency of the company (depending on the extent to which a bankruptcy trustee is able to enforce such clauses) and would not bind employees viz-à-viz third parties.

6 INSOLVENCY AND PRIVACY LAWS

If a company that operates in the intangible economy becomes insolvent it is not unlikely that the only thing of value is the data that it has collected in the course of its existence. Such data might be sold by a bankruptcy trustee or any third party that has a security interest which allows it to seize and sell such data (perhaps a security interest in a database right or a security interest in the carriers on which the data is stored). Of course, the interests of creditors may clash with privacy interests of others. Section 363(b)(1) of the U.S. Bankruptcy Code provides that a sale of customer data is only possible where the privacy policy of the company permits it. If it does not, a bankruptcy court must take a decision on any sale of such data. The terms under which this is allowed are known as the Toysmart-conditions, being the conditions under which the Federal Trade Commission allowed Toysmart, an online children's toy business, to sell its customers data in bankruptcy. Those conditions are that (1) the customer information is sold as part of a package with the debtor's other assets; (2) the buyer is in the same line of business as the debtor (referred to as a "qualified buyer"); (3) the buyer agrees to comply with the bankrupt's privacy policy with respect to the purchased customer information; and (4) the buyer notifies the affected customers and obtains their consent before using the data for any *new* uses.[19]

It seems that in Europe there is no uniform approach to the sale of personal data in cases of insolvency, with the various data protection agencies taking different approaches. In The Netherlands the position of the data protection agency seems to be that a bankruptcy trustees can justify the sale of personal data on the grounds that they are obliged to liquidate the insolvent estate, but needs the permission of the persons involved if the enterprise is not, in some way, continued.[20] That is, in my opinion, an unjustifiably restrictive condition, and one which the courts so far have not set. The court of Amsterdam, for instance, ruled that personal data can be sold in the context of an insolvency, as long as the buyer is in the same line of business as the debtor and will use the data for similar purposes. The court notes that anyone wishing to remove their data after the sale can do so by addressing such a request to the buyer.[21]

7 Conclusion

The inherent characteristics of intangible investment (the four s's: *scalability*, *sunkenness*, *spillovers* and *synergies*) make it difficult for creditors to obtain security in return for financing these investments. There is no legal innovation that will definitively solve this problem. It is simply a fact of life that the intangible economy is less suitable for debt-based financing. Certain incremental improvements can be made, particularly in the area of security in intellectual property. At the same time, privacy laws might further complicate any possibility of liquidating the valuable assets that a company operating in the intangible economy might have. For property lawyers, in any case, there is a challenge to be had in

19 M.S.P. Baxter, 'The Sale of Personally Identifiable Information in Bankruptcy', *ABI Law Review*, Vol. 27, No. 2, 2019.
20 See: https://autoriteitpersoonsgegevens.nl/sites/default/files/atoms/files/brief_aan_insolad.pdf.
21 Rechtbank Amsterdam 25 oktober 2015, ECLI:NL:RBAMS:2015:7501.

shaping the legal framework of the intangible economy, much after the example that Sjef has set!

Part VI
Notariat and Land Registration

Het Nederlandse Notariaat in een Stroomversnelling

Leon Verstappen[*]

1 Inleiding

Het notariaat is een bijzondere beroepsgroep. Notarissen staan met twee benen in de maatschappij. Het ene been is dat van de ambtenaar, het andere dat van de ondernemer. De liberalisering van het notariaat in de jaren negentig van de vorige eeuw (wat klinkt dit ver weg), heeft het notariaat flink opgeschut. De beroepsgroep is danig veranderd, niet alleen de notariële dienstverlening, maar ook notarissen zelf en de organisatie van het notariaat. Als men er zelf onderdeel van uitmaakt, dan zal men niet direct in de gaten hebben dat die verandering zich heeft voltrokken. Maar wie de cijfers ziet en vergelijkingen trekt met vroeger, kan niet anders dan tot de conclusie komen dat het nu fundamenteel anders is.[1] Waar het heengaat is ongewis, omdat alweer planen worden beraamd om de Wet op het notarisambt (Wna) al dan niet fundamenteel aan te passen.[2] Ik ben benieuwd

---

* Hoogleraar privaatrecht, in het bijzonder notarieel recht, Rijksuniversiteit Groningen.

1 In eerdere publicaties heb ik ruime aandacht geschonken aan statistische gegevens over het notariaat: L.C.A. Verstappen, 'Het notariaat in een spagaat: Over instroom en de toekomst van het notariaat.' WPNR, 6591/2004; L.C.A. Verstappen, 'The Dutch situation on regulation of notaries' In N.E.H.M. Zeegers & H.E. Bröring (Eds.), 'Professions under pressure: Lawyers and doctors between profit and public interest, Boom Juridische Uitgevers: Den Haag 2009, p. 11-27; L.C.A. Verstappen, 'The hybrid notary in a split between office and enterprise.' In A.L.B. Colombi Ciacchi, M.A. Heldeweg, B.M.J. van der Meulen, & A.R. Neerhof (Eds.), 'Law & governance: Beyond the public-private law divide?', Boom Juridische Uitgevers: Den Haag 2013, p. 25-58; L.C.A. Verstappen, 'Een kwantitatieve en kwalitatieve analyse van de notariële opleidingen in Nederland', in: 'De kwaliteit binnen het notariaat' serie Ars Notariatus, deel 163, Amsterdam: Stichting tot bevordering der notariële wetenschap Kluwer: Deventer 2016, p. 37-67. In 2020 verschijnt nog van mijn hand een overzicht van al het empirisch onderzoek over het notariaat in: Nederlandse Encyclopedie Empirical Legal Studies: Encyclopedie van 25 jaar empirisch juridisch onderzoek in Nederland.

2 Zie ook het rapport Stokkermans, te vinden op: https://www.knb.nl/notariaat-magazine-nummer-2-maart-2019 (geraadpleegd op 24 oktober 2020), en de WPNR Rode Draad met artikelen over verschillende aspecten van dit rapport: Rode draad Maatschappelijke bijdrage Notariaat: J.S.L.A.W.B. Roes, 'Praktijkhouder en notarispraktijk', WPNR 2020/7272; C. van Kordelaar, 'Actualisering notariële opleidingen en eigentijdse werkcultuur nodig om maatschappelijke bijdrage notariaat te versterken', WPNR 20207275; R. Wisse, 'Maatschappelijk effectief toezicht en tuchtrecht', WPNR 2020/7279; E.E. Minkjan, 'De KNB: de discussienota van Stokkermans en het propellermodel van Tack', WPNR 2020/7284; M.I.W.E. Hillen-Muns, 'Ook de notariële akte ontkomt niet aan modernisering', WPNR 2020/7289; L.C.A. Verstappen, 'Lees wat niet geschreven is en luister naar wat niet wordt gezegd', WPNR 2020/7291; A.H.M. Rieter, 'Een openbaar ambt op een doodlopende weg?', WPNR 2020/7293. Zie ook Stokkerman's naschrift in WPNR 2021/7321. Ook

hoe Sjef, die eertijds bij de KNB voor het notariaat dienstbaar is geweest, tegen het hedendaagse notariaat in Nederland en Europa aankijkt. De onderstaande inventarisatie zou wellicht een aanzet kunnen zijn voor een discussie. De volgende onderwerpen komen aan bod: de opleiding (paragraaf 2), het aantal (kandidaat-)notarissen (paragraaf 3), de notaris in de markt (paragraaf 4), marktwerking in het notariaat (paragraaf 5), de vergelijking met juridische dienstverleners in de vastgoedmarkt in andere Europese landen (paragraaf 6), de organisatie van de beroepsgroep (paragraaf 7) en het toezicht (paragraaf 8). Het geheel wordt afgesloten met een conclusie.

2 De (Beroeps)Opleiding

De opleiding van notarissen is sinds de jaren 50 van de vorige eeuw academisch. Met de wetenschappelijke benadering van het ambt en de ambtsuitoefening, kwam ook het notariële onderzoek op gang. Eigenlijk is dat onderzoek voor wat betreft het familie(vermogens)recht, het vastgoedrecht en het ondernemingsrecht, voornamelijk privaatrechtelijk van karakter. In die zin onderscheidt dat onderzoek zich niet van privaatrechtelijk onderzoek in het algemeen en zouden docenten privaatrecht ook notariële studenten kunnen doceren. Maar het gaat in de notariële opleiding juist om de notariële invalshoek die een bijzondere is: hoe regel ik door middel van rechtshandelingen menselijke relaties. Het notariële onderzoek richt zich vaak op wat wel en wat niet geregeld kan worden in rechtshandelingen die bij notariële akte tot stand komen. Daarbij speelt een grote rol hoe mensen omgaan met belangrijke rechtshandelingen in hun leven zoals bijvoorbeeld huwelijkse voorwaarden. Bij het werk van de notaris is heel belangrijk dat men zich realiseert dat bij rechtshandelingen altijd uiteenlopende belangen kunnen spelen waarmee rekening dient te worden gehouden, zoals bijvoorbeeld bij de afwikkeling van een nalatenschap. Belangrijk is ook de vraag welke rol de notaris in het rechtsverkeer heeft: lijdelijke en gewillige dienstverlener of poortwachter die sturend optreedt? De notaris heeft een belangrijke rol in de rechtsbedeling. Hij kan en moet soms de verwezenlijking van het recht voor de burger beïnvloeden. In die zin is hij niet alleen lijdelijk en volgzaam, hij plaatst ook soms een stopbord en stuurt ook door zijn voorlichting en advisering, bijvoorbeeld wanneer het nodig is om de zwakkere partij aan tafel te beschermen. Dat vergt meer dan alleen kennis van het privaatrecht. Het vergt ook menselijk optreden, inlevingsvermogen, begrip voor uiteenlopende belangen en het vermogen om diplomatiek op te treden, maar ook een hoog normbesef en ethisch handelen. Daarom moet aan de universiteit de basis daarvoor worden

de Beroepsopleiding Notariaat is thans onderwerp van evaluatie die mogelijk leidt tot aanpassing van het programma.

gelegd door docenten die op de een of andere manier betrokken zijn (geweest) in de notariële rechtspraktijk.

De academische opleiding moet voldoen aan bepaalde eisen die in de wet zijn geformuleerd. Deze eisen bestonden al lang en zijn met het vervallen van het Academisch Statuut opgenomen in de sectorale wetgeving voor het notariaat: art. 6 lid 3 Wna.

Dit alles in aanmerking nemende, zal het niet verbazen dat het notariële onderwijs voor een groot deel privaatrechtelijk van aard is en dat de notariëlen aanschuiven bij de reguliere studenten rechtsgeleerdheid. Slechts waar het gaat om de drie hiervoor beschreven bijzondere onderwerpen familie(vermogens)recht, vastgoedrecht en ondernemingsrecht, worden specifieke notariële vakken gegeven door doorgaans notariële docenten. Daarmee onderscheiden zich de notariële opleidingen van de gewone opleiding rechtsgeleerdheid.

De toegang tot het beroep begint bij de academische opleiding en de beroepsopleiding, omdat die vereist zijn om (kandidaat-)notaris te kunnen worden. Hoe zit het met de aantallen? Over de (beroeps)opleiding en de toegang tot het beroep heb ik een studie verricht waarvoor statistische gegevens zijn verzameld en waarvan het resultaat is gepubliceerd in de serie Ars Notariatus.[3] Deze cijfers geven de ontwikkeling in de loop der jaren weer.

Het is lastig om kwantitatieve gegevens van notariële studenten te achterhalen.[4] De trendrapportages Notariaat bevatten enkele cijfers over de ontwikkelingen rondom in- en uitstroom. Deze cijfers geven echter een beperkt beeld van een aantal jaren vlak na de invoering van de huidige wet tot aan 2006.

Voor de invoering van de bachelor- en masterstructuur bestond de populatie van studenten notarieel recht van 1999-2006 uit een percentage tussen de 3 en 4% van het totale aantal rechtenstudenten. Echter, zowel in absolute als in relatieve zin was dit percentage aan het dalen. Opmerkelijk is dat het percentage afgestudeerden ten opzichte van het totaal van alle rechtenstudenten van 1997 tot 2005 tussen de 5 en 10% ligt. Dat indiceert dat notariële studenten relatief frequenter de eindstreep halen dan de overige rechtenstudenten. Dat neemt echter niet weg dat het aantal notarieel afgestudeerden tot aan 2005 is gedaald. Deze daling heeft in 2004/2005 haar dieptepunt bereikt. De periode na 2005 laat eerst een stijging van het aantal bachelor- en masterbullen zien, waarna vanaf 2008 een daling inzet waaruit de invloed van de economische crisis blijkt. Al sinds meerdere jaren draait de economie weer goed en heeft zich het verwachte effect op de arbeidsmarkt voorgedaan: er is (weer) sprake van een flink tekort aan notarieel geschoolde juristen. Het

3 L.C.A. Verstappen, 'Een kwantitatieve en kwalitatieve analyse van de notariële opleidingen in Nederland', in: 'De kwaliteit binnen het notariaat' serie Ars Notariatus, deel 163, Amsterdam: Stichting tot bevordering der notariële wetenschap Kluwer: Deventer 2016, p. 37-67.

4 Daarbij moet men bedenken dat alle universitaire opleidingen zijn veranderd ten gevolge van de invoering van de bachelor-masterstructuur per september 2002.

is onmiskenbaar dat aanbod en vraag van afgestudeerde notariële juristen conjunctuurgevoelig zijn.

De instroom in het notariaat is min of meer ook gelijk aan de instroom in de Beroepsopleiding Notariaat. Ook de Beroepsopleiding Notariaat houdt zich de laatste jaren bezig met de vraag op welke wijze de veranderingen in het notariaat invloed uitoefenen op de beroepsopleiding voor notarissen. Nadat in 2012 de laatste herziening heeft plaatsgevonden, waarin onder meer een groter accent is komen te liggen op het ontwikkelen van vaardigheden in het programma en na het eerste jaar de mogelijkheid is geïntroduceerd om voor twee van de drie aandachtsgebieden te kiezen, is het opleidingsprogramma thans weer in discussie.

3 Het Aantal (Kandidaat-)Notarissen

Door de invoering van de huidige Wet op het notarisambt in 1999 is het notariaat in beweging gebracht. Het is interessant om te bezien hoe de liberalisering van het notariaat uiteindelijk heeft uitgepakt. Een aantal getallen op een rij.

Omdat de cijfers over aantallen (kandidaat-)notarissen constant worden bijgehouden, kan aan de hand van de door de KNB verschafte gegevens worden weergegeven wat de ontwikkeling is vanaf de invoering van de huidige Wet op het notarisambt in 1999 tot nu.

Het aantal kantoren is duidelijk afgenomen; na een opleving vanaf vlak voor de invoering van de huidige Wet op het notarisambt in 1999 tot aan 2008, is het aantal langzaam maar zeker gaan dalen, aanvankelijk wat scherper. Opvallend is dat het aantal eenmanskantoren het afgelopen decennium juist een stijgende lijn te zien geeft. Dat is wel opmerkelijk omdat de verwachting was dat het aantal juist zou dalen. Meer concurrentie zou immers de samenwerking tussen kantoren versterken: meer kennis delen en meer specialisatie voor een kwalitatief betere dienstverlening, maar ook het behalen van schaalvoordelen om goedkopere dienstverlening te kunnen aanbieden. Maar dat effect heeft de liberalisering in Nederland niet tot gevolg gehad.

Figuur 1 Aantal kantoren

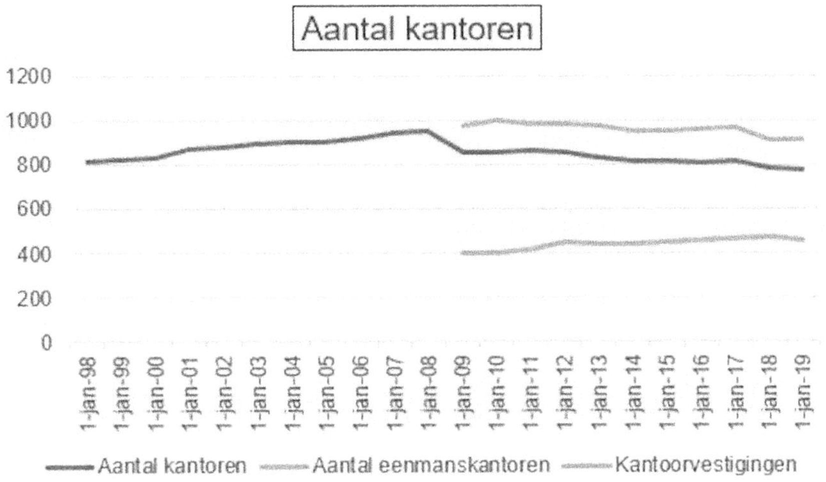

Het aantal notarissen is ten gevolge van de crisis vanaf 2008 duidelijk gedaald, om vanaf 2013 weer te stijgen. De vermindering van het aantal kantoren en het aantal vestigingen duidt op een minder grote spreiding, wat weer van belang is voor de toegankelijkheid van het notariaat. Het aantal eenmanskantoren is – anders dan werd verwacht – niet afgenomen, maar juist toegenomen. Omdat het steeds lastiger wordt om als eenmanskantoor het hoofd boven water te houden (toegenomen regelgeving, toegenomen concurrentie, toegenomen toezicht), had het voor de hand gelegen dat notarissen meer de samenwerking zouden zoeken.

Onmiskenbaar is de vaste stijgende lijn van het aantal vrouwelijke notarissen. Dat lag in 1999 op 6% en is gestegen naar bijna 27% nu, in 2020. Maar nemen we ook de toegevoegde notarissen mee in de teller en de noemer, dan is het percentage bijna 33%. Het aantal vrouwelijke kandidaat-notarissen is gestegen van 46% in 1999 naar bijna 69% nu, in 2020. Conclusie is dat de beroepsgroep feminiseert.

Figuur 2 Aantal notarissen en kandidaat-notarissen

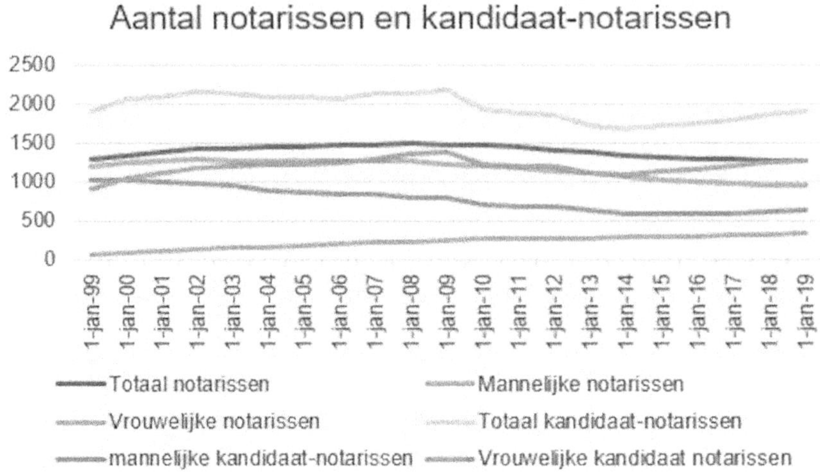

4 De KNB en de Notariële Brancheorganisaties[5]

Voor de invoering van de huidige Wet op het notarisambt was de KNB een privaatrechtelijke vereniging waarvan vrijwel elke notaris lid was. Door die invoering is de KNB omgezet in een publiekrechtelijke beroepsorganisatie met verordenende bevoegdheid. Van privaatrechtelijke vereniging die de belangen van het notariaat behartigt, naar een overheid die alleen het algemeen belang heeft te dienen. De taak van de KNB als publiekrechtelijke beroepsorganisatie is beperkt 'tot die onderwerpen, waarmee een openbaar of publiek belang is gemoeid. De behartiging van de gemeenschappelijke belangen, met name de economische belangen, van notarissen als zodanig behoort daar niet toe.', aldus de toelichting op het amendement De Koning c.s. Met deze beperking in de taakomschrijving houdt ook verband de beperking in de verordeningsbevoegdheid van de KNB. Er bestaat preventieve controle op de door de KNB vervaardigde verordeningen omdat de minister van Justitie en Veiligheid elke verordening vooraf moet goedkeuren (art. 91 lid 1 Wna). Aanvankelijk waren de enige toetsingsgronden strijd met het recht of het algemeen belang (art. 91 lid 1 Wna). Maar lid 2 van artikel 89, eveneens bij amendement ingevoerd, bepaalt daarenboven dat verordeningen geen verplichtingen of voorschriften mogen bevatten die niet strikt noodzakelijk zijn voor de verwezenlijking van het doel dat

5 Voor deze en de volgende twee paragrafen is geput uit: L.A.G.M. van der Geld, L.C.A. Verstappen, 'Het ontstaan van (branche-)organisaties in het notariaat sinds 1999', WPNR 7205/2018.

met de verordening wordt beoogd of die onnodig de marktwerking beperken. Bij reparatiewet is per 1 augustus 2004 de mogelijkheid ingevoerd om bij verordening regels te stellen betreffende de kwaliteit van de beroepsuitoefening (art. 61 lid 2 tweede volzin Wna). Direct na de revolte binnen het notariaat in 2012 ging het nieuwe bestuur naar justitie om te onderzoeken of er niet toch een mogelijkheid zou bestaan dat de KNB ook de belangen van het notariaat mocht behartigen. Bij brief van 11 juni 2012 schreef de toenmalige staatssecretaris van Veiligheid en Justitie hierover na een onderhoud met het nieuwe bestuur van de KNB: "De pbo dient zich niet uitsluitend of voornamelijk op het eigen belang te richten, maar eerst en vooral op het hogere publieke belang. [...] Het voorgaande wil niet zeggen dat het publieke belang en het groepsbelang niet zouden kunnen overlappen of samenvallen. Anders gezegd: het hogere belang kan tevens het eigen belang dienen." Met deze brief in de hand vond het toenmalige bestuur dat er in deze interpretatie van de wet, die als gezaghebbend werd ervaren, voldoende ruimte voor de KNB bestond om toch aan belangenbehartiging te doen. Daarmee was het voorstel om een nieuwe vereniging op te richten ter belangenbehartiging van het notariaat en de KNB sterk af te slanken, van de baan.[6] De vraag is echter, of de interpretatie van de staatssecretaris niet op gespannen voet met de wet en de wetsgeschiedenis staat.

Over hoe de markt heeft gereageerd en welke mogelijkheden en kansen er nog liggen heeft Barendrecht[7] onderzoek gedaan in opdracht van de KNB. In dit onderzoek, dat beperkt van opzet was, zijn de innovaties in kaart gebracht aan de hand van rapporten en databases, de juridische innovatieliteratuur, KNB strategie-documenten en een zoektocht op internet. Voorts zijn gesprekken met KNB medewerkers gevoerd, zijn twaalf (telefonische) interviews met notarissen afgenomen en werden KNB regio-bijeenkomsten bijgewoond. Het huidige notariaat is aan de hand daarvan onderscheiden in zeven bedrijfsmodellen:

1. kleine notarispraktijk in gemeente 40.000 inwoners;
2. generieke notarispraktijk met stedelijke, regionale uitstraling;
3. grotere notarispraktijk met hoge kwaliteitsaspiraties;
4. notarispraktijk in transactiepraktijk in groot advocatenkantoor;
5. netwerk: Samenwerkingsverband van kleinere kantoren;
6. niche praktijk gericht op specifieke doelgroepen en hun problemen;
7. commodity kantoor met scherpe prijzen

Twee conclusies worden getrokken. Ten eerste dat er een grote, deels onvervulde, behoefte is aan diensten waarin het notariaat een rol kan spelen. Dat het notariaat zijn beste tijd

6 De tweede auteur heeft destijds aan de KNB geadviseerd wel daartoe over te gaan omdat het wettelijke kader onvoldoende ruimte biedt voor volledige belangenbehartiging.

7 M. Barendrecht, 'Notariaat en innovatie' WPNR 2014/7030.

gehad zou hebben, of niet innovatief zou zijn, is een beeld dat volgens het onderzoek zou moeten worden bijgesteld. Er is een aantal bedrijfsmodellen die kansrijk zijn en goed aansluiten bij wat er al gebeurt. Ten tweede zit er veel spanning op de manier waarop de beroepsgroep is georganiseerd. Die organisatie is volgens het onderzoek niet erg afgestemd op de trends, de aanstormende innovaties en de uitdaging om nog beter aan de behoeften van afnemers te voldoen. Daarom wordt in de conclusies aandacht gevraagd hoe de bedrijfsmodellen het beste kunnen worden ondersteund, welke belemmeringen zij ondervinden en hoe die kunnen worden weggenomen. Die belemmeringen, de organisatie van het bedrijf en de garantie van kwaliteit richting de afnemers zijn voor ieder bedrijfsmodel weer anders, aldus het onderzoek.

5 MARKTWERKING IN HET NOTARIAAT

Sinds de invoering van de huidige Wet op het notarisambt is er veel gebeurd binnen het notariële speelveld. Ontegenzeggelijk is deze wet katalyserend geweest voor ontwikkelingen die al gaande waren. Digitalisering en nieuwe communicatiemiddelen veranderden het bureauwerk aanzienlijk, terwijl de maatschappij met mondiger burgers langzaam maar zeker een kritischer houding jegens (het werk van) de notaris innam. Daarbij ging de aandacht meer uit naar de prijs voor het notariële product en – in verband daarmee – het notariële inkomen dan naar de maatschappelijke meerwaarde van het werk van een dergelijke dienstverlener. Vóór de huidige Wet op het notarisambt waren de tarieven vast en stonden die niet in verhouding tot de verrichte werkzaamheden. Voor de ene categorie werkzaamheden waren de tarieven gemeten aan de toerekenbare kosten te hoog (vastgoedpraktijk) en voor de andere categorie werkzaamheden juist te laag (familierechtpraktijk): er vond crosssubsidie plaats.

Overheidsbeleid richtte zich aan het einde van de vorige eeuw enerzijds op verzelfstandiging van publieke dienstverlening en anderzijds op meer marktwerking in het algemeen, mede ingegeven door Europees beleid. De overheid trok zich waar dat kon terug, terwijl ondernemers en ondernemingen nadrukkelijk een rol kregen bij de behartiging van algemene belangen. Op 10 juli 1995 heeft het kabinet-Kok I over deze ontwikkelingen een standpunt ingenomen dat uitmondde in het MDW-project ('Marktwerking, Deregulering en Wetgevingskwaliteit'). De wens om tot een vernieuwing van de wetgeving rondom het beroep van notaris te komen is onder meer door het MDW-project ingegeven. De twee belangrijkste veranderingen die de Wet op het notarisambt in dit verband heeft gebracht zijn:

- de KNB werd bij wet getransformeerd van privaatrechtelijke vereniging naar een publiekrechtelijke beroepsorganisatie met verordenende bevoegdheden;

- het beschermde beroep van notaris werd geliberaliseerd om meer marktwerking te bewerkstelligen: vrije vestiging en geen vaste tarieven meer.

De discussie over de nieuwe wet in de jaren negentig van de vorige eeuw ging voornamelijk over deze twee aspecten.

Door meer regels, versterkt toezicht en handhavingsmechanismen werd het veronderstelde vertrouwen in het werk van de notaris de facto ingeruild voor georganiseerd wantrouwen. Er moest meer grip op de beroepsgroep komen. Daarvoor was nodig dat op papier kwam te staan hoe de beroepsregels precies luiden, terwijl tegelijkertijd het toezicht en de handhaving werden versterkt. Ook kreeg de notaris er meer overheidstaken bij, zoals specifieke taken in het kader van de Wet ter voorkoming van witwassen en financiering van terrorisme, hetgeen de positie van de notaris als poortwachter heeft versterkt. Marktwerking heeft mede daarom niet tot minder regels geleid, maar juist tot veel meer regulering, met name gericht op toezicht en handhaving. Niet alleen de huidige Wet op het notarisambt getuigt hiervan, maar ook de vele nieuwe uitvoeringsregels en informele beleidsregels. Zo gelden voor het werk van de notaris meer protocollen en beleidsrichtlijnen en is de rol van het Bureau Financieel Toezicht (BFT) door meer toezichtstaken uitgebreid.[8]

Voor de notaris is marktwerking van nature problematisch. Enerzijds heeft hij zijn ambtsverplichtingen; hij wordt geacht onafhankelijk en onpartijdig op te treden. Anderzijds bevindt de notaris zich vaak in een afhankelijke positie in de markt van juridische dienstverleners: anders dan fiscalisten, banken en accountants heeft hij geen structureel contact met cliënten, behoudens misschien in de zakelijke dienstverlening. Hij wordt veelal in de uitvoeringsfase ingeschakeld en staat mede daarom vaak achteraan in de rij van dienstverleners. Dat kan hem afhankelijk maken van toeleveranciers, hetgeen zijn onpartijdigheid in gevaar kan brengen. De notaris kan in voorkomende gevallen speelbal van bepaalde commerciële partijen worden. Daarnaast brengt de poortwachtersrol van het notariaat met zich dat de notaris onderzoek moet doen naar onder meer de goede bedoelingen en de integriteit van de cliënt. Mede daarom zien cliënten nogal eens niet de maatschappelijke meerwaarde van dit deel van het werk van de notaris, laat staan dat men bereid is daarvoor te betalen.

In dit speelveld moest de notaris vanaf 1999 voor minder geld meer zijn best doen om het vertrouwen te behouden, terwijl de positie van het notariaat in het maatschappelijke en politieke debat was verzwakt door een beroepsorganisatie wier verordenende bevoegdheid sterk beperkt is en die de particuliere belangen van notarissen niet (meer) mocht behartigen. De notaris moest als ondernemer laten zien dat hij zijn geld waard was,

---

8 Sinds 1 januari 2013 is sprake van integraal toezicht op notarissen, hetgeen wil zeggen dat het BFT zowel toeziet op de financiën als op de kwaliteit en de integriteit van de ondertoezichtstaanden.

en voor een groep van notarissen betekende dit dat zij zich vooral gingen toeleggen op goedkope dienstverlening.[9]

Het gevoel leefde dat kernwaarden van het notariaat - onpartijdigheid, onafhankelijkheid en integriteit - onder druk kwamen te staan. De vraag was of dit ook zijn weerslag had op de kwaliteit van dienstverlening. Met name welke rol de notaris bij financiële fraude had, kwam sterk in de belangstelling te staan. Vandaar ook de onderzoeken naar de kwaliteit van dienstverlening[10] en de rol van de notaris bij malafide vastgoedtransacties.[11]

Tegen deze achtergrond is goed te begrijpen waarom een groot deel van het empirische onderzoek over het notariaat is verricht: de overheid wil de vinger aan de pols houden, met name op twee aspecten van notariële dienstverlening: kwaliteit en prijs.

De Commissie Evaluatie Wet op het notarisambt (in de wandelgangen ook aangeduid als de commissie-Hammerstein) is op 9 juli 2004 bij besluit van de minister van Justitie ingesteld. De commissie heeft onderzocht op welke wijze de liberalisering van de notariële markt[12] in de praktijk gestalte heeft gekregen. Daarbij heeft zij gelet op de effecten van marktwerking en concurrentie en op de mogelijke gevolgen daarvan voor de ambtsuitoefening. Onderdeel van de werkwijze van de commissie was onder meer om een onderzoek in te stellen naar de gevolgen van prijsconcurrentie in het notariaat met het oog op het beoordelen van de gevolgen van marktwerking in het notariaat. Het onderzoeksbureau EIM heeft dit onderzoek uitgevoerd en daarover gerapporteerd.[13]

Een van de onderzochte veronderstellingen was dat prijsvechters slechtere dienstverlening aanboden. Het probleem was hoe de kwaliteit van notariële dienstverlening

9 Deze organisatie heeft ook onderzoek naar de marktwerking, in het bijzonder de prijsontwikkeling, binnen het notariaat uitgevoerd, maar dat is niet openbaar voor zover ik weet.

10 M.J. ter Voert, F. Zwenk, E.M.Th. Beenakkers, 'Kwaliteit in zware tijd: Marktwerking, vraaguitval en notariële dienstverlening' (Onderzoek en Beleid, nr. 296). Den Haag 2011: WODC. www.wodc.nl/binaries/ob296-volledige-tekst_tcm28-71408.pdf.

11 B. van Gestel, 'Vastgoed & fout: Een analyse van twaalf strafrechtelijke opsporingsonderzoeken naar illegale en criminele praktijken in de woningsector' (Onderzoek en Beleid, nr. 272). Den Haag 2008. www.wodc.nl/onderzoeksdatabase/illegale-praktijk-op-de-woningmarkt.aspx.; H. Ferwerda, R. Staring, E. de Vries Robbé, J. van der Bunt, 'Malafide activiteiten in de vastgoedsector: Een exploratief onderzoek naar aard, actoren en aanpak', Arnhem/Rotterdam: Advies- en Onderzoekgroep Beke/Erasmus Universiteit (2007); M.J. ter Voert, F. Zwenk, E.M.Th. Beenakkers, Kwaliteit in zware tijd: Marktwerking, vraaguitval en notariële dienstverlening (Onderzoek en Beleid, nr. 296). Den Haag: WODC. www.wodc.nl/binaries/ob296-volledige-tekst_tcm28-71408.pdf. (2011).

12 Het gaat dan vooral om drie maatregelen: de liberalisering van het benoemings- en vestigingsbeleid, de afschaffing van het verbod op het verrichten van ambtshandelingen buiten het arrondissement van vestiging en het geleidelijk vrijlaten van de tarieven.

13 Commissie-Hammerstein (Commissie Evaluatie Wet op het notarisambt) (2005). Het beste van twee werelden. Den Haag: Ministerie van Justitie. https://zoek.officielebekendmakingen.nl/kst-23706-62-b1.pdf; het EIM onderzoek is als Bijlage 2 bij dit rapport opgenomen.

te beoordelen. Wat houdt die kwaliteit precies in? En als we daarover normen kunnen opstellen, hoe gaan we die meten?

De centrale conclusie uit dit deel van het onderzoek is dat verwijzers tevreden zijn over de beweging die er is gemaakt naar meer klantgerichtheid door het notariaat. Bovendien zijn daarbij de prijzen gedaald. De kwaliteit van de akten en de zorgvuldigheid van het proces zijn op het oude niveau gebleven. 'De goedkope notaris van nu is de dure van vroeger', is een citaat dat is opgetekend tijdens deze interviews.

De prijsvechters hebben zonder uitzondering een (zeer) strak georganiseerde praktijk. Daardoor doen ze meer werk met minder mensen. Specialisatie op de vastgoedmarkt is niet aan de orde bij de prijsvechters. De familiepraktijk is juist een belangrijke aanvulling op de omzet uit de vastgoedpraktijk. De kwaliteit van de notariële dienstverlening rond het transport van registergoederen is vooral afhankelijk van het proces en zorgvuldig werken met voldoende controlemomenten. Prijsvechters wijken op deze punten niet af van andere kantoren.

Hoogst interessant is het om te bezien hoe de prijsontwikkeling van de notariële producten daadwerkelijk is geweest. Deze blijken uit de trendrapportages. Ik laat hierna een grafiek van het eindtotaal zien.

Figuur 3 Algemene tarieven notarissen (2003-2006)

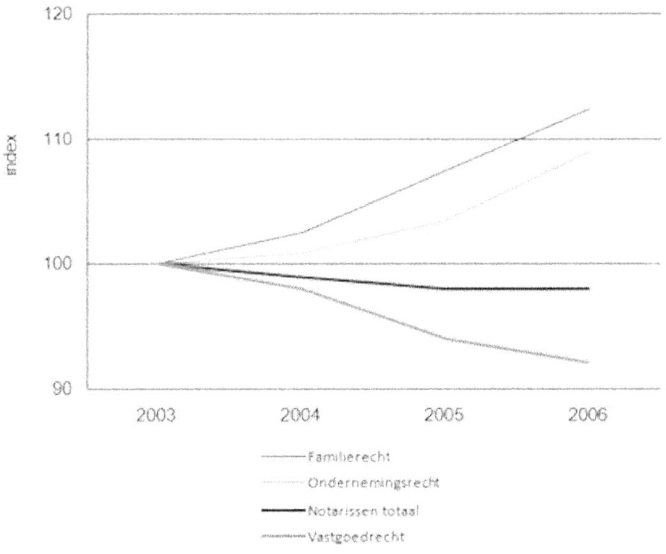

Bron: Trendrapportage Notariaat 2006 (Laclé & Ter Voert)

Uit deze grafiek blijkt heel duidelijk dat de wens tot goedkopere dienstverlening maar ten dele is uitgekomen. De vastgoedpraktijk is goedkoper geworden, maar de familie- en ondernemingspraktijk zijn daarentegen duurder geworden. In zijn algemeenheid is de notariële dienstverlening goedkoper geworden. Men bedenke daarbij dat de vastgoedpraktijk in volume en omzet veel groter is dan de familie- en ondernemingspraktijk. Doordat notarissen meer kostprijsgerelateerd in plaats van naar de waarde van de transactie zijn gaan declareren, daalde de opbrengst in de vastgoedpraktijk. Voor de levering van een doorzonwoning is de notaris vrijwel dezelfde tijd kwijt als voor de levering van een kapitale villa. De declaratie van de notaris voor deze transacties ziet er vandaag de dag dan ook nagenoeg hetzelfde eruit.

Wie hebben hiervan geprofiteerd? Dat zijn vooral de burgers die vastgoedtransacties deden in het hogere segment, het duurdere vastgoed, en dat is een betrekkelijk klein deel van de clientèle van de notaris. Daarentegen betaalt de cliënt meer voor familierechtakten, ook de cliënt met een kleine beurs. Dit is ontegenzeggelijk een nadelig effect van meer marktwerking, temeer omdat dit de toegankelijkheid van het notariaat raakt voor de burger met een kleine beurs. Oplossingen kunnen gevonden worden in nog meer concurrentie, met name door de komst van prijsvechters (de zogenoemde B-merken in het notariaat), maar ook van wat je zou kunnen noemen 'do it yourself'-notariaat, waarbij door verregaande digitalisering wordt bewerkstelligd dat de kostprijs laag gehouden kan worden. Met name wordt ingezet op standaardoplossingen voor standaardcasussen, waarbij het werk van de (kandidaat-)notaris – en dus ook diens nota – tot een minimum wordt beperkt. Een voorbeeld is de zogenoemde Hema-Notarisservice, waarbij de Hema functioneert als intermediair tussen cliënt en notaris.[14] Maar krijgt de cliënt voldoende voorlichting en advies? Klopt het product wel dat hij op semi-geautomatiseerde wijze krijgt toegediend?

6 INTERNATIONALE VERGELIJKING

Het notariaat kan ook vanuit rechtsvergelijkend perspectief worden benaderd. Daarover heeft Plaggemars dissertatieonderzoek verricht in zeventien Europese landen.[15] Deze studie bevat een vergelijking van de regulering van het beroep van notaris in zeventien Europese landen op basis van questionnaires over de karakteristieken van die notariaten aan de hand van een aantal belangrijke aspecten. Daarin kwamen aan de orde: tarieven, toegang tot het ambt, exclusieve bevoegdheden van de notaris, taken van de notaris, publiciteit door een notaris, samenwerkingsverbanden met notarissen of andere professionals, rechtsvorm,

14 https://notarisservice.hema.nl/?gclid=EAIaIQobChMIh8vP5MWO5AIVRPlRCh3N0gcyEAAYASAAEgLfG_D_BwE.

15 A.D. Plaggemars, 'Is de notaris de markt meester? (Diss. RUG), Den Haag: Boom Juridische Uitgevers 2011.

notariële regelgeving in formele zin, toezicht en tuchtrecht, overkoepelende organisatie van notarissen, aansprakelijkheid en verzekering, nascholing, centrale registers, lijdelijkheid, ministerieplicht en full-service, plaats van vestiging/standplaats/protocol van een notaris, ambtsgeheim, oudedagsvoorziening en goodwill, notaris in loondienst en in deeltijd.

De algemene conclusie die hij trekt is dat het Latijnse notariaat in de diverse beschreven landen veel gemeenschappelijke basiskenmerken heeft, ook voor wat betreft de toegankelijkheid, maar ook aanzienlijke verschillen kent.

Interessant is de vergelijking met de andere dienstverleners op dezelfde terreinen als de notaris. De meest diepgaande internationale studie is de *Conveyancing services market*,[16] verricht in 2006 door het Centre of European Law and Politics van de University of Bremen in opdracht van de directeur-generaal Competitie van de Europese Commissie. Het bevat een vergelijking van het systeem van overdracht van onroerend goed in 21 Europese landen 'integrating a legal and an economic perspective, on professional and related regulation and its impact on the efficiency and performance of the conveyancing services market'. De studie handelt onder andere over kwaliteit en kostprijs van normale vastgoedtransacties in die landen.[17] In die studie is gebruikgemaakt van nationale rapporteurs die aan de hand van een questionnaire en een survey onder 700 personen in alle 21 landen hebben uitgevoerd. Men heeft professionals en consumenten gevraagd over keuze, professionele kwaliteit, snelheid, kosten van diensten, en problemen zoals juridische geschillen tussen contracterende partijen en tussen hen en professionals. Men onderscheidde vier categorieën:

- het traditionele Latijnse notariaat: verplichte inschakeling (monopolies), numerus clausus, tarieven en strikte regulering van de markt;
- het gedereguleerde Nederlandse notariaat zonder numerus clausus, onderhandelbare tarieven en minder gereguleerde markt;
- het advocatensysteem waarin de kwaliteit wordt gereguleerd door een licentiesysteem en professioneel examen, onderhandelbare tarieven en minder regulering van de markt;
- het Scandinavische systeem van 'licensed real estate agent', die ook juridische diensten verricht, met eveneens een professioneel examen, onderhandelbare tarieven en minder regulering van de markt.

Het is al opmerkelijk dat de onderzoekers Nederland als afzonderlijke categorie hebben opgevoerd. De relevantie van dit onderzoek is dat voor het eerst de gevolgen van de

16 Ch.U. Schmid, S. Sebastian, G.S. Lee, M. Fink, L. Paterson. Conveyancing services market (COMP/2006/D3/003). (2007); https://ec.europa.eu/competition/sectors/professional_services/studies/csm_study_complete.pdf.

17 Australië, België, Tsjechië, Denemarken, Engeland en Wales, Finland, Frankrijk, Duitsland, Griekenland, Hongarije, Ierland, Italië, Luxemburg, Nederland, Polen, Portugal, Schotland, Slovakije, Slovenië, Spanje en Zweden.

liberalisering van het notariaat in Nederland in een vergelijking met andere Latijnse notariaten zichtbaar zijn gemaakt. De conclusies zijn wat Nederland betreft veelzeggend:

'Of the four types of regulatory systems examined (i.e. traditional, highly regulated Latin notary system, the deregulated Dutch notary system, the lawyer system and the Scandinavian licensed real estate agent system), the study finds that the traditional Latin notary system, which has the highest levels of restrictive regulation, including the use of fixed fees scales and numerus clausus performs the worst on all counts:

- Latin notary countries are generally more expensive than the deregulated Dutch system, the lawyer system or the Scandinavian system especially for higher value transactions (i.e. those €250,000 and over) and have some of the highest absolute legal fees (e.g. France, Belgium and Italy).
- (...)
- The Netherlands case study provides a useful insight into what happens with some deregulation of notary services and provides empirical evidence of the positive effects deregulation can have on consumer welfare. The Dutch model is a modernised version of the Latin notary system where fixed pricing and numerus clausus (two of the most radical forms of regulation) have been abolished. On pricing this has resulted in price differentiation and the possibility for consumers to negotiate on fees. The case study shows that the average consumer buying a basket of notary services is considerably better off. There has also been a rise in the number of notaries and innovation is on the up with the emergence of new business structures and the greater use of IT. Importantly quality has not been compromised and in fact the evidence points to better customer service and satisfaction as the removal of fixed fees has made notaries compete on standard of service.'

De Council of the Notariats of the European Union antwoordde overigens met een tegenrapport van Peter Murray.[18] Zijn rapport is beperkter van omvang en neemt de traditionele rechtsvergelijkende methode tot uitgangspunt, gebruikmakend van landenrapporten, waarbij acht verschillende transactietypen met elkaar zijn vergeleken. Murray komt tot wat andere conclusies dan Schmid et al.:

> 'Modern real estate conveyancing involves a number or complex and interrelated activities to meet the needs and requirements of diverse economic and regulatory interests involved in the ownership, transfer and financing of residential real estate. In all of the European jurisdictions studied the function

18 P.L. Murray, 'Real estate conveyancing in 5 European Union member states: A comparitive study.' 2007 www.dnotv.de/_files/Aktuelles/murrayreportfinal310807en.pdf.

> of effectuating transfer of title has become relatively straightforward and routine thanks to efficient systems of title registration. Complexity is lent to real estate transactions by the many legal, financial and regulatory considerations that surround and attend the transfer and the financing of the purchase. Most of the work of conveyancers deals with these considerations rather than the now relatively simple task of passing title to the property from seller to buyer.'

Murray ondergraaft daarmee de vooronderstelling dat de systemen eenvoudig te vergelijken zouden zijn, zo ongeveer als in het rapport van Schmid et al. is gebeurd:

> 'There are simply too many other variables, such as local substantive and procedural law, other professional exposures, and claims-friendliness of local legal cultures affecting these purported proxies to permit any reasonable correlation with quality or efficiency of conveyancing services.'

Murray's bevindingen komen overeen met die van Plaggemars: het notariaat in Europe is simpelweg geen eenheidsworst.

7 De Organisatie van de Beroepsgroep

Terwijl voor 1999 het notariaat een toonbeeld van een eensgezinde beroepsgroep was, met een strak geleide organisatie waar alle notarissen vrijwillig waren aangesloten, viel de organisatie van het notariaat door en na de invoering van de Wet op het notarisambt in 1999 uiteen in verschillende brancheorganisaties. Het bastion was gevallen. Het ontstaan van brancheorganisaties is niet alleen het gevolg van de nieuwe rol van de KNB en de marktwerking in het algemeen, maar ook van de steeds diverser wordende achterban in het bijzonder.

Van der Geld en ondergetekende hebben een inventarisatie naar de brancheorganisaties van het notariaat als beroepsgroep uitgevoerd.[19] Daaruit blijkt dat de invoering van de huidige Wet op het notarisambt grote invloed heeft gehad op de organisatie van de beroepsgroep als zodanig. Veel nieuwe notariële organisaties zijn destijds in het leven geroepen en ineens was er niet alleen voor de cliënt, maar ook voor de notaris veel te kiezen. Men kan thans drie categorieën notariële organisaties onderscheiden (tussen haakjes de oprichtingsdata):

19 L.A.G.M. van der Geld, L.C.A. Verstappen, 'Het ontstaan van (branche-)organisaties in het notariaat sinds 1999', WPNR 7205/2018.

1. het algemeen belang en het notariaat als zodanig dienende organisaties, voornamelijk overheidsorganisaties zoals de KNB (1843/1999) zelf, het Bureau Financieel Toezicht en de Kamers van Toezicht (1843), maar ook de Stichting Beroepsopleiding Notariaat (1987) en het Pensioenfonds Notariaat (1955);
2. algemeen georiënteerde brancheorganisaties, waarbij men kan denken aan: Netwerk Notarissen (1999), NICO Notarissen (1999), Formaat Notarissen (1999) en Nederlandse Branche Vereniging Notariaat (NBVN, 2010); deze organisaties richten zich meer op kennis- en productontwikkeling, marketing en lobby;
3. thematisch georiënteerde brancheorganisaties zoals Vereniging van Estate Planners in het Notariaat (EPN, 1999), Vereniging van Notariële Registergoed Specialisten (NRS, 2012), Vereniging van Mediators in het Notariaat (VMN, 1999), Vereniging voor Agrarisch Specialisten in het Notariaat (VASN, 2000), Vereniging van Notarieel Ondernemingsrecht Specialisten (VOC/N, 2012) en Stichting IT-notaris (IT-notaris, 2011); Deze organisaties richten zich op kennisontwikkeling en lobby op specifieke terreinen van de beroepsuitoefening.

Behalve enkele rudimentaire voorlopers zijn vrijwel alle notarissenorganisaties in de tweede en derde categorie na de invoering van de huidige Wet op het notarisambt in 1999 opgericht. Het oorzakelijk verband is evident.

Eveneens moet worden genoemd de reeds eerder vermelde studie van Plaggemars uit 2011[20] naar de kenmerken van de verschillende notariaten in Europa door het versturen van questionnaires. Zijn conclusie is hiervoor al aangegeven: de notariaten verschillen onderling sterk.

Het beeld dat over de ontwikkelingen in de organisatie van het notariaat uit dit onderzoek opkomt is dat de diversificatie in de ambtsuitoefening zich ook op organisatorisch vlak heeft doorgezet. Dat kan positief (meer diversiteit), maar ook negatief (meer versplintering) worden beoordeeld. Om naar buiten toe als beroepsgroep overtuigend over te komen is interne coördinatie van activiteiten en uitingen een *must*. Die coördinatie vindt dan ook plaats. De algemeen georiënteerde brancheorganisaties, voor zover zij aan lobby doen, houden zich vooral bezig met de vakinhoudelijke onderwerpen en niet met de lobby van de organisatie van het beroep. Maar in de media laten ook de algemeen georiënteerde brancheorganisaties naast de KNB van zich horen in het maatschappelijke debat. Omdat de achterban diverser en breder is geworden, is consensus op onderwerpen lastiger te bereiken. Dat is vooral problematisch als de politiek of de maatschappij een standpunt van het notariaat verwacht of verlangt.

20 A.D. Plaggemars, 'Is de notaris de markt meester? (Diss. RUG), Den Haag: Boom Juridische Uitgevers 2011.

8 Het Toezicht

Over het toezicht is veel te doen geweest, met name de versterkte rol van het notariaat als verlengde arm van de overheid waar het gaat om de bestrijding van fraude en criminaliteit. De commissie-Hammerstein heeft in 2005[21] reeds vastgesteld dat er, vooral binnen de beroepsgroep zelf, zorgen bestaan over de handhaving van de integriteit en de kwaliteit van de dienstverlening. Uit de *Trendrapportage 2006*[22] blijkt men voor de handhaving van de beroepsethiek primair is aangewezen op de notariële toezichthouders. Verschillende commissies wijzen echter op de tekortkomingen van in het bijzonder het tuchtstelsel en de noodzaak tot herziening. Het WODC heeft onderzoek laten doen naar de wettelijke en beroepsregelingen van onder andere het notariaat met betrekking tot de *derdenrekeningen.*[23] Over de rol van de notaris bij witwassen is het nodige te doen geweest. Het WODC heeft opdracht gegeven voor onderzoek naar *malafide activiteiten in de vastgoedsector*, om de rol van de bij vastgoedtransacties betrokken dienstverleners te achterhalen. De beroepsethiek stond vooral onder druk na de economische crisis vanaf 2008. Het WODC heeft met het rapport *Kwaliteit in zware tijd*,[24] dat in 2011 verscheen, zicht willen krijgen op de gevolgen van de crisis op onder andere de naleving van wet- en regelgeving.

De belangrijkste controlerende instelling van het notariaat is het *Bureau Financieel Toezicht* (BFT). Het bureau is thans enerzijds verantwoordelijk voor het financieel toezicht en het kwaliteits- en integriteitstoezicht op notarissen en gerechtsdeurwaarders en anderzijds voor het toezicht op de naleving van de Wet ter voorkoming van witwassen en financiering van terrorisme (Wwft) door notarissen, accountants, belastingadviseurs en administratiekantoren. Het toezicht wordt uitgevoerd door twee aparte afdelingen binnen het BFT: de afdeling notariaat/gerechtsdeurwaarders en de afdeling Wwft. Het BFT is onderwerp van verschillende onderzoeken geweest. De belangrijkste onderzoeken naar het BFT zijn verricht in 2009 en in 2018. Het onderzoek uit 2018 is verricht door SEO Economisch Onderzoek in samenwerking met Clear Conduct[25] en handelde over de doeltreffendheid en doelmatigheid van het toezicht door het BFT. Het meest recente

---

21 Commissie-Hammerstein (Commissie Evaluatie Wet op het notarisambt) (2005). Het beste van twee werelden. Den Haag: Ministerie van Justitie. https://zoek.officielebekendmakingen.nl/kst-23706-62-b1.pdf.

22 Z.D. Laclé, M.J. ter Voert, Trendrapportages Notariaat: Toegankelijkheid, continuïteit, kwaliteit en integriteit van het notariaat (Onderzoek en Beleid, nr. 265). Den Haag: WODC 2006. www.wodc.nl/onderzoeksdatabase/trendrapportage-notariaat-2006.aspx.

23 K. van Dijken, Z. Berdowski, P.H. Eshuis, De praktijk van derdenrekeningen, Den Haag: WODC 2006; IOO. https://www.wodc.nl/binaries/1287-volledige-tekst_tcm28-68634.pdf. (2006).

24 M.J. ter Voert, F. Zwenk, E.M.Th. Beenakkers, Kwaliteit in zware tijd: Marktwerking, vraaguitval en notariële dienstverlening (Onderzoek en Beleid, nr. 296). Den Haag: WODC 2011. www.wodc.nl/binaries/ob296-volledige-tekst_tcm28-71408.pdf. (2011).

25 J. Hers, W. Rougoor, C. Biesenbeek, H. van Beusekom, R. Barth, Evaluatie BFT (SEO-rapport, nr. 59). www.rijksoverheid.nl/documenten/rapporten/2018/07/13/tk-bijlage-eindrapport-evaluatie. (2018).

onderzoek *Evaluatie BFT*[26] laat zien dat het als kwalitatief degelijk wordt beoordeeld, in toenemende mate risico gestuurd en sterk gericht is op het opsporen en bestrijden van normoverschrijding.

De beroepsorganisaties van notarissen en gerechtsdeurwaarders tonen zich kritisch over het BFT. Het gaat dan voornamelijk over de keuzes en afwegingen die het BFT maakt over de opzet, de prioriteiten en de praktische uitvoering van toezicht en handhaving omdat zij niet altijd duidelijk zijn voor de notarissen en gerechtsdeurwaarders. Die willen beter begrijpen welke keuzes het BFT maakt, welke afwegingen hieraan ten grondslag liggen en welke implicaties dit met zich brengt voor de onder toezicht gestelden. Rondom vastgoedfraude spelen vele actoren, waaronder de notaris, een rol. Sinds de invoering van de Wwft is de bewustwording van die rol binnen het notariaat ontegenzeggelijk vergroot. Deze is nog versterkt door allerlei incidenten en rapporten die gaandeweg verschenen. Het gaat dan vooral om hypotheekfraude, witwaspraktijken, onder andere door ABC-transacties en verkoopcarrousel, fraude en intimidatie tijdens executieveilingen, alsmede belastingontduiking. Het is maar een greep uit het onderzoek *Malafide activiteiten in de vastgoedsector*, een exploratief en beschrijvend onderzoek naar de aard, actoren en aanpak van malafide activiteiten in het vastgoed.[27]

De notaris is duidelijk veel meer dan vroeger de poortwachter in het recht, hetgeen niet alleen nieuwe regels met zich heeft gebracht, maar ook extra toezicht en handhaving.

9 CONCLUSIE

Door de invoering van de huidige Wet op het notarisambt in 1999 is de notaris meer de markt opgejaagd, terwijl hij tegelijkertijd in zijn versterkte rol van poortwachter in het recht meer ambtelijker moet optreden. Het aanbod van notariële dienstverlening is diverser geworden door meer marktwerking en de organisatie van het notariaat is ook diverser geworden met de opkomst van brancheorganisaties. Maar er is ook veel meer diversiteit binnen de leden van de KNB, al was het alleen maar vanwege de feminisering van het ambt. Die diversiteit is niet alleen aan de bovenkant van de high-end kwalitatief hoogwaardige dienstverlening gerealiseerd, maar ook aan de onderkant met laagdrempelige, modelmatige en goedkope dienstverlening. En helaas zien wij ook meer diversiteit in gebleken notariële moraliteit bij de dienstverlening.

---

26 J. Hers, W. Rougoor, C. Biesenbeek, H. van Beusekom, R. Barth, Evaluatie BFT (SEO-rapport, nr. 59). www.rijksoverheid.nl/documenten/rapporten/2018/07/13/tk-bijlage-eindrapport-evaluatie. (2018).

27 H. Ferwerda, R. Staring, E. de Vries Robbé, J. van der Bunt, Malafide activiteiten in de vastgoedsector: Een exploratief onderzoek naar aard, actoren en aanpak. Arnhem/Rotterdam: Advies- en Onderzoekgroep Beke/Erasmus Universiteit (2007).

Het notariaat was, is en zal in beweging blijven. Soms gaat het erg langzaam, dan weer erg snel. *Panta rhei*, alles stroomt. De wereld en het notariaat zijn voortdurend in beweging. Vermijd tegen de stroom in te varen en probeer klippen te omzeilen. De vraag is welke koers het beste te varen is om het doel te bereiken waarvoor het notariaat in het leven geroepen is: rechtszekerheid en vertrouwen in het recht bieden voor justitiabelen. Recht is een in plaats en tijd bepaalde grootheid. Zo zal ook het notariaat en de notariële beroepsuitoefening ook in de toekomst blijven veranderen.

Land Register: 'Title by Registration' or 'Principle of Good Faith'?

Monika Hinteregger[*]

1 Introduction

The jubilee has always shown a keen interest in the land register laws of the European countries and the efforts towards harmonisation of the national systems at the European level. Land registers provide reliable information on property rights on real estate and are, therefore, a valuable asset for any successful market economy.[1] This also applies to the European market. Legal certainty in this regard reduces transaction costs and contributes to the effective exercise of the basic community freedoms, such as freedom of movement of people and capital and freedom of establishment, and is thus also of high importance for the smooth functioning of the single market.

Harmonisation of the land register systems is a rather challenging task due to the technicality of the matter and the great diversity of the national rules. It is therefore not surprising that substantial achievements in this area are still a long way off. Internationalisation of the real property industry and growing mobility of European nationals, however, demonstrate the need for better national registration systems in order to facilitate secured lending and cross border transactions with respect to land.

In November 2006, a first step in this direction was made by the European Land Information Service (EULIS) project. It was launched by the land registration authorities of eight European countries[2] at the annual conference of the European Mortgage Federation in Brussels with the aim to gain a better understanding of the national systems and to provide easy cross border access to the national registers. After the end of the project and the closure of the EULIS portal in May 2017, the task has been taken on by the European Land Registry Network (ELRN), established by the European Land Registry Association

* University of Graz, Austria

1 For the economic benefits of registration see World Bank Group, *Doing Business 2018: Reforming to Create Jobs*, October 2017, p. 53, available at: www.doingbusiness.org/content/dam/doingBusiness/media/Annual-Reports/English/DB2018-Full-Report.pdf (last accessed 23 November 2020).

2 England and Wales, Ireland, Lithuania, Netherlands, Sweden, Austria, Finland, and Scotland, see https://joinup.ec.europa.eu/collection/egovernment/solution/european-land-information-service-eulis/about (last accessed 23 November 2020).

(ELRA).[3] In order to promote the development and understanding of the role of land registration in real property and capital markets ELRA also implements other projects, such as CROBECO (Cross Border E-Conveyancing) concerning cross border registration in foreign land registers, or IMOLA (Interoperability Model for Land Registers) which aims to produce a model for standardized land registry output.

The rules concerning the national land registers of the European states are quite different. It is possible to distinguish between specific systems according to regional affiliation and historic legal development (England and Wales, Roman countries, Germanic countries, Scandinavian and Eastern European countries after the communist rule). All these systems differ from each other with respect to organization (affiliation to the judicial or administrative system, realfolium or personalfolium), contents (register of title or deeds register) and legal effects.[4]

From an academic point of view, it is especially this third aspect that deserves closer inspection. In order to show the difference of the effects of registration it is necessary to distinguish between two levels: the function of registration for the acquisition of the property right (constitutive or merely declaratory effect), and the effect of registration of the property right for third parties. Here, the national solutions range from guarantee of title (Torrens system) over protection of third parties in good faith (Germanic system) to no protection at all (Roman system).

The practical importance of this topic is impressively shown by the extensive discussion regarding the principle of 'title by registration' in England and Wales. There, the idea that registration itself creates the right, the so-called 'title promise' of the land register, introduced by the Land Registration Act 2002 (LRA), is subject to an intensive academic discussion. Moreover, the combination of title guarantee and the obligation of the registry to indemnity payments in case of mistaken registrations lead to a considerable increase in conveyancing fraud.[5] In England and Wales both questions, the effect of registration and

---

3 ELRA is an international non-profit organization under Belgian law, funded by the Justice Programme of the European Union. It consists of more than 30 organizations which represent the land registries of more than 25 European countries and is constantly growing. See www.elra.eu (last accessed 23 November 2020).

4 For a comprehensive overview, see European University Institute (EUI) Florence/European Private Law Forum & Deutsches Notarinstitut (DNotI) Würzburg, *Real Property Law and procedures in the European Union – General Report*, May 2005, available at: www.eui.eu/Documents/DepartmentsCentres/Law/ResearchTeaching/ResearchThemes/EuropeanPrivateLaw/RealPropertyProject/GeneralReport.pdf (last accessed 23 November 2020); A. Lodde, 'The European systems of real estate registration: an overview', *Territorio Italia*, Vol. 6, No. 1, 2016, pp. 23-42, available at: www.agenziaentrate.gov.it/portale/documents/20143/325363/sistemi+europei+Lodde+2016+en_3+Lodde_ing.pdf/3e3bdb42-db77-40ac-edb3-a01b92076131 (last accessed 23 November 2020). See also the comprehensive information on the national registers provided on the websites of ELRA and ELRN www.elra.eu.

5 Law Commission [England and Wales], *Updating the Land Registration Act 2002*, Law Com. No. 380, July 2018, p. 2, available at: https://assets.publishing.service.gov.uk/government/uploads/system/uploads/attachment_data/file/912196/Updating-Land-Registration-final_WEB_230718.pdf (last accessed

the extent of the guarantee of title that registration provides, are now (among other issues) under legislative review.[6] It might therefore be interesting to see how the English and Welsh principle of 'title by registration' relates to the Germanic principle of 'public faith'. In order to explain the systems I will first give a short outline of the Austrian and German land register and then focus on the Germanic model of public faith and compare this model to the effects of title registration under the law of England and Wales.

2 General Features of the Austrian and German Land Register

2.1 *Organisational Aspects*

Austria and Germany follow the tradition of the Middle-European land register. According to the realfolium-system, the land register consists of parcels, which form the basic unit of the register. Entry of parcels in the land register is obligatory, and there are only exceptions for public land or land that is in public ownership.[7] The land register is part of the judicial system. The land register office is a department of the local court (*Amtsgericht, Bezirksgericht*) where the parcel which is the object of the entry is situated. The recording itself is not done by a judge, but by a special court officer (*Rechtspfleger*).

The process of registration is very formalistic and follows strict rules. The registry usually acts only on application, and ex-officio registrations pose a rare exception.[8] The land register is strictly bound by the priority principle. The order of priority is determined by the point in time in which the application for the entry reached the land register, but German as well as Austrian law provide for several instruments for the alteration of the priority order by legal transaction.[9] A major difference between the two countries lies in the publicity of the register. In German law the right to inspect an entry in the land register

23 November 2020): in 2016/2017, the land registry made indemnity payments for 53 claims, totalling £5 million, see also HM Land Registry, *Annual Report and Accounts 2016 / 2017*, September 2017.

6 See Law Commission [England and Wales], *Updating the Land Registration Act 2002 – A Consultative Paper*, Consultation Paper No. 227, 2016, available at: www.lawcom.gov.uk/app/uploads/2016/03/cp227_land_registration_web.pdf (last accessed 23 November 2020) and Law Com. No. 380, 2018, pp. 251 et seq.: Chapter alteration and rectification of the register.

7 § 3 (2) German Grundbuchordnung (GBO) [German Land Register Regulations]. In Austria, land in public ownership must be entered in the land register since 2008, see § 2b Austrian Grundbuchsumstellungsgesetz (GUG) [Austrian Land Register Conversion Act]. The Austrian GUG contains the rules for the conversion of the paper-based land register to a fully electronic register.

8 See, e.g. §§ 18 (2), 53 and, 71 (2) German GBO; §§ 130 et seq. Austrian Allgemeines Grundbuchsgesetz (GBG) [Austrian Land Register Act].

9 Germany: § 879 (3) Bürgerliches Gesetzbuch (BGB) [German Civil Code]: determination of priority (*Rangvermerk*), § 880 BGB: subsequent change of priority (*Rangänderung*), § 881 BGB: reservation of priority (*Rangvorbehalt*); Austria: § 30 GBG: change of priority (*Vorrangseinräumung*), § 58 GBG: reservation of priority (*Rangvorbehalt*).

only applies to persons who can show a legitimate interest in the entry. In Austria this is only required for the inspection of the personal register, an auxiliary register to the main register which allows to search for property rights according to the name of the holder of the right. All other registers and indexes are open for the public and can also be accessed electronically via the internet.[10]

2.2 *Constitutive Effect*

In both countries registration in the land register has constitutive effect. This means that the acquisition of a property right (ownership or any limited property right, such as pledge, usufruct or servitude) requires registration of the right in the land register (§ 873 BGB, § 431 ABGB[11]). Before registration, the acquirer has only an obligatory right towards the other contracting party to the procurement of the real right.

The constitutive effect of registration only applies to the acquisition or cancellation of a real right by legal transaction (e.g. sale contract), and not if the acquisition or cancellation is effected directly by the law itself (e.g. acquisitive prescription) or by some specific judicial or administrative acts. In these cases, the registration of the owner in the land register has only declaratory effect which means that the creation or transfer of the property right does not depend on the registration of the right.

2.3 *Third Party Effect of the Land Register: The Principle of Public Faith*

A fundamental feature of the Germanic land registers is the principle of public faith. This principle is laid down by the legal presumption of the accuracy of the land register. In German law this is explicitly expressed by § 891 BGB according to which it is presumed that the person for whom a right is entered in the land register is entitled to the right. The second legal basis is § 892 BGB which provides under the title 'Public Faith of the Land Register' that 'in favor of the person who acquires a right in a parcel or a right in such a right by legal transaction, the contents of the Land Register are presumed to be correct, unless an objection to the accuracy is registered or the inaccuracy is known to the acquirer'. As a consequence, it is not the registered person, but the person who contests an entry, who bears the burden of proof that the land register is incorrect. In Austrian law this is not explicitly provided by law but deducted from several provisions (§ 1500 ABGB, §§ 62 et seq. and § 71 GBG). In Austrian doctrine this rule is generally printed with the expression

10 See § 5 (4) and § 6 (2) of the Austrian GUG.
11 Allgemeines bürgerliches Gesetzbuch [Austrian Civil Code].

'What is registered is valid' (positive side of the public faith principle) and 'What is not registered is not valid' (negative side of the public faith principle).[12]

In Austria and Germany, the entry of a right in the land register thus does not create the right, or guarantee that the right actually exists, but it only provides for the legal presumption that the registered person is entitled to the right. The entry of the right in the land register is, as was shown above, a necessary condition for the acquisition of the right (no acquisition of the property right without registration), but registration does not create or validate a non-existing or invalid property right. Whether the right is valid or not, is decided by contract law, namely the rules concerning the validity of the contract that is the basis for the transfer of the property right. In this regard it is interesting to note that this applies in both jurisdictions, although Austria and Germany have different tradition systems. Austria follows the principle of causal tradition according to which the transfer of real rights to land depends on the validity of the contract, whereas German law adheres to the principle of abstract tradition and strictly separates the contractual side of the legal transaction (*Verpflichtungsgeschäft*) from the property side (*Verfügungsgeschäft*). Contrary to Austrian law, the transfer and encumbrance of property rights does not depend on the validity of the contract but, according to § 873 BGB, on the validity of a special consensus between the transferor and transferee of the real right directed at the transfer of the right from one to another, the so-called 'real agreement' (*dingliche Einigung*). For the acquisition and loss of ownership to land § 925 BGB provides for a specific type of real agreement, called *Auflassung*, which additionally to § 873 BGB, the general provision on the real agreement, requires compliance with specific formalities. This also applies to the cancellation of a real right over land (§ 875 BGB) or the relinquishment of ownership to land (§ 928 BGB). Contrary to other real agreements, the *Auflassung* cannot be subjected to a condition or time stipulation (§ 925 (2) BGB).

The legal presumption of the accuracy of the land register is not addressed to the transferring parties, but to third parties. It allows third parties to rely on the information provided in the register and, if the register is mistaken, to acquire the property right nevertheless, provided that they are in good faith (*gutgläubiger Erwerb*). If an encumbrance (e.g. servitude) is not shown by the register the law allows for the good faith acquisition of real rights free from encumbrances (*gutgläubig lastenfreier Erwerb*). According to § 892 (1) BGB, the acquirer's good faith is destroyed if he/she, or his/her agent acting on his/her behalf, positively knew that the land register is incorrect or if an objection (*Widerspruch*) is entered in the land register. Austrian law is stricter than German law. In Austria slight negligence already destroys the good faith of the acquirer and, according to case law, the

12 R. Welser & A. Kletecka, *Grundriss des Bürgerlichen Rechts I: Allgemeiner Teil, Sachenrecht, Familienrecht*, 15th ed., Vienna, Manz, 2018, pp. 402 et seq.; G. Iro & O. Riss, *Sachenrecht: Bürgerliches Recht Band IV*, 7th ed., Vienna, Verlag Österreich, 2019, p. 62.

acquisition in good faith of the land register does not cover the gratuitous acquisition of a real right.[13]

The public faith of the land register is limited in its scope. Firstly, it only applies to the acquisition or loss of real rights by legal transaction and not if the acquisition or loss of a real right is effected by operation of law or by judicial or administrative act, and secondly, it extends only to the existence or non-existence of the registered right (and rights to such rights). It does not encompass entries that indicate merely factual or personal circumstances (e.g. size of a parcel, date of birth of the owner) and the existence or non-existence of obligatory rights to a parcel (e.g. lease) or of other rights, charges and restrictions that cannot be registered.

3 The Principle of 'Title by Registration' in English Law

For registered land, the LRA 2002 establishes that it is the entry in the land register that vests the legal estate, hence the property right, in the registered proprietor. This is deducted from Section 58 (1) of the LRA 2002 which provides that 'if, on the entry of a person in the register as the proprietor of a legal estate, the legal estate would not otherwise be vested in him, it shall be deemed to be vested in him as a result of the registration.' This means, according to the Law Commission in its 2001 Report,[14] that 'it will be the fact of registration and registration alone that confers title'. The fundamental objective of the new law was that 'the register should be a complete and accurate reflection of the state of the title of the land at any given time, so that it is possible to investigate title to land on line, with the absolute minimum of additional enquiries and inspections'.[15]

The LRA 2002, however, opens up the possibility to challenge the registered proprietor's title. This is regulated by the rules on 'alteration' and 'rectification' of the register in Schedule 4 of the LRA 2002 which enables the court and the registrar to alter the register in order to correct a mistake, to bring the register up to date, to give effect to any interest excepted from the effect of registration,[16] or to remove a superfluous entry. Conflicts between parties on title issues relate primarily to the instrument of rectification, a specific type of alteration applicable for the correction of mistakes that prejudicially affect the title of a registered proprietor. In order to protect the party who is in possession of the land, Schedule 4

---

13 M. Hinteregger, 'Commentary on prior §§ 431-446 ABGB' *in* M. Schwimann & G.E. Kodek (Eds.), *ABGB Praxiskommentar III*, 5th ed., Vienna, LexisNexis, 2020, paras. 13 et seq.

14 Law Commission [England and Wales] & HM Land Registry, Land Registration for the Twenty-First Century: A Conveyancing Revolution, Law Com. No. 271, July 2001, para. 1.10, available at: www.lawcom.gov.uk/app/uploads/2015/04/Lc271.pdf (last accessed 23 November 2020).

15 Law Commission & HM Land Registry, Law Com. No. 271, 2001, para. 1.5.

16 E.g. overriding interests which bind the proprietor although they do not appear on the register.

provides that an order for rectification shall not be made against the registered proprietor to land in his possession unless he has not consented to the amendment, or fraudulently or carelessly contributed to the mistake, or if it would for any other reason be unjust for the alteration not to be made. The requirement of possession is interpreted in a very broad sense in that physical possession of a tenant, mortgagee, licensee or beneficiary is treated as being in the possession of the registered proprietor.[17] Rectification of the register, but not alteration, can trigger a right to indemnification by the land registry for the party who in the end does not get the property, again provided that rectification did not follow from his own fraud or carelessness.[18] The land registry has then a right of recourse against the party who is at fault.The availability of indemnity is the basis of another fundamental feature of the LRA 2002, the so-called 'state guarantee of title'.[19]

The rules concerning rectification are quite unclear and highly controversial. Apart from the practical concerns regarding the increase in registration fraud and the related obligation of the land registry to pay compensation out of public funds for losses suffered,[20] there are fundamental ambiguities with respect to the contents and interpretation of the legal rules. These relate to the interpretation of the term 'mistake' in Schedule 4 of the LRA 2002,[21] the fundamental tension between the '*nemo dat*'-rule[22] of general property law and the principle of 'title by registration' in the LRA 2002,[23] and, the considerable room for

17 Section 131 of the LRA 2002. Like in the case of adverse possession there must be 'a sufficient degree of exclusive physical custody and control', see *Paton v. Todd* [2012] EWHC 1248 (Ch) (England and Wales High Court [EWHC] 11 May 2012) at para. 60.

18 See Schedule 8 of the LRA 2002.

19 Law Commission & HM Land Registry, Law Com. No. 271, 2001, para. 10.3.

20 See footnote 5 above.

21 See the discussion of 'mistake' by the Law Commission in its 2018 Report, Law Com. No. 380, 2018, paras. 13.14 et seq., 13.18.: 'The summary depends on a notion of what the registrar "would have done" if he or she had known the true or full facts'; S. Cooper, 'Regulating Fallibility in Registered Land Titles', *Cambridge Law Journal*, Vol. 72, No. 2, July 2013, pp. 341-368; R Smith, 'Assessing Rectification and Indemnity: After *Gold Harp* and *Swift 1st*', *in* A. Goymour & S. Watterson & M. Dixon (Eds.), *New Perspectives on Land Registration: Contemporary Problems and Solutions*, Oxford, Hart Publishing, 2018, p. 135.

22 '*Nemo dat quod non habet*' is a generally accepted rule of property law that a person cannot transfer a property right that he/she does not own to another.

23 A. Goymour, 'Mistaken Registrations of Land: Exploding the Myth of "Title by Registration"', *Cambridge Law Journal*, Vol. 72, No. 3, November 2013, pp. 617-650.

discretion left to the courts by the rules on rectification.[24] For instance, in *Gold Harp*[25] the Court of Appeal held that rectification comprises not only the restoration of an interest that was removed from the register by mistake, but also the power to give priority over an interest which had been registered since the mistake. In *Walker v. Burton*[26] the Court of Appeal refused rectification of a mistaken first registration against a proprietor in possession because it was 'not unjust' not to rectify.[27] It is still not clear whether the statutory right for the rightful owner to apply for alteration of the register when he is in actual occupation of the land does amount to rectification and therefore would fall under the rules on indemnification.[28] Indemnification is, however, explicitly provided in case of rectification for the proprietor of a registered estate or charge claiming in good faith under a forged disposition.[29] All these ambiguities significantly affect the main task of land registration, which is to provide legal certainty on entitlements to land, and have already given cause to reconsider the relevant rules of the LRA 2002.[30]

In the following I will show the differences in the legal effects of registration between the English and the Germanic system on the basis of two leading English court decisions that are essential for the understanding of English land register law. I will outline their contents and then examine how these cases would be solved under Austrian and German law. The cases relate to the two major issues of land register law, the effect of registration

---

24 E. Cooke, 'The Register's Guarantee of Title', 2013 *Conveyancer and Property Lawyer*, p. 344; M. Dixon, 'A Not so Conclusive Title Register?', *Law Quarterly Review*, Vol. 129, 2013, p. 320; E. Lees, 'Title by Registration: Rectification, Indemnity and Mistake and the Land Registration Act 2002', *The Modern Law Review*, Vol. 76, No. 1, 2013, p. 62; E. Lees, 'Rectification of the Register – Prospective or Retrospective?', *The Modern Law Review*, Vol. 78, No. 2, 2015, pp. 361-371; A. Goymour, 'Resolving the tension between the Land Registration Act 2002's 'priority' and 'alteration' provisions', 2015 *Conveyancer and Property Lawyer*, p. 253; SAA Cooper, 'Discretion in Property Law: A Study of Judicial Correction of Registered Title', *Legal Studies*, Vol. 38, No. 1, 2018, pp. 1-23; E. Lees, 'Guaranteed Title: No Title, Guaranteed', *in* A. Goymour & S. Watterson & M. Dixon (Eds.), *New Perspectives on Land Registration: Contemporary Problems and Solutions*, Oxford, Hart Publishing, 2018, p. 97; Smith, 2018, p. 129.

25 *Gold Harp Properties Ltd v. MacLeod* [2014] EWCA Civ 1084 (England and Wales Court of Appeal [EWCA] 29 July 2014). In Austrian and German law the case in *Gold Harp* would represent an application of the constellation referred to as the 'negative side' of the land register. Due to the fact that continental property law does not provide for leasehold as a distinctive property right the legal solution of the case under Austrian and German law is rather complicated and there is no straightforward answer.

26 *Walker v. Burton* [2013] EWCA Civ 1228 (EWCA 14 October 2013).

27 One decisive reason for this result was the applicants' lack of any title to the land concerned, see *Walker v. Burton* [2013] EWCA Civ 1228 (EWCA 14 October 2013) at 31 and 102.

28 See *Malory Enterprises Ltd v. Cheshire Homes (UK) Ltd* [2002] EWCA Civ 151 (EWCA 22 February 2002) at 68 and 85 and *Fitzwilliam v. Richall Holdings Services Limited* [2013] EWHC 86 (Ch) (EWHC 28 January 2013) where the courts attributed the original owners who were the victims of fraud beneficial ownership and the right to alteration. This view is rejected by scholarship (e.g. E. Lees, '*Richall Holdings* v *Fitzwilliam*: *Malory* v *Cheshire Homes* and the LRA 2002', *The Modern Law Review*, Vol. 76, No. 5, 2013, pp. 924-934 and Law Commission, Consultation Paper No. 227, 2016, paras. 13.42 et seq. and Law Com. No. 380, 2018, paras. 13.13. et seq.) because it bypasses the rectification and indemnification rules of the LRA 2002.

29 Schedule 8 para. 1 (2) (b) of the LRA 2002.

30 See footnote 14 above.

in case of a forged, and therefore void, disposition and the effect of registration for third parties.

4 English Case Law and Germanic Solutions

4.1 *A-B Situation*

The question which effect registration has between the registered proprietor and the person who is registered subsequently after this person shall be exemplified by the famous case of *Swift 1st Limited.*[31] In *Swift 1st* the Court of Appeal had to decide on a case of fraud. In 2006, a legal charge over Mrs. Rani's house was registered in favour of Swift 1st. The funds were advanced partly to another company (GE Money) in order to redeem a prior registered charge in favour of them and partly by cheque to Mrs. Rani. When Swift 1st took steps to enforce the charge, it came to light that both charges were a fraud committed by persons, unknown to both Swift 1st and Mrs. Rani, and that Mrs. Rani never received any of the funds. Upon order of the judge in the enforcement proceedings the entry of the charge in the land register was deleted, and Swift 1st asked the land registry for an indemnity according to Schedule 8 of the LRA 2002 which was refused by the land registry, but granted in the following lawsuit. The High Court and the Court of Appeal concluded that Swift 1st was entitled to the indemnity because they were claiming 'in good faith under a forged disposition' and that for indemnification purposes Swift 1st was 'regarded as having suffered loss by reason of such rectification as if the charge had not been forged' as provided by Schedule 8 para. 1, sub-para. 2 (b) LRA 2002.

Registration fraud is a rare event in Austria and Germany. The reason for this is most likely the fact that in both countries the land register rules require strict identity checks by public notaries before registration can take place.[32] In Austrian and German law the outcome of this case would be straightforward: The registration of Swift 1st was without any legal foundation. The unknown fraudster pretended to be Mrs. Rani, or, without any authorisation, to act in her name. As there was no consensus between the owner of the property and the recipients of the charges, both charges were null and void and the act of

31 *Swift 1st Limited v. The Chief Land Registrar* [2015] EWCA Civ 330 (EWCA 1 April 2015).

32 § 29 (1) German GBO requires for the registration or cancellation of property right a notarially authenticated authorization for registration (§ 29 GBO, *Eintragungsbewilligung*). Austrian law requires the notarial authentication of the signatures of the parties on the written contract which is the basis for the registration and, if the authorization for registration is not included in the contract, the notarial authentication of the signature of the party whose right is transferred, cancelled or encumbered on the authorization for registration (§ 31 (1) and § 32 (2) GBG). German law requires also notarial authentication for contracts on the transfer of ownership to land (§ 311b BGB).

registration did not change this legal situation. Thus, in a case like Swift 1st, the owner has the right to claim that the charge be deleted from the register. In both countries, this right can be asserted under the law of obligations,[33] but both countries also provide for a special claim under property law.

In Austria, the owner can sue the unduly registered proprietor by way of a special cancellation action (*Löschungsklage*, §§ 62 et seq. GBG),[34] which secures that the unduly registered right is deleted with retroactive effect. Moreover, the claimant can insert a special notice in the land register (*Streitanmerkung*) which prevents third parties from acquiring the unduly registered right, or any further rights on this right, in good faith from the date on which the action was brought. The cancellation action is only applicable if the defect makes the disposition void[35] or voidable.[36] If it is brought against the immediate successor the law does not provide for a specific time limit. Hence, it can be brought as long as the underlying defect can be claimed under the law of obligations (usually 3 or 30 years).

In German law, the right to correction of the land register is regulated in § 894 BGB which provides that the person whose right is not or not correctly registered, or whose right is limited by the registration of an encumbrance or restriction that does not exist, may sue the person whose right is affected by the correction for the approval of the correction (in concreto for the issue of the formal authorization of registration according to § 19 GBO). The instrument to destroy the good faith of third parties is the objection (*Widerspruch*, § 899 BGB), which is registered either by way of an interim injunction or on the basis of consent from the person whose right is affected by the correction of the land register.

In both countries the unduly registered proprietor (Swift 1st) has no right to an indemnity for its loss towards the land register or the state. Only if the deregistered proprietor can show that there was a defect (fault) on the part of the land register, he/she may claim compensation under the title of public authority liability. In a case of identity fraud, liability would rather lie with the public notary for not exercising the necessary care when performing the identity check.

---

33 In Germany, the applicable provision is § 812 BGB which regulates the claim for restitution, see J.F. Baur & R. Stürner, *Sachenrecht*, 18th ed., Munich, C.H.Beck, 2009, p. 230 (‘*Der schuldrechtliche Berichtigungsanspruch*’).

34 This specific action can only be lodged by a person whose registered right was infringed by a subsequent unduly registration.

35 E.g. incorrect entry or grounds for the invalidity of the contract, like lack of consensus or lack of legal capacity.

36 E.g. voidability of the contract because of mistake, deceit, duress.

4.2 *Effect on Third Parties: The A-B-C Situation*

The case in *Knights Construction v. Roberto Mac*[37] addressed a typical A-B-C constellation: A piece of land which, according to the chain of conveyance, belonged to Knights Construction (A) was by mistake registered in the name of the Salvation Army (B). Before the mistake was discovered, B sold the land to Roberto Mac Limited (C). After C was registered, A claimed for rectification. The Deputy Adjudicator decided in favour of A and against both B's and C's registered interest. The decision gained wide approval,[38] and it is now the prevailing understanding that rectification covers both the immediate and the subsequent consequences of a fraudulent transaction, although, as is pointed out by the Law Commission,[39] this is not yet clarified by the Court of Appeal or the Supreme Court who might still take a different approach. The consequence of this broad view of mistake is that not only B's but also C's position is object to rectification. Whether rectification is actually granted to A, however, depends on several factors, especially on the fact whether B or C is in possession of the land and whether this possessor has consented to the amendment, or fraudulently or carelessly contributed to the mistake, or if it would for any other reason be unjust for the alteration not to be made (see Schedule 4 of the LRA 2002). The party who loses the property is entitled to claim an indemnity under Schedule 8 of the LRA 2002, provided he/she did not cause, or contribute to, the loss by fraud or lack of care.

It is now largely common opinion that this solution applies when the transfer between A and B is void,[40] but, according to the Court of Appeal in *NRAM Ltd v. Evans*[41] and *Antoine v. Barclays Bank UK Plc*,[42] it does not apply to dispositions that are only voidable, because the court held that an entry that was correctly made at the time cannot become a

---

37 *Knights Construction (March) Ltd v. Roberto Mac Ltd* [2011] 2 E.G.L.R. 123 (HM Land Registry 9 February 2011) was decided by the Adjudicator to HM Land Registry (replaced by the Property Chamber of the First-tier Tribunal by the Tribunals, Courts and Enforcement Act 2007).

38 Court of Appeal in *Gold Harp Properties Ltd v. MacLeod* [2014] EWCA Civ 1084 (EWCA 29 July 2014) and in *Ajibade v. Bank of Scotland plc* [2008] EWLandRA 2006_0163 (8 April 2008), (but different obiter in *Barclays Bank plc v. Guy* [2008] EWCA Civ 452 (EWCA 9 April 2008)); Law Commission, Law Com. No. 380, 2018, paras. 13.123 et seq.

39 Law Commission, Law Com. No. 380, 2018, para. 13.40. For the future the Law Commission suggest to uphold the view that rectification should be available on the basis that the registration of C was a mistake (para. 13.134, and Recommendation 26 at para. 13.135), but suggest some amendments of the law in order to clarify the consequences when rectification of B or C is refused.

40 This includes lack of authority in agency cases: *Knightsbridge Property Development Corp (UK) Ltd v. South Chelsea Properties Ltd* [2017] EWHC 2730 (Ch) (EWHC 2 November 2017) (case comment by E. Lees, 'Agency, knowledge and good faith in land registration', 2018 *Conveyancer and Property Lawyer*, p. 76).

41 *NRAM Ltd v. Evans* [2017] EWCA Civ 1013 (EWCA 19 July 2017) (case comment by K. Lees, 'NRAM v Evans: there are mistakes and mistakes', 2018 *Conveyancer and Property Lawyer*, p. 91): Registration on the basis of a vesting order that was based on forged documents does not amount to 'mistake'.

42 *Antoine v. Barclays Bank UK Plc* [2018] EWCA Civ 2846 (EWCA 20 December 2018).

mistake because of later events. When the voidable disposition is rescinded, the register can be brought up to date under Schedule 4 para. 2 (1) (b) of the LRA 2002. As this would not constitute rectification, but only alteration, the order has no retroactivity and there is no right to indemnification.

Austrian and German law would in this case decide for the protection of C, because C acquired the property right from B by way of legal transaction and because C acted in good faith of the land register. In German law C's good faith would only be destroyed if an objection to the accuracy is already registered or if C definitely knew that the land does not belong to B. Austrian law does not protect the acquirer C if he should have known that B is not the owner (slight negligence) and if C acquired the right without consideration. A's successful cancellation action against B would in both cases (lack of good faith and gratuitous acquisition) include C and lead to the cancellation of both registrations. Moreover, in order to protect the rightful owner A from the loss of its property right, Austrian law grants A the right to include C in the cancellation action against B if A brings the action within a certain time period from the date when A is notified of B's registration.[43] If A is not notified of B's registration this time period is extended to three years.[44]

5 Conclusions

All three jurisdictions have effective registration systems for interests in land. The organizational features of the registers have, despite the different legal traditions, a lot in common. One striking difference is the function of the registrar. In Austria and Germany the registrar does not decide upon matters of law. The registrar is a legal officer of the court who carries out applications if they comply with the provided formal requirements without any power of discretion or decision making power. Disputes as to whether a property right exists, and to whom it belongs, must always be clarified in legal proceedings between the parties concerned.

When an entry is mistaken, all three systems try to achieve a balance of interest between the parties concerned. In the A-B situation Austrian and German law always protect the rightful owner and allow mistaken entries be removed from the register, and it is only in the A-B-C situation that the fact of registration plays a role for the attribution of the right between the parties concerned. In both systems the decisive element is the good faith of the third person who acquires a property right from the registered non-owner. While German law rather unconditionally protects the interests of the third person, Austrian law

43 § 63 GBG: A must enter a special notice (*Streitanmerkung*) within the appeal period and then file the cancellation action within further 60 days.

44 § 64 GBG.

tries to achieve a more balanced result between the affected interests, especially by granting the rightful owner who acts quickly enough the right to remove both B and C from the register.

English and Welsh law do not provide for such a straightforward solution of the problem. Already in the A-B situation it gives the registrar and the court a lot of discretion, and this is extended also to A-B-C cases. The decisive element here is not good faith of the person who relies on the register, but the fact of possession. Here the law is more concerned to achieve a just result in the individual case, albeit to the detriment of legal certainty. Another decisive instrument for the reconciliation of the interests of the parties concerned is the right to indemnification. Such a right is unknown in Germany and Austria, as is the view that it is the responsibility of the state to guarantee the correctness of the register also to a person who, according to the rules of property law, is not entitled to the right.

Landregistratiedata

Van wie, voor wie en waarvoor?

Jacques Vos[*]

1 CROBECO

In juni 2009 ontstonden de eerste ideeën binnen het bestuur van de Europese vereniging van landregistratieautoriteiten (ELRA)[1] voor het faciliteren van een grensoverschrijdende eigendomsoverdracht door de 'eigen' notaris. De lokale notaris zou, met gebruikmaking van moderne technologieën en bestaande (Europese)[2] regelgeving, een tweetalige akte moeten kunnen opstellen en inschrijven in de openbare registers van het land waar het registergoed gelegen is (*lex rei sitae*). In augustus van dat jaar ging een werkgroep aan de gang om een projectplan te schrijven. Crobeco was geboren.

Al snel werd gezocht naar een expert op het gebied van het rechtsvergelijkend goederenrecht. Zo kwam het dat we contact opnamen met Sjef van Erp en dat wij, Wim Louwman en ik, op twee november 2010, met Sjef en notaris Frits von Seydlitz Kurzbach, tijdens een lunchoverleg bij restaurant RossaNero in Eindhoven het idee van de eerste aanstaande grensoverschrijdende eigendomsoverdracht bespraken. Tijdens deze lunch bespraken we ook de mogelijkheid om de Nederlandse bewaarder een verklaring te laten afgeven aan zijn buitenlandse evenknie, teneinde de controles bij de inschrijving in het buitenland verder te vereenvoudigen.

De verklaring zou inhouden dat de bewaarder 'op basis van de in Nederland geldende regels geen reden ziet voor weigering van de inschrijving of plaatsing van een waarschuwing bij de overeenkomst, indien inschrijving werd verlangd in de openbare registers in Nederland en de overeenkomst betrekking zou hebben op een in Nederland gelegen onroerende zaak.' Van het stellen van de bewaardersverklaring bij het verzenden van de

---

* Bewaarder van de Dienst voor het kadaster en de openbare registers.

1 https://www.elra.eu (laatstelijk ge- raadpleegd: 20 december 2020).

2 Geconsolideerde versie van het Verdrag betreffende de Europese Unie en het Verdrag betreffende de werking van de Europese Unie 2012/C 326/01, *PB* C 326 van 26/10/2012 p. 1-0390, en vooral Verordening (EG) nr. 593/2008 van het Europees Parlement en de Raad van 17 juni 2008 inzake het recht dat van toepassing is op verbintenissen uit overeenkomst (Rome I), Verordening (EG) nr. 864/2007 van het Europees Parlement en de Raad van 11 juli 2007 betreffende het recht dat van toepassing is op niet-contractuele verbintenissen (Rome II), en Verordening (EG) nr. 44/2001 van de Raad van 22 december 2000 betreffende de rechterlijke bevoegdheid, de erkenning en de tenuitvoerlegging van beslissingen in burgerlijke en handelszaken.

akte door de Nederlandse bewaarders naar de Spaanse collega is het nimmer gekomen,[3] maar gezamenlijke lunches hebben wij sindsdien al menig maal mogen nuttigen.[4]

Kort na onze eerste gezamenlijke lunch was de eerste geslaagde grensoverschrijdende eigendomsoverdracht een feit. Deze eerste overdracht, uitgevoerd en op beeld vastgelegd[5] tijdens de eerste Crobeco-conferentie, op 25 november 2010, was één van de resultaten[6] van het twee jaar durende Crobeco[7]-project waarbij een verkenning werd uitgevoerd naar de juridische, praktische en technologische mogelijkheden om vanuit het thuisland van de koper met gebruikmaking van zijn lokale notaris de eigendomsoverdracht in het buitenland te bewerkstelligen.[8] Het project eindigde in 2012 met de oplevering van de 'Cross Border Conveyancing Reference Framework' (CCRF) en was dermate vernieuwend en succesvol dat de Europese Commissie na afronding van dit eerste project opnieuw een subsidie verstrekte, ditmaal voor het vervolgproject genaamd CROBECO II.

Ook bij dit project was Van Erp zeer nauw betrokken en werd hij veelvuldig door de leden van ELRA geroemd om de in helderheid uitblinkende presentaties.

Uiteindelijk werd een *clausus repository*, een digitale modellenbibliotheek, ingericht waarin tekstgedeelten, specifieke clausules die zien op de toepasselijke Europese verordeningen (Rome I & II en Brussel I), beschikbaar werden gesteld om gevolg en invulling te kunnen geven aan de (Europese) regelgeving die onderwerp van onderzoek

3 Gezien het onderscheid in de taken en verantwoordelijkheden van de Spaanse *registrador* en de Nederlandse bewaarder is het wellicht ook niet verwonderlijk dat de Spaanse bewaarder geen gebruik wenste te maken van deze verklaring. Immers, gezien de taken en verantwoordelijkheden van laatstgenoemde, schiet zijn Nederlandse collega (bij het registreren van een akte in de Nederlandse grondboekhouding, een aktenregistratie), tekort in de controles die nodig zijn om een garantie te kunnen geven op hetgeen op basis van deze akte dient te worden geregistreerd in de Spaanse grondboekhouding, een rechtenregistratie *in extenso*.

4 Met bijzonder veel genoegen denk ik terug aan de vele interessante discussies die wij hebben gevoerd, zowel tijdens de vele ELRA-bijeenkomsten waar Sjef als zeer gewaardeerd spreker vele malen werd uitgenodigd, al dan niet in verband met de Crobeco-projecten en de daarop volgende IMOLA-projecten, maar vooral ook aan onze discussies tijdens ontbijtgesprekken, wandelingen en diners gedurende diverse vergaderingen en conferenties. Daarbij springen de *Land and Poverty* conferenties van de Wereldbank het meest in het oog.

5 Voor een korte impressie van het Crobeco-project en de handelingen ter afronding van de eerste grensoverschrijdende overdracht via Crobeco, zie: https://www.youtube.com/watch?v=Vk7GL6A9d_0 (laatstelijk geraadpleegd: 20 december 2020).

6 Een ander vernieuwend aspect was het beschrijven van oplossingen in het Referentiekader voor Grensoverschrijdende eigendomsoverdrachten (het "Common Conveyancing Reference Framework", afgekort: CCRF). Dit CCRF kon worden opgesteld op basis van de resultaten van een aantal praktische pilots die in ELRA-verband zijn uitgevoerd. Deze pilots zagen op praktijkcasus waarbij een in Spanje gelegen registergoed via de Nederlandse bewaarder door de Nederlandse notaris werden overgedragen.

7 Een algemene beschrijving van het CROBECO-project is te vinden via: https://www.elra.eu/crobeco/ (laatstelijk geraadpleegd: 20 december 2020).

8 Een meer uitvoerige juridische beschrijving is terug te vinden in J. Vos & W. Louwman, 'De overdracht van buitenlandse onroerende zaken via de lokale notaris', *WPNR*, 6992, 2013, pp. 907-919 en: L. van Almelo, 'Vakantiehuis kopen via de eigen notaris', *Notariaat Magazine*, 5, 2012, pp. 16-17.

was (geweest) tijdens de beide opvolgende projecten en waarvan het (in sommige gevallen) noodzakelijk of raadzaam werd geacht een clausule in de akte op te nemen.

Dat niet iedereen evenzeer gediend was van de resultaten van de Crobeco-projecten bleek wel uit sommige reacties die de bewaarders, maar vooral ook Van Erp als juridisch adviseur van de projecten gedurende de looptijd van beide projecten ontvingen. Hij werd zelfs een periode 'inhoudelijk gestalkt' door een vertegenwoordiger van een buitenlands notariaat. Ook werden zijn werkzaamheden voor de KNB bij de Conseil des Notariats de l'Union Européenne in Brussel (CNUE)[9] door sommige buitenlandse notarissen bemoeilijkt. Dat moet door Sjef ongetwijfeld als bijzonder onaangenaam zijn ervaren, zeker gezien het feit dat zijn werkzaamheden (in internationaal verband) altijd gekenmerkt worden door vertrouwelijk handelen en een onafhankelijke houding, getuige ook het feit dat hij – in alle openheid – adviseur van zowel de Europese notarissen als de Europese bewaarders(vereniging) is (geweest).

ELRA was met het project en de '*three respects for*'[10] de juiste weg ingeslagen, zo blijkt wel uit een in het Notariaat Magazine[11] in diezelfde periode gepubliceerd interview met Sjef. Het interview werd namelijk voorzien van een toevoeging van het toenmalige KNB-bestuur. De reactie eindigde met de alinea:

> "Het CROBECO-project past in een verder éénwordend Europa en staat zo beschouwd wellicht voor het begin van de aanleg van een nieuwe Europese snelweg. Wanneer de snelweg er eenmaal ligt, zal hij gebruikt gaan worden. Het is aan de Europese notarissen om met elkaar aan de slag te gaan om aantrekkelijk vervoer over die snelweg mogelijk te maken. Het project CROBECO moet het notariaat in Europa een nieuwe prikkel geven om nauwer te gaan samenwerken op een praktisch niveau."

9 http://www.notaries-of-europe.eu/ (laatstelijk geraadpleegd: 20 december 2020). Vanuit informatietechnisch perspectief is het verstandig op te merken dat de CNUE gebruik maakt van een niet versleutelde verbinding tussen de server en de internetbrowser van de bezoeker. Wanneer geen gebruik wordt gemaakt van het koppelen van een beveiligde sleutel (SSL of TLS-technologie) aan de connectie van een website, bestaat het risico dat de gegevensstroom tussen de server en de bezoeker eenvoudig is uit te lezen met zogenaamde netwerk sniffers. Inloggegevens zoals wachtwoorden en persoonsgegevens die worden ingevoerd op de website zijn daarmee eenvoudig uit te lezen, waarschijnlijk de reden waarom het intranet van CNUE https://www.intranet.cnue.be/Login.aspx?ReturnUrl=%2f (laatstelijk geraadpleegd: 20 december 2020) wél is voorzien van een TLS-certificaat.

10 Het project beoogde geen wijzigingen aan te brengen in bestaande situaties en hanteerde derhalve als uitgangspunten: '*Respect for existing legislation, respect for existing technology and respect for existing responsibilities*'.

11 H. van Wermeskerken, 'European Law Institute. Werkbare oplossingen voor de praktijk', *Notariaat Magazine*, 9, 2011, pp. 14-15.

Ook de CNUE publiceerde[12] op 18 november 2011 een officieel standpuntnota ten aanzien van CROBECO. De KNB – en meer in het bijzonder de CNUE – voegde de daad bij het woord en lanceerde[13] op 11 september 2012 de notariële tegenhanger van CROBECO: het EUFides project.

EUFides heeft geresulteerd in een werkwijze waarbij de lokale notaris zich in verbinding stelt met een notaris van het land waar het registergoed is gelegen. Beide notarissen tezamen faciliteren de grensoverschrijdende eigendomsoverdracht. Inmiddels is EUFides[14] verworden tot een platform, een soort beveiligde notariële werkomgeving in de cloud[15] waar notarissen in grensoverschrijdende gevallen gebruik van (zouden) kunnen maken. Uit geen van de webpagina's van de CNUE blijkt van praktijkvoorbeelden en cijfers over casus uit de notariële EUFides-praktijk. (Ook) In ELRA-verband is CROBECO niet doorontwikkeld tot een platform voor dagelijks gebruik. De CROBECO-projecten waren destijds (mogelijk te) vooruitstrevend; zo maakten veel landen in Europa (en maken deze landen nog altijd) geen gebruik van elektronische handtekeningen. In een aantal Europese landen bestaat de eigendomsoverdracht en de registratie van rechten of akten nog altijd uit een volledig papieren proces, hoewel COVID-19 de digitalisering (ook) in die landen in een stroomversnelling lijkt te brengen.[16]

2 Elektronische handtekeningen

Uit een onderzoek onder de leden van ELRA in november 2020[17] blijkt dat veel landen nog altijd geen gebruik maken van elektronische handtekeningen of slechts voor een gedeelte van het proces van levering van een registergoed elektronische handtekeningen gebruiken. Dit laatste is overigens ook in Nederland het geval. Ondanks het gebruik door notarissen en bewaarders van gekwalificeerde elektronische handtekeningen sinds 2005,

12 http://www.notaries-of-europe.eu/index.php?pageID=4570 (laatstelijk geraadpleegd: 20 december 2020).

13 http://www.notaries-of-europe.eu//index.php?pageID=8050 (laatstelijk geraadpleegd: 20 december 2020).

14 http://www.notaries-of-europe.eu/index.php?pageID=8033 (laatstelijk geraadpleegd: 20 december 2020).

15 Opgemerkt dient te worden dat 'cloud' of 'de cloud' een synoniem is voor het internet. Wanneer een dienst wordt afgenomen door een account op een website aan te maken waar een webapplicatie achter zit, wordt die dienst afgenomen uit de cloud. 'Cloud computing' daarentegen is een techniek waarmee vele computers (CPU's) samenwerken om bronnen beschikbaar te stellen. Dat kan gaan om het opslaan en verwerken van data, het beschikbaar stellen van geheugen en processorkracht.

16 Door tal van beroepsgroepen, waaronder het notariaat en de bewaarders wordt bezien hoe, waar en wanneer digitalisering van (onderdelen van) bestaande processen kunnen worden gedigitaliseerd. Hoewel in ELRA-verband vaker onderzoek is gedaan naar het gebruik van (gekwalificeerde) elektronische handtekeningen, is in april 2020 een onderzoek verricht naar specifieke maatregelen die in de diverse lidstaten zijn ingevoerd vanwege COVID-19, zie: https://www.elra.eu/wp-content/uploads/2020/04/ELRA-Report-on-the-study-special-measures-regarding-COVID-19.pdf (laatstelijk geraadpleegd: 20 december 2020).

17 https://www.elra.eu/wp-content/uploads/2020/11/Luisa-ClodeElectronic-Signature.pdf (laatstelijk geraadpleegd: 20 december 2020).

voor zover het betreft de inschrijving van akten en stukken die hiermee verband houden, kunnen de betrokken partijen de notariële akte nog altijd niet op elektronische wijze ondertekenen.

Ruim zes jaar geleden[18] heb ik tijdens het Landelijk Notarieel Studenten Congres in Utrecht opgemerkt dat de burger in Nederland zich nog altijd moet behelpen met DigiD (www.digid.nl) voor elektronische communicatie tussen burger en overheid, terwijl in veel van de Europese lidstaten van overheidswege gekwalificeerde elektronische handtekeningen beschikbaar zijn gesteld. Deze elektronische handtekeningen zijn gebaseerd op gekwalificeerde certificaten. In veel gevallen is in de vooroplopende Europese lidstaten een elektronische identiteit voor alle ingezetenen aan deze gekwalificeerde handtekeningen gekoppeld. Met die elektronische identiteit kunnen additionele diensten worden afgenomen en wordt tegelijkertijd het rechtsverkeer optimaal bediend. Dat is Nederland nu niet het geval.

Het koppelen van additionele diensten houdt vanzelfsprekend ook een ethisch vraagstuk in. Denk alleen al aan de situatie waarin je een ticket boekt naar Washington om in November 2021 deel te nemen aan de *Land and Poverty* conferentie en waarbij je, ter preventie van het potentieel verspreiden van het Covid-19 virus, door de vliegmaatschappij wordt gevraagd om tijdens het boekingsproces jouw legitimatiebewijs te overleggen, aan welk document op elektronische wijze verbonden dient te zijn een actueel vaccinatieboekje.[19] Wanneer je dit niet elektronische document niet kunt overleggen, is het vliegen met de betreffende vliegmaatschappij[20] uitgesloten. Mocht je vervolgens toch een vliegmaatschappij hebben gevonden die deze eis niet stelt en je eenmaal voet op Amerikaanse bodem hebt gezet, word je bij de douane geconfronteerd met dezelfde vraag. Een negatief of ontkennend antwoord leidt tot een rechtstreekse vlucht terug naar Amsterdam. Om niet te hoeven wachten op een vaccinatieboekje dat is gekoppeld aan jouw legitimatiebewijs, werkt de luchtvaartsector inmiddels aan een eigen 'Coronapaspoort'. Daarbij wordt gebruik gemaakt

---

18 J. Vos, 'Zijn we al klaar voor Europees vastgoed (gerelateerde) transacties?' *in* J.W.A. Biemans, J.M. Milo, D.F.M.M. Zaman e.a. (Eds.), *Het Europees notariaat: één cohort of incoherent?*, Ars Notariatus no 158, Deventer, Kluwer, 2015, pp. 37-49.

19 NOS (2020, 16 december). RIVM: 'vaccinatiebewijs' is pas eind maart te downloaden, niet eind januari, van https://nos.nl/collectie/13850/artikel/2360888-rivm-vaccinatiebewijs-is-pas-eind-maart-te-downloaden-niet-eind-januari (laatstelijk geraadpleegd: 20 december 2020).

20 Dat dit een niet ondenkbare casus kan zijn, blijkt uit: C. Zagon, 'International travel could be revived by next year, Qantas CEO reveals', 23 november 2020, via https://9now.nine.com.au/a-current-affair/coronavirus-exclusive-the-compulsory-conditions-for-australians-to-travel-internationally-as-lockdowns-ease/e4bf2f6c-faab-46dd-8528-b7f8120ede2f?ocid=Social-ACA (laatstelijk geraadpleegd: 20 december 2020).

van een app die is ontwikkeld om te controleren op de juiste visa, met gebruikmaking van blockchaintechnologie en zonder gegevens op te slaan.[21]

Anders dan de koplopers onder de Europese lidstaten heeft de Nederlandse overheid er bij het vormgeven van de digitale overheid voor gekozen vrije marktwerking als uitgangspunt te hanteren. Het ontwikkelen en verstrekken van digitale authenticatiemiddelen dient daarmee zoveel mogelijk te geschieden door marktpartijen. Het gevolg van dit uitgangspunt is een gebrek aan gebruiksmogelijkheden (*use cases*) in de dagelijkse praktijk, in combinatie met een beperkt aantal aanbieders van gekwalificeerde elektronische handtekeningen in Nederland. Het gebruiken van meerdere identificatiesystemen past bij de nog aan te nemen Wet digitale overheid, waarbij de overheid wil bereiken dat mensen bij een overheidsplatform kunnen inloggen met producten van verschillende vertrouwensdienstverleners.[22]

Enigszins kritisch beschouwd, is voor een gekwalificeerde elektronische handtekening een tamelijk hoge aanschafprijs verschuldigd, terwijl het aantal gebruiksmogelijkheden nog altijd zeer beperkt is. Het lijkt daarmee het verhaal van de kip en het ei: zonder gebruiksmogelijkheden bestaat er bij certificatiedienstverleners geen of weinig interesse om dit type handtekeningen aan te bieden op de Nederlandse markt, waardoor het aantal aanbieders beperkt blijft en de prijs per handtekening relatief hoog blijft. Andersom vormt de relatief hoge aanschafprijs van een gekwalificeerde elektronische handtekening een drempel voor het aanschaffen, waardoor er ook geen noodzaak lijkt te ontstaan voor publieke en private dienstenaanbieders om gebruiksmogelijkheden te ontwikkelen.

Het gebrek aan een breed gebruik van gekwalificeerde elektronische handtekeningen in Nederland kan worden ervaren als een groot gemis, zeker vanuit het oogpunt van (het bevorderen van de) rechtszekerheid. Dit gemis wordt zelfs groter wanneer de (gekwalificeerde) elektronische handtekening gecombineerd wordt met zogenaamde 'digitale kluis-services', waarvan er sinds 2014 al vele initiatieven voorhanden zijn.[23]

---

21 NOS (2020, 23 november). 'Luchtvaartbranche komt met "coronapaspoort" voor reizigers', van https://www.rtlnieuws.nl/economie/bedrijven/artikel/5198828/iata-luchtvaartmaatschappij-corona-paspoort-digitaal-app-testen (laatstelijk geraadpleegd: 20 december 2020).

22 Artikel 9 in de Nota van Wijzigingen, *Kamerstukken II* 2019/20, 34972, 14, p. 2-3. Het wetsvoorstel ligt op het moment van schrijven, 20 december 2020, bij de Eerste Kamer.

23 In 2014 noemde ik als voorbeelden van dergelijke initiatieven: www.qiyfoundation.org (laatstelijk geraadpleegd: 20 december 2020). SafeGuard Encryption via www.sophos.com (laatstelijk geraadpleegd: 20 december 2020) en http://lockerproject.org/ (laatstelijk geraadpleegd: 20 december 2020). Daarbij vermeldde ik in notarieel verband eveneens www.digizeker.nl (laatstelijk geraadpleegd: 20 december 2020) en www.dataplaza.nl (laatstelijk geraadpleegd: 20 december 2020). Van deze laatste is de informatie op de website nog altijd informatief van aard. De digitale kluis van digizeker.nl is inmiddels daadwerkelijk uitgebreid met een nieuwe variant die niet alleen digitaal is beveiligd, maar ook is ondergebracht bij een Nederlandse notaris, aldus de website www.digizeker.nl. Meer informatie over die ontwikkeling is te vinden via www.nederlandsenotariskluis.nl (laatstelijk geraadpleegd: 20 december 2020).

Met IDIN (www.idin.nl) kunnen consumenten zichzelf sinds 2016 identificeren en inloggen op een elektronische omgeving bij overheidsinstanties, verzekeringsmaatschappijen en webwinkels. Om in te loggen wordt gebruik gemaakt van de inlogmethode van de bank waar de burger klant is. Opgemerkt dient te worden dat het betrouwbaarheidsniveau van het authenticatiemiddel als 'substantieel' is beoordeeld in de zin van eIDAS.[24,25] Dit houdt in dat bij de identificatieverificatie daadwerkelijk vastgesteld dient te worden dat de aanvrager een geldig, officieel document bezit met dezelfde identiteitsgegevens die gecontroleerd kunnen worden in een basisregistratie. Deze controle mag worden uitbesteed of op afstand plaatsvinden en moet een substantiële mate van vertrouwen bieden. Daarnaast is voor het middel tweefactorauthenticatie vereist, moet het middel zo ontworpen zijn dat het uitsluitend onder controle van de gebruiker gebruikt kan worden en moet sprake zijn van dynamische authenticatie:[26] de (cryptografische) gegevens voor de authenticatie veranderen bij ieder gebruik.

Het vereisen van een bestaande identificatiemethode bij het registreren en inloggen op een website, gecombineerd met biometrische technieken leidt tot het hoogste betrouwbaarheidsniveau. Het Nederlandse notariaat is druk doende met de implementatie van een 'veilig, betrouwbaar, gebruiksvriendelijk en toekomstvast online identificatiemiddel' voor burgers met een betrouwbaarheidsniveau 'hoog': NotarisID www.notarisid.nl. Met behulp van dit middel moet het voor gebruikers mogelijk worden om bij zowel publieke als private dienstenaanbieders veilig in te loggen en documenten te kunnen ondertekenen. Voor de gebruiker zijn geen kosten verbonden aan het gebruik van NotarisID; de dienstverleners (dienstenaanbieders) betalen voor het gebruik.[27] De elektronische handtekening zou ook gebruikt moeten kunnen worden voor de ondertekening van een elektronische authentieke akte.

24 Verordening (EU) nr. 910/2014 van het Europees Parlement en de Raad van 23 juli 2014 betreffende elektronische identificatie en vertrouwensdiensten voor elektronische transacties in de interne markt en tot intrekking van Richtlijn 1999/93/EG.

25 Vanaf 1 juli 2016 is de Europese eIDAS-verordening van kracht. Op grond van deze verordening gelden criteria specifieke voor de betrouwbaarheidsniveaus van authenticatiemiddelen. Er zijn drie niveaus: laag, substantieel en hoog.

26 Zie Forum Standaardisatie, 'Een handreiking voor overheidsorganisaties. Betrouwbaarheidsniveaus voor digitale dienstverlening', p. 24, online raadpleegbaar via: https://www.forumstandaardisatie.nl/sites/default/files/BFS/4-basisinformatie/publicaties/fs-handreiking-betrouwbaarheidsniveus-v4_0.pdf (laatstelijk geraadpleegd: 20 december 2020).

27 Dit is wezenlijk anders dan bij de reguliere certificatiedienstverleners, die doorgaans een aanschafprijs bij de aanvrager van het certificaat in rekening brengen.

3 Elektronische akte

Het lijkt bijna een anachronisme: een papieren akte in een hedendaagse bijna volledig digitale (werk- en privé)omgeving. Toch is het op dit moment nog niet mogelijk om een registergoed over te dragen op een volledige digitale wijze. Weliswaar vindt de inschrijving van de akte sinds invoering van WebELAN (2005) in praktisch alle gevallen langs elektronische weg plaats, de koopovereenkomst is meestal nog een overeenkomst in papieren vorm. De akte van levering is dat zonder meer in alle gevallen, nu in de huidige Nederlandse wet- en regelgeving nog niet is voorzien in de mogelijkheid van een authentieke elektronische notariële akte.

Met de komst van aanbieders van nieuwe authenticatiemiddelen zou het aantal gebruikssituaties in aantal, omvang en betekenis kunnen toenemen. De implementatie van een elektronische handtekening voor alle Nederlandse ingezetenen zal de komst van de elektronisch notariële akte wellicht bespoedigen.[28] Daarbij dient te worden opgemerkt dat het wellicht minder raadzaam is om een elektronische akte te ondertekenen met een authenticatiemiddel niveau 'substantieel'. De bewijskracht van een dergelijk middel staat immers niet gelijk aan een handgeschreven handtekening (artikel 3:15a BW). Dit heeft te maken met de eisen die aan de beveiliging van de methode van ondertekening worden gesteld. Aan een middel met niveau 'substantieel' worden minder hoge eisen gesteld dan aan een middel met niveau 'hoog'.

Naast één of meerdere aanbieders van nieuwe authenticatiemiddelen (niveau 'hoog') is het introduceren van de wettelijke mogelijkheid om een elektronische authentieke akte tot stand te laten komen noodzakelijk. Nu deze handschoen op nationaal niveau vele jaren niet is opgepakt, lijkt de oplossing uit de hoek van de Europese wetgever te komen. Van Erp heeft regelmatig opgemerkt dat – juist in de periode van crisis – door de Europese Commissie hard wordt gewerkt aan Europese eenwording en verdergaande digitalisering.

Op 31 juli 2019 is Richtlijn 2019/1151[29] in werking getreden. Deze richtlijn ziet op de oprichting langs elektronische weg van een besloten vennootschap met beperkte aansprakelijkheid. Lidstaten dienen per 1 augustus 2021 de mogelijkheid te ontsluiten om een bepaald type rechtspersoon – in Nederland is dit de besloten vennootschap met beperkte aansprakelijkheid – volledig online op te richten. Dit houdt dus in dat oprichter(s) ook

28 J. Vos, 'Zijn we al klaar voor Europees vastgoed (gerelateerde) transacties?' *in* J.W.A. Biemans, J.M. Milo, D.F.M.M. Zaman e.a. (Eds.), *Het Europees notariaat: één cohort of incoherent?*, Ars Notariatus no 158, Deventer, Kluwer, 2015, pp. 37-49.

29 Richtlijn (EU) 2019/1151 van het Europees Parlement en de Raad van 20 juni 2019 tot wijziging van Richtlijn (EU) 2017/1132 met betrekking tot het gebruik van digitale instrumenten en processen in het kader van het vennootschapsrecht.

niet verplicht is (zijn) in persoon te verschijnen voor de notaris.[30] Naast elektronische identificatie én ondertekening dient ook een elektronische akte te worden gecreëerd, op basis van online beschikbare modellen van oprichtingsakten. De invoering van deze Richtlijn lijkt dus invulling te geven aan de route om te komen tot een volledig elektronische akte.

Na de introductie van de online oprichting van de besloten vennootschap is het m.i., ondanks de werking van artikel 345 van het Verdrag van de werking van de Europese Unie,[31] niet de vraag *of* de Europese Commissie een akte met betrekking tot de totstandkoming van een (recht op een) registergoed[32] volledig online en zonder fysieke aanwezigheid van partijen tot stand wenst te laten komen, maar is het vooral de vraag *wanneer* dit het geval is en onder welke voorwaarden en in welke vorm. Het lijkt niet onwaarschijnlijk dat het vestigen van een recht van hypotheek op een registergoed als een van de meest logische vervolgstappen zal worden gezien, waarmee een relatief grote impact wordt gerealiseerd op de vier vrijheden en de hedendaagse digitale wereld.

Het gebruik van online beschikbare modellen[33] van akten heeft een zekere mate van gelijkenis en doet tot op zekere hoogte denken aan de *clauses repository* in de CROBECO-projecten en meer in het bijzonder de modelformulieren voor het aanvragen en afgeven van een Europese erfrechtverklaring als bedoeld in de Uitvoeringsverordening[34] tot vaststelling van de formulieren als bedoeld in de Erfrechtverordening.

4 ERFRECHTVERORDENING

Eén van de onderwerpen waarover Sjef en ik de afgelopen jaren veel hebben gesproken, zowel in Europees verband (ELRA) als daarbuiten, bij voorbeeld tijdens de in-house cursussen voor bewaarders, is de (inschrijving van de) Europese verklaring van erfrecht. Al tijdens een presentatie van een ambtenaar van de Europese Commissie die de

30 Zie Richtlijn (EU) 2019/1151 (voetnoot 28), Artikel 13 *octies*, met in lid 8 een uitzondering op het niet fysiek aanwezig hoeven te zijn ten aanzien van de handelingsbekwaamheid.

31 Verdrag betreffende de werking van de Europese Unie (geconsolideerde versie), (*PbEU* 2012, C 326/49).

32 Steeds vaker zien we dat nieuwe Europese regelgeving betrekking heeft op de aard van zakelijke rechten, ondanks een formele uitsluiting in de betreffende verordening. Als voorbeeld noem ik artikel 1 lid 1 onder k van de Erfrechtverordening (Verordening (EU) nr. 650/2012), waarin is bepaald dat de betreffende Verordening niet van toepassing is op de aard van de zakelijke rechten. In vergelijkbare zin ook: artikel 1 lid 2 onder g (de aard van de zakelijke rechten die rusten op vermogensbestanddelen) van de Verordening met betrekking tot het huwelijksvermogensrecht (Verordening (EU) nr. 1103/2016).

33 Zie Richtlijn (EU) 2019/1151 (voetnoot 28), Artikel 13 *nonies*.

34 Uitvoeringsverordening (EU) nr. 1329/2014 van de Commissie van 9 december 2014 tot vaststelling van de formulieren bedoeld in Verordening (EU) nr. 650/2012 van het Europees Parlement en de Raad betreffende de bevoegdheid, het toepasselijke recht, de erkenning en de tenuitvoerlegging van beslissingen en de aanvaarding en de tenuitvoerlegging van authentieke akten op het gebied van erfopvolging, alsmede betreffende de instelling van een Europese erfrechtverklaring.

concept-verordening besprak in de Algemene Ledenvergadering van ELRA in Brussel, bracht Sjef heel duidelijk naar voren dat deze verordening veel elementen bevat waarbij geen rekening is gehouden met de diversiteit van de verschillende rechtsstelsels en de bijbehorende juridische praktijken. Hij sprak daarbij de verwachting uit dat dit zou (kunnen) gaan leiden tot verschillende rechtszaken voor het Hof van Justitie van de Europese Unie. Sjef kreeg gelijk.

Inmiddels is er al veel jurisprudentie[35] door het Hof van Justitie van de Europese Unie gevormd. De meeste van deze uitspraken zijn door Sjef nader uitgelegd in de cursuscyclus die hij (destijds tezamen met Bram Akkermans) heeft aangeboden aan de Nederlandse bewaarders. Ik ga er van uit dat hij met name nog bijzondere herinneringen heeft overgehouden aan de cursus die op 22 mei 2015 plaatsvond.[36] Voorafgaand aan deze cursus zonden de bewaarders met behulp van Sjef's promovenda Katja Zimmermann, die destijds in deeltijd werkzaam was bij het Kadaster, vier vragen aan Sjef en Bram toe.

Eén van de vragen zag op de mogelijkheid een niet in Nederland bestaand zakelijk recht om te zetten naar een recht dat past in ons gesloten stelsel van zakelijke rechten. Een andere vraag zag op de autoriteit van afgifte. Beide onderwerpen zijn vanwege het stellen van prejudiciële vragen inmiddels aan het Europese Hof voorgelegd en (grotendeels) afgedaan. Maar nog steeds zorgt de (tekst van de) Verordening voor onduidelijkheden in de dagelijkse (notariële en bewaarders)praktijk en zorgt deze zelfs voor een bepaalde mate van onzekerheid. Hierbij denk ik met name aan de (on)mogelijkheid om de bevoegdheid van de autoriteit van afgifte te controleren. Recent verscheen over dit onderwerp een editorial van Van Erp's hand in het European Property Law Journal.[37] Ten tijde van het schrijven van deze bijdrage is er nog een vijftal zaken aanhangig bij het Hof van Justitie.

In zaak C-301/20,[38] ingesteld door het *Oberster Gerichtshof* in Oostenrijk, staan de geldigheid en de geldigheidsduur van de erfrechtverklaring centraal.

In de zaak die bekend is onder nummer C-422/20,[39] ingediend door het *Oberlandesgericht Köln*, gaat het (wederom) om een bevoegdheidsvraagstuk. In deze zaak waarin een Duitse erflater die laatstelijk woonachtig was in Spanje wordt (kort samengevat) de vraag gesteld of de (eerder) aangezochte (Spaanse) rechter zich uitdrukkelijk (met zoveel

35 Ik verwijs kortheidshalve naar: Uitspraak van 12 oktober 2017 in *zaak C-218/16*, *Kubicka*, ECLI:EU:C:2017:755. Uitspraak van 1 maart 2018 in *zaak C-558/16*, *Mahnkopf*, ECLI:EU:C:2018:138. Uitspraak van 6 september 2018 in *zaak C-21/17*, *Oberle*, ECLI:EU:C:2018:675. Uitspraak van 23 May 2019 in *zaak C-658/17*, WB, ECLI:EU:C:2019:444. Uitspraak van 17 januari 2019 in *Zaak C-102/18*, Brisch, ECLI:EU:C:2019:34 en Uitspraak van 16 juli 2020 in *zaak C-80/19*, *E.E.*, ECLI:EU:C:2020:569.

36 Deze cursus vond plaats op een bijzondere locatie: in een safaritent in dierenpark Apenheul in Apeldoorn. De pauze was op een zodanige wijze gepland dat we gezamenlijk de gorilla voederpresentatie konden aanschouwen.

37 S. van Erp, 'Inheritance certificates and EU law: Less European "effet utile" implies more national "pratique utile"', *European Property Law Journal*, Vol. 9, No. 2-3, 2020, pp. 67-72.

38 *UE & HC/Vararlberger Landes- und Hypotheken-Bank AG* (C-301/20).

39 *CR/RK* (C-422/20).

woorden) onbevoegd dient te verklaren, of deze beslissing van bindende aard is of niet én of – vanwege de onbevoegdverklaring van de eerder aangezochte rechter – de bevoegde rechter bevoegd is om te onderzoeken of de erflater een rechtsgeldige rechtskeuze heeft gemaakt.

Ook wordt de vraag gesteld of de bevoegd geachte rechter bevoegd is om te onderzoeken of één van de procespartijen een verzoek tot onbevoegdverklaring heeft ingediend bij de eerder aangezochte rechter. Daarbij wordt gevraagd of artikel 6 (sub a) en artikel 7 (sub a) van de Erfrechtverordening ook van toepassing zijn indien de erflater in een vóór 17 augustus 2015 opgestelde uiterste wilsbeschikking geen uitdrukkelijke of stilzwijgende rechtskeuze heeft gemaakt.

In C-387/20[40] is ten tijde van het schrijven van deze bijdrage op de website van het Hof van Justitie van de Europese Unie formeel (nog) geen informatie voorhanden. Het zou in deze casus gaan om de vrijheid om het toepasselijke erfrecht te kiezen en het toepasselijke recht te standaardiseren door middel van een rechtskeuze in verband met bilaterale overeenkomsten met derde landen en meer concrete ook de vraag of een burger van een derde land ook het recht heeft om zijn of haar nationale wetgeving te kiezen voor de rechtsopvolging bij overlijden.

In de vierde bij het Europese Hof door het Hanseatisches Oberlandesgericht Bremen aanhangige zaak,[41] waarvan formeel evenals de hiervoor besproken zaak nog geen informatie voorhanden is, staat de vraag centraal of de verklaring van verwerping die een erfgenaam aflegt bij het gerecht van een lidstaat dat bevoegd is voor zijn gewone verblijfplaats, overeenkomstig de aldaar geldende vormvereisten, rechtsgeldig wordt geacht vanaf het tijdstip waarop zij werd afgelegd (substitutie) danwel de verklaring van verwerping moet worden afgelegd bij het gerecht van een andere lidstaat dat bevoegd is om uitspraak te doen over de erfopvolging bij versterf. Daarbij zien de vervolgvragen op de vorm en termijn van verwerping en (de vorm van) het in kennis stellen van het bevoegde gerecht.

In C-277/20,[42] net als C-301/20 ingediend door het *Oberster Gerichtshof* in Oostenrijk, gaat het om de vraag of het begrip 'erfovereenkomst' zich mede uitstrekt tot een tussen twee Duitse staatsburgers met hun gewone verblijfplaats in Duitsland gesloten overeenkomst tot schenking ter zake des doods die betrekking heeft op een in Oostenrijk gelegen registergoed. Op grond van deze overeenkomst heeft de begiftigde na het overlijden van de schenker jegens de nalatenschap een verbintenisrechtelijk recht op kadastrale inschrijving van zijn eigendomsrecht. Die inschrijving zal dan kunnen geschieden op basis van die overeenkomst en de overlijdensakte van de schenker, dus zonder tussenkomst van de voor erfeniszaken bevoegde rechter. De *rechtspfleger* in Oostenrijk heeft het verzoek tot

---

40 *OKR* (C-387/20).
41 TN en NN (C-617/20).
42 *UM* (C-277/20).

tenaamstelling echter afgewezen. In beroep wordt dit standpunt gehandhaafd, weliswaar op andere gronden; de bepalingen van de erfrechtverordening waren niet van toepassing omdat in het aanbod tot sluiting van de overeenkomst de toepasselijkheid van het Oostenrijkse recht was overeengekomen. De verzoeker moest door middel van een voor kadastrale inschrijving vatbaar document aantonen dat voldaan was aan de in de overeenkomst vastgestelde opschortende voorwaarden. De overdracht op grond van de schenking ter zake des doods had niet mogen plaatsvinden voordat het huis was voltooid. Ten slotte was door het ontbreken van een dergelijk document de vervulling van de voorwaarde niet aangetoond.

In wezen lijkt deze voorwaarde op de situatie waarin de Nederlandse bewaarder weigert de eigendom over te boeken naar de nieuwe rechthebbende, indien geen verklaring van vervulling van de opschortende voorwaarde[43] wordt ingeschreven.

Het *Oberster Gerichtshof* heeft besloten de behandeling van dit beroep in *Revision* te schorsen en prejudiciële vragen te stellen aan het Europese Hof van Justitie. Het *Gerichtshof* neemt daarbij in ogenschouw de uitzondering op de toepasselijkheid van de verordening op het ontstaan, overdracht of overgang op grond van schenking (artikel 1 lid 2 onder g) en op de inschrijving van rechten op onroerende zaken (artikel 1 lid 2 onder l). Het *Gerichtshof* veronderstelt dat laatstvermelde uitzonderingsbepaling niet van toepassing is omdat de casus niet ziet op een registerrechtelijk vraagstuk maar ziet op de conflictenrechtelijke beoordeling van de overeenkomst, waarvan de beoordeling van de functionele bevoegdheid van de beslisinstantie afhangt.

Eén van de praktische problemen die de Erfrechtverordening voor de Europese bewaarders tot gevolg heeft, is de mogelijkheid van omzetting of aanpassing van onbekende zakelijke rechten in respectievelijk aan het meest gelijkwaardige zakelijke recht in de forumstaat. Indien een buitenlands zakelijk recht wordt ingeroepen in een lidstaat die het desbetreffende zakelijke recht niet kent, dan wordt dit zakelijk recht – indien noodzakelijk en voor zover mogelijk – in overeenstemming gebracht met het meest gelijkwaardige zakelijke recht in die lidstaat. Daarbij dient rekening te worden gehouden met de door dat

43 Ook de spiegelbeeldige situatie komt voor: met enige regelmaat wordt een klacht bij de bewaarder ingediend (en door de bewaarder afgewezen) met betrekking tot de situatie dat de verwerking in de basisregistratie kadaster niet juist zou zijn vanwege een akte waarin een ontbindende voorwaarde staat vermeld en deze voorwaarde inmiddels niet meer in vervulling kan gaan, bij voorbeeld door tijdsverloop. Niettegenstaande het feit dat de bewaarder erkent dat een datum reeds is verstreken en de rechtshandeling dus niet meer ongedaan kan worden gemaakt door (niet tijdige) inroeping van de ontbindende voorwaarde, blijft deze voorwaarde aangetekend in de basisregistratie kadaster. Om deze voorwaarde te verwijderen is – conform het formele negatieve (echter materieel semi-positieve) Nederlandse grondboekstelsel – een aanvullend stuk nodig waarin blijk wordt gegeven van het tijdsverloop.

specifieke zakelijke recht nagestreefde doelstellingen en belangen en de daaraan verbonden rechtsgevolgen.[44,45]

Het was niet voor het eerst dat in Europees verband werd geconcludeerd dat het principe van omzetting of aanpassing tot praktische problemen zou kunnen leiden. Van Erp heeft hier in een vroeg stadium reeds op gewezen. Bovendien bleek reeds tijdens de afsluitende CROBECO II-conferentie[46] dat het niet in alle Europese lidstaten mogelijk is om online informatie met betrekking tot de zakelijke rechten in te winnen. Waar dit wel het geval is, is het voor een (buitenlandse) raadpleger van de registratie lastig de juiste betekenis van de informatie te duiden.

Er is behoefte aan een methode of middel om toegang te krijgen tot basisinformatie over Kadasters (landregistratie autoriteiten) binnen Europa. Bovendien is de grensoverschrijdende informatie-uitwisseling tussen Europese kadasters ingewikkeld. Vandaar dat ELRA reeds tijdens de laatste (aflopende) termijn van het CROBECO-project een projectvoorstel had ingediend bij de Europese Commissie om een onderzoek te starten naar de totstandkoming van een Europees informatiemodel voor landregistratie-informatie. Het Interoperability Model for Land Registers project, afgekort tot IMOLA, zag in 2014 het levenslicht.[47]

5 IMOLA

Zoals Sjef maar al te goed bekend, zijn er veel en vaak grote verschillen te constateren tussen nationale grondregistratiestelsels en de bijbehorende nationale wet- & regelgeving. De verschillen veroorzaken dan ook een grote mate van complexiteit in geval van informatie-uitwisseling tussen Europese landregistraties, instellingen en organisaties. Deze complexiteit wordt verder vergroot door van elkaar afwijkende praktijken van landregistratie-autoriteiten en hun registraties.

Een standaardmiddel om toegang te krijgen tot basisinformatie over (alle) landregistraties binnen de Europese Unie, in combinatie met de beschikbaarheid van

44 Artikel 31 Erfrechtverordening.

45 Zie verder over art. 31 Erfrechtverordening: Bonomi A. en Wautelet P., Le droit européen des successions. Commentaire du Règlement no. 650/2012 du 4 juillet 2012, Brussel, Bruylant, 2013, pp. 479-491.

46 De datum 1 december 2014 zal (ook) Sjef waarschijnlijk aan twee zaken doen herinneren. Op die dag vond de afsluitende CROBECO II-conferentie plaats in Londen. De tweede herinnering zal zijn gevormd door een niet gepland onderdeel van deze dag: de wandeling die Sjef's promovenda Katja Zimmermann en ik samen met hem in de Engelse hoofdstad hebben gemaakt *langs* enkele van de vele Engelse pubs. Deze memorabele wandeling resulteerde in een officieel lidmaatschapsbewijs dat nadien, voorzien van enkele memorabilia in een doos, op het adres van de Maastricht Universiteit is toegezonden.

47 Ook dit project werd gesubsidieerd door de Europese Commissie, evenals de opvolgende projecten IMOLA2 en IMOLA3.

verklarend materiaal moet er toe leiden dat het begrip van buitenlandse rechtsstelsels verder verbetert.

Gedurende het eerste IMOLA-project is door de leden van ELRA, mede onder begeleiding van Sjef, diepgaand onderzoek verricht naar zogenaamde gemeenschappelijke kernpunten. Deze gemene delers bieden de mogelijkheid om een structuur te definiëren van belangrijke informatie die door de meeste kadastersystemen wordt gedeeld. In het project werd een zogenaamde ABC-structuur vastgesteld: een structuur waarbij het object, de rechthebbende en betreffende zakelijke rechten en beperkingen worden weergegeven in een overzichtelijke vorm.

Met IMOLA beoogde ELRA een model te maken voor gestandaardiseerde kadastrale output: het European Land Registry Document (ELRD), op basis van de hiervoor vermelde ABC-structuur. Om dit document te kunnen vormgeven, werd een basis gelegd voor een ontwerp op basis van technische standaarden. Door gebruik te maken van een zogenaamd XSD/ XML-schema werd een structuur van gemeenschappelijke velden (een sjabloon[48]) ontwikkeld waarin referentie-informatie kan worden opgenomen. Eenmaal verworden tot een praktisch te gebruiken systeem, zou (semi-)geautomatiseerde verwerking van informatie mogelijk moeten zijn. Daarbij zou dan gebruik kunnen worden gemaakt van gedeelde regels met metadata die zijn afgeleid van een thesaurus.

Anders gezegd, er werd onderzocht of een gestandaardiseerd formulier voor landregistratie-informatie kan worden ontwikkeld. Dat formulier zou moeten worden voorzien van een verklarende beschrijving van de informatie, teneinde een duidelijk beeld te geven van de (juridische) betekenis van de geregistreerde rechten in een andere landregistratie binnen de Europese Unie. Deze informatie zal worden verstrekt in de taal van het land waar het betreffende registergoed is geregistreerd én in de Engelse taal.

Zonder Van Erp's diepgaande en rechtsvergelijkende beschouwingen, zou mogelijkerwijs al vroeg in dit project een verkeerde weg zijn ingeslagen. Zo benadrukte Sjef de toegevoegde waarde van het principe waarbij de juridische begrippen zowel van bovenaf (top-down) als van onderaf (bottom-up) nader (dienen te) worden beschouwd. Daarmee wordt invulling gegeven aan een nauwkeurige semantische beschouwing door te werken met een *pivot*. Een pivot is in dit specifieke geval wellicht het meest betekenisvol te vertalen als een centrale begrippenlijst, waarmee op een praktische wijze invulling gegeven wordt aan het aan elkaar verbinden van de diverse nationale termen en begrippen. Zo kunnen aan het begrip 'proprietorship', als term in de pivot, de nationale begrippen 'eigentum', 'propriedad' en

48 Voor een gelijke technologische oplossing is reeds in 2006 door het Nederlandse Kadaster gekozen bij de implementatie van zogenaamde *stylesheets*, ten behoeve van de volledig geautomatiseerde verwerking van akten. Zie hiervoor meer uitgebreid (onder meer): W. Louwman, 'Toekomstige automatisering van het proces rond inschrijving in de openbare register' *JBN*, nr. 37, 2007. En W. Louwman & J. Vos, 'Automatisering van het afdoen van notariële akten door het Kadaster', *JBN, nr.* 3, 2009. En J. Vos, 'Het KIK-denken en het KIK-stotteren; stylesheets voor 'dummies', *JBN*, nr. 3, 2011.

'eigendom' eenvoudig worden gekoppeld. De toekomstig raadpleger kan vanaf het moment dat het systeem, via het e-justice portaal,[49] zal worden ontsloten niet alleen de inhoud van een specifiek vreemdtalig recht begrijpen vanwege de aangeboden vertaling naar de Engelse taal, maar dit voor hem onbekende zakelijke recht bovendien – vanwege de werking van de pivot – omgezet zien in het meest gelijkwaardige zakelijke recht in zijn eigen land. Op deze wijze kan een praktische invulling worden gegeven aan (onder andere) de omzetting of aanpassing van onbekende zakelijke rechten als bedoeld in artikel 31 van de Erfrechtverordening.

Met behulp van een dergelijk systeem zou ook invulling kunnen worden gegeven aan de verplichting voor de lidstaten op grond van artikel 32 *ter* van de Vijfde anti-witwasrichtlijn.[50] Op grond van het tweede lid van voormeld artikel dient de Europese Commissie uiterlijk op 31 december 2020 bij het Europees Parlement en bij de Raad een verslag in "waarin wordt beoordeeld of een harmonisatie van de informatie in de registers noodzakelijk is en evenredig is en of de koppeling van die registers noodzakelijk is". Dit verslag wordt, aldus het tweede lid, zo nodig vergezeld van een wetgevingsvoorstel.[51]

Het oplossen van de problemen rond het hergebruik van informatie en – meer in het bijzonder – de (veelal niet vastgelegde) verbanden tussen de gegevens in en tussen de verschillende registers, zijn de belangrijkste doelstellingen van het project. Om al deze begrippen en verbanden uit de diverse landregistratiesystemen te onderkennen, vergelijken en eenduidig te beschrijven, is een periode van twee jaar echter veel te kort; dit was ook de reden om een subsidieaanvraag in te dienen voor een vervolgproject: IMOLA2.

Tijdens dit opvolgende project werd gebruik gemaakt van een virtuele samenwerkings-omgeving, een benadering die geheel past in Van Erp's visie: het omarmen van technologische middelen. In die omgeving konden gegevens, informatie en kennis eenvoudig op elektronische wijze worden uitgewisseld. Gedurende dit project heeft Sjef meermalen een nadere juridische uiteenzetting gegeven van verschillende nieuwe technologische ontwikkelingen, waarbij de juridische implicaties van blockchain, kunstmatige intelligentie en het Internet der dingen (IoT) veelvuldig de revue zijn gepasseerd. Deze ontwikkelingen betreffen een relatief onontgonnen terrein voor juristen waarvoor Sjef en ik dezelfde interesse delen.

Voor de virtuele samenwerkingsomgeving (de Knowledge Manager) in het project is gebruik gemaakt van een gedeeld semantisch archief (Knowledge Repository) voor

49 https://e-justice.europa.eu/home.do?action=home (laatstelijk geraadpleegd: 20 december 2020).

50 Vijfde anti-witwasrichtlijn EU 2018/843. Artikel 32 *ter* verplicht de lidstaten aan de FIE's en de bevoegde autoriteiten toegang te verlenen tot informatie die het mogelijk maakt alle natuurlijke of rechtspersonen die eigenaar zijn van onroerend goed, tijdig te identificeren, onder meer door middel van registers of elektronische systemen voor gegevensontsluiting voor zover dergelijke registers of systemen beschikbaar zijn.

51 Een dergelijk voorstel zou, afhankelijk van de inhoud van dit voorstel, op gespannen voet kunnen komen te staan met artikel 345 van het verdrag van de werking van de Europese Unie.

landregistratie autoriteiten in Europa. In deze Knowledge Repository worden naast een thesaurus[52] gecontroleerde vocabulaires en woordenlijsten opgenomen en beschikbaar gesteld door middel van een webservice. Een volgende stap op weg naar een Europees landregistratie-informatiemodel is daarmee (wellicht) gezet.

In het project wordt gebruik gemaakt van een taxonomie, een conceptmodel dat aangeeft welke concepten een bredere betekenis hebben. Deze classificatie van objecten (rechten) of concepten omvat de principes die aan een dergelijke classificatie ten grondslag liggen. Op landelijk niveau heeft het Nederlandse Kadaster (een deel van) de elementen die nodig waren in de eerste twee IMOLA-projecten reeds enige jaren daarvoor gedefinieerd met behulp van Linked Data.

In het huidige IMOLA3-project maakt ELRA eveneens gebruik van de methode van Linked Data. Door het relateren van metadata kan het semantische model voor landregistratie-informatie worden vormgegeven. Op deze wijze zal duidelijk worden hoe de diverse nationale landregisters hun data laten verworden tot informatie.

6 Linked Data

Met behulp van Linked Data kunnen gestructureerde data op een zodanige wijze worden gepubliceerd dat de data onderling worden verbonden. Er wordt samenhang aangebracht tussen de diverse concepten. Elk concept wint aan betekenis wanneer er meer beschrijvingen aan worden gelinkt. Op die manier kunnen zoekopdrachten op een taalkundige wijze plaatsvinden en worden deze nauwkeuriger.

Linked Data is gebaseerd op bestaande standaard web-technologieën, zoals HTTP, RDF en URI's.[53] Hierdoor kan de informatie automatisch worden verwerkt door computers. Daarmee lijkt Linked Data zeer geschikt om overheidsinformatie, zoals landregistratie-informatie, te delen.

Berners-Lee[54] beschreef Linked Data aan de hand van vier principes al in 2006 als een component van 'Web 3.0':

- Gebruik URI's om dingen te identificeren.
- Gebruik HTTP-URI's zodat er verwezen kan worden naar deze dingen en dat ze kunnen worden opgezocht door zowel mens als machine.

52 Een thesaurus is een naslagwerk dat woorden opsomt die zijn gegroepeerd op basis van gelijkenis van betekenis, maar ook om onderscheid te maken tussen vergelijkbare woorden; het bestaat uit hiërarchische relaties tussen concepten en andere relaties.

53 URI staat voor Unique Resource Identifier en kan worden gezien als een unieke benaming voor, een unieke verwijzing naar, een 'bron' op het internet, waarbij een 'bron' kan zijn een afbeelding, een document, een (downloadbaar) bestand of zelfs een dienst of een mailbox.

54 T. Berners-Lee, 'Linked Data', 2006, note. https://www.w3.org/DesignIssues/LinkedData.html (laatstelijk geraadpleegd: 20 december 2020).

- Leg de informatie over het concept vast in een 'triple' (subject-predicaat-object), leg die triple vast en maak het gehele beschikbaar op basis van standaarden (zoals RDF en SPARQL).
- Refereer naar andere gerelateerde open-dataconcepten en neem deze op in de beschrijving. Daarmee verbetert het ontdekken van gerelateerde informatie op het internet.

Door gebruik te maken van deze vier principes kan data worden gepubliceerd *als* een webpagina in plaats van *op* een webpagina. Het World Wide Web Consortium (W3C)[55] heeft web standaarden opgesteld waarmee Linked Data kan worden opgesteld. Een voorbeeld van zo'n standaard is de SKOS-standaard,[56] die ook door ELRA in verband met het IMOLA-project wordt gebruikt.

Het grote voordeel van deze methode is, naast de herkenbaarheid van de bron, het incorporeren van de uitleg of de betekenis van de data én de meta data. De meta data kan informatie bevatten over de methode waarop de data zijn verzameld, op welk moment, door wie of welke instantie. Daarnaast is het mogelijk de mate waarin de data compleet zijn en het moment waarop deze zijn verzameld weergeven.

Linked Data definieert de samenhang tussen verschillende registers. De methode leent zich voor aanvulling van de data met ontologieën van elk register. In een dergelijke ontologie kan de samenhang van de concepten (bijvoorbeeld van 'prijs', 'goed' of 'persoon') worden gedefinieerd. Als de samenhang centraal beheerd moet blijven, kan worden volstaan met alleen de structuur van de data. Zo kan elke organisatie haar eigen samenhang op het niveau van de data zelf bepalen. Het Kadaster heeft een Linked Data model ontwikkeld en dit ook ontsloten voor een breed publiek.[57,58] Helaas is het tot op heden nog niet mogelijk gebleken om de Linked Data van het Kadaster één-op-één te gebruiken in de in opbouw zijnde Linked Data in het IMOLA-project. Het zou niet alleen vanuit het oogpunt van tijdsbesparing wenselijk zijn de gegevens vanuit de Kadaster Linked Data in de IMOLA Linked Data (en de hierna te bespreken Zorgeloos Vastgoed Linked Data) te kunnen laden;

---

55 https://www.w3.org/ (laatstelijk geraadpleegd: 20 december 2020)

56 SKOS (Simple Knowledge Organization System) is een algemeen datamodel, ontworpen voor de weergave van elk type gestructureerd en gecontroleerd vocabulaire. Daarmee is het een methode om (intern) een kennissysteem als een thesaurus te organiseren en (extern) definities van concepten te kunnen vergelijken met behulp van zaken als 'broader', 'narrower' en 'alternative label'.

57 J. Vos, 'The meaning of Land Registry data: quality, ownership and use; the Risk of Privatization of Land Administration And Blockchain's Code As Law', 2018, bijdrage ten behoeve van het (congresboek over het) 21e IPRA|Cinder congres, Cartagena de Indias (Colombia). Nog te verschijnen.

58 Vanwege wijzigingen in het informatiemodel kadaster (IMKAD), dat een levend document is, is wijziging van het Linked Data model noodzakelijk. Het is dan raadzaam een historiemodel toe te voegen aan het huidige Linked Data model.

het voorkomt bovendien de kans op discrepanties tussen (uitleg van) begrippen in meerdere Linked Data modellen en geeft een goede invulling aan het principe 'Data bij de bron'.

Vanwege de modern technologie zijn data niet langer onlosmakelijk verbonden met de context van hun toepassing; ze dragen nu hun eigen betekenis met behulp van metadata en semantiek. Nieuw bij de methodiek van Linked Data is dat deze semantiek niet meer wordt vastgelegd in databases. Door gebruik te maken van gestandaardiseerde vocabulaires kunnen computers gegevens zelf interpreteren en koppelen.

Bij het ontwerpen van een Linked Data systeem, is het van belang om drie verschillende typen 'realiteit' te onderscheiden; Brattinga en Santema[59] beschrijven hoe met Linked Data de 'natuurlijke' werkelijkheid verbonden kan worden met de institutionele werkelijkheid en hoe dit alles gepresenteerd kan worden in een administratieve werkelijkheid. Een institutioneel feit is een feit dat werkelijkheid is conform een afsprakenstelsel en wordt altijd vooraf gegaan door een aanleiding in de natuurlijke werkelijkheid en (in het geval van Linked Data altijd) opgevolgd door een administratieve gebeurtenis: het opnemen van de institutionele werkelijkheid in een (digitale) registratie. Ter verduidelijking het voorbeeld van de overdracht van een woning: het opstellen van een akte van levering door de notaris (institutionele werkelijkheid) vindt pas plaats nadat een huis wordt verkocht (natuurlijke werkelijkheid) en is pas voltooid nadat de akte is ingeschreven in de openbare registers die het Kadaster houdt (administratieve werkelijkheid). In een ideale wereld zouden deze drie werkelijkheden samenkomen op (vrijwel) hetzelfde moment. Om de administratieve werkelijkheid overeen te laten komen met de natuurlijke werkelijkheid, bestaan procesafspraken op grond waarvan de actor in de natuurlijke werkelijkheid er ook voor zorgt dat de administratieve gebeurtenis zich zal voordoen. Bij deze gedachte sluit het principe van een systeem van rechtenregistratie meer nauwgezet aan dan een systeem van aktenregistratie, zoals we dat in Nederland kennen. Dit geldt eens te meer nu in ons grondboekstelsel geen verplichting bestaat tot het vastleggen van de erfrechtelijke verkrijgingen en verkrijgingen op grond van verjaring. Vanwege het ontbreken van regels van de institutionele werkelijkheid in die situaties, verstoren verkrijgingen buiten de registers om een (vrijwel) synchroon verloop van de natuurlijke en de administratieve werkelijkheid, of, zoals Brattinga en Santema (2018) dit beschrijven: "we maken de administratieve werkelijkheid leidend bij het creëren van het institutionele feit".

De methode van Linked Data werkt met zogenaamde triples. Dit zijn korte zinnen, waarmee een relatie wordt vastgelegd tussen twee bronnen en bestaan uit een subject, een eigenschap en een object. Een voorbeeld: Sjef (subject) adviseert (predicate) ELRA (object), waarbij Sjef en ELRA beiden bronnen zijn waarnaar verwezen wordt middels een URI.

---

59 M. Brattinga & A. Santema, 'Best Practices for meaningful connected computing', Working Draft 07 november 2018. https://bp4mc2.org/20181107/ (laatstelijk geraadpleegd: 20 december 2020).

Op grond van het 'triple A-adagium' (Anybody can say Anything about Anything) ontstaat een vrijwel eindeloze informatietechnische mogelijkheid om onderwerpen en voorwerpen aan elkaar te verbinden door middel van een gezegde, zeker nu onderwerp en lijdend voorwerp een op het internet vindbare naam hebben in de vorm van een URI. Het wordt hierdoor mogelijk om data over objecten, feiten, subjecten en gebeurtenissen uit een bepaalde bron te verbinden met data uit andere bronnen.

Nu we gezien hebben dat vele (zo niet alle) landregistratiesystemen in Europa werken met een eigen ABC-structuur, een 'triple' object, subject en recht, is snel te concluderen dat de methode van Linked Data zich goed kan lenen voor het IMOLA-project. Daarmee wordt immers op een eenduidige en eenvoudige wijze inzichtelijk dat het Spaanse 'propriedad' lijkt op het Oostenrijkse recht van 'eigentum' en het Nederlandse recht van 'eigendom'. De koppelingen en verbanden tussen de diverse data(onderdelen) worden inzichtelijk via een zogenaamde *knowledge graph*, een kennismodel waarin de diverse data betekenisvol met elkaar zijn verbonden en op een visuele wijze kunnen worden gepresenteerd. Maar naast het vastleggen van een juiste betekenis en de correlatie tussen de diverse data, is het vastleggen van de juistheid en kwaliteit van de data eveneens van groot belang.

7 Meta Data & Structured Data

Molero, Barry, Hunter & Shunnar[60] verdelen data in drie soorten: gestructureerde data, semigestructureerde data en ongestructureerde data. Gestructureerde data ziet men terug in relationele database management systemen (RDBMS). Vanwege deze sterke structuren kan gebruik worden gemaakt van eenvoudige formulieren of user interfaces om de gegevens vast te leggen. Veel landregistratiesystemen maken gebruik van relationele databases en een gestandaardiseerde taal (SQL) die gebruikt kan worden voor het bevragen en aanpassen van gegevens in die databases.

Ongestructureerde data kennen dergelijke formele regels en talen niet. Zonder deze regels is (of lijkt) het meer eenvoudig om data te creëren. De keerzijde is echter dat het opslaan en vooral het terugvinden van de data meer complex is.[61] Een notariële akte, bestaande uit geheel vrije teksten, is te zien als ongestructureerde data, waar de KIK-akte[62] is te zien als een document met gestructureerde data, waar het gaat om de gegevens in het eerste deel van de akte. Semigestructureerde data zijn te beschouwen als een tussenvorm.

60 R. Molero, M. Barry, A. Hunter, T. Shunnar, 'Flexible Data Structures for Land Records', 2010. https://www.oicrf.org/-/flexible-database-structures-for-land-records (laatstelijk geraadpleegd: 20 december 2020).

61 Of zoals mijn zeer gewaardeerde collega Han Wijlens eens tegen mij zei: "Als je de registratie moeilijk maakt, maak je het de gebruiker gemakkelijker en vice versa".

62 Zie voetnoot 46.

Hierbij valt te denken aan een akte met een groot aantal (min of meer) vaststaande of gestandaardiseerde teksten, zoals de NVM koopakte. In het afsprakenstelsel Zorgeloos Vastgoed (www.zorgeloosvastgoed.nl) wordt getracht te komen tot een modeltekst koopovereenkomst die wordt voorzien van een uitleg van alle in de overeenkomst gebruikte begrippen en gegevens, onder verwijzing naar de bron middels een Zorgeloos Vastgoed Linked Data model.

Het zou niet meer dan logisch zijn in dit afsprakenstelsel aan te sluiten bij de bestaande praktijk van de KIK-akte. De makelaar zou dan bij het nemen van een inzage in de Basisregistratie Kadaster (BRK) de informatie (geleverd in XML-formaat en dus) op geautomatiseerde wijze opnemen in de koopovereenkomst en dit geheel, voorzien van de gegevens (eveneens in het XML-formaat) doorleveren aan de notaris, die vervolgens een akte van levering maakt (met behulp van een stylesheet), waardoor ook de levering voorzien wordt van een XML-bestand en ter inschrijving kan worden aangeboden bij het Kadaster. Met gebruikmaking van een slimme technologische oplossing zou kunnen worden aangegeven of de door de makelaar gebruikte informatie is gewijzigd tussen het moment van opmaken van de koopovereenkomst en het aanbieden van die akte aan de notaris. Daarmee wordt de keten verder geautomatiseerd op een geüniformeerde wijze, waarmee typefouten worden voorkomen, informatie actueel wordt gedeeld en kosten worden bespaard.[63]

Voor geo-gerelateerde informatie is GML[64] een veelgebruikt formaat. Vanwege de semigestructureerde *mark-up language* is het betrekkelijk eenvoudig om data uit te wisselen. Lemmen, Van Oosterom en Bennet[65] beschrijven dat er veel werk is verzet om te komen tot een internationaal erkende standaard voor landadministratie data. In 2012 concludeerde Lemmen[66] dat een gemeenschappelijk model voor een goed functionerend landregistratiesysteem één van de basisprincipes is van het *land administration domain*

---

63 Een verdergaande visie zou wellicht kunnen zijn een integrale herziening van de huidige aan- en verkoopprocedure, inclusief de rollen van de diverse actoren in het proces. Daarbij zou onderzocht kunnen worden of met behulp van de figuur van de (vrijwillige) veiling niet het zorgeloze karakter kan worden gerealiseerd zoals dat wordt gepoogd te bereiken met het huidige initiatief. De huidige procedure van aan- en verkoop van een woning met een 'voorlopige' koopovereenkomst, ontbindende voorwaarden, financieringsaanvragen en -voorbehouden en de voorbereiding van de akte van levering bevat meerdere momenten die voor de koper een hoog 'black-box-gehalte' hebben. Hoewel ik in 2001 schreef dat het hele systeem van veilinghuizen berust op een 'dunne' basis van vertrouwen (zie: J. Vos, 'De notaris als Trusted Third Party', afstudeerscriptie in het kader van de studie notarieel recht aan de Rijksuniversiteit Groningen, pp. 72-73) lijkt die dunne basis inmiddels verbreed door de tussenkomst van (notariële) elektronische dienstverlening, zeker waar dit ziet op doorgevoerde verbeteringen in het hedendaagse (executie)veilingproces.

64 P. van Oosterom, A. Groothedde, C. Lemmen, P. van der Molen & H. Uitermark, 'Land Administration as a Cornerstone in the Global Spatial Information Infrastructure', *IJSDIR*, 4, 2009, pp. 298-331. D. Palmer, S. Fricska & B. Wehrmann, 'Towards improved land governance', *UN-HABITAT*, 2009.

65 C. Lemmen, P. van Oosterom & R. Bennet, 'The land administration domain model', *Land Use Policy*, 49, 2015, pp. 535-545.

66 C. Lemmen, *A domain Model for Land Administration* (diss.), Delft University of Technology, Delft, 2012.

model (LADM). Dit gemeenschappelijke model wordt gevormd door een triple, bestaand uit een object, een subject en een recht. Deze ABC-structuur zien we ook terug bij het IMOLA-project.

Het lijkt raadzaam om een extra datalaag te introduceren in het huidige (Linked) Datamodel dat wordt gebruikt (Kadaster) of voorzien (IMOLA). Deze extra laag zou mijns inziens moeten inhouden *data over de data* die zijn vastgelegd. Onderdeel van die data-laag zou de *kwaliteit* van de vastgelegde data kunnen zijn. Te denken valt hierbij (ook) aan de datum waarop de data zijn verzameld, vastgelegd of vervangen door nieuwe data, inclusief een link naar deze nieuwe data. Het element *tijd*, ten behoeve van de opbouw van een historisch model, is hierbij zeker van groot belang.

Ook kan worden gedacht aan een korte *uitleg of beschrijving* van bepaalde elementen of de juridische waarde (of kwaliteit) die aan de data kan worden toegekend door de kwaliteitscontroles die destijds hebben plaatsgevonden te beschrijven.[67]

Ten slotte valt te denken aan het *doel* waarvoor de data zijn vastgelegd. Immers, dit doel is veelal de reden waarom data op een bepaalde manier geordend zijn en niet in alle gevallen eenvoudig op een juiste wijze te koppelen zijn. Zo is het Kadaster (onder meer) bronhouder van de BRK, maar beheert het daarnaast een aantal landelijke voorzieningen, waaronder de landelijke voorziening WOZ én de landelijke voorziening Basisadministratie Adressen & Gebouwen (BAG). Van beide laatstgenoemde basisregistraties zijn de gemeenten bronhouders. De Basisregistratie WOZ bevat gegevens die nodig zijn om de WOZ-waarde aan zowel een onroerende zaak te relateren als aan een belanghebbende. Deze registratie is niet openbaar, behoudens de WOZ-waarden van woningen. Die waarden zijn in te zien middels het WOZ-waardeloket.[68] De BAG bevat basisgegevens van alle adressen en gebouwen in de Nederlandse gemeenten en wordt, eveneens door het Kadaster, beheerd in een landelijke voorziening (BAG LV). De gegevens van de BAG worden ontsloten via een zogenaamde *viewer*.[69] De hiervoor genoemde basisregistraties zien alle drie op gegevens die betrekking hebben op een onroerende zaak. Elk van die registraties is ontstaan met een ander doel: de BRK geeft informatie over rechthebbenden, de WOZ over de waarde van een object en de BAG heeft als doel het uniek identificeren en aanduiden van adresseerbare objecten. Elk van deze gegevensverzamelingen hanteert een andere, unieke, zoekingang op het object. Zo hanteert de BRK de kadastrale aanduiding als zoekingang,

67 Dergelijke informatie is essentieel voor het realiseren van een actueel en zo volledig mogelijk beeld van de juridische werkelijkheid van de in de basisregistratie kadaster geregistreerde objecten en rechten. Het Kadaster heeft dit streven onder meer in haar Meerjarenbeleidsplan opgenomen en spreekt in dit verband over het 'versterken van de rechtszekerheid' en hanteert hierbij de term 'positivering'.

68 https://www.wozwaardeloket.nl/ (laatstelijk geraadpleegd: 20 december 2020). Het WOZ-waardeloket is bedoeld voor het individueel raadplegen van afzonderlijke woningen. Om te voorkomen dat dit loket wordt overbelast door massale afname, is een drempelmechanisme ingebouwd, waardoor een maximum is gesteld aan het aantal woningen dat binnen een bepaalde tijdsperiode kan worden opgevraagd.

69 https://bagviewer.kadaster.nl/ (laatstelijk geraadpleegd: 20 december 2020).

terwijl de WOZ uitgaat van een verblijfsobject en de BAG, een objectenregistratie, het adres als uitgangspunt hanteert. In de meeste gevallen is er een match en levert de koppeling geen problemen op. Echter, het komt voor dat een hoekwoning (één kadastrale aanduiding in de BRK), twee woonadressen bevat (BAG) en tezamen met de naastgelegen garage en een stukje snippergroen (3 objecten in de BRK) één te belasten object voor de onroerendezaaksbelasting (OZB) vormt. Vandaar dat het Kadaster voor de koppeling van deze drie basisregistraties – en meer in het bijzonder de koppeling tussen de BAG en de BRK – een administratieve koppeling aanbrengt en deze vervolgens controleert door een geometrische koppeling. Ook dan blijven er nog 'niet te plaatsen adressen' bestaan. Denk hierbij aan appartementsrechten in een gebouw, waarbij vervolgens een aantal van deze appartementsrechten is ondergesplitst. Aan een exacte koppeling wordt gewerkt, hoewel de praktijk weerbarstig is.

8 Openbaarheid & (on)gericht verzamelen

Over de openbaarheid van de basisregistratie kadaster en de openbare registers is met name de afgelopen jaren veel geschreven, wellicht mede vanwege het diepgaand rechtsvergelijkend onderzoek[70] dat Sjef's promovenda Anna Berlee heeft verricht naar dit vraagstuk. Sinds het verschijnen van haar proefschrift en een aantal incidenten die de persoonlijke veiligheid van een aantal personen betrof, is er veelvuldig in de media aandacht besteed aan de openbaarheid en de mogelijkheid om gegevens af te schermen. Zo zijn er meermalen Kamervragen gesteld aan de Ministers van Binnenlandse Zaken, Justitie en Veiligheid en de Minister voor Rechtsbescherming. Tijdens het plenair debat over de begroting Justitie en Veiligheid van 26 november 2020 is een (aangehouden) motie ingediend door Tweede Kamerlid Yesligöz-Zegerius c.s. over het afschermen van huisadressen in openbare registers aangehouden. De Minister van Justitie heeft geantwoord in zijn brief[71] van 17 december 2020 aan de Tweede Kamer. Hij ontraadt de motie over het afschermen van huisadressen in openbare registers onder verwijzing naar de brief van de minister van BZK van 29 juni 2018.[72] Zeer recent zijn er opnieuw Kamervragen gesteld naar aanleiding van een aantal incidenten, waarbij de Minister voor Rechtsbescherming is gevraagd zijn antwoord op één van de eerder aan hem gestelde Kamervragen te herzien

70 A. Berlee, *Access to Personal Data in Public Land Registers – Balancing Publicity of Property Rights with the Rights to Privacy and Data Protection* (diss.), Den Haag, Eleven Publishing, 2018.

71 Kamerstukken II 2020-2021, 35 570 VI (Kamerbrief 2020Z25318) Zie: https://www.rijksoverheid.nl/binaries/rijksoverheid/documenten/kamerstukken/2020/12/17/tk-motie-yesilgoz-zegerius-c-s-inzake-huisadressen-in-openbare-registers/tk-motie-yesilgoz-zegerius-c-s-inzake-huisadressen-in-openbare-registers.pdf(laatstelijk geraadpleegd: 20 december 2020).

72 Kamerstukken II 2017-2018, 32761-123.

en daarbij ook te kijken naar een uitbreiding van de afscherming van gegevens met betrekking tot wetenschappers, politici en bestuurders.[73] Ten tijde van het schrijven van deze bijdrage zijn deze vragen zijn nog niet beantwoord. Het is evident dat het vraagstuk over de openbaarheid van (adresgegevens in) de registers in relatie tot de bescherming van de persoonlijke levenssfeer nog altijd in beweging is.

Afscherming van persoonsgegevens is onder omstandigheden mogelijk geworden vanwege het op 1 juli 2019 in werking getreden artikel 37a van het Kadasterbesluit.[74] Door middel van dat artikel wordt de mogelijkheid geboden persoonsgegevens bij het Kadaster af te schermen vanwege veiligheidsoverwegingen. Voorwaarde voor afscherming is de opname van de betreffende personen op de limitatieve lijst van het Nationaal Coördinator Terrorismebestrijding en Veiligheid (NCTV) of de beveiliging van deze personen binnen of op grond van het stelsel Beveiligen en Bewaken.[75]

De inhoud van de openbare registers en de basisregistratie kadaster is in principe openbaar. De registers worden jaarlijks meer dan vierentwintig miljoen keren bevraagd, veelal in verband met aanstaande transacties die zien op onroerende zaken, maar ook in het kader van de handhaving en opsporing van specifieke (strafbare) feiten binnen Nederland.

Hèt modewoord van de laatste jaren lijkt in die laatste zin de term 'ondermijning'.[76] Om inzicht te verkrijgen in de mate van verwevenheid van de onder- in de bovenwereld en de criminaliteit het hoofd te bieden, worden (onder andere) de BRK en de openbare registers veelvuldig bevraagd. In een aantal gevallen wordt op basis van een aantal algemene of bijzondere kenmerken gevraagd om een specifieke zoekopdracht in te voeren in de kadastrale systemen. Te denken valt hierbij aan zogenaamde '*red flags*',[77] zoals kort opeenvolgende transacties, (onverklaarbare) waardesprongen tussen twee of meer transacties en transacties waarbij meer dan één object onderwerp van overdracht zijn.[78]

---

73 De vragen zijn overigens mede gericht aan de Minister van Justitie en Veiligheid, zie: https://www.tweedekamer.nl/downloads/document?id=93972e32-70d3-4a22-ac0c-5a1a8cea01ed&title=Het%20bericht%20%27Meerdere%20OMT-leden%20bedreigd%20en%20thuis%20opgezocht%27.docx (laatstelijk geraadpleegd: 20 december 2020).

74 Met dit besluit is invulling gegeven aan de wettelijke mogelijkheid van artikel 107b Kadasterwet om beperkingen te stellen aan de verstrekking van inlichtingen als bedoeld in de artikelen 99 tot en met 107 Kadasterwet.

75 Een verzoek hiertoe kan worden ingediend bij het Kadaster. Meer informatie over deze procedure is vinden via: https://www.kadaster.nl/privacy/verklaring-rechten-van-betrokkenen (laatstelijk geraadpleegd: 20 december 2020).

76 De letterlijke betekenis volgens Van Dale is 'ondergraven' of 'verzwakken'. In de wereld van opsporing, toezicht en handhaving wordt met deze term bedoeld het verweven van de onderwereld met de bovenwereld.

77 Er zijn veel overzichten van zogenaamde '*red flags*' gepubliceerd. Voor een behoorlijk volledig overzicht van risico-indicatoren verwijs ik naar: B. Unger, J. Ferwerda, H. Nelen & L. Ritzen, *Detecting Criminal Investments in the Dutch Real Estate Sector*, Dutch Ministry of Finance, 2010.

78 In die zin is er niets nieuws onder de zon. Ook voordat de term 'ondermijning' veelvuldig werd gebruikt in het kader van de bestrijding van criminaliteit werd het Kadaster op regelmatige basis al bevraagd door

Het is de vraag of de door de opsporingsinstanties gestelde vraag in al die gevallen gedragen wordt door een gelegitimeerd belang, zeker bezien vanuit het oogpunt van de bescherming van de persoonlijke levenssfeer van de personen wiens gegevens onderdeel uitmaken van een verzoek om ongerichte informatie. In zijn algemeenheid kan worden gesteld dat een dergelijk 'sleepnet' niet (snel) geoorloofd is.

Veel opsporingsinstanties[79] en toezichthouders die zich wenden tot het Kadaster vermelden als grondslag voor het verzamelen van persoonsgegevens het algemeen belang dan wel voortvloeiend uit het oogpunt van openbaar gezag. Hiermee wordt door die instanties veelal verwezen naar artikel 6, eerste lid, onder e) van de Algemene Verordening Gegevensbescherming (AVG). Voorwaarde aan deze grondslag is echter de noodzakelijkheid van de gegevensdeling voor het vervullen van de desbetreffende publieke taak. Hiervoor is een wettelijke grondslag vereist.

Bij het verstrekken van een (omvangrijke) verzameling persoonsgegevens dient een balans te worden gevonden tussen enerzijds de bescherming van de persoonlijke levenssfeer van onschuldige burgers in Nederland en anderzijds het opsporen van criminele activiteiten en het vervolgens vervolgen van de bij die feiten betrokken personen. Bij het afwegen van die belangen dient niet alleen de aanvrager zich af te vragen of de juiste balans is gevonden en er een wettelijke grondslag gevonden kan worden door het opvragen (en verwerken) van de data; ook het Kadaster dient daarbij acht te slaan op de vraag of de verstrekking kan plaatsvinden. Op grond van artikel 107c Kadasterwet dient de gegevensverstrekking voort te vloeien uit een van de doeleinden van artikel 2a van de wet en de aanvrager deze gegevens kan verwerken op één van de gronden als bedoeld in artikel 6, eerste lid, onder c tot en met f van de Algemene verordening gegevensbescherming. Als laatste voorwaarde wordt gesteld dat 'zulks is toegestaan bij algemene maatregel van bestuur'. Aan een dergelijke nadere regeling is echter nimmer invulling gegeven, reden waarom de afweging om de gegevens te verstrekken thans een lastig vraagstuk vormt.

Momenteel wordt gewerkt aan de versterking van de juridische basis[80] onder de uitwisseling van informatie en het gezamenlijk verwerken daarvan door samenwerkingsverbanden, zoals als de Infobox Crimineel en Onverklaarbaar Vermogen (iCOV), het Financieel Expertise Centrum en de Regionale inlichtingen en expertisecentra (RIEC's). Het wetsvoorstel gegevensverwerking door samenwerkingsverbanden strekt er

---

opsporingsinstanties. Eén van de meest bekende voorbeelden waarbij de bovenwereld (een gerenommeerd pensioenfonds) werd benadeeld door de onderwereld betrof de 'Klimop-zaak', zie: J. Vos, 'Fraud in the Netherlands, despite the transparent land registry system; possible preventative measures and advices taken and given be the Dutch Registrar', *XIX Congreso Mundial de Derecho Registral IPRA CINDER. 19th IPRA-CINDER World Land Registration Congress*, Chile 2014. *Tirant lo Blanch, Valencia 2016.*

79 Voor zover de gegevensverwerking niet onder de Wet politiegegevens valt.

80 Het wetsvoorstel voor een kaderwet Wet gegevensverwerking door samenwerkingsverbanden (*Kamerstukken* II, 35 447, nr. 2, 2020) is op 17 december 2020, met inachtneming van diverse moties en amendementen, door de Tweede kamer aangenomen.

onder andere toe om voor samenwerkingsverbanden voorwaarden vast te leggen waaronder de deelnemers gezamenlijk data-analyses kunnen uitvoeren, en om te komen tot oplossingen in huidige sectorale bepalingen op het gebied van informatie-uitwisseling. Daarbij wordt het mogelijk om op termijn bij Algemene Maatregel van Bestuur nieuwe samenwerkingsverbanden onder de wet te laten vallen.

Zoals de Ministers van Justitie en Rechtsbescherming zelf al concludeerden in hun brief van 23 november 2020 aan de Tweede Kamer, is het "inherent aan opsporing dat inbreuk wordt gemaakt op de privacy. Kern van opsporing is immers het verzamelen van informatie, waaronder persoonsgegevens. Daarbij moet voor ogen worden gehouden dat een inbreuk op de privacy van een verdachte of van derden (verdere) schendingen van grondrechten van slachtoffers door criminelen kan helpen voorkomen. Een rechtmatige toepassing van de wettelijke bevoegdheden levert geen schending van dat grondrecht op. Er is dan immers voldaan aan de voorwaarden die aan een inbreuk gesteld worden."

Een voorbeeld waarbij enorme hoeveelheden data uit verschillende bronnen zijn verzameld met het oog op het zichtbaar maken van patronen en het opdoen van inzichten die bijdragen aan de aanpak van ondermijnende criminaliteit, wordt gevormd door City Deal Zicht op Ondermijning.[81] Talloze zoekopdrachten kunnen worden ingevoerd in het dashboard, hoewel soms met wisselend[82] resultaat.

Ter voorkoming van het risico op onthulling van individuele gevallen en het kunnen herleiden van een casus tot een natuurlijk persoon, zijn aantallen steeds afgerond op tientallen en worden – naast enkele andere maatregelen – de uitkomsten op basis van minder dan tien waarnemingen onderdrukt.

Het is van het grootste belang dat het koppelen van enorme hoeveelheden data uit diverse bronnen op een juiste wijze kan plaatsvinden. Om dit te kunnen doen, is enerzijds kennis nodig van de data van de specifieke bronnen. Daarbij is van belang dat een bronhouder uitleg geeft over het doel, de methode en de werkwijze van het registreren van data, alvorens deze data te verwerken en te koppelen met eventuele andere bronnen en data.

Wanneer de diverse bronnen gebruik zouden maken van de Linked Data methodiek, zouden op relatief eenvoudige wijze en met een zeer geringe kans op fouten relaties kunnen worden gelegd tussen de diverse data. Een probleem hierbij wordt nog steeds gevormd door de vertrouwelijkheid van de data en de methoden om deze data te beveiligen.

81 https://www.zichtopondermijning.nl/ (laatstelijk geraadpleegd: 20 december 2020).

82 Zo verschijnt een onjuiste uitkomst bij het selecteren van de risico-indicator 'onbekende eigenaar' in combinatie met 'onbekend bij Kadaster' met betrekking tot de beschikbare informatie over het jaar 2018. Het zou voor het jaar 2018 gaan om 394.030 gevallen waarbij sprake zou zijn van het ontbreken van informatie bij het Kadaster. Dit is niet juist. Bij elk registergoed in Nederland staat een eigenaar vermeld. Het komt echter, vanwege het negatieve stelsel van grondboekhouding, wel voor dat een overleden persoon als rechthebbende staat vermeld bij een registergoed.

Om geëncrypte data te kunnen bewerken, moeten bij reguliere encryptietechnologieën de data eerst worden ontgrendeld. Door het de-crypten (ontgrendelen) van de geëncrypte data wordt de inhoud alsnog inzichtelijk. Een oplossing voor deze problematiek lijkt aanstaande met de komst van de hierna kort te behandelen relatief nieuwe vorm van encryptie en Secure Multi-Party Computation (MPC).

9 (Full) Homomorphic Encryption

Betrekkelijk nieuw en in ontwikkeling is namelijk *(Full) Homomorphic Encryption* (FHE/HE), een technologie die het toelaat dat de informatie wordt verwerkt zonder dat een sleutel nodig is om de data te ontgrendelen. Deze technologie omvat een cryptosysteem met encryptie- en decryptiefuncties die bits converteren van platte tekst naar cijfertekst, versleutelde tekst, en weer terug. Daarnaast is een evaluatiefunctie onderdeel van de technologie. Met deze functie wordt geaccepteerd dat een beschrijving of rekenactie wordt uitgevoerd op de cijfertekst. De technologie zou een uitkomst kunnen zijn voor opslag van data in de Cloud, iets waar veel organisaties zich aan hebben gewaagd, maar waarbij veel andere organisaties een argwanende houding aannemen vanwege het niet geëncrypt (kunnen) opslaan van data.

De mogelijkheden van deze encryptietechnologie lijken vrijwel eindeloos, hoewel het vanwege de benodigde rekenkracht niet waarschijnlijk lijkt dat deze technologie voor elke vorm van opslag en delen van data zal worden gebruikt.

Wanneer alle aan het samenwerkingsverband (City Deal Zicht op Ondermijning) deelnemende partijen hun data zouden versleutelen met behulp van homomorphic encryption en deze versleutelde data vervolgens zouden delen ten behoeve van het onderkennen van fenomenen die verband houden met ondermijning, blijven de verbanden bestaan (in de cijfertekst) en kunnen deze worden gebruikt bij de analyse van de versleutelde gegevens. Aangezien de data en de resultaten alleen met behulp van een decryptiesleutel kunnen worden gelezen, blijven de data van de andere organisaties vertrouwelijk. Het grote voordeel van deze methodiek bestaat hierin dat de data niet eerst ontsleuteld hoeven te worden voordat deze verwerkt kunnen worden. Bovendien staan de data op die manier uitsluitend tot de beschikking van de beheerder van de data.

Net als vele andere (combinaties[83] van) technologieën (zoals blockchain en distributed ledger technologie), is het idee (en soms zelfs de technologie) niet van een zeer recente

83 Blockchain is een combinatie van verschillende technieken. Interessant feit is dat blockchain het resultaat is van ruim veertig jaar onderzoek. D. Held, 'Planting Bitcoin – Soil' 2019, 3/4. https://www.danheld.com/blog/2019/1/6/planting-bitcoinsoil-34 (laatstelijk geraadpleegd: 20 december 2020).

datum.[84] Niettemin benoemt Gartner deze technologie als één van de *Top Strategic Technology Trends for 2021*.[85] Afhankelijk van het doel voor het verzamelen van de data en het onderkennen van fenomenen, is het de vraag of je alleen de data of ook de bijbehorende query wilt versleutelen. Immers, de onderwereld zal vooral geïnteresseerd zijn in de door de opsporingsdiensten onderkende fenomenen en profielen.

Het analyseren van data uit verschillende bronnen wordt steeds belangrijker, hoewel het delen van datasets niet (altijd) wenselijk is. Om een virtuele gezamenlijke database te realiseren, zonder de data te hoeven onthullen kan gebruik worden gemaakt van Secure Multiparty Computation (MPC). MPC is te omschrijven als een 'gereedschapskist' met cryptografische technieken die het mogelijk maakt dat meerdere partijen gezamenlijk aan data kunnen rekenen, alsof ze een gedeelde database hebben. De deelnemende partijen kunnen de data met elkaar delen, zonder dat ze de data van elkaar kunnen inzien. Gezamenlijk bepalen zij wie de uitkomst van de berekening mag inzien. De datasets worden verdeeld in gefragmenteerde datasets die worden gedeeld. Andere deelnemende partijen kunnen de data bewerken. Vervolgens worden de data weer samengevoegd tot één geheel. Het principe van Full Homomorphic Encryption (FHE) is volledig anders dan blockchain of distributed ledger technologie, ook al is FHE net als blockchain en DLT gedistribueerde technologie en worden de data gedeeld. Waar blockchain en DLT de algoritmes publiceren, is dat bij homomorphic encryption niet het geval. Daarmee is deze laatste technologie zeer geschikt voor bijvoorbeeld nationale veiligheidsdiensten.

Dit onderwerp leent zich, ondanks de relatieve onvolwassenheid[86] van de technologie – tezamen met een aantal aanpalende onderwerpen – wellicht goed voor een nadere beschouwing tijdens de *Land and Poverty Conference* in Washington, afhankelijk van het verloop van Covid-19, in 2021 (of daarna).

10 LAND AND POVERTY CONFERENTIES

Dan richt ik me nu graag direct tot Sjef. Beste Sjef, zoals we vaak al grappend concluderen, lijkt het er soms op dat je nooit van me af kunt komen. Toch rond ik af. Voor nu.

---

84 Het idee om versleutelde data te bewerken werd al in 1978 opgeworpen door MIT-medewerkers Ron Rivest, Len Adleman en Michael Dertouzos.

85 C. Panetta, 'Gartner Top Strategic Technology Trends for 2021', 2020. https://www.gartner.com/smarterwithgartner/gartner-top-strategic-technology-trends-for-2021/ (laatstelijk geraadpleegd: 20 december 2020).

86 Dat de technologie nog niet volwassen is, blijkt onder meer uit het kraken in 2014 van een eerdere versie van de op de tekentafel uitgewerkte technologie, zie: S. Bogos, J. Gaspoz en S. Vaudenay, 'Cryptanalysis of a Homomorphic Encryption Scheme', *Arcticcrypt*, 2016. https://eprint.iacr.org/2016/775 (laatstelijk geraadpleegd: 20 december 2020).

We hebben in internationaal verband bijzonder veel en vaak samen opgetrokken. Onze vriendschap, want zo zou ik onze vorm van omgang met elkaar graag kwalificeren, is ontstaan tijdens de twee Crobeco-projecten. Daarbij hebben we vaak gesproken over het gebruik van de elektronische handtekening en het veelvuldig ontbreken daarvan in internationaal verband. Vervolgens zagen we de Erfrechtverordening op ons af komen, met al zijn implicaties en (on)mogelijkheden, waarna dit concreet een invulling kreeg bij de totstandkoming van de (tot nu toe) drie IMOLA-projecten.

Mijn eerste deelname aan de Land and Poverty conferentie in Washington was in 2015, toen ik op verzoek van Klaus Deininger sprak over vastgoedfraude. Het jaar daarop veranderde het zijn van spreker in het zijn van co-host van de panels die wij vervolgens jaarlijks gezamenlijk hebben georganiseerd. In 2016 begonnen we met een paneldiscussie getiteld "Real Estate Fraud & Hacking". Het onderwerp zou ook in deze tijd van *fake news* en *deep fakes* niet misstaan. In deze *infocalyps*[87] is het soms de vraag of wij onze ogen en oren nog wel mogen geloven.

In 2017 organiseerden we een sessie over blockchaintechnologie in de vastgoedketen, waarbij we vervolgens werden gevraagd voor een aantal 'side events'. Dat de technologie niet uit het zicht is verdwenen blijkt onder meer uit de blockchainwerkgroep van het European Law Insititute waarvan jij de voorzitter bent en waaraan ik namens ELRA mag deelnemen. Mede vanwege de infocalyps en de transparantie en juiste werking van *smart contracts* lijkt het belang van trusted third parties (TTP`s) en Oracles niet af te nemen.

Het jaar daaropvolgend (2018) stelden we het thema data-eigendom centraal. Dat ook dit een uitermate nuttige exercitie is, blijkt onder meer uit de Netflix-documentaire *The Social Dilemma* en uit de *platformcalyps*: het moment waarop eigenaren van een platform niet meer vrij zijn van controle op de content die anderen op het platform plaatsen en ook daadwerkelijk verantwoordelijkheid moeten nemen voor de inhoud op het platform. Hiervoor kan men gebruik maken van algoritmes, mits deze transparant en controleerbaar zijn. Voor landregistratie-systemen is dit niet nieuw; zij werden altijd al geacht kwalitatief goede data te presenteren en te garanderen.

In 2019 verschoven we de aandacht van 'eigendom'(en beheer) van data naar privatisering van landregistraties; ook dit is nog altijd een actueel onderwerp. Het onderwerp dat we hadden bedacht voor 2020, het jaar van Covid-19, ligt nog op de plank. De conferentie werd vanwege de pandemie uitgesteld. Ik spreek de hoop uit dat we komend jaar – ten minste nog eenmaal – gezamenlijk een (of twee) sessies mogen organiseren voor de Wereldbank, tijdens de *Land and Poverty Conference 2021* en daarbij tijdens een verloren moment gedurende deze conferentie mogen wandelen over de *National Mall*, elkaar

87 N. Schick, *Deep Fakes and the Infocalypse: What You Urgently Need To Know*, Octopus Publishing Group, 2020.

verrijkend met inzichten (en voor één van beide: zere voeten[88]) en waarbij we terugblikken op uitermate interessante conferenties door de jaren heen. Ik hoop dat we de reis dan mogen afsluiten met een bezoek aan een bezienswaardigheid in de (directe) omgeving van Washington, zoals we dat eerder ook hebben mogen doen.

Sjef, Ik heb intens genoten van de vele momenten die we samen hebben beleefd; van de cursussen en lezingen die jij hebt verzorgd, maar bovenal van de *Land and Poverty conferenties* waaraan wij gezamenlijk hebben mogen deelnemen. Deze momenten zijn mij zeer dierbaar en blijven altijd in mijn gedachten. Bijzonder veel dank, Sjef, voor al die mooie, warme, momenten. Het ga je goed, blijf gezond en graag tot in Washington!

88 Een gratis advies van deze 'Noorderling': het is aan te bevelen om gymschoenen mee te nemen en aan te trekken, wanneer een wandeling op *the Mall* wederom op ons programma zou mogen komen te staan.

Part VII
Succession

Disinheritance in an Ageing Society

Antoni Vaquer[*]

1 Introduction

Disinheritance has a double meaning. In common law systems, the etymological sense prevails: disinheritance means denying someone from a share of a certain decedent's succession. If, for example, a mother disinherits her daughter, she will not receive property from her mother's estate. Nevertheless, it has to be taken into account that in the common law world – not in the civilian systems either – no one has a right to become an heir. It is true that the law establishes that the succession of a deceased is assigned to her relatives in a given order, but the decedent's will may displace statutory regulation of the succession. The rules on intestacy are default rules. Yet in civil law systems, a number of relatives have a right to obtain a share of the assets or a share of the value of the estate: the compulsory share, *réserve*, *Pflichtteil* or *legítima* grants the closest relatives, as defined by law, a share of the estate *in natura* or in money. In the civilian world, disinheritance means deprivation of the compulsory share. This term comes from Roman law times, where the compulsory share had to be attributed by means of institution of heir: "sui heredes aut instituendi sunt aut exheredandi" (Ulp. D 28, 2, 1).[1] From here the legal impossibility of appointing voluntary heirs in customary French law[2] and later in the French *Code civil*[3] or the

* Professor of private law at the University of Lleida. I am indebted to Prof. Shael Herman for comments on an earlier draft of this chapter.

1 Pasquale Voci, *Diritto ereditario romano*, vol. 2, 2nd ed., Milano, Giuffrè, 1963, p. 634.

2 Jean Domat, *Les lois civiles dans leur ordre naturel; le droit public, et legum delectus*, Paris, Chez Michel Brunet, 1735, seconde partie des successions, préface, VII, p. 305: "il n'y a pas des autres héritiers que les proches que la Coutume appelle à la succession, & qui ne donne que la qualité de légataires universels à ceux à qui on laisse par un testament (…), le nom d'héritier demeurant propre au seul héritier de sang"; Robert J Pothier, 'Traité des Successions', *in Œuvres de Pothier*, t. VIII, Paris, Videcoq-Cosse et N. Delamotte, 1845, art. IV, § p. 25: "Quoiqu'il n'y ait que la loi, par notre droit coutumier, qui fasse les héritiers, et qu'elle les fasse indépendamment de la volonté du défunt, elle lui laisse néanmoins la faculté d'exclure de sa succession ceux qui s'en sont rendus indignes, et elle ne lait point héritiers ceux qui, par un juste jugement du défunt, ont été exhérédés." But see previously Ranulf de Glanville, *Tractatus de legibus et consuetudinibus regni Angliae*, Londinum, in aedibus Richardi Toteli, s.d. [1554], liber septimus, fol. 43: "solum deus heredem facere potest non homo".

3 Art. 1003 only allowed the *legs universel*. See F. Laurent, *Principes de droit civil*, t. 12, 3rd ed., Bruxelles, Bruylant-Christoph & Co, 1878, p. 15: "lorsque le défunt laisse des réservataires, le testateur ne peut plus faire une institution d'héritier".

expression still used in Spanish law *forced heirs* to refer to those relatives entitled to the compulsory share.

This paper, combining both senses of disinheritance, principally analyses mechanisms that exclude relatives from the list of kin entitled to share in a succession, either because they are potential intestate heirs or because – in civil law countries and some mixed systems – they are entitled to the compulsory share. Specifically, the paper focuses on the demands of an ageing society.

2 An Ageing Society

Life expectancy has increased worldwide. In 1900, when the most important Civil Codes had already been enacted around Europe, life expectancy was about 40 years.[4] In 1950 the life expectancy for newborns exceeded 60 years in Europe, North America, Oceania, Japan and parts of South America.[5] Since 1970 life expectancy in OECD countries has increased on average by ten years.[6] According to the data of 2017, life expectancy was

Table 1 Life expectancy

Country	Females	Males
Latvia	79,7	69,8
Australia	85,0	81,3
USA	81,9	77,3
France	85,6	79,6
Spain	86,1	80,6
Japan	87,2	80,7

A longer life expectancy generally requires a society to allocate a lot of resources in old age. The impact on health care and long-term care spending is huge. It is expected that age-related health spending in industrialized countries will rise by around 6 to 7 percentage points of GDP between 2000 and 2050.[7]

4 Johan P Mackenbach, Caspar WN Looman, 'Life expectancy and national income in Europe, 1900-2008: an update of Preston's analysis', (2013) 42 *International Journal of Epidemiology*, pp. 1100-1110 at 1104.

5 Max Roser, Esteban Ortiz-Ospina, Hannah Ritchie *in* https://ourworldindata.org/life-expectancy (accessed 13 February 2021).

6 Veena S Raleigh, "Trends in life expectancy in EU and other OECD countries: Why are improvements slowing?", *OECD Health Working Papers No. 108*, 26 February 2019, p. 10.

7 Michael K. Gusmano, Kieke GH Okma, 'Population Aging and the Sustainability of the Welfare State', (2018) 48 S3 *The Hastings Center Report*, pp. S57-S61 at S59.

At the same time, two other factors have to be borne in mind. On the one side, the income of people depends on their age. In most EU Member States, the highest levels of net wealth were recorded for households where the reference person was aged either 55-64 years or 65-74 years.[8] If we accept that average age at maternity is above 30,[9] this implies that expectation for becoming an heir or receiving the compulsory share usually coincides with both the highest net wealth of the children and the need for more care of the parents.

On the other side, according to European statistical surveys,[10] more than 32% of elderly population lives alone. Irrespective of the particular reasons in each case, loneliness has been described as an epidemic.[11] Additionally, social isolation may be a crucial risk factor for elder abuse. Abuse may be physical, sexual, mental and/or financial. The prevalence of elder maltreatment in the European community is high. It affects at least 3% of the population.[12] In the United States financial abuse has been reported has the most common type of abuse.[13]

The last factor to take into account is the so-called revolution in family wealth transmission:[14] intergenerational wealth transmission no longer occurs primarily upon the death of the parents, but rather, when the children are growing up, hence, during the parents' lifetimes because of the investment on education and support when the children gain their independence and establish a domicile separate from their parents.[15]

Although succession law is a particularly conservative branch of law, it contains mechanisms that can improve allocation of resources in modern ageing societies. Laughing heirs are conceived as those legally entitled to inherit the property of a decedent, even though that heir is only distantly related to the deceased and is unlikely to grieve over the death. Traditionally this distance reflected the degree of kinship; today affective distance may give rise to another category of laughing heirs: that is, children and other close relatives affectively related distantly to the decedent or even those affectively unrelated to the decedent.

---

8 https://ec.europa.eu/eurostat/statistics-explained/index.php?title=Ageing_Europe_-_statistics_on_pensions,_income_and_expenditure#Wealth_and_debt_of_older_people (accessed 13 February 2021).

9 https://www.oecd.org/els/soc/SF_2_3_Age_mothers_childbirth.pdf (accessed 13 February 2021).

10 https://ec.europa.eu/eurostat/cache/infographs/elderly/index.html (accessed 13 February 2021).

11 KDM Snell, 'The rise of living alone and loneliness in history', (2017) 42 *Social History*, pp. 2-18 at 22.

12 See *European report on preventing elder maltreatment*, available at http://www.euro.who.int/__data/assets/pdf_file/0010/144676/e95110.pdf (accessed 13 February 2021), and Maria Gabriella Melchiorre, "Abuse of Older Men in Seven European Countries: A Multilevel Approach in the Framework of an Ecological Model", (2016) *PLoS ONE* 11(1).

13 Report Elder Abuse and Neglect Committee, Pennsylvania (http://www.pacourts.us/assets/files/page-543/file-4023.pdf?cb=1555891200091) (accessed 13 February 2021) using data from 2013-2014, estimates that 16,1% of all abuses are financial abuse.

14 John H Langbein, 'The Twentieth-Century Revolution in Family Wealth Transmission', (1988) 86 *Michigan Law Review* pp. 722-751.

15 However, support also extends to grown children. See Karen L Fingerman *et al*, 'Support to Aging Parents and Grown Children in Black and White Families', (2011) *The Gerontologist* pp. 441-452.

3 Disinheritance

As previously said, in the civil law, *stricto sensu*, disinheritance means deprivation of the compulsory share. Roman law made the compulsory share a duty of the decedent. Freedom of testation once unlimited was restricted on the basis of an *officium pietatis*. During the decedent's lifetime there was a sort of community or *consortium* for the family property. Hence, at death succession in favour of the children was the natural progression; if the decedent wanted to select other heirs, formal disinheritance was required.[16] In the late Republic the children were granted a share in the estate. Should the decedent disregard this duty, the children could challenge the will by means of the *querela inofficiosi testamenti*;[17] literally, the will was void because the deceased had neglected her duty.

It is crystal clear that this was a duty of the decedent. Two millennia later such an assertion is not a relic. A former French Minister of Justice, facing a question about suppressing the compulsory share in French law, replied:

> "Cette réserve assure la cohésion du groupe familial en réalisant une égalité entre les enfants quel que soit le mode d'établissement de leur filiation et en imposant au de cujus un devoir d'assistance économique envers ses proches".[18]

The French *réserve* has its origin in customary law, on the basis that the family co-owned property. The French codifiers mixed the *réserve* – the denomination was maintained in the *Code* – with the principles of the Roman compulsory share and the extension of the use of the will. The *réserve* ensured that 4/5 of the estate was transferred to the issue and therefore the interest of the family members was secured.[19] Consequently, disinheritance of the *réservataires* was not allowed.[20]

---

16 Reinhard Zimmermann, 'Compulsory Heirship in Roman Law', *in* Kenneth GC Reid, Marius J de Waal, Reinhard Zimmermann (ed.), *Exploring the Law of Succession*, Edinburgh, Edinburgh University Press, 2007, p. 27.

17 David Johnston, 'Succession', *in* id. (ed.), *The Cambridge Companion to Roman Law*, Cambridge, Cambridge University Press, 2015, pp. 199, 209; Reinhard Zimmermann, "Protection against Being Passed Over or Disinherited in Roman Law", in: Kenneth GC Reid, Marius J de Waal, Reinhard Zimmermann (ed.), *Comparative Succession Law. Mandatory Family Protection*, Oxford, OUP, 2020, pp. 6-10.

18 Mme. Christiane Taubira, JO Sénat of 18/09/2014, 2100.

19 Marta Peguera-Poch, *Aux origines de la réserve héréditaire du Code Civil: la légitime en pays de coutumes (XVIe-XVIIIe siècles)*, Aix-en-Provence, Presses Universitaires, 2009. See also Barbara Willenbacher, 'Individualism and Traditionalism in Inheritance Law in Germany, France, England, and the United States', 28 (2003) *Journal of Family History*, pp. 208-225 at 211.

20 Laurent (footnote 2), p. 19: "Les lois de la révolution (…) enlevèrent au père le droit d'exhéréder ses enfants; ceux-ci étaient donc héritiers en vertu de la loi, et ne pouvaient être privés de ce titre ni des droits qui y sont attachés". See also Philippe Malaurie, Claude Brenner, *Droit des successions et des liberalités*, 7th ed., Paris, LGDJ, 2016, § 714. The same applied to the Italian Civil Code of 1865: Francesca Bartolini, Francesco Paolo Patti, 'The freedom to disinherit children', (2018) *Zeitschrift für Europäischen Privatrecht* pp. 428-

Only the Civil codes enacted at the end of the XIX century generalized some grounds for disinheritance. However, disinheritance was deemed a private penalty and restricted to cases where the beneficiaries had seriously offended the deceased, such as killing or trying to kill her or her closest relatives, committing physical serious abuse of refusing to pay maintenance.[21] Because disinheritance was a penalty, case law had consistently considered that the grounds for disinheritance must be restrictively construed.[22]

However, it is commonly said that the foundation of the compulsory share lies on the idea of family solidarity.[23] But solidarity is reciprocal. On the one hand, usually the compulsory share is not based on necessity: each child is entitled to an equal share regardless of wealth or health.[24] Moreover, some of the classical grounds for disinheritance are unilateral, because they only affect parents.[25] In succession law, solidarity burdens only the deceased. The decedent must be obligated solidarily toward her descendants, since she has to share the estate and when she is not willing to the law imposes a transfer of a portion to the issue. As the Spanish Supreme Court said, the behaviour of the beneficiaries is a "matter for their conscience".[26] But this approach was inconsistent with the needs of an

445 at 440-442; Veronica Bongiovanni, 'La desheredación en el ordenamiento italiano a la luz de las novedades introducidas por la reforma en materia de filiación', *in* Antoni Vaquer, María Paz Sánchez, Esteve Bosch (coord.), *La libertad de testar y sus límites*, Madrid-Barcelona-Buenos Aires-Sao Paulo, Marcial Pons, 2018, p. 194.

21 For example, § 2333 BGB, art. 852-855 Spanish Civil Code.

22 For Germany, Constitutional Court judgement of 19 April 2005, and Walter Pintens, 'S and S (2005): Compulsory Portion and Solidarity', *in* Brian Sloan (ed.), *Landmark Cases in Succession Law*, Oxford, Hart, 2019, p. 328 ("The Constitutional Court underlines that very clear rules are necessary and objects to a general clause of deprivation (...) only shortcomings that are more than a disturbance of family relations can be taken into account"), or Anne Röthel, *Erbrecht*, 18th ed., München, Beck, 2020, p. 443 ("*In der Praxis ist Pflichtteilsentziehung selten erfolgreich*". For Spain, Luis Díez-Picazo, Antonio Gullón, *Sistema de derecho civil*, vol. IV, 11th ed., Madrid, Tecnos, 2012, p. 185.

23 German Constitutional Court 19 April 2005 and 26 November 2018: "einer Familiensolidarität, die in grundsätzlich unauflösbarer Weise zwischen dem Erblasser und seinen Kindern besteht".

24 The main exception is Louisiana, where only children under 24 years of age or permanently incapable of taking care of their persons or administering their estates because of mental incapacity or physical infirmity have the legal status of forced heirs; see M. Nathan Jr, 'Forced Heirship: The Unheralded 'New' Disinherison Rules', (2000) *Tulane Law Review* pp. 1027-1043, and Vincent D. Rougeau, 'No Bonds but Those Freely Chosen: An Obituary for the Principle of Forced Heirship in American Law', (2008) 3 *Civil Law Commentaries* pp. 1-37. In Spain, art. 808 Civil Code allows the stipulation of a fideicomissum where the capacity of one of the descendants has been judicially modified, so that the other descendants will only obtain their forced shares at the death of the former.

25 According to art. 854.1 Spanish Civil Code, children may disinherit their parents in case of forfeiture of parental authority, but the opposite situation, children neglecting their parents, is not expressly listed among the disinheritance clauses of art. 853. Along the same lines the suppressed § 2334 BGB.

26 Decision of 28 June 1993 (Roj: STS 17783/1993). All Spanish decisions cited may be found at http://www.poderjudicial.es/search/indexAN.jsp using the Roj number.

ageing society and therefore the widening of new grounds for disinheritance was anticipated.[27]

The change of paradigm has come with the newest codifications and reforms.[28] In 2008, the Catalan Civil Code incorporated a new ground for disinheritance in art. 451-17.2.e: "the evident and continued lack of family relationship between the deceased and the beneficiary of the compulsory share provided that it is solely imputable to the beneficiary". Hence, the law faces up to the "social or moral side" of family relationships.[29] The ground for disinheritance is qualified by two adjectives, "evident" and "continued". "Continued" means long-lasting, but also that the absence of relationship must endure until the decedent's death; "evident" embraces serious, external acts likely to be known by family and friends. Moreover, the ground for disinheritance must be exclusively imputable to the successor. Although these two requirements must be complied with, it can be said that courts validate more disinheriting clauses than before the legal amendment.[30]

Though the Spanish Civil Code has not been modified recently, the Supreme Court made a new interpretation of the ground for disinheritance enshrined in art. 853.2 concerning the "mistreatment" of the deceased, along the lines of the Catalan Civil code. The lack of family relationship without a good reason results in "psychological abuse" that, since the decision of the Supreme Court handed down on 3 June 2014,[31] is included in the notion of "mistreatment" that constitutes a valid ground for disinheritance. However, most scholars agree that disinheritance is upheld for only the most serious psychological abuse.[32]

In force from 2017, Austrian Civil Code section 776 permits reduction by half of the compulsory share where the beneficiary never had a close relationship with the deceased or their relationship has been cut off for a long period. Scholars suggest 20 years for such

27 Walter Pintens, (2001) 'Die Europäisierung des Erbrechts', *Zeitschrift für Europäisches Privatrecht* pp. 628-648 at 643.

28 See also Esther Arroyo i Amayuelas, Esther Farnós Amorós, 'Kinship Bonds and Emotional Ties: Lack of a Family Relationship as Ground for Disinheritance', (2016) *European Review of Private Law* pp. 203-222.

29 Jordi Ribot Igualada, 'Art. 451-17', *in* Joan Egea Fernández, Josep Ferrer Riba (dir.), *Comentari al llibre quart del Codi Civil de Catalunya, relatiu a les successions*, Barcelona, Atelier, 2009, p. 1400.

30 For example, disinheritance has been considered appropriate ("fair") in cases where the beneficiary had not visited for a long time the grandparents at the nursing home and during the grandfather funeral he refused to preside over it and to give a kiss to the disinheriting grandmother in front of all the attendees, or where a daughter cut off any personal contact with the disinheriting father causing him great sorrow; see for an analysis of case law Antoni Vaquer, 'Acerca del fundamento de la legítima', (2017/3) *InDret* pp. 1-28 at 13-15.

31 Roj: STS 2484/2014. Later on decisions of 30 January 2015 (Roj: STS 565/2015) and 13 May 2019 (Roj: STS 1523/2019).

32 See a sample of decisions in Vaquer (footnote 30), pp. 17-18, footnote 60. In particular, case law tends to consider that divorce of the parents implies a good reason to cut off relations with one of them.

a period of estrangement, and require that the deceased has not given a fair reason for the lack of relationship.[33]

Rooted in Chinese tradition, a similar provision appears in the Taiwanese Civil Code. According to art. 1145(5), a son may be disinherited "where he seriously ill-treated or insulted the deceased and has been forbidden to inherit by the deceased". According to Taiwanese case law, serious mental abuse may consist of purposefully not supporting a parent to whom the child owes a duty of support and failing to visit him.[34]

Although these geographically distant new regulations are a step in the right direction, they are nevertheless insufficient. The attribution of the lack of relationship exclusively to the beneficiary and the restriction to some serious cases of abuse make disinheritance unworkable in practice absent very repulsive behaviour. Despite the introduction of such a new ground for disinheritance, most courts have remained faithful to the forced share as a unilateral duty of the deceased. Moreover, ordinary situations of physical, verbal, and financial abuse do not fit the grounds of disinheritance, since they presuppose a relationship and they are not gross enough to cause the severed disturbance that the law requires.

4 UNWORTHINESS

Provided that even the newest grounds for disinheritance are not fit for situations of loneliness and usual types of abuses and neglect, unworthiness becomes relevant. Unworthiness denies succession to unworthy heirs, legatees and beneficiaries under any mortis causa title. The effects of unworthiness are not automatic, but other successors –included potential successors, i.e. those who would be called to an intestate succession if the will becomes ineffective– may challenge the testamentary or legal disposition, absent the testator's forgiveness of the wrongdoer.[35] Roman lawyers encapsulated these ideas in the phrase *indignus potest capere sed non retinere*: the qualification as unworthy does not prevent acceptance of the benefit but it does entail forfeiture of inheritance rights.

It is not only a matter of preventing the acquisition of the reserved portion. Usually the grounds for unworthiness are also grounds for disinheritance.[36] But unworthiness goes further, since an unworthy successor takes no benefit either under the will or under intestacy. Thus, unworthiness is a heavier penalty. But the conduct of the unworthy successor is also more offensive than the one required for disinheritance.

33 Bernard Eccher, *Die österreichische Erbrechtsreform*, Wien, 2017, p. 160.

34 Ya-Hui Hsu, 'Should China Adopt Taiwan's Mandatory Share Doctrine?', 29 (2010) *Penn State International Law Review* pp. 289-333 at 313.

35 Gregor Christandal, *Selbstbestimmtes Testieren in einer alternden Gesellschaft*, Tübingen, Mohr, 2016, p. 108.

36 For example, art. 852 Spanish Civil Code, 451-17.2.a) Civil Code of Catalonia, 622 Civil Code of Malta.

The grounds for disinheritance involve mainly the intentional killing or injuring of the deceased and the interference with the deceased freedom of testation. Killing and injuring are usually related to criminal offences, although not every legal system requires criminal conviction.[37] The counterpart in England is the forfeiture rule, according to which the successor who unlawfully kills the decedent is not then entitled to benefit in any way from the death of the victim.[38] The United States coined the slayer rule. Art. 2-803 of the Uniform Probate Code lays down that "An individual who feloniously and intentionally kills the decedent forfeits all benefits under this [article] with respect to the decedent's estate, including an intestate share, an elective share, an omitted spouse's or child's share, a homestead allowance, exempt property, and a family allowance. If the decedent died intestate, the decedent's intestate estate passes as if the killer disclaimed his [or her] intestate share".[39]

Interference with freedom of testation comprises destruction, forgery or concealment of a will, preventing or instigating the deceased to make a will. Other acts leading to unworthiness may be charging the deceased with a crime punishable with imprisonment, false statements and removal of parental authority.[40] None of these grounds for unworthiness are fit for the aforementioned problematic of an ageing society.

The Spanish Code civil, however, contains a rule focused on protecting specifically decedents with disabilities. It was introduced in 2003 in the framework of a legal reform intended to protect the property of disabled persons. If a successor has not cared for a disabled decedent, she is deemed unworthy to inherit. Yet care is related to art. 142 and 146 of the *Código civil* that regulate the maintenance obligation. In addition, payment of maintenance must have been claimed. Therefore, two flaws can be pointed out. On the

37 Compare art. 412-3 Civil Code of Catalonia and art. 727 French Civil Code ("those convicted") to § 539 ABGB ("*strafbare Handlung*").

38 Ian Williams, 'How does the forfeiture rule work?', *in* Birke Häcker, Charles Mitchell (ed.), *Current Issues in Succession Law*, Oxford, Hart, 2016, pp. 51-75; Alexander Learmonth, Charlotte Ford, Julia Clark, John Ross Martyn, *Williams, Mortimer and Sunnucks on Executors, Administrators and Probate*, London, Sweet & Maxwell, 2018, p. 1275 ff; Roger Kerridge, *Parry and Kerridge The Law of Successions*, 13th ed., London, Sweet & Maxwell, 2016, 14-64 ff. It is also in force in Australia, New Zealand and Canada (Ken Mackie, *Principles of Australian Succession Law*, 3rd ed., Australia, Lexis-Nexis, 2017, 9-24 ff). The *forfeiture rule* does not apply to physical, psychological, and financial abuses.

39 Robert H. Sitkoff, Jesse Dukeminier, *Wills, Trusts, and Estates*, 10th ed., New York, Wolters Kluwer, 2017, pp. 134-135; Kevin Bennardo, 'Slaying Contingent Beneficiaries', 24 (2016) *University of Miami Business Law Review* pp. 31-58 at 34-40; Carla Spivack, 'Killers Shouldn't Inherit from Their Victims-Or Should They?', 48 (2013) *Georgia Law Review*, pp. 145-226; Nili Cohen, 'The Slayer Rule', (2012) 92 *Boston University Law Review*, pp. 793-810; Peter Arant, "In Re Ests. of Swansons: The Slayer Statute and the Impact of a Guilty Plea on Collateral Estoppel in Montana", 71 (2010) *Montana Law Review* pp. 217-235 at 218-221; Sara M. Gregory, 'Paved with Good 'Intentions': The Latent Ambiguities in New Jersey's Slayer Statute', 62 (2010) *Rutgers Law Review* pp. 821-848; Karen J. Sneddon, "Should Cain's Children Inherit Abel's Property", 76 (2007) *UMKC Law Review* pp. 101-139.

40 Art. 412-3.d) and f) Civil Code of Catalonia, 463.3b *Codice Civile*, 727.3 *Code civil*, § 541.3 ABGB.

one hand, the rule applies only to persons with a disability, not generally to vulnerable testators. On the other hand, it focuses upon the non-performance of the maintenance obligation, and does not extend to neglect and abuse.[41] Moreover, courts seldom apply it. The recent decision of the Supreme Court handed down on 2 July 2019[42] illustrates the shortcomings of the legal provision. The claimant asked for a flexible construction of the rule allowing unworthiness because of the granddaughters' psychological mistreatment of their grandparents. The Supreme Court objected to the construction of the rule along the lines of the extension of the ground for disinheritance, arguing that only the legislator has the power to include new grounds for disinheritance or insert other behaviours to the existing grounds.

Therefore, none of the analysed regulations shield vulnerable decedents against neglect and most other abuses that their successors may commit. Under intestacy the rules do not consider either the potential heirs' behaviour of or the relationship between the decedent and her relatives.[43] Therefore, accurately drafted grounds of unworthiness constitute the only mechanism to protect vulnerable decedents. Abuses and neglect also affect the decedent's freedom of testation, because her state of mind does not allow her freely to decide the destiny of her estate after her death.

Legislation of certain states in the US deserves consideration. According to the California Probate Code section 259(1), any person shall be deemed to have predeceased a decedent to the extent that "It has been proven by clear and convincing evidence that the person is liable for physical abuse, neglect, or financial abuse of the decedent, who was an elder or dependent adult". The provision tackles voluntary and reckless neglect; conviction is not required. Scholars believe that the rule enshrines a feeling of fairness that takes into account the successor's behaviour.[44] In 2009, the state of Washington enacted a rule to exclude the

41 María José Azaustre Fernández, 'La falta de atención al discapacitado como causa de indignidad: de la novela 115 a las Leyes 41/2003 y 15/2015', (April 2017) *Revista Internacional de Derecho Romano* pp. 317-348; María Paz García Rubio, Marta Otero Crespo, 'Capacidad, incapacidad e indignidad para suceder', *in* Mª del Carmen Gete-Alonso y Calera (dir.), *Tratado de sucesiones*, t. I, 2nd ed, Cizur Menor, Thomson, 2016, pp. 276-277; María Teresa Martín Meléndez, 'La causa de indignidad para suceder del art. 756.7º del Código civil', *in* Andrés Domínguez Luelmo, María Paz García Rubio (dir.), *Estudios de derecho de sucesiones. Liber Amicorum T.F. Torres García*, Las Rozas (Madrid), La Ley, 2014, p. 809.

42 Roj: STS 2241/2019.

43 Shelley Kreiczer-Levy, 'Big Data and the Modern Family', (2019) *Wisconsin Law Review* pp. 349-372, who at 351 adds: "Intestate rules (...) inhibit any real chance of challenging concepts of intimacy. In other words, they do not allow for true freedom of association".

44 Kymberleigh N. Korpus, 'Extinguishing Inheritance Rights: California Breaks New Ground in the Fight against Elder Abuse but Fails to Build an Effective Foundation', 52 (2001) *Hastings Law Journal* pp. 537-578; Anne-Marie Rhodes, 'On Inheritance and Disinheritance', 43 (2008) *Real Property, Trust and Estate Law Journal* pp. 433-445 at 443-444; Seymour Moskowitz, 'Golden Age in the Golden State: Contemporary Legal Developments in Elder Abuse and Neglect', 36 (2003) *Loyola of Los Angeles Law Review* pp. 589-666; Travis Hunt, 'Disincentivizing Elder Abuse Through Disinheritance: Revamping California Probate Code § 259 and Using It as a Model', (2014) *Brigham Young University Law Review* pp. 445-475.

successor who financially abused the vulnerable decedent.[45] By contrast, the rule does not cover physical abuse. Conviction is not required. Unworthiness alike, the abuser can be forgiven by the decedent.[46] Kentucky has a similar regulation encompassing physical abuses.[47] In Maryland, "a person convicted of unlawfully obtaining property from a victim in violation of § 8-801(b) of the Criminal Law Article shall be disqualified from inheriting, taking, enjoying, receiving, or otherwise benefitting from the estate, insurance proceeds, or property of the victim, to the extent provided in § 8-801(e) of the Criminal Law Article".[48] Conviction is required and the penalty extended to will substitutes. The requirement of conviction is criticised because the isolation of most of the vulnerable decedents hinders prosecution of abusers. Usually the abuser is a close relative who controls the decedent's finances and welfare, and consequently abuses will seldom emerge.[49]

5 A New Ground for Unworthiness

5.1 *Rationale*

I have identified a series of behaviours, such as physical, psychological, and financial abuses that do not entail conviction. These behaviours, when carried out by successors, do not correspond to the traditional grounds for unworthiness and disinheritance. In particular, courts seem reluctant to extend the traditional grounds to the interests of an ageing society.

The constitutional framework has prompted the introduction of a new ground for disinheritance intended to remove abusers from succession. On the one hand, art. 2 of the European Charter of Fundamental Rights lays down that everyone has the right to respect for his or her physical and mental integrity. Specifically, art. 25 points out that the European Union recognises and respects the rights of the elderly to lead a life of dignity and

---

45 According to section 11.84.020, "No slayer or abuser shall in any way acquire any property or receive any benefit as the result of the death of the decedent, but such property shall pass as provided in the sections following". Section 11.84.010(1) defines *abuser*: ""Abuser" means any person who participates, either as a principal or an accessory before the fact, in the willful and unlawful financial exploitation of a vulnerable adult". *Financial exploitation* means "the illegal or improper use, control over, or withholding of the property, income, resources, or trust funds of the vulnerable adult by any person or entity for any person's or entity's profit or advantage other than for the vulnerable adult's profit or advantage". Vulnerable adult includes a person sixty years of age or older who has the functional, mental, or physical inability to care for himself or herself, receiving services from home health, hospice, or home care agencies.

46 Jennifer Piel, 'Expanding Slayer Statutes to Elder Abuse', (2015) *The Journal of the American Academy of Psychiatry and the Law* pp. 369-376 at 370-372.

47 Ky. Rev. Stat. § 381.280. But see Emily Irwin, "Protecting Mamaw and Her Estate: Elder Abuse Disinheritance in Kentucky", 54 (2016) *University of Louisville Law Review* pp. 307-329 at 326-328.

48 Maryland MD. Code ANN., EST. & TRUSTS § 11-111. See Irwin (footnote 47) 322-323.

49 Frances Murphy, "The 18-Bill Elder Abuse Legislative Package: The Pressure's on the House", 58 (2013) *The Wayne Law Review* pp. 1167-1191 at 1175-1188.

independence. On the other hand, the European Charter of the rights and responsibilities of older people in need of long-term care and assistance enumerates in art. 1, among others, rights to respect for human dignity and welfare, for protection of psychological and emotional welfare and protection from any form of psychological or emotional abuse or mistreatment, as well as to be protected against all forms of financial and material abuse. The violation of these rights deserves a penalty in terms of private law. It would be completely unfair that someone who has abused or neglected the decedent, even if such behaviour has no criminal consequences, could be entitled to succession. Unworthiness is the most suitable mechanism for denying abusers rights under a will or intestacy. The introduction of a new ground for unworthiness is consistent with the constitutional foundations of the European Union. Additionally, it may deter abuses and foster provision of better care for decedents.[50] Lastly, it may contribute to a more efficient allocation of resources, since those who affect the wellness of decedents and cause public social spending will not share the estate.

Some legislators are conscious that care of elders often takes place within the family and that, although its general conception as paradigm of solidarity, the forced share does not always benefit those who care for the decedent.[51] The Austrian Civil Code now contains a rule establishing a statutory legacy in favour of caregivers. According to § 677 ABGB, intestate heirs, their spouses, registered partners and cohabitants as well as their children and the cohabitant of the deceased and the cohabitant's children, who have provided care services in the last three years before death for at least six months, are entitled to a statutory legacy unless they have received a mortis causa benefit or where consideration has been agreed upon.[52] The amount of the legacy depends of the duration and circumstances of the care services (§ 678 ABGB). In Germany, the new § 2057a BGB lays down that any descendant who, as a result of not remunerated work over a long period in the household, occupation or business of the deceased, of substantial financial contributions or in another way has to a particular degree contributed to the preservation or increase of the property of the deceased, may, in the partitioning, demand adjustment between the descendants

50 Boudewijn Bouckaert, 'The Post Mortem Homo Economicus: What does He Tell Us?', *in* Christoph Castelein, René Foqué, Alain Verbeke (ed.), *Imperative Inheritance Law in a Late Modern Society*, Antwerp-Oxford-Portland, Hart, 2009, p. 96; JC Tate, 'Caregiving and the Case for Testamentary Freedom', (2008) *University of California Davis Law Review* pp. 129-193. On the deterring role see also Mariusz Zalucki, *Uniform European Inheritance Law. Myth, Dream, or Reality in the Future*, Krakow, 2015, p. 114.

51 Jens Beckert, 'Familiäre Solidäritat und die Pluralität moderner Lebensformen', *in* Anne Röthel (ed.), *Reformfragen des Pflichtteilsrecht*, Köln-Berlin-München, 2007, p. 13-15, pointed out that the amount of the forced share is not enough to incentive care within the family and that, conversely, it can benefit relatives that disregard the wellness of the decedent. As said in the text, a ground for unworthiness is preferable to disinheritance.

52 Gregor Christandal, Kristin Nemeth, 'Austrian Succession Law Rewritten: A Comparative Analysis', (2020) *European Review of Private Law*, p. 149-172 at 158.

who inherit as heirs on intestacy together with her. This special *collatio* specifically applies to descendants who cared for the deceased for a long period.[53]

Both the Austrian and the German solution imply individualisation[54] of the intestacy regime in relation to the potential heirs caring for the decedent.[55] Castelein had wondered whether consanguinity sufficed to determine the destiny of the estate or the duties of care and contribution played any role. One may wonder if this is a first crack in the foundations of the legal titles of succession.[56]

5.2 An Open Clause

A new ground for unworthiness intended to protect vulnerable decedents must be necessarily drafted in open terms. This is not the drafting tradition, for classical grounds are drafted in strict terms that correspond to criminal offences. Probably the rigid drafting of the grounds, resulting from its conception as a penalty, has hindered its adjustment to the evolution of the society in terms of life expectancy and explains its rare judicial application. On the contrary, new grounds for disinheritance such as the lack of family relationship are expressed in broader terms. Of course, legal certainty is at stake, yet openness is necessary in order that courts may assess a given behaviour and adapt to new situations consistent with the rationale of the rule. This price is worth paying if the result better protects our elders.[57]

5.3 Vulnerable Decedents

The openness of the clause becomes evident in defining a vulnerable decedent. A combination of age and health and social conditions likely will accomplish optimal results. Probably every lawyer has in mind a person whose ability to protect herself from abuse or neglect is significantly impaired through physical or mental disability or illness, old age

53 Anne Paetel, *Die erbrechtliche Ausgleichung von Pflegeleistungen und anderen Sonderleistungen - Eine Auseinandersetzung mit § 2057a BGB und dem geplanten § 2057b BGB*, Hamburg, Verlag Dr Kovač, 2009.

54 Reinhard Zimmermann, "Intestate Succession in Germany", *in* Kenneth GC Reid, Marius J de Waal, Reinhard Zimmermann (ed.), *Intestate Succession*, Oxford, Oxford University Press, 2015, p. 208.

55 See also Antoni Vaquer, 'Freedom of Testation, Compulsory Share and Disinheritance based on Lack of Family Relationship', *in* Miriam Anderson, Esther Arroyo i Amayuelas, *The Law of Succession: Testamentary Freedom*, Groningen, Europa Law Publishing, 2011, p. 95-98.

56 Kreiczer-Levy (footnote 43), who at 351 adds that "Intestate rules (…) inhibit any real chance of challenging concepts of intimacy. In other words, they do not allow for true freedom of association".

57 Thomas E. Simmons, 'A Chinese Inheritance', (2017) *Quinnipiac Probate Law Journal* p. 124-148 at 130; Cohen (footnote 39) p. 804. Also in Italy scholars advocate for a broadening of the letter of the grounds for unworthiness; see Ilenia Rapisarda, 'Appunti sull'indegnità a succedere (In attesa dell'auspicata riforma del diritto delle successioni)', (2018) *Rivista di Ditto Civile* pp. 1372-1402 at 1397-1398.

or otherwise. Therefore, the ground for unworthiness should focus on the successor's behaviour and not go into excessive details about a vulnerable decedent. Some legal systems define a dependent adult; if that is the case, the rule could speak of dependent decedents. Courts should be able to identify the targeted individuals taking into account all circumstances.

5.4 *Physical, Psychological, and Financial Abuses*

Some legislators argue that the grounds for unworthiness ought to be informed by certain criminal offences. Therefore, behaviours not leading to conviction or not matching a certain offence, although entailing abuses, cannot disqualify a successor. Emphasis must be put on the impact of the behaviour upon the decedent, not on the gravity of the offense. The statistics on elder abuse do not reflect the number of judicial decisions validating unworthiness. By contrast, some of the new grounds for disinheritance have been drafted more openly. This has not caused great inconvenience; in particular, even if it is a penalty that extinguishes a subjective right, legal certainty has not been threatened.

Hence, it is preferable expressly to incorporate in the civil codes a new ground for unworthiness covering physical, psychological and financial abuses that do not entail a criminal offence. This would be so even if there has been no prosecution; a vulnerable decedent will find it difficult to lodge a criminal complaint against a son or a daughter or a caregiver, and it is not easy to detect neglect and abuses.[58] Furthermore the behaviour may not constitute a crime in the given legal system. Codification of grounds can turn on a warning light. As Rhodes has said, "a legislative grant of discretion to a judge represents a legislative determination that the misconduct it has identified cannot be so easily located for inheritance purposes. (...) The judge is asked (...) to balance decedent's intent and public policy under the circumstances".[59]

58 A study in New York found an elder abuse incidence rate that was nearly 24 times greater than the number of cases referred to social service, law enforcement or legal authorities who have the capacity as well as the responsibility to assist older adult victims (*Under the Radar: New York State Elder Abuse Prevalence Study*, 2011, 55, available at https://ocfs.ny.gov/main/reports/Under%20the%20Radar%2005%2012%2011%20 final%20report.pdf, accessed 13 February 2021). Scholars generally suggest that official figures are likely an underestimation of the real extent of the problem; see Lia Susana Dalchman, Susana Aguas, Charmaine Spencer, 'Elder abuse', *in The International Encyclopedia of Public Health*, 2nd ed., Amsterdam, Academic Press, 2017, p. 444.

59 Anne-Marie Rhodes, 'Consequences of Heir's Misconduct: Moving from Rules to Discretion', 33 (2007) *Ohio Northern University Law Review* pp. 975-991 at 989.

5.5 *Extension to Will Substitutes*

The grounds for unworthiness should apply to both succession under a will and intestacy as well as will substitutes. The grounds for unworthiness apply to any succession title: institution of heir, legacy, compulsory portion, agreements as to succession, gift *mortis causa*, etc. Taking into account the rationale of the institution of unworthiness and its general application to succession, logically it should extend to transmission of wealth akin to succession. The Uniform Probate Code extends the slayer rule to will substitutes,[60] and this represents the way forward.

5.6 *A Change of Paradigm*

No legal amendment will be successful unless it is accompanied by a change of paradigm. Neither the compulsory share nor the right of succession is an innate right. If the paradigm decides that the closest relatives are entitled to share the estate, reforming the rules of unworthiness is nonsense. The focus must be upon the idea of solidarity. Relatives's behaviour is by no means irrelevant. Taking into account that there usually has been a transmission of wealth during the decedent's lifetime, the compulsory share and the right to intestacy must be considered as functional elements within the crisis of the welfare state that hits the most vulnerable people particularly hard.

5.7 *Drafting a Rule*

A new ground for disinheritance could be drafted in the following terms:

> "When the decedent is a vulnerable/dependent person, any individual who has physically, psychologically, or financially abused the decedent forfeits all benefits with respect to the decedent's estate, life insurances, and beneficiary designations in other instruments of transmission of wealth at death".

The legal requirements and consequences would be the same as any other ground for unworthiness. Hence, the declaration of unworthiness must be declared by any successor

60 Section 2-803. Effect of Homicide on Intestate Succession, Wills, Trusts, Joint Assets, Life Insurance, and Beneficiary Designations. John H Langbein, 'Major Reforms of the Property Restatement and the Uniform Probate Code: Reformation, Harmless Error, and Nonprobate Transfers', 38 (2012) *ACTEC Law Journal* p. 1-21 at 18: "What we did in the UPC was to extend expressly the divorce revocation statute to the will substitutes. Our guiding principle was to treat functionally comparable transfers alike. We did the same with the UPC slayer statute". As already said (footnote 48), Maryland expressly extends the version of the slayer rule that includes abuses to will substitutes

having a legitimate interest, and the decedent may forgive the successor. When unworthiness is declared, the affected successor forfeits all rights under the will, intestacy or will substitute, since the clause is ineffective. Substitution or increase of rights occurs in favour of worthy successors, so that for example, where substitution is not foreseen or representation takes no place, if one of three heirs is unworthy, each of the other two [worthy] heirs receives one half of the estate. The result would be the same if a successor is deemed to have predeceased the decedent, the usual formula under United States law.

6 Concluding Remarks

Protection of vulnerable decedents must be a priority for legislators in an ageing society. An efficient allocation of resources advocates for denying abusers benefits under a will, intestacy or will substitutes. This also corresponds to the presumed intention of the decedent, who probably would not have benefitted the abuser had she not been in the situation of vulnerability. No one should believe that she has a connatural right of succession irrespective of her behaviour towards the decedent. The introduction of a new ground of unworthiness focused on abusers of vulnerable decedents could be a valuable contribution to the welfare of elder citizens.

Reflections on "nemo pro parte testatus pro parte intestatus decedere potest"

Reinhard Zimmermann[*]

1. In Germany, as in all other European legal systems, there are two modes of succession upon death: the succession can be determined by a disposition *mortis causa* on the part of the deceased (typically a will); or it may occur according to the rules of intestate succession. Intestate succession is of a subsidiary nature – it only governs the devolution of the estate if the deceased has not exercised his right freely to dispose of it. Does this imply that testamentary succession and intestate succession cannot apply, side by side, to one and the same estate – with the effect that the intestate heirs succeed to one part of the estate, and the testamentary heirs to the other? The Roman lawyers appear to have thought so. Thus we read in Inst. 2, 14, 5: "... neque idem ex parte testatus et ex parte intestatus decedere potest". This is confirmed by a fragment, included by Justinian in the *regulae iuris antiquae*, according to which there is a natural conflict between testate and intestate succession.[1] The relevant rule is usually couched in the words "nemo pro parte testatus pro parte intestatus decedere potest".[2] Christian Friedrich Mühlenbruch recorded that "there has always been much dispute about the reason for this rule";[3] Bernhard Windscheid,

* Reinhard Zimmermann is Director at the Max Planck Institute for Comparative and International Private Law in Hamburg. All translations from German legal sources into English in this essay are his.

1 Pomponius D. 50, 17, 7: "Ius nostrum non patitur eumdem in paganis et testato et intestato decessisse: earumque rerum naturaliter inter se pugna est 'testatus' et 'intestatus'". Cicero, *De inventione*, II, XXI, [63], also has this rule in mind when he states "nec unquam factum est, ut eiusdem pecuniae alius testamento, alius lege heres esset". On the Cicero text see P. Meylan, 'Nemo pro parte testatus pro parte intestatus decedere potest', in: *Zum Schweizerischen Erbrecht: Festschrift P. Tuor*, 1946, pp. 179-200, 181-183, 191 f.

2 Ph.E. Huschke, 'Ueber die Rechtsregel: Nemo pro parte testatus pro parte intestatus decedere potest', *Rheinisches Museum für Jurisprudenz*, Vol. 6, 1834, pp. 257-369, 257 f., and K.A. von Vangerow, *Lehrbuch der Pandekten*, Vol. II, 7th edn., Marburg and Leipzig, 1867, § 397, p. 9 take this to be a foundational rule of Roman law. E. Gans, *Das Erbrecht in weltgeschichtlicher Entwicklung*, Vol. II, 1825, pp. 451-462 even saw in "nemo pro parte ..." the expression, in a nutshell, of "the entire idea of the Roman law of succession", i.e. the battle between collectivity (as respresented by the family) and individualism. E. Rabel, *Grundzüge des römischen Privatrechts*, 2nd edn., 1955, p. 203 regarded it as "a mere maxim"; *cf* also R. Zimmermann, '"Coniunctio verbis tantum": Accrual, the methods of joinder in a will and the rule against partial intestacy in Roman-Dutch and Roman law', *Zeitschrift der Savigny-Stiftung für Rechtsgeschichte (Romanistische Abteilung)*, Vol. 101, 1984, pp. 234-274 ('convenient maxim').

3 Ch.F. Glück, *Ausführliche Erläuterung der Pandekten nach Hellfeld: ein Commentar für meine Zuhörer*, 63 Vols., Erlangen, from 1790 onwards, after Glück's death continued by Ch.F. Mühlenbruch et al., Vol. 40, Erlangen, 1838, p. 145.

more pointedly, even refers to "infinite disputes".[4] And according to Otto Lenel the rule was taken to be "the great mystery of the Roman law of succession".[5]

Equally disputed is its historical development.[6] Was it based on a literalistic interpretation of a directive in the Twelve Tables on what was to happen "si intestato moritur"?[7] Was it an "indispensable complement" of the old *testamentum calatis comitiis*?[8] Did it follow from the original function of the Roman will and from the formal structure of the *testamentum per aes et libram*?[9] Or from the principle of universal succession and from the idea that the heir "on the whole continues the deceased's personality with regard

4 B. Windscheid, Th. Kipp, *Lehrbuch des Pandektenrechts*, 9th edn., 1906, § 537, n. 2; *cf.* also von Vangerow, 1867, § 397, p. 10. R. von Jhering, *Geist des römischen Rechts auf den verschiedenen Stufen seiner Entwicklung*, Part III/1, 5th edn., 1906, p. 149, stated that concerning the significance of this rule "extraordinarily much has been unearthed in our literature that is completely unhealthy and fantastic". In his 'confidential letters on contemporary legal scholarship' the rule was therefore the object of his satirical comments on the "speculative method": see *Scherz und Ernst in der Jurisprudenz*, 13th edn., 1924, reprint 1992, pp. 17-34 (directed, primarily, against Gans and Huschke). Meylan, 1946, p. 178 refers to "mille essais d'explication". Surveys about the various views can be found in Gans, 1825, pp. 455-458; Huschke, 1834, pp. 259-271; Glück/Mühlenbruch, 1838, pp. 145-151; Th. Schirmer, *Handbuch des Römischen Erbrechtes*, Part I, Leipzig, 1863, p. 54 f.; von Vangerow, 1867, § 397 (pp. 10 f.); A. Amiet, *Der praktische Grund und die juristische Begründung der Regel nemo pro parte testatus, pro parte intestatus decedere potest, Inaugural-Dissertation Straßburg* 1883, pp. 1-36. Windscheid/Kipp, 1906, § 537, n. 2; H. Dernburg, *Pandekten*, Vol. III, 6th edn. in cooperation with J. Biermann, 1901, § 57, n. 5; G. von Schmitt, *Begründung des Entwurfes eines Rechtes der Erbfolge für das Deutsche Reich*, 1879, in: W. Schubert (Ed.), *Die Vorlagen der Redaktoren für die erste Kommission zur Ausarbeitung eines Bürgerlichen Gesetzbuches, Erbrecht*, Part I, 1984, p. 157 f.; Meylan, 1946, pp. 181-186; B. Schmidlin, 'Sinn, Funktion und Herkunft der Testamentsregeln: nemo pro parte testatus pro parte intestatus decedere potest – hereditas adimi non potest', *Bullettino dell'istituto di diritto romano*, Vol. 78, 1975, pp. 71-81; G. Coppola, 'Nascita e declino dell' adagio nemo pro parte testatus pro parte intestatus decedere potest', *Teoria e storia del diritto privato*, Vol. V, 2012, 12 (pp. 1-172, under 2); A. Gómez Ródenas, 'El principio nemo pro parte testatus pro parte intestatus decedere potest: estudio sobre el origen, evulución y trascendencia en el ordinamiento jurídico actual', *Revista de derecho UNED*, Vol. 17, 2015, pp. 833-867, 836-846; W. Borysiak, 'Roman Principle nemo pro parte testatus pro parte intestatus decedere potest and the reasons of its modern rejection', *in Mater Familias – Scritti Romanistici per Maria Zabłocka*, 2016, pp. 63-83, 70-73.

5 O. Lenel, 'Zur Geschichte der heredis institutio', in: P. Vinogradoff (Ed.), *Essays in Legal History read before the International Congress of Historical Studies*, 1913, pp. 120-142, 127. *Cf.* also Dernburg, 1901, § 57, p. 100: "All of this appears to be a mystery"; F. Wieacker, 'Hausgenossenschaft und Erbeinsetzung: Über die Anfänge des römischen Testaments', in: *Festschrift der Leipziger Juristenfakultät für Heinrich Siber*, Vol. I, 1941, p. 41 (the rule "has a bad reputation for being mysterious and even monstrous").

6 M. Kaser, *Das römische Privatrecht, Erster Abschnitt*, 2nd edn., 1971, p. 677. For an extensive older discussion, see Amiet, 1883, 1-36.

7 Along the lines that, when someone has made a will even only for a part of his property, he has not died "intestatus"; *cf., e.g.*, A. Brinz, *Lehrbuch der Pandekten*, Vol. III, 2nd edn., 1886, p. 73, n. 11, relating to Table V, 3; see also Lenel, 1913, p. 127 (the rule clearly appears to have been part of the most ancient law). For a different view see, recently, Gómez Ródenas, 2015, pp. 846-853.

8 Jhering, 1906, p. 149.

9 S. Bolla, 'Beiträge zur Lehre vom Zusammentreffen mehrerer Berufungsgründe im Erbrecht', *Österreichische Juristenzeitung*, Vol. 2, 1947, pp. 88-91, 88; P. Voci, *Diritto Ereditario Romano*, Vol. I, 2nd edn., 1967, pp. 498 f.

to the property left by the latter"?[10] Are we dealing with a remnant of the old idea that several heirs originally constituted a kind of community of joint owners (*Gesamthand*)?[11] Did it relate to the Roman *favor testamenti*?[12] Is this an instance where, what had in classical Roman law been no more than a pragmatic interpretational guideline, came to be converted into a firm rule of law in the postclassical period?[13] Or are we dealing, the other way around, with a classical rule of law which was gradually abandoned in postclassical times?[14] Whatever the answer to these questions may be, it is clear that there were exceptions to this rule. One of them concerned the military will,[15] another certain instances of succession "against the will"[16] – as, for example, when *sui heredes* other than a son in the testator's power had been "passed over" (i.e, not mentioned) in the testator's will, for in such cases the will remained valid while the persons passed over were given a share in the estate next to whoever had been instituted in the will.[17] Papinian did not regard it as "absurd" in such cases that the deceased was "pro parte" taken to be "intestatus".[18]

2. An important function of the "nemo pro parte"-rule, on a practical level, seems to have been to keep the number of heirs small.[19] After all, a *pater familias* had once been

10 C.F. Koch, *Allgemeines Landrecht für die Preußischen Staaten, Kommentar in Anmerkungen*, Part I/2, 2nd edn., Berlin 1856, p. 6, n. 2. *Cf.* also Schirmer, 1863, p. 53 f. ("Since none the less the legal unity of the estate requires a disposition on the part of the testator of the whole, the legal interpretation felt compelled to extend the will, only partly expressed, to the whole"); Huschke, 1834, pp. 272-300 ("necessary indivisibility of the institution of an heir"); *cf* also Coppola, 2012, under 2 *in fine*.

11 See Zimmermann, 1984, p. 237.

12 See Meylan, 1946, p. 195.

13 F. Schulz, *Classical Roman Law*, 1951 (reprint 1992), [447]; see also Rabel, 1955, pp. 203, 216.

14 M. Kaser, *Das römische Privatrecht, Zweiter Abschnitt*, 2nd edn., 1975, pp. 476 f.

15 The words "inter paganis" (= among persons who are not soldiers) in Pomponius D. 50, 17, 7, refers to that exception; *cf.* also Ulpian D. 29, 1, 6: "... miles enim pro parte testatus potest decedere, pro parte intestatus"; Inst. 2, 14, 5. For discussion, see Huschke, 1834, pp. 326-333; Amiet, 1883, pp. 48 f. Military wills were exempted from most of the specifically Roman rules on will making; this appears to have been in order to accommodate non-Romans fighting in the army: Kaser, 1971, p. 681.

16 See, *e.g.*, Huschke, 1834, pp. 336-358; Schirmer, 1863, pp. 55-60; Voci, 1967, pp. 497 f.; Kaser, 1971, p. 677; F. Longchamps de Bérier, *Law of Succession*, 2011, pp. 55-57. Schirmer draws attention to the fact that this is just an apparent exception from the rule; the concurrence of testamentary and intestate succession is not brought about by the testator but by means of an external interference with his disposition; *cf.* also von Vangerow, 1867, § 397, p. 10: "Always, however, our rule just wants to say that a concurrence between testate and intestate heirs must not emanate from the testator himself"; C.F.A. Koeppen, *System des heutigen römischen Erbrechts*, Jena, 1862, p. 278 ("... do not fall into the scope of this rule"); Amiet, 1883, pp. 49 f.

17 Gaius inst. 2, 124.

18 Papinian D. 5, 2, 15, 2: "... nec absurdum videtur pro parte intestatum videri" (relating to a case where a son has brought the *querela inofficiosi testamenti* against two heirs and has been successful against the one but not against the other). On the text by Papinian (and on Ulpian D. 5, 2, 24) Schmidlin, 1975, pp. 70-91, 73-83.

19 See, *e.g.*, Kaser, 1971, p. 677; and see Wieacker, 1941, pp. 41 f.; Zimmermann, 1984, p. 239; A. Wacke, 'Erbrechtliche Sukzession als Persönlichkeitsfortsetzung?', *Zeitschrift der Savigny-Stiftung für Rechtsgeschichte (Romanistische Abteilung)*, Vol. 123, 2006, pp. 197-247, 234; von Schmitt, *Begründung*, 1879, p. 158, n. 3 from the previous page; J.P. Schmidt, *Itinera Hereditatis: Strukturen der Nachlassabwicklung in historisch-vergleichender Perspektive*, 2021, § 3 A.III., C.II.1. Practical considerations for maintaining the rule in clas-

permitted to appoint a single heir of his farm (and to provide for the other members of his household in other ways) in order to prevent the undesirable consequences of a farm being split up so often that its individual parts could no longer be managed profitably – a state of affairs which had been brought about because already by the time of the Twelve Tables it had been recognized that each member of a family community could request its dissolution by means of an *actio familiae erciscundae*.[20] In the course of the further development of Roman law the position of the heir (*heres*) underwent a functional change insofar as his task of winding up the estate came to be emphasized.[21] This is reflected in the idea that the institution of an heir was regarded as the foundational element of each and every will;[22] wills merely containing legacies[23] thus became inadmissible. If, when a testator disposed only of part of his estate, the rules on intestate succession had governed the remainder of the estate, clarity and concentration of the process of winding up the estate would have been seriously jeopardized.[24] This was a beneficial effect, if not the reason, for the "nemo pro parte"-rule, for the application of that rule did not lead to the will containing the disposition of only part of the estate being invalid but to that part which had not been disposed of accruing to the heir(s) determined by will.[25]

In later times it has frequently been said that that legal consequence runs counter to the deceased's intentions.[26] Such criticism, however, would appear to be unjustified in case

---

sical law are also advanced by Jhering, 1906, p. 151; Koeppen, 1862, p. 274; Amiet, 1883, pp. 50-58; *cf.* also Schulz, 1992, [447]. Other authors attributed the survival of the rule to the conservatism of the Roman lawyers; see, *e.g.*, Dernburg, 1901, § 57, p. 101: the old rule had been "incrusted" into the law.

20 Wieacker, 1941, pp. 15-25; Kaser, 1971, pp. 91-109; by way of overview see also R. Zimmermann, 'Protection against Being Passed Over or Disinherited in Roman Law', in: K.G.C. Reid, M.J. de Waal, R. Zimmermann (Eds.), *Mandatory Family Protection*, 2020, pp. 1-4.

21 For a detailed discussion, see Schmidt, 2021, § 3 A.III.

22 Gaius inst. 2, 229: "… testamenta vim ex institutione heredis accipiunt, et ob id velut caput et fundamentum intellegitur totius testamenti heredis institutio"; Inst. 2, 20, 34. See, *e.g.*, Kaser, 1971, pp. 685-690; M. Kaser, R. Knütel, S. Lohsse, *Römisches Privatrecht*, 21st edn., 2019, p. 81; J.P. Meincke, *Römisches Privatrecht*, 3rd edn., 2019, p. 81; Th. Rüfner, 'Testamentary Formalities in Roman Law', in: K.G.C. Reid, M.J. de Waal, R. Zimmermann (Eds.), *Testamentary Formalities*, 2011, pp. 1-26, 9 f.

23 Lenel, 1913, pp. 120-137; Rabel, 1955, pp. 203 f.; Kaser, 1971, pp. 107 f.

24 Von Schmitt, *Begründung*, 1879, p. 158; Schmidt, 2021, § 3 A.III.

25 Ulpian D. 28, 5, 13, 2 f.; Inst. 2, 14, 7; Kaser, 1971, p. 687. For more details, see Zimmermann, 1984, pp. 236-240.

26 See, *e.g.*, S. Stryk, *Tractatus de cautelis testamentorum*, Halle and Magdeburg, 1708, Chapter I, § 13; 'Suarez amtliche Vorträge bei der Schluß-Revision des Allgemeinen Landrechts', (*von Kamptz*) *Jahrbücher für die Preußische Gesetzgebung, Rechtswissenschaft und Rechtsverwaltung*, Vol. 41, 1833, p. 79; F. Edler von Zeiller, *Commentar über das allgemeine bürgerliche Gesetzbuch für die gesammten Deutschen Erbländer der Österreichischen Monarchie*, Vol. II, Wien and Triest, 1812, § 534; Dernburg, 1901, § 57, p. 100; F. Mommsen, *Entwurf eines Deutschen Reichsgesetzes über das Civilrecht nebst Motiven*, Braunschweig 1876, p. 145; von Schmitt, *Begründung*, 1879, p. 159; *cf.* also Borysiak, 2016, pp. 80 f. Kaser, 1971, p. 677, states that in most cases accrual conforms more closely to the (presumed) intention of the testator than intestate succession; but see also Kaser, 1975, p. 476 ("… only rarely conforms to the testator's will").

scenarios where the testator had inadvertently not disposed of his entire estate.[27] The same is true in situations where the testator had expressly disinherited his intestate heirs.[28] Apart from that the Roman lawyers may have asked themselves why, if the testator had not wanted to disinherit his intestate heirs, he had not included them in his will for the remainder of his property.[29] In view of the great significance of the institution of an heir, at any rate, they could not be regarded as having been tacitly instituted.[30] Augustin Leyser, therefore, had a point when he wrote that whoever admits the intestate heirs to succeed together with the testamentary heirs is more likely to contravene the deceased's will than he who accepts the accrual solution adopted by the Roman lawyers.[31]

3. In France the rule of "nemo pro parte testatus pro parte intestatus decedere potest" was not received, at least in the *pays de droit coutumier*;[32] in view of the fact that determination of an heir by (human) will was not regarded as acceptable[33] this is hardly surprising. The *Code civil*, therefore, describes the will as "un acte par lequel le testateur dispose ... de tout ou partie de ses biens ...".[34] The Austrian code also expressly turns against the Roman rule when it states that testamentary and intestate succession are allowed to exist side by side.[35] It thus confirms an Imperial Decree of 1789 formally renouncing the "nemo pro parte"-rule that had originally been received but then no longer applied in practice.[36] It had also not been taken to be in line with the *aequitas canonica*.[37] The latter view probably contributed to the fact that, by the 17th century, it had come to be regarded as obsolete also in other parts of Europe. The Netherlands provide a good example in that respect. "In Belgio generali consuetudine passim receptum est, ut unicuique liceat partim testato, partim intestato decedere contra dispositionem iuris Romani" is what Arnoldus

27 See also Lenel, 1913, p. 128; Meylan, 1946, pp. 191, 195; Kaser, 1971, p. 687 (text to fn. 18); Zimmermann, 1984, pp. 239 f.

28 Kaser, 1971, p. 677.

29 See Rabel, 1955, p. 216; Schulz, 1992, [447].

30 So, as far as Roman law is concerned, F.L. von Keller, *Pandekten*, 1861, § 460; von Schmitt, *Begründung*, 1879, pp. 157 f.

31 *Meditationes ad Pandectas*, Vols. V and VI, 3rd edn., Leipzig and Wolfenbüttel, 1744, Spec. CCCLXI, V.

32 See, *e.g.*, J.-Ph. Lévy, A. Castaldo, *Histoire du droit civil*, 2nd edn., 2010, [865]; Helmut Coing, *Europäisches Privatrecht*, Vol. I, 1985, p. 563; see also P. Blondel, *La transmission à cause de mort et des droits extra-patrimoniaux et des droits patrimoniaux à caractère personnel*, 1969, p. 15, drawing attention to the fact that the *droit coutumier* influenced the *droit écrit*.

33 "Institution d'héritier n'a lieu": Lévy/Castaldo, 2010, [865], [906]. This was based on the old idea that the selection of the heir is the work of God, not man: "Solus Deus heredem facere potest, non homo": see, *e.g.*, R. Zimmermann, 'Heres Fiduciarius?: Rise and Fall of the Testamentary Executor', in: R. Helmholz, R. Zimmermann (Eds.), *Itinera Fiduciae: Trust and Treuhand in Historical Perspective*, 1998, pp. 267-304, 292.

34 Art. 895 *Code civil*; see also Art. 1002 *Code civil*.

35 § 534 ABGB; on which, see von Zeiller, 1812, § 534.

36 G. Wesener, *Geschichte des Erbrechts in Österreich seit der Rezeption*, 1957, pp. 30 f. (against Bolla, 1947, pp. 88 f.)

37 Coing, 1985, p. 573.

Vinnius writes in his *Commentar on* Justinian's *Institutes*,[38] and he refers, in that respect, to Petrus Gudelinus, Paulus Christinaeus, and Franciscus Zypaeus; and at a different place he writes that this Roman subtlety was also rejected in the Northern Netherlands (and, of course, in France).[39] Groenewegen, in this context, draws attention to the fact that a concurrence of testamentary and intestate heirs is bound to exist wherever the institution of forced heirship is recognized.[40]

4. Also in Germany, according to Mühlenbruch, lawyers did not really reconcile themselves to the "nemo pro parte"-rule and "for the most part took it to be a useless Roman subtlety".[41] The question of its application was thus, he wrote, disputed.[42] But at a different place in the same volume of Glück's *Commentary* he states that exceptions from the rule can only be admitted as far as they had been recognized in Roman law.[43] Samuel Stryk, while also condemning the rule in strong terms ("absurditas subtilitatis illius Romanae", "ratione juris gentium plane non congruen[s]", "nihil Veritatis naturalis continet"),[44] did not maintain that it was not applicable.[45] Augustin Leyser expressly confirms its application. The pandectist textbooks also treat the rule as constituting valid law.[46] As far as the various "particular (statutory) laws" prevailing in late 18th and 19th century Germany are concerned, some of them expressly recognized the rule,[47] while most ignored it; occasionally it was also specifically rejected.[48] The latter position was the

38 A. Vinnius, *In quatuor libros institutionum Imperialium commentarius*, Leiden, 1709, lib. II, tit. XIV, 5, [7].

39 Vinnius, 1709, lib. II, tit. XIV, 9, [5]. And see S. van Groenewegen van der Made, *Tractatus de legibus abrogatis et inusitatis in Hollandia vicinisque regionibus*, Leiden, 1649, Inst. lib. II, tit. XIV, § 9; J. Voet, *Commentarius ad Pandectas*, Frankfurt/Oder and Halle, 1698/1704, lib. XXVIII, tit. I, I. For further references concerning Dutch law, see Zimmermann, 1984, pp. 251-254 (where attention is also drawn to the fact that in Friesland, characteristically, the "nemo pro parte"-rule was applied).

40 Groenewegen, 1649, lib. II, tit. XIV, § 9, [3].

41 *Ausführliche Erläuterung der Pandekten nach Hellfeld: ein Commentar für meine Zuhörer*, 63 Vols., Erlangen, from 1790 onwards, after Glück's death continued by Ch.F. Mühlenbruch *et al.*, Vol. 38, Erlangen, 1835, p. 80.

42 See also Coing, 1985, p. 563.

43 Glück/Mühlenbruch, 1835, p. 345.

44 1708, Chapter I, §§ 13-15.

45 In his great work *Usus modernus pandectarum, Continuatio Tertia*, 2nd edn., Halle and Magdeburg, 1713, lib. XVIII, tit. V, § VIII, Stryk merely states that according to a number of statutory laws (and to Belgian customary law) a testator can die partly *testatus* and partly *intestatus*, but he does not maintain that for the Empire.

46 This is said expressly by Windscheid/Kipp, 1906, § 537, p. 213; *cf.* also C.G. Wächter, *Pandekten* (edited by O. von Wächter), Part II, 1881, § 273 III; von Vangerow, 1867, § 397; Schirmer, 1863, p. 63, n. 37; Amiet, 1883, pp. 73 f. The Roman rule did not apply to contracts of inheritance; here the rules on intestate succession were seen to be excluded only as far as the testator's will extended: Windscheid/Kipp, 1906, § 537, p. 213; Koeppen, 1862, pp. 285-290; Schirmer, 1863, p. 63; Amiet, 1883, pp. 74-77; O. Stobbe, *Handbuch des Deutschen Privatrechts*, Vol. V, 1./2. edn., 1885, § 278 II, n. 4.

47 This was the case in the *Codex Maximilianeus Bavaricus Civilis*, Part III, Chapter III, § 9.

48 See the overview in Glück/Mühlenbruch, 1835, pp. 80-82; Stobbe, 1885, § 278 II, n. 4; von Schmitt, *Begründung*, 1879, pp. 157 f.

one adopted by the Prussian code of 1794; it allowed the testator "to provide for only part of his estate, and to leave matters with regard to the remainder to intestate succession".[49] The Saxonian Civil Code also turned away from the Roman rule as was apparent from several of its provisions;[50] and so did the Zurich Code of Private Law.[51] The reason why "nemo pro parte" was to be abandoned, according to Friedrich Mommsen,[52] was that it led to decisions which are "in flagrant conflict" with the principle, on which recognition of testamentary succession is based.[53]

5. For Gottfried von Schmitt, the author of the "Preliminary Draft" of a law of succession for the German Empire (and, by means of that Draft, the person principally responsible for shaping Book 5 of the *Bürgerliches Gesetzbuch* (BGB)) the decision could therefore no longer be subject to doubt; the testator's will must be the supreme law which, however, by retaining the Roman rule, could easily be turned into its opposite.[54] von Schmitt therefore stated by way of general principle that the testamentary heir was to succeed to the deceased's property in preference to the intestate heirs "as far as he is instituted".[55] And he added a number of rules which were intended to guide the judge as to when and to what extent

---

49 § 45 I 12 PrALR. For comment, see F. Förster, M.E. Eccius, *Preußisches Privatrecht*, Vol. IV, 7th edn., Berlin, 1897, § 251, p. 402. A different view was taken by Koch, 1856, who remarks *à propos* § 45 I 12 PrALR: "In that case intestate succession takes place". What he meant to say was that intestate succession governs the entire estate, in view of the fact that Koch regarded the institution of a person for part of the estate as the bequest of a legacy (p. 7, n. 6). He therefore wrote that the rule "nemo pro parte testatus pro parte intestatus decedere potest" only *appears* to have been abandoned (even if he concedes that it was in fact intended to be abandoned). Koch refers to Suarez' (1833) very pronounced criticism of the rule ("... preposterous, even absurd consequences", "... extremely shocking for a sound human mind") and adds, in a somewhat patronizing tone (p. 6, n. 2): "The idea which Suarez exhibits with regard to the concepts of heir, institution of the heir, and jus accrescendi, significantly reduces, right from the start, any expectation concerning his achievements as a legislator in the law of succession; whoever regards the jus accrescendi as an arbitrary invention, does not have any insight into how things really fit together". Koch's criticism of Suarez is based on the former's view of the heir as the person who "is always the successor of the deceased for the entirety (per universitatem)".

50 §§ 2011, 2014, 2174, 2176 Saxonian Civil Code; see E. Siebenhaar, *Commentar zu dem bürgerlichen Gesetzbuche für das Königreich Sachsen*, Vol. III, Leipzig 1869, pp. 226 f.

51 §§ 2076, 2085 Zurich Code of Private Law; see A. Schneider, *Das Zürcherische Erbrecht: Auf der Grundlage des Bluntschli'schen Kommentars allgemeinfaßlich erläutert*, 2nd edn., 1901, § 1008, sub 3.

52 Mommsen, 1876, p. 145. Friedrich Mommsen, not to be confused with Theodor Mommsen, was a Prussian professor and practitioner who published, in 1876, a Draft Imperial Statute concerning the law of succession, with motivations; it had been prompted by a prize contest initiated by the Law Society in Berlin. The provisions in that draft pertinent in the present context are §§ 4, 17 and 141. § 4 corresponds to § 534 ABGB.

53 Meylan, 1946, p. 179 states in general terms: "Dans nos idées modernes, la règle nemo pro parte ne se justifie évidemment à aucun égard". See previously also, from the point of view of the Law of Reason, Hugo Grotius, *De jure belli ac pacis libre tres*, reprint 1993, II, XII, XXVI: "... ea regula e solis Romanorum moribus pendeat, neque apud alios populos locum habeat."

54 von Schmitt, *Begründung*, 1879, pp. 158 f.

55 § 46, in: G. von Schmitt, *Entwurf eines Rechtes der Erbfolge für das Deutsche Reich*, 1879, in: W. Schubert (Ed.), *Die Vorlagen der Redaktoren für die erste Kommission zur Ausarbeitung eines Bürgerlichen Gesetzbuches, Erbrecht*, Part I, 1984, p. 9.

the intestate heirs could be taken into account next to the heirs instituted by the testator.[56] Again, in drafting these rules, the foremost consideration was "sola voluntas in testando spectatur".[57] In the process of the further deliberations leading up to the BGB these rules were changed,[58] but the rejection of the "nemo pro parte"-rule[59] and the pre-eminence of the testator's will in determining the legal consequences of the institution of an heir for only part of the deceased's property were (and are) no longer in doubt.[60]

It is, therefore, possible to say with Otto Lenel that, like Roman law modern German law also does not recognize a real concurrence of testate and intestate succession: the intestate heirs are only called to succeed "because we think that this corresponds to the presumed intention of the testator"[61] – while in cases where this assumption is not justified, the remainder has to accrue to the testamentary heirs. The difference from Roman law in antiquity only lies in the fact that today account is taken not only of the will expressed by the testator but also of his unexpressed will, as far as it can be gleaned from the circumstances, no matter whether it leads to the remainder of the estate going to the intestate heirs or to a proportional increase of the shares of the heirs instituted by the

56 §§ 47-52, in: von Schmitt, *Entwurf*, 1879, p. 9; for comment, see von Schmitt, *Begründung*, 1879, pp. 161-164.

57 von Schmitt, *Begründung*, 1879, p. 159.

58 In particular, § 50 of the Draft by von Schmitt became § 1790 of the First Draft of the BGB (see 'Motive', in: B. Mugdan, *Die gesammten Materialien für das Bürgerliche Gesetzbuch für das Deutsche Reich*, Vol. V, 1899, p. 34), § 1961 of the Second Draft of the BGB (see 'Protokolle', in Mugdan, 1899, p. 554), and ultimately § 2088 BGB, i.e., the rule which is normally cited for the rejection of the "nemo pro parte"-rule; see, *e.g.*, G. Otte, in: *J. von Staudingers Kommentar zum Bürgerlichen Gesetzbuch*, revised edn., 2019, § 2088, [1]; M. Rudy, in *Münchener Kommentar zum Bürgerlichen Gesetzbuch*, Vol. 11, 8th edn., 2020, [1]. But see also already §§ 1948, 1951 BGB: K. Muscheler, *Erbrecht*, 2010, [825]. § 2088 states: "(1) If the deceased has instituted only one heir and has limited that institution to a share of the estate, intestate succession ensues as far as the remainder is concerned. (2) The same applies if the deceased has instituted several heirs, limiting each of them to a share of the estate, with the shares not exhausting the entire estate". § 2089 BGB, on the other hand, provides that "if the heirs instituted by the deceased are, according to the will of the deceased, to be the only heirs, then, if each of them has been instituted for a share, and the shares do not exhaust the entire estate, the shares are to be increased proportionally." This rule is sometimes seen to apply (only) in cases where the deceased in drawing up his will has made a mistake: *Staudinger*/Otte, 2019, § 2089, [1].

59 German law, in this respect, is part of the international mainstream: the "nemo pro parte"-rule has in most countries been abandoned; see K.G.C. Reid, M.J. de Waal, R. Zimmermann, 'Intestate Succession in Historical and Comparative Perspective', in: K.G.C. Reid, M.J. de Waal, R. Zimmermann, *Intestate Succession*, 2015, pp. 442-512, 445; Borysiak, 2016, pp. 73-80. Exceptions are Catalonia and San Marino. On Catalonia (as well as Mallorca and Menorca) see S. Cámara Lapuente, 'Intestate Succession in Spain', in: Reid/De Waal/Zimmermann, 2015, pp. 96-117, 97; Gómez Ródenas, 2015, pp. 858-863. On San Marino, see M. Reinkenhof, *Die Anwendung von ius commune in der Republik San Marino*, 1997, pp. 128, 191, 262 f. Reinkenhof draws attention to the fact that the rule is practically very widely evaded by way of a codicillary clause.

60 See today, *e.g.*, D. Weidlich, in: *Palandt, Bürgerliches Gesetzbuch*, 79th edn., 2020, § 2088, [1].

61 Lenel, 1913, p. 128, n. 2.

deceased.[62] Even today, therefore, "nemo pro parte testatus pro parte intestatus decedere potest", not taken as a strict rule of law but as a maxim conveniently reflecting the pre-eminence of the testator's intention, may be said adequately to reflect the legal position in cases where the testator does not dispose of his entire estate. If he fails to do so by mistake, it is clear that the accrual solution corresponds to his presumed intention.[63] If he specifically disinherits his intestate heirs, accrual would also appear to come closer to what he would have wanted. In cases where he does not specifically disinherit the intestate heirs, various case-scenarios are imaginable. If it can be established, for example, that the testator had provisionally only disposed of part of his estate and had died before he was able to dispose of the remainder, it can often be assumed that he did not want his intestate heirs to succeed. If, on the other hand, he had quite consciously left part of his estate undisposed of, he can be seen, by implication, to have wanted to favour his intestate heirs.[64] Substantially, therefore, they succeed because the testator had wanted them to be his heirs.

If a legal system wishes to lay down a rule, it has to deal with situations where the process of interpretation does not lead to a result one way or the other. In Germany, this is § 2088 BGB: The remainder goes to the intestate heirs.[65] Swiss law also says that, if the testator has only disposed of part of his estate, the remainder falls to the intestate heirs.[66] But in Switzerland, too, the matter is in the first place one of interpretation.[67] Is the rule prevailing today in Germany and Switzerland, as well as apparently in Austria,[68] more sensible than the Roman accrual solution? This is not beyond doubt. Some more comparative research would be welcome – maybe by Sjef van Erp after his retirement?[69]

---

62 Lenel, 1913, p. 128, n. 2. *Cf.* already Leyser, 1744, Spec. CCCLXI, V, emphasizing that "quod in verbis est omissum, suppleatur ex tacita testatoris intentione". (For Leyser, the intention of the testator must be presumed to be that he "cui res adscripta fuit unica, totum patrimonium, quod defunctus eidem destinabat, assignatur". Differently, *e.g.*, Dernburg, 1901, § 57, p. 101 f.).

63 See, for example, Bayerisches Oberstes Landesgericht, *Zeitschrift für das gesamte Familienrecht*, 1990, pp. 1278 f.

64 If, however, the testator in a first will had instituted A and then, in a second will, B for half of his estate, the other half not disposed of in the second will should go to A rather than the intestate heirs; this example is provided by Lenel, 1913, p. 128, n. 2. Interestingly, this case is specifically dealt with in § 713 ABGB, though with a different result: the other half is to go to the intestate heir.

65 See, *e.g.*, *Staudinger*/Rudy, 2020, § 2088, [1] ("supplementary rule", if, by way of interpretation, no contrary will on the part of the testator can be established).

66 § 481 (1) ZGB. On Swiss law prior to the unification of private law, see Meylan, 1946, pp. 197-200.

67 D. Staehlin, in: H. Honsell, N.P. Vogt, T. Geiser, *Basler Kommentar, Zivilgesetzbuch II*, 4th edn., 2011, Art. 481, [2].

68 P. Apathy, M. Neumayr, in: H. Koziol, P. Bydlinsky, R. Bollenberger, *ABGB: Kurzkommentar*, 6th edn. 2020, § 560, [3]. The Austrian Civil Code used to have two rules of interpretation concerning accrual for cases where the testator had not disposed of his entire estate, which were regarded as unsatisfactory (see R. Welser, 'Einsetzung auf bestimmte Teile und gesetzliches Erbrecht', *Österreichische Notariatszeitung*, 1997, pp. 345-348, 345 f.) and have been deleted in the course of the reform of 2015/2017.

69 Sjef, after all, is not only one of the leading comparative property lawyers in the world, but also the author of the general report on 'New Developments in Succession Law" for the XVIIth Congress of the International Academy of Comparative Law in 2007 (Utrecht).

***

In the corridor outside of my office there is a picture showing John Fleming and his wife, Sjef, Barbara and Jim Gordley, and me. We are sitting round a table outside John Fleming's country house in the Sonoma valley. We had driven out from San Francisco for the day: I was then Robbins Collection Fellow at the University of California at Berkeley, and Sjef was also there for a period of research. The day, a sunny Saturday in the spring of 1994, was memorable, in the first place, for the kindness and the generosity of the Flemings. I also remember a car coming from the other direction with too much speed, swerving onto our lane and hitting John's car right in front of us. The culprit, a smart lawyer from San Francisco, and rather arrogant and high-handed at first, became amenable to admitting his guilt when he was told by Jim Gordley, in no uncertain terms, that he had crashed into the car of one of the world's most famous tort lawyers. But the day, now so far back, was also the beginning of my friendship with Sjef. We have met and co-operated on many different occasions since then, and it is a great pleasure to wish him well when he retires from the University of Maastricht, a place to which I am fortunate enough to have close ties.

Part VIII
Marital Property Law

De Objectieve Conflictregels van de EU Verordening Huwelijksvermogensstelsels

*Sabine Heijning**

1 Inleiding

Tussen Sjef en mij bestaat een bijzondere band. Sjef was de eerste medewerker ipr van het Notarieel Juridisch Bureau, dat een onderdeel van de Koninklijke Notariële Broederschap vormde en ik was de laatste medewerker ipr bij het bureau. De inhoud van het werk bestond uit het adviseren van (kandidaat)notarissen over vragen van ipr en buitenlands recht. In 2015 is het Notarieel Juridisch Bureau opgeheven en sindsdien ben ik verbonden aan *het* Notarieel Bureau. De inhoud van het werk is hetzelfde gebleven: praktische ipr-adviezen geven.

In 1985 schreef Sjef in de serie studiepockets privaatrecht uitgegeven door Tjeenk Willink zijn eerste boek met de titel Internationaal huwelijksvermogensrecht. Nu hij afscheid gaat nemen als hoogleraar bij de universiteit Maastricht, zal ik hem eren met een artikel over het huidige internationale huwelijksvermogensrecht.

Sinds 1985 is er veel gebeurd binnen het internationale huwelijksvermogensrecht. Er bestond toen een onderscheid tussen huwelijken waarop het Haags Huwelijksgevolgenverdrag 1905[1] van toepassing was en huwelijken waarop het verdrag 1905 niet van toepassing was. Daarnaast had de Hoge Raad nieuwe conflictregels geformuleerd in het Chelouche/van Leer-arrest,[2] maar onduidelijk was toen of die regels ook met terugwerkende kracht konden worden toegepast op huwelijken die niet onder het verdrag van 1905 vielen. Het verdrag van 1905 had namelijk geen universele werking en kon alleen worden toegepast indien verwezen werd naar het huwelijksvermogensrecht van een verdragsland. In 1985 was de tekst van het Haags Huwelijksvermogensverdrag

* Verbonden aan het Notarieel Bureau.

1 Het verdrag betreffende de wetsconflicten met betrekking tot de gevolgen van het huwelijk ten opzichte van de rechten en verplichtingen der echtgenoten in hun persoonlijke betrekkingen en ten opzichte van hun goederen gesloten te 's-Gravenhage op 17 juli 1905, Stb. 1907, 198, voor Nederland in werking getreden op 22 augustus 1912 en opgezegd per 23 augustus 1977.

2 HR 10 december 1976, NJ 1977, 275 m.nt. J.C. Schultsz.

1978[3] vastgesteld, maar het verdrag was nog niet in werking getreden. Sjef leidde de lezers langs alle obstakels en dilemma's van toen.

Op 1 september 1992 is het Haags Huwelijksvermogensverdrag 1978 in werking getreden en recent is op 29 januari 2019 de EU verordening huwelijksvermogensstelsels[4] van toepassing geworden voor Nederland en 17 andere lidstaten[5] in het kader van de voortgezette samenwerking. Kortom, de horizon van het internationaal huwelijksvermogensrecht zag er in 1985 heel anders uit dan die in 2021.

De praktijkjuristen wisten na inwerkingtreding van het verdrag 1978 mede hun weg te vinden aan de hand van het Trema rapport,[6] waarin de toenmalige conflictregels werden verduidelijkt met vele praktijkvoorbeelden. Daarmee werd bereikt dat binnen Nederland praktijkvragen op dezelfde manier werden beantwoord.

De verordening kent zoals alle EU verordeningen geen toelichtend rapport, maar wordt begeleid door Overwegingen, waarin een aantal uitgangspunten en begrippen nader worden toegelicht. In deze bijdrage zal ik mijn licht laten schijnen over de objectieve conflictregels van de verordening aan de hand van de overwegingen en de literatuur met de bedoeling te beoordelen of de praktijkjurist voldoende handvaten heeft om de conflictregels toe te passen.

2 Inhoud Objectieve Conflictregels

Als geen of een ongeldige rechtskeuze is uitgebracht door de echtgenoten, bepaalt artikel 26 lid 1 van de verordening welk huwelijksvermogensrecht van toepassing is.

> **Artikel 26**
> 1. Bij gebreke van een rechtskeuzeovereenkomst overeenkomstig artikel 22, is op het huwelijksvermogensstelsel het recht van toepassing van de staat:
> a) waar de echtgenoten na de huwelijkssluiting hun eerste gewone gemeenschappelijke verblijfplaats hebben, of, bij gebreke daarvan,
> b) waarvan beide echtgenoten op het tijdstip van de huwelijkssluiting de nationaliteit bezitten, of, bij gebreke daarvan,

3 Het verdrag inzake het recht dat van toepassing is op het huwelijksvermogensregime gesloten te 's-Gravenhage op 14 maart 1978, Trb. 1988,130.

4 Voluit geheten verordening (EU) 2016/1103 van de raad van 24 juni 2016 tot uitvoering van de nauwere samenwerking op het gebied van de bevoegdheid, het toepasselijke recht en de erkenning en tenuitvoerlegging van beslissingen op het gebied van huwelijksvermogensstelsels gepubliceerd in PbEU 2016, L 183/1.

5 Dat zijn naast Nederland: België, Bulgarije, Cyprus, Tsjechië, Duitsland, Griekenland, Spanje, Frankrijk, Kroatië, Italië, Luxemburg, Malta, Oostenrijk, Portugal, Slovenië, Finland en Zweden.

6 Werkgroep IPR van de Nederlandse Vereniging voor Rechtspraak, Knelpunten in het internationaal huwelijksvermogensrecht, Trema 1995, afl. 5, blz. 128-165.

c) waarmee de echtgenoten samen op het tijdstip van de huwelijkssluiting de nauwste band hebben, met inachtneming van alle omstandigheden.

De conflictregels uit artikel 26 lid 1 van de verordening lijken simpel:
- er wordt aangeknoopt bij het recht van de eerste gemeenschappelijke gewone verblijfplaats van de echtgenoten (sub a).
- Ontbreekt deze dan geldt het recht van de gemeenschappelijke nationaliteit van de echtgenoten (sub b).
- Ontbreekt ook deze dan geldt het recht waarmee de echtgenoten op het tijdstip van de huwelijkssluiting de nauwste banden hebben op grond van alle omstandigheden (sub c).

Ik behandel hierna de begrippen gewone verblijfplaats, eerste gemeenschappelijke gewone verblijfplaats, gemeenschappelijke nationaliteit en de nauwste band. Vervolgens ga ik onder 3 in op de exceptie gegeven in artikel 26 lid 3 van de verordening.

2.1 Gewone Verblijfplaats

De gewone verblijfplaats vormt een autonoom begrip in de Europese Verordeningen. Volgens vaste rechtspraak van het Europese Hof wordt in algemene zin onder gewone verblijfplaats verstaan, "de plaats waar de betrokkene het permanente centrum van zijn belangen heeft gevestigd met de bedoeling daaraan een vast karakter te verlenen, waarbij voor de vaststelling van de gewone verblijfplaats rekening moet worden gehouden met de feitelijke omstandigheden die voor dat begrip bepalend zijn".[7] In het bijzonder is aan dat begrip invulling gegeven in rechtspraak over de gewone verblijfplaats van minderjarigen bij de toepassing van artikel 8 van de Verordening Brussel IIbis.[8] In de uitspraak Mercredi[9] nam het hof aan dat naast de fysieke aanwezigheid van het minderjarige kind in een lidstaat, op grond van andere factoren moest worden aangetoond dat deze aanwezigheid niet tijdelijk of toevallig is en dat de verblijfplaats van de minderjarige een zekere integratie in een sociale en familiale omgeving tot uitdrukking brengt. Het hof geeft als omschrijving van de gewone verblijfplaats van de minderjarige in die uitspraak: de plaats waarmee een sociale en familiale integratie is, waarbij wordt gewezen op aspecten als duur,

7 Zie bijvoorbeeld: Hof van Justitie 26 april 2007 C-392/05 r.o. 55-57 ECLI:EU:C:2007:251 (accijns op motorvoertuigen) en Hof van Justitie 15 september 1994 C-452/93 P ECLI:EU:C:1994:332 r.o. 22 (ambtenarenrecht en ontheemdingstoeslag).

8 Verordening (EG) nr. 2201/2003 van de Raad van 27 november 2003 betreffende de bevoegdheid en de erkenning en tenuitvoerlegging van beslissingen in huwelijkszaken en inzake de ouderlijke verantwoordelijkheid, en tot intrekking van Verordening (EG) nr. 1347/2000, P. L 338.

9 Hof van Justitie van de Europese Gemeenschappen 2 april 2009 C-523/0727.

regelmatigheid, omstandigheden en redenen van verhuizing, nationaliteit van het kind, schoolbezoek, talenkennis. De rechter dient rekening te houden met alle feitelijke omstandigheden van de zaak in concreto.

Ook kan aansluiting gezocht worden bij de uitleg die de EU Erfrechtverordening[10] geeft aan het begrip gewone verblijfplaats in overweging 23:

> "Gelet op de toenemende mobiliteit van burgers en teneinde de goede rechtsbedeling in de Europese Unie te waarborgen en ervoor te zorgen dat er een echte band bestaat tussen de erfopvolging en de lidstaat waar de bevoegdheid wordt uitgeoefend, moet deze verordening erin voorzien dat de gewone verblijfplaats van de erflater op het tijdstip van zijn overlijden als algemeen aanknopingspunt geldt voor het bepalen van zowel de bevoegdheid als het toepasselijke recht. Om de gewone verblijfplaats vast te stellen, dient de aangezochte autoriteit zich een oordeel te vormen over alle aspecten die het leven van de erflater in de jaren voor zijn overlijden en op het tijdstip van overlijden hebben gekenmerkt, en daarbij alle relevante feitelijke elementen in beschouwing te nemen, in het bijzonder de duur en de regelmatigheid van de aanwezigheid van de erflater in de betrokken staat en de omstandigheden van en de redenen voor het verblijf. De aldus vastgestelde gewone verblijfplaats moet, uit het oogpunt van de specifieke doelstellingen van deze verordening, duiden op een nauwe en duurzame band met de betrokken staat."[11]

Deze overweging uit de Erfrechtverordening kan als richtsnoer dienen wat onder de gewone verblijfplaats bij de toepassing van de verordening huwelijksvermogensrecht dient te worden verstaan. Ik vorm deze voor het huwelijksvermogensrecht als volgt om:

> Om de gewone verblijfplaats van een echtgenoot op het moment van de huwelijkssluiting vast te stellen dient de aangezochte autoriteit zich een oordeel te vormen over alle aspecten die het leven van de echtgenoot op het moment van de huwelijkssluiting hebben gekenmerkt en daarbij alle relevante feitelijke elementen in beschouwing te nemen, in het bijzonder de duur en de regelmatigheid van de aanwezigheid van de echtgenoot in de betrokken staat en de omstandigheden van en de redenen voor het verblijf. De aldus vastgestelde

10 Verordening (EU) nr. 650/2012 van het Europees Parlement en de Raad van 4 juli 2012 betreffende de bevoegdheid, het toepasselijke recht, de erkenning en de tenuitvoerlegging van beslissingen en de aanvaarding en de tenuitvoerlegging van authentieke akten op het gebied van erfopvolging, alsmede betreffende de instelling van een Europese erfrechtverklaring, Pb EU L 201/207.

11 Zie voor de invulling van de gewone verblijfplaats de Conclusie van AG M. Campos Sánchez-Bordona van 26 maart 2020 inzake de zaak E.E. C-380/19, ECLI:EU:C:2020:230.

gewone verblijfplaats moet, uit het oogpunt van de specifieke doelstellingen van deze verordening, duiden op een nauwe en duurzame band met de betrokken staat.

In het huwelijksvermogensrecht dient de gewone verblijfplaats voor beide echtgenoten afzonderlijk te worden vastgesteld.

Voor de doelstelling van de verordening kan gekeken worden naar de eerste zin van overweging 49:

> "Indien er geen rechtskeuze is gemaakt, dient deze verordening, met het oog op het verenigen van voorspelbaarheid en rechtszekerheid met de realiteit waarin het paar leeft, geharmoniseerde collisieregels te introduceren om volgens een reeks aanknopingspunten te bepalen welk recht op het gehele vermogen van de echtgenoten van toepassing is."

2.2 Eerste Gemeenschappelijke Gewone Verblijfplaats

Op basis van het bovenstaande vormt zich een aardig beeld wat de gewone verblijfplaats inhoudt in het EU recht, maar daarmee is nog niet gezegd wat de *eerste gemeenschappelijke* gewone verblijfplaats van de echtgenoten inhoudt. Overweging 49 geeft de volgende toelichting op dit begrip:

> "Zo dient de eerste gemeenschappelijke gewone verblijfplaats van de echtgenoten kort na de huwelijkssluiting het eerste criterium te vormen vóór het recht van de gemeenschappelijke nationaliteit van de echtgenoten op het tijdstip waarop het huwelijk werd gesloten."

Vooralsnog weet niemand wat met 'kort' bedoeld wordt. Is sprake van een eerste gemeenschappelijke gewone verblijfplaats, als de echtgenoten zich in dezelfde staat vestigen 1 week na het huwelijk, of 1 maand of 1 jaar? Met name voor huwelijken waar één van de echtgenoten de nationaliteit bezit van een niet EU-lidstaat kan het vaak lang duren, voordat de andere echtgenoot zich in Nederland kan vestigen. Een periode van 1 jaar of langer komt in mijn adviespraktijk vaak voor.

De expertgroep van het Landelijk Overleg Vakinhoud Familie- en Jeugdrecht van de rechtbanken in Nederland (LOVF) heeft op 19 juni 2019[12] een aanbeveling gegeven, waarin

12 De aanbeveling LOVF inzake het eerste huwelijksdomicilie onder de Europese Verordening huwelijksvermogensstelsels dd. 19 juni 2019 is gepubliceerd in EB 2019/94.

aangenomen wordt dat enige rek zit tussen de huwelijkssluiting en de periode waarbinnen de echtgenoten hun eerste gemeenschappelijke gewone verblijfplaats na de huwelijkssluiting kunnen vestigen. De werkgroep stelt voor deze periode op 6 maanden[13] te stellen en slechts op grond van zeer bijzondere omstandigheden van die periode af te wijken.

Die termijn van 6 maanden was ook het uitgangspunt in de tremanormen over het Haags Huwelijksvermogensverdrag 1978.[14]

Ik hoop dat het Europese Hof van Justitie het woord 'kort' nader zal uitleggen. Voor de praktijk is deze onduidelijkheid lastig om mee om te gaan, met name omdat er bij gebreke aan nadere toelichting ruimte is voor iedere lidstaat om te bepalen wat 'kort' inhoudt.

2.2.1 Onder Één Dak

Dienen echtgenoten daadwerkelijk ook onder hetzelfde dak te wonen binnen een bepaalde staat om een gemeenschappelijke gewone verblijfplaats aan te nemen? Schrijvers nemen aan dat vestiging in dezelfde staat voldoende is en dat eenzelfde adres niet absoluut is voorgeschreven.[15] Daaraan moet wel de voorwaarde worden verbonden dat in die staat uniform recht geldt en voor verschillende gebieden binnen die staat geen afzonderlijk recht geldt. Woont bijv. binnen Spanje een echtgenoot in Madrid en de ander in Barcelona, dan is de inhoud van het huwelijksvermogensrecht van Catalonië afwijkend van het algemene Castiliaanse recht, zoals dat geldt voor Madrid.[16]

2.2.2 Duur van de Eerste Gemeenschappelijke Gewone Verblijfplaats

Een andere vraag die gesteld kan worden is hoe lang de echtgenoten in een bepaalde staat hun eerste gemeenschappelijke gewone verblijfplaats dienen te hebben. Dient die gewone verblijfplaats van enige duur te zijn en hoe lang dan? De verordening geeft daar geen nadere regels voor.

Uit overweging 23 van de Erfrechtverordening kan worden afgeleid dat de duur van de gewone verblijfplaats voorafgaande aan het overlijden van belang is om een nauwe band

13 Waarbij de expertgroep zich baseert op buitenlandse literatuur: D. Coester-Waltjen, 'Die objektive Anknüpfung des ehegüterstatus', in: A. Dutta/J. Weber (red.), Die Europäischen Güterrechtsverordnungen, C.H. Beck 2017, p. 53; B. Heiderhoff, Die EU Güterrechtsverordnungen, IPRax 2018/1 p. 5, en P. Lagarde, in: U. Bergquist e.a. (red.), The EU Regulation on matrimonial and patrimonial property, Oxford University Press 2019, p. 112).

14 Zie het rapport van de Werkgroep IPR van de Nederlandse Vereniging voor Rechtspraak, Knelpunten in het internationaal huwelijksvermogensrecht, Trema 1995, afl. 5, blz. 150.

15 Zie Frohn, WPNR 7216/2018, p. 896; D. Coester-Waltjen, Die objektive Anknüpfung des Ehegüterstatuts, in: A. Dutta/J. Weber (red.), Die Europäische Güterrechtsverordnungen (München: C.H. Beck 2017), p. 52, en The EU Regulations on the property regimes of international couples, Viarengo/Franzina (red), Cheltenham Edward Elgar publishing 2020, p. 248.

16 De vraag welk recht binnen Spanje geldt is afhankelijk van de *vecindad civil* van de echtgenoten, zie artikel 14 van de Spaanse Codigo Civil. Daarop ga ik in dit artikel niet verder in.

met die staat te verkrijgen. De duur kan volgens de Erfrechtverordening een belangrijke rol spelen. Uit de rechtspraak van het Europese Hof van Justitie over de gewone verblijfplaats van minderjarigen bij de toepassing van Brussel IIbis wordt afgeleid dat een zekere sociale integratie vereist wordt. De integratie neemt immers in het algemeen toe met de duur van het verblijf. Er is naar mijn mening niet echt een bepaalde duur aan de gewone verblijfplaats bij de toepassing van de verordening huwelijksvermogensrecht te geven, wetende dat er na de huwelijkssluiting nog zoveel kan veranderen.

Echtgenoten kunnen een nieuwe gewone verblijfplaats vestigen na de huwelijkssluiting, wanneer zij bijvoorbeeld voor werk of om economische redenen naar een ander land verhuizen. Daarbij wordt vereist dat de echtgenoten de intentie hebben om hun gewone verblijfplaats permanent in een bepaalde staat te vestigen, maar de intentie alleen is onvoldoende. De intentie dient gemanifesteerd te worden door duidelijke bewijzen, zoals bijvoorbeeld de aankoop of huur van een woning, het sluiten van een arbeidscontract enz.. Echtgenoten kunnen ook kort ergens anders gaan wonen voor bijv. werk, maar hun huis aanhouden in het land van hun eerste gemeenschappelijke gewone verblijfplaats, bijv. wanneer zij vaak terugkeren naar dat huis in weekends of vakanties. Dan kan de intentie om zich elders te vestigen ontbreken.

Weten de echtgenoten op het moment van de huwelijkssluiting dat zij binnen een periode van enkele weken of maanden zich gezamenlijk in een andere staat zullen vestigen, dan kan de eerste gemeenschappelijke gewone verblijfplaats aangenomen worden in die nieuwe staat. Ook hier speelt dat onduidelijk is, wat 'kort' betekent in overweging 49. Ik stel voor ook hier de termijn van 6 maanden aan te houden zoals voorgesteld door het LOVF.

Wat verder te denken van gepensioneerde echtgenoten die de helft van het jaar in Nederland verblijven en de andere helft in bijvoorbeeld Spanje? Ik neem aan dat het uitgangspunt is dat iedere echtgenoot één gewone verblijfplaats dient te hebben en er niet twee kan hebben.[17]

Is sprake van een onvrijwillig verblijf in een ander land, bijv. in een gevangenis of psychiatrische inrichting op basis van een gedwongen opname, dan bestaat geen intentie om in die staat te willen verblijven en wordt aangenomen dat de gewone verblijfplaats in die staat niet gevestigd wordt.[18] De intentie dient gebaseerd te zijn op de vrije wil van de echtgenoten.

Ik concludeer dat de lengte van het verblijf in een bepaalde staat geen grote rol speelt voor de bepaling van de eerste gemeenschappelijke gewone verblijfplaats, aangezien de

17 Vergelijk het arrest van het Europese Hof van Justitie, 16 juli 2020, ECLI:EU:C:2020:569, zaak C-80/19 inzake E.E.

18 Zie The EU Regulations on the property regimes of international couples, Viarengo/Franzina (red) Cheltenham Edward Elgar publishing 2020, p. 249.

intentie en het feitelijk verblijf van groter belang zijn dan de duur. Enkele weken ergens wonen, kunnen dus al voldoende zijn.[19] Zie echter ook hierna onder 3 over de exceptie van artikel 26 lid 3 van de verordening.

2.3 *Gemeenschappelijke Nationaliteit*

De tweede trede van de conflictenladder van artikel 26 lid 1 sub b van de verordening verwijst wanneer de echtgenoten geen eerste gemeenschappelijke gewone verblijfplaats hebben, naar het recht van de gemeenschappelijke nationaliteit die de echtgenoten bezitten op het moment van de huwelijkssluiting.

Het uitgangspunt is dat de echtgenoten de gemeenschappelijke nationaliteit bezitten op het moment van de huwelijkssluiting. Of een persoon een nationaliteit bezit wordt bepaald door de nationaliteitswetgeving van die staat. De verordening lijkt geen ruimte te geven om een gemeenschappelijke nationaliteit aan te nemen, indien een echtgenoot de nationaliteit van de ander verwerft binnen enkele maanden na de huwelijkssluiting, maar helemaal zeker is dat niet.[20]

In de vorige eeuw bezaten vele nationaliteitswetgevingen een regel dat de vrouw door het huwelijk van rechtswege de nationaliteit van haar man verwierf. Vele staten hebben die regel inmiddels laten vervallen, maar de regel bestaat nog steeds in een aantal staten.[21] Verkrijgt de vrouw van rechtswege de nationaliteit van de man door het huwelijk, dan neem ik aan dat sprake is van een gemeenschappelijke nationaliteit.

2.3.1 Dubbele Nationaliteit in Nederland

Er bestaan weinig vragen, indien de echtgenoten ieder dezelfde nationaliteit bezitten, bijvoorbeeld beiden echtgenoten hebben krachtens geboorte de Duitse nationaliteit en bezitten die nationaliteit op het moment van de huwelijkssluiting. Bezitten de echtgenoten meer dan één gemeenschappelijke nationaliteit, dan bepaalt artikel 26 lid 2 van de verordening dat het bepaalde in lid 1 sub b niet van toepassing is:

> Als de echtgenoten op het tijdstip van de huwelijkssluiting meer dan één gemeenschappelijke nationaliteit bezitten, is alleen het bepaalde in lid 1, onder a) en c), van toepassing.

---

19 Vergelijk bij de toepassing van artikel 4 lid 1 van het Haags Huwelijksvermogensverdrag 1978, Joppe, Huwelijksvermogensrecht, Praktijkreeks IPR, 3e herziene uitgave, 2010, p. 92.

20 Zie Frohn, WPNR 7216/2018, p. 897 en Lagarde, The EU regulation on matrimonial and patrimonial property, onder redactie van Bergquist, Damascelli, Frimston, Lagarde en Reinhartz, Oxford university press, 2019, p. 113.

21 Zo kwam ik onlangs nog de regel tegen in de nationaliteitswetgeving van Iran.

Overweging 50 geeft een nadere toelichting over de meervoudige nationaliteit:

> "Waar in deze verordening verwezen wordt naar nationaliteit als aanknopingspunt, is de vraag hoe een persoon met een meervoudige nationaliteit moet worden beschouwd een prealabele vraag die buiten de werkingssfeer van deze verordening valt en moet worden overgelaten aan het nationaal recht alsmede, indien van toepassing, internationale overeenkomsten, met volledige inachtneming van de algemene beginselen van de Unie. Deze overweging mag geen gevolgen hebben voor de geldigheid van een rechtskeuze die in overeenstemming met deze verordening is gemaakt."

Naar mijn mening heeft de gemeenschappelijke nationaliteit in ieder geval geen waarde, indien beide echtgenoten ieder dezelfde dubbele nationaliteit bezitten.[22] De verordening legt geen effectiviteits- of realiteitstoets op.[23] Dat is overigens ook het uitgangspunt van artikel 15 van het Haags Huwelijksvermogensverdrag 1978.

Voorbeeld 1 Een echtpaar trouwt op 17 juli 2019 in Turkije. Hij verblijft in Duitsland voor werk en zij woont in Nederland. Zij bezitten ten tijde van de huwelijkssluiting beiden zowel de Turkse als de Nederlandse nationaliteit. Dan kan niet één van de dubbele nationaliteit voorgaan, aangezien niet op effectiviteit of realiteit getoetst mag worden. Er is dan geen gemeenschappelijke nationaliteit. Artikel 26 lid 1 sub b kan op deze echtgenoten niet worden toegepast, en dat betekent dat moet worden bepaald met welk recht de echtgenoten de nauwste banden hebben in de zin van artikel 26 lid 1 sub c.

Maar de vraag is hoe we moeten handelen als één echtgenoot een dubbele nationaliteit bezit en de andere echtgenoot een enkele nationaliteit bezit op het moment van de huwelijkssluiting, terwijl één van die nationaliteiten dezelfde is.

Overweging 50 bepaalt dat de vraag over de gemeenschappelijke nationaliteit een prealabele vraag is en buiten de werkingssfeer van de verordening valt. Nederland kent geen nadere regels welke nationaliteit voorgaat, indien een persoon een dubbele nationaliteit bezit in andere verdragen of wetten of in Boek 10 BW. De Uitvoeringswet Verordening huwelijksvermogensstelsels en Verordening Partnerschapsvermogensstelsels[24] regelt de dubbele nationaliteit ook niet. Ik concludeer dat Nederland dergelijke nadere regels niet heeft.

---

22 Zie ook Knot, FJR 2016/56.

23 Zie ook Frohn, WPNR 7216/2018, p. 897.

24 Stb. 2018, 332.

Voorbeeld 2 Een Nederlands/Marokkaanse vrouw trouwt op 10 oktober 2020 in Marokko met een Marokkaanse man. Zij woont in Nederland en hij woont in Marokko. Er is geen sprake van een eerste gemeenschappelijke gewone verblijfplaats in de zin van artikel 26 lid 1 sub a van de verordening. Is dan sprake van een gemeenschappelijke nationaliteit in de zin van artikel 26 lid 2 sub b van de verordening?

De Nederlandse autoriteiten kunnen naar mijn mening aannemen dat de echtgenoten een gemeenschappelijke Marokkaanse nationaliteit bezitten. Er geldt dan Marokkaans huwelijksvermogensrecht.

Ook komt het voor dat echtgenoten beiden een dubbele nationaliteit bezitten, waarvan er één dezelfde is en de andere verschillend.

Voorbeeld 3 Een man die zowel de Israëlische als de Russische nationaliteit bezit, trouwt op 1 maart 2019 met een vrouw, die de Israëlische en Nederlandse nationaliteit bezit. Zij wonen niet samen. Ik neem aan dat de Israëlische nationaliteit de gemeenschappelijke nationaliteit is en het feit dat iedere echtgenoot daarnaast nog een andere nationaliteit bezit niet relevant is.

2.3.2 Dubbele Nationaliteit in Andere Lidstaten

Andere EU lidstaten die gebonden zijn aan de verordening kennen wel regels over de gemeenschappelijke nationaliteit in hun wetgeving. Ik noem er hier een aantal.

Artikel 3 § 2 van de Belgische ipr-wet bepaalt:

> De verwijzingen in deze wet naar de nationaliteit van een natuurlijke persoon die twee of meer nationaliteiten heeft, beoogt:
> 1. de Belgische nationaliteit, indien zij een van die nationaliteiten is;
> 2. in de andere gevallen, de nationaliteit van de Staat waarmee die persoon, alle omstandigheden in acht genomen, de nauwste banden heeft, inzonderheid rekening houdend met zijn gewone verblijfplaats.

Artikel 5 lid 1 van het Duitse EGBGB bepaalt:

> Wird auf das Recht des Staates verwiesen, dem eine Person angehört, und gehört sie mehreren Staaten an, so ist das Recht desjenigen dieser Staaten anzuwenden, mit dem die Person am engsten verbunden ist, insbesondere durch ihren gewöhnlichen Aufenthalt oder durch den Verlauf ihres Lebens. Ist die Person auch Deutscher, so geht diese Rechtsstellung vor.

§ 9 lid 1 van de Oostenrijkse IPR-wet bepaalt:

> Das Personalstatut einer natürlichen Person ist das Recht des Staates, dem die Person angehört. Hat eine Person neben einer fremden Staatsangehörigkeit auch die österreichische Staatsbürgerschaft, so ist diese maßgebend. Für andere Mehrstaater ist die Staatsangehörigkeit des Staates maßgebend, zu dem die stärkste Beziehung besteht.

Artikel 9 lid 9 van het Spaanse BW bepaalt:

> A los efectos de este capítulo, respecto de las situaciones de doble nacionalidad previstas en las leyes españolas se estará a lo que determinen los tratados internacionales, y, si nada estableciesen, será preferida la nacionalidad coincidente con la última residencia habitual y, en su defecto, la última adquirida.
> Prevalecerá en todo caso la nacionalidad española del que ostente además otra no prevista en nuestras leyes o en los tratados internacionales. Si ostentare dos o más nacionalidades y ninguna de ellas fuera la española, se estará a lo que establece el apartado siguiente.

Artikel 19 lid 2 van het Italiaanse BW bepaalt :

> Se la persona ha piu' cittadinanze, si applica la legge di quello tra gli Stati di appartenenza con il quale essa ha il collegamento piu' stretto. Se tra le cittadinanze vi e' quella italiana, questa prevale.

Wij zien hier dat in vele lidstaten de regel geldt voor personen met een dubbele nationaliteit dat de eigen nationaliteit voorgaat, en in andere gevallen bepaalt dient te worden welke nationaliteit de effectieve nationaliteit is.

Ik signaleer hier twee kwesties.

De eerste vraag is of daarmee in alle gevallen de eigen nationaliteit mag voorgaan. De algemene beginselen van de Europese Unie dienen volgens overweging 50 in acht te worden genomen. Artikel 18 van het Verdrag betreffende de werking van de Europese Unie (afgekort: VWEU)[25] verbiedt discriminatie op grond van nationaliteit:

25 Publicatieblad 26.10.2012 van de Europese Unie C 326/47.

> Binnen de werkingssfeer van de Verdragen en onverminderd de bijzondere bepalingen, daarin gesteld, is elke discriminatie op grond van nationaliteit verboden.
> Het Europees Parlement en de Raad kunnen, volgens de gewone wetgevingsprocedure, regelingen treffen met het oog op het verbod van bedoelde discriminaties.

Artikel 18 VWEU bepaalt dat de eigen nationaliteit niet boven die van de andere lidstaten mag worden gesteld. Dit verbod heeft consequenties voor de verordening huwelijksvermogensrecht.

Voorbeeld 4 Een Duitse man die ook de Franse nationaliteit bezit trouwt op 19 december 2019 met een vrouw, die de Franse nationaliteit bezit. Hij woont in Duitsland en zij in Frankrijk. Welk huwelijksvermogensrecht geldt er op grond van artikel 26 lid 1 van de verordening?

Aannemende dat de eerste gemeenschappelijke gewone verblijfplaats in de zin van artikel 26 lid 1 sub a van de verordening ontbreekt, dienen wij te bepalen of deze echtgenoten een gemeenschappelijke nationaliteit bezitten. De Nederlandse autoriteiten toetsen de nationaliteit van de man niet en zullen aannemen dat de echtgenoten een gemeenschappelijke Franse nationaliteit bezitten. In het Franse recht is mij geen regel bekend dat de eigen nationaliteit voorgaat en neem ik aan dat hier hetzelfde uitgangspunt geldt.

De Duitse autoriteiten zullen een ander uitgangspunt hanteren. Zij zullen aannemen op grond van artikel 5 lid 1 EGBGB dat de Duitse nationaliteit voorgaat. Dan hebben de man en de vrouw vanuit Duits gezichtspunt geen gemeenschappelijke nationaliteit.[26] De vraag is dan of daarmee geen sprake is van discriminatie van de Franse nationaliteit van de man op grond van artikel 18 VWEU. Dan zou artikel 26 lid 1 sub b wellicht niet toegepast mogen worden. Dat betekent dat de Duitse autoriteiten zullen aannemen dat de echtgenoten geen gemeenschappelijke nationaliteit bezitten in de zin van artikel 26 lid 1 sub b van de verordening. De uitkomst is dan dat artikel 26 lid 1 sub c moet worden toegepast en de Duitse autoriteiten zullen dan moeten bepalen met welke recht de echtgenoten op grond van alle omstandigheden op het moment van de huwelijkssluiting de nauwste banden hebben.

De Franse autoriteiten zullen in dit voorbeeld aannemen dat de echtgenoten een gemeenschappelijke Franse nationaliteit bezitten.

---

26 Zie Coester-Waltjen in Die Europäischen Güterrechtsverordnungen onder redactie van Dutta/Weber, Beck, 2017, p. 53-54.

Voorbeeld 5 Gaan wij terug naar het voorbeeld 2 van de twee Marokkanen, waarvan de vrouw ook de Nederlandse nationaliteit bezit. Stel zij zouden ook vermogen in Duitsland bezitten en de Duitse autoriteiten zouden moeten vaststellen welk huwelijksvermogensrecht van toepassing is, dan zou worden aangenomen op grond van artikel 5 EGBGB dat de Nederlandse nationaliteit van de vrouw haar effectieve nationaliteit is gezien haar woonplaats. Discriminatie van de nationaliteit van lidstaten in de zin van artikel 18 VWEU speelt hier niet. Dat betekent dat de echtgenoten geen gemeenschappelijke nationaliteit bezitten in de zin van artikel 26 lid 1 sub b van de verordening en dat betekent dat de conflictregel ex artikel 26 lid 2 sub c dient te worden toegepast, inhoudende dat moet worden vastgesteld met welke recht de echtgenoten op grond van alle omstandigheden op het moment van de huwelijkssluiting de nauwste banden bezitten.

Dat brengt de vraag met zich mee hoe om te gaan met het feit dat afhankelijk van de lidstaat die de ipr-regel moet toepassen er een andere uitkomst van artikel 26 lid 1 sub b van de verordening wordt gegeven? Die verschillende uitkomsten van de ipr regels zijn in strijd met de uitgangspunten van de verordening, zie overweging 49:

> "Indien er geen rechtskeuze is gemaakt, dient deze verordening, met het oog op het verenigen van voorspelbaarheid en rechtszekerheid met de realiteit waarin het paar leeft, geharmoniseerde collisieregels te introduceren om volgens een reeks aanknopingspunten te bepalen welk recht op het gehele vermogen van de echtgenoten van toepassing is."

Het Europese Hof van Justitie zou hier meer duidelijkheid in moeten aanbrengen hoe om te gaan met de gemeenschappelijke nationaliteit van echtgenoten. Nu het bepalen van de gemeenschappelijke nationaliteit aan de lidstaten wordt overgelaten, kan dat leiden tot de toepassing van verschillend huwelijksvermogensrecht in de verschillende lidstaten. Dat is niet de bedoeling van de verordening.

2.4 *De Nauwste Band*

Bezitten echtgenoten ten tijde van de huwelijkssluiting noch een eerste gemeenschappelijke gewone verblijfplaats noch een gemeenschappelijke nationaliteit, dan schrijft artikel 26 lid 1 sub c voor dat het recht van toepassing is waarmee de echtgenoten samen op het tijdstip van de huwelijkssluiting de nauwste band hebben, met inachtneming van alle omstandigheden.

Overweging 49 geeft de volgende toelichting:

> "Bij de toepassing van dit laatste criterium moeten alle omstandigheden in ogenschouw worden genomen en moet worden verduidelijkt dat deze banden in overweging moeten worden genomen zoals die bestonden ten tijde van de huwelijkssluiting."

Dit begrip is een autonoom begrip binnen het EU recht. Er mag alleen gekeken worden naar de omstandigheden zoals die waren op het moment van de huwelijkssluiting en dat betekent dat latere omstandigheden daarna geen rol van betekenis mogen spelen, bijvoorbeeld de omstandigheid dat de echtgenoten later wel zijn gaan samenwonen in een bepaalde staat.

Volgens verschillende schrijvers moet het daarbij steeds gaan om omstandigheden die beide echtgenoten betreffen, zoals de plaats waar zij samenwonen voor of na de huwelijksvoltrekking (die, niet aangemerkt kan worden als de eerste gemeenschappelijke gewone verblijfplaats op of kort na de huwelijkssluiting), de plaats waar het gemeenschappelijk vermogen is gelegen en indien zij gescheiden van elkaar wonen, de plaats waar de echtgenoten elkaar bezoeken, samen de weekends doorbrengen of vakantie houden. Verder kunnen meespelen de maatschappelijke en sociale betrekkingen (werk, studie) van de echtgenoten, hun religie en de taal die zij samen spreken.[27] Ook is van belang de intentie om als echtpaar ergens samen te wonen en de mate waarin daar uitvoering aan is gegeven. De plaats van de huwelijkssluiting is van minder belang. Dat aanknopingspunt heeft in het eerste conceptontwerp van de verordening gestaan, maar is in de definitieve tekst komen te vervallen. De lijst van omstandigheden staat niet vast, maar de omstandigheden moeten wel beide echtgenoten en hun vermogen betreffen.

Het komt vaak voor in de Nederlandse notariële praktijk dat het recht van de nauwste band moet worden vastgesteld in de gevallen dat er een huwelijk gesloten wordt met een buitenlandse echtgenoot met een nationaliteit van een niet EU-lidstaat. Het vreemdelingenrecht in Nederland is streng en wanneer de echtgenoot eerst het inburgeringsexamen moet halen alvorens hij een verblijfsvergunning kan krijgen, kan het lang duren, voordat hij in Nederland zijn gewone verblijfplaats kan vestigen.

Ook komt het voor dat de echtgenoten zich tijdens de duur van het huwelijk nooit ergens samen gevestigd hebben. Vaak zijn er weinig gemeenschappelijke factoren aanwezig bij deze categorie echtgenoten. Dan blijft vaak over het land waar zij elkaar ontmoet hebben, of het meest samen verblijven of waar het huwelijk is gesloten. De bepaling met welke staat de echtgenoten de nauwste banden hebben, is dan ook niet eenvoudig te noemen.

27 Zie Frohn, WPNR 7216/2018, p. 897-898, Coester-Waltjen in Die Europäischen Güterrechtsverordnungen onder redactie van Dutta/Weber, Beck, 2017, p. 54, en Martiny in The EU Regulations on the property regimes of international couples, Viarengo/Franzina (red) (Cheltenham Edward Elgar publishing 2020, p. 254.

Naar mijn mening heeft de plaats van het gemeenschappelijk vermogen van de echtgenoten in de praktijk weinig aanknopingswaarde. Meestal bezitten echtgenoten op het moment van de huwelijkssluiting nog geen gemeenschappelijk vermogen, tenzij zij voorafgaande aan het huwelijk al hebben samengewoond. Vermogen dat zij tijdens huwelijk gezamenlijk verkrijgen dient buiten beschouwing te worden gelaten. Het gaat immers om de nauwste banden op het moment van de huwelijkssluiting. Bovendien is de vraag of vermogen tot een gemeenschap behoort, ook afhankelijk van de vraag welk recht op het huwelijksvermogensrecht van toepassing is.

Ook op het punt hoe de nauwste band kan worden bepaald hoop ik dat het Europese Hof van Justitie nadere uitleg kan geven, aan de hand van welke omstandigheden de nauwste band kan worden vastgesteld.

3 Uitzondering lid 3 van artikel 26

De verordening introduceert in het derde lid van artikel 26 een uitzondering op de toepassing van het volgens de aanknoping aan de eerste gemeenschappelijke gewone verblijfplaats toepasselijke recht. De regel luidt:

> Bij wijze van uitzondering kan de rechterlijke instantie die bevoegd is om te beslissen in zaken betreffende het huwelijksvermogensstelsel, op verzoek van een van de echtgenoten beslissen dat het recht van een andere staat dan de staat waarvan het recht uit hoofde van lid 1, onder a), van toepassing is, op het huwelijksvermogensstelsel van toepassing is, op voorwaarde dat de verzoeker aantoont dat:
> a. de echtgenoten in die andere staat hun laatste gemeenschappelijke verblijfplaats hadden gedurende een beduidend langere periode dan in de in lid 1, onder a), bedoelde staat, en
> b. beide echtgenoten zich hebben verlaten op het recht van die andere staat bij het regelen of plannen van hun vermogensrechtelijke betrekkingen.
>
> Het recht van die andere staat is van toepassing vanaf de huwelijkssluiting, tenzij één echtgenoot het daar niet mee eens is. In dat geval sorteert het recht van die andere staat effect vanaf het tijdstip van vestiging op de laatste gemeenschappelijke gewone verblijfplaats in die staat.
> De toepassing van het recht van de andere staat laat de rechten die derden ontlenen aan het op grond van lid 1, onder a), toepasselijke recht onverlet.

> Dit lid is niet van toepassing wanneer de echtgenoten huwelijkse voorwaarden hebben gemaakt vóór het tijdstip van vestiging op de laatste gemeenschappelijke gewone verblijfplaats in die andere staat.

Overweging 51 geeft de volgende toelichting:

> Met betrekking tot de aanwijzing van het recht dat bij gebreke van een rechtskeuze en van huwelijkse voorwaarden op het huwelijksvermogensstelsel van toepassing is, dient de rechterlijke instantie van een lidstaat, op verzoek van een van de echtgenoten, in uitzonderlijke gevallen, als de echtgenoten voor een lange tijd naar de staat van hun gewone verblijfplaats zijn verhuisd, te kunnen beslissen dat het recht van die staat van toepassing kan zijn indien de echtgenoten zich erop hebben verlaten. In geen geval kan de wijziging afbreuk doen aan de rechten van derden.

De uitzondering mag alleen worden toegepast, wanneer sprake is van een eerste gemeenschappelijke gewone verblijfplaats in de zin van artikel 26 lid 1 sub a van de verordening. Waarom daar voor gekozen is, blijkt niet uit de verordening. Dat betekent dat de uitzondering niet geldt, indien bij gebreke aan een gemeenschappelijke eerste gewone verblijfplaats aangeknoopt wordt aan het gemeenschappelijke nationale recht volgens artikel 26 lid 1 sub b of het recht van de nauwste band volgens artikel 26 lid 1 sub c. Aanknoping aan de gemeenschappelijke nationaliteit en de nauwste band is dus onveranderlijk, tenzij de echtgenoten zelf daar wijziging in aanbrengen door staande huwelijk een rechtskeuze uit te brengen. Naar mijn mening is dat een gemiste kans. Zeker voor de huwelijken waarop het recht van de nauwste band van toepassing is, zou wanneer de echtgenoten later tijdens het huwelijk wel een gewone verblijfplaats vestigen, de exceptie recht kunnen doen aan de onzekerheid die eerst bestond.

3.1 Voorwaarden Gesteld aan de Exceptie Clausule

De echtgenoten of één van hen dienen/dient in een gerechtelijke procedure een beroep op de uitzondering te doen, Die procedure zal veelal een echtscheiding betreffen. 26 lid 3 verbindt twee voorwaarden aan de exceptie.

Wat betreft de voorwaarde onder a doet zich de vraag voor hoeveel langer een beduidend langere periode is dan de periode van de eerste gemeenschappelijke gewone verblijfplaats?

Overweging 51 heeft het over 'een lange tijd' dat de echtgenoten verhuisd zijn naar de staat van hun gewone verblijfplaats. Dat geeft op dit punt niet meer duidelijkheid. Coester-Waltjen geeft als voorbeelden 6 maanden tegen 2 jaar, die zij als beduidend langer aanmerkt, maar niet 20 jaar tegen 22 jaar.[28] Martiny geeft als richtsnoer dat tenminste 2/3 deel van de tijd voldoende is om te kunnen spreken van een beduidend langere periode.[29] De rechter zal enige vrijheid bezitten om aan te nemen wanneer een periode beduidend langer is, maar ook hier hoop ik dat het Europese Hof van Justitie verduidelijking van dit begrip zal geven.

Wat betreft de voorwaarde onder b doet zich de vraag voor hoe echtgenoten kunnen aantonen dat zij uit zijn gegaan van dat andere recht. Martiny noemt overeenkomsten of financiële transacties tussen echtgenoten of tussen echtgenoten en derden.[30] Lagarde noemt de verwerping of aanvaarding van een bepaalde transactie na de wijzing van hun gemeenschappelijke gewone verblijfplaats of een brief tussen de echtgenoten of een echtgenoot en de schoonouders.[31] Ik kom hier onder 3.5. op terug.

3.2 Terugwerkende Kracht

Het uitgangspunt is dat bij een geslaagd beroep op de exceptie gedurende de gehele duur van het huwelijk het recht van de nieuwe gewone verblijfplaats geldt. Is één van de echtgenoten het daar niet mee eens, dan kan de rechter ook bepalen dat het recht van die andere staat effect sorteert vanaf het tijdstip van vestiging van de laatste gemeenschappelijke gewone verblijfplaats in die staat. Dan kan het dus zo zijn dat eerst recht A van toepassing is en dan recht B. Dan krijgen die echtgenoten te maken met het zogenaamde wagonstelsel, dat wij ook kennen uit artikel 7 van het Haags Huwelijksvermogensverdrag 1978. Hoe wenselijk is dat?

Rechten van derden die ontleend zijn aan het op grond van lid 1 sub a toepasselijke recht worden onverlet gelaten, zo bepaalt artikel 26 lid 3. De terugwerkende kracht werkt niet tegenover derden. Derden zijn dus gebonden aan de uitkomst van artikel 26 lid 1 sub a. van de verordening. Moeten we concluderen dat derden wel geacht worden de regels te kennen, terwijl dat niet geldt voor echtgenoten? Zie hierna onder 3. 5.

---

28 Coester-Waltjen in Die Europäischen Güterrechtsverordnungen onder redactie van Dutta/Weber, Beck, 2017, p. 56.

29 Martiny in The EU Regulations on the property regimes of international couples, Viarengo/Franzina (red) (Cheltenham Edward Elgar publishing 2020, p. 257.

30 Martiny in The EU Regulations on the property regimes of international couples, Viarengo/Franzina (red) (Cheltenham Edward Elgar publishing 2020, p. 257.

31 Zie Lagarde, The EU regulation on matrimonial and patrimonial property, onder redactie van Bergquist, Damascelli, Frimston, Lagarde en Reinhartz, Oxford university press, 2019, p. 116.

3.3 *Beperking van een Geslaagd Beroep op de Exceptie*

Op de uitzondering is in lid 3 laatste zin een beperking aangebracht. De exceptie clausule is niet van toepassing, indien de echtgenoten huwelijkse voorwaarden hebben gemaakt vóór het tijdstip van vestiging van de laatste gemeenschappelijke gewone verblijfplaats in die eerste staat. Bevatten de huwelijkse voorwaarden een uitdrukkelijke rechtskeuze, dan komt de echtgenoten sowieso geen beroep op artikel 26 lid 3 van de verordening toe. In het geval de rechtskeuze niet geldig is of de huwelijkse voorwaarden geen rechtskeuze bevatten, komt de echtgenoten ook geen beroep op de exceptie clausule toe. Dan gelden tussen hen de huwelijkse voorwaarden binnen de kaderwet van artikel 26 lid 1 van de verordening.

Het kan natuurlijk ook zo zijn dat echtgenoten huwelijkse voorwaarden hebben gemaakt nadat zij zich in een andere staat hebben gevestigd. Er zijn rechtstelsels waarbinnen het mogelijk is met terugwerkende kracht huwelijkse voorwaarden te maken en daarmee kunnen echtgenoten regelen dat vanaf de datum van de huwelijkssluiting één bepaald stelsel tussen hen geldt. Het Nederlandse recht staat dat echter niet toe, zie artikel 1:120 BW, waarin bepaald wordt dat tijdens het huwelijk gemaakte of gewijzigde huwelijkse voorwaarden beginnen te werken op de dag, volgende op die waarop de akte is verleden. Het is mogelijk in de akte een later tijdstip aan te wijzen, maar een eerder tijdstip is niet mogelijk. Naar mijn mening behoort het tot de taak van de Nederlandse notaris het oude stelsel indien bestaande uit enige vorm van een gemeenschap, te verdelen. Dat betekent dat de notaris dan ook het toepasselijke recht zal moeten vaststellen. Ook dan is er geen ruimte om de exceptie te kunnen toepassen naar mijn mening.

3.4 *Overlijden en de Bevoegdheid van de Notaris in het Algemeen*

Een huwelijk kan naast echtscheiding ook door overlijden van één van de echtgenoten ontbonden worden. Ik neem aan dat indien er een geschil is tussen de langstlevende echtgenoot en de erfgenamen over de vraag welk huwelijksvermogensrecht van toepassing is, de rechter ook kan beslissen of er met succes een beroep op de exceptieclausule kan worden gedaan. De notaris is niet bevoegd om daarover te beslissen, tenzij hij als gerecht wordt aangemerkt. Artikel 3 lid 2 van de verordening geeft een definitie voor gerecht:

> Voor de toepassing van deze verordening wordt verstaan onder "gerecht": de rechterlijke instanties, en alle andere instanties en rechtsbeoefenaren met bevoegdheid ter zake van huwelijksvermogensstelsels, die rechterlijke functies vervullen dan wel handelen op machtiging van of onder toezicht van een rechterlijke instantie, mits deze andere instanties en rechtsbeoefenaren

> waarborgen bieden inzake onpartijdigheid en het recht van partijen om te worden gehoord en mits hun beslissingen overeenkomstig het recht van de lidstaat waar zij gevestigd zijn: a) vatbaar zijn voor hoger beroep bij of herziening door een rechterlijke instantie, en b) dezelfde rechtskracht en dezelfde rechtsgevolgen hebben als een beslissing van een rechterlijke instantie over dezelfde aangelegenheid. De lidstaten stellen de Commissie overeenkomstig artikel 64 in kennis van de lijst van de in de eerste alinea bedoelde andere instanties en rechtsbeoefenaren.

Er zijn in een aantal lidstaten die gebonden zijn aan de verordening, waar de notaris bevoegd is de echtscheiding uit te spreken en over het huwelijksvermogensrecht beslissingen te geven. Die notarissen kunnen als gerecht worden aangemerkt.

Over de vraag of de notaris een gerechtelijke autoriteit is bij de toepassing van de erfrechtverordening bestaat veel rechtsspraak.[32] De notaris in Nederland bezit geen bevoegdheden om de echtscheiding uit te spreken en beslissingen over huwelijksvermogensrecht te geven. Ik neem analoog aan de rechtspraak over de erfrechtverordening aan dat de Nederlandse notaris geen gerecht is. Als na overlijden van een echtgenoot een geschil ontstaat over de vraag of de exceptieclausule van artikel 26 lid 3 van de verordening kan worden toegepast, dan zal de rechter daarover een beslissing moeten nemen in Nederland. De notaris in Nederland is daartoe niet bevoegd.

3.5 Kritiek op de Exceptieclausule

Lagarde[33] komt met een voorbeeld van de exceptieclausule, die ik hier graag citeer, aangezien ik mijn kritiek op dit artikel meer vorm kan geven aan de hand van dit voorbeeld:

> "A United Kingdom citizen and a French citizen live in Paris and get married with no agreement or choice of law applicable to the matrimonial regime. They live there for two years, in a flat purchased by the French spouse. The UK spouse finds employment in Hamburg and settles there. The French spouse then also moves there, after selling the flat in Paris and buying another one in Hamburg, declaring themselves in the sale and purchase deeds to be married under German law. The couple then live in Hamburg for four years, and they subsequently separate and get divorced. Under which matrimonial regime

32 HvJ EU 21 juni 2018, C-20/17, ECLI:EU:C :2018 :485 Oberle, HvJ EU 23 mei 2019, C-658/17, ECLI:EU:C:2019:444 de W.B. zaak en HvJ 16 juli 2020, C-80/19, ECLI:EU:C:2020:569 de E.E. zaak.

33 Lagarde, The EU regulation on matrimonial and patrimonial property, onder redactie van Bergquist, Damascelli, Frimston, Lagarde en Reinhartz, Oxford university press, 2019, p. 117-118.

> should the spouses' assets be shared? According to the French community of acquests system or according to the German *Zugewinngemeinschaft* system? The first state of the conflict rule designates French law, being that of the first common habitual residence. This lasted two years, which is a sufficient duration. Under this law, all the acquests made by spouses would be split in half. Either spouse, in this example the French spouse given their positions in purchases and sales, may benefit from availing themselves of the German regime and thus only sharing the increase in the gains from the assets of both spouses. In the example, the French spouse is likely to succeed in requesting the application of the exception clause and enforcing, on one hand, the duration of the German common residence, twice as long as the previous common residence in France, and, on the other, the fact that the French spouse, as the UK citizen cannot dispute, had applied German law to organize their property relationships. This law will also be applied in principle, unless contested by the other spouse, as from the date of the marriage (e.g. by determining the French spouse's alienation powers during the first period) and not merely after the date of establishing the common residence in Germany."

Ik heb moeite om mij voor te stellen hoe de echtgenoten kunnen bewijzen dat zij uitgegaan zijn van het huwelijksvermogensrecht van hun later gevestigde gewone verblijfplaats. Burgers wonende in de EU-lidstaten die gebonden zijn aan de verordening huwelijksvermogensrecht horen de inhoud van Europese verordeningen te kennen. Zij behoren dus te weten dat het recht van hun eerste gemeenschappelijke gewone verblijfplaats van toepassing is op grond van artikel 26 lid 1 sub a van de verordening. Hoe kunnen de echtgenoten in het voorbeeld bij de verkoop van de woning in Frankrijk en aankoop van de woning in Duitsland verklaren dat zij gehuwd zijn volgens Duits recht? Waar is die aanname op gebaseerd?

Bij de overdracht van onroerend goed zijn in Frankrijk en Duitsland notarissen betrokken. De meeste echtgenoten zullen bij aankoop van een woning een lening bij een bank ter financiering nodig hebben. Ook dan speelt vaak de vraag welk huwelijksvermogensrecht van toepassing is. In Nederland zal de notaris bij verkoop van onroerend goed de beschikkingsbevoegdheid van de verkoper moeten controleren en zal de notaris moeten bepalen welk huwelijksvermogensrecht van toepassing is. Ik neem aan dat de notaris in Frankrijk en Duitsland eenzelfde rol heeft. Dat wil zeggen dat de notaris niet af mag gaan op de verklaringen van de echtgenoten. Dan kunnen de echtgenoten op dat punt niet te goeder trouw aannemen dat zij gehuwd zijn volgens het recht van hun later gevestigde gewone verblijfplaats.

De exceptieclausule mag alleen bij wijze van uitzondering worden toegepast zo bepaalt artikel 26 lid 3. Overweging 51 heeft het ter toelichting over 'uitzonderlijke gevallen. Die formulering komt overeen met artikel 21 lid 2 van de verordening erfrecht, waarvoor in overweging 25 een rechtvaardiging wordt gegeven dat de erflater kennelijk een nauwere banden had met een andere staat en ook een voorbeeld wordt gegeven, wanneer daar sprake van zou kunnen zijn bijvoorbeeld indien de erflater vrij kort voor zijn overlijden naar de staat van zijn gewone verblijfplaats was verhuisd en uit alle omstandigheden blijkt dat hij kennelijk een nauwere band had met een ander land. Het Europese Hof van Justitie heeft in de zaak E.E[34] bepaald dat de aangezochte autoriteit, aan de hand van een beoordeling van alle omstandigheden van het geval, moet bepalen in welke – enige – lidstaat de gewone verblijfplaats zich bevindt. De Advocaat-Generaal[35] voegt daar nog aan toe dat de uitzondering van artikel 21 van de verordening erfrecht niet mag worden toegepast, als de gewone verblijfplaats moeilijk is te bepalen. Naar zijn oordeel maakt dit duidelijk dat er geen ontkomen aan is: er moet een gewone verblijfplaats worden bepaald, hoe moeilijk dat ook is.

De autoriteit moet dus analoog redenerende altijd bepalen waar de gewone verblijfplaats van iedere echtgenoot was gelegen op het moment van de huwelijkssluiting of 'kort' daarna. Derden zijn ook aan die uitkomst gebonden. De echtgenoten zelf echter niet, wanneer zij aantonen dat zij inmiddels langer in een andere staat gewone verblijfplaats hebben gehad en zich op dat recht hebben verlaten. Hierboven heb ik aangetoond dat de echtgenoten uit het voorbeeld niet tot de conclusie hadden kunnen komen op het moment dat zij belangrijke beslissingen nemen in hun leven, zoals de verkoop en aankoop van een huis.

De rechtvaardiging om de exceptie toe te passen, wordt naar mijn mening in overweging 51 nauwelijks toegelicht. Hoe rechters de exceptie kunnen toepassen, is zo lang het Europese Hof van Justitie daarover geen nadere toelichting geeft, onzeker.[36] Het lijkt erop dat echtgenoten in de verordening beloond worden voor hun eigen onwetendheid.

4 Conclusie

Ipr huwelijksvermogensrecht is een lastige materie. Dat was het in 1985 en dat is het ook in 2021. Een degelijk ipr-advies blijft maatwerk en is noodzakelijk in een wereld die steeds internationaler wordt. Ik hoop dat met deze toelichting de lezer weer wat wijzer is geworden.

---

34 Zie EHvJ 16 jul 2020, ECLI:EU:C:2020:569, zaak C-80/19,E.E, r.o. 40.

35 Zie r.o. 59 van de conclusie van de AG Campos Sánchez-Bordona gepubliceerd op 26 maart 2020, ECLI:EU:C:2020:230.

36 Op moment van schrijven is er in Nederland nog geen enkele uitspraak over artikel 26 van de verordening gepubliceerd. Het Europese Hof van Justitie heeft ook nog geen uitspraken over dit artikel gegeven.

Part IX
Property and Technology

"Data Property": Entitlements Between "Ownership", Factual Control and Access to Commons

Christine Godt[*]

1 Technology, Fluidity and Sjef

Sjef is an inspirer; no-one catches the attention of students and colleagues like him. He picks up topics which are "in the air" and no-one fully grasps yet. His strength is to provide language and structure to unresolved issues. I got to know him in 2001 when we met subsequently at two different spots, first in Trento (discussing Comparative Intellectual Property Law), shortly afterwards in Bremen (where he taught Comparative Property Law at the Hanse Law School). We are in touch since then.

This article aims to give something back. When writing about data, I am aware that the endeavour is doomed to fail: He is the master of thinking about data.[1] He writes in 2019.[2]

> "If land registries would start to register, next to traditional data about immovables or valuable movables such as ships and aircraft, what might be

* Prof. Dr. Christine Godt, Chair for European and International Economic Law, Private Law at the Carl von Ossietzky University of Oldenburg, e-mail: christine.godt@uni-oldenburg.de. Please note that this contribution was written in the summer of 2020, prior to the publication of the Draft EU Data Package (announced for November 2020, comprising a "Data Governance Act", a "Digital Markets Act", and a "Digital Services Act").

1 S. van Erp, 'Data protection in hybrid worlds', *in* L. A. DiMatteo/M. Cannarsa/C. Poncibò (Eds.), *The Cambridge Handbook of Smart Contracts, Blockchain Technology and Digital Platforms*, Cambridge, Cambridge University Press, 2020a, pp. 233-239; S. van Erp, 'Who "Owns" the Data in a Coronavirus Tracing (And/or Tracking) App?', *in*: E. Hondius/M. S. Silva/A. Nicolussi/P. S. Coderch/C. Wendehorst/F. Zoll (Eds), *Coronavirus and the Law in Europe, Examining coronavirus-related legislation and its consequences in European states*, IntersentiaOnline, 2020b, preprint available at https://ssrn.com/abstract=3678095 (last accessed 11 September 2020); S. van Erp, 'Digital Revolution. New challenges for law: Final remarks', *in* A. De Franceschi/R. Schulze (Eds.), *Digital Revolution: New Challenges for* Law, Baden-Baden, Nomos, 2019, pp. 341-343; S. van Erp, 'Ownership of data and the numerus clausus of legal objects', *in* S. Murphy/P. Kenna (Eds.), *eConveyancing and title registration in Ireland*, Dublin, Clarus Press, 2019, pp. 125-140.

2 S. van Erp, 'The need for a common vocabulary on "data ownership"', 8 *European Property Law Journal* 2019, pp. 1-3.

> called "data passports" (i.e. land data unrelated to traditional land registration), who is then the "owner" of the passport? Or would "ownership" differ depending upon the data source (satellites, sensors in farming equipment, mobile phones), type of data (land quality, geo-spatial) and purpose (data gathering in the general interest or "precision farming")? It is vital that we start thinking about these new types of "ownership" or "entitlement". Or should we perhaps start thinking about new types of "possession"? The answers may very well be different based on (a) area of law (private law, public law), (b) type of object (tangible, intangible, digital), (c) purpose (full control, security, management), (d) nature of the data carrier (physical, human), (e) distance of data from a subject ("dispossession" by mass processing). At least a cross-linguistic common vocabulary is badly needed."

Sjef teaches property as a matrix, a metaphor for claims of assignment and protection, fragmented, proceduralised, sector adapted, but based on normative principles. He never got weary to emphasize that property is an institution which promises stability, while at the same time explaining that it is a legal institution under continuous change,[3] required to address contemporary problems and in need for procedural approaches.[4]

---

3 S. van Erp, 'Fluidity of ownership and the tragedy of hierarchy. A sign of a revolutionary evolution?', 4 *European Property Law Journal* 2015, pp. 56-80; S. van Erp, 'Contract and property law: distinct, but not separate', 2 *European Property Law Journal* 2013, pp. 240-259, he explains that novel property rights emerge on the continuum of property and contracts.

4 Often referring to the works of his dear friend André van der Walt, *see* van Erp, 2015, *supra* note 3.

At the time of writing the hot phase of public debate about "data *ownership*" is over.[5] The debate has shifted to "data *rights*",[6] summarised under the term "access".[7] Even if some policy areas stick to the term "ownership" (with or without quotation marks[8]), a broader

5 It saw its peak in about 2016/2017 with various expert working groups on the national and the EU level. The European Commission´s White Paper stands out: 'Towards a European Data Space', COM(2018) 232 final, 25 April 2018; aligned with OECD, 'Maximising the Economic and Social Value of Data', DSTI/CDEP(2016) 4, 28 October 2016. Examplary for the national debates: e.g. Germany: F. Faust, *Gutachten A zum 71. Deutschen Juristentag. Digitale Wirtschaft – Analoges Recht – Braucht das BGB ein Update?*, München, C. H. Beck, 2016; Interministerielle Arbeitsgruppe ´Digitaler Neustart´ der Justizministerien, final report available at www.justiz.nrw.de/JM/schwerpunkte/digitaler_neustart/zt_bericht_arbeits-gruppe/bericht_ag_dig_neustart.pdf (last accessed 11 September 2020); and UK: Royal Society, *Data Ownership, rights and controls: Reaching a common understanding*, Report of Seminar Contributions of 3 October 2018, available at https://royalsociety.org/-/media/policy/projects/data-governance/data-ownership-rights-and-controls-October-2018.pdf (last accessed 11 September 2020). The shifting tone is summarized by European Commission, *Synopsis Report of the Consultation on the 'Building of a European Data Economy' Initiative*, available at https://ec.europa.eu/information_society/newsroom/image/document/2017-36/synopsis_report_-_data_economy_A0EFA8E0-AED3-1E29-C8DE049035581517_46646.pdf (last accessed 11 September 2020); further expert groups are listed by H. Ullrich, 'Technology protection and competition policy for the information economy. From property rights for competition to competition without proper rights?', *Max Planck Institute for Innovation & Competition Research Paper Series*, No. 19-12, 2019, p. 24, notes 72 and 73; for further international arenas see J. Ritter/A. Mayer, 'Regulating Data as Property: A New Construct for Moving Forward', 16 *Duke Law and Technology Review* 2018, pp. 238, 265.

6 On the differentiation between 'data ownership' (exclusive exploitation right) and 'data rights' (emerging from a 'dynamic special relationship', the original says: 'Dynamische Sonderbeziehung') and granting rights of say and participation (German: Mitsprache- und Teilhaberechte) operationalized by a recognized third party effect of (bilateral) data transfer agreements with explicit reference to the model of Art. 4 sec. 4 Dir. 2016/943 (transposed to German law in 2019, § 3 Abs. 3 GeschGehG), *see* The German Data Ethics Commission (GEK, installed in Sept. 2018) issued its final report in October 2019, available at www.bmi.bund.de/SharedDocs/downloads/DE/publikationen/themen/it-digitalpolitik/gutachten-datenethikkommission.pdf?__blob=publicationFile&v=6 (last accessed 11 September 2020), pp. 85, 104, 144 (referenced to Prelimineary Drafts No. 2 (February 2019) und No. 3 (October 2019) of the ALI-ELI Principles for a Data Economy, available at www.europeanlawinstitute.eu/projects-publications/current-projects-feasibility-studies-and-other-activities/current-projects/data-economy/ [last accessed 11 September 2020]) . The envisioned goal are "distributed property rights" (in the German text version: "verteiltes Eigentum" – for German law a novel concept) encapsulated as a right to injunction and damages against a third party for acquisition, use and transfer if the person knew or could have known that the person from who the third party acquired the data used and transferred the data unlawfully.

7 Which encompasses two directions: First, the debate about industrial 're-use', *see* Ullrich, 2019, *supra* note 5, p. 21: "[...] the problem of the data economy is not so much an insufficient production of data, but an insufficient dissemination of data (complementary, improving, diversifying or even displacing) follow-on innovation in the digital economy. The catch-word is trading with and sharing of digital data, i.e. access rights, not rights of protection." Second, the debate around the shift towards the term "Datenbesitz" (which signals a title 'less than' or burdening ownership), T. Hoeren, 'Datenbesitz statt Dateneigentum', *Multimedia und Recht* 2019, pp. 5-8.

8 The term is employed in the agricultural sector. With quotation marks: European Commission, *EU Code of Conduct on agricultural data sharing by contract agreement*, April 2018, available at https://copa-cogeca.eu/img/user/files/EU%20CODE/EU_Code_2018_web_version.pdf]; without quotation marks: American Farm Bureau Federation, *US Privacy and Security Principles for Farm Data*, April 2016, available at https://www.fb.org/issues/innovation/data-privacy/privacy-and-security-principles-for-farm-data (last accessed 5 July 2020). Yet, 'classical' full ownership in the legal sense is not meant.

societal reflection has taken up momentum.[9] Being an ELI-member himself,[10] Sjef abandoned the technical term "ownership", and moved on to reflect fragmented entitlements ("belonging"[11]) and the underlying reasons. He holds on to the need to conceptualise data: "Data does not come into existence because we can show an end-user license agreement."[12] This statement responds to two groups, on the one side to those who relegate data simply to contracts,[13] and on the other side to those who call for concepts which conceptualise data as novel input factor,[14] beside of labour and capital. Assuming that the developments will be propelled by the judiciary, Sjef calls for principles of entitlements with regard to data, as the novel category beside of movables, land, claims and creative expressions.[15] In the tradition of Hohfeld, he conceives singular, but conjural rights to process, to retrieve, to use, to manage. This fundamental work is ongoing and the current article will not interfere, but only modestly aims to contribute some reflections from the IP and competition law perspective.[16]

9 Reflected by ethic committees (for the German DEK *id.*; for the European High Level Expert Group on AI which presented a consolidated version of 'Ethics Guidelines for Trustworthy Artificial Intelligence' on 8 April 2019, see https://ec.europa.eu/digital-single-market/en/news/ethics-guidelines-trustworthy-ai [last accessed 11 September 2020]), numerous conferences (e.g. ASCOLA, 25-27 June 2020), research projects (GOAL, discussed at a GOAL-Summer School 23-24 June 2020), and court decisions (inter alia BGH, KVR 69/19, decision of 23.6.2020 – *Facebook* [The Federal German Supreme Civil Court upheld the injunction of the German Antitrust Agency against Facebook to oblige users to convey internet use data which is independent from the use of the platform itself and which precludes any user choice]).

10 Sjef is a founding member of the European Law Institute (ELI) and currently involved in two of its projects. He chairs the project "Blockchain Technology and Smart Contracts", and is member of the Advisory Committee of the joint ELI and American Law Institute project "Principles for a Data Economy". ELI´s mission is to 'improve the quality of European law, understood in the broadest sense. It seeks to initiate, conduct and facilitate research, to make recommendations, and to provide practical guidance in the field of European legal development.' https://www.europeanlawinstitute.eu/about-eli/ (last accessed 7 December 2020).

11 Van Erp, 2020b, *supra* note 1.

12 S. van Erp, 'Management as Ownership of Data', *in* S. Lohsse/R. Schulze/D. Staudenmayer (Eds.), *Data as Counter Performance – Contract Law 2.0?*, Oxford/Baden-Baden, Hart/Nomos, 2020c, p. 77, at 86.

13 S. Ras Engelfriet, *Handboek ICT-contracten*, Utrecht, Ius Mentis, 2015, p. 24: "data should be regarded as by-product of a service".

14 The German Chancellor Merkel said to the participants of the annual meeting of the World Economic Forum on 24 January 2018: "Die Antwort auf die Frage ‚Wem gehören die Daten' wird letztlich darüber entscheiden, ob Demokratie, Partizipation, Souveränität im Digitalen und wirtschaftlichen Erfolg zusammengehen. [...] Wir brauchen eine Soziale Marktwirtschaft 4.0, nicht nur eine Industrie 4.0."; I. Schneider, 'Governance and digital Sovereignty in the Data Economy: Data Trusteeship instead of Data Ownership', *in* C. Godt/M. Lamping (Eds.), *A Critical Mind in the Triangle of Internal Market Law, Intellectual Property and Competition Law – Liber Discipulorum for Hanns Ullrich*, Berlin, Springer, 2021 (forthcoming), manuscript, p. 3.

15 Van Erp, 2020, *supra* note 12, p. 14.

16 Building on A. Perzanowski/J. Schultz, 'Reconciling Personal and Intellectual Property', 90 *Notre Dame Law Rev.* 2015, p. 1211. They stress the complementary tension. The reflection of classic property law versus IP law in this context is pursued in parallel by Franz Hofmann, Benjamin Raue and Herbert Zech who organised (after the submission deadline of this article) a conference on the very same topic ´Eigentum in der digitalen Gesellschaft-Perspektiven von Sacheigentum und geistigem Eigentum, 20.11.2020.

This contribution is interested in the debate: "Who "owns" data?" It neglects the issue of data as subjects[17] (software agents[18] and AI creations[19]), and also the question of conflicts of interests between multiple processors.[20] Its focus is the subject-object relation, thus the assignment function of proprietary entitlements: The central question is the construction of raw data as "incoming" resource. In Sjef's words, does the processor of data possess the data as her own (sic, was it "res nullius" beforehand?[21]) or was it someone else's data (in technical terms: [in French] "detenteur ou possesseur", [in German] "Fremdbesitz oder Eigenbesitz")?[22] The "input-question" refers to a central difference of classic property law and IP legal thinking. Broad-brushed and simplified, the default scenario of classical property law is that objects are owned (the core of the discipline circles around rules on "transfer" of title [acquisition or loss]); original acquisition[23] is today governed by public law. In contrast, the default scenario for IP law is information in the public domain. The very heart of IP laws is to define the creation of "new objects" ("inventions", "creations", "plant varieties"). A characteristic of IP-claims is that they are rather "strong", and IP-law is therefore also a law of limitations. With "raw" information ("data"), the schism between these areas of laws is put back on the table. The present article is interested in how differently conflicts of interests as the flow of information moves and transforms are framed. Up to today, conflicts of interests have only been reflected in a constitutional framing of property, based on approaches of Elsabe van der Slide (a private law property law scholar) and Josef Drexl (an IP and competition law scholar).[24] The present contribution is interested how

17 Faust, 2016, *supra* note 5.

18 G. Teubner, 'Digitale Rechtssubjekte? Zum privatrechtlichen Status von autonomen Softwareagenten', 218 *Archiv für die civilistische Praxis (AcP)* 2018, pp. 155-205.

19 A. Früh, 'Inventorship in the Age of Artificial Intelligence', *in* C. Godt/M. Lamping (Eds.), *A Critical Mind in the Triangle of Internal Market Law, Intellectual Property and Competition Law – Liber Discipulorum for Hanns Ullrich*, Berlin, Springer, 2021 (forthcoming).

20 A question which is essentially driving the debate, see the various examples in M. Barbero *et al.*, *Study on emerging issues of data ownership, interoperability, (re-)usability and access to data, and liability*, Brussels, 2017, (in the further course: 'Deloitte Study 2017'), available at https://ec.europa.eu/digital-single-market/en/news/study-emerging-issues-data-ownership-interoperability-re-usability-and-access-data-and (last accessed 11 September 2020); for the example of the automotive industry *see* J. Metzger/L. Mischau, 'Neutrale Server – Datenschutz und Datenwirtschaft im vernetzten Fahrzeug', *in* Stiftung Datenschutz (Ed.), *Daten-Debatten*, Berlin, Erich Schmidt Verlag, 2020 (forthcoming).

21 Van Erp, 2020b, *supra* note 1, p. 10.

22 S. van Erp, Oral Lecture 'Property and Technology', Online 'PropCon' Conference, 7. April 2020, referring to the claim for vindication in insolvency, as decided by the Court of Appeal (England Wales) in *Your Response Ltd. v. Datateam Business Media Ltd.* [2014] EWCA (Civ) 281 [2014], 3 WLR 887; discussed by A. Boerding *et al.*, 'Data Ownership – A Property Rights Approach from a European Perspective', 11 *Journal of Civil Law Studies* 2018, p. 350; on data in insolvency: S. Schulze, *Daten als Kreditsicherungsmittel mit Bestand in der Insolvenz*, München, UTZ Verlag, 2019, p. 19 *et seq.*

23 Most noteworthy acquisition of water, minerals, archaeological relicts, waste management, land use.

24 E. van der Sijde, *Reconsidering the Relationship between Property and Regulation: A systematic constitutional approach* (dissertation defended at the University of Stellenbosch 2015), available at http://hdl.handle.net/10019.1/97827 (last accessed 11 September 2020); J. Drexl, 'Legal Challenges of the Changing Role of Personal

the property systems absorb these concerns. It will focus on "non-personal data", governed by the EU Framework-Reg. 2018/1807, and rather on B2B contracts (acknowledging that the debate on personal data is much more advanced, due to the longstanding history of data protection since in the 70s. In addition, public media has quite well covered evolving claims emerging from personal data processed by the "big fives",[25] data accumulated in cars[26] [mostly in the context of autonomous driving[27]], and consumer protection.) This contribution puts the rather old-fashioned question of abstract allocation centre stage, and questions the position which assigns data to the processor by default.[28] It is interested in how property law versus IP law conceptualise the respective conflicts at hand.

The contribution departs from the assumption that the answer does not only lie in any of the existing areas of law, be it conventional property law, IP law, competition law or internal market law. "Data rights" require an understanding of a "*greffe*" (Amstutz[29]), a reflection about a matrix of proprietary relations, finetuned by "procedural restructuring",[30] open

---

and Non-Personal Data in the Data Economy', *Max Planck Institute for Innovation & Competition Research Papers*, No. 18-23, 2018, pp. 5-19, available at https://papers.ssrn.com/sol3/papers.cfm?abstract_id=3274519; for earlier references by the author to these pioneering works *see* C. Godt, 'Conflict Configuration', *in* C. Godt/L. Guibault/G. Van Overwalle/D. Beyleveld (Eds.), *Boundaries to Information Property*, London, Intersentia, 2021a (forthcoming); C. Godt, 'How to Stay Modern Feudalism? Comparing EU and US Methodologies in Containing Post Sale Restraints by Way of IP-Exhaustion', *in* C. Godt/M. Lamping (Eds.), *A Critical Mind in the Triangle of Internal Market Law, Intellectual Property and Competition Law – Liber Discipulorum for Hanns Ullrich*, Berlin, Springer, 2021b (forthcoming).

25 The term "The Big Five" refer to Appel, Google, Microsoft, Amazon, and Facebook; see only BGH, KVR 69/19, decision of 23.6.2020 – *Facebook.*

26 *Frankfurter Allgemeine Zeitung*, 5. May 2019, p. T1, describing six sets of car data: (1) 'necessary' data stirring the driving functions of the car removed from the individual driver´s control, (2) driver´s control over heat and light, (3) entertainment and communication (music, e-mails, connection with one´s smart home, e.g. in order to open the garage door), (4) 'surveillance' data of the car for external and internal purposes. External control can be exerted once the car escapes a prescribed geographical area, or exceeds the maximal speed limit. Internal control (or delegated internal control) can be exerted for 'enhanced' inspection (precision data about breaks and tires), (5) Some manufactured differentiate their product lines by 'digital (up-)grading' which one need to rent after a time period (months, years) of free use, (6) personalised data streams (usually submitted to 'PIC', but essentially removed from the driver´s control) to be sold to third parties (e.g. insurances).

27 Ritter/Mayer, 2018, *supra* note 5, pp. 244 *et seq.*; Metzger/Mischau, 2020, *supra* note 20.

28 Inter alia pioneering: H. Zech, Information als Schutzgegenstand, Tübingen, Mohr Siebeck, 2012, p. 386; more recently: J. Jöns, Daten als Handelsware, Baden-Baden, Nomos, 2019, pp. 226, 248; G. Wagner, § 823, in Münchener Kommentar zum BGB, 7th ed., München, C. H. Beck, 2017, para. 296.

29 A term coined by M. Amstutz/V. Karavas, 'Weltrecht: Ein Derridasches Monster', *in* G.-P. Calliess *et al.* (Eds.), *Soziologische Jurisprudenz – Festschrift G. Teubner*, Berlin, De Gruyter, 2009, pp. 647-674 (at p. 648): A *Greffe* is "a structure which works off the heterogeneity of its heterogeneous bodies and makes them disappear" (translation by the author).

30 A term coined for recent EU copyright regulations, M. Grünberger, 'From a Rights Based to a Procedural Approach: Re-Purposing the Exercise of Intellectual Property Rights', *in* C. Godt/M. Lamping (Eds.), *A Critical Mind in the Triangle of Internal Market Law, Intellectual Property and Competition Law – Liber*

to fragmentation which reflects societal embeddedness.[31] It is in search of a constitutional thinking *inside* property law. The question "Who owns it?" is understood as a metaphor. The public discourse might even frame collective or public interests as "property right".[32] This contribution aims to further entangle the different interests which risk to be mixed up or prematurely absorbed when using the single term "ownership".

2 Data – a Contested "Proprietary Object"

Sjef has been interested in the conceptualisation of data early on. At the beginning of the 2010s, when the approach prevailed that digital relationships are sufficiently governed by contracts, he referred to the *Hoge Raad*'s decision on the quasi-property status of a virtual amulet in the game *Runescape*[33] (emerging in the context of criminal law[34]), and to the protective function of property. In a similar vein, he questioned Facebook's standard terms with a property lawyer's intuition as a new form of acquisition, and followed closely the emerging judicial arguments if a Facebook account gets "bequested" by the parents after a mortal accident (suicide?) of an adolescent daughter.[35] He wrote about digital assets,[36] bitcoins,[37] blockchain based digital land registries,[38] and found interest in research work

Discipulorum for Hanns Ullrich, Berlin, Springer, 2021 (forthcoming); on the importance of reversals of proof in IP also Godt 2021b (forthcoming), *supra* note 24.

31 D. Wielsch, 'Differenzierungen des Eigentums', *in* S. Keller/S. Wiprächtiger (Eds.), *Recht zwischen Dogmatik und Theorie*, Zürich/St. Gallen/Baden-Baden, Nomos, 2012, p. 329.

32 As seen in other contexts, C. Godt, *Eigentum an Information*, Tübingen, Mohr Siebeck, 2007, at p. 436.

33 Dutch Supreme Court (Hoge Raad), decision of 31 January 2012, ECLI:NL:HR:2012:BQ9251, NJ 2012/536 (*Runescape*).

34 A case about the 'theft' of a digital theft in the game of a virtual amulet. Followed by a decision by the Cour de Cassation des Luxembourg in 2014 with regard to downloading, Luxembourg, Cour de cassation N° 17 / 2014 pénal. du 3.4.2014. Not. 6458/10/CD Numéro 3304 du registre, available at https://juricaf.org/arret/LUXEMBOURG-COURDECASSATION-20140403-1714 (last accessed 11 September 2020).

35 German Supreme Court (BGH), decision of 21. Juni 2018, Az. III ZR 183/17; reversing the Regional instance court (KG) decision of 31.05. 2017, Az. 21 U 9/16, which had reversed the first instance court's obligation to Facebook (LG Berlin, decision of 17.12.2015, Az. 20 O 172/15).

36 S. van Erp, 'Ownership of digital assets?', 5 *European Property Law Journal* 2016, pp. 73-76, J. Uitdehaag/S. van Erp, 'Digital assets', *in* M. Schmitz/P. Gielen (Eds.), *Avoris dématérialisés et exécution forcée. Digital assets and enforcement*, Editions Bruylant, 2019, pp. 175-180.

37 J. Uitdehaag/S. van Erp, 'Attachment of digital assets: crypto-currencies', *in* M. Schmitz/P. Gielen (Eds.), *Avoris dématérialisés et exécution forcée. Digital assets and enforcement*, Brussels, Bruylant, pp. 181-189.

38 S. van Erp 2019 (sura n. 1).

about (digitally bartered) proprietary empty cargo vessel space,[39] and CO_2 allowances,[40] digital bills of lading,[41] and software "grandchildren licenses" with *in rem* effects.[42]

Sjef sensed early on that data is a distinct object. He preferred the term "asset" when reflecting about "data entitlements".[43] Building on his earlier works, he is interested in conceptualising a "management right" rather than "ownership" as exclusive allocation.[44] He writes: "As to data, the degree of ownership we should try to understand is management, as the expression of access, control, portability and erasure."[45]

Today, we categorise "data" along three characteristics. The first line of arguments aims at distinguishing "data" against "information" and "facts". Sjef starts with the ISO definition of data as "reinterpretable representation of information in a formalized manner suitable for communication, interpretation, or processing."[46] Implied is the central distinction between "data" and "information" which has become standard:[47] its core is that data requires "framing",[48] which brings up questions as to "who's" and by which criteria.[49] In Marc Amstutz words: "Data Ownership merges individual and collective autonomies".[50] While jurisdictions which only accept "property" in things and creations have witnessed

39 V. Heutger, 'Derivatives in Maritime Freight: Novel Property Rights with Prospects and Pitfalls', *in* C. Godt (Ed.), *Regulatory Property Rights*, Leiden/Boston, Brill, 2017, pp. 223-234.

40 C. Godt, '"Regulatory Property Rights" – A Challenge to Property Theory', *in* C. Godt (Ed.), *Regulatory Property Rights*, Leiden/Boston, Brill, 2017, p. 33.

41 D. Saive, *Das elektronische Konnossement – Umsetzung der Anforderungen aus § 516 Abs. 2 HGB durch funktionsäquivalente Blockchain-Token*, Tübingen, Mohr-Siebeck, 2020.

42 C. Godt/J. Simon, 'In Rem Effects of Non-exclusive Sub-licenses in Insolvency', *in* C. Godt (Ed.), *Regulatory Property Rights*, Leiden/Boston, Brill, 2017, p. 207.

43 F. Faust, 'Ausschliesslichkeitsrechte an Daten', *in* Stiftung Datenschutz (Ed.), *Dateneigentum und Datenhandel*, Berlin, Erich Schmidt, 2019, p. 94; Faust, 2016, *supra* note 5.

44 Which is, in a jurisdiction such as Germany, conceived to be the core of ownership, J. Wilhelm, *Sachenrecht*, 6th ed., Berlin, DeGruyter, 2019, para. 237; C. von Bar, Gemeineuropäisches Sachenrecht, Vol. 1, München, C. H. Beck, 2015, para. 22.

45 Van Erp, 2020c, *supra* note 12, p. 93; in this attempt, he aligns with Boerding *et al.*, 2018, *supra* note 22, p. 350.

46 Van Erp, 2020c, *supra* note 12, p. 80: ISO/IEC 2382-1, revised by ISO/IEC 2382:2015 – Information technology – Vocabulary.

47 This is what Herbert Zech calls 'semantic information' (content), as distinguished from 'syntactic information' (representation of signs) and structural information (as embodied in material), Zech, 2012, *supra* note 28.

48 This is why information is not neutral. In the words of Rob Kitchin, *The Data Revolution: Big Data, Open Data, Data Infrastructure & their Consequences*, London, Sage, 2014, p. 2: "These choices reflect the human agency present in the creation of data"; M. Anzini/A.-C. Peirrat, *Data Pools as Information Exchange between Competitors: An Antitrust Perspective*, Paper submitted to the ASCOLA Conference, 25 June 2020, available at https://www.cep.eu/fileadmin/user_upload/cep.eu/Studien/cepInput_Data_pools/cepInput_Data_Pools_as_Information_Exchanges_between_Competitors_An_Antitrust_Perspective.pdf (last accessed 11 September 2020); referring to C. Jones/C. Tonetti, *Nonrivalry and the Economics of Data*, 29 August 2019, available at https://www.gsb.stanford.edu/gsb-cmis/gsb-cmis-download-auth/469311?undefined (last accessed 11 September 2020).

49 Ullrich, 2019, *supra* note 5, p. 24, at note 73.

50 M. Amstutz, 'Dateneigentum: Funktion und Form', 218 *AcP* 2018, 438, at pp. 535 *et seq.* with reference to Dan Wielsch.

tensed debates on data ownership, few jurisdictions such as Latvia[51] and Luxembourg[52] stipulated data ownership, while jurisdictions which also embrace claims as property[53] have seen a more open, but still have had controversial debate.[54] Next to data and information is the distinction of data against facts. Facts are part of the real world what implies that protection for data must be "more robust" than for facts,[55] alluding to the delineation of public domain facts and creations in copyright.[56] The distinction between data and facts positions data as a category between facts and IP: For a selected/arranged accumulation of data ("content") with substantial investment, a proprietary *sui generis* title is available under the Database Directive,[57] submitted to various exceptions (e.g. "lawful use", infra). Full-fledged copyright protection is available for data compilations with an "original selection or arrangement".[58] The second central category is the distinction between personal and "non-personal" data.[59] The idea is that personal information is attributed to the person, whereas non-personal information is – as one often reads – in the public

51 Deloitte Study 2017, *supra* note 20, p. 185.

52 Art. 567 Code de Commerce Luxembourg; critical on this legal reform F. Hoffmann, '"Dateneigentum" in der Insolvenz', *Juristenzeitung (JZ)* 2019, 960, at p. 968.

53 Such as France, Belgium, the Netherlands, Austria, Common Law.

54 Such for Austria only G. Klammer, *Dateneigentum*. Das Sachenrecht der Daten, Wien, Jan Sramek Verlag, 2019.

55 T. Scassa, *Data Ownership*, CIGI Papers No. 187 – September 2018, p. 1, referring to a Canadian court decision not verified.

56 With noteworthy borderline case for 'fictionalized facts' (attributed to the copyright holder in the case of a lexicon for the Harry Potter series of novels by the US District Court for the Southern District of New York, 575 F.Supp.2d 513 [SDNY 2008] – *Warner Bros. Entertainment, Inc. and J. K. Rowling v. RDR Books*) and 'seismic data'. In the latter case, the Alberta Court of Queen´s Bench divided seismic data about the ocean floor into two categories, 'field data' and 'processed data', distinguished from ´features of the sub-ocean landscape´. The judge found that both categories, 'field data' and 'processed data', meet the threshold of originality, since each required considerable skill and judgement for their creation (2016 ABQB 230, 38 Alta LR (6th) 48, aff´d 2017 ABCA 125, appeal denied 2017 CanLII 80435 (SCC) *Geophysical Services Inc. v. Encana Corp.*). The judge concluded that seismic data are "an expression of [the firms] views of what the image of the subsurface of the surveyed area represents." Scassa, 2018, *supra* note 55, p. 10, comments that the wording signals that the judge seemed to recognize copyright in the data themselves rather than just in the overall compilation of data.

57 Directive 96/9/EC of the European Parliament and of the Council of 11 March 1996 on the legal protection of databases, OJ 1996 L 77, p. 20.

58 Dubbed 'merger doctrine', discussed by Scassa, 2018, *supra* note 55, p. 10, in distinctions to 'factual compilations' for which copyright is denied, the leading case is US Supreme Court, 499 US 340, 111 S Ct 1282 (1991) – *Feist Publications Inc v. Rural Telefone Services Co.*

59 While this distinction appears to be strong European black letter law, Ingrid Schneider cautions that the categorization might be overstressed, Schneider, 2021 (forthcoming), *supra* note 14, pp. 3-4. This caution is warranted considering the CJEU considers also dynamic IP addresses as personal data, C-582/14, (ECLI:EU:C:2016:930).

domain.[60] Even if personal data can be bartered,[61] the person remains linked to it. This translates legally into "withdrawal rights" such as the right to erasure[62] and the "portability right" stipulated by the (public law) EU-General Data Protection Regulation (GDPR).[63] The third category refers to the distinction between consumers and businesses. Beside their "portability right" for their personal data, consumers have a porting right also for non-personal data when the contract terminates (Art. 16 sec. 4 Dir. 2019/770). Businesses do not enjoy secure mandatory access right. Art. 6 sec. 1 lit. a Reg. 2018/1807[64] obliges the Commission to "encourage and facilitate" codes of conducts which provide for a "porting right" for non-personal data, so that the transfer of data to either another or the own IT-processor becomes possible. Beyond, businesses only have a right to information under the Fairness and Transparency Regulation[65] and access claims may be argued under national contract law.[66] Yet, scholars advocate an access right for "re-use" for businesses in various forms (*infra*).

Thus, Sjef positions data in the domain of property law. His aim is to apply values of property law to the data economy, such as stability, policy choices (*inter alia* protection of commerce), leading principles (*inter alia* Numerus Clausus), and ground rules (*inter alia* nemo dat rule).[67] This is why he proposed in 2019 the (ownerless!) Québec trust as a template for fragmented management rights in data. In 2020, his thoughts circle around data as items of "dynamic property",[68] in order to counter the factual control mechanisms of processors and the current practise of ubiquitous (compulsory) contractual transfers of data entitlements.

Aside of contract and property lawyers, there are intellectual property (IP) and competition lawyers who engage in the discussion about "data ownership". IP law is

60 Deloitte Study 2017, *supra* note 20, pp. 184-185 (report about the French law). See, however *infra* 3c (agricultural data), already land related data is – in practise – attributed to the owner of the land.

61 Art. 2 sec. 7 Dir. 2019/770 of the European Parliament and of the Council of 20 May 2019 on certain aspects concerning contracts for the supply of digital content and digital service, OJ 2019 L 136, p. 1.

62 Also called the 'right to be forgotten', first acknowledged in 2014 by the CJEU in *Case 131/12, Google Spain v. Spanish Data Protection Agency and Mario Costeja González (Google Spain)*, ECLI:EU:C:2014:317; later stipulated in Art. 17 sec. 2 GDPR. In fact, the relative value of the individual prior consent (Art. 6 sec. 1 subsec. 1 lit a GDPR) vis-à-vis other parallel stipulated 'justifications for data processing', which might eventually supersede the withdrawal of the individual person, is highly controversial (cp. Art. 6 sec. 1 subsec. 1 lit. b-f GDPR).

63 Art. 17 sec. 2 and Art. 20 Reg. 2016/679 (GDPR), OJ 2016 L 119, p. 1.

64 Reg. 2018/1807 of the European Parliament and of the Council of 14 November 2018 on a framework for the free flow of non-personal data in the European Union, OJ 2018 L 303, p. 59.

65 Reg. 2019/1150 the European Parliament and of the Council of 20 June 2019 on promoting fairness and transparency for business users of online intermediation services, OJ 2019 L 186, p. 57.

66 A. Metzger, 'Access to and Porting of Data under Contract Law: Consumer Protection Rules and Market-Based Principles', *in* J. Drexl (Ed.), *Data Access, Consumer Protection and Public Welfare (Verbraucherrechtstage 2019)*, Baden-Baden, Nomos, 2020 forthcoming (manuscript pp. 9-11).

67 Van Erp, 2020c, *supra* note 12; concurrent Wagner 2017, supra note 28, para. 297.

68 Van Erp, 2020b, *supra* note 1.

associated due to the immaterial nature of data, the *factual* quasi-exclusionary nature of databases,[69] the widespread protection of algorithms,[70] and the incorporation of proprietary data[71] and business secrets[72] in databanks. In addition, the dualistic structure of copyright allows a split of personal and patrimonial interests in the same right. However, the premises of general private law on the one hand, and IP-law on the other, are very different – notwithstanding that several scholars cross the lines. While pioneering scholars such as Karl-Heinz Fezer[73] and Herbert Zech[74] early embraced the idea of "digital ownership", despite for different subjects and for different reasons, many IP lawyers remained sceptical as a matter of principle. The reason is that IP entitlements are primarily conceived as market control rights, not as control over objects. They are granted for performance, not on mere information. While firmly rooted in the property paradigm, protection of IP-rights is purpose-bound (Grünberger[75]). IP-law is all about incentives, very little about freedom. Very different to the general take on property, exclusive IP rights are conceived as exceptions to the rule of competition. This is why IP laws define the rule under which rights emerge; their grant requires justification. This balancing is reflected by limited protection terms, numerous limitations and exceptions. While often not accepted

69 H. Richter/R. Hilty, 'Die Hydra des Dateneigentums – eine methodische Betrachtung (The Hydra of "Data Property Rights" – A Methodological View)', *in* Stiftung Datenschutz (Ed.), *Dateneigentum und Datenhandel*, Berlin, Erich Schmidt, 2019, pp. 241-259 (also available at https://ssrn.com/abstract=3263404 [last accessed 11 September 2020]).

70 P. Drahos, 'TRIPS through a Military Looking Glass', *in* C. Godt/M. Lamping (Eds.), *A Critical Mind in the Triangle of Internal Market Law, Intellectual Property and Competition Law – Liber Discipulorum for Hanns Ullrich*, Berlin, Springer, 2021 (forthcoming), manuscript, p. 14.

71 Proprietary data includes data from an agricultural inputs company about its agronomic products (seeds, pesticides), the result of field tests or other exclusive information, such as fertility of soil in a particular region for land scouting services, C. Atik/B. Martens, 'Competition Problems and Governance of Non-personal Agricultural Machine Data: Comparing Voluntary Initiatives in the US and EU', Joint Research Council (JRC) Digital Economy Working Paper 2020-07 (Dec. 2020), p. 5 (available at https://ec.europa.eu/jrc/en/publication/eur-scientific-and-technical-research-reports/competition-problems-and-governance-non-personal-agricultural-machine-data-comparing (last accessed 22 December 2020).

72 Jöns, 2019, *supra* note 28, p. 236 advocates therefore a parallel constitution of data along the model of copyright, building on C. Wendehorst, 'Die Digitalisierung und das BGB', *NJW* 2016, pp. 2609-2613; and N. Härting, '"Dateneigentum" – Schutz durch Immaterialgüterrecht?', *Computer und Recht (CR)* 2016, pp. 646-649.

73 K.-H. Fezer, 'Dateneigentum der Bürger – Ein originäres Immaterialgüterrecht sui generis an verhaltensgenerierten Informationsdaten der Bürger', *Zeitschrift für Datenschutz (ZD)* 2017a, p. 99; K.-H. Fezer, Dateneigentum, MMR 2017b, p. 99; K.-H. Fezer, 'Digitales Dateneigentum – ein grundrechtsdemokratisches Bürgerrecht in der Zivilgesellschaft', *in* Stiftung Datenschutz (Ed.), *Dateneigentum und Datenhandel*, Berlin, Erich Schmidt, 2019, p. 101.

74 H. Zech, 2012, *supra* note 28; H. Zech, '"Industrie 4.0"- Rechtsrahmen für eine Datenwirtschaft im digitalen Binnenmarkt', *GRUR* 2015a, p. 1151; H. Zech, 'Daten als Wirtschaftsgut – Überlegungen zu einem "Recht des Datenerzeugers"', *CR* 2015b, p. 137.

75 Grünberger, 2021 (forthcoming), *supra* note 30.

as generic "use rights", but as "privileges" only,[76] exceptions limit the property right. The core is that IP protection is never absolute, and not related to "the information" or "the idea", but limited to the *creative* expression or the technical teaching.

The point of departure (private law vs. IP law) has several ramifications on the data debate. I shall highlight five of them. First, the public domain is an integral part of IP-reflection. Input information which does not meet the creativity threshold *remains* in the public domain (free to be used, no compensation due), protected knowledge *becomes* public domain once the protection term has expired. And even if protected, the purposes might demand public access rights by way of stipulated exceptions and privileges (for free or remunerated), and non-written access rights (under competition law).[77] The public domain may also get contractually re-constructed.[78] Different from private property lawyers, publicly available information is an elementary category for IP- and competition lawyers. Non-protection is not *per se* a problem. Whereas in property law "res nullius" has become a rare exception, IP law has remained susceptible for the attached values. Second, in contrast to property lawyers, IP-lawyers do subscribe to a different notion of "stability" since their mission is to foster economic change and innovation.[79] IP-laws point of reference is dynamic competition in which the right to exclude may unfold an advantage (the characteristic profit margin above market level). Only from the limited perspective of the right holder does the IP right provide stability in the "turmoil of competition" as long as the right lasts. The core of the IP philosophy, however, is "creative destruction" (Schumpeter[80]). It strikes a balance between the central property function (investment incentive; wealth accumulation) and free trade. Besides time limitations, the most evident institution for the legal concept of the "embeddedness of exclusive rights in competition and trade" is the principle of

76 Recently highlighted by T. Dreier, 'Caught between Post- and Neo-Colonialism – IP for Traditional Knowledge, Traditional Cultural Expressions and Indigenous Resources', *in* C. Godt/M. Lamping (Eds.), *A Critical Mind in the Triangle of Internal Market Law, Intellectual Property and Competition Law – Liber Discipulorum for Hanns Ullrich*, Berlin, Springer, 2021 (forthcoming).

77 On the four pillars of the public domain L. Guibault, 'Drawing Contours of the European Public Domain', *in* C. Godt *et al.* (Eds.) 2021, supra note 24, manuscript, p. 16; following P. Samuelson, 'Mapping the Digital Public Domain', 66 *Law & Comp. Probs* 2003, pp. 147-172.

78 L. Guibault/P. B. Hugenholtz (Eds.), *The Future of the Public Domain: Identifying the Commons in Information Law*, Alphen aan den Rijn, Kluwer Law International 2006; J. H. Reichman/P. F. Uhlir, 'The Contractually Reconstructed Research Commons for Scientific Data in a Highly Protectionist Intellectual Property Environment', 66 *Law & Comp. Probs* 2003, p. 317.

79 'Stability' as such is not a value. Entitlements are always timely limited. 'Disruptive technology' is not seen as evil, but is part of the disciplinary DNA. As Joseph Schumpeter explained in his seminal work *Business Cycles* of 1939, 'disruptive innovation' fosters growth – and this is exactly what IP-laws incentivise. Yet, IP property provides for fences in competition, and in this sense *stabilizes* the prospect on returns of investments.

80 Seminal: J. A. Schumpeter, Capitalism, Socialism and Democracy, reprint, London, Routledge, 1994 (org. 1942), pp. 82-83. The 'gale of creative destruction' describes the 'process of industrial mutation that continuously revolutionizes the economic structure from within, incessantly destroying the old one, incessantly creating a new one'.

exhaustion.[81] Exhaustion splits the original single IP-title into two: one continuing, but timely limited title to the invention/creation, and one timely unlimited property title to the single goods. It thus limits the IP-right and provides stability to the purchaser.[82] Data entitlements need to be embedded in similar ("cut-off") principles.[83] Third, IP law's perception is dynamic and sequential in time. The knowledge output of one inventor/creator is the input for the next.[84] This creates inherent fragmentation. IP laws have developed different types of fragmentation, such as the dual theory for copyright (which defines the relation of creator and economic partner) or the dependency-principle in patent law (which defines the relation of consecutive patents). Thus, fragmentation is inbuilt in IP (and not challenged as a legal concept, regardless of the legal family). The alignment of data entitlements requires a similar conceptualisation.[85] Fourth, the IP-title *may* have a value as commodity. However, this value is only a reflection of the monetary value generated in competitive markets of the copies which embody the immaterial object. In contrast, in private law, the object covered by the property title is conceptualised as embodying the value of *that* item. The underlying idea is twofold: First, the item embodies the proprietary value, and this creates stability. Second: the object provides the owner with the means to invest and generate profits (an idea which derives from "*dominium directum*" which allows the *superior* to collect rent from the person actually using the land [*inferior*]). Only the latter idea is shared with IP law in that the IP right creates an incentive that the owner takes care of his things (invests), devise means to create an economic surplus ("to manage it"), thus fostering societal growth. Only in this regard does IP law "mimick"[86] property law. Yet, data sits in the middle. As such, it has seldom a value in itself. It is the cumulative nature of big data which both, has value and can be used to further create value. This hybridity needs to be reflected in future concepts, and would be neglected if "absolute title" would be granted to the processor. Fifth, the functional embeddedness[87] is today clearly acknowledged for IP. Rights have to fulfil a public purpose. This creates an inherent tension between industrial and competition policies. The industrial policy decision is to protect immaterial goods and to grant strong entitlements (because immateriality "perpetuates"); remedies reach beyond the object itself (so-called "reach through"-claims). It is for

81 Godt, 2021b (forthcoming), *supra* note 24.

82 This argument is stressed by Perzanowski/Schultz, 2015, *supra* note 16, pp. 1217, 1249.

83 Time limitations are conceived as central to IP lawyers, Ullrich, 2019, *supra* note 5, p. 22.

84 Constituting in conjunction with spill overs the 'dual nature of knowledge externalities', D. Kim, 'Incentives for Data-Sharing as a Case on (Regulating) Knowledge Externalities', *in* C. Godt/M. Lamping (Eds.), *A Critical Mind in the Triangle of Internal Market Law, Intellectual Property and Competition Law – Liber Discipulorum for Hanns Ullrich*, Berlin, Springer, 2021 (forthcoming), manuscript, p. 7.

85 The fragmentation is evident for the dualist tradition in copyright, however, it is equally present for the bifurcation in monist traditions which distinguish the title and moral rights.

86 Van Erp, 2020b, *supra* note 1, p. 5.

87 Emphasised as 're-purposing', and operationalised by sectorial regulation, *see* Grünberger, 2021 (forthcoming), *supra* note 30.

competition law to contain the negative effects by defining limitations and cut-off rules. This complexity is an important difference to property entitlements in objects (which are today defined by "private utility"). The architecture of data entitlements would need a similar system of "checks and balances".

For all these differences, the discussion about "data ownership" unfolds differently in the IP-context compared to the purely private law context, but is by no means less controversial. Proponents of data property either call for more control of the individual (Kilian,[88] Fezer,[89] Amstutz[90]), for more incentives for investments (Zech,[91] Specht,[92] Jöns[93]), or for more creativity dependent on the sectorial specificities (Grünberger[94]). Despite the common stance as to the instrument and to the liberal underpinning, these approaches differ strongly as to *who* will be the owner (the originator for Fezer or the processor for Zech) and for which purpose (liberty for Fezer versus incentives for Zech). Opponents focus on the functioning of markets (Drexl,[95] Hilty[96]) or competition (Ullrich,[97] Schweitzer/Peitz,[98] Kerber,[99] Zimmer[100]). The central arguments are twofold. First, there is no lack of incentive to invest in databanks. Second, commodification would propel the loss of private sovereignty.[101] Taken together, a data property right would exacerbate power accumulation in the market and impede access to content data.[102] In fact, the approaches

88 W. Kilian, 'Informationelle Selbstbestimmung und Marktprozesse', *CR* 2002, p. 921.

89 Fezer, 2017a und 2017b, *supra* note 73.

90 Amstutz, 2018, *supra* note 50, p. 438.

91 Zech, 2015a, *supra* note 74; Zech, 2015b, *supra* note 74, K. Johanna/H. Zech, 'Datenbankherstellerschutz für Rohdaten?', *CR* 2017, p. 417.

92 More moderate compared to Zech: L. Specht, 'Ausschließlichkeitsrechte an Daten – Notwendigkeit, Schutzumfang, Alternativen', *CR* 2016, p. 288.

93 Jöns, 2019, *supra* note 28.

94 Grünberger, 2021 (forthcoming), *supra* note 30.

95 Drexl, 2018, *supra* note 24.

96 Richter/Hilty, 2019, *supra* note 69.

97 Ullrich, 2019, *supra* note 5, p. 25.

98 H. Schweitzer/S. Peitz, *Datenmärkte in der digitalisierten Wirtschaft: Funktionsdefizite und Regelungsbedarf*, ZEW Discussion Paper No. 17-043, 2017, available at http://ftp.zew.de/pub/zew-docs/dp/dp17043.pdf (last accessed 14 September 2020), at G; J. Crémer/Y.-A. de Montjoye/H. Schweitzer, *Competition Policy for the digital era. Final report*, Brussels, European Commission, 2019, available at https://ec.europa.eu/competition/publications/reports/kd0419345enn.pdf (last accessed at 14 September 2020).

99 W. Kerber, 'A New (Intellectual) Property Right for Non-Personal Data? An Economic Analysis', *GRUR Int.* 2016, p. 989; W. Kerber, 'Rights on Data: The EU Communication "Building a European Data Economy" from an Economic Perspective', *in* S. Lohsse *et al.* (Eds.), *Trading Data in the Digital Economy: Legal Concepts and Tools*, Baden-Baden, Nomos, 2017, p. 109.

100 D. Zimmer, 'Property Rights Regulating Data?' *in* S. Lohsse *et al.* (Eds.), *Trading Data in the Digital Economy: Legal Concepts and Tools*, Baden-Baden, Nomos, 2017, p. 101.

101 N. Wessels/A. Laubach/P. Buxbaum, 'Personenbezogene Daten in der digitalen Ökonomie – Eine wirtschaftliche und juristische Betrachtung', *in* C. Ochs (Ed.), *Die Zukunft der Datenökonomie – Zwischen Geschäftsmodell, Kollektivgut und Verbraucherschutz*, Springer 2019, pp. 11-27 (at p. 23).

102 This is why Ullrich (2019, *supra* note 5, p. 24) opposes Zech´s distinction between semantic and syntactical information. Protection of syntactical information would impede access to content information.

of Amstutz and Drexl appear rather related, despite the use of different languages and the clear opposed results. Amstutz and Drexl envision differentiated rights linked to other individuals and to collective needs. Amstutz' clearly distances his approach from Zech's. "Data are not assets but media."[103] "The IP model is diametrical in opposition to the idea of civil society data ownership".[104]

Both, property and the IP scholars take reference to economic literature which departs from the non-rivalness of data. This term resonates with the public good qualification, although the second limb of its definition (non-exclusiveness) is usually exerted by factual control. This point of departure defines the structure of the argument. Public goods are prone to market failures. Either "well-defined property rights" (Coase[105]) or regulation are required. This juxtaposition gives rise to the question how data is most efficiently used. While in legal literature it seems to be common sense, that data has become a (valuable) currency in exchange of a service, economic literature has come to reject the notion of data as a valuable object. "The marginal value of collecting additional data to built-up data bases is very low or zero. This depresses the market value of individual data."[106] "Data have no value on their own."[107] The economic rationale prevails that assigning "property" to data will not remedy, instead the concomitant "alienability" will exacerbate the problem of power accumulation. In this reasoning, economic literature is concurrent with competition and IP law.[108] It is against the backdrop of obvious shortcomings of exclusivity, anti-trust concerns and lock-ins, that "access" has become the key term which has been proposed in three different forms. The first approach advocates a self-standing entitlement directly against (*sic* "mandatory" obligation of) the processor, either based on anti-trust law with reference to a market dominant data processor,[109] or based on data as "essential

103 Amstutz, 2018, *supra* note 50, p. 528.

104 *Id.*, p. 527.

105 R.H. Coase, 'The Problem of Social Cost', 3 *Journal of Law and Economics* 1960 (October), pp. 1-44.

106 Atik/Martens, 2020, *supra* note 71, pp. 16/17 (for non-personal data), and this "explains why intermediary platforms cannot give farmers a meaningful remuneration". For the same reasoning with regard to personal data: D. Acemoglu *et al.*, *Too much data: prices and inefficiencies in data markets*, NBER Working Paper 26296, 2019.

107 Atik/Martens, 2020, *supra* note 71, p. 8: "Data have no value on their own. They become valuable when they can be used to generate more revenue in product and service markets. Capturing the value of data requires some degree of integration between upstream data and downstream product and services markets."

108 Kim, 2021 (forthcoming), *supra* note 84, p. 4.

109 See pending legislative draft for a 10th revision of the German Act against Restraints of Competition which proposes to introduce new instruments, especially Section 18(3b): Intermediation power; Section 19a: Paramount crossmarket importance for competition; Section20(1): Relative market power; *see* Federal Ministry for Economic Affairs and Energy, *Gesetzentwurf des Bundesministeriums für Wirtschaft und Energie, Entwurf eines Zehnten Gesetzes zur Änderung des Gesetzes gegen Wettbewerbsbeschränkungen für ein fokussiertes, proaktives und digitales Wettbewerbsrecht 4.0 (GWB-Digitalisierungsgesetz)*, 9. Sept. 2020, available at https://www.bmwi.de/Redaktion/DE/Downloads/Gesetz/gesetzentwurf-gwb-digitalisierungsgesetz.pdf (last accessed 18 September 2020); as advocated by academia: J. Drexl, 'Neue Regeln für die Europäische Datenwirtschaft? Ein Plädoyer für einen wettbewerbspolitischen Ansatz', *NZKart*

facility".[110] The second approach refers to contract law, either as advised terms for co-generated databases[111] ("opt-in"), as compulsory sectorial contract law,[112] or as a general (default) private law rule[113] ("opt out"). The third approach advises organisational forms of " intermediaries" ("trusted third parties") which already exist in the automotive, energy, and banking/payment sectors.[114] Even Fezer advocates a public agency to pool "data property" of citizens and function as their "representative" (evidently aside of state data protection agencies).[115] Jones/Tonetti[116] propose the pooling of property rights in consumers, Metzger/Mischau[117] stress the neutrality of third party" intermediaries for the pooling of car driving related data, Atik/Martens[118] and Kenney et al[119] report about several designs of agricultural neutral intermediaries in France, the US and the Netherlands.[120] Yet, the central problem of setting up these intermediaries is finance.[121] The probable high service costs upstream are to be factored-in against reduced costs in the future and better services downstream.

2017, 415, at p. 418; A. Metzger, 'Mehr Freiheit wagen auf dem Markt der Daten: Voraussetzungen und Grenzen eines Marktmodells für "big data"', *in* A. Dutta/C. Heinze (Eds.), *Mehr Freiheit wagen – Symposium zur Emeritierung von Jürgen Basedow*, Tübingen, Mohr Siebeck, 2018, 131 (pp. 144-145).

110 S. Esken, 'Dateneigentum und Datenhandel', *in* Stiftung Datenschutz (Ed.), *Dateneigentum und Datenhandel*, Berlin, Erich Schmidt, 2019, 73, at p. 83.

111 Principles 23-25 'Data Rights Beyond Co-Generation' of the ALI-ELI Principles for a Data Economy – Data Rights and Transactions" (last version 22. May 2020). Co-generation is broadly defined by a non-exhaustive list of circumstances which should be taken into account when stipulating contractual access and porting rights, such as that the data is necessary for the normal use, maintenance or resale of the product or service, for quality monitoring, for the understanding of the party's own operations, for the development of new products or services or for preventing a lock-in situation, as reported by A. Metzger, 2020, *supra* note 66.

112 European Commission, 'European data strategy for data', COM(2020) 66 final, 19 February 2020, p. 13.

113 Qualified as 'majoritarian default rule', by A. Metzger, 2020, *supra* note 66, while he stresses that contract of freedom has to be secured by opt-put options.

114 *See* Deloitte Study 2017, *supra* note 20, e.g. for the energy sector p. 336; a critical debate is unfolding: R. Hilty/V. Moscon, 'Online Intermediaries as a Vehicle for Acts of Unfair Commercial Practices and Trade Secrets Infringement: What Liability within the European Legal Framework?', *in* G. Frosio (Ed.), *The Oxford Handbook of Online Intermediary Liability*, Oxford, Oxford University Press, 2020, pp. 421-443.

115 K.-H. Fezer, 'Repräsentatives Dateneigentum', *in* P. Kuzev/T.Wangermann (Eds.), *Studie im Auftrag der Konrad Adenauer Stiftung e.V. zum Thema "Einführung eines besonderen Rechts an Daten"*, 2018, available at https://www.kas.de/c/document_library/get_file?uuid=f828a351-a2f6-11c1-b720-1aa08eaccff9&groupId=252038 (last accessed 14 September 2020), p. 77.

116 Jones/Tonetti, 2019, *supra* note 48.

117 Metzger/Mischau, 2020, *supra* note 20.

118 Atik/Martens 2020, *supra* note 71, p. 9, pp. 32 et seq.

119 M. Kenney/H. Serhan/G. Trystram, *Digitalization and Platforms in Agriculture: Organizations, Power Asymmetry, and Collective Action Solutions*, ETLA Working Papers No. 78, 23 April 2020, available at http://pub.etla.fi/ETLA-Working-Papers-78.pdf (last accessed 24 July 2020).

120 Which all have their trade-offs (Atik/Martens, 2020, *supra* note 71, p. 33). Cooperatives either lose their neutrality over time – or keep them with the trade-off of not providing 'full service' (cost advantages will then again depend on the respective bargaining power); cooperation with (independent) large data processors avoid self-preferencing, but cannot avoid new lock-ins.

121 Atik/Martens 2020, *supra* note 71; Schneider 2021, *supra* note 14.

In contrast to the current debate which revolves around contracts and competition, the shift in argumentation towards "access" appears to be a reflection of a shift from binary market relations towards commons. Already in 2004, Yochai Benkler picked up this stream of thought and distinguished goods with high, medium and low granularity, building on Ostrom.[122] His interest was in "sharable goods" and the gap between the costs of production and the good's capacity to meet consumption needs.[123] His reflection was fuelled by products where the purchaser "gets more than he/she needs". The conceptual core of his reflection was the "slack capacity", which he finds in "mid-grained lumpy" goods, and which allows for sharing and pooling.[124] Benkler's "granularity theorem" is helpful as far as it re-directs the reflection about data. Even if products cannot be equated with data, there are parallels, and the concept opens perspectives. One parallel can be drawn between "mid-grained" goods and accumulated data. The cumulator "sits" on more data *information* than the company could meaningfully exploit itself. This constellation calls for arrangements which allow access right in order to fully grasp the societal use potential (sharing for re-use). A parallel to "fine-grained goods" would be a contract with e.g. Spotify or Netflix. Here, the customer gets exactly as much as he/she pays for.

Yet, what about raw data? They can be qualified as "fine-grained goods" if the transfer is conceptualised as a barter against the service. But what exactly is transferred? This is at the heart of the contested debate about "data ownership"; it puts the "input question" centre stage. From the preceding literature review, it appears that IP-lawyers presume raw data as public domain, while private law proponents appear to assume an acquisition process where prior entitlements to data (of whatever nature these entitlements are) perish with processing, similar to the ideas underlying § 950 German Civil Code, and time rules such as acquisitive prescription and adverse possession. In this ambiguity, the discussion resembles the one about other types of contested input information such as "Traditional

122 Y. Benkler, 'Sharing nicely: On Shareable Goods and the Emergence of Sharing as a Modality of Economic Production', 114 *Yale Law Journal* 2004, pp. 273-358.

123 *Id.*, at pp. 207-303.

124 'Fine-grained goods' have a 'granularity' which allows consumers to buy precisely as much of the goods as they want. An example is food. The use value equals the exchange value. By contrast, 'large-grained goods' require aggregated demand across many individuals to make the purchase costs effective. The use value of an individual is much, much smaller than the exchange value. An example is a steam engine. With 'mid-grained lumpy goods' the consumer gets more of the good as he/she can afford and consumes. The use value for the individual is smaller than the exchange value. These goods have 'slack capacity', and are therefore 'shareable.'

Knowledge"[125] and biomedical information,[126] which have widely remained unsolved[127] (in more depth *infra* 4a). Yet, while the legal techniques in IP and classical property law differ,[128] the economic rationale is congruent: Property shall be assigned to the one who invests and contributes most (and does not stifle[129]) economic growth.

While IP and property law converge as regards the economic rationale, both areas differ as to how they integrate non-economic and non-individual interests. And while the conceptualisation of data is still underway, the legislator is already actively shaping the legal environment. The GDPR grants individuals with regard to personal input information a portability right and a right to be forgotten. Reg. 2018/1807 on non-personal data primarily calls for private self-regulation, but it does already stipulate a "porting right". Public sector information is framed by two directives, Dir. 96/9/EC,[130] and Dir. 2019/1024[131] (repealing Dir. 2003/98/EC[132] with effect from 17 July 2021). The latter turns away from the proprietary approach and provides for access rights for the data categories covered.[133] Thus, data entitlements are already existing. However, our understanding of the inherent balance between public and private interests, and between recognition of (other) interests and the fostering of entrepreneurial activity is lagging behind. This problem it not adequately grasped by the debate about the economic value of input data. At stake are values such as autonomy, recognition, self-determination, self-subsistency, and the question who benefits from publicly financed data. To which extent is data "public"? This raises the question of the systematic value of raw data which unfolds a public dimension and involves

125 Knowledge held by collective entities, a category not acknowledged by Western law (see for a comparative screening and G. Van Overwalle´s analysis for case 10 in C. Godt et al (2021), supra note 24. Yet, Western property systems can overcome this *problematique* by a conflict of laws approach, Godt, 2007, *supra* note 32, p. 123; C. Godt, 'Enforcement of Benefit-Sharing Duties in User Countries', *in* E. Kamau/G. Winter (Eds.), *Genetic Resources, Traditional Knowledge and the Law*, London, Earthscan, 2009, p. 419.

126 To which claims in the various European jurisdictions are regulated either as individual or collective interest, *see* Comparative Remarks for Cases 10-13 in C. Godt *et al.*, 2021, supra note 24.

127 Concomittant with ethical issues: Is the individual entitled to a share of commercial benefits and to economic damages once his/her rights get violated? While the paradigmatic case dates back to 1990 (*Moore*), the debate is still ongoing, *see* A. Clarke, *Principles of Property Law*, Cambridge, Cambridge University Press, 2020, pp. 308-325.

128 In § 950 BGB the 'incoming' object/information gets 'appropriated' ('absorbed'), in copyright, prior titles get 'cut-off' (do have no influence on the later creation), in patent law, discoveries and mathematical theories are excluded from patentability from the beginning (while sequential 'proprietary titles' are aligned via the 'dependency principle').

129 This is the assumption of patent exclusions for discoveries and mathematical theories, see Godt 2007, *supra* note 32, p. 26.

130 Dir. 96/9/EC of the European Parliament and of the Council of 11 March 1996 on the legal protection of databases, OJ 1996 L 77, pp. 20-28.

131 Dir. 2019/1024 of the European Parliament and of the Council of 20 June 2019 on open data and the re-use of public sector information (PE/28/2019/REV/1), OJ 2019 L 172, pp. 56-83.

132 Dir. 2003/98/EC of the European Parliament and of the Council of 17 November 2003 on the re-use of public sector information, OJ 2003 L 345, pp. 90-96.

133 Guibault, 2021 (forthcoming), *supra* note 77, p. 18.

public interests.[134] How can these relationships be conceptualised, and what are the consequences? Before I submit a proposal (4.), we will look into some selected cases first (3.).

3 Case Studies

3.1 *Agricultural Data*

Recital 9 Reg. (EU) 2018/1807 refers to "data on precision farming" as an example of non-personal data. Yet, detached from the legal bifurcation of personal and non-personal data, does industry, as reported by the European Commission, distinguish three types of data as follows:[135] (i) farm data (from particular farms via sensors, machines or directly about farmers), (ii) complementary data (such as weather, satellite and other environmental data, including precipitation events, evapotranspiration, and heat unit accumulation), (iii) proprietary data (about agronomic inputs performances such as seeds or pesticides).[136] While farm data is submitted to transatlantic standardisation (so called ISOBUS[137]), the attribution of these data-sets slightly differs between the EU and the US, each having set up Codes of Conduct[138] aimed at enhancing the bargaining power of farmers. For farm data, the US Chapter assigns "ownership" to "the farmer";[139] complementary data, *argumentum e contrario*, is (appropriable) public domain information; proprietary data appears to be conceived as business secret. The European equivalent (despite earlier demands[140]) does not use the term "ownership"; it assigns "the exclusive right to licence access to the data and control its downstream use or re-use" to "the originator". This term refers to the machinery,[141] and it is not clear if the originator is the owner of the device,

134 Rightfully stressed by Scassa, 2018, *supra* note 55, p. 2.

135 *Bayer/Monsanto* (Case M.8084) Commission Decision of 21 March 2018, C(2018) 1709 final, para. 2453.

136 The different flows of data is visualised by P. Noack, *Precision Farming – Grundlagen und Anwendungsfelder*, Berlin, Wichmann, 2018, p. 19.

137 Norm ISO 11783, for more technical description *see id.*

138 US Privacy and Security Principles for Farm Data 2016, and EU Code of Conduct on agricultural data sharing 2018, thoroughly juxtaposed by Atik/Martens, 2020, *supra* note 71.

139 These terms are similar to those used in the automotive sector where, on paper and as default rule, "data belongs to the vehicle owner", Ritter/Mayer, 2018, *supra* note 5, p. 245.

140 M. Kritikos, *Precision Agriculture in Europe: Legal, social and ethical considerations*, Brussels, Scientific Foresight Unit of the European Parliamentary Research Service, 2017, available at www.europarl.europa.eu/RegData/etudes/STUD/2017/603207/EPRS_STU(2017)603207_EN.pdf (last accessed 14 September 2020), p. 47.

141 The machinery is equipped with 'sensors' and 'actuators'. Sensors collect data on mechanical movements and navigation position of the machine. Actuators use data inputs to activate mechanical movements and steer the machine.

the device controller or the farmer who has rented the device.[142] Eventually, the clear point of departure in the US and the unclarities in the EU are irrelevant since both Chapters recognise alienability. In the US, Monsanto Software contracts for Fieldview limit portability to other users of the same software. Hardware and software are licensed, not sold. The hardware is to be returned at the end of the contract.[143] In the EU, "portability" is secured (but also limited) to changing services (Art. 6 Reg. 2018/1807 thus stipulates a "porting right" only); anonymized and aggregated data (thus data which is "no longer specifically identifiable") is exempt. As a matter of consequence, the legal differences do not matter *in practise*, since contracts override default principles, legal transplants from the GDPR remain mute, and transferability is in practise not only accepted, but often imposed to the provider.[144] Problems have been reported as to the transfer of behavioural and on-site data to third parties (manufacturers, insurers).[145]

3.2 *Platforms and Databases*

Large databases can be exclusive or publicly accessible. If data sets enjoy proprietary *sui generis* protection under Dir. 96/9/EC is a contingent question. The Court restricted the emergence of the database right in *British Horseracing* 2004,[146] and adjudicated little afterwards.[147] The central question which is distinct from the emergence of the right is the question of access. The originators are now given "retrieval rights", either for control, or for porting to another processor. Public discussion has shifted to third parties" right for "re-use". While re-use got regulated in three service sectors (see above), the triangular situation is largely unresolved. As far as the projected use by the third party is covered by the data originators prior informed consent ("PIC") and the transfer as such authorised

142 Atik/Martens, 2020, *supra* note 71, p. 21; also Deloitte Study 2017, *supra* note 20, pp. 223, 224; a true problem when considering the different technical devices contracted for in digital farming, for a practical account see the comparison of data generated by multicopters (aerial vehicles) and ground sensors in winter wheat cultivation, *see* C. W. Zecha, *Spatial Combination of Sensor Data deriving from Mobile Platforms for Precision Farming Applications*, PhD-thesis, University of Hohenheim, 2019, available at http://opus.uni-hohenheim.de/volltexte/2019/1629/pdf/PhD_Thesis_CWZecha_2019.pdf (last accessed 14 September 2020).

143 Para. 3.4 Climate Fieldview™ Terms of Service, available at https://climate.com/fieldview-terms-of-service (last accessed 24 July 2020).

144 Atik/Martens, 2020, *supra* note 71, pp. 34; for a competition law perspective on the Bayer/Monsanto Merger see C. Atik, Understanding the Role of Agricultural Data on Market Power in the Emerging Digital Agricultural Sector: A Critical Analysis of the Bayer/Monsanto Decision, 2020 (DOI:10.13140/RG.2.2.21178.00962), last accessed 30.9.2020.

145 Deloitte Study 2017, *supra* note 20, p. 225.

146 Judgement of 9 November 2004, *Case 203/02, British Horseracing Board v. William Hill Organisation Ltd*, ECLI:EU:C:2004:695; Judgement of 9 November 2004, *Case 46/02, Fixtures Marketing Ltd v. Oy Veikkaus Ab*, ECLI:EU:C:2004:694.

147 Guibault, 2021 (forthcoming), *supra* note 77, p. 19 with an analysis of later case law.

in advance, it might be legitimate to submit the transfer to a bilateral agreement (submitted to power imbalances). Where, however, the data set entails proprietary data or the use goes beyond the consented use scope, both parties have to renew prior informed consent of the originator.

Yet, the question of *sui generis* protection got side-lined since the CJEU acknowledged mere factual control (including the contractual restrictions) in *Ryanair*.[148] The case revolved around access of a price comparing platform to Ryanair's publicly available dataset which includes prices, flights and timetable information. Ryanair had posted that it excluded access consent for commercial re-use purposes. In a contested judgement, the Court ruled that in cases where the directive does not apply also the exemptions to the exclusive right for "lawful use" are not applicable. As criticised by Guibault, this ruling "disregards the balance mechanisms built in IP legislation, and effectively reinforces the primacy of public ordering through contracts."[149]

This problem is exacerbated when it comes to exclusive databases which exist today in all sectors. Due to their industrial (secretive) nature, little empirical data is available, and – beyond the agricultural sector – only few publications.[150] With regard to "portability", literature purports "effective arrangements" in the automotive sector, the energy sector and the banking and payments services, and in agriculture.[151] Yet, the quest for standards for access, interoperability and data quality have become the central issues of the debate of how digitalisation can be advanced.[152] The regulator responded: porting rights also for non-personal data in general have to be secured for consumers and businesses alike by member states effective by 30 May 2021.[153] Thus, where service providers process machine generated maintenance data for the owner of the machine (e.g. combustion engines data in large vessels in order to coordinate repairs on the travel way of the vessel, or elevator use data in order to manage security checks), the possibility for the machine owner to transfer data to another service provider is prospectively secured. With regard to access for re-use, specific regulation exists for the automotive sector (though selectively),[154] and

148 Judgement of 15 January 2015, *Case 30/14, Ryanair Ltd v. PR Aviation BV*, ECLI:EU:C:2015:10 (concerning 'screen scraping').

149 Guibault, 2021 (forthcoming), *supra* note 77, p. 19.

150 An informative exception is the Deloitte Study 2017, *supra* note 20, which includes a survey of ten sectors.

151 Yet improvable, cp. Atik/Martens, 2020, *supra* note 71, p. 34 et seq.; A. Metzger, 2020, *supra* note 66.

152 *See* Deloitte Study 2017, *supra* note 20, pp. 330, 331 just for an example the energy sector: access is asked for to both private and public data banks; quality in data is described as "non-duplicative, complete, real-time". More: T. Hoeren, 'Big data and the legal framework for data quality', 25 *International Journal of Law and Information Technology* 2017, pp. 26-37.

153 Art. 4 sec. 3 Dir. 2018/1807, OJ 2018 L 303, p. 59.

154 Car maintenance data are to be made accessible to independent repair shops under Reg. 715/2007/EC (OJ 2007 L 171/1) on FRAND-terms; yet, in reality the problem appears to be most acute in this sector, see Deloitte Study 2017, *supra* note 20, p. 63.

for banking and payment services.[155] Cross sectorial contracts on data transfer are known for car automotive generated data between car manufacturers and insurers.[156] It is the re-use issue which the commission scrutinizes for misuse, and for which it actively encourages "codes of conduct".[157]

3.3 *Public Sector Data*

Looking at public sector data brings us closer to the question of what the nature of input data is. Public sector information is framed by two directives, Dir. 96/9/EC and Dir. 2019/1024.[158] Art. 3 in conjunction with Art. 13 Dir. 2019/1024 provide for access rights to listed high-value public data-sets (Annex 1: geospatial, earth observation and environment, meteorological, statistics, companies and campany ownership, mobility). This directive reverses CJEU-adjudication in *Compass-Datenbank*[159] and *Freistaat Bayern*[160] on Dir. 96/9/EC, and turns away from the proprietary approach. In contrast to its preceding Dir. 2003/98, Dir. 2019/1024 gives priority to the re-use of public sector information over the public body's IP right. It also extends the "principle of open by default" to research data, which is considered by most member states as "property" of the public institution, Art. 10 Dir. 2019/1024. Thus, the directive re-installs the general public's access to what most people perceive as (collected) "public domain" material.[161] In this regard, a comparative account of public sector information in various EU member states is most informative for their differing rationales. While in some jurisdictions, private property for public institutions is taken for granted (burdened only by researchers" freedom), public finance correlates with public access and remuneration restrictions with an outspoken policy to provide access to as many people as possible.[162]

155 Dir. 2015/2366/EU on payment services in the internal market, OJ 2015 L 337/35, (so called 'PSD2'), which replaces Dir. 2007/64/EC, made service like 'Apple pay' possible; further description of how financial SMEs and start-ups use it: Deloitte Study 2017, *supra* note 20, p. 242.

156 A. Metzger, 'Digitale Mobilität – Verträge über Nutzerdaten', *GRUR* 2019, pp. 129-136.

157 European Commission, 'A European Strategy for data', COM(2020) 66 final, 19 February 2020; *Id.*, 'Towards a Common European Data Space', COM(2018) 232 final, 25 April 2018; *Id.*, 'Building a European Data Economy', COM(2017) 9 final, 10 January 2017; on all three Kim, 2021 (forthcoming), *supra* note 84.

158 Infra fn. 126 and 127.

159 Judgement of 18 July 2012 in *Case 138/11*, ECLI:EU:C:2012:449. A private entity requested access to the company register created and maintained by the Republic of Austria based on Art. 102 TFEU. The legal question was if Austria´s licencing activities were to be qualified as ´an undertaking´ within the meaning of Art. 102 TFEU, a proposition denied by the Court. The result supported Austria´s argument to have a databank right under Dir. 96/6/EC, OJ 1996 L 77/20 (its preconditions were not inquired by the court).

160 Judgment of 29 October 2015 in *Case 490/14*, ECLI:EU:C:2015:735. The Freistaat Bayern claimed injunction against a publisher for unlawfully using topographic maps, appropriating underlying data and producing touristic maps, relying on its databank right under Dir. 96/6/EC, OJ 1996 L 77/20.

161 Guibault, 2021 (forthcoming), *supra* note 77, p. 18.

162 *See* Godt *et al.*, 2021 (forthcoming), *supra* note 24, comparative remarks on case 4.

Yet in practise, weather, satellite and other environmental data, including precipitation events, evapotranspiration, and heat unit accumulation is then "owned by the party that purchases the data, e.g. in case of data on weather forecasts, the data is purchased by a software provider and transformed into an easy-to-use application for farmers".[163]

3.4 *Corona Apps, E-health Apps*

In a recent article, Sjef explores Corona Apps, and reflects about them as a specific form of e-health apps.[164] The important teaching of this article is the complex interest structure of these data. The information of a person infected by the corona virus is evidently not only purely personal information for which the infected person can claim data protection. Evidently, it is personal information of any person who met him or her. For the case of the German corona app, it is only the contact data collected by way of Bluetooth which is decentrally collected on the smartphone, and pseudonymized numbers are stored. Beyond, legitimate public health concerns exist (to be communicated and processed by public agencies). Sjef also acknowledges interests of the pharmaceutical industry and insurers, even discusses the eminent domain of territorial states. The article sheds a spotlight on the complex public nature of data.

3.5 *Interim Conclusion*

These limited examples show two things. First, the assignment of non-personal data to the factual controller is not evident. Possession may result in factual control. However, the examples show that actors in the field attribute the original title to the data provider (the contractual terms demand transfer of title, for both personal and non-personal data). The actors' language implies that the legitimate ("better") title does not rest with the processor/the possessor in the first place, as courts have assumed (also against contractual terms, cp. *supra* re *Ryanair*, stipulated exemptions not applicable) resulting in overridden re-use interests and retrieval rights. Yet, more recent EU legislation has paved the way to assign specific entitlements to the originator and to third parties. These recent developments dismantle the property language as simplistic, sometimes manipulative. It becomes evident that the language is used in two ways. Originators use classic property language (rei vindicatio) to counter the processors control, and processors use IP language to counter data originators demands (qualifying their information as "public domain").

163 Deloitte Study 2017, *supra* note 20, p. 223.
164 Van Erp, 2020b, *supra* note 1.

Second, legislation has already installed fragmented property rights. The one "who owns" may be entitled to specific rights, e.g. retrieval rights, access (re-use), use rights. These rights are of different nature and mirror different legitimations for each entitlement. In the retrospect, the Lockenean "added labour" concept (which, in consequence, would assign full title to the processor) loses persuasive power with regard to data. Recent opposition by economists, competition lawyers and consumers support the proposition that the contrary may be true. Also a focus on innovation (either with reference to anticommons[165] or to competition and existing access rights[166]) might equally prove too narrow. A second look reveals a more complex topography of data where public and competing private interests overlap.

These insights must have to be absorbed by the design of the future data constitution.

4 Elements of the Data Constitution

4.1 Preliminaries

How does a data constitution for a just, political equal, in a liberal sense free and economically prosperous society look like? As a starting point, the metaphor of "data as new oil" has to be taken more seriously.[167]

As to the object, the qualitative descriptions of "renewability" or "re-use" signal fundamental differences compared to the classical commodities. These qualifications tend to limit data to their immaterial, inexhaustible, non-rival qualities, and bring the debate home to IP law. However, this framework oversees the societal public dimension of data. Buzzwords such as smart cities/houses/energy, robots for elderly care ("e-care"), facial recognition, social scoring, aerial postal delivery, medical applications ("e-health"), e-mobility delineate the playing field, but neglect data as "building block" of the digital

165 Kim, 2021 (forthcoming), *supra* note 84, referring to the discussion when too much or too many property rights impede innovation, with reference to the seminal papers of M. Heller/R. Eisenberg, 'Can Patents Deter Innovation? The Anticommons in Biomedical Research', 280 *Science* 1998, p. 689., and M. Heller, 'The Tragedy of the Anticommons: Property in the Transition from Marx to Markets', 111 *Harvard Law Review* 1998, p. 621, on both Godt, 2007, *supra* note 32, p. 550.

166 Ullrich, 2019, *supra* note 5, p. 29.

167 Scassa, 2018, *supra* note 55, p. 1.

economy.[168] This is why Sjef calls for a more profound reflection of the "hybrid world";[169] something which is also caught in Ingrid Schneider's "four models".[170] These works call for a normative re-virement. In future deliberations, Mancusos's analysis on the different types of collective and diffuse interests might prove helpful to better understand the dimensions of data publicness.[171] This exercise will help to reflect about the *nature* of data, beyond the three specifications of the current debate (supra 2). "Publicness" refers to a disruptive characteristic of the changing society which cannot be built solely on exclusive property as we know it. A gear shift is needed, comparable in weight with accepting incorporated firms as "legal" persons, and putting them on a par to natural persons by the end of the 19th century. I submit that it is the "public connotation" which is the driving force of the digital societal change. This is why Sjef's reflections on property *structures* in data are much closer to the challenge ahead of us.

Publicness demands legitimisation. Two dimensions should guide our reflection, prosperity and social freedom. With John Rawls, legitimate wealth generation demands that efficiency gains which result in economic and social inequalities as a consequence of a capitalist division of labour finance redistributive policies.[172] Profits based on data use are either to be taxed or profits have to be shared in other ways with the (raw) data providers. With Polanyi, capitalist markets will only deliver societal freedom, when market institution are re-embedded in societal institutions. Considering that data is as much a "fictitious commodity" as land, labour and money,[173] society as a whole has to "to use the instruments of democratic governance to control and direct the economy to meet our individual and collective needs", as Fred Block rephrases Polanyi's central thrive.[174] The consequence for a data constitution is that we reflect about on how data entitlements are framed by entitlements of and responsibilities vis-à-vis others.

168 The CJEU *Cases 434/15, Elite Taxi* (ECLI:EU:C:2017:981), *320/16, Uber France* (ECLI:EU:C:2018:221), and *390/18, Airbnb Ireland* (ECLI:EU:C:2019:1112) shed light on the public policy ramifications of regulative public transport and housing policies which may override (either by EU or national regulations) the general regulations on service liberalisation. M. Inglese, *Regulating the Collaborative Economy in the European Union Digital Single Market*, Cham, Springer, 2019, p. 34 rightfully describes the status quo as 'piecemeal approach' paving the way to future litigation in other service sectors. If it "undermines" (p. 34) the completion of the EU´s Digital Single Market remains to be seen.

169 Sjef enjoys challenging his students when he exposes to them: "You are data!".

170 Schneider, 2021 (forthcoming), *supra* note 14: (1) The collective/private model (micropayments), (2) state ownership, (3) commons, (4) trust.

171 R. Mancuso, Interesses difusos: conceito e legitimação para agir, 7th ed. São Paulo, Revista dos Tribunais, 2011.

172 J. Rawls, *A Theory of Justice*, Harvard University Press, 1971. Where IT-companies do not contribute by way of withdrawing from paying taxes, this liberal manifest becomes more and more hollowed.

173 K. Polanyi, *The Great Transformation*, reprint 2nd ed., Boston, Beacon Press, 2001 (orig. 1944), Chap. 6, p. 71.

174 F. Block *in* K. Polanyi, *The Great Transformation*, reprint 2nd ed., Boston, Beacon Press, 2001, p. xxxvii.

Doctrinal elements of the data economy will be "governance" and "fragmented titles". It does not come as a surprise when social scientists and technicians work on "guidelines on algorithms" and "AI ethics".[175] These approaches are geared towards securing personal freedoms and freedoms to operate, against both full proprietary discretion and full state control. These debates are in search of governance forms for an emerging data economy. The discussion has shifted to securing "self-sovereign identity" (by way of blockchains),[176] and "data governance".[177] The general support of these projects gives evidence that society does not accept data control as full proprietary disposition. Freedoms are to be secured, not as in the 18th century, "via" property against the sovereign, but "against" entitlements dubbed "property". What is needed is, in Sjefs words, "unbundling"[178] which gives way to a fragmented structure allowing "time management of access".[179] It is this perspective which demands reforming "property" as a central societal institution for modern societies. Property as an institution has survived the transformation from feudal reign, over the industrial revolution towards the constitutionally embedded property as regulated institution. However, it underwent change. Land today is conceived as private commodity, but few owners can use it as they please. In all legal systems (yet by different doctrines), water use is detached from the title to land. Firms are private entities, but heavily governed by corporate and collective labour law. Financial assets underlie regulation. Neither knowledge nor natural resources are today submitted to the basic appropriation rule of § 950 BGB.

As to methodology, the templates of private property and IP law have to be merged, and be further developed in the light of the already emerging structures. The modern structure of IP-law (fragmented, flexible, input sensitive, public policy balanced) and the power sensitivity which property law has been cultivated for over 200 years (coalesced in values and principles) are to be brought together. Property law should take two central insight from IP law on board. First, for the proper delineation of entitlements is not enough to delimit the object. Residuary rights of upstream input providers, and freedoms of downstream users re-define the content of the entitlement. IP law takes time and the

175 As proposed from the competition law´s perspective by the OECD, Algorithms and Collusion: Competition Policy in the Digital Age, Paris, OECD, 2017, p. 50; see also the deliverables of a German Government (BMBF) funded interdisciplinary research project ´Governance von und durch Algorithmen´ (engl.: Governance of and by algorithms), available under https://goal-projekt.de/ (accessed 29.9.2020).

176 A. Giannopoulou, 'Data Protection Compliance Challenges for Self-sovereign Identity', *in* J. Prieto *et al.* (Eds.), *Blockchain and Applications: 2nd International Congress*, Cham, Springer, 2020, pp. 91-100; B. Bodo/A. Giannopoulou, 'The logics of technology decentralization – the case of distributed ledger technologies', *in* M. Ragnedda/G. Destefanis (Eds.), *Blockchain and Web 3.0: Social, Economic, and Technological Challenges*, London, Routledge, 2020, pp. 114-129.

177 Schneider, 2021 (forthcoming), *supra* note 14.

178 Van Erp, 2020b, *supra* note 1, p. 23.

179 Van Erp, 2020c, *supra* note 12.

dynamics of data flows on board. This is where traditional property law falls short: It leaves the definition of use rights all to the contractual bargain of the parties, complemented – where necessary – by public regulation. It has neglected its role to theorize legitimate use rights. Where stipulated in regulation, these were accepted as imposed. But use rights in contracts, code of conducts, collective arrangements have not been understood as societal shift from property rules to liability rules (sic. "access").[180] Second, IP law teaches how "control through the chain" can be limited by doctrine. Effective devices are developed for both bilateral contract relationships and multilateral arrangements ("barriers theory" in copyright, collective societies, clearinghouses, pooling and collective governance of rights).[181] Some projects emerged as self-governed industry initiatives,[182] others were induced by regulation,[183] others emerged from private collective societal action.[184] For all arrangements it is key to identify the individual, the collective, the diffuse, and constitutionally embedded public interests of market-oriented mass societies with regard to data.

Building on these reflections, I submit that five data principles have emanated.

4.2 *Five Data Principles*

4.2.1 Input Recognition (PIC)

The first principle that the data constitution has to take on board is the recognition of input data ("access right type 1"). Data, by default, cannot and is not assumed to be "res nullius" or "public domain". The GDPR and Dir. 2018/1807 already acknowledge prior informed consent (PIC) and retrieval rights which give credit to the value both for the person and for businesses (which encompass delivery of information, control for purpose-compliant use, correction of false second layer analysis, erasure). On the national level, regulations acknowledge clients" data "ownership" e.g. for energy consumption

180 To pick up the language of G. Calabresi/D. Melamed, 'Property Rules, Liability Rules and Inalienability: One View of the Cathedral', 85 *Harvard Law Review* 1972, p. 1089; for a contemporary reflection see D. Wielsch, 2012, *supra* note 31.

181 A. Wernick/C. Olk/M. von Grafenstein, 'Defining Data Intermediaries – A Clearer View through the Lens of Intellectual Property Governance', *Technology and Regulation* 2020, pp. 65 *et seq.*, available at https://doi.org/10.26116/techreg.2020.007 (last accessed 14 September 2020); building on G. Van Overwalle *et al.*, 'Models for Facilitating access to patents on genetic inventions', 7 *Nature Reviews Genetics* 2006, p. 143. Ingrid Schneider critizes that the data originators are not knitted into the architectural fabric, Schneider, 2021 (forthcoming), *supra* note 14, p. 25, note 118.

182 E.g. M. A. Kock/F. ten Have, 'The "International Licensing Platform-Vegetables": A prototype of a patent clearing house in the life science industry', 11 *Journal of Intellectual Property & Practice* 2016, p. 496.

183 Participation Rule for the EU Research Funding Programm 'Horizon 2020', commented by C. Godt, 'Artt. 179-190 AEUV (Forschung, technologische Entwicklung, Raumfahrt)', in M. Dauses/M. Ludwigs (Eds.), *Dauses Handbuch für Europäisches Wirtschaftsrecht*, München, Beck, 44th complement 2018, paras. 44-70.

184 Most noteworthy the open source movement for software (GPL-License), Creative Commons.

data.[185] As of 2020, it is safe to say that data originators" rights have become acknowledged by law.[186] This recognition rebuts the economic default reflex that that "data has no value";[187] they only have no *commodity* value. As elementary "bricks" for further procession they have a quintessential value.

In legal terms, the entitlement is not simply lost (model § 950 German Civil Code) or absorbed by the subsequent processor (model public domain). Recent laws rather take reference to the dual model of copyright and to structures of data protection (where personal data remains linked to the person). For non-personal data the situation appears still more complex. As far as machine generated data is concerned, the data is rather attributed to the owner of the machine or to the owner of the object tracked (*supra* 3 c and d, mirrored by the fact that service providers require data providers by contract to transfer rights for use and re-use).[188]

Beyond the initial PIC and the retrieval (erasure) right, many questions remain to be discussed. How far do consent and determination go? Can withdrawal of consent with regard to personal data be overridden by stipulated processing justifications (Art. 6 GDPR)? Should remuneration be introduced?[189] Despite the fact that Art. 9 GDPR frames how to weigh individual and collective rights in Art. 9 GDPR, there is no cogent graduation of sensitive, pure personal or non-personal nature of data in the sense that the more sensitive the information is to a person the stronger is the determination right.[190] The reason is that the reference points are different. For personal information it is human dignity protected by Art. 1 and 8 EU Charter of Fundamental Rights, Art. 8 European Convention on Human Rights and under national constitutions (such as Art. 1 German Constitution). For business interests, it is the "freedoms to operate", as protected by economic freedoms under internal market rules, competition law, Art. 16 EU Charter of Fundamental Rights and national constitutions (such as Art. 12 German Constitution). Yet, the conceptual issue appears broader. It saddles up to the debate for recognition of "input" information in related fields,

185 As reported by Deloitte Study 2017 (*supra* note 20) for the UK on p. 333.

186 Ground-braking for this shift in mind-set A. Metzger, 'Dienst gegen Daten: Ein synallagmatischer Vertrag', 216 *AcP* 2016, p. 817.

187 Atik/Martens, 2020, *supra* note 71, p. 8; Schneider, 2021 (forthcoming), *supra* note 14, p. 17.

188 For the agricultural sector supra 3c; for the energy sector Deloitte Study 2017, *supra* note 20, p. 333.

189 This proposition of Jaron Lanier is discussed by Schneider, 2021 (forthcoming), *supra* note 14, p. 9, and pp. 16-18.

190 Note the differences in data protection across Europe, and especially with regard to sensitive biomedical data. In comparison, patients and clients are attributed less control about their biomedical data than their general data. Some states only acknowledge only a one-time approval right (no right to revocation), while other do. While purposing for general data is the rule; it is the exception for sensitive medical data. E.g. Germany does not allow purposing; while many other states so, *see* Godt *et al.*, 2021 (forthcoming), *supra* note 24, comparative remarks to cases 7 and 8. This restriction of personal data sovereignty is legitimized by the research freedom and public health policies.

such as traditional knowledge of communities,[191] "property" in genetic resources of provider countries[192] (in Western terms "sovereignty"), biomedical information of patients.[193] In inverse terms, the debate take reference to limits on the appropriation of chemical compounds,[194] and the contested debate around results emanating from public research.[195] These debates recur to claims to data sovereignty by indigenous peoples,[196] data retrieval rights of private individuals or business machine owners with regard to their "data property", and they will occur with regard to re-use claims. These rights do not protect the commodity value, but a participatory right in form of a veto position. It is this characteristic which renders them highly-personal, thus mostly non-transferable as commodity (but inheritable).

4.2.2 Re-use Rights

A second principle is acknowledging use rights ("access right type 2"). Evidently, those entitlements to data are not "absolute" in the classical sense; access rights, by their nature, are relative. Neither do they depend on a pre-existing absolute right.[197] Their legitimacy stems from the characteristic of publicness of data, and the economics of the digital economy (inverse proportional returns of production costs and customers; network

191 T.R. Eimer/T. Bartels, 'From consent to consultation: Indigenous rights and the new environmental constitutionalism', 29 *Environmental Politics* 2019, pp. 235-256, available at https://doi.org/10.1080/09644016.2019.1595884 (last accessed 14 September 2020); T. R. Eimer, 'What if the subaltern speaks? Traditional knowledge policies in Brazil and India', 41 *Third World Quarterly* 2019, pp. 96-112, available at https://doi.org/10.1080/01436597.2019.1650639 (last accessed 14 September 2020); T. Kiene, *The Legal Protection of Traditional Knowledge in the Pharmaceutical Field: An Intercultural Problem on the International Agenda*, Münster, Waxmann, 2011; Dreier, 2021 (forthcoming), *supra* note 76.

192 J. Reichman, 'Why the Nagoya Protocol to the Convention on Biological Diversity Matters to Science and Industry Everywhere', *in* C. Correa, X. Seuba (Eds.), *Intellectual Property and Development: Understanding the Interfaces - Liber amicorum Pedro Roffe*, Singapore, Springer Singapore, 2019, pp. 295-314.

193 On the diverging constitution of this information among European countries, *see* comparative remarks to case 7, in Godt *et al.*, 2021 (forthcoming), *supra* note 24.

194 S. Merenyi, *Der Stoffbegriff im Recht*, Tübingen, Mohr Siebeck, 2019; S. Merenyi, 'Stoffschutz im Internationalen Jahr des Periodensystems', *Zeitschrift für Geistiges Eigentum*, 2020, pp. 42-92.

195 Godt, 2007, *supra* note 32.

196 Canada: First Nations Information Governance Centre (FNIGC), *Ownership, Control, Access and Possession (OCAP™): The Path to First Nations Information Governance*, Ottawa, FNIGC, 2014, available at https://fnigc.ca/sites/default/files/docs/ocap_path_to_fn_information_governance_en_final.pdf (last accessed 14 September 2020); and Inuit Tapiriit Kanatami (ITK), *National Inuit Strategy on Research*, Ottawa, ITK, 2018, available at https://www.itk.ca/wp-content/uploads/2018/03/National-Inuit-Strategy-on-Research.pdf (last accessed 14 September 2020); United States: US Indigenous Data Sovereignty Network, online: http://usindigenousdata.arizona.edu; New Zealand: Maori Data Sovereignty Network, online: www.temanararaunga.maori.nz; Australia: the Maiamnayri Wingara Aboriginal and Torres Strait Islander Data Sovereignty Group is active on these issues.

197 Rightfully stressed by J. Drexl, Designing Competitive Markets for Industrial Data – Between Propertisation and Access, 8 JIPITEC 257 (at 291, para. 184).

externalities).[198] The necessity to grant access rights is currently strongly driven by competition concerns,[199] either for creating new markets or containing market dominance. As envisioned by the ALI-ELI principles (supra fn. 109), the access right for re-use is conditioned by a prior relationship which justifies access ("co-generation") or competition needs as regard to a bottle-neck situation. Yet, the threshold of granting an access right cannot only be determined by the measures of competition law ("dominant position"), as Axel Metzger seems to argue.[200] The threshold is dependent on the "publicness" of the data set.

Be it for competition reasons or for the intrinsic interests of re-users, the scope of access rights depends on the scope of the collective qualities of the data, the commercial character of a given data, and the structure of the division of labour in the given sector. Their legitimacy rests on economic (individual and collective rights to operate) and public interests (such as industrial policies). Building on research about the sequential character of progress in research driven industries,[201] competition lawyers have called for access rights (sharing rights),[202] and advise the European Commission to support self-governing arrangements. They advocate standards of interoperability when collecting data and the definition of access entitlements. The European Commission responded swiftly.[203] The next step is to find a standard for when access is to be granted to continuous data.[204]

Aside of direct claims, trusted third parties/trustees/stewardships have been proposed and in some cases tested.[205] The German Data Ethics Commissions called for sectorial pilot projects.[206] Various governance options in order to mitigate competing interests are

198 Crémer/Montjoye/Schweitzer, 2019, *supra* note 98, at p. 2. With regard to network externalities they explain: "The convenience of using a technology or a service increases with the number of users that adopt it."

199 For the European debate *see* Crémer/Montjoye/Schweitzer, 2019, *supra* note 98 for the German debate see Draft proposal for the 10th Revision of the German Law against Competition Restraints (GWB), https://www.bmwi.de/Redaktion/DE/Downloads/Gesetz/gesetzentwurf-gwb-digitalisierungsgesetz.pdf.

200 A. Metzger 2020, *supra* note 66.

201 S. Scotchmer, 'Standing on the Shoulders of Giants: Cumulative Research and the Patent Law', 5 *Journal of Economic Perspectives* 1991, pp. 29-41.

202 Crémer/Montjoye/Schweitzer, 2019, *supra* note 98.

203 The catch word is 'FAIR = Findable, Accessible, Interoperable and Reusable', European Commission, 'White Paper on Artificial Intelligence – A European approach to excellence and trust', Brussels, COM(2020) 65 final, 19 February 2020, p. 8, as proposed by the Expert Group on FAIR Data, *Turning FAIR into reality – Final Report and Action Plan*, Brussels, European Commission, 2018, available at https://ec.europa.eu/info/sites/info/files/turning_fair_into_reality_1.pdf (last accessed 14 September 2020), and negotiated under the roof of the OECD, https://www.oecd.org/going-digital/ai/principles/.

204 Crémer/Montjoye/Schweitzer, 2019, *supra* note 98, p. 107.

205 Some are listed in Schneider, 2021 (forthcoming), *supra* note 14, pp. 22-25; for initiatives in the agricultural sector see Atik/Martens, 2020, *supra* note 71, pp. 32 *et seq.*; for proposals in the automotive sector: Metzger/Mischau, 2020, *supra* note 20.

206 The German Data Ethics Commission (GEK), 2019, *supra* note 6, p. 134.

discussed.[207] The problems with building up these structures is the classical collective action problem (sic motivation),[208] and structural "co-opetition" trade-offs between competition and cooperation.[209] Yet, cultural preferences might also be taken into account. The French tradition tends to work with co-ownership constructions for overlapping entitlement, the German traditions tends to prefer the assignment of "absolute" positions which are moulded into arrangements which force parties into negotiations.[210] In IP-law, the dependency principle which grants full proprietary injunction power to both subsequent patent holders is an example for the German template. It is up to the regulator to devise sectorial arrangements which fit the needs.

4.2.3 Scoping Private Sovereignty

The third principle is "Scoping Private Sovereignty". "Private Sovereignty" substitutes the word "ownership". "Private Sovereignty" implies limited autonomy and fragmentation. "Private sovereignty" is closer to the use of the term "property" in the common law tradition, and appears open for an autonomous European re-definition. While common law lawyers would agree that the factual control of the processor is a "proprietary entitlement", continental lawyers would deny. "Private sovereignty" is the power of the individual to dispose of and manage his/her data entitlement. Thus, a processor who acquired data is free to use, accumulate, analyse, sell it in the limits of the prior agreed terms and adjacent regulations. The processor may "add labour and investment", and sell the processed product with profit. The central difference to classical commodities is the following. Access entitlements remain in place and do not perish. The "adding of labour" has no effect as to full title acquisition; "access right type 1" do not fully perish. The pooling of data may transform former individual entitlements into something like a common which again gives way to "access rights type 2". Both types of limitations, though, are familiar to IP-lawyers.

For property lawyers, respective limitations are reflected in Locke's acquisition theory for natural resources. Locke argues that legitimate extraction is bound to provisos (no spoiling, only as much as necessary).[211] Natural resources can be compared with pooled data to the degree that common's nature of data collections stems from the input of many, while with natural resources the common nature is based on conflicting use of many. In

207 For design principles in general see Schneider, 2021 (forthcoming), *supra* note 14, last section 'Datentreuhänderschaft-von der Idee zur Praxis' (pp. 21-25).

208 Deloitte Study 2017, *supra* note 20, p. 225; Schneider, 2021 (forthcoming), *supra* note 14, p. 25.

209 As Atik/Martens, 2020, *supra* note 71, pp. 33-35 explain, the detrimental lock-in effects which come with proprietary integration often are linked to advantageous services or package deals.

210 E.g. German Federal Supreme Court (BGH) in *Gummielastische Masse II*, decision of 22.3.2005, Doc.No. X ZR 152/03, BGHZ 162, 342; also BGH in *Orange Book Standard*, decision of 6.5.2009, Doc.No. KZR 39/06, BGHZ 180, 312 – which requires the party who is granted a use right has to deposit a security corresponding to the sum demanded by the patent owner.

211 Explained for property law by Clarke, 2020, *supra* note 127, pp. 49 *et seq.*

this regard, similar limitations appear sensitive. The commons" quality of data collections gives rise to the need of interoperability (to be operationalized by technical standards, either collectively convened [*supra* example 3 c] or publicly imposed[212]). Thus, access rights are not only a consequence of competition policy needs. They stem from the cumulative nature of the raw data ("publicness"). In the same vein, the general acceptance of non-discrimination standards for algorithms is to be explained both by the communal origin of data and the consequences for affected individuals (comparable to the integration of discrimination standards, which were still rebutted in the 70s, but got finally "internal" private law by way of the direct impact of fundamental rights.[213])

In order to give guidance to the legal architecture of data, a general "data act" as proposed by Sjef might be helpful. It would clarify the notion of the various entitlements, and define the connecting points. In addition, it should lay down some limiting rules (*sic* "cut-off points"), such as time limitations, and doctrines equivalent to the exhaustion principle in IP, in order to mutually protect freedoms to operate.[214]

4.2.4 Publicness

The publicness of data gives rise to two separate dimensions, inherent publicness and eminent domain.

Beyond personal data, machine data or data created and funded by the state (discussed above), there is data with an inherent publicness. The number of bees in my garden is not simply a private information, nor the diversity of birds, nor the stratigraphy of the soil layers under my house. The coronavirus app spotlighted this structure (*supra* 3 d). Data has inherent public characteristics. As such, they are often commons.[215] The central teaching from this observation is the following: data does not simply "miss" commodity characteristics (for being non-rival, non-exclusive) which need to be re-sculptured by law through the assignment of a right to exclude/participation right. There is a public dimension. For personal data, this dimension is captured by the value of privacy as a building block for liberal societies. Non-personal data have a public dimension as far as the freedom to operate is concerned as a value embodied in market economies. I hereby

212 Such as the Payment Services Dir. 2015/2366, OJ 2015 L 337, pp. 35-127.

213 Again a doctrinal development which Sjef was involved in and supported by founding the *European Journal of Comparative Law and Governance*; on the doctrinal shift see A. Colombi Ciacchi, 'European Fundamental Rights and Private Litigations: Judicial Dialogue and Judicial Governance', *in* F. Cafaggi/S. Law (Eds.), *Judicial Cooperation in European Private Law*, Cheltenham/Northampton, Edward Elgar Publishing, 2017, pp. 208-222.

214 On a modern judicial re-reading of "exhaustion" in digital environments see Godt, 2021b (forthcoming), *supra* note 24.

215 Comprehensively about the modern notion of commons building on Ostrom, S. Bailey, *The Common Good in Common Goods-The Decommodification of Fundamental Resources through Law*, Ph.D.-thesis University of Gothenburg, defended 9. June 2020, publication forthcoming.

contradict the position that geographic, morphological and chemical "primary data" of land can be assigned by default to the land owner, as opposed to "computed data", especially when aggregated with other farmers' data. While "computed data" seems to be considered in the ownership of the aggregating company,[216] the claim is that "data collected from farmers should remain the property of the farmers".[217] The simplicity of the binary juxtaposition between provider and processor should be opposed. I submit that the farmer *may* hold *an* entitlement to the geological data, but he/she does not "own" it as he/she does the land – due to the public characteristics of land. He/she is "trusted" with the information. The inherent commons quality may be operationalised as the anchor for participation in the form of remuneration, if the collective is well defined and representation is possible.[218] Yet, the emerging problem of all these forms of immediate remuneration appears to be collusion. In a case such as "agricultural data", remuneration would flow from big data processors (e.g. BASF/Monsanto) to farmers representations. I submit that it is preferable to organise "societal participation" via taxes which will be spent under democratic control (and might enhance digital education and profound reflection on conflicts in digital development). The governance of inherent publicness requires a public policy which is entrusted to the state.

Very different from the "state public policies" is "state sovereignty" which some states have claimed about data on their territory.[219] This approach is embraced for COVID-19 apps e.g. by Australia, a state not suspect of being socialist.[220] This practise coincides with academic propositions such as the one of Evgeny Morozov.[221] The underlying idea is "eminent domain",[222] close to the notion of public property. The European Union has enacted harmonizing regulation, in order to contain policies in this regard.[223] Yet, the different conceptual (cultural) notions will not be fully discarded this way. Whereas in Germany, public property is a singular and exceptional category encapsulated in public law (and rejected as a special category of "property"), the recently enacted new Belgian

216 Kritikos, 2017, *supra* note 140, p. 17.
217 *Id.*, p. 47.
218 Implied by Schneider, 2021 (forthcoming), *supra* note 14.
219 Van Erp, 2020b, *supra* note 1, p. 9.
220 I owe this substantiation to Sjef. Section 94 ZC Privacy Amendment (Public Health Contact Information) Act 2020, available at https://www.legislation.gov.au/Details/C2020A00044 (last accessed 14 September 2020). If Québec conceptualises public health data stored on public health agency as 'public property' is an open question.
221 Discussed by Schneider, 2021 (forthcoming), *supra* note 14.
222 Van Erp, 2020b, *supra* note 1, p. 11.
223 Both in general for non-personal data (Reg. 2018/1807, OJ 2018 303/59), and for specific data such as Corona infections, see Commission Recommendation 2020/518 of 8 April 2020 on a common Union toolbox for the use of technology and data to combat and exit from the COVID19 crisis, in particular concerning mobile applications and the use of anonymised mobility data, OJ 2020 L114/7, in more depth van Erp, 2020b, *supra* note 1, p. 9.

Civil Code acknowledges "public property", and does not limit its management to the state.[224]

These conceptual differences have to be taken into account when pondering about "publicness" of data across Europe. Having said this, "inherent publicness" should not be confused with "eminent domain", "public property" or even "public domain" (res nullius).

4.2.5 Legitimacy and Operationalization

Legitimacy of data governance is conferred by external and internal means. Democratic decision making legitimizes public rule making by way of *external* control; transparency and actor's accountability provides for *internal* legitimation.[225] The external frame is programmed by existing rules, such as Art. 345, 114, Art. 20 EUT/Art. 326 TFEU, and pertinent IP-laws. Internal legitimacy emerges from codes of conduct, standards which respond to economic and non-economic interests and liability rules.

Aside of the "General data act" proposed by Sjef, the complexity of conflicts of interests in data might require further finetuned operationalization by sectorial rules. E-health requires a different balance between highly personal information on the one hand, and public policy on the other hand, compared to the various actors of the automotive sector (repair; e-mobility). Building on experiences in the finance and agricultural sectors, I expect further sectoral regulation emerging for health-related data (building on EC directives such as Dir. 2004/23/EC,[226] Dir. 2006/17/EC,[227] and Dir. 2006/86/EC[228]) or energy data. The frameworks for these sectorial rules may differ. Some may remain purely self-regulatory, others may emerge as specific block exemptions under competition law (e.g. for the automotive sector) and others as direct sector regulation.

224 Article 3:45 new Belgian Civil Code (adopted by Parliament on 30 January 2020), defines public property as belonging to the private domain, unless meant to be used in the public domain.

225 Scassa, 2018, *supra* note 55, p. 3.

226 Dir. 2004/23/EC of the European Parliament and the Council of 31 March 2004 on setting standards of quality and safety for the donation, procurement, testing, processing, preservation, storage and distribution of human tissues and cells, OJ 2004 L 102/48.

227 Commission Dir. 2006/17/EC of 8 February 2006 implementing Directive 2004/23/EC of the European Parliament and of the Council as regards certain technical requirements for the donation, procurement and testing of human tissues and cells, OJ 2006 L 38/40.

228 Commission Dir. 2006/86/EC of 24 October 2006 implementing Directive 2004/23/EC of the European Parliament and of the Council as regards traceability requirements, notification of serious adverse reactions and events and certain technical requirements for the coding, processing, preservation, storage and distribution of human tissues and cells, OJ 2006 L 294/32.

5 Conclusion: Framework Thinking

The analysis has shown that we neither can nor should escape the discussion on "data ownership". Yet, the term "data ownership" may not always bring the debate forward, due to unsurmountable conflicts of political interests. Against this background, an academic debate on the rationalities of why and to whom we assign entitlements to data is even more necessary. Established terms should not stand in the way, but be exploited for their historic depth. The aim of the article was to highlight the inherent "public" characteristics of data which shift the balancing exercise to include a broader set of policies and interests in an exercise of framework thinking. The tacit underlying idea is that "data entitlements" (colloquially dubbed as "ownership" or "property rights") will emerge regardless of a public debate which rejects them. They are already emerging gradually by piecemeal regulation and judicial intervention. We are better aware of these strong unfolding societal forces driven by technological development. As academics, it is our task to observe what is happening, and to accompany the process by way of a conceptual discourse among us. Sjef, we are looking forward to further inspiration!

Comparative Law and Legal Issues Arising From Distributed Ledgers and Smart Contracts

Jasper Verstappen[*]

1 Introduction

The science of comparative law constitutes one of the pillars of the European Law School in Maastricht. Several reasons have been given for the focus of the Maastricht curriculum on comparative law. One of these reasons is the idea that a lawyer who is familiar with one or more jurisdiction other than their own, is less likely to experience a 'threshold of the unfamiliar' when they encounter legal issues involving multiple legal systems.[1] Additionally, a lawyer with a background in comparative law has a broader horizon. Having a broader horizon, in the legal sense of the word, enables one to relativize one's own national jurisdiction. This allows one to look at the law as more than the legal structure of a society, but instead as one of multiple possible solutions to societal issues.[2] Moreover, a strong comparative background enables a person to use comparative law as a heuristic tool. Comparative law allows a person to view the law of different jurisdictions as alternative hypotheses about possible solutions to social problems. It has also been argued that comparative law is a useful tool for students and lawyers alike in determining which arguments are valid.[3] Lastly, the fact that courts and legislatures might base their decisions on comparative considerations increases the relevance of comparative law,[4] thereby justifying it as a focal point for students and researchers.[5]

---

* Jasper Verstappen is a Lecturer in IT Law at the University of Groningen and a PhD Researcher in European Private Law at the University of Maastricht.

1 Jaap Hage, 'Comparative Law and Legal Science', *in* Aalt Willem Heringa and Bram Akkermans (Eds.), *Educating European Lawyers*, Cambridge, Intersentia, 2011, p. 66.

2 *Ibid.* pp. 71-73.

3 *Ibid.* pp. 69-70.

4 Smits gives multiple examples of the use of comparative considerations by courts and legislatures in Jan Smits, 'Comparative Law and Its Influence on National Legal Systems', *in* Reihard Zimmermann and Mathias Reimann (Eds.), *The Oxford Handbook of Comparative Law*, Oxford, Oxford University Press, 2006, pp. 478-487.

5 Jaap Hage, 'Comparative Law and Legal Science', *in* Aalt Willem Heringa and Bram Akkermans (Eds.), *Educating European Lawyers*, Cambridge, Intersentia, 2011, p. 66.

Whilst comparative law is but one pillar of the European Law School at Maastricht University, it is a pillar to which Sjef van Erp devoted much of his career.[6] This contribution will not focus on the added value, the methodology of comparative law as such, nor on Sjef van Erp's contributions thereto. Instead, this contribution will look at the changing application of comparative law in a world characterized by accelerating technological developments. It is argued that such technological developments open new avenues for comparative legal analysis and increase its relevance. Note that the focus of the contribution will be limited to the comparative legal methodology from a contract law perspective.

Lastly, but most importantly, this contribution will investigate Sjef van Erp's views on comparative law and the role of the comparative lawyer. By doing so we can distill a vision of the purpose of comparative law and the tasks of the comparatist. Applying that vision to the new avenues for comparative legal analysis allows us to determine whether that vision holds true today and is sustainable in the future.

2 On Methodology: What is Comparative Law

The comparative methodology distinguishes itself from the study of foreign laws by the explicit attention to similarities and differences between systems of laws. Where the purpose of a study of foreign laws is to communicate the content of that foreign law to a domestic audience, the comparative method aims to deliver added value by highlighting potential advantages of the foreign legal system through the comparative perspective it takes.[7]

A condition for the execution of the comparative exercise is the identification of a 'common comparative denominator', or *tertium comparationis*.[8] The comparatist will take the *tertium comparationis* as their starting point and focus on the similarities and differences amongst the legal systems that are being compared.[9] It is at this point that one would go into the different variations of the comparative legal methodology, including the functional

6 See for example his inaugural lecture as professor of civil law and European private law: Sjef van Erp, 'European Private Law: Postmodern Dilemmas and Choices. Towards a Methods of Adequate Comparative Legal Analysis', *Electronic Journal of Comparative Law*, vol. 3, no. 1, 1999, available at: www.ejcl.org/31/abs31-1.html (last accessed 21 December 2020); and his recent publication Sjef van Erp, 'De Betekenis van de (Vergelijkende) Rechtswetenschap Voor Het Notariaat', *WPNR*, vol. 150, no. 7225, 2019, pp. 77-78.

7 John Reitz, 'How to Do Comparative Law', *The American Journal of Comparative Law*, vol. 46, no. 4, autumn 1998, pp. 617-636, 620-621.

8 Esin Örücü, 'Methodology of Comparative Law', *in* Jan Smits (Ed.) *Elgar Encyclopedia of Comparative Law*, Cheltenham, Edward Elgar Publishing, 2006, p. 442.

9 John Reitz, 'How to Do Comparative Law', *The American Journal of Comparative Law*, vol. 46, no. 4, autumn 1998, pp. 617-636, 620-621.

approach, the structural approach, and the analytical approach.[10] However, such an overview would be out of scope here. For the purposes of this contribution, general notions of the methodology will suffice.

Finally, having identified the common point of departure for the comparative analysis, the comparatist will draw explicit comparisons and all the while pay explicit attention to similarities and differences amongst the different legal systems that are under investigation. Apart from simply drawing conclusions with regard to the contents of the legal systems under investigation, the comparative methodology allows the researcher to draw two unique types of conclusions. First and foremost, this methodology allows one to highlight special and unique features of the legal systems under considerations. Secondly, regarding the issues that one is researching, the comparative methodology allows a person to draw conclusions with regard to the commonalities amongst legal systems. This latter question will lead to insight into potentially universal aspects of legal systems and insights into fundamental aspects of the particular legal issue at hand.[11]

3 ON ROLE AND PURPOSE: WHY COMPARATIVE LAW

In his inaugural lecture in 1998, Sjef van Erp outlined his views on the expectations placed on comparative lawyers. In doing so he made explicit reference to Zweigert and Kötz who argue in favor of the functional approach to the process of comparative law.[12] A comprehensive overview of 'the functional method of comparative law' cannot be given, simply because it does not exist. The functional method has been described as "a chimera, both in theory and in practice" as no single cohesive, well-established variation of the functional comparative legal methodology exists.[13] Instead a patchwork of slightly different variations of the functional approach have been created over the years. An overview of sorts is given by Ralf Michaels in the Oxford Handbook of Comparative Law.[14] A deep-dive into the variations is beyond the scope of this contribution. However, a common denominator shared by all variations of the functional approach can be distilled. The

10 For a concise overview hereof see Mark van Hoecke, 'Methodology of Comparative Legal Research', *Law and Method*, vol. 12, 2015, pp. 8-20, available at: https://biblio.ugent.be/publication/7145504 (last accessed 21 December 2020)

11 John Reitz, 'How to Do Comparative Law', *The American Journal of Comparative Law*, vol. 46, no. 4, autumn 1998, pp. 617-636, 624.

12 Sjef van Erp, 'European Private Law: Postmodern Dilemmas and Choices. Towards a Methods of Adequate Comparative Legal Analysis', *Electronic Journal of Comparative Law*, vol. 3, no. 1, 1999, available at: www.ejcl.org/31/abs31-1.html (last accessed 21 December 2020) referencing; Konrad Zweigert and Hein Kötz, *Einführung in Die Rechtsvergleichung*, 3th ed.,Heidelberg, JCB Mohr, 1996.

13 Ralf Michaels, 'The Functional Method of Comparative Law', *in* Reihard Zimmermann and Mathias Reimann (Eds.),*The Oxford Handbook of Comparative Law*, Oxford, Oxford University Press, 2006, p. 340.

14 *Ibid.*

functional approach differentiates itself from alternative variations by recognizing functionalism as a fundamental principle. Functionalism recognizes that all legal systems will be confronted with similar issues, but might solve those issues in different ways. The functional approach to comparative law therefore dictates that the comparative lawyer ought to tackle these issues free from the conceptual framework of one's own legal system.[15] A legal scholar therefore ought to free himself from national legal categorizations in order to allow himself to investigate the legal norms in their environment. For example, rather than investigating the systems by which property is transferred in legal systems, the comparatist applying the functional methodology would ask the question in which way the legal systems under consideration protect the interest of a third party recipient in good faith. This might go further than simply investigating legal norms, and may include investigating cultural norms, economic factors and political environments. The underlying aim is to discover the function of legal norms in a certain environment, by observing that these norms are not abstract constructs but rather means through which actual issues are solved.[16]

Lastly, before we consider new avenues of application of the comparative legal methodology, let us return to the role of the comparative lawyer and the purpose of comparative law in the eyes of Sjef van Erp. In his inaugural lecture, Sjef van Erp argued for a pragmatic approach to functional comparative law. This allows the comparative lawyer to strike a balance between ideal and reality, without getting lost in intellectual isolation:

> For me, the comparative-law method is above all a source of inspiration and creativity, especially when it is employed in the development of a European private law as the object of jurisprudential research. Comparing alternatives and assessing their advantages and disadvantages is an instructive process for every lawyer. In such a process, which requires an open view of the world, particularly of globalisation, and a growing awareness of mutual dependence, there is no place for intellectual purism. What is needed here is the daring to take the risk of misunderstanding or being misunderstood – a daring that must certainly be based on efforts to achieve the ideal of comparative law, but is also characterised by an open attitude and a willingness to learn from past mistakes. To this extent my approach to comparative law could be described as pragmatic.[17]

15 Uwe Kischel, *Comparative Law*, Oxford, Oxford University Press, 2019, pp. 88-89.

16 Ibid., p. 8.

17 Sjef van Erp, 'European Private Law: Postmodern Dilemmas and Choices. Towards a Methods of Adequate Comparative Legal Analysis', *Electronic Journal of Comparative Law*, vol. 3, no. 1, 1999, p. 10, available at: www.ejcl.org/31/abs31-1.html (last accessed 21 December 2020).

In his view, the comparative lawyer therefore ought to strike a balance between the ideal comparative law and the practical comparative law. This balance is to be found in the 'adequate solution'. In finding this adequate solution, the comparative lawyer ought to take six aspects into account: the object of the study, the area of the law that is being studied, the nature of the problem chosen, the extent to which the legal systems being studied are related to one another, the accessibility of material about the relevant foreign law, and the necessity in social, economic, or political terms of achieving results quickly.[18] The following paragraphs will connect this view on the comparative methodology to the development of distributed ledgers and smart contracts, and the legal issues this creates.

4 On Technology: When Technology Might be Relevant for a Comparative Lawyer

Technological developments can create novel legal issues. One such technology is smart contracts. Whilst smart contracts can exist in isolation, their full potential can only be unleashed when they exist on a distributed ledger (also known as 'a blockchain'). I will use the development of distributed ledger technology (DLT) and smart contracts as a case study. Using this case study, I will outline some of the legal issues that might be created. The focus is exclusively on issues in the area of contract law. Having outlined these legal issues, I will analyze whether the comparative methodology is suitable to tackle these issues and, if yes, whether these new developments change the role, purpose, and perspective of the methodology. Lastly, by doing so, I will be able to test the views on a postmodern role for the comparative legal methodology outlined by Sjef van Erp in his 1998 inaugural lecture.

However, before I can do so, it is essential to outline the technological developments and their functioning. An understanding of the technology is required to understand the legal issues it creates. Without a thorough understanding of the technology, the appearance, severity and impact of the legal issues will remain unclear. Moreover, without a sense of the appearance, severity, or impact of the legal issues, it is impossible to apply the comparative methodology. After all, the comparative methodology requires the identification of a *tertium comparationis* as a foundation upon which the comparative exercise is based.[19] For a question to be relevant, both from the perspective of the technological developments as well as from a comparative point of view, this foundation

18 Sjef van Erp, 'European Private Law: Postmodern Dilemmas and Choices. Towards a Methods of Adequate Comparative Legal Analysis', *Electronic Journal of Comparative Law*, vol. 3, no. 1, 1999, p. 11, available at: www.ejcl.org/31/abs31-1.html (last accessed 21 December 2020).

19 John Reitz, 'How to Do Comparative Law', *The American Journal of Comparative Law*, vol. 46, no. 4, autumn 1998, pp. 617-636, 620-621.

ought to be at least affected by the technology or created by the technology. Hence, for a question to be relevant from both the technological perspective as well as from a comparative methodological perspective, the technology must create legal issues that affect the object of the comparison. For the comparative methodology, a deep and thorough understanding of that object of comparison is essential. The appearance, impact, and severity of the legal issues, which ensure the relevance of the comparative exercise, are directly dependent on the technology and affect the *tertium comparationis*. Therefore, one has to have a certain appreciation and awareness of the technology, its functioning, and its application.

5 On Technology: Distributed Ledgers and Smart Contracts

This contribution looks at the development of distributed ledgers and smart contracts as an example of technological developments that potentially create novel legal issues and uses it as a case study. One could consider a distributed ledger as a platform without central authority. This platform allows persons to transact. Certain platforms allow for smart contracting. For a platform to allow smart contracting, a programming language with a certain complexity is required. In their very essence, smart contracts are nothing more than conditional promises; they express a condition and a result. Once the condition is fulfilled, the result is executed. An offer expressed in that programming language might express a condition of payment and a transfer as a result. A simple example of such an offer might look like this: 'if payment of 10,- is received, this smart contract code will transfer the object expressed therein.'

A short disclaimer is appropriate before I outline the technological functioning of the case study, i.e. distributed ledger technology and smart contracts. A complete outline of the technology is, for reasons of space, beyond the scope for this contribution. Instead, I shall identify five aspects by which the technology differentiates itself. Three of these aspects are based on the distributed ledger technology, whilst two are based on the smart contract technology. The former three include immutability, transparency, and pseudonimity. The latter two include automatic execution and automatic enforcement. All of these will be considered in turn.

5.1 Immutability

This first aspect relates to a unique characteristic of distributed ledgers. In principle, no single party can alter the state of the ledger. The ledger is therefore immutable. This immutability is guaranteed on two different levels, i.e. on a transaction-level and on a recordation-level. I will touch upon both.

Integrity of transactions is guaranteed through public-private key encryption. As a precursor to distributed ledgers, this system was first proposed in the context of digital currencies by David Chaum. He proposed a system in which both parties are in possession of a public key and a private key. The public key is known to anyone, whilst the private key is only known to the holder. Without going into details, this system allows parties to encrypt and decrypt data in communication amongst each other. Hereby parties effectively disguise the content of their messages from third parties.[20] Moreover, this system introduces non-repudiation amongst the parties. This means that persons who sent the data are unable to claim that they have not sent the data while preventing anyone from altering the data in transmission.[21] Immutability between parties is therefore guaranteed by public-private key encryption.

Additionally, immutability between the parties and everyone else is guaranteed through the consensus mechanism. A multitude of different consensus mechanisms exist. However, as an example we will use the first successful implementation of a distributed ledger. This implementation is based on a 2009 publication by Satoshi Nakamoto, who proposed Bitcoin as a peer-to-peer version of electronic cash.[22] The technology proposed by Nakamoto must guarantee that the entire ledger, i.e. the entire network, is in agreement about the answer to the following three questions:[23]

- Can I trust that the money is authentic and not counterfeit?
- Can I trust that the digital money can only be spent once?
- Can I be sure that no one else can claim that this money belongs to them and not me?

The consensus mechanism is the instrument that guarantees that the entire network is in agreement about the above three questions. Hence, where public-private key encryption guarantees that I can trust my counter-party, the consensus mechanism guarantees that I can rely on the state of the ledger, which answers the three questions above.

The consensus-mechanism is based on network-participants solving one-way functions. These one-way functions are mathematical functions that are easy to solve, provided the input is known, but prohibitively hard to solve if the input is unknown.[24] The bitcoin protocol provides only the output and tasks some of the network participants (the 'miners'), to find the input. Due to the nature of one-way functions, a miner can only find the input

20 David Chaum, 'Blind Signatures for Untraceable Payments', *in* David Chaum *et al* (Eds.), *Advances in Cryptology*, Boston, Springer, 1982, p. 199.

21 David Chaum and Hans van Antwerpen, 'Undeniable Signatures', *in* Gilles Brassard (Ed.), *Advances in Cryptology - CRYPTO '89 Proceedings*, New York, Springer, 1990, p. 212.

22 Satoshi Nakamoto, 'Bitcoin: A Peer-to-Peer Electronic Cash System', available at: https://bitcoin.org/bitcoin.pdf (last accessed 21 December 2020).

23 Andreas M Antonopoulos, *Mastering Bitcoin*, 2nd ed., Sebastopol, O'Reily Media, 2017, p. 3.

24 See for an overview Giovanni Die Crescenzo, 'Foundations of Modern Cryptography', *in* Dario Catalano *et al* (eds.), *Contemporary Cryptology*, Basel, Birkhäuser Verlag , 2006, pp. 92 *et seq.*

by expending a considerable amount of computing power. The output is a system-generated set of characters, known as a 'hash'. This hash is the output of the one-way function. The input to the one-way function is a set of transactions, a reference to the previous block, and a randomly generated number. By checking which input, i.e. which random number, produces the system-prescribed output, the miners are checking the validity of the transactions. Once a miner finds a solution, this solution is broadcasted as a block. All other miners check the validity of the block.[25] Once this is verified, all network participants update their ledgers in accordance with the transactions that this miner has proposed.[26] In other words, they add a block, containing verified transactions, to their chain. This system guarantees that the network is in agreement about the state of the ledger, with a minimal delay. To summarize, miners check transactions. By checking these transactions, they check that coins are authentic and not counterfeit, that coins are only spent once,[27] and that coins are not claimed by more than one person. This consensus mechanism, known as proof-of-work, guarantees the immutability of the network by way of a continuous, distributed transaction verification mechanism.[28]

Figure 1 Block transactions

25 This verification is a fairly straightforward process that requires a minimum amount of computing power: verification is done by checking whether the presented nonce, used as input, provides the prescribed hash.

26 Satoshi Nakamoto, 'Bitcoin: A Peer-to-Peer Electronic Cash System', pp. 2-4, available at: https://bitcoin.org/bitcoin.pdf (last accessed on 21 December 2020).

27 The problem of potentially spending the same coins multiple times is known as the 'double-spending' problem. Whilst a deep-dive into the solution included in the Bitcoin blockchain is beyond the scope of this contribution, it is worth noting that the process of confirming transactions includes a check on whether the transactions have been spent previously. If this is the case, the transaction will be rejected.

28 Andreas M Antonopoulos, *Mastering Bitcoin*, 2nd ed., Sebastopol, O'Reily Media, 2017, pp. 225 *et seq.*

5.2 *Transparancy and Pseudonimity*

One requirement of the consensus mechanism is that miners are able to check the validity of transactions. If miners are not able to determine whether a person had a right to make a certain transaction, the integrity of the network cannot be guaranteed. Hence, the information needs to be available. This information is contained in the blocks, that are checked by the miners prior to publication.[29] All these blocks are available to the public, they can be downloaded in bulk by synchronizing with the Bitcoin Core.[30] Alternatively one can use a Blockchain Explorer to look at the details of every single block to date, which includes all details of all transactions to date.[31] As an example, I have included below the first two transactions of the most recent confirmed block (#639843). As becomes clear, these transactions include the sender, the recipient, the time of sending, as well as the value of the transactions (black outline and text in picture added by author).

Note however, that it is impossible to identify the sender solely on the basis of the information contained in a block. On the ledger, the sender and the recipient are identified by way of their public keys. While it is impossible to identify the person behind a public key solely on the basis of the information in the block, the public keys are inherently personal. It would therefore be a mistake to consider the parties anonymous. After all, the public key acts as a sort of pseudonym by way of which the parties can be distinguished from other persons on the ledger.[32]

To summarize, all information relevant to determine the integrity of the ledger is available to the public. This information includes timestamps of transactions, recipients, senders, and values. However, the natural persons making these transactions are shielded from direct identification by their public key. Availability of the information therefore results in the ledger being transparent. Shielding the natural person behind the public key means that the ledger is pseudonymous rather than anonymous.

5.3 *Automatic Execution and Automatic Enforcement*

The first three technological aspects, discussed above, are based on the distributed ledger. Automatic execution and automatic enforcement are not created through the distributed ledger itself. Instead, they are the result of smart contracting technology that might exist on such ledgers. In order to understand the functioning of these two technological aspects,

29 Andreas M Antonopoulos, *Mastering Bitcoin*, 2nd ed., Sebastopol, O'Reily Media, 2017, pp. 225 et seq., p. 196.

30 Available at: https://bitcoin.org/nl/download (last accessed on 21 December 2020). At the time of writing, the complete dataset consists of approximately 269.82 GB.

31 Available at: www.blockchain.com/nl/explorer (Last accessed on 21 December 2020).

32 Andreas M Antonopoulos, *Mastering Bitcoin*, 2nd ed., Sebastopol, O'Reily Media, 2017, pp. 57 *et seq.*

it is necessary to first outline the political context in which smart contracts were first conceived. This political context will explain the initial aims and purposes of smart contracts.

This technology was first envisaged by Nick Szabo in a publication in Extropy Magazine, published by the Extropy Institute. Extropianism is a form of transhumanism that encompasses elements of political libertarianism.[33] Szabo was an active member of the crypto-anarchist cypherpunk movement. This movement was at the forefront of cryptocurrency developments and was very involved with extropianism. This could be explained by the political and economic goals put forward by extropianism; these are closely aligned with the political and economic goals of the cypherpunk movement. Extropianism proclaims that "an anarchist market creates free and dynamic order, while the state and its life-stealing authoritarianism is entropic."[34] The goals of the crypto-movement revolve around using technology to create instruments through which social and economic conduct becomes possible outside of the reach of government or centralized institutions.[35] It should therefore come as no surprise that Szabo, who previously published an essay entitled "Trusted third parties are security holes",[36] first proposed the concept of smart contracts in the Extropy magazine. In this publication he describes smart contracts as 'a set of promises, specified in digital form, including protocols within which the parties perform these promises'.[37]

In his publication Szabo outlines that such smart contracts allow four improvements to the contracting process. First of all, they allow parties to observe each other's performance. Secondly, they allow parties and arbiters to verify whether an obligation has been met or breached, making it much more straightforward to establish whether a burden of proof has been met. Thirdly, the smart contract gives parties control over the contents and the performance of a contract in a distributed manner in so far as it is necessary for the performance of that contract. Lastly, it minimizes the time needed for enforcement. Szabo argues that enforcement mechanisms can be automated.[38] As stated before, the result of a smart offer is specified in its code. Once the condition is fulfilled, that result is

33 Jeanine Thweatt-Bates, *Cyborg Selves: A Theological Anthropology of the Posthuman*, 1st ed, London, Routledge, 2012, p. 46.

34 *Ibid*, p. 47.

35 Julie Pitta, 'Requiem for a Bright Idea', *Forbes*, 01 November 1999, available at: www.forbes.com/forbes/1999/1101/6411390a.html#3358a52715f6 (last accessed on 21 December 2020).

36 Nick Szabo, 'Trusted Third Parties Are Security Holes', available at: https://nakamotoinstitute.org/trusted-third-parties (last accessed on 21 December 2020).

37 Nick Szabo, 'Smart Contracts: Building Blocks for Digital Markets', *Extropy*, no. 16, 1996, par. 1 available at: www.fon.hum.uva.nl/rob/Courses/InformationInSpeech/CDROM/Literature/LOTwinterschool2006/szabo.best.vwh.net/smart_contracts_2.html (last accessed 21 December 2020).

38 *Ibid*, par. 4.

effectuated automatically, rendering execution unavoidable. Enforcement is therefore automated by unavoidable performance by the technology.

This vision remained purely theoretical for a long time. It was only in 2013 that the first successful implementation of a smart contracting platform, based on a distributed ledger, became a reality. In 2013 Buterin and Wood published two papers on smart contracts. In these papers they outlined how smart contracts could be incorporated on a distributed ledger.[39] Their proposal was implemented as 'Ethereum', effectively making it the first successful implementation of a distributed smart contracting platform. We will use the Ethereum-platform as a case study for smart contracts. I will focus solely on the innovations that allow Ethereum its contracting capability.

First and foremost, contrary to the Bitcoin protocol, Ethereum is based on a programming language that is 'Turing-complete'.[40] Turing-completeness refers to the ability of the programming to solve any solvable mathematical problem.[41] Being Turing-complete gives the Ethereum platform sufficient flexibility as a platform to allow parties to program and arrange their own relations on that platform.

Secondly, in order enable smart contracts, Ethereum recognizes a special type of account. Like Bitcoin, Ethereum recognizes accounts owned by parties through their public key. On the Ethereum platform these are known as EOA's (externally owned accounts). However, contrary to Bitcoin, Ethereum also recognizes 'contract-accounts'. As opposed to the EOA's, these contract accounts include 'contract code'. Persons designing a contract-account have to write this contract code, and thereby have to *ex ante* prescribe the conditions and consequences of that code being activated. Since the language (i.e. *Solidity*) in which this contract code is written is Turing-complete, there are no software-limits on what might be programmed.[42]

The contents of the contract code are available in a contract-account and, due to the transparent nature of the platform, are available to everyone. It is therefore possible for people to understand the conditions and consequences of a contract. Moreover, it is possible for an EOA to send a message to a contract-account in order to activate the contract account. Once the conditions for execution of a contract account are fulfilled, the execution of that account happens automatically; neither the creator of the contract account nor the

---

39 Gavin Wood, 'Ethereum: A Secure and Decentralised Generalised Transactions Ledger', available at: https://ethereum.github.io/yellowpaper/paper.pdf (last accessed 21 December 2020); Vitalik Buterin, 'Ethereum White Paper – A next Generation Smart Contract & Decentralized Application Platform', available at: https://github.com/ethereum/wiki/wiki/White-Paper (last accessed 21 December 2020).

40 For an overview of what Turing-completeness means see Donald E. Johnson, *Programming of Life*, New York, Big Mac Publishing, 2010, pp. 12 *et seq* and p. 60.

41 Andreas M. Antonopoulos and Gavin Wood, *Mastering Ethereum*, Sebastopol, O'Reily Media, 2019, p. 8.

42 *Ibid*, p. 26; Vitalik Buterin, 'Ethereum White Paper – A next Generation Smart Contract & Decentralized Application Platform', p 7. Available at: https://github.com/ethereum/wiki/wiki/White-Paper (last accessed 21 December 2020).

holder of the EOA are able to prevent execution.[43] Both execution and enforcement is therefore independent of the parties. Moreover, both execution as well as enforcement is independent of any third party. Therefore, smart contracts incorporated on a distributed ledger introduce automatic execution and automatic enforcement as technological aspects.

This system provides a plethora of revolutionary new applications, including supply chain applications,[44] IoT-applications,[45] and financial services applications.[46] However, the impact on legal systems cannot be underestimated either. With the implementation of smart contracting capabilities, the vision put forward by Szabo in his 1996 essay in Extropy magazine has become a reality. In light of the previously mentioned political and economic goals of the movement of which Szabo was an active part, the impact on the legal system should be taken seriously. Incorporating self-executing instructions on a blockchain enables parties to automatically and securely transact.[47]

6 On Law: Potential Legal Issues Stemming from DLT and Smart Contracts

I have highlighted the five technological aspects that are introduced by the technology under investigation here: immutability, pseudonimity, transparency, automatic execution and automatic enforcement. I have used two case studies, namely the Bitcoin blockchain and the Ethereum platform, to elaborate on these aspects and explain their technological foundations. It is crucial to realize that these platforms are not the only platforms that exist: an abundance of different implementations has been created. Moreover, the strength of the five technological aspects is not binary: a ledger is not either completely immutable or not immutable at all; neither is it fully transparent or opaque. All these aspects exist on a spectrum. Where these five technological aspects fall on that spectrum is dependent on the particular use-case, design, and implementation of the technology in a particular instance. Some distributed smart contracting platforms might be more pseudonymous

43 Andreas M Antonopoulos, *Mastering Bitcoin*, 2nd ed., Sebastopol, O'Reily Media, 2017, p. 129.

44 Heineken, 'Hop on the Blockchain – Using Blockchain Technology to Establish a More Sustainable and Transparent Supply Chain', 22 January 2019, available at: https://www.theheinekencompany.com/newsroom/hop-on-the-blockchain (last accessed 7 December 2020).

45 See for overview Tiago M. Fernández-Caramés and Paula Fraga-Lamas, 'A Review on the Use of Blockchain for the Internet of Things', *IEEE Access*, vol. 6, 2018, pp. 32979-33001, available at: https://ieeexplore.ieee.org/document/8370027 (last accessed 7 December 2020).

46 Alexander Shelkovnikov, 'Blockchain Applications in Banking', *Deloitte*, 2016, available at: https://www2.deloitte.com/content/dam/Deloitte/ch/Documents/innovation/ch-en-innovation-deloitte-blockchain-app-in-banking.pdf (last accessed 7 December 2020).

47 Samuel Bourque and Sara Fung Ling Tsui, *A Lawyer's Introduction To Smart Contracts*, Lask, Scientia Nobilitat, 2014.; Karen Levy, 'Book-Smart, Not Street-Smart: Blockchain-Based Smart Contracts and the Social Workings of the Law', *Engaging Science, Technology, and Society*, vol. 3, 2017, pp. 1-15, 2-3

and less transparent, whilst other distributed smart contracting platforms might characterize themselves by a flexible approach toward immutability.[48] Therefore, the impact of the five technological aspects can most effectively be assessed in light of a particular implementation project. The relative infancy of the technology at the time of writing and the lack of a concrete implementation project precludes me from doing so in this contribution.

The potential impact of these five technological aspects on systems of contract law is considerable. These implications are not limited to a particular phase of the lifeline of a contract, but permeate the entire contractual process in all its aspects: including the pre-contractual phase, questions of capacity to contract, formation, interpretation, breaches, and remedies. In order to highlight both the issues as well as the application of the comparative methodology, I will focus on one of these issues in light of three European legal traditions. The following paragraph will give a short overview of whether a smart contract, prior to being activated, might be considered an offer according to French, German, and English law. I focus on these legal systems because they represent the three main European legal traditions.

6.1 *Smart Contracts as Offers in Contract Formation*

For an offer to be effective in all legal systems under consideration, several requirements have to fulfilled. First and foremost, the offer ought to contain all elements necessary for the agreement.[49] This requirement is especially clear in article 1583 of the French *Code Civil* which requires the offer to include the object and the price. Moreover, the offer must be such that it is clear that the offeror intends to be bound.[50] All legal systems distinguish between legally binding offers on the one hand, and offers 'subject to agreement', *freibleibende* offers and offers *sans engagement* on the other hand.[51]

However, offers on a distributed ledger are different from the classic offer in which an offeror expresses their intention to contract by way of an offer to an offeree. Instead an offer might be uploaded to a platform, free for any willing offeree to accept it. This therefore seems closer to offers made to the public.

48 Many smart contracting platforms are still in their very infancy. However, design choices made during development give strong indications as to the strength of their pseudonimity and immutability. Whilst a deep-dive is beyond the scope of this contribution, one could look into the EOS-initiative as a case-study of a smart contracting platform that makes alternative choices that might have a direct impact on its pseudonimity and immutability.

49 Hein Kötz, *European Contract Law*, 2nd ed, Oxford, Oxford University Press, 2017, p. 19; Nils Jansen and Reinhard Zimmermann, *Commentaries on European Contract Laws*, Oxford, Oxford University Press 2018, p. 181.

50 See also article II-4:201(1) DCFR for a reflection of these criteria.

51 See for example *Bundesgerichtshof* 8 March 1984, [1984] NJW 1885, Civ. 28 November 1968, JCP 1969.II.15797, and *Gibson v Manchester City Council* [1979] 1 WLR 295.

The French *Cour de Cassation* decided in 1969 that offers to the public bind a party upon acceptance identically to offers made to that party directly. However, this does not hold true in situations when the personal characteristics of the offeree are of interest to the offeror.[52] This might be the case in credit arrangements or employment relations.

Under English law, whether or not an offer to the public constitutes a binding legal offer is dependent on construction, meaning that a court will investigate whether the communication in a particular case provides sufficient evidence of an offerors intention to be bound,[53] an example of which might be found in *Gibson v Manchester City Council* in which Lord Diplock considers the words 'may be prepared to sell' and determines that these words bar the statement from being considered a binding offer.[54] In other instances the courts have decided that advertisements and pricelists are considered mere invitations to treat,[55] but 'offers made to all the worlds' in an advertisement for a reward are legally binding offers.[56]

In 2007 it was held that even automated mechanisms involving offers for unilateral contracts might result in binding legal agreements.[57] This exception is likely to be applicable to smart contracts, especially in light of a comparison between vending machines and smart contracts made by Szabo in 1997:

> The basic idea behind smart contracts is that many kinds of contractual clauses (such as collateral, bonding, delineation of property rights, etc.) can be embedded in the hardware and software we deal with, in such a way as to make breach of contract expensive (if desired, sometimes prohibitively so) for the breacher. A canonical real-life example, which we might consider to be the primitive ancestor of smart contracts, is the humble vending machine. Within a limited amount of potential loss (the amount in the till should be less than the cost of breaching the mechanism), the machine takes in coins, and via a simple mechanism, which makes a freshman computer science problem in design with finite automata, dispense change and product according to the displayed price. The vending machine is a contract with bearer: anybody with coins can participate in an exchange with the vendor. The lockbox and other

52 *Maltzkorn v Braquet*, Cour de cassation, Chambre civile 3, 28 November 1986.

53 Ewan McKendrick, 'Contract: In General', *in* Andrew Burrows (ed.), *English Private Law* , 3rd ed., Oxford, Oxford University Press, 2013, paras 8.05-8.06.

54 *Gibson v Manchester City Council* [1979] 1 WLR 295, 298-299.

55 *Partridge v Crittenden* [1968] 2 All ER 421; *Grainger & Son v Gough* [1896] AC 325 HL.

56 *Louisa Carlill v Carbolic Smoke Call Company* [1893] 1 QB 256 .

57 Mateja Durovic and André Janssen, 'The Formation of Smart Contracts and Beyond: Shaking the Fundamentals of Contract Law', *in* Larry DiMatteo *et all* (Eds.) *Smart Contracts and Blockchain Technology: Role of Contract Law*, Cambridge, Cambridge University Press, 2019, p. 765; *R (Software Solutions Partners Ltd) v HM Customs & Excise* (2007) 971 EWHC, par. 67.

> security mechanisms protect the stored coins and contents from attackers, sufficiently to allow profitable deployment of vending machines in a wide variety of areas.[58]

This example has strong parallels to a question tackled by Lord Denning in *Thornton v Shoe Lane Parking*. The facts concern Thornton who approached the garage in his car and noticed a red traffic light barring him entry. As he drove in and got to the appropriate place, the light turned green and a machine pushed out a ticket, which he took. Three hours later he returned and paid the charge. One of the questions for the House was whether Thornton had, through his actions and under these circumstances, accepted an offer. Lord Denning answered this question in the affirmative:

> The customer pays his money and gets a ticket. He cannot refuse it. He cannot get his money back. He may protest to the machine, even swear at it. But it will remain unmoved. He is committed beyond recall. He was committed at the very moment when he put his money into the machine. The contract was concluded at that time. It can be translated into offer and acceptance in this way: the offer is made when the proprietor of the machine hold it out as being ready to receive the money. The acceptance takes place when the customer put his money into the slot. The terms of the offer are contained in the notice placed on or near the machine stating what is offered for the money. The customer is bound by those terms as long as they are sufficiently brought to his notice beforehand, but not otherwise. He is not bound by the term printed on the ticket if they differ from the notice, because the ticket comes too late. The contract has already been made.[59]

Given the similarities between the facts of *Thornton v Shoe Lane Parking* and the functioning of smart contracts, especially in light of the subsequent case law in which these principles were extended to include contracts resulting from automatic mechanisms, it is likely that 'smart offers'[60] might be accepted as an offer for a unilateral contract.

Lastly, the German starting point is close to the English system in the sense that it is rather restrictive in accepting that offers to the public create legally binding agreements upon acceptance. Advertisements, catalogues, and window displays with a stated price are not considered binding offers. Instead, German law considers these invitations to treat

---

58 Nick Szabo, 'Formalizing and Securing Relations on Public Networks', *First Monday*, vol 2, no. 9, September 1997, Available at: https://firstmonday.org/ojs/index.php/fm/article/view/548 (last accessed 21 December 2020).

59 *Thornton v Shoe Lane Parking Ltd* (1971) 163 QB, p. 169.

60 This refers to the code of the smart contract, prior to acceptance.

(*invitatio ad offerendum*).[61] It is unlikely that a smart offer might be accepted as a legal offer under German law. Classifying the smart offer as an invitation to treat would mean that the reaction of the party who responds to the smart offer would be considered the legal offer. Furthermore, the subsequent reaction of the person who made the initial smart offer could then be classified as the acceptance.

An alternative route to give smart offers legal effect under German law might be available under certain circumstances. Given the self-executing nature of the smart contract and the manner in which the smart contract comes into being, the smart offer could sometimes be considered as an *einseitiges Rechtsgeschäft*, more specifically as an offer for a reward.[62] Acceptance thereof would constitute a unilateral agreement, which is not recognized as such under German law. The policy reason underlying this choice is that, according to German law, all contracts are bilateral in the sense that they are considered to be *zweiseitige Rechsgeschäfte*.[63] In order to ensure that offers for a reward have a certain legal recognition while guaranteeing the integrity of the German law of obligations, the German legislature has created the *Auslobung* in § 657 BGB. This instrument guarantees the integrity of the German system because it does not result in a contract, instead it results in a binding offer for a reward.[64] The *Auslobung* has been described as

> [..] ein Schuldverhältnis, das durch ein einseitiges Rechtsgeschäft, nämlich eine nicht empfangsbedürftige Willenserklärung zustande kommt, und das den einen Teil (Auslobenden) zur Zahlung einer Belohnung an denjenigen verpflichtet, der die Handlung vorgenommen hat, für die der Auslobende durch öffentliche bekanntmachung die Belohnung versprochen hat.[65]

A smart offer can be programmed as a conditional reward. Once a person, through their actions, fulfills the condition, the automated character of the smart contract ensures that the result is effectuated. Under certain circumstances, the *Auslobung* might therefore provide an alternative mechanism through which smart offers can be given legal effects under German law. Whether or not this alternative route is open depends on whether the smart contract in question could be qualified as 'offer for a reward'.

To conclude, this example shows us that smart contracts create a problem that will confront all legal systems in exactly the same way: 'can smart offers be recognized as legal

61 Stefan Leible and Matthias Lehmann, *European Contract Law and German Law*, Deventer, Wolters Kluwer Law International, 2013, p. 82.

62 Hugh Beale *et al*, *Cases Materials and Text on Contract Law*, Oxford, Hart Publishing, 2019, par. 5.3.B.

63 Basil S Markesinis, Hannes Unberath and Angus C. Johnston, *The German Law of Contract: A Comparative Treatise*, London, Bloomsbury Publishing, 2006, p. 350.

64 Richard Hyland, *Gifts: A Study in Comparative Law*, Oxford, Oxford University Press, 2009, p. 320.

65 Wolfgang Fikentscher, *Schuldrecht*, Berlin, Walter de Gruyter, 1985, p. 595.

offers?'. Additionally, this example shows that legal systems have instruments available to deal with these issues. While the instruments might be different, the end-result is the same; potential legal effects for smart offers in all legal systems. Note that, even though these three legal systems have instruments that provide a solution to this particular problem, there is no guarantee that a legal system will have a solution for all issues that distributed smart contracting platforms might create. It is very possible that a certain legal system will be confronted with lacunas in their systems of contract law created by distributed smart contracting platforms. It is exactly in these circumstances that the comparative methodology provides added value. As we saw previously, the comparative methodology allows one to look at rules from different legal systems as potential solutions to social problems. If one's own legal system provides no workable solution, one might be forced to look across the border for effective solutions.

7 Concluding Remarks: Using Comparative Law to Study the Legal Implications of Smart Contracts

One of the fundamental characteristics of information technology is its disregard for national borders and jurisdictions. Peer-to-peer network architectures, on which these platforms is based, are amorphous and grow organically.[66] States and courts have been relatively successful in enforcing the law in this environment by cooperating internationally and by lifting the veil of the technology and distilling the actual issues at hand.[67] The question is whether they will remain able to simply apply the law to issues arising on distributed platforms with smart contracting capabilities. This technology, after all, is designed with the extropian goal to operate outside the reach of government and centralized institutions.

Hence, before attempting to apply the law to issues arising in the context of distributed platforms with smart contracting capabilities, states ought to determine whether their law functions in this environment at all. To reiterate a previous example; a legal system relying heavily on retroactivity will be severely hindered in applying the law in an immutable environment. This assessment, i.e. the determination whether a certain law can be applied in a distributed environment, is extremely suitable to be conducted from a comparative legal perspective. Jaap Hage has argued that comparative law is an instrument that allows one to look at different jurisdictions as alternative hypotheses about possible solutions to

66 See for example Quang Hieu Vu, Mihai Lupu and Beng Chin Ooi, 'Architecture of Peer-to-Peer Systems' *in* Quang Hieu Vu *et al* (eds.), *Peer-to-Peer Computing*, Berlin, Springer, 2010,

67 See for example *Metallica v Napster Inc* (2001) MDL No. C 00-1369 MHP No C 00-4068 MHP (United States District Court for the Northern District of California) and; *Attorney-General v Kim Dotcom* [2013] Court of Appeal of New Zealand CA11/2013, 43 NZCA.

societal problems.[68] Therefore, applying the comparative methodology allows one to take the societal issue as a starting point and determine not only whether the applicable law is effective in dealing with the societal issue, but also to determine whether alternative approaches might be more effective.

Secondly, given the amorphous nature of these networks and the fact that they aim to facilitate transactions in situations in non-face-to-face situations, it is not unlikely that potential issues might arise in cross-border situations. As mentioned previously, the comparative legal methodology forces lawyers to familiarize themselves with one or more jurisdiction other than their own. Lawyers thus trained are less likely to experience a 'threshold of the unfamiliar'. Given the likelihood that issues arising out of distributed smart contracting platforms are likely to include elements from multiple jurisdictions, lawyers trained in the comparative methodology are better prepared for dealing with such issues.

Last but not least, policy makers and decision makers dealing with issues stemming from distributed smart contracting platforms will equally be confronted with elements from foreign legal systems. This is either because their national legal system, and potentially the European legal system as well, is ill-equipped to deal with the issues at hand, forcing the policy makers or decision makers to look at foreign law; or because concrete issues include foreign elements due to the platform's cross-border elements. Practically speaking this means that such policy makers and decision makers are forced to take elements of foreign law into account, justifying the application of the comparative legal methodology.

These developments, and the issues that they create, are likely to force legal systems to reconsider some aspects of their systems of contract law. If the technology is programmed in a way that bars the applications of the law 'as is', a legal system has a choice to either adapt the law or to not apply the law to the technology at all, thereby creating 'legal limbo'. Given the fact that the law, even in environments in which technology attempts to take over its tasks, has a role to play in light of social functions of the law, such as the protection of the weaker party and guarantee of legal certainty, it is likely that states would rather adapt the law than not apply it. Effectively this means that legal systems are forced to ask a normative question: if a certain law or doctrine cannot be applied in a distributed environment, how should the law be adapted to serve our policy considerations?

This normative question is perfectly suited to being tackled through a comparative perspective. Identifying a common problem that has been tackled with different solutions amongst legal systems, allows the comparative lawyer to assess the effectiveness of those different solutions in light of the relevant developments. These technological developments, however, are still very much in their infancy. It is impossible to predict which applications

68 Jaap Hage, 'Comparative Law and Legal Science', *in* Aalt Willem Heringa and Bram Akkermans (Eds.), *Educating European Lawyers*, Cambridge, Intersentia, 2011, pp. 65-78.

will prove successful and how strict the implementation of the five aspects will be. The legal implications, as elaborated upon before, will be dependent on the strictness of the implementation of the five technological aspects. Whilst the comparative methodology is useful in predicting the impact of the technology, as the technology matures, the emphasis of the comparative methodology will shift towards the normative aspects. Even though the technology will be maturing, and the questions with which the comparatist is confronted will be more concrete, the issues will be new, forcing the comparatist into new and uncharted territories. In doing so, as Sjef van Erp has pointed out, an academic is bound to ensure, no matter how lonely this work can be, that his thinking is ahead of his time.[69] In his inaugural lecture Sjef van Erp draws a parallel between this duty and the poem *Vorgefühl* by Rainer Maria Rilk. New avenues for comparative law increase the relevance of the methodology. The feelings expressed by the poem therefore seem as relevant in 2020 as they were in 1998, when Sjef van Erp gave his inaugural lecture:

> Da weiß ich die Stürme schon und bin erregt wie das Meer.
> Und breite mich aus und falle in mich hinein
> und werfe mich ab und bin ganz allein
> in dem großen Sturm.[70]

To summarize, this means that the comparatist is forced to apply the comparative legal methodology as a source of creativity and inspiration in light of these new and uncharted territories. Moreover, in charting these new territories, the nature of the technology and its impact on the legal systems, force us to compare alternatives and assess their advantages and disadvantages.[71] It seems that, with the application of the comparative legal methodology to the issues stemming from distributed smart contracting, we have definitively arrived in the postmodern world of comparative law that Sjef van Erp illustrated in his 1998 inaugural lecture. He rightfully observed that comparative law requires an open attitude and an open view of the world, being mindful of mutual dependencies. It would seem that technological developments push the comparatist in the direction of a pragmatic approach to comparative law in answering novel normative questions.

---

69 Sjef van Erp, 'European Private Law: Postmodern Dilemmas and Choices. Towards a Methods of Adequate Comparative Legal Analysis', *Electronic Journal of Comparative Law*, vol. 3, no. 1, 1999, p. 15 available at: https://www.ejcl.org/31/abs31-1.html (last accessed 21 December 2020).

70 Rainer Maria Rilke, *Gedichte (Aus den Jahren 1902 bis 1917)*, Frankfurt am Main, Insel Verlag, 1983, p. 179.

71 Sjef van Erp, 'European Private Law: Postmodern Dilemmas and Choices. Towards a Methods of Adequate Comparative Legal Analysis', *Electronic Journal of Comparative Law*, vol. 3, no. 1, 1999, p. 10, available at: https://www.ejcl.org/31/abs31-1.html (last accessed 21 December 2020).

Digital Property and the Law Reformer

An Essay in Honor of Professor Sjef van Erp

Christopher K. Odinet[*]

1 Introduction

The value of data has come starkly into focus in recent years, but few have been as at the forefront of this issue than has Professor Sjef van Erp. As he noted in a recent publication: "We are increasingly confronted with the rapid digitalization of our societies, even more so now that the Covid-19 pandemic forces us to work from home, pay digitally, teach courses in a setting of distance learning, etc."[1] Indeed, in largest sense imaginable, "[e]conomically valuable assets are more and more of a digital nature."[2]

This essay pays tribute to an influential scholar of property law in the digital age. I am delighted to join with others in contributing to this *liber amicorum* – a Book of Friends – to memorialize Professor van Erp's impressive career.

Sjef's career cannot be properly chronicled in these pages. It is too accomplished and too wide-reaching to be so contained. My aim here is to offer but my own modest thoughts when it comes to how Sjef's tremendous work has shaped my way of thinking and, I am most sure, the law for years to come.

I had the pleasure of meeting Sjef many years ago at the Association of Law, Property, and Society (ALPS) meeting in 2014 when I was a new assistant professor at the Southern University Law Center. I was at once taken by not only his kind demeanor and friendly manner but also by his vast knowledge and command of property law across so many jurisdictions. I endeavored from this point onward to follow his work and learn what I could from this giant in comparative law.

I next encountered Sjef while at a property law conference at the University of Cambridge in 2018. Again, he was gracious and generous with his time and expertise, helping me work through some arguments I was attempting to make in a then forthcoming book. He also mentioned that he was, at the time, holding several positions with the

---

* Professor of Law, The University of Iowa College of Law. The author thanks Morgan Jensen (Iowa Law Class of 2022) for her helpful research and editorial assistance.

1 S. van Erp, 'Access Management of Digital Assets', *European Property Law Journal*, Vol. 8, No. 3, 2019, pp. 227-230, https://doi.org/10.1515/eplj-2019-0013 [hereinafter Erp, Access Management].

2 Access Management, *supra* note 1, at 227.

European Law Institute. We quickly started talking about his work involving the law of access to digital assets across Europe and how the United States and other countries had attempted to deal with the same problem over the preceding decade. I recounted to him that I was a delegate to the National Conference of Commissioners on Uniform State Laws (commonly called the "Uniform Law Commission") in the United States. Upon my return home, I was happy to receive an email from Sjef inquiring as to whether I would like to join the project team that he was co-leading on the digital asset issue. Needless to say, I was delighted to accept.

This led to what has now been a multi-year working relationship and friendship with Sjef, who has co-led our committee's efforts with grace, extreme competence, deft skill, and unmatched expertise. I've sat in meeting rooms in both Paris and Brussels (and, more recently, via Zoom) debating the finer points of the law (both theoretical and practical) when it comes to how digital assets in their many forms can be accessed, transacted with, and manipulated by individuals and businesses.

Yet it would be a mistake to limit Sjef to merely law reform. Important as those efforts might be, Sjef is also a consummate scholar. Despite serving the European Law Institute and other professional organizations in innumerable ways (both formal and informal), he is also prolific and has been a thought-leader in every sense of the word on issues of the digital economy and property law. Indeed, he has traversed the globe many times over giving talks and papers and making the case for why jurisdictions must address data and digital assets if they want to stay relevant in the digital age.

In these pages, I endeavor to show the connection between Professor van Erp's important work in property law and digital assets and the current legal conundrums dealing with the same under US law. This Essay gives several prominent examples of how US law struggles to deal with data and related digital assets. I do this by looking to tort law, the law of crypto-assets, the law of succession, and finally the law relative to incorporeal movable property security. Throughout this discussion, I look to Sjef's research and seek to draw out themes that can help inform how courts – and law reformers – can better address digital asset issues.

2 Remarks on Digital Property and the Law

At the onset, Sjef asks the question: "Before we can look for the applicable law, we need to qualify the problem. Are digital assets "property", "contract" or of a "sui generis" nature?"[3] In the US, courts have shown a frequent propensity to look to property law in dealing with these matters.

3 Erp, Access Management, *supra* note 1, at 227.

But before exploring digital property problems in US law, I want to saw a few things about property law more broadly.[4] Property law has a tendency to cling to a persistent concept of physicality.[5] Much of property law focuses on possession[6] in the physical sense – capturing[7] or finding[8] an object or conveying[9] a physical thing. Even commercial law – a cousin to property law – has a significant commitment to the tangible.[10] The connection between physicality and property law is not at all surprising. Indeed, it is emotive.[11] It reflects our understanding of the things around us – property – in ways that matches many of our sensibilities. What we can touch, feel, and see is salient to us and therefore is more meaningful when it is handed over or taken away.

These considerations raise the issue of how exactly we should treat data and digital assets in the context of property since they lack physicality.[12] First, some definitional concerns should be addressed. I refer to "data" to mean information recorded in any electronic form or medium.[13] In turn, a "digital asset" is data in which a person has a right or interest but which does not have a physical form.[14] For instance, the narratives, videos, images, and profile information loaded to a social media account constitute data. The social media account itself is a digital asset. It may also be the case that the images and video also constitute digital assets on an individual basis, depending on whether the law accords rights in them to an individual. In his work, Sjef offers a helpful limiting

4 This Part I is drawn, some in whole and some in part, and with permission from the following text: C.K. Odinet, 'Data and the Social Obligation Norm of Property: An Essay in Honor of Professor Gregory S. Alexander', *Cornell Journal of Law and Public Policy* (forthcoming 2020), https://papers.ssrn.com/sol3/papers.cfm?abstract_id=3492648.

5 J.M. Moringiello, 'What Virtual Worlds Can Do for Property Law', *Florida Law Review*, Vol. 62, 2010, pp. 159 at 181; J.M. Moringiello, 'False Categories in Commercial Law: The (Ir)relevance of (In)tangibility', Florida State University Law Review, Vol. 35, 2007, pp. 119 at 122.

6 S. Kurtz et al., *Cases and Materials on American Property Law*, 7th ed., 2019, § 3.1-6.

7 *Id.* § 1.3.

8 *Id.* § 1.4.

9 *Id.* § 14.1-4.

10 An example of this is the entirety of Article 3 of the Uniform Commercial Code which requires a physical piece of paper for negotiable instrument law to operate. *See* U.C.C. art. 3 (American Law Institute & Uniform Law Commission 2014).

11 B. McEniery, 'Physicality and the Information Age: A Normative Perspective on the Patent Eligibility of Non-Physical Methods', *Chicago-Kent Journal of Intellectual Property*, Vol. 10, 2010 p. 106 at 129.

12 *See* Michael Pollack. "Taking data", *University of Chicago Law Review*, Vol. 86, 2019, pp. at 77-141 (giving justifications for treating data as property for Takings Clause purposes).

13 This definition of data is derived from HIPAA and is also being used in the deliberations of the American Law Institute and the European Law Institute for their principles for a digital economy project (documentation is on file with author). *See also* 45 C.F.R. § 160.103 (2019). It is used in combination with the American Bar Association's 2019 report on digital assets. *See* American Bar Association, *Digital and Digitized Assets: Federal and State Jurisdictional Issue*s, 2019. Available at: www.steptoe.com/images/content/1/9/v2/190803/ABA-Digital-Assets-White-Paper.pdf (last accessed 13 November 2020).

14 *See generally* ABA, *supra* note 13, at 25.

principle – a conceptual cabining to help guide the discussion. He notes that "data, in as far as it is pure information, can never be given legal (including proprietary)."[15]

But this observation naturally gives us pause. How do we separate the data from the asset? When do data make an asset? Can property law answer these questions? These queries are challenging; Sjef observes that "[i]t could, without exaggeration, be said that our traditional approach to property law is besieged."[16]

This assertion deserves some unpacking, and Sjef's scholarship does just that. He notes that traditional property law consists of legal relationships between a subject and a one or more other subjects with respect to a particular object.[17] Digital assets do not fit so perfectly into this framework. Digitalization has generated incredible growth in digital assets and an "incredibly fast expansion of interconnectedness and interoperability."[18] What can be an object under the traditional property regime? How do we weave in digital assets and their component parts into the existing property system? Sjef notes that, indeed, "[o]wnership of digital data seems very different from ownership of [...] land." So can the same rules apply?

To that point, a major roadblock to using traditional property law rules is explored extensively in Sjef's scholarship – it is the *numerus clausus* principle. The concept stands for the notion that "only certain objects (physical objects, monetary claims, human creativity) can be "owned.""[19] This means that the types of property rights possible are limited in number.[20] Thus, Sjef asks, "who can be a subject of data ownership?"[21] Should the *numerus clausus* principle persist or can it accommodate this new property? Sjef offers as a foundational note that "we should revisit the classical conception of private-law objects in light of the digital revolution." This means either adapting "the existing *numerus clausus* of objects to fit the new virtual reality" or else creating "a separate area of property law."[22]

---

15 S. van Erp, 'Ownership of data: the numerus clausus of legal objects', *Brigham-Kanner Property Rights Conference Journal*, Vol. 6, 2017, pp. 235-257 at 244. Available at: https://scholarship.law.wm.edu/propertyjournal/6/ (last accessed 13 November 2020). [hereinafter Numerus Clausus of Legal Objects].

16 S. van Erp, 'New IT technology: Who is a subject, what is an object of which property entitlement?', *European Property Law Journal*, Vol. 7, 2018, No. 2, pp. 145-146 at 145. Available at: https://doi.org/10.1515/eplj-2018-0006 (last accessed 13 November 2020). [hereinafter New IT]

17 S. van Erp, 'The need for a common vocabulary on 'data ownership'', *European Property Law Journal*, Vol. 8, 2019, No. 1, pp. 1-3 at 2. Available at: https://doi.org/10.1515/eplj-2019-0001 (last accessed 13 November 2020). [hereinafter New Vocabulary].

18 Erp, Numerus Clausus of Legal Objects *supra* note 15, at 235-236.

19 Erp, New Vocabulary *supra* note 17, at 2.

20 Erp, Numerus Clausus of Legal Objects *supra* note 15, at 235.

21 Erp, New Vocabulary *supra* note 17, at 2.

22 S. van Erp,, 'Digital assets as a new category within the numerus clausus of legal objects.' *in* EC Schlemmer & PH O'Brien (Eds.), *Liber Amicorum JC Sonnekus: Essays in hounour of/Huldigingsbundel vir JC Sonnekus*, Cape Town, Juta and Company (Pty) Ltd, Tydskrif vir die Suid-Afrikaanse Reg/Journal of South African Law, 2017, Vol. Special ed., pp. 421-433 at 241 [hereinafter New Category].

To explore the idea of digital assets as property – and the many policy decisions that must be made to accommodate the digital economy – the following shows how property law and digital assets and data often try to work hand-in-hand, but with varying degrees of success, in the US.

3 Digital Property and Torts

As an obvious point, data lack physicality. It is in fact this lack of physical form that I believe causes most of the problems with how the law deals with data broadly and digital assets more specifically. Consider the many ways in which the law tries to shoe-horn digital assets into property paradigms. In *Kremen v. Cohen*, the Ninth Circuit stated that a domain name is "an intangible property right" but was quick to impose physicality on the item in order to resolve the dispute by declaring that such a right was similar to "staking a claim to a plot of land" and then recording title to it in a registry system to put others on notice.[23] Similarly, US bankruptcy courts have held that rights in a domain name are deemed assets of the bankrupt estate under the theory that the registrant of the domain name has rights akin to "direct, immediate and exclusive authority over a thing" – thereby harkening to a test that relies on an analogy to physical dominion.[24] In the context of property torts, some courts have embraced the non-physicality of certain types of property to allow for recovery under conversion. The Arkansas court in *Integrated Direct Marketing, LLC v. May* stated that "[t]here is simply no reasonable basis for allowing a claim for conversion of paper documents but not for their electronically stored counterparts."[25] Courts in Indiana have similarly held that digital assets, such as information generated from the use of a computer, constitute property for theft purposes.[26]

Yet courts are not uniform in this approach and are not even consistent within the same jurisdiction. One Indiana court in 2005 held that alleged misuse of software-generated data is not actionable under "conversion, trespass, or replevin" because these kinds of causes of action "relate only to chattels themselves,"[27] while another Indiana court in 2009 held that a "website design is personal property and is subject to a conversion claim …"[28] The Tennessee court in *Wells v. Chattanooga Bakery, Inc.* refused to allow the tort claim of conversion to operate in the context of a digital image when it stated that "[c]onversion is the wrongful appropriation of another's tangible property; an action for the conversion

23 Kremen *v.* Cohen, 337 F.3d 1024, 1030 (9th Cir. 2003).
24 *In re* Larry Koenig & Assoc., No. 01-12829, 2004 WL 3244582, at *6 (Bankr. M.D. La. Mar. 31, 2004).
25 Integrated Direct Mktg., LLC *v.* May, 495 S.W.3d 73, 76 (Ark. 2016).
26 *See* State *v.* McGraw, 480 N.E.2d 552, 554 (Ind. 1985).
27 Coleman *v.* Vukovich, 825 N.E.2d 397, 408 (Ind. Ct. App. 2005).
28 Conwell *v.* Gray Loon Outdoor Mktg. Grp., Inc., 906 N.E.2d 805, 818 (Ind. 2009).

of intangible personal property is not recognized in Tennessee."[29] The Georgia court in *Internal Medicine Alliance, LLC v. Budell* similarly wed itself to a physicality requirement in holding that "[c]onversion is not available as a cause of action with regard to intangible property interests that have not been merged into a document."[30] Other states as diverse as Rhode Island,[31] Texas,[32] Illinois,[33] and Maryland[34] also eschew the possibility that an intangible right can be converted (and thereby give relief to the right holder) unless it is represented in a physical, paper form.

Sjef's work has noted the fact that physicality's role in property law causes translation problems when it comes to digital assets. After all, "objects of property were, first of all, physical things; particularly land, but also movables."[35] Much time had to pass before intangible objects – those that lacked physicality – were accepted as having economic value, such as monetary claims.[36] At that time, "[q]uestions concerning digital data were inconceivable."[37] The idea that something as amorphous as information could ever be owned was entirely unthinkable.[38]

Sjef's work has questioned these sorts of calcified rules. He notes that "in a setting of transformation the existing law might be unable to reformulate answers which were earlier given to problems and afterwards never questioned but applied as given dogmas."[39] In an influential paper that he co-authored and presented in 2016 during the annual meeting of the Netherlands Royal Society of Notaries, he advised that there may be "footholds in existing law" from which rules for digital assets can be draw, but also cautioned that any "analogous application of the rules on ownership should be carefully considered."[40] After

29 Wells *v.* Chattanooga Bakery, Inc., 448 S.W.3d 381, 392 (Tenn. Ct. App. 2014).

30 Internal Med. Alliance *v.* Budell, 659 S.E.2d 668, 675 (Ga. Ct. App. 2008)

31 Narragansett Elec. Co. *v.* Carbone, 898 A.2d 87, 97 (R.I. 2006) ("[A] conversion action will not lie for a partnership interest or other intangible property right that is not manifested by a tangible instrument, such as a written agreement, a bankbook, or a promissory note, that may, in turn, be converted.") (quoting Montecalvo *v.* Mandarelli, 682 A.2d 918, 929 (R.I. 1996)).

32 Rehak Creative Servs., Inc. *v.* Witt, 404 S.W.3d 716, 734 (Tex. App. 2013), *disapproved of by In re* Lipsky, 460 S.W.3d 579 (Tex. 2015) ("[I]ntangible property cannot be converted unless the underlying intangible right has been merged into a document that has been converted.").

33 *In re* Thebus, 483 N.E.2d 1258, 1260 (Ill. 1985) ("[T]he subject of conversion is required to be an identifiable object of property of which the plaintiff was wrongfully deprived. Money may be the subject of conversion, but it must be capable of being described as a specific chattel . . .") (reaffirmed in The Film & Tape Works, Inc. *v.* Junetwenty Films, Inc., 856 N.E.2d 612, 624 (Ill. App. Ct. 2006)).

34 Thompson *v.* UBS Fin. Servs., Inc., 115 A.3d 125, 136 (Md. 2015) ("Maryland will remain among the many jurisdictions that maintain conversion of a document as an element of conversion of intangible property[.]").

35 Erp, Numerus Clausus of Legal Objects, *supra* note 15, at 237.

36 *Id.* at 237.

37 *Id.* at 237.

38 *Id.* at 237.

39 Erp, Access Management, *supra* note 1, at 228.

40 J.H.M. van Erp & W. Loof, 'Eigendom in Het Algemeen: Eigendom Van Digitale Inhoud (titel 1). Over Digitale Inhoud Als Zaak', *in* Boek 5 BW van de toekomst: over vernieuwingen in het zakenrecht 23ff (L.C.A. Verstappen, ed., 2017) (Neth.).

all, the numerus clausus principle is tied to "legal concepts inherited over centuries and dating back to societies where land (not even personal property) was the most valuable legal object."[41] Something altogether new may be needed.

But Sjef offers hope in his writings. He observes that the law did indeed eventually accommodate contract rights, intellectual property rights, and other types of intangible rights.[42] Progress in property law is possible. Yet, he notes that these examples still have ties to the physical world.[43] Virtual property often has no physical manifestation at all – however attenuated. This means that in any future property progression, the law must do something new to accommodate virtual reality where a connection to the physical world is often absent.[44]

Although Sjef recognizes the challenge – "New property law objects do not seem to get accepted easily."[45]

4 Digital Property and Cryptoassets

Newer forms of digital assets have proven even more difficult for courts and lawmakers to define. The most prominent example are cryptoassets (also called virtual currencies) such as the likes of bitcoin.[46] The issue of whether these complex strings of 1s and 0s that some people use to pay for goods and services, and others use for investment purposes, actually constitute "property" has vexed policymakers and courts.[47] The determination has wide-ranging effects in sundry legal regimes ranging from criminal and tort law to securities, commercial, and tax law.[48]

There remains uncertainty around cryptocurrencies as a true form of property. Some commentators have critiqued treating them as property because of the semi-anonymous nature of the public access keys, meaning that there cannot be a clear claim of exclusion.[49] Other commentators wonder whether situations where no single person or entity has

41 Erp, Numerus Clausus of Legal Objects, *supra* note 15, at 245-246.

42 *Id.* at 245-246.

43 *Id.* at 245-246.

44 *Id.* at 245-246.

45 *Id.* at 246.

46 *See generally Regulating Blockchain: Techno-Social and Legal Challenges*, P. Hacker, G. Dimitropoulos, S. Eich & I. Lianos (Eds.), 2019 (explaining cryptocurrencies) ("Blockchain is a technology that facilitates value exchanges in a secure and decentralized manner, without the need for an intermediary.").

47 Perkins Coie, 'Treatment of Bitcoin Under U.S. Property Law', March 2017. Available at: www.perkinscoie.com/images/content/1/9/v5/199638/2018-Treatment-of-Bitcoin-Under-U.S.-Property-Law-White-Paper.pdf (last accessed 13 November 2020). T. Merrill & H. Smith, 'Optimal Standardization in the Law of Property: The Numerus Clausus Principle', *Yale Law Journal*, Vol. 100, 2000, p. 1 at 4.

48 Perkins Coie, *supra* note 47, at 11-14.

49 *Id.* at 14; *see also* R.J. Straus & M.J. Cleary, *The Law of Bitcoin: The United States*, J. Brito (Ed.) 2015, p. 187.

control over access to a cryptoasset – such as in situations where multiple keys are held by multiple parties and all need to agree in order to transact business – create rights that should be appropriately called property rights.[50]

Sjef's work has particular resonance here. He notes that "[d]ata ownership, in the sense of who has access, controls and can process or delete data, [is] crucial."[51] This very well crystalizes the issue with cryptoassets. These assets typically rely on either a trusted or trustless intermediary – a third party that may merely consist of computer code. And to be sure, the asset itself is mere code. The issues then are unique. As Sjef questions: "Can a judicial enforcement officer get access and hence control over a wallet with cryptocurrencies?"[52]

Sjef proposes that the way to address these types of assets as property is to better define the term control so that it becomes a term of art.[53] By building a better vocabulary of terms for talking about digital assets and transactions involving them, the law can develop with more precision and with greater efficiency. Control helps us conceptualize what is essentially a cognitive problem with possessing intangible property. With cryptoassets, the type of control and level of control present challenges, but there are other areas of the law from which we can draw inspiration from (such as with bank accounts under Article 9 of the UCC). In order to make progress, Sjef urges a concerted focus on control as the bridge over which we can cross the issue of nonpossession.

5 Digital Property and Successions

Perhaps nowhere has the law of data and digital property seen more difficulty and also more progress than in the inheritance context. For years a struggle existed between online companies and heirs of account holders for access to a decedent's online accounts. This struggle is perhaps best explained in the context of the 2017 case of *Ajemian v. Yahoo!, Inc.* In that case, Robert created a Yahoo email account for his brother John in 2002.[54] John used the account until his death in 2006.[55] Robert and another sibling, Marianne, were later appointed co-representatives of John's estate.[56] As part of administering the estate, a

50 Perkins Coie, *supra* note 47, at 15. Objections based on traceability are raised as well. *See id.*

51 S. van Erp, 'The data economy: There is no status quo ante', *European Journal of Comparative Law and Governance*, Vol. 5, No. 4, 2018, pp. 313-315 at 314-315. Available at: https://doi.org/10.1163/22134514-00504003 (last accessed 13 November 2020).

52 Erp, Access Management, *supra* note 1, at 227.

53 Erp, Numerus Clausus of Legal Objects, *supra* note 15, at 254.

54 Ajemian *v.* Yahoo!, Inc., 84 N.E.3d 766, 768 (Mass. 2017).

55 *Id.*

56 *Id.*

written request was sent to Yahoo for access to John's email account.[57] Yahoo, however, declined by stating first that it was prohibited from doing so by certain requirements of the Stored Communications Act[58] and second by declaring that Yahoo's email account terms of service gave the company complete discretion to reject an access request by a personal representative.[59] Similar arguments have been made by other online companies in the context of obtaining access to the online accounts – i.e., the data and digital assets – of decedents.[60] Here again the issue came down to whether the accounts constituted the "property" of the decedent such that it was unequivocally part of the estate.

What resulted from these disputes was a law reform effort lead by the Uniform Law Commission. The end-product was the Uniform Fiduciary Access to Digital Assets Act,[61] which attempts to address the many situations in which someone dies and leaves behind a host of digital assets ranging from "photographs, electronic investment account statements, e-mails, social media accounts, bank account statements, and so on" but where the person did not make arrangements for those they leave behind to have access to these important items.[62] The uniform act also attempts to address situations where the account holder is still alive but where a power of attorney has been executed or a guardian has been appointed. But even here, the issue of who "owns" the information was controversial and so, to avoid the ownership issue, the legislation mostly gestures toward who has "access".[63]

In the absence of special legislation like that discussed above, can existing property law (and the related law of succession) accommodate the intestate passing of digital assets? Or, as Sjef questions, must we "completely distance ourselves from the traditional notion of ownership, by focusing on data access, control and the power to delete[?]"[64] Perhaps

---

57 *Id.*

58 18 U.S.C. §§ 2701-2712 (2018); *Ajemian*, 84 N.E.3d at 768.

59 *Ajemian*, 84 N.E.3d at 768.

60 *See, e.g.*, *In re* Estate of Serrano, 54 N.Y.S.3d 564, 566 (Sur. Ct. 2017) (seeking access to a Google account); *In re* Scandalios, No. 2017-2976/A, 2019 WL 266570 (N.Y. Sur. Ct. Jan. 14, 2019) (seeking access to an Apple account); *In re* Facebook, Inc., 923 F. Supp. 2d 1204 (N.D. Cal. 2012) (seeking access to a Facebook account).

61 Nat'l Conference of Comm'rs on Unif. State Laws, Revised Fiduciary Access to Digital Assets Act (2015). Available at: www.uniformlaws.org/committees/community-home/librarydocuments?communitykey=f7237fc4-74c2-4728-81c6-b39a91ecdf22&tab=librarydocuments (last accessed 13 November 2020).

62 E.D. Barwick, Note, 'All Blogs Go to Heaven: Preserving Valuable Digital Assets Without the Uniform Fiduciary Access to Digital Assets Act's Removal of Third Party Privacy Protections', *Georgia Law Review*, Vol. 50, 2016, p. 593, at 607-08 (discussing transferability problems with online accounts); J.P. Hopkins, 'Afterlife in the Cloud: Managing a Digital Estate', *Hastings Science & Technology Law Journal*, Vol. 5, 2013, p. 209, at 212; S.D. Haworth, Note, 'Laying Your Online Self to Rest: Evaluating the Uniform Fiduciary Access to Digital Assets Act', *University of Miami Law Review*, Vol. 68, 2014, p. 535 at 537; E.H. Capel, 'Conflict and Solution in Delaware's Fiduciary Access to Digital Assets and Digital Accounts Act', *Berkeley Technology Law Journal*, Vol. 30. 2015, p. 1211 at 1242.

63 *See* 'The Revised Uniform Fiduciary Access to Digital Assets Act (RUFADAA)', *NOLO*. Available at: https://www.nolo.com/legal-encyclopedia/ufadaa.html (last visited Apr. 17, 2019).

64 Erp, Access Management, *supra* note 1, at 229.

specific legislation is inevitable. Not all types of digital assets are the same. A social media account should perhaps be treated differently than an email account.

Sjef offers a solution in his scholarly writings on the matter. His sensible policy prescription is to create different categories of digital assets and engage in a balancing of interest to determine who should have access and on what basis.[65] He offers that "[d]ecisive factors will be: the need for data protection, tradability because of economic value and the required interest of the person(s) asking for access."[66] For illustration, Sjef notes that we might have different access rules among "heirs, legatees and professionals such as notaries."[67] More specifically: "what requirements does an heir, executor, legatee or notary acting on behalf of such persons," need to meet in order to be "entitled to gain access and how must such access procedurally be given shape?"[68] Rather than run from it, Sjef sees the complexity of digital assets as an invitation to create nuanced rules that can make this complexity workable.

6 DIGITAL PROPERTY AND SECURITY

And to be sure, it is not just courts that have difficulty in dealing with data and digital assets. Legislators and law reform groups find the task difficult as well. As an example, consider the use of digital assets in secured lending.[69] The law in this area (Article 9 of the Uniform Commercial Code or just "UCC 9") suffers from major structural weaknesses in dealing with collateralizing data/digital assets.

In terms of what kind of property *can* be the subject of a UCC 9 security interest, the law sets forth a number of collateral-specific categories, ranging from equipment and inventory, to instruments and investment property.[70] In most cases parties use these broad categories to describe the collateral rather than overly detailing the particulars of the property in question.[71] The category most relevant for a discussion of data or digital assets is that of "general intangibles."[72]

---

65 *Id.* at 230.
66 *Id.* at 230.
67 *Id.* at 230.
68 *Id.* at 230.
69 C.K. Odinet, 'Bitproperty and Commercial Credit', *Washington University Law Review*, Vol. 94, 2017, p. 649 at 676.
70 *See* C.K. Odinet, 'Testing the Reach of UCC Article 9: The Question of Tax Credit Collateral in Secured Transactions', *South Carolina Law Review*, Vol. 64, 2012, p. 143, at 154- 155; *see also* L.E. Denonn, *Secured Transactions Under the UCC 36*, 1965.
71 T.M. Anderson *et al.*, 'Attachment and Perfection of Security Interests Under Revised Article 9: A "Nuts and Bolts" Primer', *American Bankruptcy Institute Law Review*, Vol. 9, 2001, p. 179, at 187-189.
72 *See* U.C.C. § 9-102(a)(42) (2015); *see also* Odinet, *supra* note 69, at 681.

First, as a broad matter the way in which all general intangibles are collateralized is fairly uniform.[73] Debtors, through a security agreement, grant an interest to the creditor in their "general intangibles," and then creditors file a financing statement describing the same in the UCC records of the jurisdiction.[74] From the perspective of UCC Article 9, nothing else need be done.[75] However, the process is not quite as simple as the law of secured transactions suggests.[76] Despite seemingly treating intangible assets as property on the front end, the UCC does not actually treat them as having the attributes of true property on the back-end.[77]

The reason for this mismatch is because many online accounts (i.e., digital assets) are comprised chiefly of license entitlements.[78] The interplay of this concept creates significant difficulty in making data collateralization viable. While UCC section 9-408 attempts to blunt the effects of anti-assignment clauses in license agreements, the actual rights that a creditor can take in such forms of property are quite weak and, in the end, undercut the very value that the secured party seeks to capture.[79]

To see this assertion play-out, consider the standard terms and conditions agreements for Facebook,[80] Twitter,[81] YouTube,[82] and PayPal.[83] They all describe the relationship between the platform and the user as being that of licensor and licensee and further explicitly prohibit the licensee from assigning their rights to anyone else. Likewise, most domain name agreements contain similar provisions.[84] Collectively, these agreements signify that most all digital assets (despite how property-like we might consider them) are in fact not *really* property in the traditional sense and cannot be used as collateral without the consent of the actual platform company. In fairness, UCC section 9-408 attempts to deal with these anti-assignment clauses in license agreements by rendering them null. Any provision that

73 *See* W.D. Warren & S.D. Walt, *Secured Transactions in Personal Property*, 2007, pp. 363-64.

74 *See id.*

75 *Id.*

76 *See* Odinet, *supra* note 69, at 681-82.

77 *Id.*

78 A license is "[a] permission, [usually] revocable, to commit some act that would otherwise be unlawful." 'License', *in Black's Law Dictionary*, 11th ed., 2019

79 Odinet, *supra* note 69, at 695.

80 'Terms of Service', *Facebook*, § 4.5.4. Available at https://www.facebook.com/terms.php (last revised Apr. 19, 2019) ("You will not transfer any of your rights or obligations under these Terms to anyone else without our consent."); *id.* § 3.3.1 ("The license will end when your content is deleted from our systems.").

81 'Twitter Terms of Service', *Twitter*, § 4. Available at https://twitter.com/en/tos (last revised May 25, 2018).

82 'Terms of Service', *YouTube*, §§ 5.A, 13. Available at: https://www.youtube.com/static?template=terms (last revised May 25, 2018).

83 'PayPal User Agreement', *PayPal*. Available at: https://www.paypal.com/us/webapps/mpp/ua/useragreement-full (sections titled "Intellectual Property" and "Miscellaneous") (last revised Sept. 3, 2019).

84 *See* Odinet, *supra* note 69, at 696 n.321.

attempts to prohibit the granting of a security interest in a general intangible (even if a license right) is considered ineffective, per the law.[85]

However, section 9-408 makes a rather hollow promise. Although the anti-assignment clause may be ineffective, UCC Article 9 provides no way for the secured creditor to actually make *use* of the collateral once a default has occurred. The creditor will naturally want to take control of the digital asset upon the debtor's default and, as soon as possible, move to dispose of it to generate funds for satisfaction of the debt. However, that is impossible under the current scheme, as UCC section 9-408 makes clear that the licensor need not pay the slightest attention to the creditor or its supposed rights.[86] What value does the creditor then have in a digital asset if it cannot compel the licensor to recognize the creditor's security interest in the so-called property?[87]

Further, the creditor, aside from being unable to make a disposition of the collateral, cannot itself make use of the digital asset.[88] If, for example, a debtor that provided its inventory and general intangibles as collateral defaults, the creditor can certainly seize the physical inventory. However, it would *not* be able to take control of the company's website or social media accounts under the theory that the assets are merely license rights.[89] Indeed, it might very well be possible for the debtor to continue using the digital assets even after the creditor has seized the debtor's computers.[90]

This raises the issue of access as much as anything. Sjef asks: "Can collections of data be collateral for a loan?"[91] Is this even possible?

But there is another layer of complexity here. We can imagine, as Sjef's work has acknowledged, that "a distinction could perhaps be made between access questions in a non-forced and a forced setting."[92] In saying non-forced, Sjef means situations involving voluntary agreements for the giving of security over an item – like the security agreement example above involving the social media accounts.[93] This can be compared to the forced setting, where a creditor demands access, regardless of the wishes of the so-called owner, in order to enforce a right.[94] We can think of a judgment rendered against a debtor and the judgment creditor seeking to enforce that judgment through the seizure and

---

85 *See* U.C.C. § 9-408(a) (2015).

86 U.C.C. § 9-408 cmt. 2 ("However, under subsection (d), the secured party (absent the licensor's agreement) is not entitled to enforce the license or to use, assign, or otherwise enjoy the benefits of the licensed software, and *the licensor need not recognize (or pay any attention to) the secured party.*") (emphasis added).

87 S.D. Walt, 'Uncertainty About Free Assignment: Payment and General Intangibles Under Article 9', *Journal of Payment Systems Law*, Vol. 2, 2006, p. 4 at 16.

88 U.C.C. § 9-408(d)(5) (2015).

89 *See id.*

90 *See id.* § 9-408 cmt. 2.

91 Erp, Access Management, *supra* note 1, at 227.

92 *Id.* at 229.

93 *Id.* at 229.

94 *Id.* at 229.

monetization of digital assets. Sjef offers that we cannot think of one case without also considering the other. Is it right that the law of article 9 addresses license rights (even if unsatisfactory) and the general law of unsecured creditors does not?

***

In sum, the rise of digital assets and the layperson's sense of ownership over them has challenged property law in significant ways. Legal conundrums involving data and digital assets arise in the context of taxation, international law, intellectual property, searches and seizures, the takings clause, legal theory, and much more.[95] Yet, despite the lack of physicality that so historically has defined traditional property law, courts and lawmakers still show a propensity to nevertheless use property constructs to define the rules that govern data and digital assets – even when these constructs are an awkward or even ineffective fit.

7 CONCLUSION

Treating data as a form of property is not just a wishful theory or a hypothetical for conjecture. In fact, it is starting to happen even now.

Yet, at the same time that the law is embracing forms of data as property, the foundations of such treatment remain relatively ethereal. What does it mean to say that data or digital assets are property? How should we think about data as a type of asset like a type of personalty? Can we use existing property rules to understand data or do we have to branch off and develop something new? And, even if we do treat forms of data as property, what significance does it have for how we create, alienate, and otherwise transact with our data and the data of others?

Many of these questions remain unanswered or at least not fully explained. Professor Sjef van Erp's work helps us get there by challenging us to think more deeply and critically about digital assets and data as property. He notes that "[a] balance will have to be sought between stability and change, between when existing law can be preserved and when new, creative solutions are needed."[96] But as he is circumspect, he is also bold. Sjef challenges that "[p]roperty law is in need of a new paradigm, which reflects the hybrid world in which we live ..."[97] His fearlessness in meeting the challenges of the digital economy is indeed inspiring. He very well admits that "[t]he interface between IT developments and property law may result in either traditional property law being adapted to the virtual world around

95 *See supra* note 38 and accompanying citations.
96 Erp, Access Management, *supra* note 1, at 228.
97 *Id.* at 228.

us" or, as he readily admits could be the case, "in completely abandoning existing law, while replacing it both as to content and approach."[98] In either case, "we should not be afraid to develop the law further than what we inherited."[99]

I close this essay in honor of Professor Sjef van Erp with a quote from his scholarship. Indeed, short as it may be, this statement best exemplifies his energy, his passion, his infectious spirit. All who know him will nod and smile as they read it, being able to easily imagine him saying these words as though he was before them: "The effects of IT developments on property law will be enormous. The debate has only just begun!"[100]

98 Erp, New IT, *supra* note 16, at 146.

99 Erp, Numerus Clausus of Legal Objects, *supra* note 15, at 256 ("This virtual world demands a rethinking of classical property law, particularly the numerus clausus of legal objects.").

100 Erp, New IT, *supra* note 16, at 146.

The Fourth Industrial Revolution (4IR) and the Law: Challenges and Opportunities

Wian Erlank[*]

1 Introduction

Quite often the law tends to lag behind even the slowly turning wheels of justice. This might have been acceptable, or at least tolerable for most of human history, but unfortunately it cannot be allowed to continue like this. Society is rapidly changing due to technological developments and breakthroughs, many of which are considered to be "disruptive", and while the law tends to be reactive to such changes, the development of the law to catch up to these changes tends to be slow, and grudging. Perhaps it is the view that the law is unchanging, fixed and certain – for which we can thank the concept of the so-called "black letter law", and even legal positivism. However, the ever increasing tempo of technological development and the associated societal change now highlights the swiftly increasing gap between what people do in everyday life, and how the law either ignores this or is so far behind, that by the time the law starts to address a new development, that same development has already been superseded by a new one.

Jeong aptly addresses the frustration of the law lagging behind technological development by noting the following:

> The tech industry has long despaired of the law's inability to comprehend it, making much of the legal system's struggle to keep up with the rapid pace of progress. The belief that the law will never "catch up" to technology is borne in part of tech exceptionalism, a libertarian elitism that derides any kind of legal or regulatory impediment as Luddism. But it's also fueled by genuine frustration with the state of law.[1]

---

* Prof. Dr. Wian Erlank. Hons(BA) (Classical Lit), LLB, LLM (International Trade Law), LLD (Stell). Advocate of the High Court of South Africa, Professor of Law at North-West University, South Africa. Email: wian.erlank@nwu.ac.za. ORCHID ID: orcid.org/0000-0001-7796-1254. This work is based on the research supported in part by the National Research Foundation of South Africa (Grant Number 119432). Any opinion, finding and conclusion or recommendation expressed in this material is that of the author(s) and the NRF does not accept any liability in this regard.

1 Jeong S "The Judge's Code" 19 Oct 2017 *The Verge* at https://www.theverge.com/2017/10/19/16503076/oracle-vs-google-judge-william-alsup-interview-waymo-uber (last accessed 08 Dec 2020).

Of course, the idea that the law is immutable and never changes is a total fallacy, as any student of (legal) history will be able to tell you. The law over the ages has constantly been in flux, slowly developing and changing as the centuries tick by. The law today is not the same as existed 200 years ago or 2000 years ago. There are similarities, yes, but in most cases the differences are clear. I have often marvelled at the seemingly narrow-minded view of many of my practicing colleagues (and even some academics) who tend to be very resistive to change. It often seems as if the legal scholar views the concept and content of "the law" from the perspective of the *lege lata*, or law as it is, at the moment that they complete their studies. Yes, invariably some developments might happen – a new judgment might create new case law (in our common law traditions) or an act might be amended, repealed or replaced; but the bulk of the content of the law remains the same throughout the working life of the lawyer, especially if such lawyer is not someone who specialises in an area of law where there is a lot of development. The basic tenets of contract, marriage, divorce, and deeds transfer, amongst others, remain relatively stable for the duration of the lawyer's lifetime. I won't even go into the conceit of some lawyers that "their" legal system, or national law is the best, and better than every other country's law, purely since that is what they were first indoctrinated with as students at law school. Perhaps one can blame this on the decreasing importance of such subjects as legal history, comparative law and – shall I dare say it – Latin – in the modern law curriculum. Inarguably many lawyers will never in their careers need to know much about the historical development of a certain legal principle or the way in which the law is applied in a different jurisdiction, but without such content in the curricula, or at least the sensitization that other valid options exist, the rich knowledge and understanding of the law as a science is reduced to the level of a technician operating a piece of equipment, without understanding how and why it functions in a certain way. But enough of that for the moment. In a round-about way I now come to the reason for choosing this topic as a contribution to Sjef van Erp's Festschrift.

Anyone who knows Sjef is well aware that his research, much like my own, is always on the cutting edge of legal developments, especially when they are related to new technological developments. While it can reasonably be expected of me, being a bit younger than Sjef, to keep abreast of new developments in law and technology,[2] one would not expect it of Sjef being a baby boomer, who should quite comfortably be able to fondly reminisce about the good old typewriters and index cards in the library.

When I first contemplated writing my doctoral dissertation on the topic of Property in Virtual Worlds, Andre van der Walt, quite correctly informed me that he considered Sjef to be the best person to mentor me on the subject. Sjef's depth of knowledge of the arcana of interaction between law and technology was, and still is prodigious, I still consider Sjef to be one of the few people who really understands the complexities of my own research

2 Since I grew up with computer games, home computers and email as part of everyday life.

and he remains a key figure in consulting when I write about new things, which he always seems to know more about than I do! As such, Sjef is the opposite of the stagnant positivistic black letter lawyer. He has been actively contributing to the development of the law towards the ideal not only of catching up with technological development, but to try and keep abreast of it.

With this in mind, I would like to share a little vignette that Sjef told me about.

A few years ago, at a national meeting of Dutch conveyancers, Sjef gave a keynote on the technological developments that are taking place with regard to transfer and registration of deeds. Here he expounded on the possibilities of the use of (amongst others) blockchains for such transfers and the associated efficiencies that digitalisation brings to the process. The audience was interested, but afterwards, some (older) attendees noted wryly that if they will have to deal with such new developments in practice, they will rather retire early.

That somewhat fatalistic attitude of the older conveyancers, set in their ways and comfortable in their expertise of a field of law that barely changed from the time they completed their legal studies, highlights the inherent problem facing the lawyer of the future.[3] In a nutshell, the reality of the new normal that we can expect of law in the future, is constant and large scale change. In contrast to this, one must keep in mind that the practicing of conveyancing has remained essentially the same for the past few hundred years, with the biggest change to conveyancing being the digitalisation of deeds and the deeds-registry. While this digitalisation was a rather big developmental step in conveyancing, and bearing in mind that many countries still have not settled into the effective use of digital based record keeping; it does not come close to the huge change that Sjef noted will be coming. Hence it makes sense that now that technology has started to aggressively disrupt the practice of conveyancing in such a glaring way, some would rather retire than try to adapt to new developments and procedures, immense as they may be.

This example of the changes to the (practice of) law (still very much experimental at that stage of Sjef's presentation, but now a firm reality) forms part of the wider extremely disruptive period which we are now entering, called the Fourth Industrial Revolution, which will be discussed in more detail together with the previous three revolutions a bit later on.

While the concept of the "Fourth Industrial Revolution" (4iR) is encountered more and more in both academic and popular media, it is not something that has received a lot of attention from the perspective of its possible or probable effects on the legal field at large and the teaching of law in particular. This paper intends to provide a brief background discussion of the concept of the 4iR and the disruptive effects that we could expect on

3 Here I include all practicing legal professionals who are active now and not at leisure to retire.

society. The disruptive aspect of the industrial revolutions form a central theme since it highlights that an industrial revolution goes hand in hand with radical changes in the day to day status quo of how we as society approach, amongst other issues, labour and work. In casu, this paper takes a forward look at this disruption, some of the possible negative consequences, as well as the possible opportunities for society at large, the legal field and the teaching of law during this period of upheaval.

2 Background to the Fourth Industrial Revolution

It will be good to first look at what an industrial revolution is comprised of. As such, Kayembe and Nel, defines the concept of an industrial revolution as follows:

> [An] Industrial revolution could be argued to be a major development, change, or transformation that has taken place in the history of human society; from the use of machines, telecommunications, electricity, to new developments in the form of technology.[4]

Since we are discussing the Fourth Industrial Revolution, it is important to take some notice of the ones preceding it.[5] If we were to look at the essential characteristics of each of these Industrial Revolutions,[6] they could be listed as follows.[7] The First Industrial Revolution (1iR) concerned the advent of mechanical production. The Second Industrial Revolution (2iR) followed from the first by improving mechanical production and moving to electrically powered mass production. The Third Industrial Revolution (3iR) stemmed from the development of and incorporation of the internet and automated production. This has now once again moved on to the Fourth Industrial Revolution (4iR) brought about by the ubiquity of connectedness, the Internet of Things (IoT) and machine (or Artificial Intelligence) driven Industries and production.

In other words, the order of Industrial Revolutions are:

- 1st Mechanical production
- 2nd Electrically powered mass production

4 Kayembe C and Nel D "Challenges and Opportunities for Education in the Fourth Industrial Revolution" 2019(11)3 *African Journal of Public Affairs* 80.

5 For more detail on the progression of the industrial revolutions, see Kayembe C and Nel D "Challenges and Opportunities for Education in the Fourth Industrial Revolution" 2019(11)3 *African Journal of Public Affairs* 81-83.

6 See in general Agarwal H and Agarwal R "First Industrial Revolution and Second Industrial Revolution: Technological Differences and the Differences in Banking and Financing of the Firms" 2017(2)11 *Saudi Journal of Humanities and Social Sciences* 1062-1066.

7 See Mukhova I "A lawyer in the fourth industrial revolution" 2018(18)10 *Without Prejudice* 30.

- 3rd Internet and automated production
- 4th Connected & IoT, AI & machine driven

Each of these will briefly be discussed in more detail below.

2.1 The First Industrial Revolution (1iR)

As mentioned above, the First Industrial Revolution essentially came about from the use of mechanical production. Spanning a period from the middle ages to approximately 1780, the 1iR was mainly based in Britain, and developments included the improving of the ease of travel and transportation via the development of canal and eventually rail networks; the appearance of stock exchanges and the "rise of banks, financiers, and private investment ...".[8] The invention of the steam engine and mechanisation opened up new ways of production, and these technological changes spilled over to new ways to do business, deal with social issues; as well as "new possibilities, responsibilities and abilities".[9] This led to the fact that those countries who embraced the 1iR and the improvement of infrastructure that resulted from this grew their economies and flourished, while those who did not, were left behind.

Of note here is the fact that following in the footsteps of Britain, many European countries embraced the revolution, and this led to many of those societies changing "dramatically from lower income households to rich countries".[10]

Kayembe and Nel summarise the disruptive effect of the 1iR as follows:

> The 1iR was so successful that it brought European countries out of the Dark Ages ... [and] gave European countries supremacy over other parts of the world ... [it] was a step in the right direction for human civilisation.[11]

8 Kayembe C and Nel D "Challenges and Opportunities for Education in the Fourth Industrial Revolution" 2019(11)3 *African Journal of Public Affairs* 80.

9 Kayembe C and Nel D "Challenges and Opportunities for Education in the Fourth Industrial Revolution" 2019(11)3 *African Journal of Public Affairs* 81.

10 Kayembe C and Nel D "Challenges and Opportunities for Education in the Fourth Industrial Revolution" 2019(11)3 *African Journal of Public Affairs* 80.

11 Kayembe C and Nel D "Challenges and Opportunities for Education in the Fourth Industrial Revolution" 2019(11)3 *African Journal of Public Affairs* 80.

2.2 The Second Industrial Revolution (2iR)

Building on the developments of the 1iR, the 2iR saw the introduction and uptake of electrically powered mass production. It brought further technological innovation in the form of the invention of (use of) electricity which directly led to increased production due to a move away from steam as the method of mechanical power. In essence the electrically powered machine was the star of the 2iR.[12]

2.3 The Third Industrial Revolution (3iR)

The 3iR introduced a shift away from the mechanical aspects of the previous industrial revolutions due to the influence and increasing sophistication of computing, the rise of the internet and uptake of automated production. From the mid 1900's there were advancements in manufacturing, logistics of distribution and the exploitation of new forms of energy.[13] As such the development of nuclear power and the wide scale development and use of electronics are highlighted by Kayembe and Nel, who also note that many parts of the world started to catch up with the head-start made by Europe during the previous industrial revolutions.[14]

2.4 The Fourth Industrial Revolution (4iR)

Finally, the 4iR[15] keeps building on the developments of the previous three industrial revolutions, and is driven by such developments as intelligent machines which automatically perform complex tasks that is facilitated by networking with each other. Of special importance here is the fact that in terms of the Industrial (or production) aspects, these industrial processes increasingly need little to no human intervention. Even more significant is that apart from the fact of little to no intervention being needed, increasingly there is less and less human oversight needed over these processes. The Fourth Industrial Revolution is characterised by a plethora of components, developments and features, many of which

12 Kayembe C and Nel D "Challenges and Opportunities for Education in the Fourth Industrial Revolution" 2019(11)3 *African Journal of Public Affairs* 81.

13 Kayembe C and Nel D "Challenges and Opportunities for Education in the Fourth Industrial Revolution" 2019(11)3 *African Journal of Public Affairs* 81.

14 Kayembe C and Nel D "Challenges and Opportunities for Education in the Fourth Industrial Revolution" 2019(11)3 *African Journal of Public Affairs* 81.

15 The 4iR is also often referred to as Industry 4.0 in the business world. See Kayembe C and Nel D "Challenges and Opportunities for Education in the Fourth Industrial Revolution" 2019(11)3 *African Journal of Public Affairs* 82.

are discrete technologies. Schwab,[16] who is considered to have kickstarted the discussion about the Fourth Industrial Revolution and the fact that we might be in the early stages of it, highlights the following aspects:

> [The] confluence of emerging technology breakthroughs, covering wide-ranging fields such as artificial intelligence (AI), robotics, the internet of things (IoT), autonomous vehicles, 3D printing, nanotechnology, biotechnology, materials science, energy storage and quantum computing, to name a few.[17]

Many more aspects and technologies can be described under the umbrella of the Fourth Industrial Revolution, and these will continue to increase as new technologies are developed and embraced.

The Fourth Industrial revolution will (once again) be disruptive, to both the job market as well as the nature of work (amongst many other areas).[18] As with the previous industrial revolutions the changes in the nature of available work, as well as the way in which such work is performed, will directly influence the nature of labour (jobs). In other words both jobs and the skills needed to do those jobs will change. Butler-Adam notes that the nature of work and the job market will constantly, and at an increasing pace, continue to change. As example of a disruptive (but seemingly innocuous) effect of this, he uses the example of asking a child what job they would like to do when they grow up. While we can all identify with this, the reality of the disruption caused by the 4iR will mean that by the time the child finishes school and is ready for the labour market, "a large portion of current job types will have disappeared; and as many (if not more) jobs, presently not defined, will have become both every day and essential".[19] This also applies to the number of available jobs. In this sense it will once again have a similar impact on the labour market (and economy) as the previous industrial revolutions.

On an optimistic note, it was estimated in 2018, that in the next three year period the increasing use of AI systems alone would have resulted in a net job-market win due to a half a million more jobs being created, than will be lost.[20] While on the pessimistic side, is

---

16 Schwab K *The Fourth Industrial Revolution* 2016 (World Economic Forum, Geneva). See also his subsequent work Schwab K and Davis N *Shaping the Future of the Fourth Industrial Revolution* 2018 (World Economic Forum, Geneva).

17 Schwab K *The Fourth Industrial Revolution* 2016 (World Economic Forum, Geneva). Introduction.

18 Butler-Adam "The Fourth Industrial Revolution and education" 2018 (114)5-6 *South African Journal of Science* 1.

19 Butler-Adam "The Fourth Industrial Revolution and education" 2018 (114)5-6 *South African Journal of Science* 1.

20 Butler-Adam "The Fourth Industrial Revolution and education" 2018 (114)5-6 *South African Journal of Science* 1. See also Marlin D "Millenials, This is How Artificial Intelligence Will Impact Your Job For Better and Worse" 16 Jan 2018 *Forbes* at https://www.forbes.com/sites/danielmarlin/2018/01/16/millennials-this-is-how-artificial-intelligence-will-impact-your-job-for-better-and-worse/?sh=7d8488734533.

was estimated that 37% of millennials are at risk of redundancy, and that half of all current work activities could be automated in the next 10 to 30 years.[21] Muhkova notes that the changes brought on by the 4iR could result in an automation of a third of all activities in 60% of all current occupations.[22] This automation will of course result in the correlative reduction of jobs. Therefore, large numbers of people would need to a) find new jobs and/or b) learn new skills for current (or new) jobs and industries which will emerge from these changes. This aspect of either re-skilling, (or upskilling) as well as the focus on transferable skills is of key importance for making a success of the student of the future.

It is important to highlight two specific aspects of the disruptive consequences of industrial revolutions at this point. As noted by Kaymbe and Nel, it "changes government policies and the way the government provides services to various communities, and influences both the social and economic aspects of society."[23] While Stearns notes that

> [t]he expression "industrial revolution" as a generic term refers to the emergence, during the transition from a preindustrial to an industrial society of modern economic growth – that is, a sustained and substantial increase of gross domestic product (GDP) per capita in real terms."[24]

Essentially this underscores the fact that failure to exploit the opportunities presented by an industrial revolution will mean losing out on economic growth and wealth for a nation.

As alluded to above, one of the big challenges for surviving and possibly flourishing during (and after) the Fourth Industrial Revolution would be to proactively identify and then actively harness the new job opportunities; else it could (would) result in even more and increased severe social inequality and unemployment at a national as well as global scale.[25] Abusedra notes that if humans want to remain relevant and "not only unemployed, but unemployable", we should take a proactive role in shaping the technology and disruption – which could "reduce the fear of losing jobs to technology".[26] In order to

---

21 Marlin D "Millenials, This is How Artificial Intelligence Will Impact Your Job For Better and Worse" 16 Jan 2018 *Forbes* at https://www.forbes.com/sites/danielmarlin/2018/01/16/millennials-this-is-how-artificial-intelligence-will-impact-your-job-for-better-and-worse/?sh=7d8488734533. See also Manyika et al "A future that works: Automation, Employement, and Productivity" McKinsey Global Institute at https://www.mckinsey.com/featured-insights/digital-disruption/harnessing-automation-for-a-future-that-works/de-de#.

22 Mukhova I "A lawyer in the fourth industrial revolution" 2018(18)10 *Without Prejudice* 30.

23 Kayembe C and Nel D "Challenges and Opportunities for Education in the Fourth Industrial Revolution" 2019(11)3 *African Journal of Public Affairs* 80.

24 Stearns P N *Oxford Encyclopedia of the modern World* 2008 (Oxford University Press, Oxford) 158.

25 Kayembe C and Nel D "Challenges and Opportunities for Education in the Fourth Industrial Revolution" 2019(11)3 *African Journal of Public Affairs* 89.

26 Abusedra A "Law must be adapted for the Fourth Industrial Revolution" 26 Dec 2019 *Thehill.com* at https://thehill.com/opinion/technology/475937-law-must-be-adapted-for-the-fourth-industrial-revolution.

facilitate this Mukhova[27] identifies the need for partnerships between government, academia and business to upskill people so as to harness the new opportunities that emerge from the revolution; and for legal reform to make this happen.[28]

Apart from the above, the ongoing challenge of reforming and updating the law, to keep up with changing technology and new inventions, will need to be seriously addressed. One possible solution for this would be to delegate this continuous, and sped up, development to a technocratic-legal-academic corps of people; since it is doubtful if career politicians and populistic legislators can ever be up to this task, purely due to a lack of technical expertise in the underlying technologies that drive development.

New markets and industries that are created as a consequence of the Fourth Industrial Revolution will necessitate increased need for legal services from the legal profession at large. Additionally, the effect of the changes to the current and remaining (surviving) industries and the societal consequences of technological development in general, will also unlock new opportunities for the legal profession. For example, one can look at the plethora of legal issues and new opportunities for legal professionals that have been (and are still being) created by the legal ramifications caused by BREXIT. It will take decades to untangle the legal mess in general and especially with regard to trade between the UK and the EU. Another area where lawyers are now increasingly busying themselves, is with compliance with new privacy rules concerning the use, exploitation, storage, transfer and ownership of data. The advent of the GDPR[29] in the EU and the POPI[30] act in South Africa, has created a whole new market for legal specialisation and earning potential as clients struggle to understand and comply with new regulations. Not to mention the increasing volume of litigation due to contraventions of the regulations by the juggernaut IT companies that control and exploit personal data for personal gain.[31] For these large companies, but also for much smaller ones, in the future mitigation of (legal) risk will continue be a big item,

27 See Mukhova I "A lawyer in the fourth industrial revolution" 2018(18)10 *Without Prejudice* 30.

28 In order to achieve this, perhaps some form of compulsory on the job (and continuous education) training could be implemented by governments. But one would need to guard against mills of repetitive seminars or training sessions purely for rote continuous profession education (CPE) points. This would also be a clear opportunity for Universities and faculty to develop programmes for such training and to be thought leaders in the area.

29 EU *General Data Protection Regulation* (GDPR) Regulation (EU) 2016/679.

30 *Protection of Personal Information Act* 4 of 2013 (POPI).

31 See for example Lomas N "French Court slaps down Google's appeal against $57 GDPR fine" 19 June 2020 *TechCrunch* at https://techcrunch.com/2020/06/19/french-court-slaps-down-googles-appeal-against-57m-gdpr-fine/; Ritzer C "First multi-million GDPR fine in Germany: €14.5 million for not having a proper data retention schedule in place" 12 November 2019 *Data Protection Report* at https://www.dataprotectionreport.com/2019/11/first-multi-million-gdpr-fine-in-germany-e14-5-million-for-not-having-a-proper-data-retention-schedule-in-place/; Satariano A "Facebook loses antitrust decision in Germany over Data collection" 23 June 2020 *New York Times* at https://www.nytimes.com/2020/06/23/technology/facebook-antitrust-germany.html.

but lawyers will need to work as (or together with) analysts to embrace big data and understand possible legal ramifications before they conceivably happen.

3 Legal Practice and the 4iR

On a side note it bears mentioning that the use of LegalTech (legal technology) is increasingly used to improve the speed & efficiency of the legal process, both in the legal practise as well as the courts.[32] As more and more aspects of legal practise gets shifted online or can be done digitally, the LegalTech will bolster the speed and effectiveness of legal practitioners by taking away some of the drudgery of everyday repetitive tasks. The same applies to the courts;[33] although in practice it would seem as if many courts (including in South Africa) are struggling to move on from an archaic prohibitively costly, onerous and inefficient paper-based document, filing and case management system.[34] Some serious political backbone and funding (that does not disappear into state-capture and corruption) will be needed for this. I would recommend a purely performance and penalty-based provisioning system for this.

AI and automation will be able to free legal professionals from menial tasks and allow them to focus on "higher value-added services" to clients.[35] This will, however, have an impact on specifically such jobs as para-legal and legal-secretariat based jobs. The legal profession will not be too severely negatively affected by automation and AI, but we should recognise that some aspects will become automated and some line-items that have been billable will fall away.[36]

4 The 4iR and Legal Education

This brings us to what is needed to continue to teach and practice in the legal professions – lifelong learning, keeping up with the increasing amounts of changes in the law and procedures as well as with general technological innovations. Kayembe & Nel note that the 4iR holds both challenges and opportunities for education with the potential to

---

32 Mukhova I "A lawyer in the fourth industrial revolution" 2018(18)10 *Without Prejudice* 31.

33 See for example Cross M "Computer says win: funder ties up with case prediction startup" 2020 *The Law Society Gazette* at https://www.lawgazette.co.uk/practice/computer-says-win-funder-ties-up-with-case-prediction-startup/5105383.article.

34 See Broughton T "COVID-19: Some judges refuse to use their own computers during lockdown" 28 May 2020 GroundUp at https://www.groundup.org.za/article/covid-19-some-judges-refuse-use-their-personal-computers-hearings-during-lockdown/.

35 Mukhova I "A lawyer in the fourth industrial revolution" 2018(18)10 *Without Prejudice* 31.

36 Mukhova I "A lawyer in the fourth industrial revolution" 2018(18)10 *Without Prejudice* 31.

transform society for the better.[37] This could be done by embracing " ... different components of the 4iR, such as IoT, 3D printing, quantum computing and AI"[38] to transform the education sector in such a way that it can offer solutions to new challenges.

Kayembe and Nel[39] with reference to Butler-Adam[40] highlight the fact that the implications of the 4iR for education is focussed more on the aspects of developments in the curricula, as well as teaching and learning, rather than on the replacement of teaching staff with "robotic tutors". As Mukhova[41] notes "[m]achines are tactical, but humans are strategic – while machines will speed up processes and make onerous tasks easier, humans will always guide the process."[42]

Butler-Adam postulates that the success of a member of society and as an employee (here I would add – student) during the 4iR, is dependent on knowledge in the three areas of "numeracy, literacy and an understanding of how the world operates."[43] In fact I think that Butler-Adam manages to capture the essence of what we need to focus on in the development of curricula and the future teaching of law in the following statement:

> Students studying the **basic and applied sciences** need also to understand the **political and social natures** of the world in which they live. For the same reasons, students who study the **humanities and social sciences** need to understand at least the foundations on which **AI is based and operates**." (own emphasis).[44]

In other words, multidisciplinary knowledge is of cardinal importance and one cannot remain closeted in one's own silo of expertise. While this statement is inarguably correct, I would just broaden Butler-Adam's limiting reference to AI, so as to include the technical foundations of the most important technologies that drive the changes in society, essentially being an acceptable level of digital literacy. This sentiment is supported by Kayembe and

37 Kayembe C and Nel D "Challenges and Opportunities for Education in the Fourth Industrial Revolution" 2019(11)3 *African Journal of Public Affairs* 87.

38 Kayembe C and Nel D "Challenges and Opportunities for Education in the Fourth Industrial Revolution" 2019(11)3 *African Journal of Public Affairs* 87.

39 Kayembe C and Nel D "Challenges and Opportunities for Education in the Fourth Industrial Revolution" 2019(11)3 *African Journal of Public Affairs* 87.

40 Butler-Adam "The Fourth Industrial Revolution and education" 2018 (114)5-6 *South African Journal of Science* 1.

41 Mukhova I "A lawyer in the fourth industrial revolution" 2018(18)10 *Without Prejudice* 31.

42 See also Taparia H "The Future of College is Online, and It's cheaper" 25 May 2020 *New York Times* at https://www.nytimes.com/2020/05/25/opinion/online-college-coronavirus.html?action=click&module=Opinion&pgtype=Homepage.

43 Butler-Adam "The Fourth Industrial Revolution and education" 2018 (114)5-6 *South African Journal of Science* 1.

44 Butler-Adam "The Fourth Industrial Revolution and education" 2018 (114)5-6 *South African Journal of Science* 1.

Nel who argue that "[d]igital literacy is a basic prerequisite for students to develop adaptive capabilities to participate in the global digital society ...".[45]

In the future, preparing students (and staff) for those new skills required in the workplace of the future will need flexible and adaptable education and training systems.[46] Once more, we will need to constantly evaluate what we teach, how we teach it and from where[47] we teach it.

Without going into too much detail, Toolan[48] mentions some examples, noted below, of how the current developments in technological capabilities are already disruptively influencing the law and the legal profession. For example, Cleveland in the United States of America is using Artificial Intelligence for helping to make determinations of suitability of candidates to be released in bail applications.[49] While one of the arguments in favour of using AI for such determinations is that it reduces the influence of bias from judges, some studies have shown that the opposite can happen where the AI itself can be biased, due to various factors.[50] As another example some judges are either already dabbling in programming or learning to code to empower themselves to better understand the intricacies of highly technical litigation before them.[51] It goes to illustrate that without knowledge outside of the accepted legal curriculum, neither judges, nor legal council will be able to effectively participate in a case that deals with technological issues.[52] It also bears mentioning that we currently, as well as in the past, had judges and council experienced in specialist technical matters, (for example patent lawyers who often also have an engineering background), this used to be the exception. However, in the future, as the developments of the 4iR overwhelms us, it would be the rule, rather than the exception

45 Kayembe C and Nel D "Challenges and Opportunities for Education in the Fourth Industrial Revolution" 2019(11)3 *African Journal of Public Affairs* 97. (Emphasis added).

46 Abusedra A "Law must be adapted for the Fourth Industrial Revolution" 26 Dec 2019 *Thehill.com* at https://thehill.com/opinion/technology/475937-law-must-be-adapted-for-the-fourth-industrial-revolution.

47 Since working from home has become the new norm, the hidden consequences of this practice needs to be kept in mind. See Shearmur R "Remote work: Employers are taking over our living spaces and passing on the costs" 18 Jun 2020 The Conversation at https://theconversation.com/remote-work-employers-are-taking-over-our-living-spaces-and-passing-on-costs-140610; as well as Helman C "Some Hidden Energy Costs of 'Working From Home' During the Outbreak" 18 Mar 2020 *Forbes.com* at https://www.forbes.com/sites/christopherhelman/2020/03/18/some-hidden-energy-costs-of-working-from-home-during-the-outbreak/#79a9fe7128e6.

48 Toolan N "3 Ways the Fourth Industrial Revolution is disrupting the Law" 2018 (Apr) at https://www.weforum.org/agenda/2018/04/three-ways-the-fourth-industrial-revolution-is-disrupting-law/.

49 Anon "Artificial Intelligence is coming for both judges and defendants" 31 Jan 2018 New York Post at https://nypost.com/2018/01/31/artificial-intelligence-is-coming-for-both-judges-and-defendants/

50 Angwin, Larsen and Mattu "Machine Bias" 23 May 2016 *ProPublica* at https://www.propublica.org/article/machine-bias-risk-assessments-in-criminal-sentencing.

51 Jeong S "The Judge's Code" 19 Oct 2017 *The Verge* at https://www.theverge.com/2017/10/19/16503076/oracle-vs-google-judge-william-alsup-interview-waymo-uber.

52 See also Rawlinson P "Will lawyers become extinct in the age of automation?" 29 March 2018 *World Economic Forum* at https://www.weforum.org/agenda/2018/03/will-lawyers-become-extinct-in-the-age-of-automation/.

that legal disputes will deal with very technical issues or at least with the new technologies that are being embraced. This means that the lawyer of the future would need to be relatively well informed about the principles of the technologies, and also be a life-long learner, constantly keeping up to date with new developments.

Doepker postulates that the student of the future will have to ask a number of difficult questions when considering their options for higher education.[53] One of these is: "Will my education allow me to balance technical skills at risk of being replaced by automation, with timeless "soft" skills?" These soft skills can also be referred to as "transferable skills", i.e skills that you are able to use for multiple different possible careers. Another question asks whether the envisioned education will prepare the student for a career, and whether that career will still exist by the time the student is ready to join the labour market.[54] Kayembe and Nel[55] also note the importance of appropriate skills for the successful implementation of the 4iR in education and mention with reference to Gray[56] that approximately 35% of skills which are currently seen as important for success in the workplace will change in the future.

Doepker[57] underscores the need for rethinking higher education and mention some changes and interventions that have already been proven to show promise. The first of these suggested changes are to condense the higher education experience. The second, to do away with the focus on credentials. The third is to align incentives of students and educational institutions. For example, this can be done by using so-called Income Share Agreements (ISAs) for funding students to alleviate the rising burden of student debt and unaffordable tuition. The fourth change is to forge stronger ties between industry and education. In the case of law, this should not necessarily be confined to legal practice, but rather be expanded to include the wider industry. This will also become more and more pertinent for law students and academics to better understand the functioning and needs

---

53 Doepker M "5 Ways students can graduate fully qualified for the Fourth Industrial Revolution" 2019 (Jan) *World Economic Forum* at https://www.weforum.org/agenda/2019/01/how-students-can-graduate-qualified-for-fourth-industrial-revolution.

54 Doepker M "5 Ways students can graduate fully qualified for the Fourth Industrial Revolution" 2019 (Jan) *World Economic Forum* at https://www.weforum.org/agenda/2019/01/how-students-can-graduate-qualified-for-fourth-industrial-revolution. See also Anon "Artificial Intelligence: The Fourth Industrial Revolution and the need for improved employee representation" 2018 (Mar) *Norton Rose Fullbright* at https://www.nortonrosefulbright.com/en-za/knowledge/publications/4166fdcd/artificial-intelligence-the-fourth-industrial-revolution-and-the-need-for-improved-employee-representation.

55 Kayembe C and Nel D "Challenges and Opportunities for Education in the Fourth Industrial Revolution" 2019(11)3 *African Journal of Public Affairs* 88.

56 Gray A "The 10 skills you need to thrive in the Fourth Industrial Revolution" 2016 World Economic Forum at https://www.weforum.org/agenda/2016/01/the-10-skills-you-need-to-thrive-in-the-fourth-industrial-revolution/.

57 Doepker M "5 Ways students can graduate fully qualified for the Fourth Industrial Revolution" 2019 (Jan) *World Economic Forum* at https://www.weforum.org/agenda/2019/01/how-students-can-graduate-qualified-for-fourth-industrial-revolution.

of the (non-legal) industry. The fifth and final suggested change is to implement project-based learning. Doepker (while discussing modern careers and higher education in general and not law specifically) notes that:

> Modern careers require creativity, critical thinking, interpersonal skills, writing ability, presentation skills, and negotiation.

They also require:

> Crafting and presenting a reasoned argument, asking the right questions and seeking out the answers – these are skills that must be taught in combination with any sort of technical education.

It is encouraging that all of these skills are skills that already form part of the core curriculum of law and that we already teach to our students. Note, however, that these skills should also be taught to students undertaking a technical education – once again highlighting the multidisciplinary aspect of education for the future.

When it come to the necessary skillset in the current industrial revolution, Butler-Adam notes the following:

> [P]eople must have the skills required to implement, manage and work with the new technology, and with one another. And, not least, to be **problem solvers**, to be **adaptable**, and to be able to **express themselves in both the written and spoken word** – and to make the kinds of ethical and moral decisions that are not ever likely to become successful elements of AI.[58] (own emphasis)

I would also like to highlight the importance of not forgetting that lecturers and academics also need to acquire these same skillsets and knowledge as precondition for them being able to teach these skills to students. This will mean ongoing education for our legal educators as well. Since academics are already grossly overburdened with work, some prerequisites will need to be put into place to facilitate their acquisition of new skills and expertise of which one of the most important will be the reduction of administrative burdens and unnecessary bureaucracy such as "marking of tests and reporting absences.[59]

---

58 Butler-Adam "The Fourth Industrial Revolution and education" 2018 (114)5-6 *South African Journal of Science* 1.

59 Kayembe C and Nel D "Challenges and Opportunities for Education in the Fourth Industrial Revolution" 2019(11)3 *African Journal of Public Affairs* 90.

In other words, it should be possible to embrace the innovative technological developments of the 4iR to reduce the burden on teaching staff. But this, of course, will also necessitate an increase in government funding for universities to empower them to do this. Hopefully one of the effects of the disruption of the 4iR would be that the current trend of reducing funding for education and research and trying to run education as for-profit institutions will stop, since one can never justify attempting to measure the value of a good education by using business metrics and evaluating the worth of educational staff in terms of cost-to-company. In much the same way that countries outside of Europe were left behind during previous Industrial Revolutions, the same will happen to countries who do not aggressively invest in upskilling their current generation citizens who are active in the labour market. Even more so if proper investment and planning for the effective capacity building of teaching staff and the next generation of economically active citizens are not funded.

The skillset of the future student should be of such a nature that they would be able to transfer between different jobs throughout their careers and easily adapt to changes in the labour market caused by the developments of the 4iR.

With this necessity of a multidisciplinary approach to education in mind, the need for students (including law students) to have transferable skillsets as mentioned above; as well as the need for law students to have a foundational knowledge of the technologies driving the developments of the 4iR, I would like to propose the following two changes to the way in which we design our legal curriculum.

The first one is to embrace the dual-degree system used in the United States for legal education. In this case it would mean that law will always be followed as a second degree in addition to another preceding degree. The idea is that this will help produce lawyers who have a wider knowledge and some multidisciplinary background of other scientific areas (including other social sciences).

The second suggested change could be immediately implemented in jurisdictions following the straight LLB education of a single legal degree. At the moment students at most universities can choose between various optional introductory subjects from other disciplines (normally confined to the social sciences), such as political sciences, various languages, and philosophy, amongst others, which they normally take in their first year in addition to legal subjects. The recommendation is that several foundational technical or technological subjects should be included as mandatory subjects as part of the legal curriculum (or at the very least be optional in addition to the ones from social sciences). Examples of such subjects could be informatics, introduction to computer programming/artificial intelligence/machine learning/databases/networking/computer maintenance and repair etc. These and similar subjects will be of immediate use to the current student and will be of increasing importance for the student of the future who will need to understand at least the basics of the technologies underlying the disputes that they will deal with.

Finally, to conclude, I want to bring us back to the older conveyancer who contemplated throwing in the towel in the vignette mentioned by Sjef at the start. The lecturer, student and lawyer of the future will need to be adaptable, embrace constant change and development, be cognisant of the fact that what is true today will not be true tomorrow, have flexible, transferable skill sets, be a life-long learner, be inquisitive and adaptable and ready to embrace new opportunities during the disruptions caused by the Fourth Industrial Revolution. In a nutshell, he or she should not be like the conveyancer mentioned above, he or she should be like Sjef.

Rights in Co-Generated Data – A New Data Ownership Debate?

Christiane C. Wendehorst[*]

In Europe, there has been a quite lively debate about 'data ownership'. Sjef van Erp has been a major protagonist in this debate, sometimes bringing much-needed clarity into a discussion where people were frequently talking past each other. In doing so, he was benefitting from many decades as the doyen of European property law and from a wealth of experience in the international domain. In this paper, I would like to outline the 'co-generated data' approach as a possible alternative to approaches taken so far.

1 Setting the Scene: The 'Data Ownership' Debate

It is unclear whether the origins of the debate lie in European academic discourse or in a campaign launched by the industry, notably the German automobile industry that was worrying about the protection of IoT data collected through connected cars. Be that as it may, 'data ownership' has, for almost a decade, been one of the most controversial topics in the emerging body of 'digital law', and even more so after the European Commission mentioned the option of introducing a 'data producer's right' at EU level in its 2017 Communication on 'Building a European Data Economy'.[1] From the very beginning, authors had very different things in mind when discussing 'data ownership'. Not only did they approach the topic from the perspective of different stakeholder groups, but also the notion of what 'ownership' means was anything but clear. Ideas ranged from a new copyright-like intellectual property right that would allow industries the exclusive monetarisation of data generated with the help of their products,[2] to something akin to ownership in tangible property,[3] to cloudy notions of 'better control' for consumers and a 'fair share' in the profits derived from the data generated through their activities.[4] Sjef

---

* Professor of Law at the University of Vienna.

1 Communication from the Commission of 10 January 2017 – Building a European Data Economy, COM(2017) 9 final, p. 10 ff.

2 Herbert Zech, 'Information as a tradable commodity', in: Alberto De Franceschi (ed.), *European Contract Law and the Digital Single Market* (Intersentia 2016), p. 51 ff.

3 Thomas Hoeren, 'Dateneigentum – Versuch einer Anwendung von § 303a StGB im Zivilrecht', 2013 *Multimedia und Recht*, p. 486 ff.

4 Karl-Heinz Fezer, *Repräsentatives Dateneigentum* (Konrad Adenauer Stiftung 2018), p. 84 ff.

van Erp has recently stressed that common law notions of property rights, referring to a bundle of rights rather than to one single 'absolute right', may be better suited to fit the needs of the data economy.[5] Most recently, he has pointed to the Québec trust as a form of ownerless property with a stress on management that might be a model for the conceptualisation of ownership of data.[6]

The concept of exclusive ownership rights in data that might be comparable to ownership in tangible property or to intellectual property rights is problematic in various respects. For intellectual achievements protected by traditional IP rights it is usually rather obvious that it is the creator who deserves protection, and who that creator might be (with controversies as to details, such as concerning the work-for-hire doctrine). In the case of mere data, this is not clear at all as it is by and large four classes of persons that might be seen as having a legitimate claim to the data:[7] the subjects of the information, the persons by whose immediate activity the information was recorded, the persons who have assembled or otherwise processed the information, and the persons who have created the means by which information was recorded and who have often initiated the recording. Assigning intellectual property rights to one of these classes of persons at the expense of the others in a one-size-fits-all fashion would seem inappropriate, and assigning them jointly to all classes of persons would end in paralysis.[8] Even more importantly, the question arises why the law should assign exclusive rights in data to anybody. A really convincing case for why we need data ownership for functioning data markets has not yet been made, and these markets seem to be functioning well without it.[9] It is clear that those investing in data have an interest in their investment being protected, but trade secrets law demonstrates that such investment protection is possible without exclusive ownership rights. Given that anyone dealing with data has already a plethora of legal restrictions to consider, adding yet another layer of complexity might suffocate the data economy rather than boosting it.[10] Last but not least it is also unclear why data ownership would lead to a fair share for consumers in the wealth created with data – data ownership would be contracted away by

---

5 Sjef van Erp, 'Who "Owns" the Data in a Coronavirus Tracing (and/or Tracking) App?', in Ewoud Hondius, Andrea Nicolussi, Marta Santos Silva, Pablo Salvador Coderch, Christiane Wendehorst and Fryderyk Zoll (eds.), *Coronavirus and the Law in Europe* (Intersentia Online Publishing 2020).

6 Sjef van Erp, 'Management as Ownership of Data', in Sebastian Lohssee, Reiner Schulze and Dirk Staudenmeyer (eds.), *Data as Counter-Performance – Contract Law 2.0?* (Nomos 2020), p. 77 ff.

7 See, for example, Lothar Determann, 'No one owns data', 2019 *Hastings Law Journal* (70), p. 1, 28 ff.

8 Andreas Wiebe, 'Protection of industrial data – a new property right for the digital economy?', 2016 *GRUR International*, p. 877, 882 f.

9 See Wolfgang Kerber and Jonas Severin Frank, 'Data Governance Regimes in the Digital Economy: The Example of Connected Cars', SSRN ID 3064794, p. 46, who argue that it is not clear if a market failure exists.

10 Opinion of the German Data Ethics Commission (2019), p. 105, available via https://www.datenethikkommission.de.

individuals very much like other entitlements are contracted away.[11] And if it is not contracted away (e.g. if the regime is mandatory and administrated by collective societies) prices would inevitably rise, i.e. privacy-conscious individuals would cross-subsidise those producing most data, and doubtful incentives for vulnerable groups of the society would be created.[12]

If we think of data ownership as something akin to ownership in tangible items problems arise already at a more theoretical level. While it may be possible to qualify the physical manifestation of data on a medium as 'quasi-tangible' and deal with it under traditional property law,[13] the fact that data can be multiplied within fractions of a second at basically no cost, and are commonly characterised as a 'non-rival resource', means that the practical significance of this qualification is limited. At the end of the day it may be the exclusive nature of the right itself that makes 'ownership' in a more traditional sense a less than ideal concept for the phenomenon of data.

2 THE NOTION OF CO-GENERATED DATA AS DEVELOPED BY THE ALI-ELI PRINCIPLES

In 2017, the American Law Institute (ALI)[14] and the European Law Institute (ELI)[15] embarked on a joint project in the area of the data economy.[16] It was launched as a 'principles' project, which means, in ALI terms, that the standards developed are primarily addressed to legislatures, administrative agencies, or private actors, but also to courts insofar as the data economy is an emerging area that is so new that there is little established law.[17] Principles may suggest best practices for these institutions. Given that the data economy is such a vast area, the project was later narrowed down to two focal issues: data transactions and data rights. While data transactions are basically data contracts, such as for the supply of data, or for services with regard to data (including contracts with intermediaries and equivalent institutional arrangements), data rights are entitlements of a very special type specifically tailored to data. Principles 18 to 23 reflect the most important type of data rights, which are data rights based on the notion of co-generation of data. A

11 Wolfgang Kerber and Jonas Severin Frank, 'Data Governance Regimes in the Digital Economy: The Example of Connected Cars', SSRN ID 3064794, p. 46.
12 Opinion of the German Data Ethics Commission (2019), p. 105 available via https://www.datenethikkommission.de.
13 Gregor Klammer, *Dateneigentum – Das Sachenrecht der Daten* (Jan Sramek 2019), p. 27 ff.
14 https://www.ali.org/projects/show/data-economy/.
15 https://europeanlawinstitute.eu/principles-for-a-data-economy/.
16 https://principlesforadataeconomy.org/.
17 The American Law Institute, *Capturing the Voice of The American Law Institute: A Handbook for ALI Reporters and Those Who Review Their Work* (The American Law Institute 2015), p. 4.

common denominator of these rights is that they find their justification in the share which a party had in the generation of the data that is at stake. In contrast, Principles 24 to 27 deal with data rights afforded to a party for the public interest, including for ensuring fair and efficient competition.

2.1 *Co-Generation*

Principle 19 is about the notion of co-generated data. 'Co-generation' of data is a normative notion that does not coincide with any notions of 'generation' of data that may be used in a more technical context. There are largely four different types of contributions to the generation of data, which correspond to the classes of parties already mentioned above.

The first way in which a party may contribute to the generation of data is by being the subject of the information coded in the data (e.g. personal data, or data relating to a particular business and its activities), or by being the owner or operator of the subject of that information (e.g. data relating to the maintenance status of a building). Being the subject of the information may, from the point of view of European legal systems, and at least as far as natural persons are concerned, even be the strongest form of contribution that potentially trumps other forms of contribution. While, from a technical point of view, such a person would not be considered as having any share in the 'generation' of data unless that person has at the same time contributed to recording the binary code, the law may take a broader perspective, and has already done so in some areas.[18]

Another form in which a party may contribute to the generation of data is by pursuing an activity by means of which data has been produced (e.g. driving a connected car) or by being the owner or operator of a device by means of which data has been produced (e.g. owning a connected car that is rented out to others).[19] Needless to say, also processing existing data in order to obtain derived or inferred data[20] falls under this category as many ways of processing existing data lead to the generation of 'new' data.

The activity of collecting, assembling and combining data may be considered as a sub-category of the latter, or as a separate type of contributing to the generation of data. The latter view seems to be preferable, as it is often very different parties that produce and that collect data. In any case, the value and practical utility of data largely depends on its

18 See Article 4(1) GDPR, Regulation (EU) 2016/679 of the European Parliament and of the Council of 27 April 2016 on the protection of natural persons with regard to the processing of personal data and on the free movement of such data, and repealing Directive 95/46/EC, OJ C 2016/119, p. 1.

19 See Herbert Zech, 'Information as a tradable commodity', in: Alberto De Franceschi (ed.), *European Contract Law and the Digital Single Market* (Intersentia, 2016), p. 51, 75 who wanted to tie his 'data producers right' to the economically responsible operator of equipment that generates the data.

20 See OECD, *Enhancing Access to and Sharing of Data – Reconciling Risks and Benefits for Data Re-Use Across Societies* (OECD 2019), p. 29 f.

combination with other data, and there are massive effects of scale. This is without prejudice to the fact that creating a database may even qualify for copyright or sui generis database protection.[21]

Still another form of contributing to the generation of data is by developing or producing a computer program or other relevant element of a product or service by means of which data has been generated (e.g. producing a connected car), or maybe only investing in the development of such an element.

The significance of the share that a party has had in the generation of data depends, to a certain extent, on the type of contribution (i.e. which and how many of the factors listed are fulfilled). The factors are listed in the order of their relative weight; this does, however, not mean an absolute order of priority, but a factor that figures lower in the list normally needs to be present to a higher degree in order to have the same force as a factor that figures higher. Very often, more than one factor is present in a particular case, e.g., where a party generates data by driving their connected car, such data is at the same time identifiable to that party and to a device owned by that party. The share also depends on the remoteness of the contribution. For instance, where an individual provides personal data to a controller the share in the provided data is extremely high, but once the data has been processed, or even pseudonymised or anonymised, the share may become negligeable. To some degree the share also depends on the specificity of the contribution (e.g., where the same contribution could have been made by any other party, this has less weight than when a contribution is specific for a particular party).

Of course, the relative share which a party has in the generation of data depends on the contributions of other parties (e.g., the controller that has processed data in order to obtain derived data, or that has inferred data from other data, may have a significant share in the generation of that data, the extent of that share depending on similar factors as the ones just mentioned). Contributions of a party that are insignificant in the circumstances do not lead to data being considered as co-generated by that party.

2.2 *The Five-Factor-Test*

Principle 19 identifies five factors to be considered in determining whether it is appropriate to afford to a party a data right. They are: (a) the share which the party seeking access had in the generation of the relevant data; (b) the weight of grounds which that party can put forward for being afforded the data right; (c) the weight of any legitimate interests the controller or a third party may have in affording or denying the data right; (d) any imbalance

21 See Article 7(1) of the Database Directive, Directive 96/9/EC of the European Parliament and of the Council of 11 March 1996 on the legal protection of databases, OJ L 1996/77, p. 20.

of bargaining power between the parties; and (e) any public interest. It is to be noted that public interests may both be an argument for and against granting access. These five factors must be balanced against one another in a flexible manner. For instance, if the ground a party brings forward for granting an access right has particular weight, it may compensate for a relatively insignificant contribution to data generation.

The most controversial among these factors, which was added by the project Reporters only after some discussion, is that of imbalance of bargaining power. On the one hand, it is a standard justification for legal systems to interfere with private ordering for the protection of vulnerable groups, such as consumers or authors with regard to their works, and it is a fundamental point in competition law. However, one might also say that it is absorbed by the other factors, namely by the legitimate interests to be put forward by the respective parties and the public interest. One important reason for adding imbalance of bargaining power as a separate factor was to prevent that big companies claiming access to data from small companies, or from consumers, abuse the Principles.

It is also important to stress that data rights that are afforded predominantly for the public interest and without regard to the share which a party had in the generation of the data, or where that share plays a non-material role, should not be considered rights in co-generated data. It is sometimes difficult to draw a clear line between the two types of data rights. For instance, an independent repair shop's right to access vehicle data held by a vehicle manufacturer[22] may be analysed as the car owner's right in the data co-generated by the car owner, or as the right of a competitor in a downstream market who does not have any share in the generation of the vehicle data.

Apart from the decision whether or not to grant a data right, there is also the decision about the modalities of that right, such as with regard to formats, timing, security measures (including for the protection of third parties), and whether access must be provided for free or in return for appropriate remuneration.[23] Strictly speaking, the two decisions cannot be seen as being entirely detached from each other. For instance, the impossibility of taking appropriate steps for the protection of third parties may, ultimately, be a reason not to grant a data right that would otherwise have to be granted, and remuneration may serve to balance otherwise existing legitimate interests of the controller in denying the data right.

22 See Articles 61 ff. of the Type Approval Regulation, Regulation (EU) 2018/858 of the European Parliament and of the Council of 30 May 2018 on the approval and market surveillance of motor vehicles and their trailers and of systems, components and separate technical units intended for such vehicles, OJ L 2018/151, p. 1.

23 Compulsory licensing in return for remuneration, based on certain key principles, such as fair, reasonable and non-discriminatory (FRAND) terms, is being discussed as a general solution to issues of data access, see COM(2017) 9 final, p. 13. Such rules already exist e.g. in Article 63(1) Type Approval Regulation or Articles 23(1) and 24(2) of the Electricity Directive, Directive (EU) 2019/944 of the European Parliament and of the Council of 5 June 2019 on common rules for the internal market for electricity and amending Directive 2012/27/EU, OJ L 2019/158, p. 125.

2.3 Nature of the Data Rights Under the ALI-ELI Principles

Principle 18 describes the rights in co-generated data as reflecting considerations of fairness. Their implementation by courts or legislators should therefore primarily occur within frameworks associated with fairness, which differ from jurisdiction to jurisdiction. In many legal systems implementation will occur by means of interpretation of the contract, where such a contract between the parties exists, applying principles such as that of good faith and fair dealing or rules such as that of unfair contract terms control. The Principles do not seek to indicate precisely how a jurisdiction should deal with the matter, leaving the matter to domestic law. This also applies with regard to the question whether, and under what conditions, data rights may be waived or varied by agreement.

3 FOUR KEY RIGHTS

Looking somewhat closer at the nature of the data rights in question, there are four key types of rights that may arise from the fact that a person has a share in the generation of data, together with the other factors, as described above. It is in particular rights to get access to co-generated data, or even to port data, that are being recognized to an increasing extent in data-specific legislation and case law worldwide. Another important data right may be the right to require that a party desist from processing of data, which can go as far as to include a right to request erasure of data. Additional data rights recommended by the Principles are the rights to require correction of incorrect or incomplete data, and, very exceptionally, to require an economic share in profits derived from the use of data.

3.1 Access and Portability Rights

In practice, access rights and related rights are the most important data rights in co-generated data. Access to data is considered to be key for many companies to be able to participate in the modern economy. It is of utmost importance not only for understanding and improving one's own business operations, but also for research and for the development of new products and services, for a better choice between different suppliers, and many other purposes.

'Access' to data is a rather broad term, and it may mean different things. The weakest form of access is that of merely receiving proof of the type of data held, and of their broad content.[24] However, access normally implies being able to view or retrieve data, including by automated means. Even this form of access to data is sometimes insufficient for satisfying

24 See Article 15 GDPR.

the legitimate interests of the party relying on the right, and transfer of data to that party or a third party may be required as well. The strongest form of an access right is that of data portability,[25] which means that the party entitled to the right is not only entitled to being transferred the data, but also to having the data transferred to third parties.[26] This occurs in a format that immediately allows the third party to start processing the data in more or less the same way as the original controller did. Needless to say, there are also different shades of portability. In particular, an important difference is that between one-off and continuous or even real-time portability.[27]

Principle 20 of the ALI-ELI Principles spells out in more detail what could be a legitimate ground on which the party seeking access may rely, without listing such grounds in an exhaustive manner.

The first 'standard ground' a party might rely on is that of access to user-generated data, i.e. data generated by a party through the use of a product or service. In the relationship between a user and a controller of user-generated data the user is often n the weaker position because it is in need of the product or service supplied and has already paid the full price to the supplier. It is mainly within the discretion of the controller to what extent data that is necessary for the use of the commodity will be stored in external locations outside the user's sphere of control. Where the user needs the data, such as for repair and maintenance, or even for simple use, it may be tempting for the controller to withhold the data, either in order to press the user for extra remuneration, or for other reasons, including forcing the user to buy a new product. Suppliers of connected products can even control the resale of products even where the law would normally not allow them to do so. Thus, Principle 20 suggests that where the user needs the data for the normal use, maintenance or re-sale by the user of a product or service consistent with its purpose and the controller can be expected to have foreseen and accepted this, the user should (subject to the five-factor-test) have an access right.

Another standard ground a party seeking access to co-generated data could rely on is quality monitoring and improvement by a supplier. A supplier, e.g. of components, may even need such access for being able to fulfil its duties vis-à-vis the controller itself, but still, controllers may have a motivation to withhold the data. They might do so, e.g., because

25 See Article 20 GDPR. Similar rights also exist in other Sector-Specific Legislation, e.g. Article 61 ff. Type Approval Regulation, or Article 66 f. Payment Sector Directive 2, Directive (EU) 2015/2366 of 25 November 2015 on payment services in the internal market, amending Directives 2002/65/EC, 2009/110/EC and 2013/36/EU and Regulation (EU) No 1093/2010, and repealing Directive 2007/64/EC, OJ L 2015/337, p. 35.

26 See Article 20(2) GDPR: "In exercising his or her right to data portability pursuant to paragraph 1, the data subject shall have the right to have the personal data transmitted directly from one controller to another, where technically feasible."

27 See Inge Graef, Martin Husovec and Jasper van den Boom, 'Spill-Overs in Data Governance: Uncovering the Uneasy Relationship Between the GDPR's Right to Data Portability and EU Sector-Specific Data Access Regimes', 2020 *Journal of European Consumer and Market Law*, p. 3, 11 f.

they are planning to develop a similar product or service and drive the initial supplier out of its business, or they may simply not be prepared to cope with the extra burden of separating data so that no trade secrets of their own are disclosed. Again, Principle 20 suggests considering an access right in particular where this is necessary for quality monitoring or improvement by the supplier of a product or service consistent with duties of that supplier and the controller can be expected to have foreseen and accepted this.

Still another standard situation is that of establishing facts and analysing business operations. For example, a party that has contributed to the generation of data may need this data in litigation with a third party, or in order to identify the source of a serious incident apparently caused by their product, or simply to understand better their own operations with a view to improving them. It is in particular where such need is urgent and where establishing facts could not possibly harm any interests of the controller that Principle 20 suggests access should be granted.

The most controversial ground proposed by Principle 20 is that of access being necessary for the development of a new product or service by a party where such development was, in the light of that party's and the controller's previous business operations, the type of their respective contributions to the generation of the data, and the nature of their relationship, to be seen primarily as a business opportunity of that first party. As such, a party that has already engaged in a particular business does not have priority when it comes to developing new products and services in the same or an adjacent area, and competition is good for innovation. However, it is precisely where there is no effective competition and one party uses its position and bargaining power to monopolize huge amounts of data, fencing off other businesses that may be as well-equipped, or even much better equipped, to exploit the data's economic potential, that denial of access is undesirable.

Last but not least, Principle 20 clarifies that also the prevention of 'lock-in' effects in general may be a reason to grant an access right, up to full portability. This standard ground overlaps to some degree with other standard grounds, but given that this notion is very much underlying Article 20 of the GDPR it seemed worth being listed separately and independently.[28]

3.2 *Rights to Require Desistance*

The second most important data right is arguably that to require desistance from a particular data use. Whether it is appropriate under the facts and circumstances to provide a party with such a right is determined by consideration of the five factors listed above, but Principle

28 The 'minimisation of lock-in effects' is also listed as one of the main objectives of the European Commission for a future EU framework for data access, see COM(2017) 9 final, p. 12.

21 explains in more detail what should count as a legitimate interest or ground for requiring a controller of data to desist from using co-generated data. Very much like access, desistance may come in different degrees. Ultimately, it may even mean an obligation to erase data.

According to Principle 21, grounds that may give rise to a party's right to require that the controller desist from using co-generated data include situations in which that use is causing significant harm to that party. In addition to significant harm, it is a condition that the controller's purpose of use is inconsistent with the purpose for which that party was induced to contribute to the generation of the data, and that the party could not reasonably have been expected to contribute to the generation of the data if it had known or foreseen the purpose. There may also be cases where a party has given, or would have given, consent, e.g. due to particular vulnerabilities, but obtaining that consent was incompatible with doctrines that vindicate important public policies, such as rules against unfair exploitation.

An illustration provided by the comments to Principle 21 is that of a farmer (or, to escape any specific rules for personal data under the GDPR, of a farm corporation) that uses a smart tractor, which collects data on the weather, on soil quality, on insecticides and fertilizers used, and other circumstances related to the farmland. Any contribution to the generation of that data by the farmer is made for the purpose of precision farming. Using the data for building up a database for investors in farmland, possibly leading to a situation where investors have better knowledge of the true value of farmland than the farmers themselves, would be inconsistent with the purpose for which the contribution was made and may cause significant economic harm to the farmers. This is why a farmer could not reasonably have been expected to consent freely to such kind of use, and why a farmer might require that the controller desist from such data use.

3.3 *Rights to Have Data Corrected*

Principle 22 deals with grounds that, subject to the five-factor-test, may give rise to a party's right to require that the controller correct errors in co-generated data. Again, this should include situations in which control or processing of the incorrect data may cause more than insignificant harm to that party's or another party's legitimate interests. While normally the controller itself has an interest in improving the quality of data controlled, there may be situations in which the controller happens not to care, but another party who has co-generated the data does care. It is for these situations that a right to require correction may be afforded. Among the legitimate interests the controller may raise in denying the request are the costs and efforts of correction and the potential effectiveness of such correction in preventing loss to the party seeking the correction.

4 Right to Receive a Share in Profits Derived

While, for many people, a right of individuals to receive a fair economic share in the monetary value created with the help of their data, is the most important right discussed under the heading of 'data ownership' or similar headings,[29] the ALI-ELI Principles take a very cautious approach in this respect.

Principle 23 stresses that a party is normally not entitled to an economic share in profits derived by another party from the use of co-generated data unless there is a contractual or statutory basis for such a claim or it is part of another type of individual arrangement. Only very exceptionally may a party be entitled to an economic share in profits derived by a controller of co-generated data from use of the data. This could be the case when that party's contribution to the generation of the data was so unique that it cannot, from an economic point of view, be substituted by contributions of other parties or caused that party significant effort or expense. However, this is not enough. Rather, it is also a requirement that profits derived by the controller are exceptionally high and that the party seeking an economic share was, when its contribution to the generation of the data was made, not in a position to bargain effectively for remuneration.

One of the main reasons for not affording a general right to a share in profits is that introducing claims for remuneration on a broad scale would require ubiquitous measurement of data flows and make life for businesses and consumers alike much more complicated. Calculation of reimbursements and payment management would itself mean additional costs. Given that businesses are likely to pass the additional costs on to their customers in the form of higher prices it would result in privacy-conscious customers subsidising other customers. Further considerations include the creation of inappropriate incentives for vulnerable groups of the society to generate and disclose as much data as possible for economic reasons.

5 The Multi-Relational Dimension of Data Rights

In recent years, the multi-relational dimension of data has rightly been stressed by many authors.[30] It has become widely accepted that the bilateral paradigm underlying the GDPR and other legal instruments dealing with data is inadequate to fully address the problems of data use. Among the points that are frequently made is the point that dispositions of one data subject with regard to 'their' data affects also other individuals, not least because

29 Karl-Heinz Fezer, *Repräsentatives Dateneigentum* (Konrad Adenauer Stiftung 2018), p. 84 ff.

30 For an explanation see only Jeni Tennison (Open Data Institute), *Individual, collective, and community interests in data* (2020), available via http://www.jenitennison.com/2020/12/27/individual-collective-community.html.

the processing of the data of one individual allows inferences to be drawn with regard to other individuals.[31] So the 'horizontal' relationship among the various data subjects or – in the words of the Principles – the various parties contributing to the generation of data needs to be included in the equation.

5.1 *Rights in Co-Generated Data as an Answer to the Multi-Relational Nature of Data*

To a certain extent, the concept of rights in co-generated data is perfectly suited to address the multi-relational nature of data and data use. This is so because the very idea of co-generated data is that many different parties have contributed to the generation of data in different roles, but of course also in similar roles, such as when various data subjects are involved. Also, legitimate interests of third parties are one of the factors that need to be considered in each and every case under the five-factor-test. This is so at two levels, at the level of the decision whether or not to afford a data right, and at the level of determining the modalities, e.g. whether access to data is granted only in a secured environment or only against remuneration. Last but not least, when it comes to a right to require desistance from data use, also harm caused to third parties counts as relevant harm that may give rise to such a data right.

5.2 *Collective Data Rights*

Whether only individual parties who have themselves contributed to the generation of data (or their successors in interest) can rely on rights with regard to co-generated data or whether also groups of persons, such as the citizens of a particular State, can do so, is not fully answered by the Principles. In the comments, the Reporters reveal that they tend to believe there are such things as collective data rights, and that they might follow similar considerations, but that collective data rights are beyond the scope of the Principles. In fact, analysing in more depth the existence and conditions of collective data rights may go way beyond what the current ALI-ELI project is dealing with, and delve deeply into such intricate problems as 'indigenous data sovereignty'[32] or 'digital colonialism'.[33] Yet, collective

31 See Philipp Hacker, *Datenprivatrecht* (Mohr Siebeck 2020), p. 64 ff. with further references.

32 GIDA, *CARE Principles for Indigenous Data Governance*, available via https://www.gida-global.org/care; United States Indigenous Data Sovereignty Network, *Indigenous Data Governance Principles*, available via https://nnigovernance.arizona.edu/sites/default/files/resources/US%20Indigenous%20Data%20Sov%20Principles%20Working%20File.pdf.

33 Government of India, *Report by the Committee of Experts on Non-Personal Data Governance Framework*, available via https://static.mygov.in/rest/s3fs-public/mygov_159453381955063671.pdf; Thomas Ramge and

rights in (collectively) co-generated data may be one of the most promising research topics to follow from the concepts introduced by the Principles.

5.3 *Beyond the Scope: Unfair Algorithmic Practices*

It is, however, clear that rights in co-generated data cannot solve all problems associated with data. In particular, they only give rights to parties who have, in one role or the other, contributed to the generation of data. They do not give any rights to parties who are just indirectly affected by data use, such as by the deployment of artificial intelligence (AI) that has been trained with the help of other people's data. One could reflect for a moment whether someone who is affected by AI because the AI was trained with the data of another individual that belongs to the same class of individuals may have some kind of right based on some notion of 'group rights'. However, it is clear that this would be a rather artificial analysis, and it would not carry far where the algorithmic system has not been trained with data but coded in a more traditional way – the latter reveals that the use of data is incidental in such constellations and can easily be replaced by other factors.

The reason why the Principles are not giving any rights to parties affected by AI and other algorithmic decision-making is not that the Reporters believe such rights should not exist, quite on the contrary. It is just something that is not within the scope of the Principles inasmuch as the Principles are Principles for a Data Economy, and not AI Principles. Recent approaches made, inter alia, by the Japanese Ministry for Economy, Trade and Industry (METI)[34] and by the German Data Ethics Commission[35] confirm that the 'data perspective' and the 'algorithm perspective' are two closely related, overlapping, and yet not wholly identical perspectives. The situation where someone is negatively affected by intelligent software is clearly something to be dealt with under the algorithm perspective, as are the problems of discrimination, unreasonable inferences,[36] exploitation of vulnerabilities, manipulation, or total surveillance. Such practices are to be qualified as 'unfair algorithmic practices'[37] or prohibited AI practices that should be banned as such

Viktor Mayer-Schönberger, *Machtmaschinen – Warum Datenmonopole unsere Zukunft gefährden und wie wir sie brechen* (Murmann 2020), p. 183 ff.

34 METI, *Contract Guidelines on Utilization of AI and Data – Data Section* (2018), available via https://www.meti.go.jp/press/2019/04/20190404001/20190404001-1.pdf.

35 Opinion of the German Data Ethics Commission (2019), p. 105, available via https://www.datenethikkommission.de.

36 Sandra Wachter and Brent Mittelstadt, 'A Right to Reasonable Inferences, Rethinking Data Protection in the Digital Age', 2019 *Columbia Law Review*, p. 494 ff.

37 Jens-Peter Schneider and Christiane Wendehorst, *Response to the public consultation on the White Paper: On Artificial Intelligence - A European approach to excellence and trust* (2020), available via https://www.europeanlawinstitute.eu/fileadmin/user_upload/p_eli/News_page/2020/ELI_Response_AI_White_Paper.pdf.

under upcoming legislation on AI,[38] but not within legislation dealing more specifically with data.

6 CONCLUSION

The ALI-ELI Principles for a Data Economy have introduced the notion of co-generated data and rights in such co-generated data, and the concept is gaining widespread recognition, such as by the German Data Ethics Commission,[39] the European Commission,[40] and the Global Partnership on AI (GPAI).[41] These rights are data-specific and do not correspond to any clear-cut category of rights we have been dealing with for the past centuries in non-digital environments. They are not contractual, as they may exist between parties without any contractual link, and they do not reflect ownership notions in the traditional sense, because traditional notions of ownership do not work well with resources of a non-rival nature. The data rights dealt with under the Principles, and in particular the access or portability right, fulfil functions similar to those fulfilled by ownership with regard to traditional rivalrous assets. However, the notion of data rights recommended by the Principles is not identical to that of ownership, nor to that of property rights. Unlike intellectual property rights, rights in co-generated data do not afford their holder a clearly defined range of rights against everyone else to do something or to omit doing something, but rather the data rights depend very much on the parties involved, and on the particular situation. The Principles reflect a policy that whoever has contributed to the generation of data should generally have some rights of co-determination with respect to its use and some rights to share in the utility and value it generates. Whether or not the bundle of rights in co-generated data constitutes 'property' or 'ownership' is not a concern of the Principles, but left to the doctrinal debate that may follow the Principles' publication.

38 White Paper on Artificial Intelligence – A European approach to excellence and trust, COM(2020) 65 final.

39 Opinion of the German Data Ethics Commission (2019), p. 85 ff., available via https://www.datenethikkommission.de.

40 Communication from the Commission to the European Parliament, the Council, the European Economic and Social Committee and the Committee of the Regions – 'A European strategy for data', COM(2020) 66 final, p. 8, 13.

41 GPAI Data Governance Working Group, *A Framework Paper for GPAI's work on Data Governance* (2020).

Part X
Sjef in Data

A Digital Selfie

Gijs van Dijck[*]

1 Introduction

Who is Sjef van Erp? In this contribution, I try to define Van Erp by means of a topic he has become extremely passionate about: data. I have collected data of Van Erp and conducted empirical analyses on his publication output, the type of output, and how his output evolved over time. Because I have been amazed by the amount of travelling Van Erp has done, I also collected information about his traveling patterns. To my knowledge, I am the first having collected and analyzed data about him, thereby opening a new line of research and significantly advancing the body of academic knowledge.

Regarding the data collection, I have taken the output information from Maastricht University's electronic publication repository. Consequently, I rely on self-reported data of when Van Erp started working at Maastricht University – the publication data therefore only include data as of 1998 (appointment in September 1997). Having been part of several of Van Erp's appraisal meetings, in which he has always followed through on his promises to update the publication output, and having known Van Erp as a very diligent colleague, I am confident that the data are correct and reliable. For some output, however, I could not immediately figure out what the contribution was about. My command of the Spanish, Polish, Italian, and Russian language are mostly non-existent. In fact, I sometimes had difficulties determining the language of the publication. I used web translation services in these instances to solve this issue. In some instances, the content of the publications was inspected. Considering that various publications are books or book chapters, I sometimes had to inspect the paper version for some publications. Fortunately, Van Erp has stalled part of his book collection in my office.

Van Erp's work calendar information was inspected for determining his travel data. Somewhat surprisingly, calendar data were available as of 2011. Also here, the diligent nature of Van Erp made me feel sufficiently confident that the obtained calendar data are reliable. I considered collecting pre-2011 data from through Prof Emer van Erp-Jacobs, a historian whose skillset perfectly matches the objective. However, the application of a

---

* Professor of Private Law, Maastricht University. Thanks to Stephan Mulders for feedback on the GDPR analysis and Marcus Meyer for help with connection different data sheets in the visualization software (Tableau). Mistakes are, as always, for the author.

proportionality and necessity test led to the conclusion to not ask Prof Emer van Erp-Jacobs. No other methods of obtaining the pre-2011 data were deemed feasible.

Before the data collection, I had to ask myself whether I am allowed to use Van Erp's publication and travel data. Perhaps they are copyright-protected, and surely there are issues of data protection, given that all data and results are identifiable.

2 Is It Allowed To Use the Data?

The legality of using the data has at least two dimensions: a copyright and a privacy dimension. Copyright law aims to protect the creative form of the information, not data as such. One could argue that the publication data I aim to use are generated and produced in a creative form that does fall under the protection of copyright law, as the data have been collected and processed in a way that adds value to the raw data. Assuming the information can be qualified as a creative form that falls under the protection of copyright law, the *Digital Single Market (DSM) Directive*[1] comes to my rescue, as the Directive allows text and data mining, at least for purposes of scientific research, as long as lawful access to the data can be obtained and appropriate levels of security are applied.[2] Lawful access was obtained, given that the data are available online for anyone with access to the Internet.[3] The same goes for the calendar data, since I, through my secretary, have access to the calendar data.[4] Furthermore, I submit that the purpose of my contribution qualifies as scientific research. Recital 159 of the DSM Directive defines scientific research in a broad manner, in my opinion sufficiently broad to cover my analysis, which will be published, follows academic standards of how to conduct research, and contributes to the body of knowledge, in this case to a better understanding or application of how to analyze and visualize scientific output of an author.

1 Directive (EU) 2019/790 of the European Parliament and of the Council of 17 April 2019 on copyright and related rights in the Digital Single Market and amending Directives 96/9/EC and 2001/29/EC.

2 Article 3(1): "Member States shall provide for an exception to the rights provided for in Article 5(a) and Article 7(1) of Directive 96/9/EC, Article 2 of Directive 2001/29/EC, and Article 15(1) of this Directive for reproductions and extractions made by research organisations and cultural heritage institutions in order to carry out, for the purposes of scientific research, text and data mining of works or other subject matter to which they have lawful access". Article 3(2): "shall be stored with an appropriate level of security and may be retained for the purposes of scientific research, including for the verification of research results".

3 Possible contractual exclusions would have been unenforceable by Article 7(1): "Any contractual provision contrary to the exceptions provided for in Articles 3, 5 and 6 shall be unenforceable".

4 The secretary would under the GDPR be considered a processor.

However, Article 28 of the DSM Directive does prescribe that the processing of personal data must comply with the *General Data Protection Regulation* (GDPR).[5] Under the GDPR, 'personal data' means:

> "any information relating to an identified or identifiable natural person ('data subject'); an identifiable natural person is one who can be identified, directly or indirectly" (Article 4 GDPR).

Information about the author's publications falls under this definition, since it contains the name of the author and possible co-authors, which is information that is clearly identifiable, even after pseudonymization. This particularly applies to the author of interest here. It would be difficult to deny I am writing about Van Erp in the context of his *Liber Amicorum*, even when I replace his name in the data by a token.

The identifiability of data does not necessarily exclude prohibit processing data, with processing referred to as:

> "(...) any operation or set of operations which is performed on personal data or on sets of personal data, whether or not by automated means, such as collection, recording, organisation, structuring, storage, adaptation or alteration, retrieval, consultation, use, disclosure by transmission, dissemination or otherwise making available, alignment or combination, restriction, erasure or destruction" (Article 4(2) GDPR).

Article 6 GDPR provides justifications for lawfully processing data:

a. Consent by the data subject.
b. Processing is necessary for the performance of a contract to which the data subject is entering into or to which the subject is party.
c. Processing is necessary for compliance with a legal obligation to which the controller is subject.
d. Processing is necessary for protecting the vital interests of the data subject of another natural person.
e. Processing is necessary for the performance of a task carried out in the public interest or in the exercise of official authority vested in the controller.
f. Processing is necessary for the purposes of the legitimate interests pursued by the controller or by a third party, except when the interests are overridden by fundamental

5 Regulation (EU) 2016/679 of the European Parliament and of the Council of 27 April 2016 on the protection of natural persons with regard to the processing of personal data and on the free movement of such data, and repealing Directive 95/46/EC (General Data Protection Regulation).

rights and freedoms of the data subject. (This does not apply to public authorities in the performance of their tasks.)

My impression is that research into persons is commonly conducted on influential persons of the past who have deceased once the research is conducted. It is not necessary to ask deceased persons for consent, as only living persons can have personal data (recital 27 GDPR). Although data about deceased individuals can in fact be personal data, the GDPR does not apply to the personal data of deceased persons (Figure 1).

Figure 1 Skeleton[6]

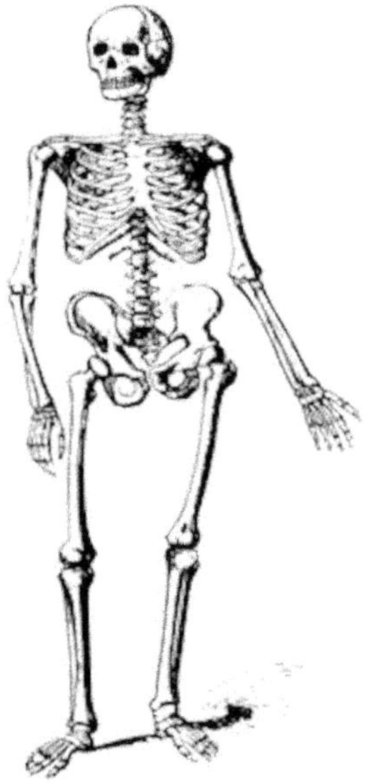

Van Erp, however, is fortunately not deceased. In fact, he is very much alive, which is further evidenced by the array of activities he is involved in: from being a deputy-judge to teaching courses and publishing papers and reports. Consequently, it is possible to ask Van Erp for consent.

Consent must be "unambiguous" and fit for purpose. The 'fit for purpose' requirement generally poses a challenge for scientific research, since "[i]t is often not possible to fully identify the purpose of personal data processing for scientific research purposes at the

6 Image taken from pixabay.com (https://pixabay.com/vectors/bones-buried-dead-skeleton-skull-1297457/, last accessed 5 August 2020). The image is not copyright protected.

time of collection" (Recital 33). In this instance, I do not see a challenge here, considering that the purpose of processing the data is rather clear: write a book contribution in which I analyze scientific output and travel information related to Van Erp.

I could simply not collect information of co-authors and ask permission to Van Erp to use 'his' publication output data. However, this would defeat the purpose of the *Liber Amicorum*, which is traditionally written without the knowledge of the Professor Emeritus to-be. I would therefore prefer a justification for processing the personal data on a different basis than it being consent.

Two options come to mind when it comes to allowing research as a basis for processing: considering myself as a controller or a third party, where a controller is defined as:

> "the natural or legal person, public authority, agency or other body which, alone or jointly with others, determines the purposes and means of the processing of personal data" (Article 4(7) GDPR,

and a third party (i.e. me as a Maastricht University employee, with which I have an authority relationship) as:

> "a natural or legal person, public authority, agency or body other than the data subject, controller, processor and persons who, under the direct authority of the controller or processor, are authorised to process personal data" (Article 4(8) GDPR).

The information I am interested in has already been collected by Maastricht University, although likely not for the purpose of this contribution, and perhaps not even for purposes of scientific research. The latter surely applies to the calendar data.

The most applicable situation is one of secondary processing. Article 6(4) of the GDPR allows processing of already collected data not based on the data subject's consent ("processing for a purpose other than that for which the personal data have been collected"). In addition, the re-purposing needs to be deemed lawful. I would argue that, in this instance, "processing is necessary for the performance of a task carried out in the public interest" (Art. 6(1)(e) GDPR). Scientific research is a task carried out in the public interest, which is said to be a compatible lawful processing operation:

> "(...) further processing for archiving purposes in the public interest, scientific or historical research purposes or statistical purposes should be considered to be compatible lawful processing operations" (Recital 50).

Furthermore, it could be claimed that "processing is necessary for the purposes of the legitimate interests pursued by the controller or by a third party" (Article 6(1)(f)) GDPR. Recitals 47 and 157 suggest that scientific research can be considered such an interest. Recital 47 states that "[t]he processing of personal data for direct marketing purposes may be regarded as carried out for a legitimate interest". From this, it can be inferred that scientific research would also qualify as a legitimate interest, particularly when taking Recital 157 into consideration, which highlights the benefits of research on personal data: "researchers can obtain new knowledge of great value" (focusing on medical research), "research results can be enhanced" (with registry research), "enables researchers to obtain essential knowledge about the long-term correlation of social conditions", and, importantly, "[i]n order to facilitate scientific research, personal data can be processed for scientific research purposes, subject to appropriate conditions and safeguards set out in Union or Member State law". Additionally, a legitimate interest could exist where there is a "relevant and appropriate relationship between the data subject and the controller". A work relationship, as is the case with van Erp, could qualify as such a relationship. Nevertheless,

> "[a]t any rate the existence of a legitimate interest would need careful assessment including whether a data subject can reasonably expect at the time and in the context of the collection of the personal data that processing for that purpose may take place. The interests and fundamental rights of the data subject could in particular override the interest of the data controller where personal data are processed in circumstances where data subjects do not reasonably expect further processing" (Recital 47).

A balancing test will therefore need to take place in order to determine whether processing personal data can be based on the 'legitimate interest' ground.

Moreover, I need to apply the compatibility test specified in Article 6(4) of the GDPR, which holds that if the processing of the data is based on a different purpose than consent was obtained for, whether it is because a public task is carried out (Article 6(1)(e) GDPR) or because there is a legitimate interest (Article 6(1)(f) GDPR), it needs to be ascertained that the processing is compatible with the purpose for which the personal data were initially collected. This requires taking into account:

- "any link between the purposes for which the personal data have been collected and the purposes of the intended further processing". The publication data are collected for reporting purposes and, presumably, for marketing and visibility purposes. These purposes, particularly the first, relate to the purpose of this contribution: to examine trends and patterns in the publication output of a particular author. This is different for the calendar data. Those data were collected for scheduling and availability purposes, not for analysis purposes. It is not unthinkable that a data subject like Van Erp would feel uncomfortable with colleagues accessing his work calendar (which is why the data was gathered by the secretary who already had access to the data) and his traveling information for other purposes than scheduling and availability. However, the purpose of processing the data was to describe the data in a neutral (or positive) and non-harmful way.

- "the context in which the personal data have been collected, in particular regarding the relationship between data subjects and the controller". The data were collected in the context of the organization and execution of ordinary work processes related to academic research and education. The data subject has relationships with the controllers and processors (Maastricht University as employer; secretary as colleague; me as colleague). This is a context of high-trust, where information is expected to be used and shared for reasonable purposes.
- "the nature of the personal data, in particular whether special categories of personal data are processed, pursuant to Article 9, or whether personal data related to criminal convictions and offences are processed, pursuant to Article 10". No special data as meant in these provisions were processed.
- "the possible consequences of the intended further processing for data subjects". No negative consequences are envisioned as a result of the processing or the findings. This could be different had I intended to conduct the analyses to negatively portray Van Erp. There is no reason to do that, and even if I wanted to, it would be impossible in a convincing way, considering his outstanding reputation.
- "the existence of appropriate safeguards, which may include encryption or pseudonymisation" (Art. 6(4) GDPR, also Art. 89(1) GDPR). Safeguards are not necessary, especially regarding the publication data, as it is publicly available on the Maastricht University website. With respect to the calendar information, the data were processed by a secretary who already had access to Van Erp's work calendar. The processing took place with the sole purpose of analyzing travel information (dates and travel destination). The data have been stored on a work server and will be permanently deleted upon publication of the Liber Amicorum.

Based on the DSM Directive and the GDPR, I see no objection to the repurposing of the data without the subject's consent. I expect the conclusion to be the same for the names of possible co-authors. Although the names of co-authors were collected, these were not further processed or analyzed.

Do I need to inform Van Erp about the processing? The Dutch GDPR Implementation Law (UAVG) determines that chapters III-VII GDPR do not apply to academic expressions (art. 43 UAVG). If the chapters were applicable, Article 12(1) of the GDPR prescribes that I (or the UM, as a controller) would need to "take appropriate measures" to inform data subjects of the processing activities and of their right to access, rectify, erase, and object

(Article 13(2)) as well as the storage period. This would need to be done at the time the data is first collected and "in a concise, transparent, intelligible and easily accessible form, using clear and plain language" (Article 12(1)). Even if the provision would be applicable to me, meeting this obligation is no longer possible, since the data have been collected, starting in the late 90s.

Article 13(3), also not applicable, would require the controller to inform the data subject about the new purpose and the aforementioned rights in instances where the controller desires to further process data for a different purpose. However, Recital 33 stipulates that data subjects should give consent to only "certain areas of research or parts of research projects to the extent allowed by the intended purpose". Importantly, Article 14 provides for an exemption in instances where "the provision of such information proves impossible or would involve a disproportionate effort", which, according to Recital 62, "could in particular be the case" in the context of scientific research. Additionally, an exemption applies when providing notice would "likely to render impossible or seriously impair the achievement of the [research] objectives".

Considering the surprise nature of a *Liber Amicorum*, it was decided to inform Van Erp about the further processing when the book will be presented to him. If he objects and desires to have his data erased, this request is unlikely to be granted, given that the relevant GDPR provisions are not applicable, and even if they were, erasure could endanger my obligations to be transparent about the data that I collected (Article 17(3)(d) GDPR). Invoking Article 21 of the GDPR (object to processing) would, if it were applicable, stand a better change, although it can be overridden if the processing is necessary for the performance of a task carried out for reasons of public interest" (Article 21(6)), which, I would believe, covers academic research. Recital 45 prescribes that the carrying out of a public interest should have a basis in Union or Member State law. However, this

> "does not require a specific law for each individual processing. A law as a basis for several processing operations based on a legal obligation to which the controller is subject or where processing is necessary for the performance of a task carried out in the public interest or in the exercise of an official authority may be sufficient" (Recital 45).

Although Dutch law does not define what is a 'public task', it follow from the *Wet op het Hoger Onderwijs* (WHW), Article 1.3 in particular, that scientific research falls under "carrying out a public task".[7] I therefore believe it is safe to assume that the data will not

7 See also J.J.C. Kabel, P.B. Hugenholtz, Chr. A. Alberdingk Thijm, D.J.B. Bosscher, *Kennisinstellingen en informatiebeleid Lusten en lasten van de publieke taak*, Amsterdam, Instituut voor Informatierecht, 2001, par 1.2.4.

have to be deleted. It is important to mention here that the calendar data used for this contribution will be permanently deleted as soon as the *Liber Amicorum* will have been published.

3 RESULTS

3.1 Number of Publications

A total of 154 publications were found. A categorization by output type reveals that Van Erp mostly wrote book chapters and conference proceedings, followed by journal articles.

Figure 2 Number Publications (per output type)

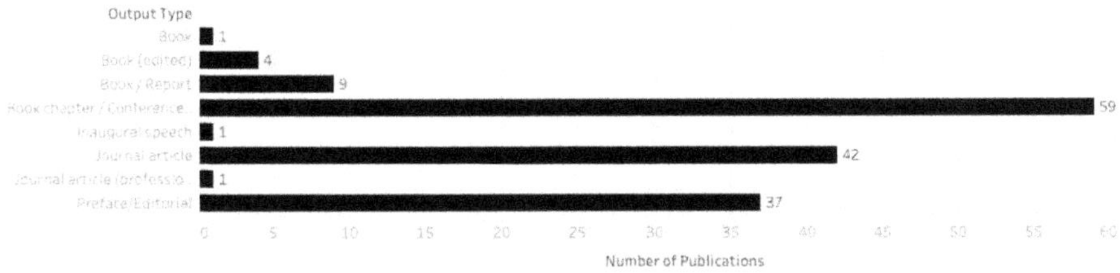

The 37 prefaces / editorials were not further included in subsequent analyses.

Maastricht University might have started to worry towards the end of 2000. No publications followed his 1998 inaugural lecture in 1999 and 2000, but the numbers sharply increased in 2001 (n=6) and in 2002 (n=7), and they have remained stable after that (Figure 3).

Figure 3 Number Publications (per Year), Prefaces and Editorials Excluded

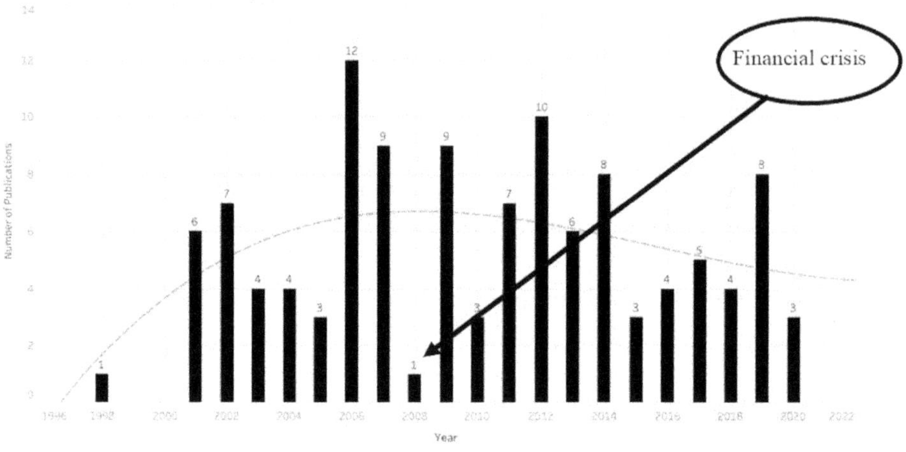

The pattern seems a bit erratic, with years with high number of publications alternating with years containing fewer publications. However, such a trend is common within academia, as authors sometimes work on papers that originate from the same idea. This is no different for Van Erp, which can be illustrated by a project on real and personal security that resulted in conference proceedings, a book chapter, and a journal article (all in 2002).

When observing the trend line, it may seem as if the number of publications has gone down over the years (Figure 3). A figure with a linear trend line (rather than a polynomial one) gives a more positive story (Figure 4).

Figure 4 Number Publications (per Year, Linear Trend Line), Prefaces and Editorials Excluded

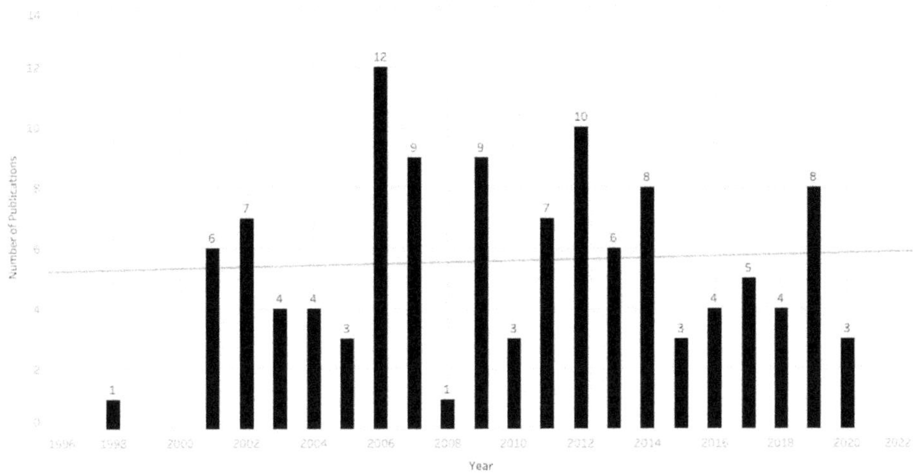

Importantly, the trend lines are not statistically significant, which entails that there is insufficient support for the claim that the differences in the association between the number of publication and the year in which the publications were published are meaningful. The proper conclusion is therefore that the empirical evidence suggests that number of publications has remained relatively stable over time.

3.2 *Language*

Van Erp's chair is titled "Professor of Civil Law and European Private Law". The European component in the chair title creates the expectation of a European, and consequently of publications that at least in part will be in English (not in Dutch). Indeed, a non-national focus follows from the publication data. Firstly, Van Erp has published in ten languages, including in Russian (n=2), Polish (n=1), Czech (n=1), French (n=1), Spanish (n=1), and Italian (n=1). Secondly, many reports and publications are written in the English language (n=72), with the number of publications in English exceeding the number of Dutch publications (n=36). Thirdly, many publication titles, such as 'Comparative property law' (2006), 'Contract and property law: distinct, but not separate' (2013), and 'Ownership of data: the numerus clausus of legal objects' (2017), strongly suggest a European, transnational, or global approach.[8]

The question arises whether the international focus has always been the case. In legal academia in the Netherlands, internationalization had not taken off, at least not until after 2003.[9] Comparing the number of publications in Dutch and English for each year, it becomes clear that Van Erp already started publishing in English in the early stages of his career, and that the number of English publications has slightly increased (not statistically significant) over the years (Figure 5). The same goes for the publications in Dutch (very slight increase, not statistically significant) (Figure 5).

Figure 5 Number Publications per Year, in Dutch and English, Prefaces and Editorials Excluded

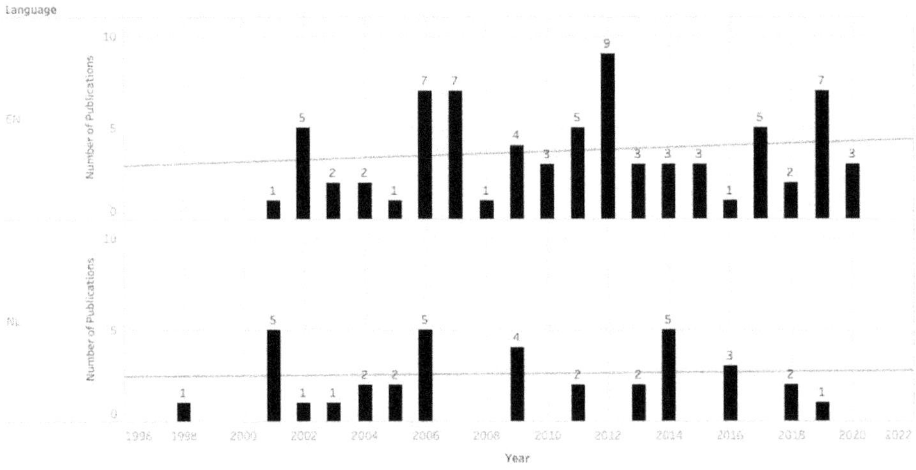

Similar results were obtained when looking at trends of the publications in Dutch and English, respectively, as percentages of the total number of publications.

In my talks with Van Erp, terms such as digital assets, digital data, data access, and data ownership have frequently come up. This made me wonder when he became interested in these (and other) topics, and whether his interests have remained stable over time. I therefore categorized his publications. The categorization consisted of an iterative process

8 For an overview of his publications, see https://cris.maastrichtuniversity.nl/en/persons/sjef-van-erp (last accessed 6 August 2020).

9 *Oordelen over rechten. Rapport Commissie Voorbereiding Onderzoeksbeoordeling Rechtsgeleerdheid*, VSNU, 2003 ("Van een werkelijk internationaal forum is althans voor de meeste rechtsgebieden (men hoede zich voor ongenuanceerde generalisaties) nog maar in beperkte zin sprake").

in which initial categories were drafted and later adjusted. Based on an inspection of the title of the publication and the journal in which it was published, each publication was assigned to the topic that was deemed most suitable.[10] For instance, the publication titled 'Civil and common property law: caveat comparator – The value of legal historical-comparative analysis' was labeled as 'Property Law'. Although one could also argue such titles could be categorized as 'Legal Research Methodology', the Property Law label deemed more fit. Furthermore, sometimes a publication could be assigned to multiple areas of the law. For instance, the title 'Positive duties in the grey area between contract and property law' suggests that the publication is at the intersection of two fields, in this case property law and contract law. With a variety of areas of the law that Van Erp has focused on, it was decided to label a publication under 'Property Law' if it addressed property law, also if other areas of the law were addressed. If the publication concerned digital property law, then it was labeled as 'Digital Property Law' and not as 'Property Law'.

The categorization resulted in four topics: Legal Research Methodology, Property Law, Digital Property Law, and Other. I could have taken a more granular approach, with more categories, which would do more justice to Van Erp's interest beyond property law (e.g. private international law, contract law). However, this would result in a large number of topics with few observations per category, which makes it more difficult to observe trends in his output. Moreover, the categorization would have become more arbitrary if a more granular approach would have been followed, as it would have been difficult to assign publications to sub-fields, and even to properly and convincingly define sub-fields.

When looking at how the four topics developed, Van Erp's career at Maastricht University started with laying the groundwork for a methodology for conducting research in the field of comparative property law and European private law in general. These methodological contributions particularly focused on the sources of European private law, as suggested by titles such as 'European Union Case Law as a Source of European Private law; a comparison with American Federal Common Law', 'Europees privaatrecht en rechtsvergelijking'. From 2002, Van Erp's research in the field took off, with a, on average, stable number of publications over the years, at least until 2015 (Figure 6).

10 Creating a series of binary variables was considered, with each variable measuring one topic. This possibility was ultimately not selected, as it would make the total number of publications less salient (i.e. adding up the total numbers for each binary variable would exceed the total number of publications).

Figure 6 Topic Distribution over Years, Prefaces and Editorials Excluded

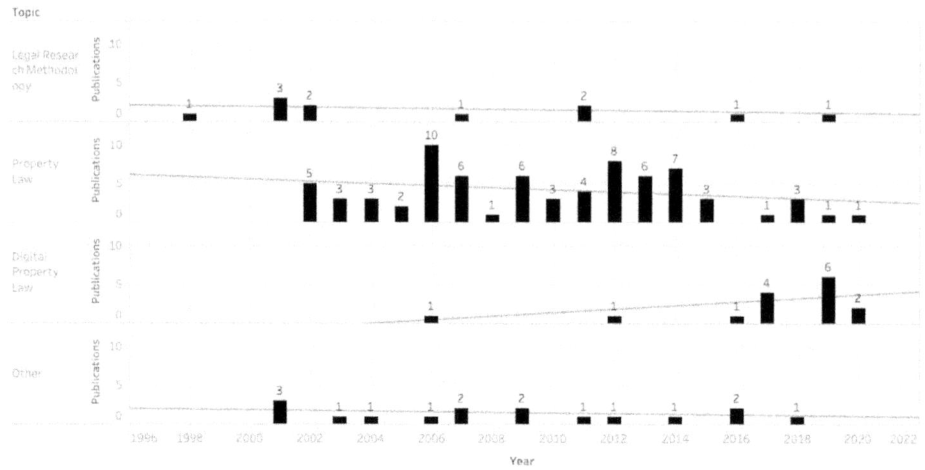

Van Erp has addressed a range of topics, in both Dutch and English (and other languages). These topics include an analysis of mortgage law,[11] security,[12] succession law,[13] and land law.[14] As mentioned above, his publications have often been at the intersection of property law and a quite impressive number of other areas of the law, including tort law,[15] contract

11 J.H.M. van Erp, 'A Comparative Analysis of Mortgage Law: Searching for Principles', *in* M.E. Sáncheze Jordán & A. Gambarro (Ed.), *Land Law in Comparative Perspective*, (Dordrecht,) Kluwer Law International, 2002, p. 69-86.

12 E.g. J.H.M. van Erp, 'Personal and real security', *in* J.M. Smits (Ed.), *Elgar Encyclopedia of Comparative Law*, 2nd ed., (Cheltenham,) Edward Elgar Publishing, 2012, p. 647-660, J.H.M. van Erp, 'Security interests: A Secure Start for the Development of European Property Law', *in* M. Hinteregger, T. Boric (Ed.), *Sicherungsrechte an Immobilien in Europa*, (Vienna/Berlin,) LIT Verlag, 2009, p. 3-39.

13 E.g. J.H.M. van Erp, 'New developments in succession law', *in* K. Boele-Woelki & J.H.M. van Erp (Ed.), *General reports of the XVIIth congress of the International Academy of Comparative Law/Rapports Généraux du XViie congrès de l'Académie Internationale de Droit Comparé*, (Bruxelles/Utrecht,) Bruylant/Eleven International Publishing, 2007, p. 73-94, J.H.M. van Erp, 'The new Dutch law of succession', *in* K.G.C. Reid, M.J.D. Waal & R. Zimmerman (Ed.), *Exploring the law of succession. Studies national, historical and comparative*, (Edinburgh,) Edinburgh University Press, 2007 p. 193-208.

14 E.g. J.H.M. van Erp, B. Akkermans, *Towards a Unified System of Land Burdens?*, (Antwerp,) Intersentia, 2006.

15 E.g. J.H.M. van Erp, 'Different Degrees of Convergence: A Comparison of Tort Law (Example: Fairchild v. Glenhaven Funeral Services) and Property Law', *Electronic Journal of Comparative Law*, 2002, J.H.M. van Erp, 'The EU Succession Regulation: a possible source for Member State 'Francovich' liability?', *European Property Law Journal*, No. 3, 2014, p. 211-214.

law,[16] private international law,[17] EU Law,[18] and the Draft Common Frame of Reference (DCFR).[19]

A shift in focus can be observed after 2015, when his focus shifted from general property law research to research on, what I refer here to as, 'Digital Property Law'. Van Erp mostly started working on access and ownership of data and other digital assets, while also working on cryptocurrencies and online elements of land registries.[20] Signs of the interest in digital aspects of property law can, however, already be observed in 2006, when Van Erp started writing about property and virtual property, raising the question "whether certain rules on property law might perhaps also apply to specific relationships that exist with regard to the use of computers and computer networks, next to the protection that is nowadays given by intellectual property law" and "[g]iven, that virtual property can exist, which property rights could then be applicable?".[21] Later, in 2012, Van Erp published a journal article on cross-border electronic conveyancing in a property law context.[22] (Admittedly, I had to read the article to learn what that meant. It turned out to address the topic of the digitalization of transfer and mortgage deed, secured with electronic signatures.)

While most of Van Erp's work has focused on property law related matters, I was not able to categorize two publications under one of the three aforementioned categories. These 'other' publications concern contract law[23] and the possibility of a European civil

16 J.H.M. van Erp, 'Positive duties in the grey area between contract and property law', *in* S. Bartels & M. Milo (Ed.), *The content of the real right*, (Nijmegen,) Wolf Legal Publishers, 2004, p. 149-162.

17 E.g. J.H.M. van Erp, B. Akkermans, 'Optioneel Goederenrecht en Internationaal Privaatrecht (IPR)', *in* M. Hesselink, M. Loos, A.V. Hoek, A. Salomons (Ed.), *Groenboek Europees contractenrecht: Naar een optioneel instrument?*, (Den Haag,) Boom Juridisch, 2011, p. 105-124, S. van Erp, 'Lex rei sitae: The territorial side of classical property law', *in* Godt, C. (Ed.), *Regulatory property rights: The transforming notion of property in transnational busisness regulation.* (Leiden,) Brill | Nijhoff, 2017, p. 61-81, S. van Erp, K. Zimmermann, 'The impact of recent EU conflicts of law regulations on land registration', *in* G. Muller, R. Brits, B.V. Slade, & J. van Wyk (Ed.), *Transformative Property Law: Festschrift in honour of AJ van der Walt*, (Cape Town,) Juta and Company (Pty) Ltd, 2018, p. 318-340.

18 J.H.M. van Erp, 'EU Charter of Fundamental Human Rights and property rights', *in* D. Wallis, S. Allanson (Ed.), *European property rights and wrongs*, (Brussels,) Wallis, 2011, p. 44-49, S. van Erp, 'Article 345 TFEU: A framework for European property law', *in* E. Lauroba Lacasa & J. Tarabal Bosch (Ed.), *El derecho de propriedad en la construcciön del derecho privado Europeo*, (Valencia,) Editorial Tirant Lo Blanch, 2018, p. 59-70.

19 E.g. J.H.M. van Erp, 'DCFR and property law: the need for consistency and coherence', *in* R. Schulze (Ed.), *Common Frame of Reference and existing EC contract law*, (Munich,) Sellier European Law Publishers, 2009, p. 257-269, J.H.M. van Erp, 'Symposium Book X (Trusts) of the DCFR. A Dutch perspective', *Edinburgh Law Review*, 2011, p. 479-482.

20 See https://cris.maastrichtuniversity.nl/en/persons/sjef-van-erp for examples.

21 J.H.M. van Erp, 'Servitudes: The borderline between contact and (virtual) property', *in* J.H.M. van Erp, B. Akkermans, *Towards a unified system of land burdens?*, (Antwerp,) Intersentia, 2006, p. 3, 5.

22 J.H.M. van Erp, 'Cross-border electronic conveyancing: overcoming problems with negative and positive integration in European property law', *European Property Law Journal*, No. 1, 2012, p. 3-9.

23 J.H.M. van Erp, 'A European 'culpa in contrahendo' doctrine? Towards a model of contract as a legal relationship and situation-specific duties to inform', *in* S. Espiau Espiau, A. Vaquer Aloy (Ed.), *Bases de un Derecho Contractual Europeo/Bases of a European Contract Law*, (Valencia,) Brant La Blanch, 2003, p. 67-

code.[24] Particularly his focus on contract law is understandable, given, among other things and as explained in one of his publications,[25] the interplay between contractual rights and property rights, for example regarding the idea of contractual rights creating third-party effect.

3.3 *Co-Authorship*

I have known Van Erp as someone who has a broad interest and who is also interested in others. This led me to hypothesize that I would find quite some papers in which he collaborated with others. This turns out to be correct. In 28% (33 of the 117) of his publications (excluding prefaces / editorials) a co-author was involved. Interestingly, although team science is only now starting to get some traction in legal academia, the number of co-authors in Van Erp's publications particularly peaked in the beginning of his professorship (Figure 7).

Figure 7 Co-Authorship over the Years, Prefaces and Editorials Excluded

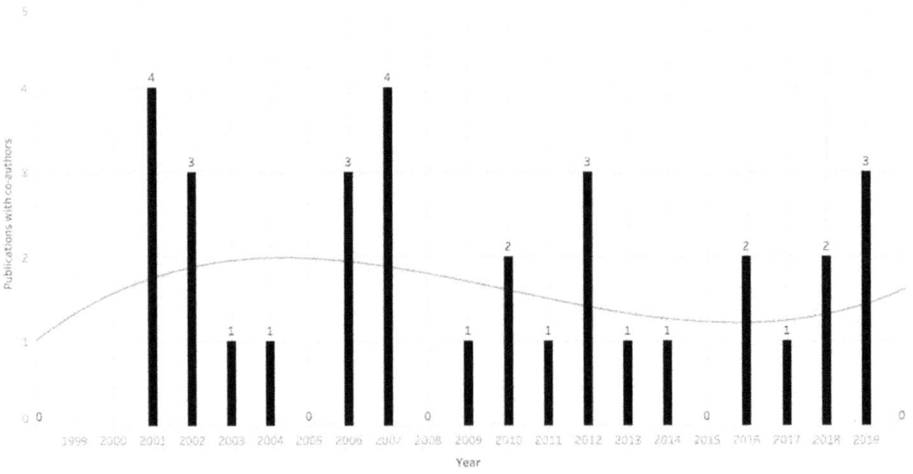

77, J.H.M. van Erp, 'The pre-contractual stage', *in* A. Hartkamp, M. Hesselink, E. Hondius, C. Mak, E.D. Perron (Ed.), *Towards a European Civil Code*, (Nijmegen,) Ars Aequi Libri, p. 493-513.

24 J.H.M. van Erp, 'Wordt het nieuwe BW ten dele vervangen door een Europees BW?', *Weekblad voor Privaatrecht, Notariaat en Registratie*, 2001. p. 773-775, J.H.M. van Erp, 'Komt er dan toch een Europees BW?', *Weekblad voor Privaatrecht, Notariaat en Registratie* 2009/6784, p. 101-104.

25 J.H.M. van Erp, 'Contract and property law: distinct, but not separate', *European Property Law Journal*, No. 3, 2013, p. 240-259.

3.4 Open Access

Open access? Not so much. Only two publications, both on ownership of data in relation to the numerus clausus of legal objects, are openly accessible through the university repository.[26] The good news is that this can still be remedied. At least Van Erp will have something to do once he reaches his emeritus status.

3.5 Air Miles

Van Erp has visited many places throughout his career for work-related purposes (Figure 8).

Figure 8 Work Travel Destinations, World (since 2010, not including the Netherlands)

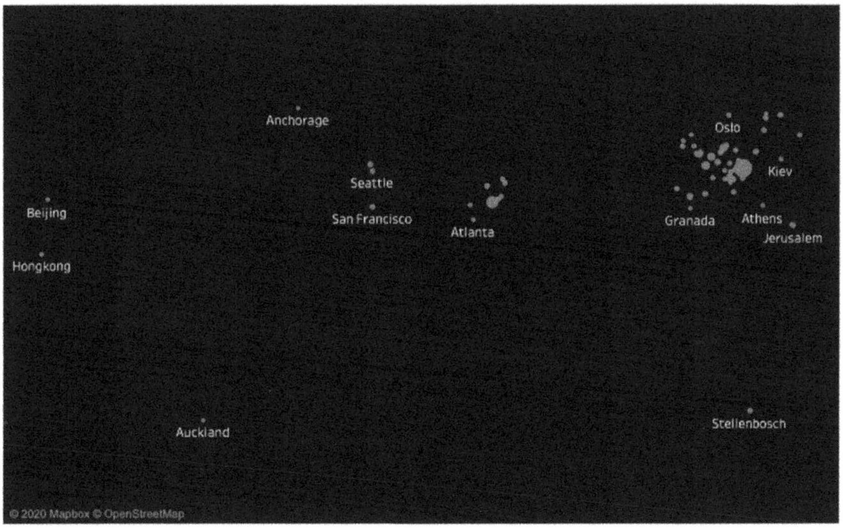

In North America, his visits to Washington, DC (n=15) stand out, first for the purpose of attending *Association for Law, Property and Society* (ALPS) conferences, later also for conferences and meetings of the *American Law Institute* (ALI) and the *WorldBank* (Figure 9).

26 S. van Erp, 'Ownership of data: the numerus clausus of legal objects', *Brigham-Kanner Property Rights Conference Journal*, No. 6, 2017, p. 235-257, S. van Erp, 'Ownership of data and the numerus clausus of legal objects', *in* UNCITRAL (Ed.), *Modernizing international trade law to support innovation and sustainable development: Proceedings of the congress of the United Nations Commission on International Trade Law*, (Vienna,) United Nations, Vol.4, 2017, p. 69-80.

Figure 9 Work Travel Destinations, North America (since 2010)

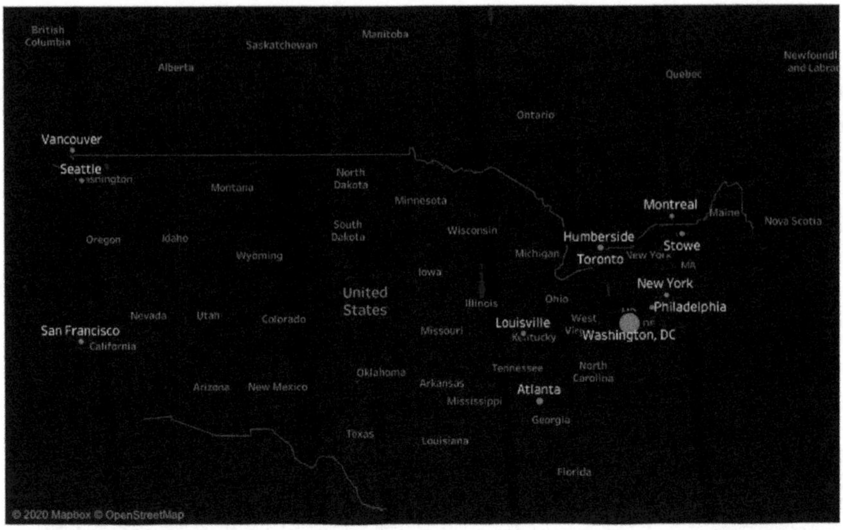

Note: Anchorage, Alaska was visited (n=1) but not displayed in the figure.

In Europe, his involvement in and vice-presidency of the *European Law Institute* (ELI) clearly shows, considering that his visits to Vienna (n=32) outnumber the visits to other destinations (Figure 10).

Figure 10 Work Travel Destinations, Europe (since 2010, not including the Netherlands)

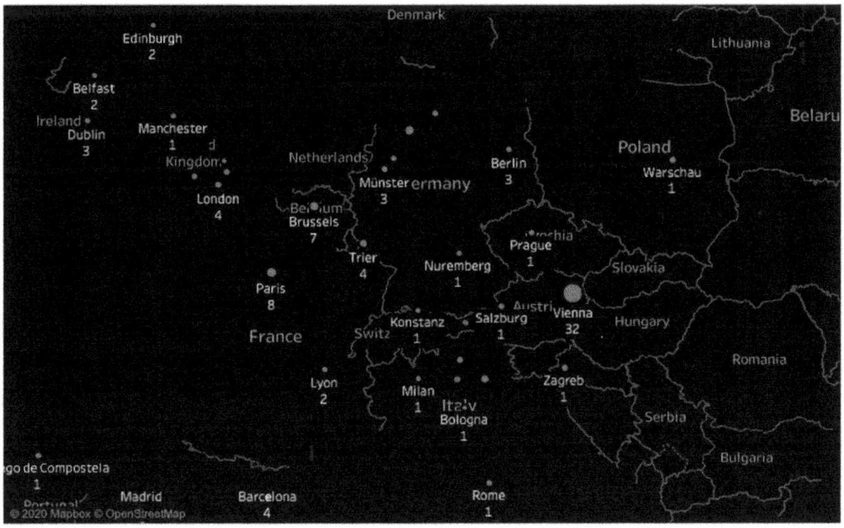

Note: Athens, Greece was visited (n=2) but not displayed in the figure.

Trends in the destinations over time were explored, but not found. Since 2010, Van Erp has maintained a stable traveling career.

3.6 *Correlation Air Miles and Output*

Finally, the question emerges whether Van Erp's travel behavior correlated with his academic output, more specifically his number of publications. For this, his yearly number of publications was compared with the number of kilometers traveled on a yearly basis (Figure 11). Although the figure might suggest a somewhat negative relationship (less publications when traveling more), the relationship is extremely weak and not statistically significant ($r = .01$, $p = .99$). This suggests that the productivity in terms of research output has not been affected much by the traveling done.

Figure 11 Relationship Number of Publications (top) – Number of Travel Kilometers (bottom) per year (editorials/prefaces excluded)

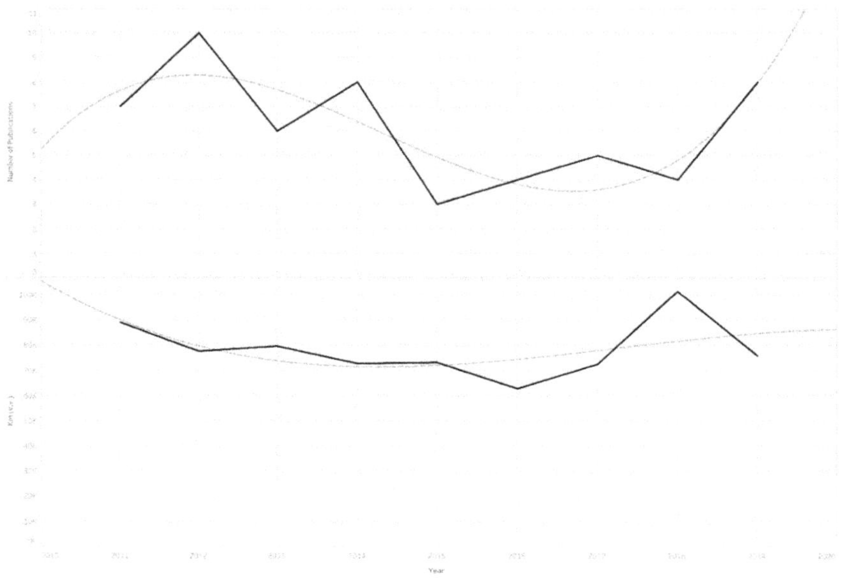

4 Conclusion

I have tried to describe Van Erp in terms of longitudinal data I could retrieve. Some of the findings do confirm my personal impressions: his broad interest in a variety of topics, having been productive throughout his appointment at Maastricht University, and having had an extended network over the world. The inspection of his publications reveal that he has focused on at least two topics that I consider transformative: European property law and digital property law. Van Erp has helped laying the foundation for these fields. His pioneering spirit, combined with his warm personality, have made him a great colleague to work with. I hope he will appreciate this unconventional contribution to his *Liber Amicorum*, and if not, I am sure he will let me know.

01010011011010100110010101100110*

*Anna Berlee***

Figuur 1 Meest gebruikte woorden in 135 publicaties van Van Erp tussen 1991-2020

---

* Dit is 'Sjef' in binaire code uitgedrukt. Een computer kan nullen of enen lezen en dus alles wat je op een computer doet, inclusief tekst, wordt weergegeven in een reeks nullen of enen. Het gaat om een 'ASCII tekst' weergegeven in 1'en en 0'en. Zie voor de tekst zelf het vakje 'output' bij CyberChef: https://gchq.github.io/CyberChef/#recipe=From_Binary('None')&input=MDEwMTAwMTEwMTEwMTAxMDAxMTAwMTAxMDExMDAxMTA (Laatstelijk geraadpleegd: 1 December 2020).

** Senior adviseur bij de Autoriteit Persoonsgegevens, maar bovenal voormalig promovenda van Sjef van Erp en Bram Akkermans. Het stuk is op persoonlijke titel geschreven.

Anna Berlee

1 Inleiding

Bij een emeritaat past het om terug te blikken op al het werk dat is verzet. Wanneer dat werk uit meer dan een half miljoen woorden bestaat, zoals bij Sjef van Erp, is het haast onbegonnen werk om het allemaal door te lezen. Aangezien Van Erp zich de laatste paar jaar steeds meer is gaan richten op de juridische kwalificatie van 'data' of 'gegevens' leek het me een mooi moment om het werk van Sjef aan een eigen data-analyse te onderwerpen. Hierin kunnen we dan wellicht wat interessante patronen ontdekken en mooie ontwikkelingen in aantreffen. De bijdrage van Gijs van Dijck in dit *Liber amicorum* doet iets soortgelijks, maar veel beter. Daarom doe ik het anders. De bijdrage is in tegenstelling tot die van Van Dijck in het Nederlands, minder wetenschappelijk en met meer plaatjes. Dit alles om te zien of ik wat interessants kan halen uit de woorden die Van Erp heeft gebruikt.

1.1 Disclaimer

Ik heb me niet gehouden aan de spelregels die horen bij deugdelijk wetenschappelijk onderzoek. Alles uit dit stuk moet dan ook met een grove hoeveelheid zout worden genomen – en geen enkele deugdelijke conclusie kan worden gebaseerd op het hieronder omschrevene, behalve dat Sjef van Erp veel heeft geschreven en dat dit vaak over het recht ging.

1.2 'Methode' en plan van aanpak

In totaal heb ik 135 van Van Erp's werken weten te verzamelen. Het gaat hierbij om ruim meer dan 1000 pagina's aan geformatteerde tekst. Bij elkaar goed voor meer dan een half miljoen woorden, die samen ruim 4 miljoen tekens vormen.[1] En dit terwijl ik Sjef nog nooit heb gehoord over RSI-klachten.

Net als Van Dijck ben ik de verzameling begonnen bij zijn eigen gerapporteerde lijst van publicaties. Deze 154 publicaties waren echter lang niet alles dat ik digitaal heb kunnen vinden van Van Erp. De zelf gerapporteerde publicaties waren alleen dun bezaaid voor de jaren 1990-2000. Ik heb wat meer van die tijd kunnen vinden door het archief van het WPNR te doorzoeken. Dit bracht me op het idee om in Legal Intelligence gewoon eens zijn naam in te toetsen. Dit bleek niet bijzonder verstandig, omdat er nog een J. van Erp bestaat die ook veel schrijft in het Nederlands, namelijk Judith van Erp, hoogleraar in

1 Het waren er 4125619.

Utrecht.[2] Gelukkig zijn haar publicaties gemakkelijk te herkennen aangezien die veelal over toezicht gaan. Problematischer was het werk van kandidaat-notaris J.L.M. van Erp die ook over het goederenrecht heeft geschreven in het huisblad van de goederenrecht juristen: het WPNR. Die moest ik er dus uit filteren. Ook heb ik gebruik gemaakt van het zoeken door scholar.google.com, SSRN.com en was het online archief van het European Journal of Comparative Law and Governance - waar Van Erp gelet op zijn rol als editor-in-chief veelvuldig in schreef - een goede plaats om zijn artikelen en editorials te vinden. Hoewel ik dus niet alle stukken van Van Erp die hij zelf opgevoerd heeft op cris.maastrichtuniversity.nl heb kunnen achterhalen kwam ik uiteindelijk uit op een mooie verzameling van 135 werken. Dit is dus, zoals eerder aangegeven niet een mooie spreiding van werk dat hij daadwerkelijk heeft gepubliceerd, omdat veel - vaak boekhoofdstukken - niet digitaal te vinden waren.

134 van de gevonden 135 teksten waren in PDF en dat is handig voor het werken met opgemaakte tekst, maar verschrikkelijk om data analyse op toe te passen. Alles moest dus eerst omgezet worden in 'platte tekst' ofwel in .txt bestanden.[3] Daarna heb ik ieder bestand voorzien van een jaartal in de bestandsnaam. Dit maakte het mogelijk om de bestanden samen te voegen op jaartal en per 5 jaar.

Ik heb alleen maar gebruik gemaakt van software en diensten op websites die gratis te gebruiken zijn.[4]

2 Sjef van Erp in Data

2.1 *Wat zegt hij veel*

Voor simpele data analyse hoeft u helemaal geen ingewikkelde programma's te downloaden of te gebruiken. Zo heeft uw computer een mooi programma waarmee u op de 'command

2 Zij zat ook per ongeluk in twee van de 154 titels op cris.

3 Hiervoor heb ik zowel *pdftotext* gebruikt als *pdf2txt* en automator.app gebruikt. Ik kwam er nadat de bijdrage voltooid was achter dat iemand het prachtige *rigrep-all* heeft gemaakt (https://github.com/phiresky/ripgrep-all, laatstelijk geraadpleegd 1 december 2020), waarmee deze hele exercitie van omzetten naar platte tekst niet nodig bleek voor veel van de toepassingen hieronder, aangezien hiermee ook door PDF bestanden kan worden gezocht. Al doende leert men, zullen we maar zeggen.

4 De 'Terminal.app' & 'Automator.app' op MacOS en www.monkeylearn.com; https://personality-insights-demo.ng.bluemix.net/; en https://www.ibm.com/cloud/watson-natural-language-understanding (allen laatstelijk geraadpleegd: op 1 december 2020).

line' kunt werken en veel simpele data analyse al kunt uitvoeren.[5] Zo is heel gemakkelijk te achterhalen hoeveel woorden en tekens Van Erp in zijn werk heeft gebruikt. Hiervoor zijn alle 135 bestanden in 1 samengevoegd genaamd 'Alles.txt'.[6]

```
wc Alles.txt
```

Dit leverde op voor mij het volgende resultaat op:

```
17970 595458 4199230 Alles.txt
```

Waarbij 17970 staat voor het aantal regels in het bestand, 595458 voor het aantal woorden en 4199230 voor het aantal tekens.

Vervolgens is het wellicht interessant om per jaartal de 15 meest gebruikte woorden te halen uit het werk van Van Erp. Daarvoor heb ik het volgende stukje code gebruikt:

```
tr -c '[:alnum:]' '[\n*]' < 2000.txt | sort | uniq -c | sort -nr | head -100
```

Dit ziet er al meer uit als iets dat in een film als 'hacking' wordt omschreven. Maar eigenlijk is het heel gemakkelijk. Wat dit doet is het bestand 2000.txt (ieder jaartal had een eigen .txt bestandje) te bekijken en daar de woorden die erin werden gebruikt te 'tellen' en te sorteren op hoe vaak ze voorkomen (van vaak naar weinig) en de 100 meest voorkomende woorden te tonen. Ik moest hiervoor 100 gebruiken, omdat 15 niet werkt, want je wilt niet weten hoe vaak 'de', 'het', 'en', en 'een' voorkomen in een tekst. Dat zijn natuurlijk totaal niet relevante woorden. Ik wilde weten welke inhoudelijke woorden het meest werden gebruikt. Daarom liet ik er 100 zien en ben zelf door de resultaten heen gelopen en gekeken welke bij elkaar stonden.

Als Member los stond en State en/of States iets verder op, dan voegde ik dit samen tot Member State(s). Net als right en rights tot right(s). Dat geeft wel een iets vertekend beeld. Want de computer telt alleen woorden en niet combinaties daarvan.[7] Aangezien dit toch niet een wetenschappelijke exercitie was, liet ik me hier niet door tegenhouden. Het is overigens wel mogelijk om dit eruit te filteren en op woordcombinaties te zoeken.

---

5 Alles wat ik heb gedaan was op een Unix systeem (MacOS in mijn geval), dus niet Windows. Dat betekent overigens niet dat dit niet op een Windows PC had kunnen worden gedaan, zeker wel, alleen dan pak je het net wat anders aan.

6 Dat kan gemakkelijk door in de map met alle .txt bestanden het volgende in te voeren: cat *.txt Alles.txt.

7 Daarbij zoekt hij ook *precies* op die combinatie van letters. Dus right en Right worden als twee verschillende gezien. Ook dat is op te lossen trouwens.

Dan is er nog het bijkomende probleem van de betekenis van woorden. Het woord 'will' is een doodnormaal woord in het Engels maar kan ook een relevant woord zijn voor iemand als Sjef van Erp, die tevens schrijft over testamenten welke vertalen naar 'will' in het Engels. Ik heb 'will' uiteindelijk niet opgenomen maar wel 'common' omdat ik weet dat Van Erp vaak schrijft over common law systems en civil law systems. Terwijl 'common' natuurlijk ook gewoon 'gebruikelijk' kan betekenen en dus niet relevant hoeft te zijn. Daarbij is ook belangrijk op te merken dat hoe minder data ik had voor een jaar, hoe minder relevant de uitkomst eigenlijk is. Zo had ik voor 2008 maar één publicatie om op terug te vallen, dus ook dat geeft een wat vertekend beeld.

Met dit alles in het achterhoofd kunnen we kijken naar de eerste resultaten.

Tabel 1 2000 t/m 2005

	2000	2001	2002	2003	2004	2005
1	Law	Law	Law	Law	Law	Law
2	European	Federal	European	Property	Recht	Surety
3	Recht	European	Right(s)	Right(s)	Europesese	European
4	Studenten	Court	Recht	European	Registration	Principal
5	Comparative	Case	Europese	Civil	Goederenrecht	Agreement
6	Private	Common	Pledge	Security	European	Principle
7	Opleiding	US	Property	Charge	Interest	Credit
8	System	Member States	Claim	Right(s)	Richtlijn	Property
9	Mixed	National	Mortgage	Dutch	Internationaal	Directive
10	Diefstal	Europese	Private	Ownership	System	Debtor
11	University	Private	Security	Civil Code	Comparative	Accessority
12	Netherlands	Community	Case	Common	Information	Creditor
13	Europese	Liability	Common	Floating	Security	Security
14	Studie	Courts	Ownership	Netherlands	Registry	Obligation
15	Common	Recht	Civil	Absolute	National	Contract

Tabel 2 2006 t/m 2011

	2006	**2007**	**2008**	**2009**	**2010**	**2011**
1	Law	Law	European	Law	Law	Law
2	Property	National	Financial	Property	Property	Property
3	Right(s)	Succession	Market	European	European	European

4	Agreement	Report	Member States	Right(s)	Registered	Contract
5	Land	European	Law	Ownership	Together	English
6	Lessor	Comparative	Credit	Model	Member State(s)	DCFR
7	Case	Property	Mortgage	Rules	Marriage	Right(s)
8	Contract	Family	Europa	Contract	Common	Case
9	European	Country	Integration	System	Private	Trust
10	Owner	Surviving	Crisis	Transfer	Matrimonial	Right(s)
11	Parties	Spouse	Europe	Security	Partnership	Common
12	Surety	Right(s)	Directive	DCFR	Relationship	Recht
13	Rights	Children	Measures	Classical	Civil	Comparative
14	Software	Systems	Internal	Land	Union	System
15	Servitudes	Private	Contract	Member State(s)	Model	Ownership

Tabel 3 2012 t/m 2016

	2012	2013	2014	2015	2016
1	Law	Law	Law	Law	Digitale
2	Property	Property	Europese	Property	Recht
3	Right(s)	European	Erfrechtverklaring	European	Inhoud
4	European	Contract	Recht	Right(s)	Law
5	Land	Right(s)	Notaris	Netherlands	Eigendom
6	Ownership	Private	Verordening	Convention	Goederen
7	Security	Mortgage	Public	Ownership	Software
8	Person	MERS	Erfrecht	Comparative	European
9	Contract	Member State(s)	European	Model	Gemeenschap
10	Common	Ownership	Information	Dutch	Property
11	Object	Land	Right(s)	Islands	Verkoop
12	Case	System	Autoriteit	System	Zaak
13	Civil	National	Rechter	Cape Town Convention	Rechtsvergelijking
14	Personal	Parties	Property	Carribean	Licentie
15	Owner	Integration	EU	Private	Auteursrecht

Tabel 4 2017 t/m 2020

	2017	2018	2019	2020
1	Law	Recht	Data	Data
2	Property	Europese	Property	Law
3	European	Law	Law	Property
4	Lex rei site	Data	Land	EU
5	Rule	Nederlandse	Right(s)	European
6	Land	Land	Object	Ownership
7	Use	Inschrijving	Information	Right(s)
8	Public	Erfrecht	Physical	Object
9	System	EU	Right(s)	Public
10	Rights	Notaris	Digital	Personal
11	Regulation	Erfrecht	Person	Information
12	Registration	Verordening	Token	Private
13	Member State(s)	Verklaring	Personal	World
14	Subject	Zaak	Ownership	Physical
15	Case	European	Personal	Protection

2.2 *Van Erp is een echte goederenrecht jurist*

Wat kunnen we nu halen uit deze informatie? Het is overduidelijk dat Van Erp graag over het recht schrijft. Stipt op één staat immers 'Law' als meest voorkomende woord, jaar naar jaar. Om te kijken hoe vaak een bepaald woord voorkomt kunnen we het volgende invoeren:

```
grep -o -i law Alles.txt | wc -l
```

Dan komen we er achter dat Van Erp maar liefst 8738 keer law/Law gebruikt in zijn stukken.[8] Property staat ook erg hoog aangeschreven, en dit komt op een totaal van 3436 keer. Van Erp is dus een echte goederenrecht jurist. Maar dit betekent niet dat hij zijn oude liefde, het verbintenissenrecht is vergeten. Hij heeft maar liefst 1845 keer het woord contract opgeschreven.[9]

We kunnen natuurlijk hetzelfde trucje nog eens doen met zijn meest gebruikte woorden, en zo zien welke woorden het vaakst worden gebruikt van de meest gebruikte woorden. Maar interessanter is om dit gewogen te doen. Dus alle woorden van rij 1 15x mee te tellen,

8 Met of zonder hoofdletter. De -i zorgt ervoor dat hoofdletter of kleine letter niet uitmaakt.

9 Met of zonder hoofdletter. Inclusief alle keren dat contracts of contractual is opgeschreven.

rij 2 14x, enzovoorts tot rij 15 welke we 1x meetellen. Dan uit die resulterende lijst woorden te tellen welke het vaakst voorkomen.

Dat levert het volgende lijst op: Law; European; Property; Right(s); Recht; Land; Ownership; Contract; Europese; Private; Data; Member State(s); System; Comparative; Common. Hieruit zou men kunnen concluderen dat Van Erp in het Nederlands het vaak heeft over de invloed van het Europese recht op het goederenrecht.[10] In het Engels komt Europees recht en de invloed van Europa op lidstatelijk recht ook vaak terug, het is dus geen wonder dat we dit in deze reeks terug zien. Daarnaast heeft Van Erp het vaak over het meest omvangrijke zakelijke recht; het eigendomsrecht en eigendom meer in het algemeen. We zien bij de 15 meest voorkomende woorden bijvoorbeeld niet 'Pledge' terug, of 'Mortgage/Hypothec' of 'usufruct'. Het gaat Van Erp vaak om het primaire goederenrechtelijke recht, en niet die beperkte rechten. Hoewel deze rechten natuurlijk wel vallen onder het vaak gebruikte 'System'. Daarnaast zien we ook 'Land' terugkomen, wat ook geen verbazing wekt, aangezien Sjef vaak schrijft over de perikelen inzake de registratie van goederenrechtelijke rechten ten aanzien van land. Het is dan ook geen wonder dat zijn werk ook veel door notarissen wordt gelezen. Zijn enorme interesse de laatste paar jaren voor de goederenrechtelijke kwalificatie van gegevens/data zien we ook terug in de gewogen lijst. Het zou me niets verbazen dat als we deze exercitie nog eens doen in 2030 dat 'data' dan nog een stuk hoger staat in de gewogen lijst.[11]

2.3 *Van Nederlands naar Engels*

Interessant wellicht is ook dat de focus van Van Erp's publiek breder is geworden met de jaren. Een 'word cloud' van zijn publicaties tussen 1991-1996 en een uit 2001-2006 laten een prachtige ommezwaai zien van een concentratie op het recht in het BW en een sterke verbintenisrechtelijke focus, naar een duidelijke voorkeur voor het schrijven in het Engels en het Europees goederenrecht.

10 Daarnaast is van belang dat Data zowel in het Nederlands als Engels hetzelfde betekenen.

11 Ik verwacht namelijk niet dat Van Erp de pen neerlegt nu hij met emeritaat is. Ik hoop het ook niet.

Figuur 2 Word cloud van publicaties tussen 1991-1996

Figuur 3 Word cloud van publicaties tussen 2001-2006

2.4 *Sentimentanalyse*

We kunnen aan de hand van wat ingewikkeldere tekstanalyse software, of 'algoritmen', namelijk de zogenaamde 'sentiment analysis' ook kijken of Sjef positieve, neutrale, of negatieve taal bezigde in zijn stukken.

Sentiment analysis algoritmen zijn niet primair bedoeld om het werk van wetenschappers te beoordelen of te analyseren. Vaker wordt het ingezet door bedrijven, en naar verluidt ook regeringen, om social media mee te monitoren, om te kijken hoe er wordt gesproken over het merk, een bepaald product, of beleid. Ook kunnen reviews van producten of bedrijven worden geanalyseerd, of commentaar op fora of onder video's of nieuwsberichten om zo vooraf te filteren welke berichten nadere menselijke analyse behoeven of waar een product manager wat mee moet.

Desalniettemin heb ik ze toch gebruikt en kunnen we er leuke informatie uithalen.

Tabel 5 Is Van Erp positiever geworden door de jaren heen?

Periode	Positief/Neutraal/Negatief sentiment in tekst?	Hoe zeker was het algoritme van die kwalificatie?
1991-1996	Positief	86.6%
1997-2000	Positief	58.2%
2001-2005	Positief	73.5%
2006-2010	Positief	83.6%
2011-2015	Positief	99.8%
2016-2020	Positief	84.2%

Sjef blijkt uit deze analyses, zoals ik hem ook ken, een zeer positief ingestelde man te zijn. Wanneer je zijn stukken over een paar jaar bekijkt, dan zie je dat het altijd als positief wordt bestempeld door het algoritme, en dat het zelfs met bijna 100% zekerheid kan stellen dat Van Erp tussen 2011-2015 positief was in zijn publicaties. Ik dacht bij het zien van deze resultaten eerst dat misschien het algoritme niet goed werkte, maar als we bijvoorbeeld 4 publicaties uit 2020 even naast elkaar leggen en individueel door het algoritme laten beoordelen zien we dat de uitkomst per stuk wel degelijk kan verschillen.

Tabel 6 Sentiment analyse 4 losse artikelen

Titel	Positief/Neutraal/Negatief sentiment in tekst?	Hoe zeker was het algoritme van die kwalificatie?
Are land registers becoming online intermediary platforms of land data?	Negatief	86.7%
Data Protection in Hybrid Worlds	Positief	49.0%
European property law: Competence, integration and effectiveness	Positief	84.2%
Who 'owns' the data in a coronavirus tracing (and/or tracking) app?	Neutral	53.8%

We kunnen naast hele artikelen ook individuele zinnen aan een dergelijke analyse onderwerpen. Dat maakt het mogelijk om te kijken met welk sentiment Van Erp spreekt in zinnen waarin hij 'property' of 'contract' noemt. Om alle regels waarin een bepaald woord voorkomt te verzamelen kan het volgende gebruikt worden:

```
grep -i property Alles.txt > property.txt
```

Dit kopieert de hele regel waarin het woord 'property' voorkomt in het nieuwe bestand 'property.txt'.[12] Dat kan dan weer door het sentimentanalyse algoritme worden bekeken.

Wanneer we een zin met zowel 'property' als 'contract' willen vinden moet het net een beetje anders.

```
grep -i 'property.*contract\|contract.*property' Alles.txt > pc.txt
```

Dat kan natuurlijk ook met andere combinaties. Omdat we zien dat Van Erp zich de laatste jaren steeds meer richt op 'data' en de goederenrechtelijke status van gegevens, heb ik die ook meegenomen in de analyse.

Tabel 7 Sentiment analyse op regels met specifieke woorden of woordcombinaties

Woord in een regel	Positief/Neutraal/Negatief sentiment?	Hoe zeker was het algoritme van die kwalificatie?
Property	Negatief	75.8%
Contract	Negatief	55.3%

12 Wederom onafhankelijk van hoofdletter gebruik.

Zowel 'property' als 'contract' in dezelfde regel. Niet een van de twee.	Positief	90.4%
Data	Positief	87.6%
Zowel 'property' als 'data' in dezelfde regel.	Positief	94.4%
Zowel 'contract' als 'data' in dezelfde regel.	Positief	40.3%

Interessant is dus dat Van Erp zich niet positief lijkt te uitten over het goederenrecht of goederen in het Engels, en ook niet bijzonder over contracten. Maar wanneer je ze samen neemt komt daar juist wel weer een positief beeld uit. Nóg zekerder is het algoritme van de positiviteit waarmee Van Erp zich uit over de combinatie van 'property' en 'data' in een zin. Zekerder in ieder geval dan de combinatie 'contract' en 'data'. Zou hieruit wellicht ook een voorkeur voor een goederenrechtelijke benadering van gegevens kunnen worden afgeleid?

Er bestaan meer soorten algoritmen, en IBM's Watson kan in plaats van positief/neutraal/negatief, onderverdelen in Sadness/Joy/Fear/Disgust/Anger. De versie die ik gebruikte kon voornamelijk goed met enkele artikelen omgaan en daar keywords uithalen en het bijpassende sentiment berekenen. Daarom zocht ik eerst alle stukken die ik had waarin het woord 'data' terugkwam. In de folder (in de terminal app) met alle stukken die ik had met Van Erp's stukken in .txt kan dan het volgende worden ingetoetst:

```
grep -i -l 'data' *.txt
```

Ofwel, zoek alle .txt bestandjes door in deze folder en zoek naar het woord 'data' met of zonder hoofdletter en laat de bestandsnamen zien van de bestanden waarin dit woord voorkomt. De inhoud van die bestanden kon ik dan door het algoritme 'halen'. Het algoritme herkende 'data ownership' als een eigen Keyword, en daarbij kon het algoritme de volgende emoties halen. Hieronder een selectie.

Tabel 8 Met welke emotie sprak Van Erp over 'data ownership'?

Title	Sadness	Joy	Fear	Disgust	Anger
The need for a common vocabulary on 'data ownership'	14.91%	12.09%	16.03%	4.41%	5.59%
Data Protection in Hybrid Worlds	8.43%	42.51%	8.94%	6.08%	13.3%
Who 'owns' the data in a coronavirus tracing (and/or tracking) app?	20.32%	11.27%	2.95%	0.19%	1.4%

De sterkste emoties blijken uit Van Erp's stuk over 'Data Protection in Hybrid Worlds' waarin hij overwegend vrolijk sprak over 'data ownership' maar ook direct met de meeste 'woede', ook al bleef dat bij 13,3 procent, het is na vrolijkheid de eerstvolgende emotie waarmee hij het vaakst 'spreekt' over het onderwerp data eigendom. Wat we hiermee moeten weet ik ook niet precies. Interessanter vind ik dat het meevalt met de mate van angst waarover hij praat als het gaat om eigendom van data in dat stuk. Het lijkt dus alsof je hieruit – zonder het stuk daadwerkelijk te lezen – zou kunnen aflezen dat Van Erp positief staat tegenover het accepteren van eigendom van data. Dit terwijl hij hierover aanzienlijk minder positief gestemd is wanneer het gaat om eigendom van data in het kader van de vraag wie de rechthebbende is bij contact-tracing apps die worden ingezet om het coronavirus te bestrijden. Daar wordt de vrolijkheid ondergraven door een meer triestere emotie. Dit kan te maken hebben met het onderwerp dat voor velen een zeer trieste aangelegenheid betreft: het coronavirus. Maar aangezien het algoritme specifiek ziet op de manier waarop Van Erp praat over 'data ownership', moet het een andere oorzaak hebben. Wat deze precies is, komen we niet achter aangezien het algoritme dit niet uitlegt. Het blijft in zoverre een 'black box' waar dit op gebaseerd is.

2.5 Wat zeggen Van Erp's teksten over hemzelf?

We hebben hiervoor gezien hoe over het sentiment waarmee Van Erp praat over bepaalde onderwerpen. Maar wat zeggen zijn woorden eigenlijk over *Sjef* zelf? Ook daar blijkt een algoritme of twee voor te bestaan. IBM's Watson kan ons hierin voorzien.[13] Wanneer we het 'Alles.txt' documentje door IBM's 'Personality Insights' halen krijgen we een 'very strong analysis' die zelfs als 'statistisch relevant' wordt beschouwd door IBM's Watson. Het gaat hier om een 'High quality assessment of someone's personality'. Watson heeft het volgende over Sjef van Erp te vertellen:

> **IBM's Watson – Summary – Personality Insights of Sjef van Erp based on his work:**
> You are heartfelt. You are philosophical: you are open to and intrigued by new ideas and love to explore them. And you are authority-challenging: you prefer to challenge authority and traditional values to help bring about positive changes.
> You are motivated to seek out experiences that provide a strong feeling of discovery.

13 https://personality-insights-demo.ng.bluemix.net (Laatstelijk geraadpleegd: 1 december 2020).

> You are relatively unconcerned with tradition. And you prefer activities with a purpose greater than just personal enjoyment.

Dat zijn mooie woorden van een algoritme. Het zijn ook woorden die ik zelf zou hebben kunnen gebruikt om Sjef te omschrijven. Ik ken hem als een zeer vriendelijke, open, vrijwel exclusief goedgemutste man die bovenal enorm leergierig is. Dat blijkt dus ook uit zijn werk, volgens Watson.

Hij heeft binnen het goederenrecht, af en toe gefungeerd als een pionier. Iemand die als een van de eersten duikt in het rechtsvergelijkend goederenrecht, Europees goederenrecht en vragen over de goederenrechtelijke kwalificatie van data. Het was daarmee ook soms wat onontgonnen terrein en ik zou Van Erp willen omschrijven als iemand die als eerste het pad uitstippelde, waarna velen volgden. Hierbij stootte hij soms tegen wat heilige huisjes van het Nederlandse goederenrecht, in het bijzonder wanneer hij het had over de invloed van het Europese recht op het (Nederlandse) goederenrecht. Ook kan ik beamen dat Van Erp altijd open heeft gestaan voor nieuwe ideeën en theorieën over hoe het goederenrecht werkte of behoorde te werken. Dat leverde tussen ons mooie discussies op en waarbij we vaak beiden met 'huiswerk' eindigden omdat we geen tijd meer hadden om door te praten, maar we nog wel zoveel moesten uitzoeken. Ik verliet dan vaak Sjef's kantoor vol enthousiasme dat werd gematcht door een even zo enthousiaste Sjef.

Terug naar het algoritme. Het algoritme splitst vervolgens de persoonlijkheid uit in enkele subonderdelen en scoort daarop de schrijver van de teksten. Ik haal er wat mooie uit:

Openness: 100%

Hieronder vallen bijvoorbeeld Intellectual curiosity, waar Sjef ook 100% op scoort, maar ook 'Adventurousness' met 74%. Het gaat hier om hoe open iemand staat voor nieuwe ervaringen. Sjef's enorm hoge score betekent dat hij intellectueel nieuwsgierig is en bereid is om nieuwe dingen uit te proberen.

Conscientiousness: 83%

Hieronder valt onder andere hoe gedisciplineerd iemand is. Hoe hoger de score hoe gedisciplineerder maar ook hoe plichtsgetrouwer en hoe meer iemands drive van binnenuit komt en niet zozeer gedreven door invloeden van buiten.

Introversion/Extraversion: 66%

Hoe hoger hoe energieker en des te duidelijker de binding met buiten is. Hoe hoger hoe assertiever iemand is ook binnen een groep. Kan goed praten in groepen en voelt zich daarin op zijn gemak.

Emotional range: 2%

Hierbij wordt expliciet opgemerkt dat de demo waar ik gebruik van maakte '*cannot diagnose a mental illness*'. Ik schrok eerst toen ik die score zag, tot ik de uitleg las. Hoe lager hoe beter blijkt. Lager betekent juist dat iemand kalmer is en niet zo snel uit z'n lood is geslagen.

3 Conclusie

Wat kunnen we nu uit dit alles leren? Zoals ik hier al in het begin voor waarschuwde, in ieder geval niets dat wetenschappelijk onderbouwd is. Dat weerhoudt me er echter niet van enkele dingen op te merken.

Allereerst over de mogelijkheden van het gebruik van data-analyse voor wetenschappelijk onderzoek, met name in de voorfase. In het bijzonder lijkt het mogelijk – wanneer gedegen uitgevoerd – dat men sentimentanalyse en emotieanalyse misschien zou kunnen inzetten bij tekstanalyses van grote hoeveelheden stukken om zo te kunnen 'scannen' wanneer iemand zich positief of negatief uitlaat over een bepaald onderwerp. Dit kan een eerste schifting in 'voor' en 'tegen' argumenten wellicht mogelijk maken over bijvoorbeeld een onderwerp als 'eigendom van data'. Vooral ook op een manier die toegankelijk is. Zo heb ik gebruik kunnen maken van gratis demoversies van krachtige software, waarbij het enige dat ik hoefde te doen wat tekst te kopiëren en plakken. Dat kan iedere student, promovendus of onderzoeker. Ik wil hier uitdrukkelijk niet suggereren dat de teksten niet daadwerkelijk gelezen hoeven te worden, maar het kan wellicht handig zijn een grootschalig onderzoek wat gerichter te maken.

Als tweede, wat vertelt dit alles ons nu over Sjef van Erp. Ik vond het mooi te zien dat de sentimentanalyse een overweldigend positief beeld gaf van hoe hij zich uit in zijn werk. En dat hij die positiviteit al vanaf het begin van zijn carrière uitte en nooit is verloren. Daarnaast kwam er een prachtige analyse van Sjef's persoonlijkheid uit het algoritme rollen. Het is mooi te zien dat de manier waarop ik Sjef ken ook duidelijk spreekt uit zijn eigen geschreven teksten.

Sjef is dus in data net als in het echt.

www.ingramcontent.com/pod-product-compliance
Ingram Content Group UK Ltd.
Pitfield, Milton Keynes, MK11 3LW, UK
UKHW051317180926
15262UKWH00021B/499

9 789462 361973